Dieter Arnold

Fachwörterbuch
Messen und Ausstellungen

Dieter Arnold

Fachwörterbuch Messen und Ausstellungen

Deutsch – Englisch / English – German

Deutscher Fachverlag

Bibliografische Information Der Deutschen Bibliothek

Die Deutsche Bibliothek verzeichnet diese Publikation in der Deutschen Nationalbibliografie; detaillierte bibliografische Daten sind im Internet über http://dnb.ddb.de abrufbar.

Reihe Edition m&a
ISSN 1438-8626
ISBN 3-87150-950-7
© 2006 by Deutscher Fachverlag GmbH, Frankfurt am Main.
Alle Rechte vorbehalten.
Nachdruck, auch auszugsweise, nur mit Genehmigung des Verlages.
Umschlag: idüll, Frankfurt am Main
Umschlagfoto: Messe Frankfurt GmbH, Frankfurt am Main
Satz: UCMG, Kiew
Druck und Bindung: Wilhelm & Adam, Heusenstamm

Vorwort

Die Beteiligung an internationalen Messen erfordert heute eine Verständigung, die überwiegend auf Englisch verläuft. Dabei ist die Kommunikation in englischer Sprache vielfach bereits bei den vorbereitenden Aufgaben wie der Suche und Auswahl von geeigneten Veranstaltungen, bei der Anmeldung, der Platzwahl, der Standplanung und dem Standbau erforderlich.

Vor diesem Hintergrund wurde die Fachterminologie des vorliegenden Wörterbuchs insbesondere den Teilnahmebedingungen, den Anmeldeformularen und Formblättern der internationalen Messeveranstalter entnommen. Aber auch Dokumentationen von Organisationen der Messewirtschaft sowie von Zulieferern und Dienstleistern wurden berücksichtigt.

Die Unterscheidung zwischen britischem und amerikanischem Englisch ist jeweils separat angegeben, obwohl die Anwendung im alltäglichen Sprachgebrauch auf Messen und Ausstellungen fließend ist.

Der Autor ist für Anregungen, Verbesserungen und Ergänzungen dankbar.

Köln, im Juli 2006

Dieter Arnold

1 Deutsch – Englisch
German – English

Teil I: Deutsch – Englisch
Part I: German – English

Der deutsch-englische Teil des Wörterbuchs verwendet folgende Abkürzungen:

Genusbezeichnungen: m – Maskulinum (der)
  f   – Femininum (die)
  n – Neutrum (das)
  pl – Plural (die)

sowie GB – britisches Englisch
  US – amerikanisches Englisch

A

Abbau *(m)* dismantling, removal, teardown
Abbauausweis *(m)* dismantling pass, pass for dismantling staff
abbauen dismantle, remove, tear down
Abbauende *(n)* dismantle deadline, end of dismantling period, end of removal time
Abbaukarte *(f)* dismantling ticket, removal ticket
Abbaupersonal *(n)* dismantling personnel, removal staff
Abbaurichtlinien *(f, pl)* dismantle rules, provisions on stand dismantling
Abbautermin *(m)* dates for dismantling
Abbauzeit *(f)* dismantling times, removal period
Abbauzeit *(f)*, **verlängerte** dismantle time extension
abbestellen cancel
Abbestellung *(f)* cancellation
Abbild *(n)* copy; (Bild) picture
Abbildung *(f)* reproduction, picture, illustration
abblenden screen, dim
Abdampf *(m)* exhaust steam
Abdeckfolie *(f)* plastic covering, protective sheeting
Abdeckprofil *(n)* cover profile
Abdeckstopfen *(m)* end cap
Abdichtung *(f)* seal
Abdruck *(m)* reprint, reproduction
abdunkeln dim
Abendanzug *(m)* dinner suit
Abendkleidung *(f)* evening dress
Abfahrt *(f)* departure, start
Abfahrtszeit *(f)* departure time, time of departure
Abfall *(m)* waste, garbage (US), rubbish (GB)

Abfall *(m)*, **wiederverwertbarer** recyclable waste
Abfallbehälter *(m)* waste container, trash can (US), rubbish bin (GB)
Abfallbeseitigung *(f)* waste disposal
Abfallbeutel *(m)* waste bag, waste collection bag, trash bag (US)
Abfalleimer *(m)* waste bin, garbage can (US), rubbish bin (GB), litter bin (GB)
Abfallentsorgung *(f)* waste disposal
Abfallgesetz *(n)* waste management legislation, waste law
Abfallsammlung *(f)*, **sortenreine** presorted waste collection, waste sorting for collection
Abfertigung *(f)* (Flughafen etc.) check-in, registration; (Güter) forwarding
abfließen flow-off
Abflug *(m)* start, take-off, departure
Abflugdatum *(n)* departure date
Abflugzeit *(f)* departure time, time of departure
Abfluss *(m)* (Wasser) outlet
Abflussleitung *(f)* waste pipe
Abflussrohr *(n)* drain pipe, waste pipe
Abfuhr *(f)* removal
Abgas *(n)* exhaust gases, waste fumes
abgasarm with low exhaust emission, low-emission
Abgasleitung *(f)* exhaust pipe
Abgasreinigung *(f)* purification of exhaust gases
abgepackt packaged, prepacked
abgerundet round, rounded
abhanden kommen get lost
Abhängegurt *(m)* suspension strap
Abhängeseil *(n)* (Draht) suspension wire
Abhängestab *(m)* suspension rod
Abhängung *(f)* suspension
abhobeln plane down, plane off
Abholdienst *(m)* pick up service

abholen call for, come for, pick up; (Dinge) collect, fetch
abklemmen pinch off, disconnect
Abkommen *(n)* agreement
Abkommen *(n)* **treffen** come to an agreement
abkühlen cool down
abkürzen (kürzen) shorten; (Gespräch etc.) abridge; (Aufenthalt etc.) cut short
Abkürzung *(f)* (Weg, Zeit) short cut; (Gespräch etc.) abridg(e)ment, abbreviation
abladen unload
Ablauf *(m)* (Frist etc.) expiry of the deadline, expiration; (Flüssigkeit) drain, outlet
Ablauf *(m)*, **programmierter** programed operation (US), programmed operation (GB)
ablaufen (Frist etc., Flüssigkeit) run off, run out
Ablehnung *(f)* refusal, rejection
ablesen (Manuskript, Zähler etc.) read
abliefern deliver; (übergeben) hand over
Ablieferung *(f)* delivery
Abluft *(f)* waste air
abmelden (Anmeldung etc.) cancel
Abmeldung *(f)* cancellation, withdrawal; (EDV) sign-off
abmessen measure
Abmessung *(f)* measurement
Abnahme *(f)* **von Messegut** receiving of exhibition materials, inspection of exhibition goods
Abnahmebescheinigung *(f)* acceptance certificate, inspection certificate
Abnahmeprüfung *(f)* acceptance test
abnehmbar removable
abräumen clear away, remove; (Tisch) clear the table
abrechnen account for, cash up, invoice

Abrechnung *(f)* accounting, billing, settlement, settlement of accounts, statement, statement of accounts, invoicing
Abrechnungstag *(m)* accounting day, settlement day
Abrechnungszeitraum *(m)* accounting period
Abreise *(f)* departure; (vom Hotel) check-out
Abreisedatum *(n)* date of departure
abreisen depart, leave
Abreisetag *(m)* day of departure
Absage *(f)* cancellation; (Ablehnung) refusal
absagen cancel, call off
absägen saw off
Absatz *(m)* (Handel) sales, turnover; (Text) paragraph
Absatzanalyse *(f)* sales analysis
Absatzdiagramm *(n)* sales chart
absatzfähig saleable, marketable
Absatzfähigkeit *(f)* saleability
Absatzgebiet *(n)* market, trading area, marketing area
Absatzgeschwindigkeit *(f)* rate of sales
Absatzkanal *(m)* distribution channel, channel of sales
Absatzmöglichkeit *(f)* sales opportunity, market opportunity
Absatzplan *(m)* sales plan, sales budget, distribution plan
Absatzpolitik *(f)* sales policy, distribution policy
Absatzpotenzial *(n)* sales potential
Absatzprognose *(f)* sales forecast
Absatzsteigerung *(f)* sales increase
Absatzvolumen *(n)* sales volume
Absatzweg *(m)* trade channel, distribution channel
Absatzzahlen *(pl)* sales figures
Absatzziel *(n)* sales target, marketing objective
absaugen suck off

abschalten cut off, switch off, turn off, disconnect
Abschaltstrom *(m)* cut-off current
abschicken send, post
Abschied *(m)* parting, farewell
Abschirmung *(f)* shield, shielding
Abschlagszahlung *(f)* part payment
abschleifen grind down, grind off
abschleppen tow, tow off
Abschleppkosten *(pl)* towing charge
abschließbar lockable
abschließen lock, lock up; (beenden) complete
Abschluss *(m)* end, conclusion; (Geschäft) business deal
Abschlusspressekonferenz *(f)* closing press conference
abschrägen slope, bevel
abschrauben screw off, unscrew
abschreiben (Buchung) amortize, charge off, depreciate, write down, write off
Abschreibung *(f)* amortizement, depreciation, write off, writing off, allowance for depreciation
Abschreibungssatz *(m)* depreciation rate, rate of depreciation
abschrubben scrub
absenden send, send off, dispatch, forward; (Post) mail (US), post (GB)
Absender *(m)* sender, dispatcher
Absicht *(f)* intention
Absichtserklärung *(f)* letter of intent
absolut absolute, total; (völlig) complete
abspeichern (EDV) save, file
Absprache *(f)* arrangement
absprachegemäß as agreed
abspülen rinse; (abwaschen) wash up, do the dishes
Abstand *(m)* (Raum) distance; (Zeit) interval
Abstandshalter *(m)* distance connector
abstauben dust

abstellen put down; (Energie, Wasser) cut off, turn off; (Maschine) switch off, stop
abtauen (Kühlgerät) defrost
abteilen divide; (Wand etc.) partition off
Abteilung *(f)* department, division
Abteilung *(f)* **für Öffentlichkeitsarbeit** public relations department
Abteilungsleiter(in) *(m/f)* department head, department manager, department manageress, head of department
Abtransport *(m)* transportation
abtransportieren transport, take away
abtrennen separate, divide off, take off; (abschneiden) cut off
Abtropfwanne *(f)* drip tray
Abverkauf *(m)* sale
Abwärme *(f)* waste heat
abwärts down
Abwasch *(m)* washing-up
abwaschen wash off; (Geschirr) wash up
Abwasser *(n)* waste water, sewage
Abwasseranschluss *(m)* drain connection
Abwasserbeseitigung *(f)* wastewater disposal
Abwasserentsorgung *(f)* sewage disposal
Abwasserleitung *(f)* sewerage
Abweichung *(f)* difference, deviation, variance
abwerten devalue, devaluate
Abwertung *(f)* devaluation
abwesend absent, out, not in
Abwesenheit *(f)* absence
Abwicklung *(f)* handling, completion, settlement
Abzeichen *(n)* badge
abziehen substract, deduct; (Preis) take off; (Rabatt) discount
Abzug *(m)* (Reduktion) allowance, deduction, discount; (Foto) copy, print, proof; (Dampf, Gas) duct, escape, outlet

Abzug *(m)*, **ohne** without deduction
abzugsfähig deductible
abzugsfähig, nicht non-deductible
Abzugshaube *(f)* extractor hood
Abzugsrohr *(n)* offlet
Abzweigdose *(f)* conduit box
Achslast *(f)* axle load
Achteck *(n)* octagon
achteckig octagonal
Acrylglas *(n)* acrylic glass
Adapter *(m)* adapter, adaptor
administrativ administrative
Adressanhänger *(m)* address label
Adressat *(m)* addressee
Adressbuch *(n)* directory
Adresse *(f)*, **vollständige** full address
Adressenverzeichnis *(f)* address list, mailing list
adressieren address
Agentur *(f)* agency
Aggregat *(n)* aggregate, unit
Akkumulator *(m)* **(Akku)** accumulator, storage battery
Akkuschrauber *(m)* storage battery screwdriver
Akontozahlung *(f)* payment on account
Akte *(f)* file, record, document
Aktentasche *(f)* briefcase
Aktion *(f)* campaign
Aktionszone *(f)* staging area
aktualisieren bring up to date, update
Aktualisierung *(f)* update, updating
aktuell up to date, current, topical
Akustik *(f)* acoustics
Akzentbeleuchtung *(f)* key lighting
akzeptabel acceptable
akzeptieren accept; (zustimmen) agree to
Alarmanlage *(f)* alarm system
alkoholfrei nonalcoholic
Alleinstellung *(f)* island position
Alleinunterhalter(in) *(m/f)* solo entertainer
Alleinvertretung *(f)* sole agency
Alleskleber *(m)* all-purpose glue

Allgemeinbeleuchtung *(f)* general lighting
Allgemeine Deutsche Spediteurbedingungen *(f, pl)* General Conditions of Contract of German Forwarding Agents
allgemeinverbindlich generally binding
alljährlich annual, yearly
Allzweck- all-purpose
altbekannt well-known
altbewährt well-tried
alternativ alternative
Alternative *(f)* alternative
Altersgruppe *(f)* age group
altmodisch old-fashioned
Alufolie *(f)* aluminium foil, tin foil
Aluminiumknoten *(m)* aluminium node
Aluminiumleiter *(f)* aluminium ladder
Aluminiumprofil *(n)* aluminium extrusion
Aluminiumrohr *(n)* aluminium tube
Aluminiumstab *(m)* aluminium rod
Ambulanz *(f)* (Krankenwagen) ambulance; (Klinik) outpatients, outpatients department
Ampere *(n)* ampere
Amperemeter *(n)* ammeter
Amperestunde *(f)* ampere-hour
amtlich official
analog analogous; (EDV) analog (US), analogue (GB)
Analogrechner *(m)* analog computer (US), analogue computer (GB)
Analyse *(f)* analysis
analysieren analyze (US); analyse (GB)
anberaumen arrange, fix; (verabreden) appoint
anbieten offer, make an offer
Anbieter *(m)* provider, supplier, bidder, marketer; (Vertrag) offerer, offeror
anbringen (befestigen) fix, fasten
ändern alter, change, modify
andersherum the other way round
Änderung *(f)* alteration, change, modification

Andrang *(m)* crowd, rush, run, throng of people, congestion
Anfahrt *(f)* (Zufahrt) approach
Anfahrtsplan *(m)* **zur Messe** route to the exhibition
Anfahrtsweg *(m)* access route, approach road, driveway
anfertigen make; (herstellen) manufacture
anfordern ask for, demand, request
Anforderung *(f)* demand, request
Anforderungszettel *(m)* request slip
Anfrage *(f)* inquiry (US); enquiry (GB); (Ersuchen) request
Angebot *(n)* offer; (Waren) supply; (Preis) quote, bid
Angebot *(n)* **und Nachfrage** *(f)* supply and demand
Angebot *(n)*, **beschränktes** limited offer
Angebot *(n)*, **bindendes** binding bid, binding offer, binding tender
Angebot *(n)*, **festes** firm offer
Angebot *(n)*, **unverbindliches** without obligation, not binding offer
Angebotspreis *(m)* supply price
Angel *(f)* (Tür) hinge
Angelegenheit *(f)* affair, matter
Angelegenheit *(f)*, **geschäftliche** business matter
angemessen suitable, appropriate, adequate; (Preis) reasonable
angeschlossen connected, linked-up
Angestellte(r) *(f/m)* employee
Angestellte(r) *(f/m)*, **leitende(r)** executive, top executive
angrenzen border
Anhang *(m)* appendix
Anhänger *(m)* (PKW, LKW) trailer
anheben lift, lift up
Animation *(f)* (Darstellung) animated view
ankleben stick on, stick to
anklopfen knock
Ankündigung *(f)* announcement
Ankunftsdatum *(n)* date of arrival

Ankunftszeit *(f)* time of arrival
Anlass *(m)* cause; (Gelegenheit) occasion
anlässlich on the occasion of
Anleitung *(f)* directions, instructions
anliefern deliver
Anlieferung *(f)* delivery
Anlieferung *(f)* **von Messegut** delivery of exhibition materials
Anlieferung *(f)*, **kostenfreie** free delivery
Anmeldebestätigung *(f)* registration confirmation
Anmeldeformular *(n)* registration form, application form
Anmeldegebühr *(f)* registration fee, application fee
anmelden announce; (beantragen) apply for; (Zoll) declare
Anmeldeschluss *(m)* closing date for application, closing date for entries, closing deadline for registration
Anmeldung *(f)* (Messebeteiligung etc.) registration; (Antrag) application
Anmeldung *(f)* (von Musikwiedergabe) **bei der GEMA** application to the performing rights society
Anmeldung *(f)*, **Zurücknahme der** cancellation of registration, withdrawal of registration
Anmietung *(f)* leasing, renting, hiring
Annahme *(f)* acceptance
Annonce *(f)* advertisement
annullieren annul, cancel
anordnen (arrangieren) arrange; (anweisen) order, direct
Anordnung *(f)* (Arrangement) arrangement, grouping, layout, composition; (Anweisung) order, direction
anpassen adapt, adjust, fit
Anpassung *(f)* adaption, adjustment
anrechenbar chargeable
anrechnen (berechnen) charge; (gutschreiben) credit, allow, take into account

anregen stimulate, encourage; (vorschlagen) suggest
Anregung *(f)* stimulation, encouragement; (Vorschlag) suggestion
Anreise *(f)* journey, journey there
anreisen travel, arrive
Anreisetag *(m)* day of arrival
Anruf *(m)* (Telefonat) call, phone call, telephone call
Anrufbeantworter *(m)* answering machine, telephone answering machine
anrufen (telefonieren) call, ring
Ansage *(f)* announcement
Ansammlung *(f)* accumulation; (Menschen) gathering, crowd; (Zusammenstellung) collection
Anschaffung *(f)* purchase, acquisition
Anschaffungskosten *(pl)* purchase cost
anschalten switch on, turn on
anschaulich clear
Anschauungsmaterial *(n)* visual aid
Anschlagbrett *(n)* billboard, noticeboard
anschließen (Strom etc.) connect
Anschluss *(m)* (Strom etc.) connection
Anschlussarmatur *(f)* connection fitting
Anschlüsse *(m, pl)*, **technische** service connections
Anschlussflug *(m)* connecting flight
Anschlusskabel *(n)* connecting cable
Anschlussleistung *(f)* (Strom) total electrical loading, total voltage
Anschlussleitung *(f)* connection line; (Gas/Wasser) connection pipe
Anschlusspreis *(m)* connection price
Anschlussstück *(n)* connection piece
Anschlusswert *(m)* (Strom) connected load
Anschlusswinkel *(m)* connecting angle
Anschlusszug *(m)* connecting train
anschrauben screw on
Ansehen *(n)* reputation, prestige, standing

Ansicht *(f)* view; (Meinung) opinion, view; (Zeichnung) drawing; (Aufriss) elevation, projection
Ansichtsskizze *(f)* view sketch
Ansichtszeichnung *(f)* view drawing
ansprechen speak to, talk to, address
Ansprechpartner(in) *(m/f)* contact partner, contact person, person to talk to, person to contact
Anspruch *(m)* claim
anspruchsvoll demanding, ambitious, pretentious
Anstecknadel *(f)* pin
ansteigen (anwachsen) increase; (sich erheben) rise; (eskalieren) escalate
anstrahlen floodlight, illuminate
anstreichen paint
Anstreicher *(m)* painter
Anstrich *(m)* painting
Ansturm *(m)* run, rush, onrush
Antenne *(f)* antenna (US), aerial (GB)
Antennenanschluss *(m)* antenna connection (US), aerial connection (GB)
Antrag *(m)* application
Antragsformular *(n)* application form
Antragsteller(in) *(m/f)* applicant
Antriebsaggregat *(n)* drive assembly
Antwortcoupon *(m)* reply coupon
Antwortkarte *(f)* reply card
anweisen instruct, direct, order; (Summe) remit
Anweisung *(f)* instruction, direction, order; (Summe) remittance
anwenden use, make use of
Anwender(in) *(m/f)* user
Anwendersoftware *(f)* (EDV) application software, user software
Anwendung *(f)* use, usage, application
Anwendungsbeispiel *(n)* example of use
Anwendungsvorschrift *(f)* directions for use, instructions for use
Anwesenheit *(f)* attendance, presence
Anwesenheitsliste *(f)* attendance list, attendance register

Anzahlung *(f)* advance, deposit, payment on account
Anzeige *(f)* advertisement
anzeigen (Skala etc.) indicate
Anzeigenblatt *(n)* advertising paper, advertising journal, freesheet, free paper
Anzeigenkampagne *(f)* advertising campaign
Anzeigenkosten *(pl)* advertising rate
Anzeigenpreis *(m)* advertising rate
Anzeigenraum *(m)* advertising space
Anzeigenschluss *(m)* closing date, copy date
Anzeigenspalte *(f)* advertisement column
Anzeigentarif *(m)* advertising rate
Anzeigenwerbung *(f)* press advertising
anziehen (Besucher) attract, draw; (Schraube etc.) tighten; (Kleidung) put on
Anziehung *(f)* attraction
Anziehungskraft *(f)* force of attraction, appeal
Anzug *(m)* suit
Apparat *(m)* appliance, machinery, device, gadget
Applaus *(m)* applause
Arbeitsablauf *(m)* workflow
Arbeitsausweis *(m)* working pass
Arbeitsbedingungen *(f, pl)* operating conditions, working conditions
Arbeitsbelastung *(f)* workload
Arbeitsbühne *(f)* working platform
Arbeitserlaubnis *(f)* work permit
Arbeitsessen *(n)* working lunch, working dinner
arbeitsfähig able for work, fit for work
Arbeitsgemeinschaft *(f)* team, working group, working pool
Arbeitshandschuhe *(m, pl)* working gloves
arbeitsintensiv labor-intensive (US), labour-intensive (GB)

Arbeitskleidung *(f)* work clothes, working clothes
Arbeitsklima *(n)* work climate
Arbeitskraft *(f)* worker, labor force (US), labour force (GB)
Arbeitskräfte *(f, pl)* labor (US), labour (GB), manpower, workforce
Arbeitskräfte *(f, pl)*, **ungelernte** unskilled labor (US), unskilled labour (GB), unskilled manpower, unskilled workers
Arbeitsmitteln *(n, pl)*, **Einsatz von** use of working aids
Arbeitsmittelreinigung *(f)* tool cleaning
Arbeitsniederlegung *(f)* strike, walkout
Arbeitspapiere *(n, pl)* working papers
Arbeitsplatte *(f)* work panel
Arbeitsplatz *(m)* (Stelle) job; (Ort) work place
Arbeitsraum *(m)* workroom
arbeitsscheu work-shy
Arbeitsschluss *(m)* end of work
Arbeitsschutz *(m)* industrial safety, maintenance of industrial health and safety standards
Arbeitsschutzvorschriften *(f, pl)* health and safety regulations
Arbeitssicherheit *(f)* industrial health, occupational health and safety, job security
arbeitssparend labor-saving (US), labour-saving (GB)
Arbeitsstunde *(f)* man hour
Arbeitstag *(m)* working day
Arbeitsteilung *(f)* division of labor (US), division of labour (GB)
arbeitsunfähig disabled, unfit for work
Arbeitsunfall *(m)* industrial accident
Arbeitsunterweisung *(f)* job instruction
Arbeitsvermittlung *(f)* employment agency
Arbeitsvertrag *(m)* employment contract, contract of employment
Arbeitsvorbereitung *(f)* operations scheduling

Arbeitszeit *(f)* working hours
Architekt *(m)* architect
architektonisch architectural
Archivbild *(n)* library picture
Ärger *(m)* trouble
Argument *(n)* argument
argumentieren argue
Armatur *(f)* fitting
arrangieren arrange
Artikel *(m)* (Schriftstück) article; (Ware) article, item; (Produkt) product
Arzt *(m)* doctor, physician
ärztliche Hilfe *(f)* medical assistance, medical care
ärztliches Attest *(n)* medical certificate, doctor's certificate
Ascher *(m)* ashtray
Aspekt *(m)* aspect
ästhetisch aesthetic
asymmetrisch asymmetric, asymmetrical
Atmosphäre *(f)* atmosphere
Attraktion *(f)* attraction
attraktiv attractive
Attrappe *(f)* dummy; (Schaupackung) dummy pack; (Schaustück) show piece
Audioanlage *(f)* audio set
Audiomischer *(m)* audio mixer
audiovisuell audiovisual
Aufbau *(m)* (Stand) building, set-up, setting up, construction, erection, installation
Aufbauanleitung *(f)* assembly instructions, installation instructions
Aufbauausweis *(m)* pass for assembly, installation labor pass (US), installation labour pass (GB)
Aufbaubeginn *(m)* installation start, start of construction, start of setting up
aufbauen (Stand) build, erect, construct, assemble, set up
Aufbauhöhe *(f)* construction height, structure height
Aufbaukarte *(f)* installation pass, labor pass (US), labour pass (GB), setting-up ticket

Aufbaupersonal *(n)* construction staff, assembly staff, setting-up personnel
Aufbaurichtlinien *(f, pl)* installation rules, provisions on construction, provisions on setting up
Aufbauschluss *(m)* installation deadline
Aufbauten *(pl)* superstructure
Aufbautermine *(m, pl)* construction dates, erection dates, installation dates
Aufbauzeit *(f)* construction times, build-up period
Aufbauzeit *(f)***, verlängerte** installation time extension
aufbewahren keep; (Wertsachen) look after
Aufbewahrung *(f)* keeping, storage, left luggage office
Aufbewahrungsschein *(m)* baggage ticket (US), luggage ticket (GB)
aufblasen blow up
aufdrehen (Hahn etc.) turn on; (Schraube) unscrew
Aufdruck *(m)* imprint
aufdrucken print on
Aufenthalt *(m)* stay, stop
Auffangbehälter *(m)* spill basin
Aufführung *(f)* performance, show
Aufführungsrechte *(n, pl)* performing rights
Aufgabe *(f)* task, function, job, assignment
Aufgeld *(n)* surcharge
aufhängen hang up, hang on
Aufklebeadresse *(f)* gummed address
aufkleben glue on, stick on; (Foto) mount
Aufkleber *(m)* sticker
aufladen (Güter) load; (Batterie) charge
Auflage *(f)* (Buch) edition; (Zeitung) circulation; (Bedingung) condition; (Vorschrift) regulation; (Schicht) layer; (Stütze) rest, support
Auflage *(f)***, verkaufte** net paid circulation

Auflagebügel *(m)* (Regalboden etc.) shelf support
Auflagewinkel *(m)* (Regalboden etc.) supporting angle
Auflaufposition *(f)* (Messestandlage) high-traffic location
Auflösung *(f)* (Bild) resolution
Aufmachung *(f)* (Darstellung) presentation; (Druck) layout; (Kleidung) outfit
Aufmaß *(n)* **vor Ort** measurement on site
aufmerksam attentive
Aufmerksamkeit *(f)* attention
Aufnahme *(f)* (Foto) photo, photograph; (Aufnehmen) taking, shot, shooting; (Ton) recording, sound recording
Aufplanung *(f)* allocation of stand space
Aufplanungsbeginn *(m)* start for allocation of stand space
Aufpreis *(m)* extra charge, surcharge
aufräumen tidy, tidy up
aufrecht erect, upright
aufregen excite, upset
Aufregung *(f)* excitement
aufreihen line up
aufrichten set upright
Aufriss *(m)* (Zeichnung) elevation
aufrollen roll up, unroll
Aufschlag *(m)* surcharge, additional charge, extra charge
aufschließen unlock, open
aufschrauben unscrew
Aufschrift *(f)* inscription
Aufsehen *(n)* **erregen** attract attention, cause a sensation
Aufseher(in) *(m/f)* attendant, supervisor
Aufsicht *(f)* supervision
Aufsichtsperson *(f)* supervisor
Aufsichtspflicht *(f)* duty of supervision, obligatory supervision
aufspannen spread, spread out
aufstellen (Exponat etc.) install, set up; (anordnen) arrange; (postieren) place; (Leiter) raise

Aufstellkosten *(pl)* installation costs
Aufstellung *(f)* (Liste etc.) list, table, survey; (Maschine etc.) installation, setting up
aufstocken scale up
auftauen (Tiefkühlkost etc.) defrost
Auftrag *(m)* order
Auftrag *(m)* **erteilen** place an order
Auftraggeber(in) *(m/f)* client, customer, purchaser
Auftragsbestätigung *(f)* (vom Kunden) confirmation; (vom Anbieter) acknowledgement
Auftragsbuch *(n)* order book
Auftragseingang *(m)* incoming orders
Auftritt *(m)*, **imagebildender** image building appearance
Aufwand *(m)* expenditure; (Kosten) cost, expense
aufwändig costly, expensive
Aufwandsentschädigung *(f)* expense allowance
Aufwartefrau *(f)* charwoman
Aufwärtsentwicklung *(f)* upward trend
Aufwendung *(f)*, **außerordentliche** extraordinary expenses, extraordinary expenditure
aufzählen enumerate, list; (aufführen, spezifizieren) specify
Aufzählung *(f)* enumeration
aufzeichnen record; (Video) tape, video-tape; (Tonband) tape, tape-record
Aufzeichnung *(f)* (Notiz) note; (TV etc.) recording
Aufzug *(m)* elevator (US), lift (GB)
Augenschraube *(f)* eyebolt
AUMA (Ausstellungs- und Messe-Ausschuss der Deutschen Wirtschaft e.V.) Association of the German Trade Fair Industry
AUMA-Auslandsmesseprogramm *(n)* AUMA Trade Fair Data Worldwide
AUMA-Gebühr *(f)* AUMA fee
ausarbeiten work out

Ausbau *(m)* expansion, extension; (Festigung) consolidation
ausbauen expand, extend
ausbessern mend, repair
Ausdruck *(m)* printout
ausdrucken print out
Ausfachmaterial *(n)* infill materials
Ausfahrt *(f)* exit
Ausfall *(m)* (Defekt) failure, breakdown; (Veranstaltung) cancellation of the event
ausfallen (Defekt) fail, break down; (Veranstaltung) be cancelled
ausführen carry out
Ausfuhrlizenz *(f)* export license (US), export licence (GB)
Ausfuhrpapiere *(n, pl)* export documents
ausfüllen (Antrag etc.) fill in, fill out
Ausgabe *(f)* (Herausgabe) handing out, distribution; (Zeitschrift etc.) issue, number; (Kosten) expenses, costs; (Computer) output
Ausgang *(m)* way out, exit; (Ergebnis) outcome
Ausgangspunkt *(m)* starting point, base
Ausgangstor *(n)* exit gate
Ausgangstür *(f)* exit door
ausgeben (weggeben) give out, hand out, distribute; (Geld) spend
ausgebucht booked up, fully booked
ausgenommen except, excepting, with the exception of
ausgesucht select, exquisite
Ausgleichsboden *(m)* adjustable floor
Ausguss *(m)* sink, outlet
aushandeln bargain
Aushang *(m)* notice, bulletin
aushelfen help out
Aushilfe *(f)* help; (Person) temporary help, part-timer
Aushilfskraft *(f)* temporary worker, (coll.) temp
Auskunftsbüro *(n)* information office
Auskunftsschalter *(m)* information desk

ausladen unload
Auslage *(f)* (Kosten) expense; (Waren) display
Ausland *(n)* foreign countries
Ausländer(in) *(m/f)* foreigner
ausländisch foreign
Auslandsbesucher *(m, pl)* international attendees
Auslandsbeteiligung *(f)* foreign participation, international participation
Auslandsdelegation *(f)* inward mission
Auslandsfachbesucher *(m, pl)* international trade attendance
Auslandsgespräch *(n)* international call
Auslandskrankenschein *(m)* proof of foreign medical coverage
Auslandskrankenversicherung *(f)* health insurance for abroad
Auslandskunde *(m)* foreign customer
Auslandskundin *(f)* foreign customer
Auslandsmesse *(f)* foreign exhibition, foreign fair, foreign trade fair
Auslandsmesseförderung *(f)* foreign exhibitions sponsoring
Auslandsmesseprogramm *(n)* foreign exhibitions program (US), foreign exhibitions programme (GB)
Auslandsüberweisung *(f)* overseas transfer, overseas bank transfer
Auslandsvertretung *(f)* overseas representation
Auslassungspunkt *(m)* **für Abhängungen** suspension point
Auslaufmodell *(n)* phase-out model
Ausleger *(m)* (Kran) boom
Auslegestrahler *(m)* cantilever spotlight, spot mounted on arm
Auslegeware *(f)* (Teppichboden) floor coverings
ausleihen lend, lend out, loan
ausleuchten illuminate
ausliefern hand out, hand over, deliver
Auslieferung *(f)* (Ware) delivery
auslosen draw, draw lots
auslösen (Kamera) release

Auslöser *(m)* trigger; (Kamera) release, shutter-release
Auslosung *(f)* draw
Ausmaß *(n)* size, dimensions
ausmessen measure, measure out
Ausnahme *(f)* exception
ausnahmsweise as an exception, by way of exception, once, for once
auspacken unpack, unwrap
ausräumen (Stand etc.) clear, clear out
ausrichten align
Ausrichtung *(f)* alignment
ausrollen (Teppichbahn etc.) unroll, roll out
Ausrufanlage *(f)* public address system
ausrufen (Ausrufanlage) call out, have s.o. paged
Ausrüstung *(f)* equipment
Aussage *(f)* statement
ausschalten (Licht etc.) switch off, turn off; (Strom) cut out
Ausschalter *(m)* circuit breaker
ausschlaggebend decisive
ausschließlich exclusive, exclusively
Ausschluss *(m)* (von Veranstaltung etc.) exclusion
Ausschluss *(m)* **der Gewährleistung** exclusion of warranty, exclusion of seller's warranty, exclusion of liability
Ausschluss *(m)* **von Ausstellern** exclusion of exhibitors
Ausschluss *(m)* **von Exponaten** exclusion of exhibits
ausschmücken decorate
ausschneiden cut out, clip
Ausschnittdienst *(m)* clipping service, press cutting agency
ausschreiben (Projekt) invite tenders
Ausschreibung *(f)* invitation of tenders, invitation to bid
Ausschreibung *(f)***, öffentliche** public invitation to bid, invitation to make an offer, advertised bidding
Ausschuss *(m)* (Gremium) committee

Ausschussmitglied *(n)* committee member
Ausschusssitzung *(f)* committee meeting
Aussehen *(n)* looks, appearance
außen outside, on the outside; (von außen) from outside, from the outside; (nach außen) outwards
Außenanstrich *(m)* outside coating
Außendienst *(m)* field work, external duty
Außendienstmitarbeiter(in) *(m/f)* field worker, sales representative
Außenecke *(f)* external corner, outer corner
Außengewinde *(n)* screw on the outer side
Außenhandel *(m)* external trade, foreign trade, overseas trade
Außenwerbung *(f)* outdoor advertising
außergewöhnlich exceptional, unusual, uncommon
außerhalb outside, out of
außerordentlich extraordinary, unusual, outstanding, remarkable
Aussicht *(f)* view
aussparen leave open
Aussparung *(f)* (Lücke) gap, cut out
ausstatten equip, fit out, furnish
Ausstattung *(f)* equipment, outfit, furnishing; (Gestaltung) design
Ausstattung *(f)* **eines Stands** stand furnishing, stand outfitting
Ausstattungsvariante *(f)* design variation
Aussteifungsprofil *(n)* reinforcing profile
ausstellen exhibit, show, display
Aussteller *(m)* exhibitor
Aussteller *(m, pl)***, ausländische** foreign exhibitors, international exhibitors
Ausstelleranalyse *(f)* exhibitor analysis
Ausstellerausweis *(m)* exhibitor card, exhibitor pass
Ausstellerbefragung *(f)* exhibitor survey

Ausstellerbeirat *(m)* exhibitor advisory board, exhibitor committee
Ausstellerbetreuung *(f)* advice for exhibitors
Ausstellerdatenbank *(f)* exhibitors' data base
Ausstellereinladung *(m)* exhibitors' invitation; (Schlussveranstaltung) end-of-show party
Ausstellerfirmen *(f, pl)* exhibiting firms
Ausstellerfrequenz *(f)* exhibitor participation frequency
Ausstellerinformation *(f)* exhibitor information, exhibitor advisories
Ausstellerkarte *(f)* exhibitor ticket
Ausstellerkarten *(f, pl)*, **zusätzliche** additional exhibitor passes, additional exhibitor tickets
Ausstellerliste *(f)* exhibitor list
Ausstellerparkplatz *(m)* exhibitor carpark
Ausstellerservice *(m)* services for exhibitors
Ausstellerservicemappe *(f)* exhibitors' service kit, exhibitors' service folder
Ausstellerstruktur *(f)* exhibitor structure, exhibitor makeup
Ausstellerverzeichnis *(n)* index of exhibitors, list of exhibitors
Ausstellerverzeichnis *(n)*, **alphabetisches** alphabetical list of exhibitors
Ausstellerzahl *(f)* number of exhibitors
Ausstellung *(f)* exhibition, exposition, fair, show
Ausstellung *(f)* **besuchen** attend an exhibition, attend a fair
Ausstellung *(f)*, **nationale** national exhibition, national fair
Ausstellung *(f)*, **regionale** local exhibition, local fair, regional exhibition, regional fair
Ausstellung *(f)*, **überregionale** supraregional exhibition, supraregional fair, supraregional show

Ausstellungsbereiche *(m, pl)* exhibition grouping, exhibition sections
Ausstellungsbeteiligung *(f)* exhibition participation
Ausstellungsbudget *(n)* exhibition budget
Ausstellungsdauer *(f)* show duration
Ausstellungsfläche *(f)* exibition area
Ausstellungsfläche *(f)*, **belegte** booked exhibition area, rented stand space
Ausstellungsfläche *(f)*, **Zuweisung der** space assignment, stand space assignment, stand allocation, stand space allocation
Ausstellungsgelände *(n)* exhibition grounds, fair grounds
Ausstellungsgut *(n)* exhibits, exhibit materials, exhibition goods
Ausstellungsgüter *(n, pl)*, **vereinbarte** agreed exhibits
Ausstellungshalle *(f)* exhibition hall
Ausstellungskatalog *(m)* exhibition catalog (US), exhibition catalogue (GB)
Ausstellungskomitee *(n)* exhibition committee
Ausstellungslaufzeit *(f)* exhibition period
Ausstellungsleitung *(f)* exhibition management
Ausstellungsort *(m)* (Veranstaltungsort) venue; (Dokument) place of issue
Ausstellungsprogramm *(n)* exhibition program (US), exhibition programme (GB)
Ausstellungsraum *(m)* exhibition room, show room
Ausstellungsschluss *(m)* close of the exhibition, close of the fair
Ausstellungsstand *(m)* stand, booth, exhibition stand
Ausstellungstagung *(f)* exhibition congress, conference and exhibition
Ausstellungsveranstalter *(m)* exhibition organizer, show organizer

Ausstellungsversicherung *(f)* exhibition insurance, fair insurance
Ausstellungswagen *(m)* promotion mobile
Ausstiegsluke *(f)* hatch, escape hatch
Austausch *(m)* exchange
austauschbar exchangeable, interchangeable
austauschen exchange; (ersetzen) replace, substitute
ausüben practise (US), practice (GB)
Ausverkauf *(m)* sale, clearance sale, selling off
ausverkaufen clear off, sell out
Auswahl *(f)* selection; (Sortiment) assortment; (Auslese) choice; (Reihe) range; (Vielfalt) variety
Auswahl *(f)* **von Messen** choise of exhibitions, selection of exhibitions
Auswahl *(f)*, **reichhaltige** wide selection
auswählen choose, select
Ausweis *(m)* pass, card
ausweisen identify
Ausweisnummer *(f)* I.D. number, identity number
Ausweispapiere *(n, pl)* identity papers, identification papers
ausweiten expand
auswerten analyse, evaluate
Auswertung *(f)* analysis, evaluation
Auswirkung *(f)* effect, consequence
Auszeichnung *(f)* (Preisgewinn) award; (Ware) labelling
Auszugsplatte *(f)* pull-out shelf
Autoanhänger *(m)* trailer
Autoausfahrt *(f)* exit drive
Autoeinfahrt *(f)* way in
Automat *(m)* dispenser, vending machine
Autoverleih *(m)* car rental (US), car hire (GB)
Autovermietung *(f)* car rental service (US), renting of cars (US), car hire service (GB)

B

Bagger *(m)* excavator
Bahnenware *(f)* (Teppich) off-the-roll carpeting
Bahnfahrkarte *(f)* railroad ticket (US), railway ticket (GB)
Bahnfracht *(f)* rail carriage, rail freight
Bahnhof *(m)* railroad station (US), railway station (GB)
Bahntarif *(m)* railroad rates (US), railway rates (GB)
Bahnverbindung *(f)* train connection
Balken *(m)* beam
Balkendecke *(f)* ceiling with wooden beams, timbered ceiling
Balkendiagramm *(n)* bar chart
Balkenkonstruktion *(f)* timber-frame construction
Ballon *(m)* balloon
Band *(n)* ribbon; (Musikband) band; (Isolier-, Klebe-, Tonband) tape
Bandaufnahme *(f)* tape-recording
Bandmaß *(n)* tape measure, measuring tape
Bandsäge *(f)* band-saw
Bankautomat *(m)* cash dispenser
Bankett *(n)* banquet
Bankettraum *(m)* banquet room
Bankkonto *(n)* bank account
Banknote *(f)* bill (US), banknote (GB), currency note (GB)
Banküberweisung *(f)* bank transfer
Banner *(n)* banner, standard
bar cash
Bar *(f)* nightclub, bar
bar bezahlen pay cash
Bargeld *(n)* cash, cash on the hand, hard cash, ready cash
bargeldlos cashless, non-cash
Barhocker *(m)* barstool
Barhocker *(m)* **mit Lehne** bar stool with backrest

Barmöbel *(pl)* bar furniture
Bartheke *(f)* bar, bar counter
Barzahlung *(f)* cash payment, payment in cash
Basis *(f)* base, basis
Basisausstattung *(f)* basic fittings; (Stand) basic stand package
Basiseintrag *(m)* (Katalog etc.) basic entry
Basisjahr *(n)* base year
Batterie *(f)* battery
batteriebetrieben battery operated
Batterieladegerät *(n)* battery charger
Bau *(m)* construction, structure; (Gebäude) building
Bauabnahme *(f)* construction inspection, acceptance of construction work
Bauanfrage *(f)* building request, construction request
Bauarbeiten *(pl)* construction work
Bauaufsichtsbehörde *(f)* building supervisory board
Bauaufsichtsbestimmungen *(f, pl)* construction regulations
Baubeschreibung *(f)* building description, construction specification
Bauelement *(n)* building component, construction component, structural element
Baugenehmigung *(f)* construction permit, construction permission, building approval, planning and building permission
Bauhöhe *(f)* construction height
Bauhöhe *(f)* **des Stands** stand height
Baukastensystem *(n)* modular system
Baumaterial *(n)* building material
Bauordnung *(f)* building regulations
Bauordnungsamt *(n)* building authority, construction authority, department of building
Bauplan *(m)* architect's plan, building plan
Bauschutt *(m)* building waste, construction debris

Baustelle *(f)* building site, construction site
Baustoff *(m)* building material, construction material
Baustoffe *(m, pl)*, **leicht entflammbare** highly flammable materials, high fire risk materials
Baustoffe *(m, pl)*, **nichtbrennbare** nonflammable materials
Baustoffe *(m, pl)*, **normalentflammbare** normal-flammability materials
Baustoffklassen *(f, pl)* construction materials classification
Bauten *(m, pl)*, **fliegende** portable constructions, portable structures
Bauten *(m, pl)*, **nicht genehmigte** non-approved structures
Bauweise *(f)* type of construction
Bauweise *(f)*, **mehrgeschossige** multi-story building (US), multi-storey building (GB)
beabsichtigen intend, plan, aim at
beachten pay attention to, note; (Regelung, Vorschrift) observe
Beachtung *(f)* attention; (von Regelung, Vorschrift) observing
beanstanden object to, complain about
Beanstandung *(f)* objection, complaint
beantragen apply for
bearbeiten work on
Bearbeitung *(f)* handling, working
Bearbeitungsgebühr *(f)* charge for handling, handling charge, processing fees
beaufsichtigen supervise
Beaufsichtigung *(f)* supervision
beauftragen engage, instruct, charge with, commission
Bedarf *(m)* need, requirement, demand
Bedarf *(m)* **an Arbeitskräften** manpower requirement
Bedarfsanalyse *(f)* demand analysis
bedauern regret
bedeutend important, considerable, great

Bedeutung *(f)* **von Messen** importance of exhibitions, show impact and status
bedienen (Maschine) operate, run; (Kunden) attend, serve, wait on
Bedienung *(f)* service; (Lokal) waiter, waitress, attendance; (Technik) operation
Bedienung *(f)* **inbegriffen** service included
Bedienung *(f)* **nicht inbegriffen** service not included
Bedienungsanleitung *(f)* instructions for use, operating instructions, operating manual
Bedienungspersonal *(n)* attendants, service staff
Bedienungszuschlag *(m)* service charge, extra charge for service
Bedingungen *(f)* conditions, terms
Bedürfnis *(n)* need
beeindrucken impress
beeinträchtigen abridge, detract, impair, interfere
Beeinträchtigung *(f)* abridgement, detraction, impairment, encroachment, infringement
beenden conclude, close, end, finish
Beendigung *(f)* conclusion, close, end; (Abschluss) completion
befahrbar passable
Befahrbarkeit *(f)* trafficability
befestigen fasten, fix
Befestigung *(f)* fastening, fixing
Befestigung *(f)* **im Hallenboden** fixing to the hall floor, floor anchoring
Befestigungspunkt *(m)* **für Abhängungen** suspension point
Befestigungsschiene *(f)* fixing rail
beflaggen flag
befördern convey, transport, forward
Beförderung *(f)* (Transport) conveyance, transport, transportation, forwarding, shipment; (Rang) promotion
Beförderungsband *(n)* conveyer belt

Beförderungskosten *(pl)* transport charges, haulage
Beförderungsmittel *(n)* means of transportation
befragen canvass, interview
Befragte(r) *(m/f)* informant, interviewee, respondent
Befragung *(f)* interview; (Erhebung) survey; (Öffentlichkeit) public opinion poll
befristet limited, restricted
Befugnis *(f)* authority, authorization
befugt authorized
Begegnung *(f)* meeting
begleiten accompany
Begleitperson *(f)* accompanying person
Begrenzung *(f)* limiting, limitation, restriction
begrüßen greet, welcome
Begrüßung *(f)* greeting, welcome
Begrüßungsansprache *(f)* welcoming speech
Begrüßungsgetränk *(n)* welcome drink
Behälter *(m)* container, bin
behaupten claim, maintain, say
Behauptung *(f)* claim, maintenance, assertion
beheizen heat
beherbergen accommodate, lodge, put up
behindern hinder, hamper, obstruct
beidseitig double sided; (auf beiden Seiten) on both sides
Beifall *(m)* applause,
Beifall *(m)* **spenden** applaud
Beilage *(f)* supplement, enclosure, insert
beilegen enclose, insert
beiliegend enclosed
Beipackzettel *(m)* instructions, instruction leaflet
Beirat *(m)* advisory board, advisory council
Beisammensein *(n)* gathering, get-together
Beispiel *(n)* example

Beispiel *(n)*, **zum** for example, for instance
beispielsweise for example, for instance
Beißzange *(f)* pliers, a pair of pincers
Beistelltisch *(m)* occasional table
Beitrag *(m)* (Geld) contribution; (Mitgliedschaft) fee; (Versicherung) premium
bekannt known, well-known
bekannt machen, jdn. introduce s.o.
Bekannte(r) *(f/m)* acquaintance
Bekanntgabe *(f)* announcement, publication
Bekanntheit *(f)* awareness
Bekanntheitsgrad *(m)* customer awareness, name recognition, degree of fame
bekleben (mit Klebstoff) paste over; (mit etw. bekleben) paste on, stick on, stick onto
bekräftigen confirm
Bekräftigung *(f)* confirmation
beladen load
Beladungsgrenze *(f)* maximum load
Belag *(m)* covering; (Überzug) coating; (Brot etc.) filling; (Brotaufstrich) spread
Belastbarkeit *(f)* maximum capacity, load-bearing capacity
Belastbarkeit *(f)* **des Hallenbodens** hall floor loading capacity, hall floor load-bearing capacity
Belastung *(f)* (Last) load, loading
Belastungswert *(m)* load-bearing capacity, load value, loading value
Beleg *(m)* (Quittung) receipt; (Schein) voucher
Belegexemplar *(n)* author's copy, specimen copy
beleuchten light, light up, illuminate
Beleuchtung *(f)* lights, lighting, illumination
Beleuchtungseffekt *(m)* lighting effect, illumination effect

Beleuchtungseinspeisung *(f)* lighting inlet
Beleuchtungskonzept *(n)* lighting concept
Beleuchtungskörper *(m)* lighting appliance
Beleuchtungsstärke *(f)* illumination level
Belichtung *(f)* (Kamera) exposure
beliefern supply
Belieferung *(f)* supply
belüften ventilate
Belüftung *(f)* ventilation
Belüftungsanlage *(f)* ventilation system
bemängeln complain, criticize, fault
bemerken notice; (äußern) remark
bemerkenswert remarkable
Bemessung *(f)* **der Standgröße** determination of stand size
benachrichtigen advise, inform, notify
Benachrichtigung *(f)* advice, notification
benötigen need, require; (dringend) be in urgent need
Benutzer(in) *(m/f)* user
benutzerfreundlich user-friendly
Benutzerhandbuch *(n)* handbook, user handbook, operating manual, user's guide
Benutzername *(m)* (Computer) user name
Benutzeroberfläche *(f)* (Computer) user interface, system interface
Benutzeroberfläche *(f)*, **grafische** graphical user interface
Benutzung *(f)* use
Benutzungsgebühr *(f)* fee, charge
beobachten observe, watch
bequem comfortable; (gelegen) convenient; (leicht) easy
Bequemlichkeit *(f)* comfort, convenience, ease
beraten advise
beraten lassen, sich ask s.o.'s advise
beraten werden get advice

beratend advisory, consultative, consulting, deliberative
Beratung *(f)* advice, consultation, counseling (US), counselling (GB), consultancy
Berechnung *(f)* calculation
Berechnung *(f)*, **ohne** free of charge
Berechnung *(f)*, **statische** static calculation, technical calculation
Berechnung *(f)*, **überschlägige** estimate, rough estimate
berechtigt authorized, entitled, legitimate
Berechtigung *(f)* authorization, legitimacy, right
Bereich *(m)* area
bereitstellen provide, supply, make available
Bereitstellung *(f)* provision
Bericht *(m)* report
berichten report
Berieselung *(f)* (Musik etc.) constant stream, constant exposure
berücksichtigen consider, take into consideration
Berücksichtigung *(f)* consideration
Beruf *(m)* occupation, profession
Besatzung *(f)* (Stand etc.) crew
beschädigen damage
Beschädigung *(f)* damage, damaging
Beschädigung *(f)*, **mutwillige** malicious damage
Beschaffung *(f)* obtaining, procurement, procuring
Beschäftigung *(f)* activity, engagement; (Tätigkeit) occupation; (Beruf) employment
Bescheid *(m)* note, notice; (Antwort) answer; (Mitteilung) information
bescheinigen certify, attest; (Empfang) acknowledge receipt
Bescheinigung *(f)* attestation, certificate, certification
beschicken (Messe) exhibit a fair
Beschickung *(f)* (Messe) fairgoing

Beschilderung *(f)* signposting
Beschlag *(m)* (Tür) mounting
beschließen decide
Beschluss *(m)* decision, resolution
beschränken limit, restrict
Beschränkung *(f)* limitation, restriction
beschreiben describe
Beschreibung *(f)* description, specification
beschriften inscribe; (Umschlag) address; (Leergut etc.) mark
Beschriftung *(f)* inscription
Beschwerde *(f)* complaint
beschweren, sich complain
beschwichtigen appease, calm, calm down
Beseitigung *(f)* removal; (Abfall) disposal
Besen *(m)* broom
besetzt full, full up, occupied; (Platz) taken; (Telefon) engaged
Besetztzeichen *(n)* engaged signal, engaged tone
Besichtigung *(f)* visit, inspection
besonders especially, particulary, chiefly
besprechen discuss, talk over
Besprechung *(f)* (Unterredung) discussion; (Sitzung) conference
Besprechungskabine *(f)* conference cabin, conference cubicle
Besprechungszimmer *(n)* conference room, meeting room
Bestand *(m)* (Lager) stock
Bestandskontrolle *(f)* inventory control, stock control
Bestandteil *(m)* component, part, constituent part
Bestätigung *(f)* acknowledgement, confirmation; (Bescheinigung) certificate
Bestätigung *(f)*, **schriftliche** written acknowledgement
Besteck *(n)* cutlery
Bestellbuch *(n)* order book
bestellen order
Besteller *(m)* orderer

Bestellformular

Bestellformular *(n)* order form
Bestellung *(f)* booking, order
Bestellung *(f)*, **telefonische** order by telephone
Bestellvordruck *(m)* order form
bestimmen determine
Bestimmung *(f)*, **gesetzliche** legal regulation
Bestrebung *(f)* attempt, endeavor (US), endeavour (GB); (Zweck, Absicht) aim
bestreiten contest, dispute; (leugnen) deny
bestücken equip, fit, provide
Bestückung *(f)* equipment
Bestuhlung *(f)* seating
Besuch *(m)* visit; (kurzer Besuch) call; (Teilnahme) attendance
Besucher *(m, pl)*, **ausländische** visitors from abroad
Besucher(in) *(m/f)* visitor, caller, guest
Besucherakquisition *(f)* canvassing, visitor canvassing
Besucheranalyse *(f)* attendance analysis, visitors profile
Besucherbefragung *(f)* visitor interview, visitor survey
Besucherinformationssystem *(n)* visitor information system
Besucherkarte *(f)* visitor pass
Besuchermasse *(f)* mass audience
Besucherprospekt *(m)* visitor brochure, visitors leaflet
Besucherqualität *(f)* audience qualification
Besucherstatistik *(f)* attendance statistics
Besucherstruktur *(f)* audience profile
Besucherwerbung *(f)* attendance promotion
Besucherzahl *(f)* number of visitors
Besucherzulassung *(f)* visitor admittance, visitor authorization
Besuchsbericht *(m)* visit report, call report
Besuchshäufigkeit *(f)* call frequency

Besuchsplanung *(f)* call planning
Besuchszeit *(f)* visiting hours
beteiligen an, sich participate in, take part in
Beteiligung *(f)* **an einer Ausstellung** show participation
Beteiligung *(f)* **an einer Messe** fair participation
Beteiligung *(f)*, **individuelle** individual participation
Beteiligung *(f)*, **offizielle** official participation
Beteiligungsförderung *(f)* participation promotion
Beteiligungsformen *(f, pl)* participation forms
Beteiligungskosten *(pl)* participation costs
Beteiligungsziele *(n, pl)* participation goals, objectives of participation
Betrachtung *(f)*, **fotorealistische** photo-realistic view
Betrag *(m)* amount, sum
betreten (Stand etc.) step on, enter, go into
betreuen look after
Betrieb *(m)*, **mittelständischer** medium-sized enterprise
Betriebsanleitung *(f)* operating instructions
Betriebsdruck *(m)* line pressure, supply pressure
Betriebskosten *(pl)* operating costs, operational costs, running costs
Betriebsleitung *(f)* management, top management
Betriebssicherheitsverordnung *(f)* Industrial Safety Ordinance, Operational Safety Ordinance
Betriebssystem *(n)* (EDV) operating system
Betriebstemperatur *(f)* operating temperature
Betriebsverbot *(n)* (Geräte, Anlagen) operating prohibition

Betriebsvorschrift *(f)* (Geräte, Anlagen) operating regulation
beurteilen judge
bevollmächtigen authorize
Bevollmächtigung *(f)* authorization
bevorraten keep in stock, store, stock up
Bevorratung *(f)* provision with stocks, stockpilling
bevorzugen prefer; (begünstigen) favor (US), favour (GB)
bewachen guard, watch
Bewachung *(f)* guarding, security, surveillance
Bewachungsgesellschaft *(f)* security company
Bewachungspersonal *(n)* security guards, security personnel
Bewachungsunternehmen *(n)* security company, security service
bewährt well-tried, tried and tested
bewegen move; (in Bewegung setzen) set sth. going
beweglich movable, mobile; (agil) agile
Beweis *(m)* proof, evidence
beweisen prove
bewerten assess, judge; (einschätzen) rate
Bewertung *(f)* assessment, judgement; (Einschätzung) rating, valuation
Bewilligung *(f)* allowance, approval, permission
bewirten cater for, entertain
Bewirtung *(f)* entertaining, entertainment, hospitality, service
Bewirtungsabfall *(m)* catering waste, hospitality waste
Bewirtungskosten *(pl)* entertainment expenses, hospitality expenses
Bewirtungszone *(f)* attendance area, hospitality area
Bezahlung *(f)* payment
Beziehung *(f)* relations, relationship
Bezirksleiter *(m)* area manager

bezugsfertig (Stand etc.) ready for use, ready for occupancy
Bezugsquellennachweis *(m)* trade directory, trade register, dealer tie-in
Bier *(n)* beer
Bier *(n)* **vom Fass** beer on tap, draft beer (US), draught beer (GB)
Bier *(n)*, **dunkles** dark beer, porter, stout beer
Bier *(n)*, **englisches** ale, pale ale
Bier *(n)*, **helles** lager, light beer
Bierdeckel *(m)* beer mat
Bierdose *(f)* beer can
Bierfass *(n)* beer barrel
Bierflasche *(f)* beer bottle
Biergarten *(m)* beer garden
Bierglas *(n)* beer glass
Bierkasten *(m)* beer crate
Bierkeller *(m)* beer cellar
Bilanz *(f)* balance, balance sheet
Bild *(n)* picture; (Foto) photo; (Gemälde) painting
Bild- und Tonaufnahme *(f)* photography, video and audio recording
Bildauflösung *(f)* resolution
Bildausgabegerät *(n)* imaging output device
Bildbearbeitung *(f)*, **digitale** digital treatment of pictures
Bildeingabegerät *(n)* imaging input device
Bildmischer *(m)* video mixer
Bildplatte *(f)* video disc
Bildschärfe *(f)* picture resolution, picture definition
Bildschirm *(m)* screen
Bildschirmgerät *(n)* visual display terminal
Bildspeicher *(m)* picture memory
Bildspeichersystem *(n)* picture storage system
Bildsplitwand *(f)* (Multivision) split screen
Bildstörung *(f)* interference

Bildtafelhalter *(m)* graphic panel retainer
Bildteilersystem *(n)* (Multivision) image splitting system
Bildungsmesse *(f)* educational fair
Bildunterschrift *(f)* caption, legend, underline
Bildverarbeitung *(f)* image processing
billig cheep; (Preis) low, low-priced
Billigung *(f)* approval
Binnenmarkt *(m)* domestic market, home market
BIP *(n)* **(Bruttoinlandsprodukt)** GDP (Gross Domestic Product)
Bitte *(f)* request
bitten ask, ask for; (ersuchen) request
Blatt *(n)* (Papier) leaf, sheet; (Zeitung) paper; (Seite) page
Blattsäge *(f)* pad saw
Blende *(f)* (Kamera) aperture; (Stand) fascia, fascia board, trim panel
blenden (Licht) dazzle; (täuschen) deceive
Blendenautomatik *(f)* automatic aperture control
Blendenbeschriftung *(f)* fascia inscription, fascia board inscription
Blendring *(m)* (Lampe) anti-glare ring
Blickfang *(m)* eyecatcher
Blickkontakt *(m)* eye contact, visual contact
Blickwinkel *(m)* point of view
blinken gleam, glitter, sparkle; (aufblitzen) flash
Blisterhaken *(m)* pre-pack bracket
blitzen (Foto) flash, use flash
Blitzlicht *(n)* flash, flashlight
Blitzlichtaufnahme *(f)* flash shot
Blockbuchstabe *(m)* block letter
Blockschrift *(f)* block letters
Blockstand *(m)* island stand, island site, shell scheme booth
Blumendekoration *(f)* floral decoration
Blumenschale *(f)* jardiniere, flower bowl

Blumenstrauß *(m)* bouquet, bunch of flowers
Blumenvase *(f)* vase
Boden *(m)* (Erde) ground; (Fußboden) floor
Bodenbelag *(m)* floor covering
Bodenbelastung *(f)* floor load
Bodenbelastung *(f)***, maximale** maximum floor load
Bodenfläche *(f)* floor space
Bodenfreiheit *(f)* ground clearance
Bodenkanal *(m)* trench, duct, floor duct
Bodenschutz *(m)* ground protection
Bodenunebenheit *(f)* unevenness of the floor
Bogen *(m)* arc, arch, bow, curve; (Wölbung) vault; (Papier) sheet
bogenförmig arched
Bohle *(f)* plank, thick board
bohren bore; (mit Bohrer) drill
Bohrer *(m)* drill
Bohrloch *(n)* drill hole
Bohrschablone *(f)* drilling jig, drilling template
Bohrung *(f)* drilling
Boiler *(m)* water heater, boiler
Bolzen *(m)* bolt
Bolzenschussgerät *(n)* bolt setter, stud gun
Bonität *(f)* financial standing, credit-worthiness
Bonus *(m)* bonus
Botschaft *(f)* (Nachricht) message; (Land) embassy
Branchenadressbuch *(n)* classified directory, trade directory, yellow pages
Branchenkenntnis *(f)* trade knowledge
Branchentelefonbuch *(n)* classified telephone directory, yellow pages
branchenüblich usual in the trade
Branchenverzeichnis *(n)* classified directory, trade directory, yellow pages
Brand *(m)* fire
Brand *(m)* **geraten, in** catch fire
Brandgefahr *(f)* fire hazard

Brandschaden *(m)* fire damage
Brandschutz *(m)* fire prevention, fire protection, fire precautions
Brandschutzbestimmungen *(f, pl)* fire safety protection regulations
brandschutztechnische Bestimmungen *(f, pl)* fire prevention regulations
brandschutztechnische Einrichtungen *(f, pl)* fire protection equipment
Brandschutztor *(n)* fire safety door
Brandverhalten *(n)* **von Baustoffen, Bauteilen (DIN 4102)** flammability of construction material and components (DIN 4102)
Brandverhaltens *(n)*, **Klassifizierung des** fire properties classification
Brauch *(m)* common usage, custom, practice
Break-Even-Punkt *(m)* breakeven point
Brecheisen *(n)* crowbar
breit broad
Breitbandkabel *(f)* broadband cable
Breitbandverteilernetz *(n)* broadband distribution network
Breite *(f)* breadth, width
brennbar combustible; (leicht brennbar) flammable; (entzündbar) inflammable
brennbar, leicht flammable
brennbar, nicht non-flammable
brennbare Baustoffe *(m, pl)* flammable materials
brennbare Flüssigkeiten *(f, pl)* flammable liquids
brennen burn, be on fire
Brennpunkt *(m)* focus
Brennweite *(f)* focal length
Brett *(n)* board; (Regalbrett) shelf
Briefbogen *(m)* sheet of writing paper
Briefgebühr *(f)* letter rate
Briefkopf *(m)* letter head
Briefpapier *(n)* letter paper
Brieftasche *(f)* wallet
Briefumschlag *(m)* envelope

Briefwechsel *(m)* correspondence
Briefwerbung *(f)* direct-mail advertising
Broschüre *(f)* booklet, pamphlet
Brötchen *(n)* bun, roll; (belegt) filled roll
Brotzeit *(f)* elevenses, mid-morning snack
Bruch *(m)* break, breaking; (Schaden) breakage
Bruch *(m)* **gehen, zu** break
bruchfest unbreakable
bruchsicher breakproof
Brüstung *(f)* balustrade
Bruttoausstellungsfläche *(f)* gross exhibition area
Bruttoeinnahmen *(f, pl)* gross receipts
Bruttoerlös *(m)* gross earnings
Bruttogewicht *(n)* gross weight
Bruttogewinn *(m)* gross profit
Bruttoinlandsprodukt *(n)* **(BIP)** Gross Domestic Product (GDP)
Bruttosozialprodukt *(n)* **(BSP)** Gross National Product (GNP)
Bruttoumsatz *(m)* gross sales
BSP *(n)* **(Bruttosozialprodukt)** GNP (Gross National Product)
Buchablage *(f)* bookshelf
buchen (vorbestellen) book, reserve; (einschreiben) enter, make an entry
Buchhaltung *(f)* accounting, book-keeping; (Abteilung) accounts department
Büchsenbier *(n)* canned beer (US), tinned beer (GB)
Büchsenleiste *(f)* pin socket panel
Büchsenmilch *(f)* canned milk (US), tinned milk (GB), evaporated milk
Büchsenöffner *(m)* can opener (US), tin opener (GB)
Buchstabe *(m)* letter
Buchstabe *(m)*, **großer** capital letter
Buchstabe *(m)*, **kleiner** small letter
Buchung *(f)* (Vorbestellung) booking, reservation; (Einschreibung) entry
Buchung *(f)* **von Mitarbeitern** booking of staff

Buchung *(f)* **von Standpersonal**
  booking of stand personnel
Budget *(n)* budget
budgetieren budget
Budgetierung *(f)* budgeting
Budgetkontrolle *(f)* budgetary control
Büfett *(n)* buffet, refreshment bar
Büffet *(n)*, **kaltes** cold buffet
Bügelservice *(m)* pressing service
Bügel-Transportwagen *(m)* roll cage
Bühne *(f)* stage
Bühnenbeleuchtung *(f)* stage lighting
Bühnenbild *(n)* stage set
Bühnenleuchte *(f)* stage floodlight
Bundesimmissionsschutzgesetz *(n)*
  Federal Emissions Control Act
bündig (in Fluchtlinie) flush
bunt (farbig) colored (US), coloured (GB); (vielfarbig) colorful (US), colourful (GB), multicolored (US), multicoloured (GB)
Büromaterial *(n)* office supplies
Büromöbel *(pl)* office furniture
Bürste *(f)* brush
Busbahnhof *(m)* bus station
Bushaltestelle *(f)* bus stop
Buslinie *(f)* bus line, bus route
Bußgeld *(n)* fine

C

Camcorder *(m)* camcorder
Cappuccino *(m)* cappucino
Cateringunternehmen *(n)* caterer
Cave-Technik *(f)* **zur virtuellen Darstellung** Cave automatic virtual environment
CD-Spieler *(m)* CD player
CE-Zeichen *(n)* CE symbol, CE mark
Champagner *(m)* champagne
Chance *(f)* chance
Charakter *(m)* character

Charterflug *(m)* charter flight
chartern charter
Checkliste *(f)* check list
Chef *(m)* chief, boss, head
Chefkonstrukteur(in) *(m/f)* chief designer
Chefredakteur(in) *(m/f)* editor-in-chief
Chefsekretärin *(f)* executive assistant, personal assistant, executive secretary, private secretary
Chemikalien-Verbotsverordnung *(f)* Chemical Prohibition Ordinance
Chip *(m)* chip
Chromgestell *(n)* chrome-plated frame
Cocktail *(m)* cocktail
Cocktailglas *(n)* cocktail glass
Code *(m)* code
codieren codify, code, encode
Computerarbeitsplatz *(m)* work station
Computerausdruck *(m)* computer listing
Computerdatei *(f)* computer file
computergesteuert computer-controlled
computergestützt computer-aided
computergestützte Zeichnung *(f)* CAD (computer-aided design)
Computergrafik *(f)* computer graphics
computerisieren computerize
computerlesbar computer-readable
Computernetzwerk *(n)* computer network
Computerprogramm *(n)* computer program (US), computer programme (GB)
Computersatz *(m)* computer typesetting
Computersimulation *(f)* computer simulation
Computersprache *(f)* computer language
Computersystem *(n)* computer system
Computervirus *(m)* computer virus
Computerzeichnung *(f)* CAD (computer-aided design)

Container *(m)* container
Containerladung *(f)* container load
Containerstand *(m)* container stand
Containerstapler *(m)* container carrier truck
Containerstellfläche *(f)* container space
Containerterminal *(m, n)* container terminal, container berth
Convenienceprodukte *(n, pl)* convenience goods
Couch *(f)* couch
Couchtisch *(m)* coffee table
Coupon *(m)* coupon
Couvert *(n)* envelope

D

Dach *(n)* roof
Dachbalken *(m)* roof beam
Dachgesellschaft *(f)* holding company, parent company
Damentoilette *(f)* ladies, ladies room (US), ladies restroom (US), ladies' lavatory (GB), ladies' toilet (GB)
Dampf *(m)* steam
daneben beside, next to
Dankesworte *(pl)* words of thanks
darbieten perform
Darbietung *(f)*, **akustische** acoustic performance
Darbietung *(f)*, **musikalische** musical presentation
Darbietung *(f)*, **öffentliche** public performance
Darbietung *(f)*, **optische** visual performance
darlegen explain, show, state
Darlehen *(n)* credit, loan
Darstellung *(f)*, **dreidimensionale** three-dimensional design, three-dimensional image

Darstellung *(f)*, **grafische** graph, illustration
Darstellung *(f)*, **visuelle** visualization
Datei *(f)* file, data file
Daten *(pl)* (Technik) data; (Angaben) facts
Datenabruf *(m)* data retrieval
Datenanschluss *(m)* data connection
Datenaufbereitung *(f)* data preparation
Datenausgabe *(f)* data output
Datenaustausch *(m)* data exchange
Datenautobahn *(f)* information superhighway
Datenbank *(f)* data bank
Datenbasis *(f)* database
Datenblatt *(f)* data sheet
Dateneingabe *(f)* data input
Datenerfassung *(f)* data accumulation, data acquisition, data capture, data collection
Datenfernübertragung *(f)* data transmission
Datenfernverarbeitung *(f)* teleprocessing
Datenhandschuh *(m)* data glove
Datenleitung *(f)* data line
Datenmonitor *(m)* data monitor
Datennetz *(n)* data network
Datennetz *(n)*, **externes** external network
Datenschutz *(m)* data protection
Datensicherheit *(f)* data integrity
Datensicherung *(f)* backup
Datensichtgerät *(n)* visual display unit
Datenspeicherung *(f)* data storage
Datnträger *(m)* data carrier, data medium
Datenübermittlung *(f)* data transfer
Datenübertragung *(f)* data transmission
Datenübertragungsrate *(f)* data transmission speed
Datenverarbeitung *(f)* data processing

Datenverarbeitungsprogramm *(n)* program for data processing (US), programme for data processing (GB)
Datum *(n)* date
Dauer *(f)* **der Ausstellung** duration of the exhibition
Dauer *(f)* **der Messe** duration of the fair
Dauerausstellung *(f)* permanent exhibition
Dauerbetrieb *(m)* continuous operation, non-stop operation
dauerhaft lasting, permanent
Dauerkarte *(f)* season ticket, all-days pass
Debatte *(f)* debate
debattieren debate, discuss
Decke *(f)* (Raum) ceiling
Decke *(f)*, **geschlossene** closed ceiling
Deckel *(f)* lid, cover; (Schraubdeckel) cap, screw cap; (Buch) cover
Deckenabhängung *(f)* ceiling suspension
Deckenarten *(f, pl)* ceilings, ceiling types
Deckenarten *(f, pl)*, **zugelassene** approved ceiling types
Deckenbalken *(m)* ceiling beam
Deckenbeleuchtung *(f)* ceiling lighting
Deckenelement *(n)* ceiling element
Deckenfluter *(m)* ceiling floodlight
Deckenkonstruktion *(f)* ceiling construction
Deckenleuchte *(f)* ceiling lamp
Deckenraster *(n)* ceiling cell, ceiling grid
Deckenstrahler *(m)* ceiling-mounted spotlight
Deckungsbeitrag *(m)* contribution margin, contribution pricing
defekt defective, faulty
Defekt *(m)* defect, fault
Defizit *(n)* deficit
Dekoelement *(n)* decorator element, decorative object
Dekor *(n)* decoration; (Raumdekor) decor
Dekoration *(f)* decoration

Dekorationsmaterial *(n)* decorative material, decorator material
dekorativ decorative
dekorieren decorate; (Schaufenster) dress
Delegation *(f)* delegation
Delle *(f)* dent
dementieren deny
Demokassette *(f)* demo tape
Demontage *(f)* dismantling, disassembly, take down
Design *(n)* design
Designer(in) *(m/f)* designer
Desinteresse *(n)* indifference, lack of interest
desinteressiert indifferent
Dessert *(n)* dessert, sweet dish
Detail *(n)* detail
Deutsche Zentrale *(f)* **für Fremdenverkehr** Central Office of German Travel
Deutscher Fremdenverkehrsverband *(m)* German Tourist Association
Deutscher Hotel- und Gaststättenverband *(m)* German Hotel and Catering Association
Devise *(f)* (Wahlspruch) motto
Devisen *(f, pl)* foreign currency, foreign exchange
Devisenkurs *(m)* exchange rate, rate of exchange
Dezibel *(n)* decibel
Dezimalsystem *(n)* decimal system
diagonal diagonal
Diagonalkreuz *(m)* diagonal cross
Diagramm *(n)* chart, diagram, graph
Diakasten *(m)* slide box
Dialeuchtkasten *(m)* light box for slides, light box for transparencies
Dialogmarketing *(m)* dialog marketing (US), dialogue marketing (GB)
Diapositiv *(n)* slide, transparency
Diaprojektion *(f)* slide projection
Diaprojektor *(m)* slide projector

Diarahmen *(m)* slide frame
Diät halten be on a diet
Diätkost *(f)* dietary food
dicht (Leitung etc.) tight; (Gefäß etc.) leakproof
Dichtung *(f)* (Abdichtung) seal, packing
Dichtungsmaterial *(n)* sealing compound, packing material
Dichtungsscheibe *(f)* washer
Diebstahl *(m)* theft
diebstahlsicher theftproof
Diebstahlsicherung *(f)* theft protection, anti-theft device
Diebstahlversicherung *(f)* insurance against theft
Dienst *(m)* **haben** be on duty
Dienstleister *(m)* service provider, supplier of services
Dienstleistung *(f)* service
Dienstleistungen *(f, pl)*, **sonstige** other services
Dienstleistungen *(f, pl)*, **technische** technical services
Dienstleistungsgewerbe *(n)* service industries
Dienstleistungsvertrag *(m)* service contract
Dienstreise *(f)* business trip, official trip
Differenz *(f)* difference
differenzieren differentiate, make distinctions
diffizil difficult
Digitalanzeige *(f)* digital display
Digitaldruck *(m)* digital printing
digitalisieren digitize
Digitalkamera *(f)* digital camera
Diktiergerät *(n)* dictating machine
Dimmer *(m)* dimmer
Dimmerschalter *(m)* dimmer switch
Direktflug *(m)* direct flight
Direktion *(f)* management, directorate
Direktor(in) *(m/f)* director, executive director, general manager
Direktorium *(n)* board of directors

Direktverkauf *(m)* direct selling
Direktwerbung *(f)* direct advertising
Diskette *(f)* disk, floppy disk, diskette
Diskettenlaufwerk *(n)* disk drive
Diskontpreis *(m)* discount price
Diskontsatz *(m)* discount rate
Diskussion *(f)* discussion
diskutieren discuss
Display *(n)* display
Display System display system
Display *(n)*, **drehendes** rotating display
Displaywand *(f)* display wall
disponieren make arrangements, plan ahead
Distanzhalter *(m)* distance piece
Distanzzarge *(f)* distance beam
Distribution *(f)* distribution
Diversifikation *(f)* diversification
diversifizieren diversify
Dokument *(n)* document
Dokumentation *(f)* documentation
dokumentieren document
dolmetschen interpret
Dolmetscher(in) *(m/f)* interpreter
Doppelboden *(m)* double floor, raised floor
Doppelseite *(f)* spread, double-page spread
Doppelstecker *(m)* two-way adaptor, two-way adapter
doppelt double; (Technik) dual, twin, duplex
Doppelzimmer *(f)* double room, twin-bedded room
Dose *(f)* can (US), tin (GB)
Dosenbier *(n)* canned beer (US), tinned beer (GB)
Dosenmilch *(f)* canned milk (US), tinned milk (GB)
Dosenöffner *(m)* can opener (US), tin opener (GB)
Draht *(m)* wire
Drahtmodell *(n)* wire model
Drahtseil *(n)* wire cable
drapieren drape

draußen outside; (im Freien) in the open air
Dreck *(m)* dirt, filth, stuff
dreckig dirty, filthy
drehbar rotatable, rotating, revolving
Drehbühne *(f)* revolving stage, turnable stage
drehen turn; (Film) shoot
drehen, sich rotate
Drehstrom *(m)* three-phase current, 3-phase current, three-phase power, 3-phase power
Drehstromanschluss *(m)* three-phase power connection, 3-phase power connection
Drehstuhl *(m)* swivel chair
Drehtür *(f)* revolving door
dreidimensional three-dimensional (3-D)
3-D-Darstellung *(f)* 3-D design, 3-D image
Dreieck *(n)* triangle
dreieckig triangular
Dreieckknoten *(m)* triangle node
Dreieckträger *(m)* triangular truss section
dringend urgent
Dringlichkeit *(f)* urgency; (größte Dringlichkeit) first priority, top priority
drinnen inside, indoors
dröhnen boom, roar
Druck *(m)* (Belastung) pressure, stress; (Papier) printing
Druck- und Flüssiggasanlagen *(f, pl)* compressed and liquefied gas systems
Druckabfall *(m)* drop in pressure, pressure drop
Druckanstieg *(m)* increase in pressure, pressure increase
Druckauflage *(f)* gross circulation, print run
Druckbehälter *(m)* pressure container, pressure tank, pressure vessel
Druckbuchstabe *(m)* block letter, printed letter

druckempfindlich sensitive to pressure
drucken print
drücken press, squeeze
Drucker *(m)* printer
Druckerei *(f)* printing establishment, printing office, printing works
Drückergarnitur *(f)* door handle set
Druckfahne *(f)* proof, galley proof
Druckfehler *(m)* misprint, printer's error, typographical error
Druckgas *(n)* pressurized gas
Druckgasanlage *(f)* pressurized gas system
Druckgasflasche *(f)* pressurized gas bottle
Druckgeräteverordnung *(f)* Pressure Container Ordinance
Druckknopf *(m)* (Auslöser) push button
Drucklegung *(f)* going to press, printing, press date
Druckluft *(f)* compressed air
Druckluftanschluss *(m)* compressed air connection
Druckluftbehälter *(m)* compressed air cylinder
Druckluftnetz *(n)* compressed air system
Druckluftrohr *(n)* pressure pipe
Druckluftversorgung *(f)* compressed air supply
Druckmedien *(n, pl)* printed media
Drucksache *(f)* printed material, printed matter, printed paper
Drucksachengebühr *(f)* printed papers reduced rate
Druckschrift *(f)* brochure
Druckunterlage *(f)* printing material
Druckzeile *(f)* printed line
Dübel *(m)* dowel, peg, plug, treenail
dübeln dowel, peg, plug
dunkel dark
Dunkelheit *(f)* darkness
dünn thin
Dunst *(m)* steam
Dunstabzugshaube *(f)* extractor hood

durchbiegen bend
Durchbiegung *(f)* bending
durchdacht reasoned
durchdenken think through, reason, reason out
Durcheinander *(n)* confusion; (Unordnung) mess
Durchfahrt *(f)* passage
Durchfahrt verboten! No thoroughfare!
Durchfahrtshöhe *(f)* vertical clearance, clearance height
Durchfahrtsschein *(m)* passage pass, passage ticket
Durchführungsgesellschaft *(f)* official participation contractor
Durchgang *(m)* gateway, pass, passage
Durchgang verboten! No thoroughfare!
Durchlauferhitzer *(m)* instantaneous water heater, continuous flow water heater
durchlesen read through
Durchmesser *(m)* diameter
durchrechnen calculate
Durchsage *(f)* announcement
Durchsageanlage *(f)* public address system
durchsagen announce
Durchschnitt *(m)* average
Durchschnitt *(m)*, **im** on an average
durchschnittlich average, on an average
Durchschnittswert *(m)* average value
Durchschreibeblock *(m)* carbon-copy pad
Durchschrift *(f)* copy
Durchzug *(m)* draft (US), draught (GB)
Dusche *(f)* shower, douche
Duschkabine *(f)* shower cubicle
Duschraum *(m)* shower room
Düse *(f)* nozzle
duzen address s.o. with „du"
DVD-Laufwerk *(n)* DVD drive
DVD-Spieler *(m)* DVD player

E

Echtzeit *(f)* (EDV) real time
Ecke *(f)* corner
eckig angular, square
Eckplatz *(m)* corner seat
Eckstand *(m)* corner stand, corner booth
Eckverbinder *(m)* corner connector
Edelstahl *(m)* stainless steel
Edelstahlspüle *(f)* steel sink
EDV (elektronische Datenverarbeitung) EDP (electronic data processing)
EDV-Abteilung *(f)* computer department
EDV-Anlage *(f)* EDP equipment
EDV-Branche *(f)* data processing business
EDV-System *(n)* EDP system
Effekt *(m)* effect
Effektbeleuchtung *(f)* effect lighting, decorative lighting
effektiv actual, effective
Effektivität *(f)* effectiveness
effektvoll effective
Ehrengast *(m)* guest of honor (US), guest of honour (GB)
eigen own, of one's own
Eigengewicht *(n)* net weight
Eigenkapital *(n)* equity, equity capital, owner's equity
Eigenmarke *(f)* own brand
Eigenschaft *(f)* quality; (Merkmal) characteristic, feature; (techn. Merkmal) property
Eigentum *(n)* property, ownership
Eigentümer(in) *(m/f)* proprietor, owner
Eilauftrag *(m)* rush order
Eilbrief *(m)* express letter, special delivery letter
eilig hasty, hurried
Eilzustellung *(f)* express, special delivery
Eimer *(m)* bucket, pail

Einband *(m)* (Buch) cover; (Front) front cover page; (Rückseite) back cover page
Einbau *(m)* installation, fitting; (Einbau-) built-in, fitted
einbauen built in, install, fit
Einbaugefriergerät *(n)* built-in freezer
Einbauherd *(m)* built-in cooker
Einbaukühlschrank *(m)* built-in refrigerator
Einbauofen *(m)* built-in oven
Einbauspülmaschine *(f)* built-in dishwasher
Einbaustrahler *(m)* built-in spotlight
Einbettzimmer *(n)* single room, single bedroom
einblenden fade in, slot in
Einblendung *(f)* fade in, intercut
einbrennlackiert powder-coated
Einbringung *(f)* bringing in
Einbruch *(m)* burglary
Einbruchsdiebstahl *(m)* burglary
einbruchsicher burglar proof
Einbruchsverhütung *(f)* burglary prevention
Einbruchsversicherung *(f)* burglary insurance
Einbuße *(f)* loss
einchecken check in
Eincheckschalter *(m)* check-in counter
Eindruck *(m)* impression
eindrucksvoll impressive
Einfahrt *(f)* entrance, entry, driveway
Einfahrt verboten! No entry!
Einfahrtschein *(m)* entrance pass, entry permit
Einfahrtsgenehmigung *(f)* entrance permit
Einfahrtsregelung *(f)* entrance regulations
Einfahrtstor *(n)* entrance gate
einfarbig unicolor (US), unicolour (GB), unicolored (US), unicoloured (GB), of one color (US), of one colour (GB)
einfügen fit, fit into, insert, inset

Einfuhr *(f)* import
Einfuhr *(f)*, **temporäre** temporary importation
einführen (Ware) import; (Produkt) introduce
einführen, jdn. introduce s.o.
Einfuhrgenehmigung *(f)* import licence
Einführung *(f)* (Import) importation; (Markt) launching; (Vorstellung) introduction
Einführungskampagne *(f)* introductory campaign, launching campaign
Einführungspreis *(m)* introductory price, advertising price
Einführungstermin *(m)* introductory date, launching date
Einfuhrverbot *(n)* import ban
Einfuhrzoll *(m)* customs duty, import duty
Eingabedaten *(pl)* (EDV) input data
Eingang *(m)* entrance, way in; (Zutritt) entry
Eingangsdatum *(n)* date of receipt
eingebaut built-in
eingeben (EDV) enter
eingetragen registered
Eingriffe *(m, pl)* **in die Bausubstanz** violations of structural integrity
einhaken hook in
Einhängehaken *(m)* **zur Abhängung** suspension hook
einheimisch domestic, local, native
Einheit *(f)* unit
einheitlich (gleichförmig) uniform, homogeneous; (genormt) standard, standardized
Einkauf *(m)* buying, purchase, purchasing
Einkäufer *(m)* buyer
Einkäuferausweis *(m)* buyer's pass
Einkaufsabteilung *(f)* buying department, purchasing department
Einkaufsleiter *(m)* head buyer, purchasing manager

Einkaufspreis *(m)* purchase price
einkleiden fit s.o. out
Einkleidung *(f)* (Standmitarbeiter) staff clothing, staff fitting out, staff outfitting
Einkünfte *(pl)* income, earnings
einladen (Gäste etc.) invite; (Güter) load
einladend inviting
Einladung *(f)* invitation
Einladungsaktion *(f)* invitation action, invitation campaign
Einladungsbrief *(m)* letter of invitation
einlagern store
Einlagerung *(f)* storage, storing, warehousing
Einlass *(m)* admission, admittance
Einlassregelung *(f)* admittance regulation, admission rules
einmalig unique
Einnahme *(f)* receipt, income, revenue
einpacken (Koffer etc.) pack; (in Papier etc.) wrap up; (Paket etc.) pack up
einrahmen frame
Einreise *(f)* entry
Einreisebestimmungen *(f, pl)* entry regulations
Einreisegenehmigung *(f)* entry permit
einreisen enter; (in ein Land) enter a country
Einreiseverbot *(n)* refusal of entry
Einreisevisum *(n)* entry visa
einrichten (ausstatten) fit out; (möblieren) furnish; (gestalten) form, shape, fashion
Einrichtungen *(f, pl)*, **technische** technical devices
Einrichtungsidee *(f)* idea for fitment
einsatzbereit operational, ready for use
Einsatzmöglichkeit *(f)* range of application
einschalten turn on, switch on
Einschaltquote *(f)* audience rating, ratings
einschränken restrict; (begrenzen) limit

Einschränkung *(f)* restriction; (Begrenzung) limitation
Einschreibebrief *(m)* registered letter
Einschreibegebühr *(f)* registration fee
Einschreibung *(f)* registration
Einschubprofil *(n)* insert profile
einseitig (eine Seite) one-sided, single-sided; (eine Partei) unilateral
Einsendeschluss *(m)* closing date
einsparen save
Einsparung *(f)* saving, economy
einspeisen feed, feed in
Einspeiser *(m)* feeder
Einspeiserbrücke *(f)* feeder bridge
Einspeisungsstück *(n)* feed connector piece, main connector piece
Einspruch *(m)* objection, protest
Einstandspreis *(m)* cost price
einstellbar adjustable
einstellen (beenden) stop, discontinue; (Zahlung) suspend; (Gerät etc.) adjust, set; (Mitarbeiter) take on staff, hire (US)
Einstellknopf *(m)* control knob
Einstiegsluke *(f)* hatch, access hatch
einstöckig one-story (US), one-storey (GB)
einstufen classify, grad
eintragen enter, register, list
Eintragung *(f)* (Katalog etc.) entry, registration, listing
Eintragungsbescheinigung *(f)* registration certificate
eintreffen arrive
eintreten enter
Eintritt *(m)* entry
Eintritt frei! Admission free!
Eintritt verboten! Keep out!, No entry!
Eintrittskarte *(f)* entrance ticket, admission ticket, ticket of admission
Eintrittskarte *(f)*, **ermäßigte** reduced ticket
Eintrittskarte *(f)*, **gültige** valid admission ticket
Eintrittskartengutschein *(m)* admission voucher, free pass

Eintrittspreis *(m)* admission price, entrance price, charge for admission
einverstanden sein (mit jdm.) agree with s.o.; (mit etw.) agree to sth.
Einverständnis *(n)* consent
Einwand *(m)* objection
einwandfrei perfect
Einweg- disposable, one-way, non-returnable
Einwegflasche *(f)* one-way bottle, non-returnable bottle
Einweggeschirr *(n)* disposable dishes
Einwegteppich *(m)* disposable carpet
Einwegverpackung *(f)* non-returnable packing
einweisen brief, introduce
einwickeln wrap up
einzeichnen sketch in
Einzelanfertigung *(f)* special design
Einzelaufstellung *(f)* (Liste) itemized list
Einzelaussteller *(m)* individual exhibitor
Einzelbeteiligung *(f)* single participation
Einzelgewicht *(n)* unit weight, special weight
Einzelhandel *(m)* retail trade
Einzelhandelsgeschäft *(n)* retail shop, retail outlet
Einzelhandelspreis *(m)* retail price
Einzelhändler *(m)* retail dealer, retailer
Einzelheit *(f)* detail
einzeln anführen specify, itemize
Einzelperson *(f)* individual
Einzelteil *(n)* component, part
Einzelzimmer *(n)* single room
Einzelzimmerzuschlag *(m)* single room supplement
einzigartig unique
Ein-Zimmer-Suite *(f)* junior suite
Eiserzeuger *(m)* ice maker
eisgekühlt chilled, iced
eiskalt ice cold; (Ware) chilled
Eiswürfel *(m)* ice cube
Eiswürfelbereiter *(m)* ice cube machine, ice cube maker

elastisch elastic, flexible
Elektriker(in) *(m/f)* electrician
Elektrizitätsversorgung *(f)* electricity supply, power supply
Elektroanschluss *(m)* electric power connection, electrical connection, connection of electricity
Elektroanschlusspreis *(m)* electric power connection price, electrical connection price
Elektroantrieb *(m)* electric drive
Elektroboiler *(m)* electric boiler
Elektroherd *(m)* electric cooker
Elektroinstallation *(f)* electrical installations, electrical installation work
Elektrokabel *(n)* electric cable
Elektrokochplatte *(f)* electric hot-plate
Elektromotor *(m)* electric motor
Elektronik *(f)* electronics
elektronische Datenverarbeitung *(f)* **(EDV)** electronic data processing (EDP)
Elektroofen *(m)* electric oven
Elektroschaltanlage *(f)* electro control panel
Elektroschock *(m)* electric shock, electroshock
Elektrotechnik *(f)* electrical engineering
elektrotechnisch electrotechnical
Elektroversorgung *(f)* electrical supply
Elektroverteiler *(m)* electric distribution box, electrical distribution box
Elektroverteilung *(f)* electrical distribution, distribution wiring
eloxiert anodized, clear anodized
E-Mail *(f)* e-mail, electronic mail
E-Mail-Adresse *(f)* e-mail address
Empfang *(m)* (Veranstaltung, Person) reception; (Sache) receipt
Empfang *(m)* **nehmen, in** receive
Empfänger *(m)* consignee, recipient
Empfangsbereich *(m)* reception area
Empfangsbestätigung *(f)* acknowledgement of receipt
Empfangsdame *(f)* receptionist

Empfangskomitee *(n)* reception committee
Empfangsraum *(m)* reception room
empfehlen recommend
empfehlenswert recommendable
Empfehlung *(f)* recommendation; (Referenz) reference
Empfehlungsschreiben *(f)* letter of recommendation
empfindlich sensitive
Empore *(f)* gallery
Endabnehmer *(m)* ultimate buyer, end consumer, end user
Ende *(n)* (Zeit) end; (Abschluss) ending; (Schluss) close
Ende *(n)*, **offenes** open end
Endergebnis *(n)* final result
Endhaltestelle *(f)* terminus, terminal stop
Endreinigung *(f)* final cleaning
Endstromverbraucherkreis *(m)* end current load circuit
Endstück *(n)* end piece
Endsumme *(f)* total
Endtermin *(m)* deadline, final day
Endverbraucher *(m)* end user, end consumer
Endverstärker *(m)* output amplifier
Energiebedarf *(m)* energy demand, energy requirement
Energiekosten *(pl)* energy costs
Energiekostenpauschale *(f)* energy cost lump sum
Energieverbrauch *(m)* consumption of energy, energy consumption
Energieverschwendung *(f)* waste of energy
Energieversorgung *(f)* energy supply, power supply
eng narrow
Engländer *(m)* (Werkzeug) adjustable wrench, monkey wrench
Engpass *(m)* bottleneck
entfernen (wegnehmen) remove
Entfernen *(n)* (Exponate etc.) removal

entfernen, sich leave, go away
entflammbar inflammable
entflammbar, leicht highly flammable
entgegengesetzt (Lage etc.) opposite; (Meinung etc.) contrary, opposed
enthalten contain
entkorken uncork
entladen unload
entleeren empty
Entlüftung *(f)* de-aeration, airing, ventilation
entrollen unroll
entscheiden decide
Entscheidung *(f)* decision
Entscheidung *(f)*, **rationale** rational decision
Entscheidungskriterium *(n)* deciding factor
Entscheidungsprozess *(m)* decision-making process
Entscheidungsträger(in) *(m/f)* decision-maker
Entschluss *(m)* decision
entschuldigen excuse
Entschuldigen Sie! Excuse me!, Sorry!
entschuldigen, sich apologize
Entschuldigung *(f)* excuse
entsorgen dispose of
Entsorgung *(f)* disposal
Entsorgung *(f)* **von Bewirtungsabfällen** food service waste disposal
Entsorgung *(f)* **von Küchenabfällen** kitchen waste disposal
Entsorgung *(f)* **von Produktionsabfällen** construction waste disposal
Entsorgung *(f)* **von Sonderabfällen** hazardous waste disposal
Entsorgung *(f)* **von Standbauteilen** stand components waste disposal
Entsorgung *(f)* **von Verpackungsmaterial** packing waste disposal
Entsorgung *(f)* **von Wertstoffen** reusable waste recycling
Entsorgungskonzept *(n)* waste disposal concept

Entsorgungskosten *(pl)* waste disposal costs
Entsorgungsunternehmen *(n)* waste disposal company
entweichen (Gas etc.) escape; (Flüssigkeit) leak
entwerfen sketch, outline
entwickeln develop, work out; (Vorstellung) evolve
Entwicklung *(f)* development
Entwicklungsstadium *(n)* stage of development
Entwurf *(m)* (Zeichnung) sketch, outline; (Plan) plan, blueprint; (Gestaltung) design
Entwurfsskizze *(f)* sketch, outline
Entwurfsstadium *(n)* planning stage
entzündbar inflammable
entzündbar, leicht highly inflammable
erden earth, ground
Erdgeschoss *(n)* ground floor, first floor
Erdung *(f)* earthing, grounding
ereignen, sich happen, take place, occur
Ereignis *(n)* event, occurrence; (Kunst etc.) happening
Erfahrung *(f)* experience; (Technik) know how
Erfahrungsaustausch *(m)* exchange of experience
Erfolg *(m)* success; (Ergebnis) result
erfolglos unsuccessful, without success
erfolgreich successful
Erfolgsaussichten *(f, pl)* chances of success
Erfolgskontrolle *(f)* efficiency review; (Werbung) result testing
erfolgversprechend promising
erforderlich necessary, required; (unabdingbar) essential
Erfordernis *(n)* requirement
erforschen study, research
erfragen ask, inquire
Erfrischung *(f)* refreshment
Erfrischungsgetränk *(n)* cool drink, soft drink

Erfüllungsort *(m)* place of fulfillment (US), place of fulfilment (GB), place of performance
Erfüllungsort *(m)* **und Gerichtsstand** *(m)* place of fulfillment and court of jurisdiction (US), place of fulfilment and court of jurisdiction (GB), place of performance and court of jurisdiction
ergänzen complete; (hinzufügen) add, supplement
ergänzend complementary, additional, supplementary
Ergebnis *(n)* result
erhalten get, receive
Erhebung *(f)* (Befragung) inquiry
erhöhen increase, scale up
erinnern an, jdn. remind s.o. of
erinnern an, sich remember s.o., remember sth.
Erinnerungstest *(m)* recall test
erklären explain
Erklärung *(f)* explanation
erkranken fall ill, fall sick
Erkrankung *(f)* disease, illness, sickness
erlauben allow, permit
Erlaubnis *(f)* permit, permission
erledigen attend to, carry out, finish, settle
Erledigung *(f)* settlement
Erlös *(m)* proceeds, revenue
ermächtigen authorize, empower
Ermächtigung *(f)* authorization
Ermahnung *(f)* admonition
ermäßigen reduce, cut
Ermäßigung *(f)* reduction
eröffnen open
Eröffnung *(f)* opening
Eröffnungsrede *(f)* inaugural address
Eröffnungsveranstaltung *(f)* opening ceremony
erproben test, try
erprobt experienced, well tried; (bewährt) proven
Ersatz *(m)* replacement, substitute

Ersatzlampe *(f)* extra bulb
Ersatzteil *(n)* replacement part, spare part
Ersatzteildienst *(m)* spare parts service
Erscheinungsbild *(n)* appearance, image
Erscheinungsbild *(n)* **des Stands** general stand appearance
Erscheinungsdatum *(n)* date of publication, publication date
erschöpft exhausted
ersetzen replace, substitute
ersparen save
Ersparnis *(f)* saving
erstatten refund, reimburse
Erstattung *(f)* refund, refunding, reimbursement
Erstauftrag *(m)* initial order, original order, pilot order
Erstaussteller *(m)* new exhibitor
erste Hilfe *(f)* first aid
erstklassig first-class, first-rate, high-grade
erstmals for the first time
ersuchen request
Ertrag *(m)* income, earnings, proceeds, return, revenue, yield
Ertragssteigerung *(f)* increase of effiency
erwarten expect; (warten auf) wait for; (entgegensehen) await
Erwartung *(f)* expectation
erweitern (vergrößern) enlarge; (Aktivitäten etc.) expand; (Betrieb etc.) extend
Erweiterung *(f)* (Vergrößerung) enlargement; (Aktivitäten etc.) expansion; (Betrieb etc.) extension
Erwerb *(m)* acquisition, purchase
erwerben acquire, purchase
erzeugen produce
Erzeugnis *(n)* product, produce
Espressomaschine *(f)* espresso machine, espresso maker

Essen *(n)* (Kost) food; (Mahlzeit) meal; (Gericht) dish
Essengutschein *(m)* luncheon voucher, meal voucher
Etage *(f)* floor
Etat *(m)* budget
Etikett *(n)* label, sticker, tag
etikettieren label
EU-Mitgliedsland *(n)* EU member state
EU-Norm *(f)* EU standard
EU-Richtlinie *(f)* EU directive
Europäische Union *(f)* **(EU)** European Union (EU)
Eurocheck *(m)* Eurocheck (US), Eurocheque (GB)
Eurocheckkarte *(f)* Eurocheck card (US), Eurocheque card (GB)
Event *(n)* event, special event
exakt accurate, exact, precise
Exemplar *(n)* specimen; (Buch) copy; (Muster) sample; (Zeitung etc.) issue
exklusiv exclusive, select
Exklusivrecht *(n)* exclusive rights, exclusivity
expandieren expand
Expansion *(f)* expansion
Experte *(m)* expert, specialist
Explosionsgefahr *(f)* danger of explosion
explosionsgefährliche Stoffe *(m, pl)* explosive materials, explosive substances
Explosionsschutzdokument *(n)* explosion protection document
explosiv explosive
Exponat *(n)* exhibit
Exponatschild *(n)* exhibit sign
Exponatversicherung *(f)* exhibit insurance
Export *(m)* export, exportation
Exportabteilung *(f)* export department
Exportanteil *(m)* export content
Exportartikel *(m)* export article, export item
Exportbedingungen *(f, pl)* export terms

Exporteur *(m)* exporter
Exportgenehmigung *(f)* export permit
exportieren export
Exportland *(n)* exporting country
Exportleiter(in) *(m/f)* export manager
Exportmesse *(f)* export goods exhibition, export goods fair, export show
Exportmodell *(n)* export model
Exportverbot *(f)* export ban
Exportzoll *(m)* export duty
Extras *(pl)* optional extras
Exzenterspannschloss *(n)* eccentric tension lock

F

Fabrikant *(m)* manufacturer
Fabrikat *(n)* article, product
Fabrikation *(f)* manufacture, manufacturing, production
fabrizieren manufacture, make
Fachausdruck *(m)* technical term
Fachausstellung *(f)* special-interest exhibition, special-interest fair, special-interest show
Fachbegriff *(m)* technical term
Fachbeirat *(m)* advisory committee
Fachberater(in) *(m/f)* technical adviser
Fachberatung *(f)* expert advice, technical advice
Fachbesucher *(m, pl)* trade audience
Fachbesucher(in) *(m/f)* specialized visitor, trade visitor
Fachbesucherprospekt *(m)* trade visitor brochure
Fachbesucherstrukturtest *(m)* trade visitors profile, trade audience audit
Fachbesuchertag *(m)* trade visitor day, trade admittance day
Fachboden *(m)* (Regal) shelf

Fachbodenhalter *(m)* (Regal) shelf support
Fachfrau *(f)* expert, specialist, professional, professional women
Fachgebiet *(n)* specialist field, area of expertise, area of practice
Fachkenntnis *(f)* expert knowledge, special knowledge
Fachkraft *(f)* specialist, qualified employee, qualified worker, skilled worker; *(f, pl)* qualified personnel
fachkundig competent, expert, professional
Fachmann *(m)* expert, specialist, professional, professional man
fachmännisch competent, expert, specialist, technical, professional
Fachmesse *(f)* trade fair, business fair
Fachpersonal *(n)* qualified personnel
Fachpresse *(f)* trade press, technical press
fachsimpeln talk shop
Fachsymposium *(n)* industry symposium, scientific symposium
Fachübersetzer(in) *(m/f)* technical translator
Fachverband *(m)* trade association, professional association
Fachwissen *(n)* specialized knowledge, know-how, expertise
Fachwörterbuch *(n)* specialist dictionary, specialized dictionary
Fachzeitschrift *(f)* professional journal, trade journal, trade magazine
fähig able, capable
Fähigkeit *(f)* ability, capability
Fähnchen *(n)* pennant
Fahne *(f)* flag, banner
Fahnenabzug *(m)* galley-proof
Fahnenmast *(m)* flagpole
fahrbar mobile
Fahrer *(m)* driver
Fahrgast *(m)* passenger
Fahrgeld *(n)* fare
Fahrgemeinschaft *(f)* car pool

Fahrkarte *(f)* ticket
Fahrkartenautomat *(m)* automatic ticket machine
fahrlässig negligent; (unachtsam) careless
Fahrlässigkeit *(f)* negligence; (Unachtsamkeit) carelessness
Fahrlässigkeit *(f)***, grobe** gross negligence
Fahrplan *(m)* timetable, schedule
Fahrpreis *(m)* fare
Fahrpreisermäßigung *(f)* fare reduction, reduced fare
Fahrstuhl *(m)* elevator (US), lift (GB)
Fahrt *(f)* drive, ride
Fahrtkosten *(pl)* travelling expenses
Fahrzeit *(f)* running time, travel time
Fahrzeug *(n)* vehicle
Faktorenanalyse *(f)* factor analysis
Faktura *(f)* bill
fakturieren invoice
fällig (Zahlung) due, due for payment, payable
fällig werden become due, fall due
Fälligkeit *(f)* due date, maturity, maturity date, settlement date
Fälligkeitsdatum *(n)* date of maturity, settlement date
Fallstudie *(f)* case study
falsch false, wrong
fälschen fake, falsify
Fälschung *(f)* fake, faking, falsification, forgery, forging
Faltblatt *(n)* leaflet, folder
Faltdisplay *(n)* folding display, foldable display
Faltkarton *(m)* folding cardboard box
Falttür *(f)* folding door
Fantasie *(f)* fantasy, imagination
fantastisch fantastic
Farbabzug *(m)* color print (US), colour print (GB)
Farbandruck *(m)* color proof (US), colour proof (GB)
Farbanstrich *(m)* paint, coat of paint

Farbaufnahme *(f)* (Foto) color photo (US), colour photo (GB); (Film) color film (US), colour film (GB)
Farbbeilage *(f)* color supplement (US), colour supplement (GB)
Farbdruck *(m)* color print (US), color printing (US), colour print (GB), colour printing (GB)
farbecht colorfast (US), colourfast (GB)
farbenfroh colorful (US), colourful (GB)
Farbenlehre *(f)* chromatology
Farbfernseher *(m)* color television (US), color TV (US), colour television (GB), colour TV (GB)
Farbfotografie *(f)* color photography (US), colour photography (GB)
Farbgebung *(f)* coloring (US), colouring (GB), tinting
farbig colored (US), coloured (GB), chromatic, polychrome
Farbkarte *(f)* color card (US), colour card (GB)
Farbkopierer *(m)* color photocopier (US), colour photocopier (GB)
Farbmonitor *(m)* color monitor (US), colour monitor (GB)
Farbmuster *(n)* color swatch (US), colour swatch (GB)
Farbpalette *(f)* color range (US), colour range (GB), range of colors (US), range of colours (GB)
Farbskala *(f)* color chart (US), colour chart (GB)
Farbton *(m)* hue, shade; (Tönung) tint
Faserplatte *(f)* fiberboard (US), fibreboard (GB)
Fassade *(f)* front, facade
Fasshahn *(m)* tap
Fassung *(f)* (Lampe) socket; (Version) version
Fassungsvermögen *(n)* capacity
Fax *(n)* fax
faxen fax
Federspannvorrichtung *(f)* spring-tighting device

43

fegen sweep, sweep clean
Fehlbetrag *(m)* deficit
Fehlentscheidung *(f)* wrong decision
Fehlentwicklung *(f)* undesirable development
Fehler *(m)* mistake; (Mangel, Defekt) fault; (Irrtum) error
fehlerfrei accurate, faultless, perfect
fehlerhaft faulty, incorrect, imperfect
Fehlerquote *(f)* error rate
fehlschlagen fail, go wrong
Feierabend *(m)* end of work, closing time
feilen file
feilschen haggle
Feinabstimmung *(f)* fine tuning
Feineinstellung *(f)* fine adjustment
Feinheit *(f)* fineness
Feinschmeckerrestaurant *(n)* gourmet restaurant
Fensterscheibe *(f)* pane, window pane
Fernbedienung *(f)* remote control
Ferngespräch *(n)* long-distance call
ferngesteuert remote-controlled
Fernlast *(f)* distance freight
Fernschreiber *(m)* teleprinter, teletype
Fernsehbildschirm *(m)* screen, TV screen
Fernseheinschaltquote *(f)* television ratings
Fernsehen *(n)* **übertragen** telecast, televise; (senden) broadcast
Fernsehgerät *(n)* television set, televiewer
Fernsehkamera *(f)* TV camera
Fernsehspot *(m)* TV spot
Fernsehwerbung *(f)* TV advertising
Fernsehzuschauer(in) *(m/f)* viewer, television viewer
Fernsprechanlage *(f)* telephone installation
Fernsprechanschluss *(m)* telephone connection
Fernsprecheinrichtung *(f)* telecommunication equipment
Fernsprechgebühr *(f)* telephone charge
Fernsprechnummer *(f)* telephone number
Fernsprechzelle *(f)***, öffentliche** public call box
Fertigbauweise *(f)* prefabricated construction
fertigbringen manage
Fertigmontage *(f)* final assembly
Fertigstand *(m)* complete stand, prefabricated stand, shell scheme booth
fertigstellen finish, complete
Fertigstellung *(f)* completion
Fertigteil *(n)* prefabricated part, finished part, assembly units
fest firm, fixed, solid, tight
Festakt *(m)* ceremony
festbinden tie up
Festbrennweite *(f)* fixed focal lense
Festhalle *(f)* banqueting hall, festival hall
festhalten hold on, hold tight, grip
Festigkeit *(f)* strength
festkleben stick, stick to
festklemmen jam, squeeze, pinch
festlegen (Preis, Termin etc.) define, determine, fix, schedule
festmachen (befestigen) fix, fasten; (vereinbaren) fix, settle
Festplatte *(f)* hard disk
Festplattenlaufwerk *(n)* hard disk drive
Festpreis *(m)* fixed price
Festredner(in) *(m/f)* main speaker
Festsaal *(m)* banqueting hall, banquet room, festival hall
festschrauben screw on, screw in tight
festsetzen arrange, fix, set
Feststellschraube *(f)* fixing screw
Fettdruck *(m)* bold print, bold typeface, bold-faced type
fettgedruckt printed in bold type
feucht damp, moist; (Luft) humid
Feuchtigkeit *(f)* damp, dampness, moistness, moisture; (Luft) humidity

Feuer *(n)* fire; (für Zigarette) light
Feueralarm *(m)* fire alarm
Feuergefahr *(f)* fire hazard, fire risk, danger of fire
feuergefährlich combustible, flammable, inflammable
Feuerlöscher *(m)* fire extinguisher
Feuermelder *(m)* fire alarm; (automatischer Melder) fire detector
Feuernotruf *(m)* emerging fire service, emergency phone number
Feuerschaden *(m)* fire damage
Feuerschutz *(m)* fire prevention
Feuerschutzmittel *(n, pl)* flame-proofing agents
feuerschutztechnische Einrichtungen *(f, pl)* fire protection equipment
feuerschutztechnische Geräte *(n, pl)* firefighting equipment
Feuertreppe *(f)* fire escape
Feuerversicherung *(f)* fire insurance
Feuerwache *(f)* fire station
Feuerwehr *(f)* fire brigade
Feuerwehrbewegungszone *(f)* fire service movement zone, emergency services movement zone
Feuerzeug *(n)* lighter, cigarette lighter
Filmproduktionsgesellschaft *(f)* film production company
Filmvorführung *(f)* movie performance (US), film performance (GB)
Filter *(m, n)* filter
Filterkaffee *(m)* filter coffee, filtered coffee
Filterpapier *(n)* filter paper
Filterzigarette *(f)* filter cigarette, filter-tipped cigarette
Filzstift *(m)* felt pen, felt-tip pen
finanziell financial
finanzieren finance
Finanzierung *(f)* financing
Finderlohn *(m)* finder's reward
Fingerspitzengefühl *(n)* sure instinct, tact

Firma *(f)* firm, company, corporation, enterprise, establishment
Firmenangaben *(f, pl)* company details
Firmenemblem *(n)* logo
Firmenerscheinungsbild *(n)* corporate design (CD)
Firmengemeinschaftsausstellung *(f)* joint exhibit
Firmengemeinschaftsstand *(m)* joint stand
Firmengrundeintrag *(m)* (Katalog) basic company entry
Firmenhomepage *(f)* company website
Firmenimage *(n)* corporate image
Firmenleitung *(f)* management, corporate management
Firmenlogo *(n)* company logo
Firmenname *(m)* company name, corporate name
Firmenporträt *(n)* company portrait
Firmenprofil *(n)* company profile
Firmenruf *(m)* goodwill
Firmenschild *(n)* company nameplate, company sign
Firmsitz *(m)* company headquarters
Firmenstempel *(m)* company stamp
Firmenvertretungen *(f, pl)* (am Stand etc.) companies represented
Firmenverzeichnis *(n)* trade directory
Firmenwagen *(m)* company car
Firmenwerbung *(f)* corporate advertising
Firmenzeichen *(n)* logo, logotype, trade sign
FI-Schutzschalter *(m)* FI protective switch
Fixierleiste *(f)* fixing plate
Fixierstück *(n)* fixation part
Fixkosten *(pl)* fixed costs, fixed expenses
FKM (Gesellschaft zur Freiwilligen Kontrolle von Messe- und Ausstellungszahlen) Society for Voluntary Control of Fair and Exhibition Statistics

FKM-Fachbesucherstrukturtest *(m)*
FKM trade attendance audit,
FKM trade visitors profile
Flachbildschirm *(m)* flat screen
Flächenbelegungsplan *(m)* space assignment plan, floor plan
Flächenlast *(f)* area loading, distributed load, distributed weight
Flächenmaß *(n)* square measure, unit of square measure, surface measurement
Flächenmiete *(f)* space rate, space rent (US), space hire (GB)
Flächenwunsch *(m)* space request, stand space required
Flachleitung *(f)* flat cable
Flachträger *(m)* flat truss section
Flagge *(f)* flag
Flamme *(f)***, offene** naked flame
Flansch *(m)* flange
Flasche *(f)* bottle
Flaschenbier *(n)* bottled beer
Flaschenkühlschrank *(m)* bottle cooling cabinet
Flaschenöffner *(m)* bottle opener
Flaschenpfand *(n)* bottle deposit
Flaschenwein *(m)* bottled wine
Flaschenzug *(m)* pulley, block and pulley
Flash-Memory-Karte *(f)* flash memory card, compact flash card
Flaute *(f)* slack period
Fleck *(m)* (Flecken) spot, stain
flexibel flexible
fliehen escape, flee, run away
Fliese *(f)* tile
Fliesenboden *(m)* tiled floor
Fliesenleger *(m)* tiler
Fließgrafik *(f)* flow graph
Flip Chart *(n)* flip chart
Flop *(m)* flop
Fluchtweg *(m)* escape route
Flugblatt *(n)* flier, leaflet, handbill
Flugbuchung *(f)* air booking
Flügelmutter *(f)* wing nut

Flügelschraube *(f)* thumbscrew, wingscrew
Flügeltür *(f)* double door
Fluggastgebühr *(f)* airport service charge
Fluggastterminal *(n)* passenger terminal
Fluggesellschaft *(f)* airline, airline company
Flughafenempfangsgebäude *(n)* airport terminal building
Flughafengebühren *(f, pl)* airport charges
Flughafenhotel *(n)* airport hotel
Flughafenrestaurant *(n)* airport restaurant
Flughafensteuer *(f)* airport tax
Flughafentransfer *(m)* airport transfer
Fluginformation *(f)* flight information
Fluglinie *(f)* airline
Flugnummer *(f)* flight number
Flugpassagier *(m)* air passenger
Flugpauschalreise *(f)* inclusive air journey
Flugplan *(m)* flight schedule, timetable
Flugplanänderung *(f)* change of flight schedule
Flugpreis *(m)* air fare
Flugreise *(f)* air journey
Flugschalter *(m)* flight desk
Flugschein *(m)* plane ticket
Flugschein *(m)***, offener** open-air ticket
Flugscheinverkaufsstelle *(f)* air ticket issuing office
Flugsicherheit *(f)* air safety
Flugsteig *(m)* gate
Flugstrecke *(f)* air route
Flugverbindung *(f)* air connection, connecting flight
Flugverspätung *(f)* flight delay
Flugzeit *(f)* flight time, flying time
Flugzeugankunft *(f)* arrival by air
Flugziel *(n)* flight destination
fluoreszieren fluoresce

Flurförderzeug *(n)* lift truck, material handling equipment
Flussdiagramm *(n)* flow chart, flow diagram
Folgekosten *(pl)* follow-up costs
Folgeschaden *(m)* consequential damage, secondary damage
Folie *(f)* foil; (Plastik) film
Folienbuchstaben *(m, pl)* adhesive lettering, stick-on letters
fordern demand
fördern promote, support
Förderprogramm *(n)* promotional program (US), promotional programme (GB), sponsoring program (US), sponsoring programme (GB)
Forderung *(f)* demand
Förderung *(f)* **von Messebeteiligungen** show participation sponsoring
Form *(f)* form; (Gestalt) shape; (Technik, Mode) design, styling
Formalien formalities
Format *(n)* format; (Größe, Umfang) size; (persönliches Format) auhority, celebrity
formatieren (EDV) format
Formblatt *(n)* form, order form
formell formal
formlos shapeless, formless; (zwanglos) casual, informal
formstabil non deforming
Formular *(n)* form
Formular *(n)* **ausfüllen** fill in a form
Formular *(n)*, **vorgedrucktes** printed form
formulieren formulate
Formulierung *(f)* formulation, phrasing, wording
formvollendet perfect, perfect in form, perfectly shaped
forschen research, do research work
Forschung *(f)* research
Fortschritt *(m)* advance, progress
fortschrittlich advanced, progressive

fortsetzen continue
Forum *(n)* forum; (Podium) platform
Foto *(n)* **machen** take a photo
Foto- und Filmerlaubnis *(f)* photography and film permit
Fotograf *(m)* photographer
Fotografie *(f)* photography
Fotografie *(f)*, **digitale** digital photography
Fotografier- und Filmverbot *(n)* photography and film restrictions, prohibition of photography and film
fotografieren photograph, take a photo, take pictures
Fotografieren verboten! Photographing not allowed!
Fotokopie *(f)* photocopy
fotokopieren photocopy
Fotokopiergerät *(n)* photocopier
Fotomodell *(f)* model
Fotomontage *(f)* photomontage
Fotosatz *(m)* photo composition
Foyer *(n)* foyer, lobby, lounge
Fracht *(f)* freight, load; (Luft-, Schiffsfracht) cargo
Frachtbrief *(m)* bill of freight, bill of lading, shipping bill, consignment note, waybill
frachtfrei carriage free, carriage paid, freight prepaid
Frachtgut *(n)* freight; (Luft-, Schiffsfracht) cargo
Frachtkosten *(pl)* carriage expenses, freight, freight charges, cost of freight, truckage
Fragebogen *(m)* questionnaire, survey sheet
fraglich in question; (ungewiss) uncertain
fraglos undoubtedly, unquestionable
fragwürdig doubtful, questionable
Fräse *(f)* milling machine, shaper
fräsen mill, mill-cut, mould, shape
freiberuflich self-employed, freelance
Freiexemplar *(n)* free copy

Freigelände *(n)* outdoor area, open-air site, open air grounds; (Messe) open exhibition area, outdoor exhibition area, uncovered exhibition area
Freigepäck *(n)* free baggage (US), free luggage (GB), allowed baggage (US), allowed luggage (GB), free baggage allowance (US), free luggage allowance (GB)
freihalten keep, keep free
Freihalten! Keep clear!
Freikarte *(f)* free ticket, complimentary ticket
Freischaltung *(f)* connection activation, connection enabling, connection release
freiwillig voluntary
Freizeichen *(n)* dial tone (US), dialling tone (GB)
fremd strange; (unbekannt) unknown
Fremdenverkehrsamt *(n)* tourist office, tourist information office
Fremdwährung *(f)* foreign currency
Frisch gestrichen! Wet paint!
Frischwasser *(n)* fresh water
Frist *(f)* deadline, period, period of time, time limit
fristgemäß in time, within the prescribet time limit, within the period stipulated
Front *(f)* front, frontage
Frontblende *(f)* fascia board, fascia panel
Frontseite *(f)* front side
Fruchtsaft *(m)* fruit juice, squash
Frühbucherrabatt *(m)* advance rates, early booking discount, early reservation discount
Frühjahrsmesse *(f)* spring fair, spring trade fair, spring exhibition, spring show
Frühstücksraum *(m)* breakfast room
frühzeitig early; (vorzeitig) premature
Fuge *(f)* joint
Führerschein *(m)* driver's license (US), driving licence (GB)

Führerscheinentzug *(m)* revocation of the driver's license (US), revocation of the driving licence (GB)
Fuhrpark *(m)* car pool, fleet, fleet of cars, fleet of trucks
Führung *(f)* leadership, guidance; (Besichtigung) guided tour; (Unternehmen) management, top management, directors; (Vorsprung) lead
Führungsebene *(f)* management level
Führungskraft *(f)* executive, executive manager
Führungskräfte *(f, pl)* management staff, executives
Fuhrunternehmen *(n)* haulage company, trucking contractor
Fullservice-Agentur *(f)* full service agency
Fundament *(n)* foundations
Fundbüro *(n)* lost property office
Funksprechgerät *(n)* walkie-talkie
Funktion *(f)* function
funktionieren function, work
Furnier *(n)* veneer
Fusion *(f)* merger
fusionieren merge
Fußausleger *(m)* foot bracket
Fußboden *(m)* floor
Fußbodenbelag *(m)* floor covering, flooring
Fußgängerbrücke *(f)* pedestrian bridge
Fußteller *(m)* footplate

G

Gabelstapler *(m)* forklift truck
Gage *(f)* fee
Galerie *(f)* gallery
Gang *(m)* (Halle) aisle; (Durchgang) passage, passageway, passing through
Gangnummer *(f)* aisle number

ganz *(vollständig)* entire, whole, coplete, total; *(intakt)* intact
ganzseitig full-page
Garantie *(f)* guarantee
garantieren guarantee
Garderobe *(f)* *(Raum)* checkroom (US), cloakroom (GB); *(Kleidung)* clothes, wardrobe
Garderobenfrau *(f)* checkroom attendant (US), cloakroom attendant (GB)
Garderobenmarke *(f)* checkroom ticket (US), cloakroom ticket (GB)
Garderobenständer *(m)* coat rack
Garderobenstange *(f)* clothes rod
Gardine *(f)* curtain
Gasanschluss *(m)* gas connection
Gasfeuerzeug *(n)* gas lighter
Gasflasche *(f)* gas cylinder
Gasleitung *(f)* gas main, gas pipe
Gast *(m)* guest
Gäste *(m, pl)* **bedienen** serve, attend to, wait on
Gästebetreuung *(f)* customer assistance
gastfreundlich hospitable
Gastfreundschaft *(f)* hospitality
Gastgeber(in) *(m/f)* host(ess)
Gasthaus *(n)* restaurant, inn; *(Wirtshaus)* pub (GB)
Gastlichkeit *(f)* hospitality
Gastnation *(f)* guest nation
Gastronomie *(f)* gastronomy, catering trade
gastronomische Versorgung *(f)* food service, catering, catering service, gastronomic accommodation
Gaststätte *(f)* restaurant
Gebäck *(n)* cakes, pastry, pastries; *(Kekse)* cookies (US), biscuits (GB)
Gebälk *(n)* beams, timberwork
Gebäude *(n)* building
Gebetsraum *(m)* prayer room
Gebiet *(n)* area, region, district
Gebietsleiter(in) *(m/f)* area manager
Gebinde *(n)* arrangement

Gebläse *(n)* fan
gebogen bent, curved
Gebrauch *(m)* use, usage, application
gebrauchen use, make use of; *(anwenden)* apply
Gebrauchsanleitung *(f)* directions for use, instructions for use
Gebrauchsgüter *(n, pl)* utility goods, durables, consumer durables, durable consumer goods, articles of everyday use
Gebrauchsmuster *(n)* registered design
Gebrauchsmusterschutz *(m)* protection of registered design
Gebühr *(f)* charge, fee
Gebühren *(f, pl)* **für Mitaussteller** co-exhibitor charge, co-exhibitor fees
Gebührenanzeige *(f)* call charge display, call charge indicator
gebührenpflichtig chargeable, subject to charges
Gedankenaustausch *(m)* exchange of ideas
Gedeck *(n)* cover
Gedeckpreis *(m)* cover charge
Gedränge *(n)* crowd; *(Ansturm)* rush
Gefahr *(f)* danger; *(Bedrohung)* threat; *(Risiko)* risk
gefährden endanger
Gefährdung *(f)* endangering
Gefahrenherd *(m)* source of danger
Gefahrgut *(n)* dangerous goods
gefährlich dangerous; *(riskant)* risky
gefahrlos safe, not dangerous
Gefahrstoff *(m)* dangerous substance
Gefahrstoffverordnung *(f)* Dangerous Substances Ordinance
Gefäß *(n)* vessel, container, receptacle
Gefrierschrank *(m)* upright freezer, upright freezer cabinet
Gefriertruhe *(f)* freezer, deep freezer, chest freezer
Gegensatz *(m)* contrast
Gegenstand *(m)* article, item, thing, object

gegenüber opposite, across the way
gegenüberliegen be opposite, face
gegenüberliegend opposite, facing
Gegenvorschlag *(m)* counterproposal
gegenwärtig present
gegenzeichnen countersign
Gehalt *(n)* salary, pay
Gehäuseabdeckung *(f)* case cover, housing cover
Geheimnummer *(f)* secret number
Gehörschutz *(m)* ear muff, ear protectors
Gehrung *(f)* miter (US), mitre (GB)
Gehweg *(m)* footpath
Geistesgegenwart *(f)* presence of mind
Gelände *(n)* grounds, terrain, site
Geländeplan *(m)* site map, site plan
Geländer *(n)* rail; (Treppe) banisters, handrail; (Stange) railing; (Balkon) balustrade
Gelbe Seiten *(pl)* yellow pages
Geldausgabe *(f)* expenditure, financial expenditure
Geldautomat *(m)* cash dispenser, ATM (automatic teller machine), autoteller
Geldbetrag *(m)* amount of money, sum of money
Geldschein *(m)* bill (US), note (GB), banknote (GB)
Geldstrafe *(f)* fine
Geldumtausch *(m)* change, exchange, money exchange, conversion, exchange of money
Geldwechsel *(m)* currency exchange, money exchange
Gelegenheit *(f)* occasion, opportunity, chance
gelegentlich occasional
Gelenkprofil *(n)* angle connector, hinged profile
Gelenkverbinder *(m)* movable hinge
Geltung *(f)* (Ansehen) prestige; (Bedeutung) weight; (Gültigkeit) validity
Geltungsdauer *(f)* period of validity

GEMA (Gesellschaft für musikalische Aufführungs- und mechanische Vervielfältigungsrechte) Society for Musical Performing and Mechanical Reproduction Rights
GEMA-Gebühren *(f, pl)* GEMA fees
Gemeinkosten *(pl)* overheads, overhead costs, overhead charge, fixed costs, on costs
gemeinsam common; (gemeinschaftlich) joint
Gemeinschaftsausstellung *(f)* joint exhibition
Gemeinschaftsstand *(m)* joint stand, joint exhibition stand, group stand
Gemeinschaftsstandbeteiligung *(f)* joint stand participation
Gemeinschaftsstandorganisator *(m)* joint stand organizer
Gemeinschaftsstandteilnehmer *(m)* joint stand exhibitor, joint stand participant
Gemeinschaftsunternehmen *(n)* joint venture
Gemeinschaftswerbung *(f)* associate advertising, cooperative advertising, group advertising
genau accurate, exact, precise
Genauigkeit *(f)* accuracy, exactness, precision
genehmigen approve; (zulassen) permit; (amtlich) authorize
Genehmigung *(f)* approval; (Zulassung) permission, permit; (amtlich) authorization
Genehmigung *(f)*, **behördliche** official approval, official permission, official authorization
Genehmigung *(f)*, **schriftliche** written approval, written authorization, written permission
Genehmigungsantrag *(m)* permit application
genehmigungspflichtig requiring official approlval

Genehmigungsvermerk *(m)* approval stamp, authorization certificate
geneigt inclined, sloping
genormt standardized
Gepäck *(n)* baggage (US), luggage (GB)
Gepäck *(n)*, **sperriges** bulky baggage (US), bulky luggage (GB)
Gepäckabfertigung *(f)* baggage processing (US), luggage processing (GB), check-in, handling of baggage (US), handling of luggage (GB)
Gepäckaufbewahrung *(f)* baggage room (US), luggage room (GB), left-luggage office (GB)
Gepäckaufbewahrungsschein *(m)* baggage check (US), luggage ticket (GB), receipt for registered luggage (GB)
Gepäckausgabe *(f)* baggage claim (US), handing out of baggage (US), handing out of luggage (GB)
Gepäckschließfach *(n)* baggage locker (US), luggage locker (GB)
Gepäckstück *(n)* item of baggage (US), piece of luggage (GB)
Gepäckversicherung *(f)* baggage insurance (US), luggage insurance (GB)
gepflastert paved
Geprüfte Messe- und Ausstellungsdaten *(pl)* audited show statistics
Gerade *(f)* straight line
geradeaus straigt ahead
geradlinig straight
Gerät *(n)* device, gadget, appliance; (Ausrüstung) equipment
Geräte *(n, pl)*, **elektrische** electrical appliances
Gerätesicherheitsgesetz *(n)* equipment safety law, law on equipment safety
geräumig roomy, spacious
Geräusch *(n)* sound; (störend) noise
Geräuschbelästigung *(f)* acoustic nuisance, noise molestation
Geräuschdämpfung *(f)* noise reduction

Geräuschkulisse *(f)* background noise
geräuschlos noiseless
Geräuschpegel *(m)* noise level
geräuschvoll noisy; (laut) loud
gerecht fair, just
Gericht *(n)* (Speise) dish, meal; (Gang) course
Gerichtsstand *(m)* place of jurisdiction, legal domicile, venue
gering little, marginal, slight, small
geringfügig minor, insignificant
Geruch *(m)* smell, odor (US), odour (GB)
Geruchsbelästigung *(f)* odor nuisance (US), odour nuisance (GB), odor molestation (US), odour molestation (GB)
gerundet rounded
Gerüst *(n)* scaffold
gesamt entire, total, whole
Gesamtansicht *(f)* general view
Gesamtbetrag *(m)* total amount
Gesamteindruck *(m)* general impression
Gesamtkosten *(pl)* total costs
Gesamtübersicht *(f)* general survey
Gesamtzahl *(f)* total number
Gesamtzahl *(f)* **registrierter Messen und Ausstellungen** total number of registered fairs and exhibitions
Geschäft *(n)* business, trade; (Handel) deal, business deal, bargain, transaction; (Laden) store (US), shop (GB)
geschäftig busy, active
geschäftlich business, on business, commercial
Geschäftsabschluss *(m)* deal, business deal
Geschäftsadresse *(f)* business address
Geschäftsausgaben *(f, pl)* expenses
Geschäftsaussichten *(f, pl)* business outlook
Geschäftsbedingungen *(f, pl)* terms of business, business conditions

Geschäftsbedingungen (f, pl), Allgemeine general terms of business
Geschäftsbericht *(m)* company's report, business report, annual report
Geschäftsbesuch *(m)* business call
Geschäftsbeziehungen *(f, pl)* business connections, business relations
Geschäftsbrief *(m)* business letter
Geschäftserfahrung *(f)* experience in business, business experience, business knowledge
Geschäftsergebniss *(n)* company result, operating result, trading result
Geschäftsessen *(n)* business lunch, business meal
geschäftsfähig legally competent, legally responsible, competent to contract
Geschäftsfeld *(n)* business segment
Geschäftsfrau *(f)* businesswoman
Geschäftsfreund *(m)* associate friend, business friend
geschäftsführend acting, executive, managing
Geschäftsführer(in) *(m/f)* manager, manageress, business manager, managing director
Geschäftsführung *(f)* management, business management
Geschäftsgebahren *(n)* business methods, business manners
Geschäftsgewinn *(m)* business gain, business profit, commercial profit
Geschäftsinhaber(in) *(m/f)* owner of a company; (Laden) proprietor
Geschäftsjahr *(n)* business year, trading year; (Finanzen) accounting year, financial year
Geschäftsleitung *(f)* management, business management
Geschäftsleute *(pl)* businesspeople
Geschäftsmann *(m)* businessman
geschäftsmäßig businesslike
Geschäftsreise *(f)* business trip, business travel

Geschäftsrückgang *(m)* business recession, downturn
Geschäftstätigkeit *(f)* business activity, business operations
Geschäftsverbindung *(f)* business connection, business relation
Geschäftsverkehr *(m)* business dealings, commercial intercourse
Geschäftszweig *(m)* business line, line of business, trade, trade section
geschätzt estimated
Geschenk *(n)* gift, present
Geschenkgutschein *(m)* gift coupon, gift voucher
Geschirr *(n)* kitchenware, dishes
Geschirrspülmaschine *(f)* dishwasher
Geschirrspülmaschine *(f)*, **gewerbliche** commercial dish washer
Geschirrtuch *(n)* tea towel
Geschmacksmusterschutz *(m)* protection of registered designs
Geschoss *(n)* (Gebäude) floor
Geschwindigkeit *(f)* speed
Geschwindigkeitsbeschränkung *(f)* speed limit
Geschwindigkeitsüberschreitung *(f)* speeding, exceeding the speed limit
Gesellschaft *(f)* association, company, corporation, society
Gesellschaft *(f)* **für musikalische Aufführungs- und mechanische Vervielfältigungsrechte (GEMA)** Society for Musical Performing and Mechanical Reproduction Rights, German Performing Rights Society
Gesellschaft *(f)* **mit beschränkter Haftung (GmbH)** limited company, limited liability company (Ltd.)
Gesetz *(n)* **zur Förderung der Kreislaufwirtschaft und Sicherung der umweltverträglichen Beseitigung von Abfällen** Law on the Promotion of Closed-Loop Recycling Systems and Safeguarding of Environmentally Compatible Waste Materials Disposal

gesetzlich legal; (gesetzmäßig) lawful, legitimate; (vorgeschrieben) statutory
gesetzlich geschützt patented
Gespräch *(n)* conversation, talk; (Telefon) call, telephone call
Gesprächsthema *(n)* subject of conversation, topic of conversation
Gestaltung *(f)* design, form, forming, shaping
Gestaltungsvielfalt *(f)* design variety
gestrichen painted
gesundheitsschädlich harmful to health, injurious to health, unhealthy
Getränk *(n)* beverage, drink
Getränk *(n)***, alkoholfreies** soft drink
Getränkeautomat *(m)* drink dispenser
Getränkebecher *(m)* drinking cup
Getränkedienst *(m)* beverage service, drinks service
Getränkekarte *(f)* list of beverages
Getränkeschankanlage *(f)* beverage dispensing system, drinks dispensing system
getrennt separate
gewährleisten ensure, guarantee
Gewährleistung *(f)* guarantee
Gewalt *(f)* force
gewaltsam forcible, by force, forcibly
Gewerbe *(n)* trade, industry
Gewerbeausstellung *(f)* trade exhibition, trade fair
Gewerbekühlschrank *(m)* commercial refrigerator
Gewerbekühlschrank *(m)***, verglaster** glazed commercial refrigerator
Gewerbeordnung *(f)* industrial legislation
Gewerbezweig *(m)* branch of trade, branch of industry
gewerblich commercial, industrial, trade
Gewerkschaft *(f)* union, trade union, labor union (US), labour union (GB)
Gewicht *(n)* weight; (Last) load
Gewicht *(n)* **pro Quadratmeter** weight per square meter (US), weight per square metre (GB)
Gewindebohrer *(m)* tap, screw tap
Gewindebuchse *(f)* threaded bushing
Gewindedraht *(m)* threaded wire
Gewindehülse *(f)* threaded sleeve
Gewindeplättchen *(n)* threaded plate
Gewindestift *(m)* threaded bolt, threaded pin
Gewinn *(m)* earnings, income, profit, surplus
Gewinn *(m)* **nach Steuern** profit after tax, after-tax income
Gewinn- und Verlustrechnung *(f)* profit and loss account, profit and loss statement
Gewinn *(m)* **vor Steuern** earnings before taxes, profit before taxes, pretax profit
gewinnbringend profitable, profit-making
gewinnen (siegen) win; (Zeit etc.) gain; (Geld etc.) get
Gewinnschwelle *(f)* breakeven point
Gewinnspanne *(f)* profit margin
Gewinnspiel *(n)* (Auslosung) draw; (Ausspielung) lottery
Gewohnheit *(f)* habit
gewöhnlich (üblich) ordinary; (vulgär) common
gewölbt arched, vaulted
Gewühl *(n)* crowd, throng
Girlande *(f)* garland
Gitter *(n)* grid; (Holzgitter) lattice
Gitterelement *(n)* grid panel
Gitterrost *(n)* grate
Gitterträger *(m)* crossbeam girder
Glanz *(m)* gleam, shine, gloss, luster (US), lustre (GB)
glänzen gleam, shine
glänzend shining, glossy; (brilliant) brilliant
Glanzlicht *(n)* highlight
Glasbausystem *(n)* glass display system

Glasboden *(m)* (Regalbord) glass board
Glasbrüstung *(f)* glass railing
Gläserspülmaschine *(f)* glass-washing machine
Gläserspülmaschine *(f)***, gewerbliche** commercial glass-washing machine, commercial dishwasher for glasses
Glashalter *(m)* glass retainer
Glasplatte *(f)* glass top
Glasreinigung *(f)* glass cleaning
Glasscheibe *(f)* glass pane, pane of glass
Glasschneider *(m)* glass cutter
Glastür *(f)* glass door
Glasvitrine *(f)* glass showcase
Glaszuschnitt *(m)* glass cut
glatt smooth
glaubwürdig credible, reliable
gleich same, equal; (ähnlich) similar
Gleitschuh *(m)* roller runner
glitzern glimmer, glitter
Glühbirne *(f)* bulb, light bulb
Gottesdienst *(m)* service, divine service
Grafik *(f)* graphic, graphic arts
Grafik-Designer(in) *(m/f)* graphic designer, graphic artist
Grafikkarte *(f)* graphics card
gratis gratis, free, free of charge
Gratisexemplar *(n)* **des Ausstellungskatalogs** free copy of exhibition catalogue
Gratisprobe *(f)* free sample
Gremium *(n)* committee
Grenze *(f)* (Grenzlinie) boundary; (Land) border, frontier; (Begrenzung) limit
grenzen (angrenzen) border
Grenzformalitäten *(f, pl)* frontier formalities
Grenzkontrolle *(f)* border control
Grenzkosten *(pl)* marginal costs
Grenzübergang *(m)* border crossing, border crossing-point, frontier crossing, frontier crossing-point
Griff *(m)* handle
Großabnehmer *(m)* bulk purchaser

großartig great, marvelous (US), marvellous (GB); (hervorragend) splendid
Großauftrag *(m)* bulk order, large order
Großbild *(n)* blow-up, poster
Großbildprojektor *(m)* large screen projector
Großbildschirm *(m)* large screen
Großbuchstabe *(m)* capital, capital letter
Größe *(f)* size; (Ausmaß) dimensions
Großeinkäufer *(m)* bulk buyer
Großflächenwerbung *(f)* billboard advertising, poster panel advertising
Großformat *(n)* large format, large size
großformatig king-size
Großfoto *(n)* large photo
Großhandel *(m)* wholesale, wholesale trade
Großhandelspreis *(m)* wholesale price
Großhandelsrabatt *(m)* wholesale discount
Großhändler *(m)* wholesaler
Großkolbenlampe *(f)* globe-type bulb
Großmesse *(f)* major exhibition, big exhibition, megashow; (Unternehmen) big exhibition company, major exhibition corporation
Großmesseplätze *(m, pl)* major exhibition venues
Grundabmessung *(f)* site dimension
Grundanstrich *(m)* priming coat
Grundausstattung *(f)* (Messestand) basic stand package, basic stand equipment, basic stand fittings
Grundbeleuchtung *(f)* general lighting
Grundeintrag *(m)* **im Katalog** basic catalog entry (US), basic catalogue entry (GB)
Grundfläche *(f)* floor space
Grundgebühr *(f)* basic rate, standing charge
Grundlage *(f)* basis, foundation
gründlich thorough

Grundmietpreis *(m)* basic space rate, basic rent
Grundreinigung *(f)* initial cleaning, preliminary cleaning
Grundriss *(m)* ground plan, plan view
Grundriss *(m)*, **maßstabsgerechter** scale floor plan
Grundriss *(m)*, **vermaßter** dimensional floor plan
Grundrissplan *(m)* ground plan, plan view
grundsäzlich fundamental, in principle
Gründungsjahr *(n)* year of foundation
Grüne Versicherungskarte *(f)* international motor insurance card
Gruppe *(f)* group; (Arbeitsgruppe) team
Gruppenbesichtigung *(f)* group visit
Gruppendiskussion *(f)* group discussion
Gruppenermäßigung *(f)* group discount
Gruppenführung *(f)* group tour
Gruppenreise *(f)* group journey, group travel
Gruppenstand *(m)* group stand
Gruppentarif *(m)* group rate
GS-Zeichen *(n)* GS safety mark
gültig valid
Gültigkeit *(f)* validity
Gültigkeitsdauer *(f)* period of validity
Gummipuffer *(m)* rubber bump
Gummiring *(m)* rubber o-ring
Gummischlauch *(m)*, **stahlummantelter** steel-sheathed rubber pipe
Gummistopfen *(m)* rubber stopper
günstig attractive, advantageous, favorable (US), favourable (GB); (preiswert) good value; (passend) convenient
Gurt *(m)* belt, strap
Gurtband *(n)* waistband
Güter *(n, pl)*, **verbrauchssteuerpflichtige** goods subject to excise duty, excisable goods
Gütezeichen *(n)* mark of quality, quality label, quality mark
Gutschein *(m)* coupon, voucher

H

haftbar liable
haften (kleben) adhere, stick
haften für be liable
Haftpflicht *(f)* liability
Haftpflichtversicherung *(f)* liability insurance
Haftung *(f)* liability
Haftung *(f)*, **beschränkte** limited liability
Haftung *(f)*, **unbeschränkte** unlimited liability
Haftungsausschluss *(m)* exclusion of liability
Haftungsbeschränkung *(f)* limitation of liability
Haftungsumfang *(m)* extend of liability
Haken *(m)* hook
Hakenschraube *(f)* clip bolt
halbautomatisch semiautomatic
halbdunkel half dark, semi-dark, dusky, dimly-lit
Halbdunkel *(n)* semi-darkness
halbhoch half high, medium-high
halbieren halve, divide
Halbjahr *(n)* half-year
Halbkreis *(m)* semicircle
Halbpension *(f)* half-board
halbrund semicircular
Halbrund *(n)* semicircle
halbseitig half page
halbtags half-day
Halle *(f)* hall; (Hotel) foyer, lobby, lounge
Hallenaufplanung *(f)* hall planning, hall space layout planning
Hallenaufsicht *(f)* hall inspector, hall supervisor, hall security
Hallenaufzug *(m)* hall elevator (US), hall lift (GB)
Hallenbelegungsplan *(m)* hall space assignment plan, hall reservation plan
Hallenbereich *(m)* hall section

Hallenboden *(m)* hall floor
Hallenbruttofläche *(f)* gross hall space
Hallendeckenabhängung *(f)* suspension from the hall roof
Halleneingang *(m)* hall entrance
Hallenelektriker *(m)* official hall electrical contractor, hall electrician
Hallenfußboden *(m)* hall floor
Hallengang *(m)* hall aisle, hall gangway, hall passage
Hallengliederung *(f)* hall arrangement
Hallenhöhe *(f)* hall height
Halleninformationssystem *(n)* hall information system
Halleninspektor *(m)* hall inspector
Hallenkapazität *(f)* hall capacity
Hallenkran *(m)* hall crane
Hallenmaß *(n)* hall dimensions
Hallenmeister *(m)* hall inspector
Hallennummer *(f)* hall number
Hallenpfeiler *(m)* hall column, hall pillar
Hallenplan *(m)* hall plan
Hallensäule *(f)* hall column, hall pillar
Hallenstromversorgung *(f)* hall power supply
Hallenstütze *(f)* hall support
Hallentaxi *(n)* hall taxi
Hallentor *(n)* hall door
Hallentormaß *(n)* hall door dimensions
Hallenübersichtsplan *(m)* general hall plan
Hallenwand *(f)* hall wall
Hallenzufahrt *(f)* hall access route
Halogenstrahler *(m)* halogen spotlight
Haltbarkeit *(f)* durability; (Stabilität) solidity; (Lebensmittel) keeping quality; (Lagerfähigkeit) shelf life
Haltbarkeit *(f)***, begrenzte** perishability
Haltebügel *(m)* supporting loop
Haltegurt *(m)* strap
Halteklammer *(f)* fixing clip
halten (festhalten) hold; (behalten) keep; (beibehalten) maintain; (stützen) support

Haltering *(f)* holding ring
Halterung *(f)* holding device
Halteverbot *(n)* no stopping, no stopping zone
Halteverbotszeichen *(n)* no stopping sign
Hammer *(m)* hammer, mallet
Hammerkopfschraube *(f)* hammerhead screw
hämmern hammer
Handbuch *(n)* handbook, manual
Handel *(m)* commerce, business, trade, trading; (Geschäft) bargain, deal, transaction
Handel *(m)* **treiben** deal, trade, do business
handeln act; (geschäftlich) deal, trade, bargain, do business
Handelsgesetzbuch *(n)* **(HGB)** German Commercial Code
Handelskammer *(f)* Chamber of Commerce, Chamber of Trade
Handelsmarke *(f)* brand, trademark, retail label
Handelsmesse *(f)* commercial fair, trade fair
Handelspartner *(m)* trading partner
Handelsrecht *(n)* commercial law, mercantile law
Handelsregister *(n)* commercial register, trade register
Handelsspanne *(f)* operating margin, operating price margin, trade margin
handelsüblich customary, usual in trade
Handelsvertreter(in) *(m/f)* sales representative
Handelsvertretung *(f)* commercial agency
Handelsware *(f)* merchandise for resale
Handfeger *(m)* brush
Handfeuerlöscher *(m)* hand-held fire extinguisher
handgearbeitet handmade
Handgepäck *(n)* hand baggage (US), hand luggage (GB)

Handgriff *(m)* handle, grip
handhaben handle, manage; (Maschine) operate
Handhabung *(f)* handling; (Maschine) operation
Handlauf *(m)* handrail
Handlaufprofil *(n)* handrail extrusion
Handlauf-Wandbefestigung *(f)* handrail wall fixing bracket
Händler *(m)* dealer, trader
Händlerrabatt *(m)* trade discount
handlich handy
Handlungsbevollmächtigte(r) *(f/m)* authorized agent, authorized clerk, registered manager
Handlungsvollmacht *(f)* limited commercial authority, limited authority to act and sign
handschriftlich handwritten
Handsender *(m)* handheld transmitter
Handtuch *(n)* towel
Handwagen *(m)* cart
Handwaschbecken *(f)* washbasin
Handwerk *(n)* craft, handycraft, craft business, trade
Handwerker(in) *(m/f)* craftsman, craftswoman, tradesman, workman
Handwerkskammer *(f)* chamber of handicrafts
Handwerksmesse *(f)* small industries fair, handicrafts fair
Handwerkszeug *(n)* tools
Handy *(n)* cell phone (US), mobile (GB), mobile phone (GB)
Handzettel *(m)* handbill
Hängeleuchte *(f)* hanging lamp, hanging light
hängen hang; (herabhängen) hang from
hängen an hang on
Hängeschelle *(f)* suspension clamp
Hängeschrank *(m)* wall cabinet
Hartfaserplatte *(f)* fiberboard (US), hardboard (GB)
Haube *(f)* hood
häufig frequent, frequently, often

Hauptabsperrventil *(n)* main stop valve
Hauptanschluss *(m)* (Strom) electric main connection; (Telefon) main line
Hauptausgang *(m)* main exit
Hauptaussteller *(m)* main exhibitor, primary exhibitor
Hauptbahnhof *(m)* central station, central railway station
Haupteinfahrt *(f)* main entrance
Haupteingang *(m)* main entrance
Hauptgang *(m)* (Gastronomie) main course
Hauptgericht *(n)* (Gastronomie) main course, main dish
Haupthahn *(m)* (Wasser) main tap
Hauptleitung *(f)* (Strom) mains; (Wasser, Gas) main pipe
Hauptsache *(f)* main point, most important thing
hauptsächlich chief, main, principal
Hauptschalter *(m)* main switch
Hauptschlüssel *(m)* passkey, master key
Hauptsicherung *(f)* main fuse
Hauptwasseranschluss *(m)* water main connection
Haushaltskühlschrank *(m)* household refrigerator
Hausmesse *(f)* in-house trade show, private trade show
Hausordnung *(f)* house rules, rules of the house
Hausrecht *(n)* domestic authority, domestic rights, domiciliary rights
Hauszeitschrift *(f)* house journal, house magazine
Hebebühne *(f)* lifting platform, platform lift
Hebel *(m)* lever
Hebelriegelschloss *(n)* lever bolt lock
heben lift, raise; (hochziehen) hoist
Hebevorrichtung *(f)* lifting equipment, hoisting gear
Hebezeug *(n)* lifting gear, hoist
Hefter *(m)* file, folder

heftig fierce, violent; (intensiv) intense; (vehement) vehement
Heftklammer *(f)* paper clip
Heftmaschine *(f)* stapler
Heftpflaster *(n)* adhesive plaster, sticking plaster
Heftzwecke *(f)* drawing-pin, thumbtack
Heimatanschrift *(f)* home address
Heimatstadt *(f)* home town, native town
Heimcomputer *(m)* home computer
Heimreise *(f)* journey home, homeward journey, return trip
Heiße Theke *(f)* food hot display unit
heißlaufen overheat, run hot
Heißluft *(f)* hot air
Heißluftherd *(m)* convection oven
Heißluftofen *(m)* hot-air oven
Heißwasser *(n)* hot water
Heißwasserboiler *(m)* water heater
Heißwasserspeicher *(m)* storage water heater
Heizanlage *(f)* heating system
Heizlüfter *(m)* fan heater
Heizplatte *(f)* hotplate
Heizung *(f)* heating, central heating
helfen help, aid; (behilflich sein) assist
hell light, bright
Helligkeit *(f)* brightness; (Licht) lightness
Henkel *(m)* handle
herablassen lower, let down
heraufziehen pull up
herausfordern challenge
Herausforderung *(f)* challenge
Herausgeber *(m)* publisher
herausragen (heraustehen) jut out; (überragen) tower above
Herbstmesse *(f)* fall fair (US), fall exhibition (US), autumn fair (GB), autumn exhibition (GB)
Herkunftsland *(n)* country of origin
Herkunftszertifikat *(n)* certificate of origin

Herrentoilette *(f)* gents, men's toilet, men's restroom (US), gentlemen's cloakroom (GB), gentlemen's lavatory (GB), men's lavatory (GB)
herstellen make, manufacture, produce
Hersteller *(m)* manufacturer, producer
Herstellerfirma *(f)* manufacturers
Herstellerpreis *(m)*, **empfohlener** manufacturer's recommended price
Herstellkosten *(pl)* manufactoring costs, production costs
Herstellung *(f)* manufacture, production
Herstellungsprogramm *(n)* manufacturing program (US), manufacturing programme (GB)
Herstellungsprozess *(m)* industrial process
Herstellungsverfahren *(n)* manufacturing method, manufacturing process
herunterhängen hang down
hervorragend outstanding; (ausgezeichnet) excellent
Hilfe *(f)* aid, assistance, help
Hilfeleistung *(f)* aid, assistance, help
Hilfestellung *(f)* aid; (Unterstützung) support
hilflos helpless
hilfreich helpful; (nützlich) useful
Hilfsarbeiter(in) *(m/f)* unskilled worker
hilfsbereit helpful, ready to help
Hilfsdienst *(m)* auxiliary service
Hilfskraft *(f)* help, helper, assistant
Hilfsmittel *(n)* aid
Hin- und Rückfahrschein *(m)* return ticket, roundabout ticket
Hin- und Rückflug *(m)* return flight, outward and inward flight
Hin- und Rückreise *(f)* outward and homeward journey, outward and homeward voyage

Hin- und Rückreisepreis *(m)* return fare
Hinfahrt *(f)* journey there, outward journey, outward voyage
Hinflug *(m)* outward flight
Hinreise *(f)* journey there, outward journey, outward voyage
hinstellen put, put down
hinten at the back, at the rear; (nach hinten) to the back
hinter (Ort) behind; (Zeit) after
Hinterbandkontrolle *(f)* pitch monitoring
hintereinander (Reihenfolge) one behind the other; (zeitlich) one after the other
Hintergrund *(m)* background
Hintergrundmusik *(f)* background music
Hintertür *(f)* back door
Hinweis *(m)* **für Aussteller** notice to exhibitors
Hinweisschild *(n)* sign
hinzufügen add
Hitze *(f)* heat
Hobel *(m)* plane
hobeln plane
hoch high; (Gestalt) tall
Hochbetrieb *(m)* intense activity, peak period, peak time
hochentwickelt higly advanced, highly developed
Hochformat *(n)* vertical format
Hochfrequenzgerät *(n)* high-frequency equipment
Hochgarage *(f)* multi-story garage (US), multi-storey garage (GB), multi-storey car park (GB)
Hochglanz *(m)* high polish
hochkant end up, on end
Hochleistungs- heavy-duty
Hochleistungsdiaprojektor *(m)* high-power slide projector
Hochrechnung *(f)* projection, projected result

Hochsaison *(f)* high season
Hochspannung *(f)* high tension, high voltage
Hochspannungskabel *(n)* high-voltage cable
Höchstbelastung *(f)* maximum load
Höchstgebühr *(f)* maximum fee
Höchstgeschwindigkeit *(f)* maximum speed
Höchstgewicht *(n)* maximum load, weight limit
Höchstpreis *(m)* maximum price
Hochtechnologie *(f)* high technology
Hochvitrine *(f)* large glass display cabinet, large glass display showcase
Hochvoltlampe *(f)* HV bulb
hochwertig high quality, high-grade quality, high value
hochziehen draw up, pull up
Hocker *(m)* stool
hoffentlich hopefully, hope so, let's hope so
höflich polite; (zuvorkommend) courteous
Höflichkeit *(f)* politeness, courteousness, courtesy
Höhe *(f)* height; (Niveau) level; (Wert) amount
Höhe *(f)* **von Exponaten, maximale** maximum exhibit height
Höheneinstellung *(f)* (Regalböden etc.) height adjustment
Höhenjustierbarkeit *(f)* (Ständer etc.) vertical adjustment
höhenverstellbar vertically adjustable
Höhepunkt *(m)* highlight, high spot
Höhere Gewalt *(f)* act of God, force majeure
hohl hollow
Hohlkehle *(f)* groove
Hohlkehlprofil *(n)* groove profile
Hohlraum *(m)* hollow space
holen fetch, get; (abholen) take away; (jmd. abholen lassen) send for s.o.
Holografie *(f)* holography

Hologramm *(n)* holograph
Holz *(n)* wood; (Bauholz) timber
Holzbearbeitung *(f)* woodworking
Holzbearbeitungsmaschine *(f)* woodworking machinery
Holzfachboden *(m)* (Regal) wooden board
Holzklotz *(m)* block of wood
Holzkonstruktion *(f)* timber construction
Holzleiste *(f)* wooden ledge
Holzsockel *(m)* timber pedestal
Holzstrebe *(f)* wooden strut
Honorar *(n)* fee
hörbar audible
Hörer *(m, pl)* listeners
Hörerschaft *(f)* listeners
Hörfunk *(m)* radio
horizontal horizontal
Horizontalauflösung *(f)* horizontal resolution
Horizontalfrequenz *(f)* horizontal frequency
Horizontalfuge *(f)* horizontal gap
Hostess *(f)* hostess
Hostessendienst *(m)* hostess service
Hotel *(n)* **der gehobenen Mittelklasse** upper-bracket hotel
Hotel *(n)* **erster Klasse** first-class hotel
Hotel *(n)* **garni** residential hotel, lodging house, bed and breakfast
Hotel *(n)* **internationaler Klasse** hotel of international standard
Hotel- und Gaststättenführer *(m)* hotel and restaurant guide
Hotelarrangement *(n)* hotel package
Hotelbelegung *(f)* hotel booking, hotel occupancy
Hoteldirektion *(f)* hotel management
Hotelempfangshalle *(f)* lobby, hotel lobby
Hotelführer *(m)* hotel guide
Hotelgast *(m)* hotel guest
Hotelkette *(f)* hotel chain
Hotelkosten *(pl)* hotel costs

Hotelnachweis *(m)* hotel information service
Hotelrechnung *(f)* hotel bill
Hotelreservierung *(f)* hotel booking
Hotelreservierungsservice *(m)* hotel reservation service
Hotelrestaurant *(n)* hotel diningroom
Hotelunterkunft *(f)* hotel accommodation
Hotelverzeichnis *(n)* hotel register
Hubgerät *(n)* lifting device
Hubkraft *(f)* lifting capacity
Hubstapler *(m)* forklift, forklift truck
Huckepacktransport *(m)* piggy-back freight
Hülle *(f)* cover; (Briefhülle) envelope
Hutablage *(f)* hat shelf
Hydrant *(m)* hydrant
Hydraulik *(f)* hydraulics
Hygiene *(f)* hygiene
hygienisch hygienic

I

ideenreich full of ideas
Identifikationsnummer *(f)* ID number
Illumination *(f)* illumination
illuminieren illuminate
Illustration *(f)* artwork; (Darstellung) illustration
illustrieren illustrate
Image *(n)* image
Imagepflege *(f)* image cultivation
Imbiss *(m)* luncheonette, snack
Imbissstube *(f)* snack bar, snack counter
Imitation *(f)* imitation
Impfbestimmungen *(f, pl)* inoculation requirements
impfen inoculate, vaccinate
impfen lassen, sich be vaccinated
Impfung *(f)* inoculation, vaccination
Impfzeugnis *(n)* certificate of vaccination

imponieren impress
imponierend impressive
Importerlaubnis *(f)* import permit
Importeur *(m)* importer
Importfirma *(f)* importer, import company
Importgenehmigung *(f)* import license (US), import licence (GB)
Importgüter *(n, pl)* imports, imported goods
Importlizenz *(f)* import license (US), import licence (GB)
imprägnieren impregnate
Imprägnierung *(f)* impregnation
Impressum *(n)* imprint
Improvisation *(f)* improvisation
improvisieren improvise
Impuls *(m)* impulse
Impulskauf *(m)* impulse purchase
inbegriffen, alles all included, everything included
Inbetriebnahme *(f)* (Maschine, Anlage) put into operation; (Geschäft etc.) start-up
Inbusschlüssel *(m)* Allen key
Inbusschraube *(f)* Allen screw
Index *(m)* index
Indikator *(m)* indicator
indirekt indirect
individuell individual
Industrie- und Handelskammer *(f)* chamber of industry and commerce
Industrieausstellung *(f)* industries exhibition, industries fair
Industriegebiet *(n)* industrial area, industrial estate
Industriegüter *(n, pl)* manufactured goods, manufactured products, industrial goods, industrial products, manufactures
Industriemesse *(f)* industries exhibition, industries fair
Industrieverband *(m)* federation of industries
Industriezweig *(m)* branch of industry

infolge as a result of, owing to
infolgedessen as a result, consequently, because of that
Information *(f)*, **technische** technical information
Informationsbroschüre *(f)* information brochure
Informationsdienst *(m)* information service
Informationsmaterial *(n)* information, informational material
Informationsquelle *(f)* source of information
Informationsstand *(m)* information stand; (Empfang) information desk
Informationssystem *(n)*, **elektronisches** electronic information system
Informationstechnik *(f)* information technology
Informationszentrum *(n)* information center (US), information centre (GB)
Infotainment *(n)* infotainment
Infotheke *(f)* information counter, information desk
Infrastruktur *(f)* infrastructure
Inhaber(in) *(m/f)* owner, proprietor
Inhalt *(m)* contents; (Broschüre etc.) content, subject, matter; (Volumen) volume, capacity
Inhaltserklärung *(f)* list of contents
Inhaltsverzeichnis *(n)* list of contents, table of contents
Inklusivpreis *(m)* all-in price, all-in rate, inclusive terms
Inland *(n)* inland; (gegenüber Ausland) home
inländisch domestic, home
Inlandsabsatz *(m)* domestic sales, home sales
Inlandsflug *(m)* internal flight
Inlandsgeschäft *(n)* domestic business
Inlandsmarkt *(m)* domestic market, home market
Inlandsnachfrage *(f)* domestic demand
Innenansicht *(f)* interior view

Innenarchitektur *(f)* interior design
Innenausbau *(m)* interior design, interior fitting, interior works
Innenausstattung *(f)* interior decoration, interior furnishings
Innenbeleuchtung *(f)* interior lighting
Innendienst *(m)* office duty, office work
Innendienstmitarbeiter(in) *(m/f)* office worker
Innenecke *(f)* inner corner, internal corner, inside corner
Innenraum *(m)* interior
Innensechskant *(m)* hexagonal recess
Innensechskantschlüssel *(m)* hexagonal recess
Innenseite *(f)*, **vordere** inside the front cover
Innenüberwachung *(f)* indoor surveillance
innerbetrieblich in-house, internal
innerhalb inside, within
Innovation *(f)* innovation
insbesondere specially, especially, in particular, particulary
Inserat *(n)* advertisement, ad
Inserent *(m)* advertiser
inserieren advertise
insgesamt alltogether, in all
Insolvenz *(f)* failure, insolvency; (Überschuldung) bankruptcy
Inspektion *(f)* inspection; (Auto) service
Instabilität *(f)* instability
Installateur(in) *(m/f)* (Klempner(in)) plumber; (Elektriker(in)) electrician
Installation *(f)* installation
installieren install
Instandhaltung *(f)* maintenance
Institution *(f)* institution
instruieren instruct
Instrument *(n)* instrument; (Werkzeug) tool
Instrumentenbrett *(n)* instrument panel
intensivieren intensify
Interesse *(n)* **haben** be interested
Interessensgebiet *(n)* field of interest

Interessent *(m)* interested person, interested party
Internetanschluss *(m)* internet access
Internetpressefach *(n)* internet press box
Internetzugang *(m)* internet access
Interview *(n)* interview
Interview *(n)*, **strukturiertes** guided interview
interviewen interview
Interviewer *(m)* interviewer
Intranet *(n)* intranet
investieren invest
Investition *(f)* investment
Investitionsgüter *(n, pl)* capital goods
Investitionsgütermesse *(f)* capital goods exhibition, capital goods fair
Investor *(m)* contributor of capital, investor
irreführen mislead
irreführend misleading
irren, sich be mistaken, be wrong
Irrtum *(m)* error
ISDN ISDN (Integrated Services Digital Network)
Isolierband *(n)* insulating tape
isolieren insulate
Isolierung *(f)* insulation
Ist-Kosten *(pl)* actual costs

J

Jahresabschluss *(m)* annual accounts, annual statement of accounts, annual accounts statement, year-end accounts
Jahresbericht *(m)* annual report
Jahresbilanz *(f)* annual balance sheet
Jahresgewinn *(m)* annual earnings, annual net profit
Jahresumsatz *(m)* annual sales, annual turnover
jährlich annual, yearly

Jalousettenhalter *(m)* blind retainer
Jalousie *(f)* blind, window shades
jederzeit any time, always
Job-Messe *(f)* job fair
Journalist *(m)* journalist
Joystick *(m)* joystick
Jugendliche(r) *(f/m)* young person, youth

K

Kabel *(n)* wire, cable
Kabelanschluss *(m)* cable connection
Kabelbinder *(m)* cable clip
Kabelfernbedienung *(f)* cable remote control
Kabelführung *(f)* (Verkabelung) wiring
Kabelgraben *(m)* cable trench
Kabelklemme *(f)* cable clamp, cable clip
Kabine *(f)* cabin, cubicle
Kabinendecke *(f)* cabin ceiling, cubicle ceiling
Kabinengröße *(f)* size of cabin, size of cubicle
Kaffee *(m)* **kochen** make coffee
Kaffee *(m)* **mit Milch** white coffee, coffee with milk
Kaffee *(m)* **mit Sahne** coffee with cream
Kaffee *(m)*, **schwarzer** black coffee
Kaffeefilter *(m)* coffee filter
Kaffeekanne *(f)* coffeepot
Kaffeelöffel *(m)* coffee spoon
Kaffeemaschine *(f)* coffeemaker, coffee machine, coffee percolator
Kaffeepause *(f)* coffee break
Kaffeetasse *(f)* coffee cup
Kalender *(m)* calendar; (Taschenkalender) diary
Kalenderjahr *(n)* calendar year
Kalenderwoche *(f)* calendar week

Kalkulation *(f)* calculation, cost estimating, costing
kalkulieren calculate
Kälte *(f)* cold
Kälteanlage *(f)* refrigeration plant
Kältemittelverdichter *(m)* refrigerant compressor
Kältesatz *(m)* refrigerating unit system
Kältesatz *(m)*, **luftgekühlter** air-cooled refrigerating system
Kältesatz *(m)*, **wassergekühlter** water-cooled refrigerating unit system
Kältetechnik *(f)* refrigeration technology
Kamerafahrt *(f)* camera movement
Kamerafahrt *(f)*, **vorgegebene** pre-defined camera movement
Kampagne *(f)* campaign
Kanal *(m)* canal, duct; (Entwässerung) drain; (Abwasser) sewer; (TV) channel
Kanalisation *(f)* severage system
Kanister *(m)* can, metal container
Kännchen *(n)* jug
Kanne *(f)* can; (Kaffee, Tee) pot
Kante *(f)* edge
Kante *(f)*, **abgerundete** radiussed edge
Kante *(f)*, **gerundete** radiussed edge
Kantenriegel *(m)* flush bolt
Kantenschutz *(m)* edge protection
Kantenschutzprofil *(n)* edge protection extrusion
Kantholz *(n)* squared timber
Kantine *(f)* canteen
Kapazität *(f)* capacity
Kapitalgesellschaft *(f)* incorporated firm, public limited company, plc, PLC
kaputt broken, kaput; (Maschine) out of order
Karte *(f)* (Besucher) card; (Theater, Bahn etc.) ticket; (Landkarte) map
Kartei *(f)* card file, card index
Kartenschalter *(m)* ticket counter
Karton *(m)* cardboard, carton, pasteboard
kaschieren (überziehen) laminate, line, glue

Kasse *(f)* (Bank etc.) cashdesk; (Supermarkt) cash point, check-out; (Theater etc.) box office
Kassenbeleg *(m)* sales check, sales receipt
Kassenschalter *(m)* paybox, pay desk, pay cash desk, pay cashier's desk
Kassette *(f)* (Medien) cassette; (Sammelpackung) pack set
Kassierer(in) *(m/f)* cashier
Kasten *(m)* box, case, coffer
Katalog *(m)* catalog (US), catalogue (GB)
Kataloganzeige *(f)* catalog advertisement (US), catalogue advertisement (GB), catalog ad (US), catalogue ad (GB)
Katalogeintragung *(f)* catalog entry (US), catalogue entry (GB)
Katalogfreiexemplar *(n)* free catalog (US), free catalogue (GB)
Katalogklappseite *(f)* catalog gatefold (US), catalogue gatefold (GB), catalog flap (US), catalogue flap (GB)
Katalognachtrag *(m)* catalog supplement (US), catalogue supplement (GB)
Katalognummer *(f)* catalog number (US), catalogue number (GB)
Katalogpreis *(m)* catalog price (US), catalogue price (GB)
Katalogredaktion *(f)* catalog editor (US), catalogue editor (GB)
Katalogrückseite *(f)* catalog back cover (US), catalogue back cover (GB)
Katalogseite *(f)* catalog page (US), catalogue page (GB)
Kauf *(m)* buying, purchase
Kaufabsicht *(f)* purchase intention
kaufen buy, purchase
Käufer(in) *(m/f)* buyer, purchaser
Käuferschicht *(f)* group of buyers
Kauffrau *(f)* businesswoman
Kaufkraft *(f)* buying power, purchasing power, spending power

käuflich purchasable
Kaufmann *(m)* (Geschäftsmann) businessman, merchant; (Händler) trader
kaufmännisch business, commercial
Kaufoption *(f)* purchase option
Kaufpreis *(m)* buying price, purchase price, selling price
Kaufvertrag *(m)* contract of sale, sales contract
Kaution *(f)* security, key money, deposit
kehren sweep
Keil *(m)* wedge
keilförmig wedge-shaped
Kellner(in) *(m/f)* waiter, waitress
kennen know
kennen, jdn. be acquainted with, be familiar with
kennenlernen get to know, become acquainted with
Kennkarte *(f)* identity card
Kenntnis *(f)* knowledge
Kenntnis *(f)* **nehmen, zur** take note of
Kennwort *(n)* code name; (EDV) password
Kennziffer *(f)* key number, reference number
Kette *(f)* chain; (Reihe) line, string
Kettensäge *(f)* chain saw
Kilowatt *(n)* kilowatt
Kilowattstunde *(f)* kilowatt hour
Kindergarten *(m)* kindergarten; (Kleinkinder) nursery school
Kindertagesstätte *(f)* day nursery, kindergarten
Kirchencenter *(n)* church center (US), church centre (GB)
Kiste *(f)* box, case; (Lattenkiste) crate
Kitchenette *(f)* (Kleinküche) kitchenette
Kitsch *(m)* kitsch
kitschig kitschy
Klammer *(f)* clip, cramp; (Heftklammer) staple
Klang *(m)* sound

Klangfarbe *(f)* tone color (US), tone colour (GB)
klappbar folding
Klapptisch *(m)* folding table
klären clear, purify; (abklären) clear up, clarify
Klarsichthülle *(f)* clear plastic folder
klassifizieren classify; (einstufen) grade
Klausel *(f)* clause
Klebeband *(n)* adhesive strip, adhesive tape
kleben glue, paste
Klebstoff *(m)* adhesive; (Leim) glue
kleiden clothe, dress
Kleiderbügel *(m)* clothes hanger, coat hanger
Kleiderhaken *(m)* coat hook
Kleidung *(f)* clothes
Kleinanzeige *(f)* classified ad, small ad
Kleinbus *(m)* minibus
Kleingeld *(n)* small coin, small change, loose change
Kleintransporter *(m)* pickup, pickup truck
Kleister *(m)* paste
kleistern paste
Klemme *(f)* (Klammer) clip; (Zwinge) clamp
klemmen jam; (quetschen) pinch, sqeeze
Klempner(in) *(m/f)* plumber
Klimaanlage *(f)* air conditioning system
Klimagerät *(n)* air conditioner
klimatisiert air-conditioned
Klimatisierung *(f)* air conditioning
Kneifzange *(f)* pliers, pair of nippers, pair of pincers
Kneipe *(f)* pub
Kneipenbummel *(m)* pub crawl
Knoten *(m)* node
Knotenachse *(f)* node axis
Koaxialkabel *(n)* coaxial cable
Kochnische *(f)* kitchenette
Kochplatte *(f)* hotplate

Kochtopf *(m)* pot, cooking pot, saucepan
koffeinfrei decaffeinated, without caffeine
Koffer *(m)* bag, case, suitcase
Kollege *(m)* colleague
kollegial cooperative
Kollegin *(f)* colleague
Kollizettel *(m)* pack label
Kombinationsschloss *(f)* combination lock
Komfort *(m)* (Bequemlichkeit) comfort
Kommanditgesellschaft *(f)* limited partnership, limited commercial partnership, private limited partnership, public limited partnership
Kommentar *(m)* commentary; (Stellungnahme) comment
kommentieren comment on
Kommission *(f)* committee
Kommunikation *(f)* communication
Kommunikationsdienstleistung *(f)* communication service
Kommunikationssystem *(n)* communicating system
Kommunikationsweg *(m)* channel of communication
Kompaktküche *(f)* kitchenette; (vorgefertigt) kitchenette unit
Kompatibilität *(f)* compatibility
kompetent competent
Kompetenz *(f)* competence
Komplettmessestand *(m)* complete stand, completely equipped stand
Komplettpreis *(m)* package price
Komplettstand *(m)* complete stand, completely equipped stand
Komplikation *(f)* complication
kompliziert complicated
Kompressor *(m)* compressor
Kondensmilch *(f)* condensed milk, evaporated mik
Kondition *(f)* condition
Konfekt *(n)* sweets, confection

Konfektionsständer *(m)* clothing stand
Konferenz *(f)* conference, meeting
Konferenzraum *(m)* conference room, meeting room
Konferenzschaltung *(f)* conference circuit
Konferenztisch *(m)* conference table, round table
Konformitätserklärung *(f)* declaration of conformity
Kongress *(m)* congress; (Tagung, Versammlung) convention
Kongressausstellung *(f)* congress and exhibition
Kongressprogramm *(n)* congress program (US), congress programme (GB)
Konjunktur *(f)* economic activity, economic situation, economic trends
Konjunkturaussichten *(f, pl)* business outlook, economic prospect
Konkurrent *(m)* competitor, rival
Konkurrenz *(f)* competition, rivalry
Konkurrenzerzeugnis *(n)* competing product, competitive product, rival product
konkurrenzfähig competitive
Konkurrenzfähigkeit *(f)* competitiveness
Konkurrenzfirma *(f)* rival firm
Konkurrenzkampf *(m)* competitive struggle, rat race
Konkurrenzklausel *(f)* restraint clause, restraining clause, non-competitive clause
konkurrenzlos unrivaled (US), unrivalled (GB)
Konkurrenzmarke *(f)* rival brand
Konkurrenzpreis *(m)* competitive price
Konkurrenzprodukt *(n)* rival product
Konkurrenzunternehmen *(n)* competitor
konkurrieren compete

Konkurs *(m)* insolvency; (Zahlungsunfähigkeit) liquidation; (Überschuldung) bankruptcy
konsequent consequent, consistent, logical; (unbeirrt) firm, resolute
Konsequenz *(f)* consequence; (Beharrlichkeit) consistency
Konserve *(f)* preserve, preserved food, tinned food
Konservendose *(f)* can (US), tin (GB)
Konsole *(f)* console, bracket, shelf bracket
Konsolenträger *(m)* bracket support
konstant constant
konstruieren construct, build; (entwerfen) design
Konstrukteur(in) *(m/f)* design engineer, designer
Konstruktion *(f)* construction; (Entwurf) design
Konstruktionsfehler *(m)* constructional fault
Konstruktionssoftware *(f)* construction software
Konsulat *(n)* consulate
Konsum *(m)* consumption
Konsument(in) *(m/f)* consumer
Konsumentenbefragung *(f)* consumer survey
Konsumforschung *(f)* consumer research
Konsumgüter *(n, pl)* consumable goods, consumer goods
Konsumgütermesse *(f)* consumer goods fair, consumer goods exhibition
Konsumneigung *(f)* propensity to consume
Kontaktanbahnung *(f)* contact generation, lead generation
Kontaktbildschirm *(m)* touch-sensitive screen, touch screen
kontaktfreudig sociable
Kontingent *(n)* quota
kontinuierlich continuous
Konto *(n)* account

Kontrastregler *(m)* contrast control
Kontrastverhältnis *(n)* contrast ratio
Kontrolle *(f)* control, inspection, check; (Überwachung) supervision
Kontrolle *(f)* **von Messe- und Ausstellungszahlen** auditing of show statistics
Kontrolle *(f)*, **unter** under control
Kontrollfrage *(f)* control question
Kontrollgerät *(n)* controlling device
kontrollierbar controllable; (überprüfbar) verifiable
kontrollieren check, control
Kontrolllampe *(f)* pilot lamp
Kontrollliste *(f)* checklist
konventionell conventional
Konzept *(n)* concept
Konzeption *(f)* conception
Konzeptioner *(m)* designer
Konzern *(m)* group, affiliated group, group of companies, concern, combine, trust
Konzession *(f)* concession, license (US), licence (GB)
konzessionierte Fachfirma *(f)* licensed speciality contractor
Kooperation *(f)* cooperation
kooperieren cooperate
Kopfende *(n)* head
Kopfhörer *(m)* headphones
Kopfhörerleiste *(f)* headphone panel
Kopfschmerz *(m)* headache
Kopfschmerztablette *(f)* headache tablet
Kopfstand *(m)* (Messestand) peninsula stand, two-corner stand, end-of-row booth
Kopierdienst *(m)* copying service
Kopierer *(m)* copier, photocopier
Kopierladen *(m)* copy shop
Kopierpreis *(m)* copy price
Korkenzieher *(m)* bottle screw, corkscrew
Körperschaftssteuer *(f)* corporate tax, corporation tax, corporation income tax

Körpersprache *(f)* body language
Körperverletzung *(f)* bodily injury
Korrektur *(f)* correction
Korrekturfahne *(f)* proof, galley proof
Korrespondenz *(f)* correspondence
Korrespondenzsprache *(f)* language for the correspondence
kosten (Geld) cost; (Zeit) take; (probieren) taste
Kosten *(pl)* charge, cost, costs; (Ausgaben) expenditure, expense, expenses; (Auslagen) outlays
Kosten *(pl)* **tragen** bear the costs
Kostenanalyse *(f)* cost analysis
Kostenaufwand *(m)* cost, expenditure
Kostenberechnung *(f)* costing
Kostenbeteiligung *(f)* cost sharing, sharing of costs
kostendämpfend cost-cutting
kostendeckend cost-covering
Kostenersparnis *(f)* cost saving
Kostenfaktor *(m)* cost factor
Kostenfrage *(f)* question of costs
kostengünstig cost-effective
kostenintensiv cost-intensive
Kostenkontrolle *(f)* cost control, expense control, cost monitoring
kostenlos at no charge, free, free of charge, without charge, gratuitous
Kosten-Nutzen-Analyse *(f)* cost-benefit-analysis
kostenpflichtig chargeable, liable to pay the costs, subject to a charge
Kostenplanung *(f)* budgeting, cost planning
Kostenrechnung *(f)* cost accounting
Kostenrentabilität *(f)* cost effectiveness
Kostensenkung *(f)* cost cutting, cost reduction
kostensparend cost-saving
Kostensteigerung *(f)* cost increase
Kostenstelle *(f)* cost center (US), cost centre (GB)
Kostenüberwachung *(f)* expense control

Kostenvoranschlag *(m)* estimate, cost estimate, forecast, cost forecast
Kostprobe *(f)* taste, sample
kostspielig costly, expensive
Kostüm *(n)* costume
Kraft *(f)* strength, force, power
Kraftanstrengung *(f)* effort
Kraftfahrer *(m)* driver, motorist
Kraftfahrzeug *(n)* motor vehicle
kräftig strong, sturdy, robust, powerful
Kraftstoff *(m)* fuel
Kraftstoffleitung *(f)* fuel pipe
Kraftstoffverbrauch *(m)* fuel consumption
Kragarm *(m)* cantilever
Kragarmleuchte *(f)* cantilever floodlight, clamp-on floodlight
Kran *(m)* crane
Kran- und Hebefahrzeuge *(n, pl)* cranes and lifting equipment, hoisting equipment
Kranbahn *(f)* craneway
krank sick, ill, diseased
Krankenhaus *(n)* hospital
Krankenkasse *(f)* health insurance company
Krankenversicherung *(f)* health insurance, medical insurance
Krankheit *(f)* illness, sickness, disease
Krankmeldung *(f)* notification of illness, notification of sickness
krankschreiben file a medical certificate
kratzfest scratch-resistant
Krawatte *(f)* tie
Krawattennadel *(f)* tie-pin
kreativ creative
Kreativität *(f)* creativity
Kredit *(m)* credit, loan
Kredit *(m)* **gewähren** grant a credit
Kredit *(m)*, **kurzfristiger** short credit, short-term credit
Kreditauskunft *(f)* credit information, banker's reference
Kreditbetrag *(m)* credit sum, loan amount
Kreditbürgschaft *(f)* loan guarantee
Kreditgeber *(m)* creditor; (Bank) lender
Kreditkarte *(f)* credit card
Kreditnehmer *(m)* borrower, debtor
kreditwürdig creditworthy
Kreditwürdigkeit *(f)* creditworthiness, credit rating, credit standing
Kreis *(m)* circle
Kreisabschnitt *(m)* segment
Kreisausschnitt *(m)* sector
Kreisdiagramm *(n)* pie chart
kreisförmig circular
kreisrund circular
Kreissäge *(f)* circular saw
Kreuzschlitzschraube *(f)* recessed head screw
kreuzweise crosswise
Kriterium *(n)* criterion
Kritik *(f)* criticism
kritisch critical
kritisieren criticize
krumm crooked, warped; (verbogen) bent
Kubikmeter *(m, n)* cubic meter (US), cubic metre (GB)
Küchenabfall *(m)* kitchen waste, kitchen garbage (US)
Küchenausstattung *(f)* kitchen fittings
Kücheneinheit *(f)* kitchen unit, kitchenette
Kücheneinrichtung *(f)* kitchen furniture and fittings, kitchen equipment, outfit for kitchens
Küchengeschirr *(n)* kitchenware
Küchenhilfe *(f)* kitchen help, kitchenmaid
Küchenpersonal *(n)* kitchen personnel, kitchen staff
Küchentuch *(n)* kitchen towel
Küchenutensilien *(f, pl)* kitchenware, kitchen utensils
Kugel *(f)* ball

kugelförmig globular, spherical
Kugellautsprecher *(m)* spherical speaker
Kugelschreiber *(m)* ballpoint pen
kühl chilly, cool
kühl lagern store cool
Kühl-/Gefrierkombination *(f)* combination freezer-refrigeration
Kühlanlage *(f)* cooling plant, cooling system, refrigerating plant, refrigerating system
Kühlauslage *(f)* cooling display, refrigerated display
Kühlbehälter *(m)* cooling container
Kühlcontainer *(m)* refrigerated container
kühlen chill, cool, refrigerate
Kühlfahrzeug *(n)* vehicle for refrigerated transport
Kühlhaus *(n)* cold-store, cold-storage depot
Kühlhauslagerung *(f)* cold storage
Kühlinsel *(f)* refrigerated island site cabinet
Kühlkuppel *(f)* refrigerated cupola
Kühlmöbel *(m)* refrigerated cabinet
Kühlraum *(m)* cold room, cold-storage room
Kühlregal *(n)* multi-deck refrigerated commercial cabinet, refrigerated vertical cabinet
Kühlschrank *(m)* refrigerator, fridge, icebox (US)
Kühlschrank *(m)* **mit Tiefkühlfach** refrigerator with low temperature compartment
Kühlschrank *(m)* **mit verglaster Tür** refrigerator with glazed door
Kühlservierwagen *(m)* refrigerated trolley
Kühltheke *(f)* refrigerated service counter
Kühltruhe *(f)* refrigerated open top display cabinet
Kühlung *(f)* cooling

Kühlvitrine *(f)* refrigerated display cabinet
Kühlzelle *(f)* portable cold room
Kunde *(m)* customer
Kunde *(m)*, **potenzieller** potential customer, prospective customer
Kundenbedürfnisse *(n, pl)* customer needs
Kundenberatung *(f)* customer advisory service
Kundenbetreuung *(f)* customer care, customer support, customer assitance
Kundenbonität *(f)* customer's solvency
Kundendienst *(m)* after-sales service, backup service, customer service
Kundendienstabteilung *(f)* customer service department
Kundendienstmechaniker(in) *(m/f)* service engineer
Kundenkartei *(f)* list of customers
Kundenkredit *(m)* customer credit
Kundenkreis *(m)* clientele
Kundennutzen *(m)* customer value
Kundenorientierung *(f)* customer orientation
Kundenprofil *(n)* customer profile
kundenspezifisch customized
Kundentreue *(f)* customer loyalty
Kundenwunsch *(m)* customer's request
Kundenzufriedenheit *(f)* customer satisfaction
Kundin *(f)* customer
Kundschaft *(f)* clientele
Künstler(in) *(m/f)* artist; (Darsteller) actor, actress, performer
künstlerisch artistic
Kunstlicht *(n)* artificial light
Kunststoff *(m)* synthetic material, plastic, plastic material
kunststoffbeschichtet plastic-coated, synthetic-laminated
Kunststoffclip *(m)* plastic clip

69

Kunststoff-Distanzscheibe *(f)* plastic spacer
Kunststoff-Klemmschraube *(f)* plastic set screw
Kunststoffpflanze *(f)* artificial plant
Kunststoffstab *(m)* plastic tube
Kuppel *(f)* cupola, dome
Kupplungsstutzen *(m)* coupling stud
Kupplungsteil *(n)* coupling part
Kurbel *(f)* crank, handle
Kurierdienst *(m)* courier service, delivery service, parcel delivery service
Kursbuch *(n)* railroad guide (US), railroad timetable (US), railway guide (GB), railway timetable (GB)
Kurve *(f)* curve
Kurzbericht *(m)* brief report; (Kurzfassung) summary
kurzfristig short-dated, short-term
Kurzschluss *(m)* short circuit
Kürzung *(f)* shortening; (Kosten etc.) cut
kW-Anschlussleistung *(f)* kw consumption

L

Lack *(m)* lacquer, varnish; (Einbrennlack) enemal
Lackfarbe *(f)* varnish, varnish paint
lackieren varnish
Ladegerät *(n)* battery charger
laden (Güter; Computer) load; (Batterie) charge
Laden *(m)* (Geschäft) store (US), shop (GB)
Ladeneinrichtung *(f)* shopfittings
Laderampe *(f)* loading ramp
Ladeschein *(m)* carrier's receipt, bill of lading

Ladung *(f)* cargo, lading, load, cargo load
Lage *(f)* (Ort) location; (Situation) situation
Lageplan *(m)* site plan
Lager *(n)* stock, store, storage, storehouse, warehouse
Lagerbestand *(m)* stock, inventory, goods on hand
lagerfähig storable
Lagergebühr *(f)* storage, storage charge
Lagerhaltung *(f)* storage, storekeeping, warehousing
Lagerhaltungskosten *(pl)* warehouse charges
Lagerhaus *(n)* storehouse, warehouse
lagern store, keep, warehouse; (im Kühlhaus) coldstore
Lagerort *(m)* location of goods, storage location
Lagerraum *(m)* stockroom, storeroom
Lagerstelle *(f)* **für Leergut** storage area for empties
Lagerung *(f)* storage, warehousing
Lamelle *(f)* lamella, slat
Lamellenprofil *(n)* slat profile
laminieren laminate
Lampe *(f)* lamp
Lampenfassung *(f)* socket, lamp socket
Länderpavillon *(m)* national pavilion
Landessprache *(f)* national language
landesüblich customary, in accordance with local customs
Landeswährung *(f)* national currency
Landgasthof *(m)* country inn
Landwirtschaftsausstellung *(f)* agricultural fair, agricultural show, country fair, country show
Landwirtschaftsmesse *(f)* agricultural fair, agricultural show, country fair, country show
Länge *(f)* length
Längenmaß *(n)* linear measure, long measure

längerfristig long-range, longer-term
Langfeldleuchte *(f)* fluorescent light
langfristig long-term
langlebig long-lived, durable
länglich long, longish, oblong
Längsachse *(f)* longitudinal axis
Längsschnitt *(m)* longitudinal section
Langzeitmiete *(f)* long-term rent
Lappen *(m)* cloth, rag
Lärm *(m)* noise; (Radau) row
Lärmbelästigung *(f)* noise disturbance, noise pollution
lärmen be noisy, make much noise
Lärmpegel *(m)* noise level
Lasche *(f)* loop
Laseranlage *(f)* laser equipment, laser system
Laserzeiger *(m)* laserpointer
Last *(f)* load, charge, weight
Last *(f)*, **flächig aufgelagerte** distributed load
Lastenaufzug *(m)* freight elevator (US), freight lift (GB), goods elevator (US), goods lift (GB)
Lastenverteilung *(f)* load distribution
Lastwagen *(m)* truck (US), lorry (GB)
Lastwagenanhänger *(m)* trailer, truck trailer
Lastwagentransport *(m)* motor transport, truckage
Lastzug *(m)* trailer, truck, truck trailer
Latte *(f)* lath, slat
Lattenverschlag *(m)* crate
Laufkran *(m)* travelling crane
Laufrolle *(f)* roller, castor
Laufschiene *(f)* guide rail, track
Laufschuh *(m)* runner
Laufzeit *(f)* duration, running time
Laufzeitreinigung *(f)* interim cleaning
laut loud; (lärmend) noisy
Lautsprecher *(m)* speaker, loudspeaker
Lautstärke *(f)* loudness, volume, sound volume
Lautstärkeregler *(m)* volume control
Layout *(n)* layout

LCD-Projektor *(m)* LCD projector
Leasingvertrag *(m)* leasing agreement
lebensgefährlich extremely dangerous, highly dangerous
Lebenshaltungskosten *(pl)* cost of living, living expenses
Lebensmittel *(n, pl)* food, foodstuffs, groceries, provisions
Lebensmittelgeschäft *(n)* grocer's, grocery store (US), food store (US), grocery (GB), food shop (GB)
Lebensmittel-Hygiene-Verordnung *(f)* Food Hygiene Ordinance
Lebensmittelüberwachung *(f)* food supervision
Lebensversicherung *(f)* life assurance, life insurance
Leckanzeiger *(m)* leak indicator
LED-Bidschirm *(m)* LED screen
leer empty; (Stand, Stelle etc.) vacant
leeren empty
Leergewicht *(n)* dead weight, unladen weight
Leergut *(n)* empties, returned empties, empty packaging
Leergutlagerung *(f)* storage of empties
Leergutmanipulation *(f)* empties handling
Leerpackung *(f)* dummy
Leerstand *(m)* (unbesetzter Stand) empty stand, vacant stand
legal legal, lawful
Legitimation *(f)* legitimation; (Bevollmächtigung) authorization
Lehrgang *(m)* course
leicht (Gewicht) light; (einfach) easy
Leichtheadset *(n)* light headset
leider unfortunately
Leiharbeiter(in) *(m/f)* casual worker
Leiharbeitnehmer(in) *(m/f)* agency worker
leihen borrow; (ausleihen) lend; (mieten) rent (US), hire (GB)
Leihgebühr *(f)* rental charge (US), hire charge (GB)

Leihgerät *(n)* rental equipment (US), hired equipment (GB)
Leihgeschirr *(n)* rental dinnerware
Leihmöbel *(pl)* rental furniture
Leim *(m)* glue
leimen glue, glue together
Leinwand *(f)* screen, projection screen
leise quiet; (Ton) low, soft
Leistung *(f)* (Tat) performance; (Auto, Strom) power
Leistung *(f)***, elektrische** electrical loading, electrical power
Leistungsaufnahme *(f)* (Strom) power consumption, power input
leistungsfähig able, capable, efficient
Leistungsfähigkeit *(f)* efficiency
Leistungsschau *(f)* competitive exhibition, competitive show
Leistungsumfang *(m)* scope of services
leiten be in charge of, direct, lead, manage
leitend executive, guiding, leading, managing
Leiter *(f)* ladder
Leiter(in) *(m/f)* leader, head, manager, manageress, director, managing director
Leiter(in) *(m/f)***, technische(r)** chief engineer
Leitfaden *(m)* guide
leitfähig conductive
Leitmesse *(f)* lead fair, main fair, flagship fair
Leitung *(f)* leading, leadership, guiding; (Geschäft) management, control; (Veranstaltung) organization; (Verwaltung) administration; (Verbindungsleitung) connection; (Gas, Strom, Wasser) main, pipe, pipeline; (Strom, Telefon) wire; (Telefon) line; (Versorgungsleitung) supply line, utility line
Leitungsnetz *(n)* (Gas, Strom, Wasser) mains system
Leitungsrohr *(n)* main, pipe

Leitungsverlegung *(f)* supply line installation, utility line installation
Leuchte *(f)* light, lamp
leuchten shine; (aufleuchten) flash; (glänzen) gleam, sparkle
Leuchtenanschluss *(m)* lamp connector
Leuchtfarbe *(f)* fluorescent, luminous paint
Leuchtkasten *(m)* light box, illuminated case
Leuchtkraft *(f)* brightness
Leuchtreklame *(f)* illuminated advertising, luminous advertising
Leuchtschrift *(f)* illuminated letters
Leuchtstofflampe *(f)* fluorescent lamp
Licht *(n)* **anmachen** turn on the lights
Licht *(n)* **ausschalten** switch off the lights
Lichtband *(n)* strip lighting
Lichtbildervortrag *(m)* slide lecture
Lichtbildvorführung *(f)* slide show, slide presentation
Lichtdecke *(f)* luminous ceiling
Lichtdesign *(n)* illumination design
lichtdurchlässig light-transmissive, permeable to light
Lichteffekt *(m)* lighting effect
lichtempfindlich sensitive to light
Lichtempfindlichkeit *(f)* sensitivity to light; (Film) speed
Lichtgehäuse *(n)* lightcase
Lichtgestaltung *(f)* lighting design
Lichtleitung *(f)* light circuit, lighting wire
Lichtquelle *(f)* source of light
Lichtraster *(n)* light grid
Lichtsäule *(f)* luminous column
Lichtschalter *(m)* light switch
Lichtschranke *(f)* photoelectric barrier
Lichtstab *(m)* lighting tube
Lichtstärke *(f)* (Intensität) luminous intensity; (Leuchtkraft) brightness; (Glühbirne) wattage
Lichtstrahl *(m)* beam of light

lichtundurchlässig opaque
Lichtverhältnisse *(n, pl)* lighting conditions
Lieferant *(m)* provider, supplier; (Speisen und Getränke) caterer
Lieferauftrag *(m)* delivery order
lieferbar available
Lieferbedingungen *(f, pl)* delivery terms, terms of delivery
Lieferkosten *(pl)* delivery costs
liefern (ausliefern) deliver; (versorgen) supply; (besorgen) provide
Lieferplan *(m)* delivery schedule
Lieferpreis *(m)* delivery price, supply price
Lieferschein *(m)* delivery note
Liefertermin *(m)* delivery date
Lieferung *(f)* (Auslieferung) delivery; (Versorgung) supply
Lieferung *(f)* **frei Haus** free delivery
Lieferung *(f)* **gegen Zahlung** payable on delivery, delivery versus payment
Liefervertrag *(m)* delivery contract
Lieferwagen *(m)* truck (US), pickup (US), pickup truck (US), van (GB), delivery van (GB)
Lieferzeit *(f)* delivery time, time of delivery
Liegegeld *(n)* demurrage
Lift *(m)* lift, elevator
Liftboden *(m)* raised floor
Limonade *(f)* lemonade
Lineal *(n)* ruler
Linie *(f)* line
Linienbus *(m)* regular bus, scheduled bus
Linienflug *(m)* scheduled flight
Liquidität *(f)* liquidity, solvency
Liste *(f)* list
Listenpreis *(m)* list price
Liter *(m)* liter (US), litre (GB)
Literatur *(f)*, **technische** technical literature
Lizenz *(f)* license (US), licence (GB)
Lizenzgeber *(m)* licensor

Lizenzinhaber *(m)* license holder (US), licence holder (GB)
Lizenznehmer *(m)* licensee
Lizenzvertrag *(m)* licensing agreement
LKW truck (US), lorry (GB)
LKW-Abstellplatz *(m)* truck parking space, trailer parking area
LKW-Anhänger *(m)* trailer, truck trailer
LKW-Anhängerabstellplatz *(m)* truck park, trailer park, truck parking area, trailer parking area
LKW-Transport *(m)* motor transport, truckage
Loch *(n)* hole
Lochblech *(n)* perforated sheet metal, perforated steel panel
Lochblechboden *(m)* (Regal) perforated board
lochen punch; (perforieren) perforate
Locher *(m)* punch, perforator
Lochschiene *(f)* slotted profile, slotted boring bar
Lochung *(f)* perforation
Lochwand *(f)* perforated panel
Lochzange *(f)* punch pliers
Lockartikel *(m)* bait, loss-leader
locker loose
lockern loosen; (Seil etc.) slacken
Lockvogelwerbung *(f)* bait advertising, bait and switch advertising, loss-leader advertising
Löffel *(m)* spoon
Logistik *(f)* logistics
Logo *(m)* logo, logotype
lohnend paying, profitable; (nützlich) worthwhile
Lohnkosten *(pl)* manpower costs, labor costs (US), labour costs (GB), cost of labor (US), cost of labour (GB), wage costs
Lohnsteuer *(f)* wage tax
Lokal *(n)* (Restaurant) restaurant; (Kneipe) pub (GB)
Lokalpresse *(f)* local paper, local press
Lokalzeitung *(f)* local newspaper

löschen (Feuer) extinguish; (EDV-Speicher) clear, delete; (Daten, Band) erase
Löschfahrzeug *(n)* fire engine
lose loose; (locker) slack
lösen remove, detach
loslassen let go of
losschrauben unscrew
Lösung *(f)* (Problem etc.) solution
Lösung *(f)*, **individuelle** individual solution
Lösungsmittel *(n)* solvent
löten solder
Lötkolben *(m)* soldering iron
lotrecht perpendicular, vertical
Lücke *(f)* gap
lückenhaft gappy, full of gaps
lückenlos without gaps; (vollständig) complete
Luftballon *(m)* balloon
Luftballons *(m, pl)*, **gasgefüllte** gas-filled balloons
luftdicht airtight
lüften air, ventilate
Lüfter *(m)* ventilator
Luftfahrtgesellschaft *(f)* airline
Luftfeuchtigkeit *(f)* humidity
Luftfracht *(f)* air cargo, air freight
Luftfrachtbrief *(m)* air bill of lading, air waybill
Luftfrachtgebühren *(f, pl)* air freight charges, air cargo charges
Luftfrachtkosten *(pl)* air freight costs, air cargo costs
luftgekühlt air-cooled
Luftkühler *(m)* air cooler
Luftpostbrief *(m)* air letter
Luftpostpaket *(n)* air parcel
Luftschacht *(m)* air shaft
Lüftung *(f)* airing
Lüftungs- und Klimaanlage *(f)* ventilation and air conditioning system
Lüftungsanlage *(f)* ventilation system
Luftverkehrsgesellschaft *(f)* airline

Luftzug *(m)* draft (US), draught (GB)
Luke *(f)* hatch
Lumen *(n)* lumen
Luxusartikel *(m)* luxury article; (Güter) luxury goods
Luxushotel *(n)* luxury hotel

M

Magazin *(n)* (Lager) warehouse, store, storeroom, depot; (Zeitschrift) magazine, periodical
magisch magic
magnetisch magnetic
Mahl *(n)* meal
mahnen (ermahnen) admonish, urge; (Zahlung anmahnen) demand payment, send a reminder
Mahnung *(f)* (Ermahnung) admonition; (Zahlungserinnerung) reminder
malen paint
Maler(in) *(m/f)* painter
Malerarbeit *(f)* painting
Management *(n)* management
Mangel *(m)* (Knappheit) lack, shortage, scarcity; (Defekt) defect, fault
mangelhaft (unbefriedigend) insufficient, inadequate, unsatisfactory; (fehlerhaft) faulty, defective
Mängelrüge *(f)* notice of defect
Mannequin *(f)* mannequin, model
Mannschaft *(f)* team, crew
Mantel *(m)* coat
manuell manual
Mappe *(f)* (Aktentasche) briefcase; (Hefter) folder
MARATEL-Bildschirm *(m)* MARATEL screen
MARATEL-Scheibe *(f)* MARATEL screen
Marge *(f)* margin, spread
marginal marginal, incremental

Marke *(f)* (Fabrikat) make, type; (Ware) brand, sort
Markenartikel *(m)* branded article, genuine article, proprietary article, branded goods, proprietary goods
Markenbekanntheit *(f)* brand awareness, brand familiarity
Markenfabrikat *(n)* proprietary make
Markenimage *(n)* brand image
Markenname *(m)* brand name, trade name
Markenschutz *(m)* protection of trademarks
Markenzeichen *(n)* trademark
Marketingetat *(m)* marketing budget
Marketingfachfrau *(f)* marketing specialist, marketer
Marketingfachmann *(m)* marketing specialist, marketer
Marketingkonzept *(n)* marketing concept
Marketingleiter(in) *(m/f)* marketing manager
Marketingmix *(n)* marketing mix
Marketingplan *(m)* marketing plan
Marketingstrategie *(f)* marketing strategy
markieren mark
Markierung *(f)* marking
Markt *(m)***, potenzieller** potential market
Marktanalyse *(f)* market analysis
Marktanteil *(m)* market share, share of the market, slice of the market
Marktbefragung *(f)* market survey
Marktentwicklung *(f)* market development
marktfähig marketable
Marktforschung *(f)* market research
Marktführer *(m)* market leader
Marktlücke *(f)* gap in the market
Marktnische *(f)* market niche
Marktpotenzial *(n)* market potential
Marktpreis *(m)* price, market price
Marktprognose *(f)* market forecast

Marktsättigung *(f)* market saturation
Marktsegment *(n)* market segment
Marktsegmentierung *(f)* market segmentation
Markttendenz *(f)* market trend
Markttest *(m)* market test, market testing
Marktumfrage *(f)* market survey
Marktuntersuchung *(f)* market study, market survey
Marktwert *(m)* market value
Marktzugang *(m)* access to the market
Maschine *(f)* **bedienen** operate a machine
maschinell mechanical
maschinenlesbar computer readable, machine readable
Maschinenschaden *(m)* mechanical breakdown, mechanical fault
Maß *(n)* measure; (Ausmaß, Größe) measurements; (Raum) dimensions
Maß *(n)***, lichtes** clear dimension, clear width
Maß *(n)***, metrisches** metric scale
Maßband *(n)* tape measure
Masse *(f)* (Menschen) crowd
Masse *(f)***, breite** masses
Maßeinheit *(f)* measure
Massenandrang *(m)* huge crowd, crush, terrible crush
Massenartikel *(m)* mass-produced article
Massenfertigung *(f)* mass production
maßgebend decisive; (Aussage etc.) authoritative
maßgeblich decisive; (Aussage etc.) authoritative
Maßnahme *(f)* measure, step
Maßnahmepaket *(n)* set of measures
Maßstab *(m)* (maßstäbliche Relation) scale; (Zollstock) rule, folding rule; (Vorgabe) standard, yardstick
maßstabsgerecht true to scale
Mast *(m)* mast; (Leitungsmast) pylon

Material *(n, pl)*, **leicht entflammbares** high flammable material, readily flammable material
Materialkosten *(pl)* cost of materials
Materiallager *(n)* stock of materials, materials stock
Materialtransport *(m)* materials handling
matt dull; (Foto etc.) mat; (Glühbirne) opal; (Glas) frosted; (Licht) dim
Mattglas *(n)* frosted glass
Mausklick *(m)* mouse click
maximal maximum
Maximalgeräuschpegel *(m)* maximum noise level
Maximum *(n)* maximum
mechanisch mechanical, mechanized
mechanisieren mechanize
Mechanismus *(m)* mechanism
Mediaforschung *(f)* media research
Mediaplan *(m)* media plan, media schedule
Medien *(n, pl)* media
Medien *(n, pl)*, **audiovisuelle** audiovisual media
Medien *(n, pl)*, **elektronische** electronic media
Medien *(n, pl)*, **neue** new media
Mehrarbeit *(f)* extra work, overtime
Mehrausgaben *(f, pl)* additional expenditure
Mehrbedarf *(m)* extra demand
Mehreinnahmen *(f, pl)* additional revenue
mehrfach several, multiple; (wiederholt) repeated
Mehrfachstecker *(m)* multiple adapter, multiple adaptor, multiple plug
mehrfarbig multicolored (US), multicoloured (GB)
Mehrgeräteanschluss *(m)* multi-device connection
mehrgeschossig multi-story (US), multi-storey (GB)
Mehrheit *(f)* majority

mehrjährig of several years, multi-year
Mehrkosten *(pl)* additional costs, extra costs
Mehrpreis *(m)* extra, surcharge
mehrsprachig multilingual
Mehrweg- returnable, reusable
Mehrwegteppich *(m)* returnable carpet, reusable carpet
Mehrwertsteuer *(f)* **(MwSt.)** Value Added Tax (VAT)
Mehrwertsteuer *(f)*, **gesetzliche** statutory value added tax
Mehrwertsteuerbefreiung *(f)* exemption from VAT, zero-rating, zero rate
mehrwertsteuerfrei exempt from VAT, zero-rated
Mehrwertsteuerrückerstattung *(f)* VAT refund
Mehrwertsteuervergütung *(f)* VAT refund
Mehrzahl *(f)* majority
Mehrzweck- multipurpose
Meilenerwerb *(m)* earning of miles
Meilenguthaben *(n)* mileage balance
Meilenkonto *(n)* mileage account
meinen think, mean
Meinung *(f)* opinion, view, thinking
Meinungsaustausch *(m)* exchange of ideas, exchange of views
Meinungsforscher(in) *(m/f)* canvasser, pollster
Meinungsforschung *(f)* opinion research, public opinion research
Meinungsumfrage *(f)* canvassing, opinion poll, opinion survey
melden (ankündigen) announce; (berichten) report
Meldepflicht *(f)* obligatory registration, compulsory registration, duty of notification
meldepflichtig obliged to register, subject to registration
Memorandum *(n)* memorandum; (Memo) memo
Menge *(f)* quantity; (Personen) crowd

Mengenrabatt *(m)* bulk discount, bulk volume discount, bulk quantity discount
Menü *(n)* menu
menügesteuert menu-driven
Merkblatt *(n)* instruction leaflet
merken (erfassen) notice
merken, sich remember
Merkmal *(n)* characteristic
messbar measurable
Messe *(f)* fair, trade fair, exhibition, show
Messe *(f)* **im Freigelände** outdoor exhibition, outdoor fair, open air exhibition
Messe *(f)* **veranstalten** organize an exhibition, organize a fair, organize a trade fair
Messe *(f)***, internationale** international trade fair
Messe *(f)***, nationale** national exhibition, national fair
Messe *(f)***, regionale** local exhibition, local fair, regional exhibition, regional fair
Messe *(f)***, technische** technical exhibition, technical fair, machinery fair
Messe *(f)***, überregionale** supraregional exhibition, supraregional fair, supraregional show
Messe- und Ausstellungsversicherung *(f)* trade fair and exhibition risk insurance
Messearbeitsamt *(n)* exhibition job center (US), exhibition job centre (GB), exhibition labor office (US), exhibition labour office (GB)
Messearchitekt *(m)* exhibition architect, exhibition constructor
Messearchitektur *(f)* exhibition architecture
Messeausweis *(m)* exhibition pass, fair pass, trade fair pass
Messebau *(m)***, individueller** individual stand building

Messebaufirma *(f)* stand constructor, exhibit constructor, exhibit contractor
Messebausystem *(n)* stand construction system
Messebauunternehmen *(n)* stand constructor, exhibit constructor, exhibit contractor
Messebedarf *(m)* exhibition supplies
Messebeirat *(m)* exhibition committee, advisory council
Messebericht *(m)* report on exhibition, report on fair, show report, show review, post-show report
Messebesuch *(m)* fair attendance, show attendance
Messebesucher(in) *(m/f)* visitor, fairgoer, fair dealer
Messebesuchsbericht *(m)* visitor report
Messebeteiligung *(f)* fair participation, trade fair participation
Messebeteiligung *(f)***, Nutzen der** benefits of the fair participation
Messebeteiligungsziele *(n, pl)* goals of trade fair participation, show participation goals, fair participation targets
Messebudget *(n)* exhibition budget
Messebüro *(n)* (Veranstalter) exhibition management office, fair, management office, show management office; (Stand) stand office
Messeconsulter *(m)* exhibition consultant, fair consultant
Messedesigner *(m)* stand designer, exhibit designer
Messedisplay *(n)* exhibition display, stand display
Messeeinladung *(f)* visitor invitation
Messeelektriker(in) *(m/f)* official electrical contractor
Messeempfang *(m)* exhibition reception, fair reception, show reception
Messeerfolg *(m)* exhibition success, fair success, participation success

Messeerfolgskontrolle *(f)* exhibition success survey, fair success survey
Messeetat *(m)* exhibition budget, fair budget, show budget
Messefernsehen *(n)* TV show coverage
Messeformblatt *(n)* exhibition form
Messefotograf *(m)*, **offizieller** official exhibition photographer, official fair photographer, official show photographer
Messefreigelände *(n)* open exhibition area, outdoor area, open-air site
Messefunktionen *(f, pl)* exhibition functions, fair functions
Messegastkarte *(f)* exhibition guest card, fair guest card, guest pass
Messegastronomie *(f)* site catering
Messegebäude *(n)* exhibition building, fair building
Messegebäude *(n)*, **eingeschossiges** single-story exhibition building (US), single-storey exhibition building (GB)
Messegelände *(n)* exhibition grounds, fair grounds, fair site
Messegesellschaft *(f)* exhibition company, exhibition corporation
Messegut *(n)* exhibition materials, exhibition properties
Messe-Haftpflichtversicherung *(f)* exhibitor's liability insurance, exhibitor's third-party insurance
Messehalle *(f)* exhibition hall
Messehomepage *(f)* show homepage, official show homepage
Messehostess *(f)* show hostess
Messeinflation *(f)* inflation of exhibitions, event inflation
Messeinformationssystem *(n)* show information system, show guide
Messeinfrastruktur *(f)* exhibition infrastructure
Messekalender *(m)* exhibition calendar, fair calendar, calendar of events

Messekatalog *(m)* exhibition catalog (US), exhibition catalogue (GB), fair catalog (US), fair catalogue (GB)
Messekomitee *(n)* exhibition committee, fair committee
Messekonzept *(n)* exhibition concept, fair concept
Messekosten *(pl)* costs of the exhibition, costs of the fair
Messelager *(n)* site depot, site warehouse
Messelaufzeit *(f)* duration; (Tagesöffnung) open hours
Messeleitung *(f)* exhibition management, fair authorities
Messelogistik *(f)* exhibition logistics, fair logistics, show logistics
Messemarketing *(n)* exhibition marketing, fair marketing, show marketing
Messemarkt *(m)* exhibition market
messen measure
Messenacharbeit *(f)* exhibition follow-up work, fair follow-up work
Messeneuheit *(f)* exhibition innovation, fair innovation
Messenutzencheck *(m)* exhibition benefit check, fair benefit check
Messeordnung *(f)* exhibition rules and regulations, fair rules and regulations
Messeplatz *(m)* venue
Messeradio *(n)* show radio
Messeranking *(n)*, **internationales** international exhibition rankings
Messeregularien *(pl)* exhibition rules and regulations
Messerestaurant *(n)* exhibition restaurant
Messeschluss *(m)* (Uhrzeit) closing time; (Schlusstag) closing day
Messeserver *(m)* site server
Messeshuttle *(n)* exhibition shuttle
Messespediteur *(m)* fair forwarding agent, fair carrier, show forwarder

Messespedition *(f)* fair forwarder, show carrier
Messestand *(m)* stand, exhibition stand, booth, stall
Messestand *(m)*, **mehrgeschossiger** multi-storied stand structure
Messestandauftritt *(m)*, **repräsentativer** high-image stand design
Messestandbau *(m)* exhibition stand construction; (im Freien) outdoor stand construction
Messestandkonzept *(n)* stand concept
Messestands *(m)*, **Größe des** stand size
Messestands *(m)*, **Lage des** stand location, stand placement
Messestands *(m)*, **Typ des** stand type
Messeteilnehmer(in) *(m/f)* participant
Messetermin *(m)* exhibition date, show date
Messetransfer *(m)* show transfer
Messetransparenz *(f)* show transparency
Messetyp *(m)* type of exhibition, type of fair, kind of exhibition, kind of fair
Messeüberblick *(m)* exhibition overview
Messeveranstalter *(m)* exhibition organizer, fair organizer, exhibition promoter, fair promoter
Messeversicherung *(f)* exhibition insurance, fair insurance
Messewirtschaft *(f)* expo industry
Messezeit *(f)* fairtime
Messezeitung *(f)* exhibition daily, fair daily, show daily
Messeziele *(n, pl)* exhibition targets, fair targets
Messeziele *(n, pl)*, **Definition der** definition of exhibition targets
Messeziele *(n, pl)*, **operative** strategic exhibition targets, strategic fair targets
Messeziele *(n, pl)*, **quantitative** quantitative exhibition targets, quantitative fair targets

Messinstrument *(n)* measuring instrument
Messung *(f)* measurement
Meter *(m)* meter (US), metre (GB)
Methode *(f)* method
Mietauto *(n)* rental car (US), hire car (GB), hired car (GB)
mietbar leasable, rentable (US)
Miete *(f)* lease, rent (US), hire (GB)
mieten lease, rent (US), hire (GB)
Mietgebühr *(f)* rental charge (US), rental fee (US), hire charge (GB)
Mietgeräte *(n, pl)* rental equipment
Mietkauf *(m)* hire purchase
Mietmessestand *(m)* rental stand, rental exhibition stand
Mietmöbel *(pl)* rental furniture
Mietmöbelanbieter *(m)* furniture rent company
Mietmobiliar *(n)* furniture rental
Mietpreis *(m)* rent, rent price, rental charge (US), rental rate (US), hire charge (GB), hire payment (GB)
Mietstand *(m)* rental stand
Mietsystemstand *(m)* rental system stand
Mietvereinbarung *(f)* terms of rent
Mietvertrag *(m)* lease agreement, lease contract, rental agreement, rental contract
Mietwagen *(m)* rental car (US), hire car (GB), hired car (GB)
Mikrofon *(n)* microphone
Mikrofon *(n)*, **drahtloses** cordless microphone, wireless microphone
Mikrofon *(n)*, **eingebautes** built-in microphone
Mikroprozessor *(m)* microprocessor
Mikrowellengerät *(n)* microwave, microwave oven
Milchglas *(n)* frosted glass
Milchkaffee *(m)* white coffee
Milchkännchen *(n)* milk jug
Millimeterpapier *(n)* graph paper, squared paper

minderwertig inferior, of inferior quality, low-grade
Mindestanforderung *(f)* minimum requirement
Mindestbeitrag *(m)* minimum contribution
Mindestbeleuchtung *(f)* minimum lighting
Mindestbetrag *(m)* minimum amount
Mindestbreite *(f)* minimum width
mindestens at least
Mindestgebühr *(f)* minimum charge, minimum fee
Mindesthaltbarkeitsdatum *(n)* sell-by date
Mindestquerschnitt *(m)* (Leitungen) minimum diameter
Mindeststandgröße *(f)* minimum stand size
Mindestzahl *(f)* minimum number
Mineralwasser *(n)* mineral water, soda water, table water
Minibar *(f)* mini-bar
Minicontainer *(m)* minicontainer
minimal minimal, minimum, negligible
Minimum *(n)* minimum
Minuszeichen *(n)* minus sign
Mischkonzern *(m)* conglomerate
Mischpult *(n)* mixing desk, mixer, audio mixer
Mischung *(f)* mix, mixture
Mischverstärker *(m)* mixing amplifier
missachten disregard, ignore
Missachtung *(f)* disregard
missbilligen disapprove
Missbilligung *(f)* disapproval
Misserfolg *(m)* failure, flop
Missgeschick *(n)* bad luck, misfortune, mishap
misslingen fail
Missverständnis *(n)* misunderstanding
Mitarbeit *(f)* collaboration, cooperation
mitarbeiten collaborate, cooperate
Mitarbeiter(in) *(m/f)* employee
Mitarbeiter(in) *(m/f)*, **freie(r)** contract worker, freelance worker, freelancer
Mitarbeiterschulung *(f)* staff training
Mitarbeiterstab *(m)* staff
Mitaussteller *(m)* co-exhibitor, secondary exhibitor
Mitausstellerentgelt *(n)* co-exhibitor charge
Mitausstellergebühr *(f)* co-exhibitor fee
mitbenutzen share
Mitbewerber *(m)* competitor
miteinander with each other, together
Mitglied *(n)* member
Mitglied *(n)* **der Geschäftsleitung** member of the top management team, member of the management
Mitgliederversammlung *(f)* general meeting
Mitgliedschaft *(f)* membership
mitmachen take part in, join in, cooperate
Mitnahmeset *(n)* take-away set
mitnehmen take along
Mittagessen *(n)* lunch
mittags at noon, lunchtime
Mittagspause *(f)* lunch break, lunch hour
Mittagszeit *(f)* lunch time
Mitte *(f)* middle
mitteilen inform, notify
Mitteilung *(f)* information, communication, message, notification, report
Mittel *(n)* (Verfahren) method, way; (Hilfsmittel) means
Mittel *(n, pl)*, **flüssige** liquid assets, liquid funds, cash
Mittelboden *(m)* (Regal etc.) middle shelf
mittelfristig medium-term
Mittelgurt *(m)* (Treppe, Brüstung) middle girder
mittelmäßig average, mediocre
Mittelpunkt *(m)* center (US), centre (GB); (Brennpunkt) focus

mittels through, by means of
Mittelstand *(m)* small and medium-sized enterprises (SMEs)
Mitteltheke *(f)* intermediate counter
Mittelungspegel *(m)* mean level
Mittelwert *(m)* average, average value
mittendrin right in the middle
mitverantwortlich jointly responsible
Mitverantwortung *(f)* joint responsibility, share of the responsibility
Mitverschulden *(n)* contributory negligence
mitwirken cooperate; (mitarbeiten) collaborate; (beteiligt sein) be involved
Mitwirkung *(f)* cooperation
Mixbecher *(m)* shaker
Möbel *(pl)* furniture
Möbelrolle *(f)* castor wheel
Mobiliar *(n)* furniture, furnishings
Mobilleuchte *(f)* mobile light
Mobiltelefon *(n)* cell phone (US), mobile phone (GB)
Möblierung *(f)* furnishing
Mode *(f)* fashion
Modell *(n)* model, design; (techn. Nachbau) mock-up; (Mode) fashion model
Modell *(n)*, **maßstabsgerechtes** scale model
Modellbaukasten *(m)* model kit
Modem *(n)* modem
Moderation *(f)* moderation, presentation
Moderator(in) *(m/f)* moderator, presenter
moderieren moderate, present
modernisieren modernize, bring up to date
modifizieren modify
Modifizierung *(f)* modification
modisch fashionable, stylish
Modul *(n)* module
modular modular
Mogelpackung *(f)* deception package, deceptive packaging

Möglichkeit *(f)* possibility; (Gelegenheit) opportunity; (Aussicht) chance
Monitor *(m)* monitor
Monitorsplitwand *(f)* monitor split wall
Monitorwand *(f)* monitor wall
Monoeingang *(m)* mono input
Monopol *(n)* monopoly
Monopolist *(m)* monopolist
Montage *(f)* mounting, fitting, installation; (Zusammenbau) assembling, assembly
Montageplan *(m)* assembly program (US), assembly programme (GB)
Montageversicherung *(f)* installation insurance
Montagevorschrift *(f)* assembly regulation
Montagezeit *(f)* build-up time
Monteur *(m)* assembler, fitter, mechanic
montieren assemble, fit, install, mount
Montur *(f)* uniform
Motiv *(n)* cause, motive, reason
Motivation *(f)* motivation
Motivforschung *(f)* motivational research
motivieren motivate
Motor *(m)* engine, motor
Motorsäge *(f)* power saw
Motto *(n)* motto
Muffe *(f)* sleeve
Mulde *(f)* hollow
Müll *(m)* waste, refuse, garbage (US), rubbish (GB)
Müllabfuhr *(f)* waste collection, garbage collection (US), refuse collection (GB)
Müllbeseitigung *(f)* waste disposal, garbage disposal (US), refuse disposal (GB)
Müllcontainer *(m)* waste container, garbage container (US), rubbish container (GB)
Mülleimer *(m)* garbage can (US), rubbish bin (GB)
Müllentsorgung *(f)* garbage disposal (US), refuse disposal (GB)

Mülltonne *(f)* trashcan (US), dustbin (GB)
Mülltrennung *(f)* waste separation, garbage separation (US)
Multimediaschau *(f)* multimedia show
Multiplikator *(m)* multiplier
Multivisionsschau *(f)* multivision, multivision show
Mundpropaganda *(f)* verbal propaganda
Mund-zu-Mund-Werbung *(f)* word-of-mouth advertising
Münze *(f)* coin
Münzeinwurf *(m)* coin slot
Münztelefon *(n)* coin phone, coin-operated phone
musikalisch musical
Musiker(in) *(m/f)* musician
Musikkapelle *(f)* band
Musikuntermalung *(f)* incidental music
Musikwiedergabe *(f)* music performance, music reproduction
Muskelkater *(m)* aching muscles, sore muscles, stiffness
Muster *(n)* (Probe) sample, specimen; (Stoff) design, pattern
Mustermesse *(f)* samples fair
Musterschutz *(m)* protection of registered designs
Muttergesellschaft *(f)* parent company, holding company
Muttersprache *(f)* native language
mutwillig malicious

N

nachahmen imitate, copy
Nachahmung *(f)* imitation
Nachahmung *(f)***, unerlaubte** pirating, piracy; (Plagiat) plagiarism
Nachbar *(m)* neighbor (US), neighbour (GB)
Nachbarschaft *(f)* neighborhood (US), neighbourhood (GB)
Nachbarschaftszone *(f)* (Standumfeld) neighboring zone (US), neighbouring zone (GB)
Nachbarstand *(m)* neighboring stand (US), neighbouring stand (GB)
Nachbau *(m)* copying, reproduction
nachbauen copy, reproduce
nachbessern touch up
nachbestellen reorder, repeat an order, place a repeat order
Nachbestellung *(f)* reorder, repeat order
Nachbildung *(f)* copy, imitation, reproduction, replica
nachdenklich thoughtful, pensive
Nachdruck *(m)* (Äußerung) emphasis; (wiederholter Druck) reprint
nachdrücklich emphatic
Nachdrucksrecht *(n)* right of reproduction
nacheinander one after another
Nachfassaktion *(f)* follow-up campaign
Nachfassbrief *(m)* follow-up letter
nachfassen follow up
Nachfasswerbung *(f)* follow-up advertising
Nachfolge *(f)* succession
Nachfolgemodell *(n)* follow-up model, successor
Nachfolger(in) *(m/f)* follower, successor
Nachfrage *(f)* demand
Nachfrage *(f)***, effektive** effective demand
Nachfrage *(f)***, potenzielle** potential demand
Nachfrageanalyse *(f)* demand analysis
nachfragen ask, enquire
Nachfrist *(f)* extension, extension of time, respite, additional respite
Nachgebühr *(f)* surcharge; (Zustellung) excess postage
Nachholbedarf *(m)* backlog demand

nachholen make up for, catch up on
Nachholen *(n)* **der Veranstaltung** rescheduling of the event
nachlassen (zurückgehen) decrease; (Preis etc.) reduce; (Geschäft) slack off, slacken
nachlässig careless, negligent, sloppy
Nachlässigkeit *(f)* carelessness, negligence, sloppiness
nachliefern supply subsequently
nachmachen imitate, copy
Nachmessegeschäft *(n)* post-show business
nachmessen check, measure again
Nachnahme *(f)* cash on delivery
Nachnahme *(f)*, **per** cash on delivery (C.O.D.)
Nachnahmegebühr *(f)* cash on delivery charge (C.O.D. charge)
Nachnahmesendung *(f)* cash on delivery parcel (C.O.D. parcel)
Nachporto *(n)* additional postage, excess postage, postage due
nachprüfbar verifiable
nachprüfen check, reexamine
Nachricht *(f)* message; (kurze Mitteilung) note
Nachrichten *(f, pl)* news
Nachrichtenagentur *(f)* news agency
Nachrichtendienst *(m)* news service
Nachschlüssel *(m)* duplicate key
nachsehen gaze after, have a look; (überprüfen) check, inspect; (nachschlagen) look up
Nachsendeadresse *(f)* forwarding address
nachsenden forward
Nachtarbeit *(f)* nightwork
Nachtarbeitserlaubnis *(f)* night-work permit, night-working permit
Nachtbus *(m)* night bus
Nachteil *(m)* disadvantage
nachteilig disadvantageous
Nachtflug *(m)* night flight
Nachtisch *(m)* dessert, sweets

Nachtklub *(m)* cabaret, nightclub
Nachtlokal *(n)* nightclub, night spot
Nachtportier *(m)* night concierge, night porter
Nachtrag *(m)* supplement
Nachtreinigungspersonal *(n)* nightcleaner
Nachtruhe *(f)* night's rest
Nachtschicht *(f)* nightshift
Nachttarif *(m)* night rate, night tariff
Nachtwache *(f)* night watch, night duty
Nachtwächter *(m)* night watchman
Nachtzeit *(f)* night-time
Nachtzug *(m)* night train
Nachweis *(m)* (Beweis) proof, evidence; (Zeugnis) certificate
Nachweis *(m)*, **statischer** structural calculation, structural analysis, structural report
nachweisbar verifiable, provable, demonstrable
nachweisen prove
nachweislich provable
Nachwirkung *(f)* after-effect
nachzahlen pay later; (zuzahlen) pay extra
nachzählen check
Nachzahlung *(f)* additional payment; (Zuzahlung) extra payment
Nadeldrucker *(m)* dotmatrix printer
Nagel *(m)* nail
nageln nail
nagelneu brand-new, first-hand
Nahaufnahme *(f)* (Film) close-up
nahe close, near, nearby
Nähe *(f)* nearness, proximity
nähen sew
Nahrung *(f)* food
Nahrungsmittel *(n)* food, foodstuff
Nahverkehr *(m)* local traffic, short-distance traffic
Nähzeug *(n)* sewing kit
Namensliste *(f)* list of names
Namensschild *(n)* badge, nameplate, name tag

Namenszug *(m)* (Unterschrift) signature
namhaft (erheblich) considerable; (bekannt) well-known
Nässe *(f)* wetness
Nässe *(f)* **schützen, vor** keep dry
Nationalfeiertag *(m)* national holiday
Nationalflagge *(f)* national flag
Nationalhymne *(f)* national anthem
Nationalität *(f)* nationality
natürlich natural; (selbstverständlich) of course
Naturschutz *(m)* protection of nature, nature conservation
Nebelmaschine *(f)* fog machine
neben (örtlich) beside, at the side of, by the side of, close to, near to; (außer) apart from, besides
Nebenanschluss *(m)* telephone extension
Nebenausgaben *(f, pl)* accessory charges, extras, incidentals
Nebenausgang *(m)* side exit
nebenbei besides
Nebeneffekt *(m)* side effect
nebeneinander side by side
Nebeneingang *(m)* side entrance
Nebengebäude *(n)* adjoining building; (Anbau) annex
Nebenkosten *(pl)* additional charge, incidental charges
Nebenprodukt *(n)* by-product, spin-off
Nebensache *(f)* minor matter
nebensächlich minor, unimportant
negativ negative
Negativ *(n)* negative
Neigung *(f)* (Winkel) incline, inclination
Neigungswinkel *(m)* angle of inclination
nennen name; (anführen) quote
nennenswert worth mentioning
Nennleistung *(f)* (Strom) nominal capacity, rated output
Nennspannung *(f)* (Strom) rated voltage
Neonleuchte *(f)* neon light

Neonschrift *(f)* neon sign
netto net, clear
Nettoausstellungsfläche *(f)* net exhibition space, net exhibition area
Nettobetrag *(m)* net amount
Nettoerlös *(m)* net revenue
Nettoertrag *(m)* net yield
Nettofläche *(f)* net space, net area
Nettogewicht *(n)* net weight
Nettogewinn *(m)* net profit, clear profit
Nettomarge *(f)* net margin
Nettopreis *(m)* net price
Nettoreichweite *(f)* net cover, net reach
Nettoumsatz *(m)* net sales, net revenue
Netzanschluss *(m)* mains connection
Netzbetreiber *(m)* network provider
Netzgerät *(n)* mains-operated unit, mains receiver
Netzplantechnik *(f)* network planning technique
Netzspannung *(f)* mains voltage
Netzstecker *(m)* mains plug, power plug
Netzteil *(n)* mains adaptor, mains unit
Netzwerk *(n)* network
Netzwerk *(n)*, **kabelloses lokales** Wireless LAN (WLAN)
Netzwerk *(n)*, **lokales** Local Area Network (LAN)
neuartig new, novel
Neuauflage *(f)* new edition
Neuentwicklung *(f)* innovation
Neuerung *(f)* innovation
Neugliederung *(f)* reorganization
Neuheit *(f)* innovation, novelty
Neuordnung *(f)* reorganization
Neuregelung *(f)* revision
neutral neutral
neuwertig as good as new, practically new
neuzeitlich modern
Nicht berühren! Don't touch!
Nicht öffnen! Do not open!
Nichtbeachtung *(f)* disregard; (von Vorschriften) nonobservance

nichtig (rechtlich) invalid, void; (unbedeutend) trifling, trivial; (null und nichtig) null and void
nichtig erklären nullify
Nichtraucher(in) *(m/f)* non-smoker
Nichtraucherbereich *(m)* non-smoking area
Nichtverfügbarkeit *(f)* unavailability
Nichtzutreffendes streichen! Delete which is inapplicable!, Delete where non-applicable!
Niederlassung *(f)* branch office
Niedervoltanlage *(f)* low-voltage system
Niedervoltlampe *(f)* low-voltage bulb
niedrig low
Niedrigpreis *(m)* low price, cut price
nirgendwo nowhere, not anywhere
Nische *(f)* niche, recess
Nitroverdünnung *(f)* cellulose thinner
Niveau *(n)* level, standard
nivellieren level, level out
Noppe *(f)* nap
Norm *(f)* standard
normal normal, standard
Normalarbeitszeit *(f)* normal working hours, standard working hours, regular working time
normalerweise normally
Normalfall *(m)* normal case
Normalfall *(m)*, **im** normally
Normalhöhe *(f)* normal height, standard height
normalisieren normalize
Normalkostenrechnung *(f)* standard costing
Normalverteilung *(f)* normal distribution
Normalzustand *(m)* normal state
Normelement *(n)* standard unit
normen standardize
Normhöhe *(f)* standard height
normieren standardize
Normknoten *(m)* standard node
Normlänge *(f)* standard length
Normung *(f)* standardization
Normwandler *(m)* standard converter

Normwandlung *(f)* standard conversion
Notarzt *(m)* emergency doctor, doctor on call
Notarztwagen *(m)* emergency ambulance
Notausgang *(m)* emergency exit
Notausstiegsöffnung *(f)* escape hatch
Notbeleuchtung *(f)* emergency lighting
Notfall *(m)* emergency
Notfallräumung *(f)* emergency evacuation
Nothilfe *(f)* emergency help
nötig necessary
Notiz *(f)* memorandum, note
Notizen *(f, pl)* **machen** take notes
Notlösung *(f)* temporary solution
Notruf *(m)* (Telefon) emergency call
Notrufsäule *(f)* emergency telephone
Notstromaggregat *(n)* emergency generator, emergency generating set
Notstromversorgung *(f)* emergency power supply
Notverband *(m)* first-aid dressing
notwendig necessary
Notwendigkeit *(f)* necessity
Novum *(n)* new, novelty
Nuance *(f)* nuance, shade
null und nichtig null and void
Nullwachstum *(n)* zero growth
nummerieren number
Nummerierung *(f)* numbering
Nummernschild *(n)* number plate
Nut *(f)* chase, flute, groove; (Kerbe) slot
nutzbringend profitable, useful
Nutzeffekt *(m)* efficiency
nützen be of use, be useful, be of advantage, benefit
Nutzen *(m)* advancement, advantage, benefit, value
Nutzer(in) *(m/f)* user
Nutzfläche *(f)* usable area, usable floor space
Nutzhöhe *(f)*, **lichte** clear usable height

Nutzlast *(f)* maximum load, payload
nützlich useful; (hilfreich) helpful
Nützlichkeit *(f)* utility
nutzlos useless
Nutzungsgebühr *(f)* royalty

O

oben above; (nach oben) up, upwards; (am oberen Ende) at the top
obenauf on top, on the top, uppermost
Ober *(m)* waiter
Oberbau *(m)* upper structure
Oberfläche *(f)* surface
Oberflächenausführung *(f)* surface finish
oberflächlich superficial
Obergeschoss *(n)* upper floor
Obergurt *(m)* (Treppe, Brüstung) top girder
oberhalb above
Oberkante *(f)* top edge, upper edge
Oberkante *(f)* **Hallenboden** floor level
Oberlicht *(n)* high window
Objekt *(n)* object
Objektbeleuchtung *(f)* key lighting
objektiv objective
Objektiv *(n)* lens, objective
Objektivität *(f)* objectivity
obligatorisch obligatory, compulsory, mandatory
Ofen *(m)* stove; (Backofen) oven
offen open; (Stelle) vacant; (aufrichtig) frank; (unentschieden) undecided
offen bleiben remain open
offenbar apparently, evidently; (offensichtlich) obvious
Offene Handelsgesellschaft *(f)* **(OHG)** general partnership, general ordinary partnership
offensiv offensive

öffentlich public
Öffentlichkeit *(f)* public
Öffentlichkeitsarbeit *(f)* public relations (PR)
offerieren offer
Offerte *(f)* bid, offer, tender
offiziell official
Öffner *(m)* opener
Öffnung *(f)* opening
Öffnungszeiten *(pl)* opening times, opening hours, business hours, hours of business
Öffnungszeiten *(pl)*, **allgemeine** general business hours, general opening hours
Offsetdruck *(m)* offset, offset printing
Ohm *(n)* ohm
Ökologie *(f)* ecology
ökologisch ecological
Ökonomie *(f)* economy, economics
ökonomisch economic; (sparsam) economical
Ökosteuer *(f)* green tax
Öldruck *(m)* oil pressure
ölen oil, lubricate
Ölfarbe *(f)* oil color (US), oil colour (GB), oil paint
Omnibus *(m)* bus; (Reisebus) coach
Omnibusumfrage *(f)* omnibus survey
Onlineangebot *(n)* online marketing
Onlineanmeldung *(f)* online registration
Onlinebestellsystem *(n)* online ordering system
Onlinebestellung *(f)* online purchasing
Onlinebuchung *(f)* online registration
Onlinekatalog *(m)* online catalog (US), online catalogue (GB)
operativ operational
opponieren oppose
opportun opportune
optieren opt
Optik *(f)* optics; (Foto) lens, lens system
optimal optimal

Optimierung *(f)* optimization
Option *(f)* option
Optionsfrist *(f)* option deadline
optisch optical, visual,
Orangensaft *(m)* orange juice
ordentlich tidy, orderly, neat
Ordermesse *(f)* buyers' show
ordnen put in order; (regeln) order, organize, regulate; (sortieren) arrange
Ordner *(m)* (Personal) security staff, steward; (Akte) file
Ordnung *(f)* order
Ordnung *(f)* **halten, in** keep in order
ordnungsgemäß in due form, regular, regulary, orderly, according to the rules
ordnungswidrig irregular
Organigramm *(n)* organigram, organization chart
Organisation *(f)* organization
Organisationsplan *(m)* organization chart, organigram
Organisator *(m)* organizer
organisatorisch organizational
organisieren organize
original original
Original *(n)* original; (Medien) master
originell original; (geistreich) witty
Ornament *(n)* ornament
Ort *(m)* place, point, spot; (Austragungsort) venue; (Örtlichkeit) locality
örtlich local
Ortsbesichtigung *(f)* site inspection, on-site inspection, local survey
Ortsgespräch *(n)* local call
Ortskenntnis *(f)* local knowledge
Ortsnetzkennzahl *(f)* area code
ortsüblich in accordance with local customs, customary in a place
Ortszeit *(f)* local time
Öse *(f)* eye, eyelet
oval oval

P

Päckchen *(n)* package, small parcel
packen (einpacken) pack; (festhalten) grab, seize
Packpapier *(n)* wrapping paper
Packung *(f)* pack, packet, package, banded pack
Packzettel *(m)* packing list, packing slip
Paket *(n)* parcel, package, packet
Paketgebühren *(f, pl)* parcel rates
Paketpost *(f)* parcel post
Palette *(f)* (Transport) pallet; (Auswahl) range
Palette *(f)***, breite** (Waren etc.) wide range
palettieren palletize
Panelbreite *(f)* panel width
Panelsystem *(n)* panel system
Papier *(n)* (Schreibpapier) paper; (Ausweis) papers, identity papers
Papiereinzug *(m)* (Drucker) paper feed
Papierkorb *(m)* waste paper basket
Papierserviette *(f)* paper napkin
Papierstau *(m)* (Drucker) paper jam
Papiertaschentuch *(n)* tissue, paper handkerchief
Papiertragetasche *(f)* paper carrier
Pappbecher *(m)* paper cup
Pappe *(f)* cardboard
Pappkarton *(m)* cardboard box, carton
Pappteller *(m)* paper plate
Paragraf *(m)* (Abschnitt) paragraph; (Gesetz) section; (Bestimmung) article; (Klausel) clause
parallel parallel
Parallele *(f)* parallel, parallel line
Parameter *(m)* parameter
Parkdeck *(n)* parking level
Parken verboten! No parking!
Parkfläche *(f)* parking place
Parkgebühr *(f)* parking fee, parking tax

Parkhaus *(n)* multistory car park (US), multistorey car park (GB)
Parklücke *(f)* parking gap
Parkmöglichkeit *(f)* parking facilities
Parkplatz *(m)* car park, parking place, parking lot; (bewacht) guarded car park
Parkplatzangebot *(n)* parking facilities, available parking space
Parkplatzkarte *(f)* car park ticket, car park reservation ticket
Parkscheibe *(f)* parking disc
Parkschein *(m)* parking ticket, parking permit
Parkstreifen *(m)* lay-by
Parkuhr *(f)* parking meter
Parkverbot *(n)* prohibition to park, No parking!
Parkwächter *(m)* park keeper, car park attendant, parking attendant
Parterre *(n)* ground floor, first floor
Partner(in) *(m/f)* associate, partner
Partnerschaft *(f)* partnership
Partyzelt *(n)* party tent
Pass *(m)* passport
Passabfertigung *(f)* passport inspection
Passage *(f)* passage; (Geschäfte) arcade
Passagier *(m)* passenger
Passant *(m)* passer-by
passen fit; (einpassen) fit in, fit into
passend (praktisch) convenient; (passgenau) fitting; (Farbe etc.) matching; (genehm) suitable
passieren (vorbeigehen) pass; (geschehen) happen
Passierschein *(m)* pass, permit
Passkontrolle *(f)* passport control, passport inspection
Passstück *(n)* adaptor, adapter, fitting piece
Passvorschriften *(f, pl)* passport regulations
Passwort *(n)* password
Paste *(f)* paste
Patent *(n)* patent

Patent *(n)* **angemeldet, zum** patent pending
Patent *(n)*, **angemeldetes** patent applied for, patent pending
Patentanmeldung *(f)* patent application
Patentanspruch *(m)* patent claim
patentiert patented
Patentrecht *(n)* patent law, patent right
Patentverletzung *(f)* patent infringement
Patrone *(f)* cartridge
pauschal overall; (geschätzt) estimated; (Preis etc.) all-in, all-inclusive
Pauschalbetrag *(m)* flat sum
Pauschale *(f)* inclusive charge, flat rate, lump sum
Pauschalgebühr *(f)* flat rate, inclusive rate
Pauschalpreis *(m)* flat rate, flat rate price, all-in price, inclusive fare, inclusive price
Pauschalreise *(f)* package tour
Pause *(f)* (Papier) copy, blueprint, tracing; (Ruhepause) break, pause, rest
pausenlos incessant, uninterrupted, nonstop
pausieren pause, have a break, take a break
Pavillon *(m)* pavilion
Pendelbus *(m)* shuttle bus
Pendeltür *(f)* swing door
Pendelverkehr *(m)* shuttle service
Pension *(f)* guest house, private hotel, boarding house, bed and breakfast, pension
perfekt perfect; (Abschluss etc.) settled
Perfektion *(f)* perfection
perfektionieren perfect, make perfect
Peripheriegerät *(n)* (EDV) peripheral
Person *(f)*, **wichtige** Very Important Person (VIP)
Personal *(n)* personnel, staff
Personal *(n)*, **eigenes** own staff
Personalabteilung *(f)* personnel department
Personalausweis *(m)* identity card

Personalbedarf *(m)* manpower requirements, staff requirements
Personalbeschaffung *(f)* staffing, staff resourcing, recruitment of staff
Personalcomputer *(m)* home computer, personal computer
Personaleinweisung *(f)* staff briefing
Personalengpass *(m)* manpower shortage, staff shortage, shortage of staff
Personalien *(f, pl)* personal data, particulars
Personalkosten *(pl)* personnel costs, employment costs, staff costs
Personalplanung *(f)* manpower planning
Personalschulung *(f)* staff training
Personalvermittlung *(f)* (Agentur) employment agency, recruitment agency
Personenaufzug *(m)* elevator (US), lift (GB)
Personenfunkdienst *(m)* radio paging service
Personengesellschaft *(f)* limited company, partnership
Personenrufanlage *(f)* paging system, radiopaging system
Personenrufempfänger *(m)* paging receiver, radiopaging receiver
Personenrufgerät *(n)* radiotelephone, beeper
Personenschaden *(m)* personal injury, injury to persons
Personentransport *(m)* passenger carriage, passenger services
Personenwagen *(m)* motor car, passenger car
persönlich personal
Persönlichkeit *(f)* personality
Perspektive *(f)* perspective; (Zeichnung) perspective drawing; (Aussichten) prospects
perspektivisch in perspective
Pfahl *(m)* post

Pfand *(n)* (Flaschen etc.) deposit; (Finanzen) pawn, security
Pfand *(n)* **zahlen** pay a deposit
Pfandflasche *(f)* returnable bottle
Pfandregelung *(f)* deposit regulations
Pfeiler *(m)* pillar; (Säule) column
Pflanze *(f)* plant
Pflanzgefäß *(n)* planter
Pflicht *(f)* duty
Pflock *(m)* peg
Pforte *(f)* gate, door
Pförtner *(m)* gatekeeper, gateman, porter, doorman
Pfosten *(m)* post
Phase *(f)* phase
Phon *(n)* phon
Phonzahl *(f)* decibel level
Photosatz *(m)* phototypesetting
Phrase *(f)* phrase
Piktogramm *(n)* pictogram
Pinnwand *(f)* pinboard, notice board
Pinsel *(m)* brush
Plagiat *(n)* plagiarism
plagiieren plagiarize, pirate
Plakat *(n)* bill, poster, placard
plakatieren placard
Plakatwerbung *(f)* poster advertising
Plakette *(f)* badge
plan flat, plane, level
Plan *(m)* plan, project, blueprint; (Zeit etc.) schedule; (Absicht) intention
Plan *(m)*, **vermaßter** dimensional drawing, dimensional plan
Plane *(f)* tarpaulin, awning
planen plan; (Zeit) schedule
planieren grade, level
Planierraupe *(f)* bulldozer
Planke *(f)* board, plank
planlos aimless, unsystematic, without plan
planmäßig planned, systematic, according to plan; (Zeit) scheduled, on schedule
Planung *(f)* planning

Planung (f), kurzfristige short-term planning
Planung (f), strategische strategic planning
Planungsstadium (n), im in the planning stage
planvoll methodical, systematic
Planziel (f) target
Plasma-Display (n) plasma display
Plasma-Flachbildschirm (m) plasma flat screen
Plasma-Wandbildschirm (m) plasma screen
Plastik (n) plastic; (Kunst) sculpture
Plastiktasche (f) plastic bag
Platte (f) (Wand, Boden) panel; (Regal, Holz) board; (Glas, Metall) sheet; (Stein) ledge; (Keramik) tile; (Tisch) table top
Plattenhalter (m) panel connector
Plattenkonstruktion (f) panel construction
Plattenlaufwerk (n) (EDV) disk drive
Plattenstärke (f) panel thickness
Platten-Tischherd (m) table-top cooker
Plattform (f) platform
Platz (m) (Ort, Rang) place; (Sitz) seat; (Raum) room, space; (Punkt, Stelle) spot; (Bau, Lage) site
Platzanzahl (f) number of seats
platzieren place, position
Platzierung (f) (Standplatz etc.) placement, positioning
Platzierungsvorschlag (m) (Standplatz etc.) placement proposal, positioning proposal
Platzkarte (f) seat reservation card, seat reservation ticket, reserved seat ticket
Platzmangel (m) lack of space
Platztausch (m) (Messestand etc.) exchange of place, change of location, place swap
Platzzusage (f) space confirmation
Platzzuteilung (f) space assignment, allocation of space

plaudern chat, have a chat
plausibel plausible
Pleite (f) bankruptcy
Pleite (f) machen go bankrupt
Plexiglas (n) acrylic plastic
plombieren (versiegeln) seal, seal with lead
pneumatisch pneumatic
Podest (n) platform, podium
Podesthöhe (f) platform height
Podium (n) platform, podium, rostrum
Podiumsdiskussion (f) panel discussion
polieren polish
Politur (f) polish
Polizeikontrolle (f) police check
Polizeistation (f) police station
Polster (n) upholstery
polstern upholster
Polster-Schalenstuhl (m) shell-type chair upholstered
Polstersessel (m) easy chair, armchair, high back rest upholstered
Polsterstuhl (m) upholstered chair
populär popular
porös porous
Portal (n) portal
Portier (m) porter
Portion (f) portion; (Anteil) amount
Portmonee (n) purse
Porto (n) postage
portofrei post-free, postpaid, postage paid
Portogebühr (f) postal rate
portopflichtig liable to postage
Porzellangeschirr (n) china, porcelain
Position (f) position
Positionierung (f) positioning
Post (f) mail (US), post (GB)
Post (f), elektronische electronic mail, e-mail
Postamt (n) post office
Postanweisung (f) money order, postal order
Posten (m) (Ware) lot, quantity
Poster (n) poster

Postfach *(n)* P.O. box
Postgebühr *(f)* postage rate, postal charges
postlagernd poste restante
Postleitzahl *(f)* ZIP code (US), postcode (GB)
Postpaket *(n)* parcel, postal packet
Postwertzeichen *(n)* stamp, postage stamp
Postwurfsendung *(f)* bulk mail, direct mail, direct-mail advertising, mailing piece
Potenzial *(n)* potential
potenziell potential
PR-Abteilung *(f)* PR department
prächtig splendid, magnificent
Präferenz *(f)* preference
pragmatisch pragmatic
prägnant succinct, terse, pithy
Praktikant(in) *(m/f)* trainee
praktisch practical
praktizieren practise (US), practice (GB)
Prämie *(f)* (Gewinn) award, prize; (Belohnung) reward; (Vergütung) bonus; (Versicherung) premium
prämieren award a prize to, give an award to
Präsent *(f)* gift, present
Präsentation *(f)* presentation
Präsentationsmöbel *(f)* showcase
Präsentationstechnik *(f)* presentation technology
präsentieren present
Präsenz *(f)* presence
Präsident(in) *(m/f)* president; (Vorsitzende(r)) chairman, chairwoman
Präsidium *(n)* presidency, presiding committee
Praxis *(f)* practice; (Erfahrung) experience
präzise precise, exact
Präzision *(f)* precision
Preis *(m)* price, charge, rate; (Auszeichnung) award

Preis *(m)* **erhöhen** increase price, raise price
Preis *(m)* **pro Quadratmeter** square meter space rate (US), square metre space rate (GB)
Preis *(m)* **senken** cut price, lower price, reduce price
Preis *(m)*, **angemessener** reasonable price
Preis *(m)*, **ermäßigter** reduced rate, reduced price
Preis *(m)*, **konkurrenzfähiger** competitive price
Preisabsprache *(f)* common pricing, price fixing, price agreement
Preisänderung *(f)* change in prices
Preisänderungen *(f, pl)* **vorbehalten** prices subject to change, prices subject to alteration
Preisangabe *(f)* price, price quotation, quotation of prices
Preisangebot *(n)* **machen** quote
Preisanstieg *(m)* rise in prices, price increase, escalation of prices
Preisaufschlag *(m)* extra charge, price supplement, supplementary charge, mark-up
Preisausschreiben *(n)* competition, contest
Preisbildung *(f)* pricing, price fixing, price formation
Preisbindung *(f)* price control, price maintenance
Preisbindung *(f)* **der zweiten Hand** resale price maintenance (RPM)
Preisbindung *(f)*, **vertikale** resale price maintenance (RPM)
Preise *(m)* **auf Anfrage** prices on request
Preisempfehlung *(f)* recommended price
preisempfindlich price-sensitive
Preisentwicklung *(f)* price trend
Preiserhöhung *(f)* price increase
Preisermäßigung *(f)* price cut, price reduction

Preisfestsetzung *(f)* price fixing, pricing
Preisführerschaft *(f)* price leadership
Preisgefälle *(n)* price differential
Preisgefüge *(n)* price structure
preisgekrönt award-winning, prize-winning
Preisgericht *(n)* jury
Preisgleitklausel *(f)* escalator clause, escalation clause
preisgünstig good value, low-priced
Preisherabsetzung *(f)* markdown
Preisheraufsetzung *(f)* mark-up
Preiskalkulation *(f)* pricing
Preisklasse *(f)* price category, price range
Preiskontrolle *(f)* price control
Preiskrieg *(m)* price war
Preislage *(f)* price range
preislich in price
Preisliste *(f)* price list, scale of prices
Preisliste *(f)***, bebilderte** illustrated price list
Preisnachlass *(m)* price reduction, discount, rebate
Preisniveau *(n)* price level
Preisobergrenze *(f)* price ceiling
Preispolitik *(f)* price policy, pricing policy
Preisschild *(n)* price label, price tag
Preisschwankung *(f)* price fluctuation, fluctuation of price
Preissenkung *(f)* price cut, price markdown, price reduction, reduction of the rates
Preissteigerung *(f)* rise in prices, price increase, advance in price
Preissturz *(m)* sudden drop in prices
Preisträger *(m)* prizewinner
Preisunterschied *(m)* price difference, price differential
Preisverleihung *(f)* prize-winning presentation
preiswert low-priced, good value, inexpensive
Preiszugeständnis *(n)* price concession
Presse *(f)***, überregionale** national press

Pressearbeit *(f)* press relations
Presseausschnittdienst *(m)* clipping service, press cutting agency
Presseausweis *(m)* press card
Pressebericht *(m)* press report, press coverage
Pressebetreuung *(f)* press service
Pressebüro *(n)* press agency, press office
Presseempfang *(m)* press reception
Presseerklärung *(f)* statement to the press, press release
Pressefach *(n)* press box, press distribution box
Pressefoto *(n)* press photo
Pressefotograf(in) *(m/f)* press photographer
Presseführer *(m)* press guide
Presseinformation *(f)* press briefing
Pressekonferenz *(f)* press conference
Pressemappe *(f)* press folder, press kit
Pressemeldung *(f)* press report, news item
Pressemitteilung *(f)* press release, handout
Pressenotiz *(f)* short announcement
Pressereporter(in) *(m/f)* reporter, press reporter
Pressespiegel *(m)* press review
Pressesprecher(in) *(m/f)* press officer, spokesman, press spokesman, spokeswoman, press spokeswoman
Pressestimmen *(f, pl)* press commentaries
Pressezentrum *(n)* press center (US), press centre (GB)
Pressluft *(f)* compressed air
Prestige *(n)* prestige
Primärdaten *(pl)* primary data
Primärforschung *(f)* field research
Prinzip *(n)* principle
Prinzip *(n)*, **aus** on principle
prinzipiell on principle; (grundsätzlich) in principle
Priorität *(f)* priority

Prioritäten *(f, pl)* **setzen** establish priorities
privat private; (persönlich) personal
Privatadresse *(f)* home address
Privatangelegenheit *(f)* private matter
Privatgespräch *(n)* private conversation
Privileg *(n)* privilege
PR-Kampagne *(f)* PR campaign
pro Jahr *(n)* per annum
pro Meter *(m)* per meter (US), per metre (GB)
pro Stück *(n)* a piece
pro Stunde *(f)* per hour
pro Tag *(m)* per day
Probe *(f)* (Auftritt) rehearsal; (Versuch) test, trial, tryout; (Kostprobe, Stichprobe) sample
Probeabzug *(m)* print, proof
Probeaufnahme *(f)* (Film) screen test
Probeexemplar *(n)* sample, specimen copy
Probelauf *(m)* test run, trial run
proben practise (US), practice (GB)
Probepackung *(f)* trial package
Probeseite *(f)* specimen page
probeweise on trial, on trial basis, on approval
probieren try; (Lebensmittel) taste; (prüfen) test
problematisch problematic
Problemkreis *(m)* complex of problems
problemlos unproblematic, problem free, trouble-free, without difficulties
Problemlösung *(f)* problem solving
Produkt *(n)*, **konkurrenzfähiges** competitive product
Produktakzeptanz *(f)* product acceptance
Produktanalyse *(f)* product analysis
Produktbekanntheit *(f)* product awareness
Produkteigenschaft *(f)* product features
Produkteinführung *(f)* product introduction, product initiation, product launch

Produktentwicklung *(f)* product development
Produktforschung *(f)* product research
Produktgestaltung *(f)* product design
Produktgruppe *(f)* product category, product line, product range
Produktgruppeneintrag *(m)* (Messekatalog) product category listings
Produktgruppenverzeichnis *(n)* (Messekatalog) product category index
Produkthaftung *(f)* product liability
Produktidee *(f)* product idea
Produktimage *(n)* product image
Produktionskapazität *(f)* production capacity, productive capacity
Produktionskosten *(f)* production costs, manufacturing costs
Produktionsstätte *(f)* factory, production facility
produktiv productive
Produktivität *(f)* productivity, technical efficiency
Produktkonzept *(n)* product concept
Produktlebenszyklus *(m)* product life cycle
Produktlinie *(f)* product line, product range
Produktmanagement *(n)* product management
Produktmanager(in) *(m/f)* product manager, brand manager
Produktmix *(n)* product mix
Produktpalette *(f)* array of products, product range, range of products
Produktpositionierung *(f)* product positioning
Produktqualität *(f)* product quality
Produktsicherheitsgesetz *(n)* product safety law
Produktstrategie *(f)* product strategy
Produktverbesserung *(f)* product improvement
Produktvorführung *(f)* product presentation

Produktwerbung *(f)* product advertising
Produzent *(m)* producer
produzieren make, produce, fabricate
professionell professional
Profil *(n)* profile
profilieren profile, contoure
profiliert (Person) distinguished, distinctive, clear cut
Profilstütze *(f)* profile support
Profilverlängerung *(f)* profile extension
Profit *(m)* profit
profitabel profitable
Profit-Center *(n)* profit center (US), profit centre (GB)
profitieren profit, benefit
Proformarechnung *(f)* proforma account
Prognose *(f)* prognosis, projection, prediction, forecast, forecasting
Prognose *(f)***, kurzfristige** short-range forecast, short-term forecast
Prognose *(f)***, mittelfristige** medium-term forecast
prognostizieren predict, forecast
Programm *(n)* program (US), programme (GB), plan; (Zeitplan) schedule
programmgemäß according to plan
programmierbar programmable
programmieren program (US), programme (GB)
Programmiersprache *(f)* programming language
Programmierung *(f)* programming
Programmsteuerung *(f)* (EDV) program control (US), programme control (GB)
Projekt *(n)* project
projektieren project
Projektingenieur *(m)* project engineer
Projektion *(f)* (Film etc.) projection; (Vorausschau) projection
Projektionsfläche *(f)* projection area
Projektionslicht *(n)* projection light
Projektionsscheibe *(f)* projection screen

Projektleiter(in) *(m/f)* project leader, project manager
Projektmanagement *(n)* project management
Projektor *(m)* projector
Projektstudie *(f)* case study, feasibility study
projizieren project
Pro-Kopf- per head, per capita
Prokura *(f)* procuration
Prokurist(in) *(m/f)* authorized representative, attorney
prominent prominent
Prominenz *(f)* notables, prominent figures, public figures, top people, civic heads
Promotion *(f)* promotion
prompt prompt, quick; (sofort) immediate
Propaganda *(f)* propaganda, publicity
propagieren propagate
Propangas *(n)* propane, propane gas
Proportion *(f)* proportion
Prospekt *(m)* brochure, prospectus
Prospektkasten *(m)* literature dispenser
Prospektmaterial *(n)* descriptive material
Prospektspender *(m)* brochure dispenser
Prospektständer *(m)* brochure stand, literature rack
Prost! Your health!, Cheers!
Protokoll *(n)* record, minutes; (EDV) protocol
Protokoll *(n)* **führen** keep the minutes, take the minutes
Protokollchef *(m)* chief of protocol
protokollieren record, keep the minutes, take the minutes, give record of
Prototyp *(m)* prototype
Provision *(f)* commission
provisorisch provisional
Prozentsatz *(m)* percentage
Prozessor *(m)* (EDV) processor

Prozesssteuerung *(f)* process control
Prüfbescheid *(m)* inspection report
prüfen (Kenntnisse etc.) examine; (mustern) inspect; (ausprobieren) test; (überprüfen) check
Prüfung *(f)* (Kenntnisse etc.) examination; (Musterung) inspection; (Erprobung) test, tresting; (Überprüfung) check, checking
Prüfungszeugnis *(n)* certificate
Prüfverfahren *(n)* method of testing, testing procedure
Prüfzeichen *(n)* test mark
Prüfzeichenverordnung *(f)* inspection mark legislation, test mark ordinance
Prüfzeugnis *(n)* inspection certificate, test certificate
Publikation *(f)* publication
Publikum *(n)* public; (Zuhörer, Zuschauer) audience
Publikumserfolg *(m)* great popular success, success with the public
Publikumstage *(m, pl)* public days, open to public
publizieren publish
Publizität *(f)* publicity
Pult *(n)* desk, lectern
Pultdach *(n)* desk roof
Pulver *(n)* powder
Pulverbeschichtung *(f)* powder coating
pulverlackiert powder coated
Pumpe *(f)* pump
pumpen pump
Punkt *(m)* point; (kleiner Punkt) dot; (Satzzeichen) full stop; (Diskussion) item, point
Punktlast *(f)* point load, spot load, concentrated load
pünktlich punctual, on time, on shedule
Punktstrahler *(m)* spot light
punktuell selective
pur pur
Putz *(m)* (Wand) plaster, coating
putzen clean

Putzfrau *(f)* cleaner, cleaning lady, scrubwoman
Putzkolonne *(f)* team of cleaners
Putzlappen *(m)* cloth
Putzmittel *(n)* cleaning agent, cleanser
Putztuch *(f)* cloth
Putzzeug *(n)* cleaning things
Pyramide *(f)* pyramid
pyramidenförmig pyramidal, pyramid-shaped

Q

Quadrat *(n)* square
quadratisch (Form) square; (Mathematik) quadratic
quadratische Konstruktion *(f)* square section structure
quadratisches Deckenfeld *(n)* square ceiling panel
Quadratmeter *(m)* square meter (US), square metre (GB)
Quadratmeterpreis *(m)* (Messestand) square meter space rate (US), square metre space rate (GB)
Qualität *(f)***, erstklassige** first-class quality
qualitativ qualitative
Qualitätsarbeit *(f)* quality work, high-quality work, quality workmanship, high-quality workmanship
qualitätsbewusst quality-conscious
Qualitätserzeugnis *(n)* quality product, high-quality product
Qualitätskontrolle *(f)* quality control
Qualitätssicherung *(f)* quality assurance, quality protection
Qualitätsstandard *(m)* quality standard
Qualitätsware *(f)* quality articles, high-quality articles, quality goods, high-quality goods
Qualm *(m)* smoke, dense smoke

qualmen smoke
qualmig smoky
quantifizieren quantify
Quantität *(f)* quantity
quantitativ quantitative
Quartal *(n)* quarter
Quartier *(n)* accomodation, lodging, quarters
Quartiernachweis *(m)* accommodation service
quasi quasi, as it were, to a certain extent, in a way, virtually
Quelle *(f)* (Ursprung) source
quer crossways, crosswise
quer über across, diagonally
Querschnitt *(m)* cross section
Querschnittszeichnung *(f)* sectional drawing
Querverweis *(m)* cross reference
quetschen squeeze
quietschen squeak, squeal
Quintessenz *(f)* essence, quintessence
quittieren give a receipt, acknowledge
Quittung *(f)* receipt, receipt for payment, acknowledgement
Quittung *(f)*, **gegen** on receipt
Quittungsblock *(m)* receipt book
Quittungsformular *(n)* receipt form
Quote *(f)* quota; (Statistik) proportion
quotieren be listed, be quoted
Quotierung *(f)* quotation

R

Rabatt *(m)* discount, markdown, rebate, reduction
Rabattstaffel *(f)* discount schedule, graduated discount scale
Radarfalle *(f)* radar trap, radar speed trap
Radarkontrolle *(f)* radar control, radar speed check

radieren erase, rub out
Radiergummi *(m)* rubber, eraser
Radio *(n)*, **im** on the radio
radioaktiv radioactive
radioaktivem Material *(n)*, **Umgang mit** handling radioactive material
radioaktives Material *(n)* radioactive material
Radioaktivität *(f)* radioactivity
Radius *(m)* radius
ragen tower, loom over
rahmen frame; (Diapositiv) mount
Rahmen *(m)* frame; (Diapositiv) mount
Rahmenabkommen *(n)* basic agreement, skeleton agreement
Rahmenbedingungen *(f, pl)* basic conditions, general conditions, general setting, general framework
Rahmendisplay *(n)* integrated frame display
Rahmenkonstruktion *(f)* frame construction, frame layout
Rahmenprogramm *(n)* accompanying program (US), accompanying programme, supporting program (US), supporting programme (GB), fringe program (US), fringe programme (GB), fringe events
Rahmenrichtlinien *(f, pl)* guidelines
Rahmenveranstaltung *(f)* supporting event
RAL-Farbkarte *(f)* RAL color range (US), RAL colour range (GB)
RAL-Sonderfarbe *(f)* RAL special color (US), RAL special colour (GB)
Rampe *(f)* ramp
Rampenlicht *(n)* footlights
Rand *(m)* edge, border, fringe, rim, brink; (Seitenrand) margin
Randbemerkung *(f)* marginal note, passing remark
Randplatte *(f)* end panel
Randzone *(f)* marginal zone
Rang *(m)* grade, rank, ranking, status, standing, position

Rangfolge *(f)* order of rank, ranking, order of precedence, priority
Rangliste *(f)* ranking list, ranking table
rar rare, scarce
rasant fast; (Entwicklung) rapid
rasch fast, quick, speedy, swift
Rast *(f)* rest, repose; (Pause) break
Raster *(n)* (Gitter) grid; (TV, Druck) raster, raster screen
Rasterdecke *(f)* cell ceiling, grid ceiling
Rastermaß *(n)* screen line dimension
rastlos restless
Rat *(m)* advice; (Vorschlag) suggestion; (Empfehlung) recommendation
Rate *(f)* (Zahlung) installment (US), instalment (GB); (Wachstum etc.) rate
Ratenzahlung *(f)* deferred payment, deferred instal(l)ment, payment by instal(l)ments, instal(l)ment payment
Ratgeber *(m)* adviser; (Buch) guide, reference book
rational rational
rationalisieren rationalize, streamline
Rationalisierung *(f)* rationalization, streamlining
rationell rational; (Wirtschaft) efficient, economical
ratlos helpless
Ratlosigkeit *(f)* helplessness
ratsam advisable, wise
Rätsche *(f)* ratchet
Ratschlag *(m)* counsel, advice, piece of advice
Rauchabzug *(m)* smoke outlet
Rauchen verboten! No smoking!
Rauchentwicklung *(f)* formation of smoke
Raucher(in) *(m/f)* smoker
Rauchmelder *(m)* smoke alarm
Rauchverbot *(n)* smoking ban
Rauhfasertapete *(f)* woodchip paper, woodchip wallpaper
Raum *(m)* room; (Gebiet) area; (Platz) space
Raum *(m)*, **umbauter** interior space

Raumaufteilung *(f)* (Messehalle etc.) floor plan
räumen clear, clear away; (Notfall) evacuate; (verlassen) leave
Raumgestaltung *(f)* interior design
Raumhöhe *(f)* room height
Rauminhalt *(m)* capacity, volume
räumlich spatial, three-dimensional; (Akustik) stereophonic
Raummaß *(n)* dimensions, cubic measure, solid measure
Raummeter *(m)* cubic meter (US), cubic metre (GB)
Raumpflegerin *(f)* cleaning lady, cleaner
raumsparend space-saving
Raumteiler *(m)* partition
Raumtrenner *(m)* room divider
Räumung *(f)* clearing, clearance; (Notfall) evacuation
Räumung *(f)* **des Stands** clearing the stand
Räumungstermin *(m)* **des Geländes, letzter** site vacation deadline
reagieren react, respond
Reaktion *(f)* reaction, response, feedback
real actual, real, realistic
realisierbar feasible, realizable
realisieren realize, carry out
Rechenschaft *(f)* **ablegen** account for
Rechenzentrum *(n)* computer center (US), computer centre (GB)
Recherche *(f)* investigation, search
recherchieren investigate, search
rechnen calculate
Rechner *(m)* (EDV) computer
Rechnergeschwindigkeit *(f)* (EDV) computing speed
rechnergesteuert (EDV) computer-controlled
rechnergestützt (EDV) computer-aided, computer-assisted, computer-based
Rechnerzeit *(f)* (EDV) computer time

Rechnung *(f)* account, bill, invoice, check
Rechnung *(f)* **ausstellen** bill, invoice
Rechnung *(f)* **bezahlen** settle an account
Rechnungsanschrift *(f)* invoicing address
Rechnungsbetrag *(m)* invoice amount, invoicing amount, amount of a bill, amount charged, total
Rechnungsdatum *(n)* date of invoice
Rechnungsjahr *(n)* accounting period, financial year, fiscal year
Rechnungspreis *(m)* invoice price
Rechnungsprüfer(in) *(m/f)* accountant
Rechnungsstellung *(f)* invoicing
recht (richtig) right
Recht *(n)* law
Recht *(n)* **haben** be right
Rechteck *(n)* rectangle
rechteckig rectangular
rechtfertigen justify, vindicate
Rechtfertigung *(f)* justification, vindication
rechtlich legal, lawful
rechtmäßig legal, lawful, legitimate, rightful
Rechtmäßigkeit *(f)* legality, lawfulness, legitimacy, rightfulness
Rechtsabteilung *(f)* legal department, legal section
Rechtsanspruch *(m)* legal claim, legal title
Rechtsbeistand *(m)* advocate, counsel, legal advice
Rechtsberatung *(f)* legal advice, legal counselling
rechtsbündig ranged right
Rechtsfall *(m)* case, law case, legal case
Rechtsgeschäft *(n)* legal transaction
rechtsgültig legally valid
rechtskräftig legally effective, final, valid
Rechtsschutz *(m)* legal protection

Rechtsschutz *(m)***, gewerblicher** industrial property protection, protection of industrial property rights
Rechtsstreit *(m)* lawsuit, legal action
rechtsverbindlich legally binding
Rechtsverfahren *(n)* legal procedure
rechtswidrig illegal, unlawful
Rechtswidrigkeit *(f)* illegality
rechtwinklig right-angled, rectangular
rechtwinklige Konstruktion *(f)* rectangular structure
rechtzeitig punctual, in time
recyceln recycle
recyclingfähige Stoffe *(m, pl)* recyclable materials
Recyclingfähigkeit *(f)* recyclability
Redakteur(in) *(m/f)* editor
Redaktion *(f)* editorial board, editorial staff
redaktionell editorial
Rede *(f)* speech, address
Rede *(f)* **halten** make a speech
redegewandt eloquent
redigieren edit
Redner(in) *(m/f)* speaker
Rednerpult *(n)* speaker's desk
reduzieren reduce, decrease, lower, mark down
Reduzierung *(f)* reduction, marking down
reell honest, solid; (annehmbar) decent
Referat *(n)* report, lecture, paper
Referenz *(f)* reference
referieren report, lecture, give a lecture, give a paper
reflektieren reflect
Reflektor *(m)* reflector
Reflektorlampe *(f)* reflector bulb
Regal *(n)* shelves, shelf unit, rack
Regalauszeichnung *(f)* shelf labeling (US), shelf labelling (GB), shelf price
Regalboden *(m)* shelf
Regalboden *(m)* **aus Glas** shelf of glass
Regalboden *(m)* **aus Holz** shelf of timber

Regalboden *(m)* **aus Lochblech** shelf of perforated sheet metal
Regalfläche *(f)* shelf space
Regalleiste *(f)* channel strip
Regalsystem *(f)* shelving system
Regalsystemteil *(n)* shelving system component
Regalwand *(f)* wall lined shelf units
Regel *(f)* rule
regelbar adjustable, controllable
regelmäßig regular; (wiederkehrend) periodical
regeln regulate; (Angelegenheiten) arrange
Regelung *(f)* (Vorschrift) regulation; (Vereinbarung) arrangement; (Technik) control
regelwidrig irregular, against the rules
regenerieren regenerate, revive
Regenschirm *(m)* umbrella
Regionalsender *(m)* local radio station
Register *(n)* register, table of contents
registrieren register, record
Registrierung *(f)* registration, recording
Registrierungsgebühr *(f)* registration fee, recording fee
Regler *(m)* control, controller
Regress *(m)* recourse
regresspflichtig liable to recourse, liable for compensation
regulär (geregelt) regular; (normal, üblich) normal, standard
regulierbar adjustable
regulieren regulate, adjust; (Rechnung) pay, settle
Regulierung *(f)* regulation; (Technik) adjustment; (Rechnung) payment, settlement
reiben rub
Reibung *(f)* friction
reibungslos trouble-free, smooth
reich rich, wealthy
reichen give, hand, pass

reichhaltig rich
reichlich abundant, ample, plentyful, plenty of
Reichweite *(f)* reach; (Funk) range; (Empfangsbereich) coverage
Reihe *(f)* line, row; (Spektrum) range
Reihenfolge *(f)* order, sequence, succession
Reihenstand *(m)* in-line stand, row booth, row stand
rein pure; (sauber) clean, clear
Reinfall *(m)* disaster, flop
Reingewinn *(m)* clear profit, net profit, net income
Reinheit *(f)* purity, cleanness
reinigen clean
Reiniger *(m)* cleaner
Reinigung *(f)* cleaning
Reinigung *(f)***, tägliche** daily cleaning
Reinigungsarbeiten *(f, pl)* cleaning work
Reinigungskosten *(pl)* cleaning expenses, service charge for cleaning
Reinigungsmittel *(n)* cleaning supply, detergent
Reinigungspersonal *(n)* cleaners, cleaning personnel
Reinmachefrau *(f)* cleaning lady
Reiseabrechnung *(f)* travel expense statement
Reiseagentur *(f)* tourist agency
Reiseapotheke *(f)* portable medicine-case, first-aid kit
Reiseauskunft *(f)* travel information
Reisebestätigung *(f)* trip confirmation
Reisebüro *(n)* tourist agency, travel agency
Reisedauer *(f)* duration of journey
Reiseführer *(m)* (Buch) guide, guidebook, itinerary
Reisegepäck *(n)* baggage (US), luggage (GB)
Reisegepäckversicherung *(f)* baggage insurance (US), luggage insurance (GB)
Reisekosten *(pl)* traveling expenses (US), travelling expenses (GB)

Reiseleiter(in) *(m/f)* courier, tour conductor, tour manager, travel supervisor
Reisespesen *(pl)* travel expenses, travel charges
Reisespesen-Tagessatz *(m)* per diem allowance
Reiseveranstalter *(m)* tour operator, tour organizer, travel organizer
reißen drag, pull, tear
Reißzwecke *(f)* drawing pin
Reklamation *(f)* complaint
Reklame *(f)* advertising, promotion, publicity; (Anzeige) advertisement
Reklame *(f)* **machen** advertise, promote, publicise
Reklamepostsendung *(f)* junk mail
Reklamezettel *(m)* handbill, leaflet
reklamieren claim, complain; (zurückverlangen) reclaim
Relaunch *(m)* relaunch
relevant relevant
Rendite *(f)* return, rate of return, yield, effective yield
rennen run, rush, dash
Renommee *(n)* prestige, reputation
renommiert prestigious, renowned
renovieren renovate
Renovierung *(f)* renovation
rentabel cost-efficient, commercially viable, profitable, profit-making
Rentabilität *(f)* profitability, viability
reparabel reparable, repairable
Reparatur *(f)* repair
Reparaturkosten *(pl)* cost of repairs, repair costs
Reparaturwerkstatt *(f)* workshop; (Auto) garage
reparieren fix, repair
Report *(m)* report
Reportage *(f)* report
Reporter *(m)* reporter
Repräsentant(in) *(m/f)* representative
Repräsentationswerbung *(f)* prestige advertising

repräsentativ representative, prestigious
repräsentieren represent
Reproduktion *(f)* reproduction
reproduzieren reproduce
Reprovorlage *(f)* reproduction proof
Reserve *(f)* reserve; (Vorrat) stockpile
reservieren book, make a reservation, reserve
reserviert booked, reserved
Reservierung *(f)* reservation
Reservierungsbestätigung *(f)* reservation confirmation
Resonanz *(f)* resonance, feedback
respektieren respect
Ressort *(n)* department
Rest *(m)* rest; (Überrest) remnant; (Überbleibsel) oddment
Restabfall *(m)* leftover waste
Restaurant *(f)* restaurant
restlich remaining
Restposten *(m)* oddments, remaining stock
restriktiv restrictive
Reststoffe *(m, pl)* residual materials, residual substances
Resultat *(n)* result
resultieren result
Retrospektive *(f)* retrospect
retten save, rescue
Rettung *(f)* rescue; (Entkommen) escape; (Bergung) recovery
Rettungswagen *(m)* ambulance, rescue vehicle
Rettungsweg *(m)* escape route, rescue route
retuschieren retouch, touch up
revidieren revise, overhaul
Revision *(f)* revision, overhaul
Revisionsöffnung *(f)* inspection opening
Rezeption *(f)* reception area, reception desk, front desk
Rezession *(f)* recession
Rhetorik *(f)* rhetoric

richten (lenken) direct; (Licht etc.) turn; (vorbereiten) prepare; (urteilen) judge
richtig right, correct; (genau) accurate
richtiggehend veritable
Richtigkeit *(f)* accuracy, correctness
Richtlinie *(f)* code of practice, directive, guideline, regulation
Richtlinien *(f, pl)*, **technische** technical guidelines, technical regulations
Richtpreis *(m)* guide price, target price, recommended price
Richtung *(f)* direction, course
richtungweisend guiding, trendsetting
Richtwert *(m)* guide value
riechen smell
Riegel *(m)* bolt, bar
Rille *(f)* groove
Ring *(m)* ring
Ringbuch *(n)* ring binder
ringförmig ring-like
ringförmig umschließen encircle
Ringknoten *(m)* ring node
Ringleitung *(f)* circular main
Rinne *(f)* groove
Risiko *(n)* risk; (geschäftlich) hazard
Risiko *(n)*, **auf eigenes** at one's own risk
Risikofaktor *(m)* risk factor
risikolos risk-free, without risk
risikoreich risky
riskant risky
riskieren risk
Riss *(m)* (Wand etc.) crack, breach, break, gap; (Stoff, Papier) tear, rent, rip
ritzen scratch; (einritzen) carve
Rivale *(m)* rival
rivalisieren compete
Rivalität *(f)* rivalry
robust robust
roh raw; (unverarbeitet) rough
Rohbau *(m)* shell
Rohr *(n)* tube; (Leitung) pipe; (Kanal) duct
Rohrbruch *(m)* burst pipe
Rohrdurchmesser *(m)* tube diameter
Röhre *(f)* tube; (Leitung) pipe; (TV) valve
Rohrleitung *(f)* conduit, pipe
Rohrleitungsmaterial *(n)* piping material
Rohrschelle *(f)* pipe clamp, pipe clip
Rohrzange *(f)* pipe wrench
Rohstoff *(m)* raw material
Rohzustand *(m)* crude state
Rolle *(f)* roll; (Möbel, Laufrolle) castor
rollen roll; (aufrollen) roll up
Rollenspiel *(n)* role play
Rollgeld *(n)* carriage, drayage, haulage, wheelage, trucking charges
Rollstuhl *(m)* wheelchair, invalid chair, invalid rolling chair
Rollstuhlfahrer(in) *(m/f)* spastic
rollstuhlgerecht suitable for wheel chairs
Rolltreppe *(f)* escalator
ROM ROM (Read Only Memory)
Röntgenanlage *(f)* X-ray equipment
Röntgenstrahlen *(m, pl)* X-rays
rosten rust, get rusty
rostfrei rustproof, stainless
Rotation *(f)* rotation
Rotationsdruck *(m)* rotary printing
rotieren rotate
Rotwein *(m)* red wine
Route *(f)* route
Routine *(f)* routine
routinemäßig routine, as a matter of routine
routiniert experienced
Rückansicht *(f)* back view
Rückantwort *(f)* reply; (Antwortschreiben) business reply card, business reply mail
Rückbestätigung *(f)* reconfirmation
Rückblende *(f)* (Film) flashback
Rückblick *(m)* review, retrospect, retrospective glance
rücken move
rückerstatten refund, reimburse

Rückerstattung *(f)* rebate, refund, repayment, reimbursement
Rückerstattung *(f)* **der Mehrwertsteuer** VAT refund
Rückfahrkarte *(f)* return ticket
Rückfahrt *(f)* return journey
Rückflug *(m)* return flight
Rückflugbestätigung *(f)* confirmation of return flight
Rückfracht *(f)* back freight, return cargo, return freight
Rückfrage *(f)* checkback
rückfragen check
Rückgabe *(f)* return
Rückgaberecht *(n)* right of return
Rückgang *(m)* decline, downturn, drop, fall
rückgängig machen revoke, annul, cancel
Rückgebäude *(n)* rear building
Rückhalt *(m)* support
Rückinformation *(f)* feedback
Rückkauf *(m)* repurchase
Rückkehr *(f)* return
Rücklagen *(f, pl)* reserves, savings
Rücklagen *(f, pl)*, **stille** hidden reserves
rückläufig dropping, declining, decreasing
Rücklicht *(n)* rear light
Rücknahme *(f)* taking back, repurchase; (Recht) abandonment, withdrawal
Rücknahmevereinbarung *(f)* buy-back agreement
Rückprojektion *(f)* rear projection
Rückprojektionsbox *(f)* rear projection box
Rückprojektions-Splitwand *(f)* rear projection split screen
Rückreise *(f)* return journey
Rückschau *(f)* look back, review, retrospective, retrospect, retrospection
Rückschlag *(m)* setback
Rückschluss *(m)* conclusion

Rückseite *(f)* (Stand) rear of the stand; (Druck) back page, back side, reverse page, reverse side
Rücksendung *(f)* return
Rücksicht *(f)* consideration
Rücksichtnahme *(f)* consideration
rücksichtslos inconsiderate
Rücksichtslosigkeit *(f)* lack of consideration, inconsiderateness
rücksichtsvoll considerate, thoughtful
Rücksitz *(m)* backseat
Rücksprache *(f)* consultation
Rückstand *(m)* (Zahlung etc.) arrears, lag behind; (Arbeit) backlog, work backlog
rückständig backward
Rückständigkeit *(f)* backwardness
Rücktritt *(m)* (vom Vertrag etc.) withdrawal; (vom Amt etc.) resignation
Rücktrittsfrist *(f)* escape period, period of withdrawal
Rücktrittsgebühr *(f)* withdrawal fee
Rücktrittsrecht *(n)* right of withrawal
Rückumschlagseite *(f)* back, back cover
rückvergüten refund
Rückvergütung *(f)* rebate, refund
rückversichern reinsure
Rückversicherung *(f)* reinsurance
Rückwand *(f)* back wall, rear wall
rückwärtig back, rear
rückwärts backwards
Rückweg *(m)* way back
rückwirkend backdated; (rechtlich) retroactive
rückzahlbar repayable
Rückzahlung *(f)* back payment, rebate, reimbursement, repayment
Ruf *(m)* (Rufen) call; (Achtung) reputation
Rufanlage *(f)* paging system
Rufnummer *(f)* telephone number, number
Ruhe *(f)* (Erholung) rest; (Stille) quiet; (Schweigen) silence; (Emotion) calm, calmness

Ruhe bewahren! Keep quiet!
ruhelos restless
Ruhepause *(f)* break, rest
Ruheraum *(m)* rest room
Ruhestörung *(f)* disturbance of the peace
Ruhetag *(m)* day of rest
Ruhezone *(f)* recreation area, rest area, resting place
ruhig quiet; (gelassen) calm
rund round
Rundbau *(m)* rotunda
Rundblick *(m)* panorama
Runddach *(n)* circular roof
Runde *(f)* (Personenkreis) circle; (Rundgang) round
Rundelement *(n)* curved part
Rundfunk *(m)* radio, broadcasting
Rundfunksender *(m)* radio station
Rundgang *(m)* round, tour
rundherum all round, all around
Rundrohr *(n)* round extrusion
Rundschreiben *(n)* circular, circular letter
Rundstab *(m)* rod bracket
Rundummagazin *(n)* (Diaprojektor) carousel slide tray
rutschfest slip-proof, non-slip
rutschig slippery
rutschsicher non-slip
Rutschsicherung *(f)* slip-proof security
rütteln shake

S

Sachkenntnis *(f)* expertise, expert knowledge, knowhow
sachkundig competent, expert, well-informed, knowledgeable
sachkundige Beratung *(f)* expert advice, expert guidance
sachlich factual, objective
Sachschaden *(m)* material damage, damage to property, property damage
Sachverhalt *(m)* facts, circumstances
Sachverständige(r) *(f/m)* expert, specialist
Sachverständigengutachten *(n)* specialist report
Sachverständiger *(m)*, **unabhängiger** independent expert
Saft *(m)* juice
Saftpresse *(f)* juice extractor, squeezer
Säge *(f)* saw
Sägeblatt *(n)* saw blade
sägen saw
Sahne *(f)* cream
Saison *(f)* season
saisonal seasonal
Saisonschwankung *(f)* seasonal fluctuation, seasonal variation
Sakko *(n)* jacket, coat, sports jacket, sports coat
Saldo *(m)* account balance, balance of account
Sammelauftrag *(m)* bulk order
Sammelbegriff *(m)* comprehensive term
Sammelfahrschein *(m)* group ticket
Sammelladung *(f)* consolidation, consolidated shipment, groupage, mixed consignment
sammeln collect
Sammelplatz *(m)* meeting place, assembly point
Sandpapier *(n)* sandpaper
Sandwich *(n)* sandwich
Sandwichplatte *(f)* sandwich panel
sanitär sanitary
Sanitärcontainer *(m)* sanitary container
sanitäre Anlagen *(f, pl)* sanitary facilities
Sanitärtechnik *(f)* sanitary technology
Sanitäter(in) *(m/f)* ambulance, first-aid attendant
Sanitätsstation *(f)* first-aid post, medical center

Satellitenfernsehen *(n)* satellite television
Sattelschlepper *(m)* road tractor, truck, articulated lorry (GB), semitrailler
Sättigung *(f)* (Markt etc.) saturation
Sättigungsgrad *(m)* degree of saturation
Satzspiegel *(m)* type area
Satzung *(f)* statutes, statutes and articles
satzungsgemäß statutory, in accordance with the statutes, according to the statutes
sauber clean, tidy; (gepflegt) neat
saubermachen clean, clean up, tidy, tidy up
Säuberung *(f)* cleaning
Sauerstoffflasche *(f)* oxygen cylinder
saugen suck; (staubsaugen) vacuum
Säuglingsbetreuung *(f)* baby care
Saugpumpe *(f)* suction pump
Saugrohr *(n)* suction pipe
Säule *(f)* column, pillar
Säulendiagramm *(n)* bar chart
säumig defaulting, late, tardy
Säumniszuschlag *(m)* delay penalty
S-Bahn *(f)* suburban railway, suburban train
schaben scrape
Schablone *(f)* stencil, template
Schacht *(m)* drain
Schachtel *(f)* box
schaden damage, harm
Schaden *(m)* damage; (Person) harm, injury; (Technik) defect; (Versicherung) claim, damage
Schaden *(m)* **erleiden** suffer damage
Schaden *(m)***, körperlicher** harm, injury
Schadenanzeige *(f)* notice of claim
Schadenbegrenzung *(f)* damage containment, limiting of the damage
Schadenersatz *(m)* damages, damages compensation, compensation in damages, compensation for damage, damage claim, claim for damages, claim of compensation

Schadenersatz *(m)* **leisten** pay compensation; (Versicherung) idemnify
Schadenersatzanspruch *(m)* claim for damages, damage claim
Schadenersatzklage *(f)* action for damages
schadenersatzpflichtig liable for damages
Schadenfall *(m)* event of loss
Schadenhaftung *(f)* liability for damages
Schadenhöhe *(f)* extend of damage
Schadenversicherung *(f)* casualty insurance, indemnity insurance
schadhaft damaged, faulty, defective
schädigen damage
schädlich damaging, harmful
Schadstoff *(m)* harmful substance, pollutant
schaffen create, make
Schale *(f)* bowl, dish
Schall *(m)* sound
Schalldämmung *(f)* sound insulation
schalldämpfend sound deadening
Schallpegel *(m)* noise level
schallschluckend sound absorbing, noise absorbing
Schaltbild *(n)* wiring diagram
schalten switch
Schalter *(m)* (Bank etc.) counter; (Ein/Aus-Schalter) switch
Schalter *(m)***, elektrischer** electric switch
Schalterstunden *(pl)* business hours
Schaltkreis *(m)* switching circuit
Schaltplan *(m)* wiring diagram
Schalttafel *(f)* switchboard
Schaltuhr *(f)* timer
scharf sharp
Scharfeinstellung *(f)* (Kamera) focusing (US), focussing (GB)
schärfen sharpen
scharfkantig sharp-edged
Scharnier *(f)* hinge
Schatten *(m)* shadow

schätzen (abschätzen) appraise; (einschätzen) assess, value, estimate, guess; (hoch schätzen) appreciate, respect
Schätzung *(f)* (Abschätzung) appraisel; (Einschätzung) estimate, guess; (Bewertung) rating, valuation; (Hochschätzung) appreciation, estimation
schätzungsweise approximately, roughly
Schau *(f)* show
Schau *(f)* **stellen, zur** exhibit, display, present
Schaubild *(n)* chart, diagram, graph
Schauer *(m)* (Regen) shower
Schaufel *(f)* shovel
schaufeln shovel
Schaufenster *(n)* shop window
Schaufensterdekoration *(f)* shop window decoration, window display, window dressing
Schaukasten *(m)* display case, display cabinet, showcase
Schaumlöscher *(m)* foam fire extinguisher
Schaumstoff *(m)* foam material
Schaupackung *(f)* display pack, dummy, dummy pack
Schauplatz *(m)* scene, site
Schauraum *(m)* showroom
Schauvitrine *(f)* glass cupboard, showcase
Scheck *(m)* check (US), cheque (GB)
Scheckkarte *(f)* bank card, check card (US), cheque card (GB)
Scheibe *(f)* disk; (Glasscheibe) pane; (Unterlegescheibe) washer
Schein *(m)* (Papier) slip; (Bescheinigung) certificate; (Geld) bill (US), note (GB)
scheinen shine
Scheinwerfer *(m)* floodlight, spotlight
scheitern fail
Schelle *(f)* bell; (Rohrschelle) clamp
Schema *(n)* diagram, scheme

schematisch schematic, systematic
Schemel *(m)* stool, footstool
schemenhaft shadowy
schenken give, give as a present
Scherbeneiserzeuger *(m)* flake ice maker
Schere *(f)* scissors
Scherenarbeitsbühne *(f)* scissor platform lift
Scherz *(m)* joke
scherzen joke
scherzhaft joking, humorous
Scheuerbürste *(f)* scrubbing brush
Scheuerlappen *(m)* floor cloth, scouring cloth
Scheuerleiste *(f)* skirting board
scheuern scour, scrub
scheußlich dreadful, horrible
schichten stack, stock, pile, pile up, layer
schichtweise in layers, by shifts
schick elegant, smart, chic, stylish
schicken dispatch, send; (mit der Post) mail (US), post (GB)
schieben push; (an einen anderen Ort) shift
Schiebetür *(f)* sliding door
Schiebetürprofil *(n)* sliding door profile
Schiebetürrahmen *(m)* sliding door frame
schief oblique; (krumm) crooked
Schild *(n)* sign; (Preisschild) ticket; (Etikett) label
Schildchen *(n)* tag
schildern describe
Schilderung *(f)* description
Schirm *(m)* umbrella
Schirmherr(in) *(m/f)* patron, patroness
Schirmherrschaft *(f)* patronage
Schirmständer *(m)* umbrella stand
Schlafgelegenheit *(f)* sleeping accomodation
Schlag *(m)* blow, stroke
schlagartig sudden, abrupt
Schlagbohrer *(m)* percussion drill
schlagfertig quick-witted

Schlagwort *(n)* slogan
Schlagzeile *(f)* head, headline
Schlamperei *(f)* sloppiness
Schlange *(f)* (Menschen) queue, line
Schlange stehen queue up, stand in line
schlau clever, smart
Schlauch *(m)* hose; (Auto) tube
Schlauchverbindung *(f)* hose connector
Schlaufe *(f)* loop
schlecht bad; (Leistung etc.) poor
Schleichwerbung *(f)* camouflaged advertising
schleifen grind, whet; (Holz) sand
Schleifmaschine *(f)* grinding machine
schleppen lug, drag along; (abschleppen) tow
schließen close, shut; (zuschließen) lock, lock up
Schließfach *(n)* safe deposit box; (Gepäck) locker, left-luggage locker
schließlich eventually, finally
Schließung *(f)* (Veranstaltung etc.) closing, closure
schlimm bad; (scheußlich) nasty
schlimmstenfalls at worst
Schlinge *(f)* loop, noose
Schlips *(m)* tie, necktie
Schlitz *(m)* slit; (Automat) slot
Schlitzprofil *(n)* slotted profile
Schlitzstab *(m)* slotted tube
Schloss *(n)* (Tür) lock
Schlosseinbau *(m)* lock installation
Schlosser *(m)* locksmith
schludern work sloppily
Schluss *(m)* end
Schlussabrechnung *(f)* final account
Schlüssel *(m)* key
schlüsselfertig (Stand etc.) turnkey, ready for occupancy
schlüsselfertiger Stand *(m)* turnkey stand
Schlüsselposition *(f)* key position, prominent position
Schlussfolgerung *(f)* conclusion

Schlussrechnung *(f)* final accounts, final invoice
Schlusssitzung *(f)* closing session, final session
Schlusstermin *(m)* closing date
Schlusswort *(n)* closing words, closing remarks
Schlusszeile *(f)* base line
schmecken taste
schmeißen throw, chuck; (Tür) slam, bang
Schmerz *(m)* ache, pain
schmerzen ache, hurt, pain
Schmerzensgeld *(n)* compensation for non-pecunary damage, compensation for immaterial damage, compensation for personal suffering, damages for pain and suffering
schmerzhaft painful; (betrüblich) sad
schmerzstillend painkilling
Schmerztablette *(f)* painkiller
Schmiere *(f)* (Fett, Öl) grease, lubricant
schmieren smear; (Fett) grease; (Öl) lubricate; (Brot) butter; (Butter) spread
Schmierfett *(n)* grease
Schminke *(f)* make-up
schminken make up
schmirgeln sand, sandpaper
Schmirgelpapier *(n)* sandpaper
Schmuck *(m)* jewelry (US), jewellery (GB), jewels; (Dekoration) decoration
Schmutz *(m)* dirt, filth, mud
schmutzig durty, filthy
Schmutzkante *(f)* dust-trap
Schnalle *(f)* buckle, clasp
Schnäppchen *(n)* bargain, snip
Schnappschuss *(m)* snapshot
Schnaps *(m)* spirits, hard liquor
Schnapsglas *(n)* brandy glass
schneeweiß snow-white
Schneidbrennner *(m)* cutting torch
Schneidemaschine *(f)* meat slicer
schneiden cut
Schneiderei *(f)* tailor's, dressmaker's

Schnelldrucker *(m)* high-speed printer
Schnellgaststätte *(f)* quick lunch restaurant, quick service restaurant, fast food restaurant
Schnellhefter *(m)* letter file, spring folder
Schnelligkeit *(f)* speed, rapidity
Schnellimbiss *(m)* snack-bar, self-service snack-bar
Schnitt *(m)* cut
Schnittbild *(n)* cross section, sectional view
Schnittstelle *(f)* (EDV) interface
Schnittsteuereinheit *(f)* (EDV) edit control unit
Schnittwunde *(f)* cut
Schnittzeichnung *(f)* section, sectional drawing, sectional view
Schnur *(f)* cord, string
schräg oblique, slanting; (geneigt) sloping
Schrägboden *(m)* (Regal) sloping shelf
Schräge *(f)* incline, slant, slope
Schrägkonsole *(f)* (Regal) inclined bracket
Schrägstrich *(m)* oblique stroke
Schramme *(f)* scratch
schrammen scrape, scratch
Schrank *(m)* cupboard
Schranke *(f)* bar, barrier, gate
Schrankküche *(f)* kitchenette module, portable kitchenette
Schrankvitrine *(f)* cupboard showcase
Schraubdeckel *(m)* screw cap
Schraube *(f)* screw
Schraube *(f)* **und Mutter** *(f)* bolt and nut
schrauben screw
Schraubendreher *(m)* screwdriver
Schraubenschlüssel *(m)* wrench, spanner
Schraubenzieher *(m)* screwdriver
Schreibarbeit *(f)* desk work, paperwork
Schreibblock *(m)* pad, writing pad

Schreibbüro *(n)* letter service
Schreiben *(n)* writing, letter; (kurze Mitteilung) note
Schreibmaschine *(f)* typewriter
Schreibpapier *(n)* note paper, writing paper
Schreibtisch *(m)* desk
Schreibunterlage *(f)* desk pad
Schreiner *(m)* carpenter, joiner
Schrift *(f)* writing; (Handschrift) handwriting; (Typografie) type, typography; (Schriftzeichen) script, characters; (Broschüre) leaflet
Schriften *(f, pl)*, **computergeschnittene** computer-cut types
Schriftgenerator *(m)* video type writer
Schriftgrad *(m)* typesize
schriftlich written, in writing
Schriftstück *(n)* document, paper, momorandum
Schrifttyp *(m)* type
Schriftwechsel *(m)* correspondence
Schritt *(m)* step
Schrott *(m)* scrap metal
schrottreif ready for the scrap heap
schrubben scrub
Schrubber *(m)* scrubbing brush
schrumpfen shrink; (abnehmen) decline
Schrumpffolienverpackung *(f)* blister pack, bubble pack
Schrumpfpackung *(f)* shrink wrapping
Schrumpfung *(f)* shrinking, shrinkage; (Abnahme) decline
Schub *(m)* push, thrust
Schuber *(m)* slipcase
Schubfach *(n)* drawer
Schubkasten *(m)* drawer
Schubkraft *(f)* thrust
Schublade *(f)* drawer
Schukostecker *(m)* earthed-pin plug, safety plug, shockproof plug
Schuld *(f)* guilt, blame, fault, liability; (Geld) debt
Schuld *(f)* **haben** be at fault

schulden, jdm. etw. owe s.o. sth.
Schulden *(f, pl)* **machen** get into debt, run into debt, incur debts
Schulden *(f, pl)* **zahlen** pay off one's debts, pay back a debt
Schulden *(f, pl)* debt, liabilities
schuldenfrei debt-free, free of debts
schuldhaft culpable
schuldig guilty; (verantwortlich) responsible, to blame
schuldlos innocent
Schuldner *(m)* debtor
Schulung *(f)* training
Schulung *(f)* **des Standpersonals** stand staff training
Schulungskurs *(m)* course of training, training course
Schürfwunde *(f)* abrasion, graze
Schutt *(m)* rubble
schütteln shake
schütten pour
Schutz *(m)* protection
Schutzanzug *(m)* protective clothing, protective suit
Schutzbrille *(f)* safety goggles, protective goggles
Schutzeinrichtung *(f)* protective device
schützen protect, safeguard
schützend protective
Schutzgitter *(f)* protective barrier
Schutzhandschuh *(m)* protective glove
Schutzhelm *(m)* safety helmet
Schutzhülle *(f)* protective cover
Schutzkleidung *(f)* protective clothing
Schutzleiste *(f)* protective strip
schutzlos unprotected
Schutzmarke *(f)* trademark
Schutzmarke *(f)***, eingetragene** registered trademark
Schutzmaske *(f)* mask, protective mask
Schutzmaßnahme *(f)* precaution, safety precaution
Schutzschalter *(m)* overload protection switch, protective circuit breaker
Schutzvorrichtung *(f)* safety device

schwach weak; (stagnierend) slack
Schwäche *(f)* weakness, faintness
Schwachstelle *(f)* weak point
Schwachstrom *(m)* low-voltage current
Schwarzarbeit *(f)* illicit work, unrecorded employment, moonlighting
schwarzarbeiten work in the black, work in the black economy, work on the side, moonlight
Schwarzarbeiter *(m)* moonlighter
Schwarzweiß- black-and-white
Schweißbrenner *(m)* welding torch
schweißen weld
Schweißer *(m)* welder
Schweißnaht *(f)* welded seam
Schwelle *(f)* (Tür) threshold
Schwenkadapter *(m)* swivel adaptor
schwenkbar swivelling
schwenken turn, swing, swivel, slew
schwer heavy
schwer entflammbar fire-resistant
schwer entflammbare Stoffe *(m, pl)* fire-resistant materials, flameproof materials
Schwerarbeit *(f)* heavy labor (US), heavy labour (GB)
Schwergut *(n)* deadweight cargo
Schwerlastplatte *(f)* heavy load panel
schwerwiegend grave, serious
Schwiele *(f)* callus
schwierig difficult, hard
Schwierigkeit *(f)* difficulty, trouble
Schwund *(m)* decline, decrease, leakage, shrinkage
sechseckig hexagonal
Sechskantmutter *(f)* hexagon nut
Sechskant-Schraubenzieher *(m)* Allen wrench
Seefracht *(f)* ocean freight
Segment *(n)* segment
segmentieren segment
sehenswert worth seeing
Sehenswürdigkeit *(f)* object of interest, sight

seidenmatt semi gloss
Seife *(f)* soap; (Stück Seife) cake of soap
Seil *(n)* rope
Seilabhängung *(f)* rope suspension, cable suspension, wire suspension
Seilabspannung *(f)* rope tension, cable tension, wire tension
Seilknoten *(m)* cable node
Seilschloss *(n)* wire lock
Seilstütze *(f)* cable support
Seilunterspannung *(f)* cable subtension
Seilverspannung *(f)* cable bracing
Seite *(f)* (Buch etc.) page; (örtlich) side
Seitenansicht *(f)* side view
Seitenausgang *(m)* side exit
Seiteneingang *(m)* side entrance
Seitenpreis *(m)* page rate
seitenverkehrt the wrong way round
Seitenwand *(f)* side wall
seitlich lateral, side
seitwärts sideways, at the side
Sekretär(in) *(m/f)* secretary
Sekt *(m)* sparkling wine; (Champagner) champagne
Sektglas *(n)* champagne glass
Sektkelch *(m)* champagne flute
Sektor *(m)* sector, field
sekundär secondary
Sekundärdaten *(pl)* secondary data
Sekundärforschung *(f)* desk research
Selbstbausatz *(m)* DIY kit, do-it-yourself kit
Selbstbedienung *(f)* self-service
Selbstbedienungsrestaurant *(n)* self-service restaurant, cafeteria
Selbstklebeetikett *(n)* self-sticking label, self-adhesive label
selbstklebend self-adhesive
Selbstkosten *(pl)* direct cost, prime cost, own cost
Selbstkostenpreis *(m)* cost price
selbstständig independent; (Beruf) self-employed, self-sufficient, freelance

Selbstständigkeit *(f)* independence; (beruflich) self-employment
selbsttragend self supporting
selbstverständlich natural, obvious, self-evident
selten rare, scarce
Selterswasser *(n)* soda water
seltsam strange, odd, queer
Seminar *(n)* seminar
senden (Ware) send, dispatch, forward; (Radio, TV) broadcast, telecast, transmit
Sendung *(f)* (Ware) consignment, dispatch, shipment; (Radio, TV) transmission; (Programm) program (US), programme (GB)
Senkblei *(n)* plumb line
senken sink; (absenken) lower
senkrecht vertical
Senkrechte *(f)* vertical
Senkschraube *(f)* countersunk screw
Senkung *(f)* (Preis etc.) cut, reduction; (Kürzung) retrenchment
Sensation *(f)* sensation
sensationell sensational
Sensor *(m)* sensor
separat separate
Separatwachdienst *(m)* special security service
Serie *(f)* series
Serie *(f)* **gefertigt, in** mass-produced, serialized
seriös serious, respectable
Service *(m)* service
Serviceabteilung *(f)* maintenance department
Servicebroschüre *(n)* service booklet
Serviceleistungen *(f, pl)* services
Servicepaket *(n)* service package
servieren serve
Serviette *(f)* napkin
Sessel *(m)* easy chair, armchair
Showdarbietung *(f)* show, entertainment show
sicher safe; (gesichert) secure; (gewiss) certain

Sicherheit (f) safety, security; (Gewissheit) certainty
Sicherheit (f), **öffentliche** public security
Sicherheitsabstand (m) safe distance, safe clearance, safety distance, safety clearance
Sicherheitsbeleuchtung (f) safety lighting
Sicherheitsbestimmungen (f, pl) safety rules, safety regulations
Sicherheitsbestimmungen (f, pl), **technische** technical safety regulations
Sicherheitseinrichtung (f) safety device, safety equipment
Sicherheitsglas (n) safety glass
sicherheitshalber as a precaution
Sicherheitskontrolle (m) security check
Sicherheitsmaßnahme (f) safety measure, precaution, safety precaution
Sicherheitspersonal (n) security staff
Sicherheitsrisiko (n) security risk
Sicherheitsschloss (n) safety lock
sicherheitstechnische Einrichtungen (f, pl) safety equipment
Sicherheitsvorschriften (f, pl) safety regulations
sichern secure
sicherstellen (sichern) secure; (garantieren) guarantee
Sicherung (f) (Vorsichtsmaßnahme) securing, protection, safeguarding; (Vorrichtung) safety device; (Strom) fuse
Sicherungsautomat (m) (Strom) automatic circuit breaker
Sicherungskasten (m) (Strom) fuse box
Sicherungsplatte (f) reinforcing plate
Sicht (f) sight, view
sichtbar visible; (offensichtlich) noticeable, evident
Sichtschutz (m) sight screen
Sieb (n) sieve; (für Sand etc.) riddle, screen; (für Flüssigkeiten) strainer

Siebdruck (m) screen print, screen printing, silk screen printing
Signal (n) signal
signalisieren signal
Signal-Rauschabstand (m) signal ratio, noise ratio, signal-to-noise ratio
Signatur (f) signature
Signet (n) signet, trademark
signieren sign
Silikon (n) silicon
simpel simple; (einfach) plain
simulieren (technisch) simulate; (vortäuschen) feign, sham
simultan simultaneous
Simultandolmetscher(in) (m/f) simultaneous interpreter
sinken sink; (Temperatur, Kosten etc.) decrease, fall, drop, go down
Siphon (m) siphon
Sirene (f) siren
Situation (f) situation
Sitz (m) seat; (Firmensitz) headquarters; (juristisch) legal domicile, registered office
Sitzecke (f) corner unit
Sitzgelegenheit (f) seat, seating accomodation
Sitzkissen (n) cushion
Sitzlehne (f) seat back
Sitzordnung (f) seating plan
Sitzplatz (m) seat, seating
Sitzplatzreservierung (f) seat reservation
Sitzung (f) conference, meeting
Sitzungsbericht (m) minutes
Sitzungsraum (m) conference room
Sitzungssaal (m) conference hall
Sitzungszimmer (n) meeting room
Skala (f) scale; (Spektrum) range
Skelettkonstruktion (f) framework construction
skeptisch skeptical (US), sceptical (GB)
Sketch (m) sketch
Skizze (f) sketch; (Entwurf) draft
skizzenhaft sketchy

skizzieren sketch, outline
Skonto *(n)* cash discount
SMS *(f)* Short Message Service; (Versand) text messageing
Snackbar *(f)* cafeteria, snack-bar
Sockel *(m)* (Basis) base, basis; (Unterbau) basis, pedestal
Sockelblende *(f)* base cover plate
Sodawasser *(n)* soda water
Sodawasserbereiter *(m)* soda water maker
Sofortbildkamera *(f)* instant camera
Soforthilfe *(f)* emergency aid
Sofortlieferung *(f)* immediate delivery
Sofortmaßnahme *(f)* immediate action, immediate measure
Sofortprogramm *(n)* immediate program (US), immediate programme (GB)
Software *(f)* software
Softwarepaket *(n)* software package
Sog *(m)* suction
sogenannt so-called
Solarenergie *(f)* solar energy
Solartechnik *(f)* solar technology
Solarzelle *(f)* solar cell
solide solid, substantial
Soll *(n)* (Buchhaltung) debit; (Vorgabe) target
Soll-Ist-Vergleich *(m)* target-actual comparison, performance report
Sollvorgabe *(f)* target, set point
Sollzinsen *(m, pl)* debit interest, interest charge
solvent able to pay, solvent
Solvenz *(f)* ability to pay, solvency
Sommerpause *(f)* summer break
Sonderabfall *(m)* hazardous waste
Sonderanfertigung *(f)* special design
Sonderangebot *(n)* bargain, special bargain, special offer
Sonderaufbauten *(pl)* special structures
Sonderausgabe *(f)* (Zeitung, Zeitschrift) special edition
sonderbar strange, odd, peculiar
Sonderbedingungen *(f, pl)* special terms
Sonderbeilage *(f)* special supplement
Sonderbericht *(m)* special report
Sonderbewachung *(f)* special guarding
Sonderfahrt *(f)* special ride, special trip
Sonderfall *(m)* special case
Sonderkonditionen *(f, pl)* special conditions, special terms
Sonderkonstuktion *(f)* special construction
Sonderlänge *(f)* special length
Sonderleistung *(f)* special feature
Sondermüll *(m)* hazardous waste
Sondermülldeponie *(f)* hazardous waste depot
Sondernummer *(f)* (Zeitschrift etc.) special edition
Sonderposten *(m)* special item
Sonderpreis *(m)* bargain rate, special price, special rate
Sonderrabatt *(m)* special discount
Sonderregelung *(f)* special provision
Sonderreinigung *(f)* special cleaning
Sonderschau *(f)* special show
Sonderschau *(f)* **mit Informationszentrum** special show and information center
Sonderstellung *(f)* special position
Sondertisch *(m)* bargain counter
Sonderveranstaltungen *(f, pl)* **der deutschen Wirtschaft** special German business events
Sonderwache *(f)* special stand security (service)
sondieren find out, sound out
Sonn- und Feiertage *(pl)* Sundays and holidays, Sundays and public holidays, nonbusiness days
Sonntagsarbeit *(f)* Sunday working
sonor sonorous
Sorge *(f)* care, worry; (Besorgnis) concern
sorgen für see too, look after, take care
sorgen, sich be worried, worry

Sorgfalt *(f)* care
sorgfältig careful, thorough
sorglos careless
Sorte *(f)* sort, kind, type
sortieren sort
Sortiment *(n)* assortment, choise of goods, range of goods, collection, product mix, sales mix
Sortimentsbreite *(f)* product range
Sortimentserweiterung *(f)* extension of product range
Sozialabgaben *(f, pl)* social contributions, social security contributions, social payments
Sozialversicherung *(f)* social insurance, social insurance security, social security
Spachtel *(m)* spatula
Spalt *(m)* crack
Spalte *(f)* (Material) crack; (Zeitung) column
spalten split; (Holz) chop, cleave
Spanne *(f)* (Gewinn etc.) margin; (Zeit) while
spannen stretch, tighten
Spannhaken *(m)* tender hook
Spannmutter *(f)* locknut
Spannprofil *(n)* tightening profile
Spannschloss *(n)* tension lock, turnbuckle
Spannung *(f)* tension, electric tension, voltage, electric potential
Spannungsmesser *(m)* voltmeter
Spannungsprüfer *(m)* voltage detector
Spannweite *(f)* span, clear span, span width
Spanplatte *(f)* chipboard
sparen save
Sparkasse *(f)* savings bank
Sparmaßnahme *(f)* economy measure, savings measure
Sparpackung *(f)* economy pack, economy-sized packet
sparsam economical, thrifty
Sparsamkeit *(f)* economizing, thrift

spaßen joke
spaßeshalber just for fun
Spatel *(m)* spatula
spätestens at the latest
Spediteur *(m)* carrier, freight carrier, forwarder, freight forwarder, forwarding agent, haulage contractor, haulier, transport agent
Spedition *(f)* freight forwarder, forwarding agent, carrier, carrier haulage, haulage firm, haulage company, drayage contractor
Speditionsauftrag *(m)* forwarding order
Speditionskosten *(pl)* carrying charge, haulage costs
Speditionsrecht *(n)* freight forwarding legislation
Speicher *(m)* (EDV) memory, store
Speicherfunktion *(f)* (EDV) memory function
speichern (EDV) store
Speicherplatz *(m)* (EDV) storage space
Speicherung *(f)* (EDV) storing, storage
Speiseeisvitrine *(f)* icecream freezer
Speisekarte *(f)* menu
Speisen *(f, pl)* food; (Gericht) dish, meal
Speisen *(f, pl)*, **frische** dishes prepared to order
Speisen *(f, pl)*, **kalte** cold dishes
Speisen *(f, pl)*, **warme** hot dishes
Speisentransportkiste *(f)* food transport box
Speiseraum *(m)* dining room
Speisesaal *(m)* dining hall
Spektakel *(n)* fuss, racket, row, shindy
Spektrum *(n)* spectrum
Sperre *(f)* (Schranke) barrier; (Straße) barricade, roadblock; (Technik) lock, stop, stoppage
sperren (schließen) close; (versperren) shut; (Straße) block; (Technik) block, lock, stop
Sperrfrist *(f)* blocking period, waiting period

Sperrgut *(n)* bulky goods, measurement freight, measurement goods
Sperrholz *(n)* plywood
sperrig bulky
Sperrmüll *(m)* bulk rubbish, bulky refuse
Sperrstunde *(f)* closing time
Sperrung *(f)* blocking, closing, stopping
Spesen *(pl)* expenses
Spesenpauschale *(f)* expense allowance
Spezialarrangement *(n)* special arrangement
spezialisieren specialize
Spezialisierung *(f)* specialization
Spezialist *(m)* specialist
Spezialität *(f)* specialty (US), speciality (GB)
Spezialmesse *(f)* special-interest fair
speziell special, specific
Spezifikation *(f)* specification
spezifisch specific
spezifizieren specify; (Kosten etc.) itemize
spezifizierte Abrechnung *(f)* itemized account
Spezifizierung *(f)* specification, itemization
Spiegel *(m)* mirror
Spiegelfolie *(f)* mirror foil
spiegeln mirror, shine, reflect
Spiegelreflexkamera *(f)* reflex camera, mirror reflex camera
Spiegelung *(f)* reflection
Spind *(m)* locker
Spindeltreppe *(f)* spiral staircase
spionieren spy
Spirale *(f)* spiral, coil
Spiralfeder *(f)* coil spring
spiralförmig spiral
Spirituosen *(f, pl)* spirits
spitz pointed
spitz zulaufen taper
Spitze *(f)* point, top
Spitzenbelastungszeit *(f)* peak hours
Spitzenjahr *(n)* peak year

Spitzenkraft *(f)* highly qualified worker, top-level executive, high achiever, top hand
Spitzenleistung *(f)* top-rate performance
Spitzenqualität *(f)* top quality
Spitzenreiter *(m)* hit, leader; (Verkauf) top seller
Spitzentechnik *(f)* advanced technology
Spitzentechnologie *(f)* high-advanced technology, state-of-the-art technology
Spitzhacke *(f)* axe, pick axe
spitzwinklig acute, acute-angled
Splitter *(m)* splinter
sponsern sponsor
Sponsor *(m)* sponsor
Sponsoring *(n)* sponsorship
spontan spontaneous
Spontankauf *(m)* impulse buy, impulse purchase
sporadisch sporadic
Sprachkenntnis *(f)* knowledge of languages, linguistic proficiency
Spray *(n)* spray
Sprechanlage *(f)* intercommunication system, intercom
Sprecher(in) *(m/f)* announcer, speaker, spokesman, spokeswoman
Sprechfunkgerät *(n)* radiotelephone, walkie-talkie
Sprechtaste *(f)* talking key
Sprinkleranlage *(f)* sprinkler system
Sprinklerschutz *(m)* sprinkler protection
spritzen (Flüssigkeit) squirt, splash; (Farbe) spray
Spritzer *(m)* splash
spritzlackieren spray, spray-paint
Spritzpistole *(f)* spray gun
Spruchband *(n)* banner
Sprühdose *(f)* aerosole, aerosole can, spray can
sprühen spray, sprinkle
Spülbecken *(n)* sink
Spüle *(f)* sink unit

113

spülen wash up
Spülmaschine *(f)* dishwasher
Spülmaschine *(f)* **für Gläser** glass-washing machine
Stab *(m)* (Stange) rod, bar; (Mitarbeiter) staff, team
Stabdiagramm *(n)* bar chart
Stabdurchmesser *(m)* tube diameter
stabil firm, stable, steady, solid, sturdy
stabilisieren stabilize
Stabilisierung *(f)* stabilization
Stabilität *(f)* firmness, stability
Stabsfunktion *(f)* staff function
Stadium *(n)* stage
Stadtbahn *(f)* city railway
Stadtbüro *(n)* town office
Stadtplan *(m)* city map, town map, map of the town
Stadtrundfahrt *(f)* city tour, city sightseeing tour
Stadtviertel *(n)* district, quarter
Stadtzentrum *(n)* city center (US), city centre (GB), town center (US), town centre (GB)
Staffelpreis *(m)* differential price, graduated price, sliding price
Stagnation *(f)* stagnation
stagnieren stagnate
Stahlband *(n)* steel strip
Stahlblech *(n)* sheet of steel
Stahlrohr *(n)* steel tube
Stahlrohrmöbel *(n)* tubular steel furniture
Stahlseil *(n)* steel cable
Stahlstab *(m)* steel tube
Stahlträger *(m)* steel girder
Stammhaus *(n)* company headquarters, company head office
Stammkunde *(m)* regular customer
Stammkundschaft *(f)* regular customers
Stand *(m)* stand, booth, stall
Stand *(m)* **mieten, gemeinsam einen** rent a stand jointly (US), hire a stand jointly (GB)

Stand *(m)*, **firmeneigener** exhibitor's own stand, individual stand
Stand *(m)*, **gegenüberliegender** facing stand
Stand *(m)*, **mobiler** mobile stand
Standabbau *(m)* stand breakdown, stand dismantling, stand takedown, stand teardown
Standabbauzeit *(f)* stand dismantling time
Standabmessungen *(f, pl)* stand dimensions
Standaktivitäten *(f, pl)* stand activities
Standansicht *(f)* stand view
Standard *(m)* standard
Standardanschluss *(m)* (Strom etc.) standard connection
Standardausführung *(f)* standard design
Standardausrüstung *(f)* standard equipment
Standardbedingungen *(f, pl)* standard conditions
Standardgröße *(f)* standard size
standardisieren standardize
Standardisierung *(f)* standardization
Standart *(f)* stand type
Standascher *(m)* ashtray stand
Standatmosphäre *(f)* stand ambience
Standaufbau *(m)* stand assembly, stand construction, stand erection, stand installation, stand setup
Standaufbauten *(pl)* stand structures, stand constructions
Standaufbauzeit *(f)* stand assembly time, stand construction period, stand setting-up time
Standaufnahme *(f)* stand photo
Standausstattung *(f)* stand equipment, stand furnishing, equipment for the exposition booth
Standausstattung *(f)*, **zusätzliche** additional stand equipment, additional stand furnishings
Standbau *(m)* stand construction

Standbau *(m)*, **zweigeschossiger** double-decker stand structure, two-story stand structure (US), two-storey stand structure (GB)
Standbaubestimmungen *(f, pl)* stand construction regulations
Standbauelemente *(n, pl)* stand construction elements, stand construction fittings
Standbaugenehmigung *(f)* stand construction approval
Standbauhöhe *(f)* stand height, height of stand structures
Standbauhöhe *(f)*, **maximale** maximum stand height, maximum overall stand height, maximum height of stand structures
Standbaukosten *(pl)* stand construction expense
Standbaumaterialien *(n, pl)* stand construction materials
Standbaureststoffe *(m, pl)* stand construction waste
Standbaurichtlinien *(f, pl)* stand assembly instructions, stand construction instructions
Standbausystem *(n)* structural stand system
Standbauteile *(n, pl)* stand components
Standbauten *(m, pl)*, **eingeschossige** single-story stands (US), single-storey stands (GB)
Standbauvorschriften *(f, pl)* stand construction regulations
Standbauweise *(f)*, **doppelstöckige** double-decker stand, two-story stand structure (US), two-storey stand structure (GB)
Standbegrenzungswand *(f)* stand partition wall
Standbereiche *(m, pl)*, **geschlossene** closed-in stand areas
Standbeschriftung *(f)* stand lettering
Standbestätigung *(f)* stand confirmation

Standbesucher(in) *(m/f)* stand visitor
Standbetrieb *(m)* stand organization
Standbetriebskosten *(pl)* stand operating costs, stand running expenses
Standbewachung *(f)* stand guard, stand security, stand security staff
Standbewachung *(f)*, **firmeneigene** exhibitor's own security personnel, exhibitor security staff
Standbewirtung *(f)* stand hospitality
Standblende *(f)* fascia, fascia board, trim panel
Standbreite *(f)* stand width
Standcatering *(n)* stand catering
Standdach *(n)* stand roof
Standdecke *(f)* stand ceiling
Standdesign *(n)* stand design
Standdienstplan *(m)* stand duty roster
Standeinweisung *(f)* stand walkthrough
Standentwurf *(m)* stand draft, stand blueprint, draft of the exhibition stand
Ständer *(m)* rack
Standerdung *(f)* earthing of stand
Standfläche *(f)* stand area, stand space
Standfläche *(f)*, **gewünschte** required stand area, stand space requested
Standfläche *(f)*, **reine** raw stand space
Standfläche *(f)*, **vermietete** leased stand area, leased stand space, rented exhibition area
Standgenehmigung *(f)* stand approval
Standgestaltung *(f)* stand design, stand layout
Standgrenze *(f)* stand boundary, stand limits
Standgrenze *(f)*, **rückseitige** rear boundary of stand
Standgröße *(f)* stand dimensions, stand size
Standhilfe *(f)* stand help
Standhöhe *(f)* stand height
ständig constant, continuous, permanent

Standinformation *(f)* (Empfang) stand reception desk
Standkoje *(f)* stand cabin, stand cubicle
Standkonzept *(n)* stand concept
Standkosten *(pl)* stand costs
Standlage *(f)* stand location, stand placement, stand position
Standlage *(f)*, **bevorzugte** preferred stand location
Standleiter(in) *(m/f)* stand captain, stand manager
Standleitung *(f)* stand administration, stand management, conductor of the exhibition stand
Standmaterial *(n)* stand materials
Standmiete *(f)* stand rent, space rent, stall rental
Standmietkosten *(pl)* stand rental expenses
Standmietpreis *(m)* stand rental charge, stand rental fee
Standmietvertrag *(m)* stand rental contract
Standmobiliar *(n)* stand furnishings
Standmodell *(n)* stand scale model
Standnachbar *(m)* neighboring stand (US), neighbouring stand (GB)
Standnummer *(f)* stand number
Standnummerierung *(f)* stand numbering
Standnutzung *(f)* stand use
Standort *(m)* location
Standortwahl *(f)* choice of location
Standpersonal *(n)* stand staff, stand personnel
Standplan *(m)* stand layout plan
Standplanung *(f)* stand planning
Standpunkt *(m)* point of view
Standreinigung *(f)* stand cleaning
Standreinigung *(f)*, **tägliche** daily stand cleaning
Standservice *(m)* stand service
Standsicherheit *(f)* stand safety
Standskizze *(f)* stand sketch

Standtausch *(m)* exchange of stands, stand space swap
Standtelefon *(n)* stand telephone
Standtiefe *(f)* stand depth
Standtrennwand *(f)* stand dividing wall
Standtyp *(m)* stand type
Standüberdachung *(f)* stand covering, stand roofing
Standüberdachungsmaterial *(n)* stand covering material, roofing material
Standversicherung *(f)* stand insurance
Standvitrine *(f)* floor showcase, free standing display cabinet
Standzähler *(m)* stand meter
Standzeichnung *(f)* stand drawing
Standzuteilung *(f)* stand allocation, stand space allocation, stand space assignment
Standzuteilung *(f)*, **Wünsche für die** requirements for stand location
Stange *(f)* bar, rod
Stapel *(m)* pile, stack
stapelbar stackable
stapeln stack, pile up
Stapler *(m)* forklift, forklift truck
Starkstrom *(m)* heavy current, high-voltage current, power current
Starkstromleitung *(f)* power line
Starkstromtechnik *(f)* heavy-current engineering
statisch static
Statistik *(f)* statistics
statistisch statistical
Stativ *(n)* tripod
stattfinden take place
Staub *(m)* dust
Staub wischen dust
Staubsauger *(m)* vacuum cleaner
Staubschutzleiste *(f)* dust proof rail
Stauraum *(m)* storage space
Steckdose *(f)* socket, wall socket
Steckdosenabgang *(m)* socket outlet
Steckdosenleiste *(f)* socket bar
Stecker *(m)* plug
Steckkontakt *(m)* plug, plug connection

Steckschlüssel *(m)* box spanner, socket wrench
Steckschuh *(m)* accessory shoe
Stecksystem *(n)* pin connection modules
Steg *(m)* footpath, gangplank
Stegreif *(m)* **reden, aus dem** make an off-the-cuff speech
Stegreif *(m)* **spielen, aus dem** improvise
Stegreif *(m)***, aus dem** off-the-cuff
Stehempfang *(m)* standing reception
Stehleiter *(f)* stepladder
stehlen steal
Stehplatz *(m)* standing room, standing place
Stehtisch *(m)* lean-on table
steigen (Preise etc.) go up, rise, increase
steigern increase, raise
Steigerung *(f)* rise, increase, intensification
Steigung *(f)* rise, ascent, gradient, slope
Stelle *(f)* (Ort) place; (Punkt) spot, point
Stellenvermittlung *(f)* employment agency
Stellfuß *(m)* levelfoot
Stellring *(m)* adjustable ring
Stellschraube *(f)* adjusting screw
Stellung *(f)* (Beruf) job, position; (Ansehen) status, standing
Stellungnahme *(f)* comment, opinion, statement
stellvertretend acting, deputizing
Stellvertreter(in) *(m/f)* deputy, representative, substitute
Stellvertretung *(f)* agencsy, representation
Stemmeisen *(n)* mortise chisel, crowbar
Stempel *(m)* stamp
Stenogramm *(n)* shorthand dictation, shorthand notes
Stenografie *(f)* stenography, shorthand
stenografieren write shorthand
Stereo *(n)* stereo
Stereoanlage *(f)* stereo system
Stereoeingang *(m)* stereo input
Stereoquelle *(f)* stereo source
stetig continuous, steady
Stetigkeit *(f)* steadyness, constancy, continuity
Steuer *(f)* duty, tax, imposition
Steuerabzug *(m)* tax deduction
Steuerbefreiung *(f)* exemption from tax, tax exemption
steuerbegünstigt tax-privileged, tax-sheltered, eligible for tax relief
Steuerermäßigung *(f)* tax allowance, tax reduction
Steuererstattung *(f)* tax rebate, tax refund
steuerfrei tax-free, free of tax, exempt from tax
Steuerfreibetrag *(m)* allowance, tax-free allowance
Steuergerät *(n)* controller
Steuerpult *(n)* control desk
Steuersatz *(m)* tax rate, rate of taxation
Steuertaste *(f)* (EDV) control key
Steuerung *(f)* (Prozess) control, control system
Stichflamme *(f)* jet of flame, tongue of flame, flash
Stichprobe *(f)* check, spot check, sample, random sample
Stichprobe *(f)***, repräsentative** representative sample
Stichprobenverfahren *(n)* sampling
Stichsäge *(f)* fret saw
Stichtag *(m)* effective day, qualifying date, deadline
Stickstoff *(m)* nitrogen
Stift *(m)* peg, pin
Stil *(m)* style
Stilllegung *(f)* closing down, closure, shutdown
Stirnseite *(f)* front, front side, face
Stirnwand *(f)* end wall, front wall
Stockwerk *(n)* floor, story (US), storey (GB)
Stoffbahn *(f)* length of material

Stoffbezug *(m)* cloth cover
Stördienst *(m)* fault-clearing service, complaint service
stören disturb
Störfall *(m)* breakdown, trouble, incident, disruptive incident
stornieren cancel, reverse
Stornierung *(f)* cancellation, reversal, reversing
Stornierungsgebühr *(f)* cancellation fee, reversal fee
Stornokosten *(f)* cancellation costs, reversal costs
Störung *(f)* disturbance; (Technik) defect, breakdown, trouble, fault
störungsfrei undisturbed, trouble-free
Storyboard *(n)* storyboard
stoßfest shockproof
Stoßzeit *(f)* peak period; (Verkehr) rush hour
strafbar punishable, liable to prosecution
Strafe *(f)* punishment, penalty; (Geldstrafe) fine
Strafe *(f)* **zahlen** pay a fine
straff taut, tight
straffen tauten, tighten
Straffung *(f)* streamline
Strahlenschutz *(m)* radiation protection
Strahlenschutzverordnung *(f)* Radiological Protection Order
Strahler *(m)* spotlight
strapazierfähig heavy-duty
Straßenkarte *(f)* road map
Strategie *(f)* strategy
strategisch strategic
Strebe *(f)* prop, strut
streichen (Wand etc.) paint; (entfallen) cancel, cut, delete, erase, withdraw
Streichung *(f)* cancellation, withdrawal; (Geld etc.) cut; (Schriftzeile etc.) deletion
Streifen *(m)* stripe, strip
Streit *(m)* contest, controversy, dispute, quarrel

streiten quarrel
Streuplanung *(f)* media buying
Streuung *(f)* (Medien) spread
Strich *(m)* (Feder, Pinsel) stroke; (Linie) line
Strichcode *(m)* bar code
Strichdiagramm *(n)* line chart, line graph
Strichzeichnung *(f)* line drawing
Strom *(m)* current
Stromanschluss *(m)* connection to the mains
Stromanschlusskosten *(pl)* power installation costs
Stromausfall *(m)* power failure
Stromerzeuger *(m)* generator, electrical generator set
stromführend live
stromführendes Kabel *(n)* live wire
Stromkabel *(n)* power cable
Stromkreis *(m)* circuit, electrical circuit
Stromnetz *(n)* power supply system
Stromquelle *(f)* source of power
Stromrechnung *(f)* electricity bill
Stromschiene *(f)* electrical rail, lighting track
Stromschienenadapter *(m)* adaptor for lighting tracks, adapter for lighting tracks
Stromstärke *(f)* current intensity, strength of the electric current
Stromstoß *(m)* electric shock
Stromverbrauch *(m)* electrical consumption, electricity consumption, power consumption
Stromversorgung *(f)* power supply
Stromzähler *(m)* electric meter
Struktur *(f)* structure
Stück *(n)* item, piece, unit
Stückchen *(n)* small piece
Stückgut *(n)* break bulk cargo, general cargo, loose cargo, parcel service
Stückkosten *(pl)* unit cost, cost per unit
Stückliste *(f)* list of materials
Stückpreis *(m)* unit price, price for one

Stückzahl *(f)* number of items, number of pieces
Studie *(f)* study, survey
Studiostrahler *(m)* studio spotlight
Stufe *(f)* (Bau) step; (Rang) grade; (Niveau) level
stufenförmig stepped, stairshape
stufenlos einstellbar fully adjustable
Stülpkarton *(m)* cardboard box
stundenweise by the hour, for a few hours at a time
stündlich hourly, every hour
Sturz *(m)* drop, fall, plunge, slump
stürzen drop, fall, tumble, plunge
Stützbalken *(m)* supporting beam
Stütze *(f)* support, prop, strut
stützen support, prop, shore up
stützenfrei post-free, without posts
stützenfreie Überbauung *(f)* post-free structure
Stützmauer *(f)* retaining wall, supporting wall
Stützpfeiler *(m)* buttress
Styropor *(n)* Polystyrene
Subunternehmer *(m)* subcontractor
Subvention *(f)* subsidy, grant
subventionieren subsidize
Sucher *(m)* (Kamera) viewfinder
Suchfunktion *(f)* (EDV) search function
Suchlauf *(m)* (Radio) search
Suggestivfrage *(f)* suggestive question, leading question
Summe *(f)* aggregate, amount, total, sum
Supermarkt *(m)* supermarket
Suppe *(f)* soup
Suppenwärmer *(m)* soup warmer
surren buzz, hum, whirr
Surrogat *(n)* substitute
Süßspeise *(f)* sweet dessert
Süßstoff *(m)* sweetener
Symbol *(n)* symbol
Symbole *(n, pl)* **im Messebau** stand construction symbols
Symmetrie *(f)* symmetry

symmetrisch symmetrical
Sympathie *(f)* liking, sympathy
synchron synchronous
synchronisieren synchronize
Synchronisierung *(f)* synchronization
synonym synonymous
System *(n)* system
Systembauteil *(n)* system component, modular system component
Systemhersteller *(m)* system manufacturer
Systemmessebau *(m)* modular stand construction
Systemmessebauhersteller *(m)* exhibition system manufacturer
Systemmessestand *(m)* system exhibition stand
Systemnut *(f)* system groove
Systemprofil *(n)* system profile
Systemstand *(m)* system stand
Systemwand *(f)* system wall
Szene *(f)* scene

T

tabellarisch tabulate, tabular, in tabular form
Tabelle *(f)* table
Tablett *(n)* tray
Tablette *(f)* pill, tablet
Tabulator *(m)* (EDV) tabulator, tab
Tafel *(f)* board; (Holz) panel; (Bild) plate
Tafelwasser *(n)* mineral water, table water
Tag- und Nachtdienst *(m)* 24-hour service, round-the-clock service
Tagesaufnahme *(f)* (Foto) daytime shot
Tageskarte *(f)* day ticket; (Restaurant) menu of the day, today's menu
Tageskasse *(f)* booking office, ticket office

Tageslicht *(n)* daylight
Tageslichtprojektor *(m)* daylight projector, overhead projector
Tagesordnung *(f)* agenda
Tagesordnungspunkt *(m)* agenda item, item on the agenda
Tagessatz *(m)* daily rate
Tagung *(f)* conference, congress, convention, session
Tagungshalle *(f)* conference hall
Tagungsort *(m)* venue, conference venue
Tagungsraum *(m)* conference room, convetion room
Tagungszentrum *(n)* convention center (US), convention centre (GB)
Taktik *(f)* policy, tactics
taktisch tactical
Tank *(m)* tank
tanken tank up, fill up
Tankstelle *(f)* petrol station
Tanzvorführung *(f)* dancing show
Tapete *(f)* wallpaper
Tapetenkleister *(m)* wallpaper paste
tapezieren paper, wallpaper
Taraschein *(m)* tara form, tara slip
Tarif *(m)* rate, scale of charges; (Zoll) tariff
Tariflohn *(m)* standard wage, negotiated standard wage, standard wage rate, negotiated standard wage rate
Tarifvertrag *(m)* wage agreement, collective labor agreement (US), collective labour agreement (GB), collective bargaining agreement
Tasche *(f)* (Handtasche) bag; (Aktentasche) briefcase
Taschenhalter *(m)* bag holder
Taschenkalender *(m)* pocket diary
Taschenmesser *(n)* pocket knife
Taschenrechner *(m)* hand calculator, pocket calculator
Taschenschirm *(m)* collapsible umbrella
Tasse *(f)* cup
Tastatur *(f)* keyboard, keys

Taste *(f)* key, button
Tastenknopf *(m)* key button
Tätigkeit *(f)* action, activity; (Beruf) occupation
Tätigkeitsgebiet *(n)* field of activity
Tatsache *(f)* fact
tatsächlich actual, factual, real
Tausch *(m)* exchange, swap, switch
tauschen exchange, switch; (Ware) barter
täuschen deceive, mislead
Täuschung *(f)* deception
Taxe *(f)* (Gebühr) rate, fee; (Steuer) tax
Taxi *(n)* taxi, cab
Taxifahrer *(m)* taxi driver, cab driver
Taxigebühr *(f)* taxi charge, cab charge
Taxistand *(m)* taxi rank, cab stand
Technik *(f)* engineering, technology, technique
Technik *(f)*, **neueste** advanced engineering
Techniker(in) *(m/f)* engineer, technician
technisch technical, technological
Technischer Überwachungsverein *(m)* Technical Control Board
Technologie *(f)* technology
Technologien *(f, pl)*, **neue** new technologies
technologisch technological
Tee *(m)* **mit Milch** tea with milk
Tee *(m)* **mit Zitrone** tea with lemon
Teebeutel *(m)* teabag
Teegebäck *(n)* tea cakes, biscuits
Teekanne *(f)* teapot
Teetasse *(f)* teacup
TEE-Zug *(m)* TEE train
Teil *(m)* part, piece, portion; (Bestandteil) component, element; (Anteil) share
Teilansicht *(f)* partial view
Teilbetrag *(m)* partial amount
teilen divide; (aufteilen) share
Teilerfolg *(m)* partial success
Teilhaber(in) *(m/f)* associate, partner, co-partner

Teilnahme *(f)* participation; (Anwesenheit) attendance
Teilnahmebedingungen *(f, pl)* conditions of participation
Teilnahmebedingungen *(f, pl)*, **allgemeine** general conditions of participation
Teilnahmebedingungen *(f, pl)*, **allgemeiner Teil der** general section of the conditions for participation
Teilnahmebedingungen *(f, pl)*, **Anerkennung der** acceptance of the conditions for participation
Teilnahmebedingungen *(f, pl)*, **besondere** specific event conditions, special conditions of participation
Teilnahmebedingungen *(f, pl)*, **besonderer Teil der** special section of the conditions of participation
Teilnahmebedingungen *(f, pl)*, **grundsätzliche** basic conditions of participation
teilnahmeberechtigt eligible
Teilnahmebestätigung *(f)* confirmation of participation, confirmation of acceptance
Teilnahmegebühr *(f)* participation fee
Teilnahmeverzicht *(m)* opting-out
teilnehmen attend, participate, take part
Teilnehmer(in) *(m/f)* participant
Teilnehmerliste *(f)* list of participants
Teilnehmerzahl *(f)* number of participants
Teilschaden *(m)* partial damage
Teilzahlung *(f)* part payment
Teilzahlungskauf *(m)* installment sale, hire purchase
Telefax *(n)* fax, telefax
telefaxen fax, send by fax
Telefaxgerät *(n)* fax, faxmachine, telefax machine
Telefaxteilnehmer(in) *(m/f)* fax subscriber, telefax subscriber
Telefon *(n)*, **schnurloses** cordless phone

Telefonanlage *(f)* telephone equipment, telephone installation
Telefonanruf *(m)* call, phone call
Telefonanschluss *(m)* telephone connection
Telefonanschluss *(m)*, **analoger** analog telephone connection (US), analogue telephone connection (GB)
Telefonanschluss *(m)*, **digitaler** digital telephone connection
Telefongebühr *(f)* (Grundgebühr) telephone charge, telephone rental; (Gesprächsgebühr) call charge
Telefongespräch *(n)* phone conversation, phone call
telefonieren phone, make a phone call
telefonisch telephonic, by phone, over the phone
Telefonkabel *(n)* phone cable, telephone cable
Telefonkarte *(f)* phonecard
Telefonleitung *(f)* line, telephone line
Telefonnummer *(f)* phone number, telephone number
Telefonrechnung *(f)* phone bill, telephone bill
Telefonverbindung *(f)* phone connection, telephone connection
Telefonzelle *(f)* phone box, telephone box
Telekommunikation *(f)* telecommunications
Telekopie *(f)* fax
Teleobjektiv *(n)* telephoto lens
Teller *(m)* dish, plate
Tellergericht *(n)* one course meal
Tellerspender *(m)* plate dispenser
Temperatur *(f)* temperature
Tempo *(n)* tempo, speed, rate, pace
Tempolimit *(n)* speed limit
temporär temporary
Tendenz *(f)* tendency, trend
tendieren tend
Teppich *(m)* carpet

Teppichbahnenware *(f)* off-the-roll carpeting
Teppichboden *(m)* carpet, fitted carpet, carpeting
Teppichfliese *(f)* carpet tile
Teppichklebeband *(n)* carpet tape, carpet adhesive tape
Teppichplatte *(f)* carpeting tile
Teppichreinigung *(f)* carpet cleaning
Termin *(m)* time, date, deadline; (Verabredungstermin) appointment
Termin *(m)* **festsetzen** fix a date, set a date
Termin *(m)***, frühestmöglicher** earliest possible date
Terminal *(n)* terminal
Termindruck *(m)* time pressure
termingemäß on schedule
termingerecht in due time, on schedule
Terminierung *(f)* timing
Terminkalender *(m)* appointments book, appointments diary, calendar
Terminplan *(m)* date plan, timetable, schedule, time schedule
Test *(m)* test
testen test, try out
teuer costly, expensive; (lieb) dear
Teuerung *(f)* rise in prices
Teuerungsrate *(f)* rate of price increases
Text *(m)* text
Texter *(m)* copywriter
Textverarbeitung *(f)* word processing
Textverarbeitungsprogramm *(n)* word processing program, word processor
Textverarbeitungssystem *(n)* word processing system
Theke *(f)* (Lokal) bar; (Laden) counter
Thema *(n)* (Gedanke) theme; (Gegenstand) subject; (Gespräch) topic
Theorie *(f)* theory
Thermometer *(n)* thermometer
Thermostat *(m)* thermostat
These *(f)* thesis
Tiefe *(f)* depth; (Überlegungen etc.) deepness, profundity

Tiefenschärfe *(f)* depth of focus
Tiefgarage *(f)* underground car park
tiefgefroren deep-frozen
tiefgekühlt frozen
Tiefkühlfach *(n)* freezing compartment
Tiefkühlfahrzeug *(n)* frozen food vehicle
Tiefkühlinsel *(f)* frozen food island site cabinet
Tiefkühlkost *(f)* frozen food
Tiefkühllagerraum *(m)* frozen food storage room
Tiefkühlmöbel *(n)* frozen food storage cabinet, deepfreeze equipment
Tiefkühlregal *(n)* frozen food multi-deck vertical tier cabinet
Tiefkühlschrank *(m)* vertical frozen food display cabinet
Tiefkühlschrank *(m)* **mit Glastür** upright freezer with glassdoor
Tiefkühltheke *(f)* frozen food counter
Tiefkühltruhe *(f)* chest freezer, chest type frozen food storage cabinet
Tiefkühlvitrine *(f)* frozen food sales cabinet
Tiefkühlzelle *(f)* portable frozen food room
Tipp *(m)* tip
Tischdecke *(f)* tablecloth
Tischkühlschrank *(m)* tabletop refrigerator
Tischler *(m)* joiner
Tischlerplatte *(f)* joiner panel
Tischplatte *(f)* tabletop
Tischreservierung *(f)* table reservation
Tisch-Tiefkühlschrank *(m)* tabletop frozen food storage cabinet
Tischtuch *(n)* tablecloth
Titel *(m)* title
Titel *(m)* **führen** have a title
Titelbild *(n)* cover, cover picture
Titelblatt *(n)* front page, title page
Titelgenerator *(m)* title generator
Titelseite *(f)* front page

T-Net ISDN-Anschluss *(m)* analog and ISDN telephone connections (US), analogue and ISDN telephone connections (GB)
Toast *(m)* (Trinkspruch) toast
Tochtergesellschaft *(f)* subsidiary company, subsidiary corporation, affiliated company, associated company
Toilette *(f)* toilet, lavatory (GB)
Toilette *(f)***, öffentliche** public convenience, public lavatory (GB)
Toilettenpapier *(n)* toilet paper
tolerant tolerant
Toleranz *(f)* tolerance
tolerieren tolerate
Tombola *(f)* tombola, raffle
Ton *(m)* sound
Tonangel *(f)* microphone boom
Tonaufnahme *(f)* audio recording, sound recording
Tonausfall *(m)* loss of sound
Tonband *(n)* tape
Tonbandaufnahme *(f)* tape recording
Tonbandgerät *(n)* tape recorder
Tonbildschau *(f)* audiovisual slide show
Tonfrequenz *(f)* audio frequency
Tonicwasser *(n)* tonic, tonic water
Tonkopf *(m)* sound head
Tonnage *(f)* tonnage
Tonne *(f)* (Gefäß) barrel, cask; (Gewicht) ton
Tonregler *(m)* tone control
Tonsäule *(f)* sound column
Tonspur *(f)* sound track
Tonstudio *(n)* recording studio
Tontechniker(in) *(m/f)* sound engineer, sound technician
Tonträger *(m)* sound carrier
Topf *(m)* pot
Topfpflanze *(f)* potted plant
Tor *(n)* gate, door
Tordurchfahrtshöhe *(f)* freight door height
Toreinfahrt *(f)* entrance gate
Torwache *(f)* gate staff, gate security
Torxschraube *(f)* torx head screw
Torxschraubendreher *(m)* torx head screw driver
Torxwinkelschlüssel *(m)* torx head wrench
Totalausfall *(m)* dead loss
Touristenklasse *(f)* economy class
Tragbahre *(f)* stretcher
tragbar portable
Tragegriff *(m)* handle
tragen carry; (Schulden etc.) bear; (Kleidung) wear
tragend supporting
Träger *(m)* support; (Holz) beam; (Eisen) girder; (Veranstaltung etc.) organizer, promoter
Tragetasche *(f)* bag, carrier bag
tragfähig capable of bearing
Tragfähigkeit *(f)* carrying capacity, load capacity
Tragfähigkeit *(f)* **des Hallenbodens** hall floor loading capacity
Trägheitsmoment *(n)* moment of inertia
Traglast *(f)* load, load-bearing capacity
Traglufthalle *(f)* air-supported building, air hall
Trainer(in) *(m/f)* trainer, coach
trainieren train, coach
Training *(n)* training
Transaktion *(f)* transaction
transferieren transfer
Transformator *(m)* transformer
transformieren transform
Transit *(m)* transit
Transitgüter *(n, pl)* transit goods, goods in transit
Transithalle *(f)* transit lounge
Transitverkehr *(m)* transit traffic
transparent transparent
Transparent *(n)* banner, transparent
Transport *(m)* transport, transportation, truckage, conveyance, haulage, shipment

transportabel transportable, portable, moveable
Transportband *(n)* conveyor belt
Transportdokument *(n)* transport document, transportation document
Transporteur *(m)* carrier
transportfähig moveable, transportable
Transportfahrzeug *(n)* transporter
Transportgenehmigung *(f)* transport permit
transportieren transport, forward, convey, carry
Transportkiste *(f)* transport case
Transportkosten *(pl)* carriage, transport charges, transportation charges, freight charges
Transportmittel *(n)* transport means, means of transport
Transportpapiere *(n, pl)* accompanying documents, transport documents, transporting documents, shipping documents
Transportrolle *(f)* castor
Transportschaden *(m)* damage in transit
Transportunternehmen *(n)* carrier, forwarding company, haulage contractor, haulage firm
Transportverlust *(m)* loss in transport
Transportversicherung *(f)* transport insurance
Transportvertrag *(m)* contract of carriage
Trapezdach *(n)* trapezoid roof
Traverse *(f)* cross beam
treffen meet
Treffpunkt *(m)* meeting place, meeting point
Treibgas *(n)* fuel gas
Treibstoff *(m)* fuel
Trend *(m)* tendency, trend
Trendanalyse *(f)* trend analysis
Trendwende *(f)* trend reversal, change in trend
Trennblatt *(n)* dividing card
trennen divide, separate, segregate

Trennfuge *(f)* dividing groove
Trennung *(f)* separation, segregation, division
Trennwand *(f)* dividing wall, partition wall
Treppe *(f)* stairs, staircase
Treppenabsatz *(m)* landing
Treppenaufgang *(m)* stairway
Treppengeländer *(n)* banister
Treppenneigung *(f)* staircase gradient
Treppenstufe *(f)* stair, step
Treppenwange *(f)* stair stringe
Treuhänder(in) *(m/f)* fiduciary, trustee
treuhänderisch fiduciary
Tribüne *(f)* platform, rostrum, gallery, stand
Trichter *(m)* funnel
Trikot *(f)* tricot, jersey, shirt
Trinkgeld *(n)* tip
Trinkgeld *(n)* **geben** tip
Trinkspruch *(m)* toast
Trinkwasser *(n)* drinking water
Trinkwasserkühler *(m)* drinking water cooler
Trittleiter *(f)* stepladder
Trittschallfilter *(m)* low-cut filter
Trockeneis *(n)* dry ice
Trockner *(m)* drier
tropfen drip, drop
Tropfen *(m)* drop
Trugschluss *(m)* fallacy
Truhe *(f)* chest, trunk
T-Shirt *(f)* T-Shirt
T-Stück *(n)* T-piece
Tube *(f)* tube
Tuch *(n)* cloth
Tünche *(f)* whitewash
tünchen whitewash
Tuner *(m)* tuner-amplifier
Tunnel *(m)* tunnel
Tüpfelchen *(n)* dot
Türangel *(f)* door hinge
Türanschlag *(m)* door stop
Türanschlagprofil *(n)* door stop extrusion

Türband *(n)* hinge plate
turbulent turbulent
Türgriff *(m)* handle, door handle
Türklinke *(f)* handle, door handle
Turm *(m)* tower
Turnus *(m)* turn, rota, rotation
Turnusänderung *(f)* change of rotation
turnusgemäß rotational, by rotation
Türpfosten *(m)* door post
Türrahmen *(m)* door frame
Türscharnier *(n)* door hinge
Türschild *(n)* door plate
Türschloss *(n)* lock, door lock
Tüte *(f)* bag, paper bag
Typ *(m)* model, type
Typenschild *(n)* type plate
typisch typical
Typographie *(f)* typography

U

U-Bahn *(f)* subway (US), underground (GB)
üben practise (US), practice (GB)
Überangebot *(n)* glut, oversupply, surplus
überarbeiten revise, rework
überbelichten overexpose
Überbelichtung *(f)* overexposure
überbewerten overestimate, overrate, overstate, overvalue
überbieten outbid
überblenden (Film, Dia) dissolve, fade over
Überblendprojektion *(f)* dissolve projection
Überblendsteuereinheit *(f)* dissolve control unit
Überblick *(m)* (Sicht) view; (Sache) overview, survey; (Zusammenstellung) summary
überblicken overlook, survey

überbringen deliver, bring
Überbringung *(f)* delivery
überbuchen overbook
überdachen roof over
überdacht roofed, covered
überdehnen overstretch
überdenken consider, reconsider, think over, rethink
überdimensional oversize
Überdruck *(m)* (Kessel etc.) excess pressure, overpressure; (Drucksachen) overprint
übereinander on top of the other
übereinkommen agree, come to an agreement, reach an agreement
Übereinkunft *(f)* agreement, arrangement, understanding
übereinstimmen agree, correspond; (Farben etc.) match
übereinstimmen, nicht disagree
Übereinstimmung *(f)* agreement, conformity, consensus, consistency, correspondence
Übereinstimmung *(f)* **mit, in** in accordance with
überfüllt crowded, overcrowded; (Lager etc.) overstocked
Übergabe *(f)* delivery, handling over, handover
übergeben deliver, hand over
Übergepäck *(n)* excess baggage (US), excess luggage (GB)
Übergepäckzuschlag *(m)* excess baggage fee (US), excess luggage fee (GB)
Übergewicht *(n)* overweight
übergewichtig overweight
überhöht excessive, too high
Überkapazität *(f)* excess capacity, overcapacity
überladen overload
Überlänge *(f)* exceptional length
überlassen give up, leave up, relinquish, let s.o. have sth., leave sth. to s.o.

Überlassung *(f)* **von Standfläche** stand subletting
überlasten (Gewicht) overload; (Arbeit etc.) overburden, overwork, overstretch
Überlastung *(f)* (Gewicht) overload; (Arbeit etc.) overstrain
Überlegung *(f)* consideration, reflection
übermalen paint over
übermäßig excessive, exorbitant
übermitteln convey, transmit
Übermittlung *(f)* conveyance, transmission
übernachten sleep, spend the night
Übernachtung *(f)* overnight stay
Übernachtungsmöglichkeit *(f)* overnight accommodation
Übernachtungspreis *(m)* overnight charge
Übernahme *(f)* acquisition, takeover
Übernahmeangebot *(n)* bid, takeover bid, tender offer
übernehmen take over
überprüfen check, screen, inspect, test, review
Überprüfung *(f)* checking, check, check-up, inspection, screening, search, review
überragen tower above
überreden persuade
Überredung *(f)* persuasion
Überredungskunst *(f)* powers of persuasion
überregional nationwide, supraregional
Überreste *(m, pl)* remains, remnants
Überschlagsrechnung *(f)* rough calculation
Überschrift *(f)* heading, headline, leading line, title
Überschuss *(m)* surplus, overage
Überseemärkte *(m, pl)* overseas markets
Überseetransport *(m)* overseas shipment

übersehen (nicht sehen) fail to notice; (nicht beachten) ignore
Übersetzer(in) *(m/f)* translator
Übersetzung *(f)* translation
Übersetzungsbüro *(n)* translating agency
Übersetzungsdienst *(m)* translation service
Übersetzungsfehler *(m)* error in translation
Übersicht *(f)* (Überblick) overall view; (Darstellung) survey, outline, summary
übersichtlich clear
Übersichtlichkeit *(f)* clarity, clearness
überspielen (aufnehmen) record
überstreichen coat
Überstunden *(f, pl)* overtime, overtime hours
Überstundentarif *(m)* overtime rate
übertragbar transferable, negotiable
übertragen transfer; (Aufgabe etc.) assign, delegate; (Technik) transmit; (Sendung) broadcast
Übertragung *(f)* transfer; (Aufgabe etc.) assignment, delegation; (Technik) transmission; (Sendung) broadcast
Übertragung *(f)* **des Stands** assignment of the stand
Übertragung *(f)* **von Standfläche** transfer of stand space
überwachen supervise, survey, check, control, monitor
Überwachung *(f)* supervision, control, inspection, monitoring; (rechtlich) surveillance
Überwachungskamera *(f)* surveillance camera
Überwachungsrekorder *(m)* surveillance recorder
überweisen transfer
Überweisung *(f)* transfer, transmission, remittance
überzeugen convince, persuade
überzeugend convincing

Überzeugung *(f)* conviction, persuasion
Überzeugungskraft *(f)* persuasive power, power of persuasion
Überzug *(m)* cover, coat, coating
üblich customary, usual, normal, standard
Uhr *(f)*, **rund um die** around the clock
Ultimatum *(n)* ultimatum
umändern alter, modify
Umbau *(m)* rebuilding, reconstruction, conversion; (Organisation) reorganization
umbauen alter, redesign, rebuild; (Organisation) reorganize
umbenennen rename
umbuchen change one's booking, change one's reservation; reclassify
Umbuchung *(f)* adjusting entry, reclassification; (Reise etc.) change a reservation (Kosten etc.) rebooking, reposting, payment transfer
Umbuchungsgebühr *(f)* amendment fee, alteration fee
umdrehen turn over, turn round
Umdrehung *(f)* **pro Minute** revolutions per minute
Umdrehungszahl *(f)* revolutions per minute
Umfang *(m)* (Fläche) area; (Größe) size; (Zahl) amount; (Ausmaß) extend; (Volumen) volume
umfangreich extensive, large-scale
Umfeld *(n)* surroundings, associated area
Umfrage *(f)* survey, enquiry, inquiry
Umfrage *(f)*, **demoskopische** public opinion poll
umfunktionieren convert, turn
Umgangssprache *(f)* colloquial language, colloquial speech
umgeben surround
Umgebung *(f)* environs, surroundings
umgehen bypass; (vermeiden) avoid; (Recht) evade

umgehend immediate
Umgehungsstraße *(f)* bypass
umgekehrt reversed
umgestalten alter, remodel, reshape, redesign
Umkleidekabine *(f)* changing cubicle
umkleiden change, change one's clothes
Umkleideraum *(m)* changing room
umladen reload, transship
Umladungsgebühr *(f)* reloading charge
Umlage *(f)* distribution of cost, contribution, levy
umleiten detour, divert, reroute
Umleitung *(f)* detour, diversion
Umleitungsschild *(n)* detour sign
ummanteln screen up
umorganisieren reorganize, shake up
umranden border, edge
Umrandung *(f)* border
umrechnen convert
Umrechnung *(f)* conversion
Umrechnungskurs *(m)* exchange rate, rate of exchange, conversion rate
Umrechnungstabelle *(f)* conversion table
Umriss *(m)* outline, contour
Umrisszeichnung *(f)* contour drawing
Umsatz *(m)* turnover, billing, sales, volume, transaction
Umsatzbeteiligung *(f)* participation in sales
Umsatzdiagramm *(n)* sales chart
Umsatzentwicklung *(f)* sales trend
Umsatzkurve *(f)* sales curve
Umsatzplus *(n)* increase in turnover
Umsatzprognose *(f)* sales forecast, predicted sales
Umsatzrückgang *(m)* decline in sales, drop in sales
Umsatzstatistik *(f)* sales statistics
Umsatzsteigerung *(f)* sales increase, increase in sales
Umsatzsteuer *(f)* sales tax, turnover tax

Umsatzsteuer *(f)*, **Antrag auf Vergütung der** VAT refund application
Umsatzvolumen *(n)* sales volume
umschalten switch over, change over
Umschalttaste *(f)* (Computer) shift-key
Umschlag *(m)* (Transport) transshipment; (Brief) envelope; (Katalog etc.) cover; (Ware) handling, turnover, turnaround
Umschlagplatz *(m)* trade center (US), trade centre (GB), trading center (US), trading centre (GB), transshipment point, place of transshipment
Umschlagseite *(f)* cover page
Umschlagseite *(f)*, **dritte** inside back cover
Umschlagseite *(f)*, **erste** front cover
Umschlagseite *(f)*, **vierte** back cover
Umschlagseite *(f)*, **zweite** inside front cover
umsonst (kostenlos) for nothing, free, free of charge; (vergeblich) in vain
Umstand *(m)* circumstance, fact, factor
Umständen *(m, pl)*, **unter** possibly, perhaps
umständlich complicated
Umtausch *(m)* exchange
umtauschen exchange; (Geld) change
U-Musik *(f)* light music
Umweg *(m)* detour, roundabout way
Umwelt *(f)* environment
Umweltbelastung *(f)* environmental burden, environmental load, environmental pollution, ecological damage
umweltbewusst environmentally aware, environmentally conscious, conservation-conscious
Umweltbewusstsein *(n)* environmental awareness
umweltfreundlich ecologically friendly, environmentally friendly, nonpolluting
Umweltrichtlinien *(pl)* environmental regulations

Umweltschaden *(m)* environmental damage
umweltschädlich harmful to the environment, ecologically harmful
Umweltschadstoff *(m)* pollutant
Umweltschutz *(m)* protection of the environment, environmental control, environmental protection, environmental conservation, pollution control
Umweltschutzgesetz *(n)* environmental protection law
Umweltverschmutzung *(f)* pollution, environmental pollution, pollution of the environment
umweltverträglich ecologically compatible
unachtsam careless, inattentive
Unachtsamkeit *(f)* carelessness, inattentiveness
unangemeldet unannounced
unangemessen inadequate, inappropriate, unreasonable, unsuitable
unangenehm unpleasant
unannehmbar unacceptable
Unannehmlichkeite *(f)* trouble
unauffällig inconspicuous
unaufmerksam inattentive, thoughtless
Unaufmerksamkeit *(f)* inattention, inattentiveness, thoughtlessness
unaufschiebbar urgent
unbeabsichtigt unintended, unintentional
unbeachtet unnoticed
unbeanstandet unobjected, not objected
unbeantwortet unanswered
unbedacht thoughtless, unconsidered
unbedenklich safe, harmless, completely harmless
unbedeutend insignificant, unimportant, negligible
unbedingt absolute, unconditional
unbefahrbar impassable

unbefriedigend unsatisfactory
unbefristet open-end, open-ended, unlimited
unbefugt unauthorized
Unbefugte(r) *(f/m)* unauthorized person
unbegreiflich incomprehensible
unbegrenzt unlimited
unbegründet unfounded, groundless
unbehindert unhindered
unbekannt not known, unknown, unfamiliar
Unbekannte(r) *(f/m)* unknown person, stranger
unbekümmert carefree, unconcerned
unbelichtet unexposed
unbeliebt unpopular
unbemerkt unnoticed
unbenutzt unused
unbeobachtet unobserved
unbequem uncomfortable, inconvenient
Unbequemlichkeit *(f)* uncomfortableness, inconvenience, discomfort
unberechenbar incalculable, unpredictable
unberechtigt unauthorized
unberechtigterweise without authority, without good reason
unbeschädigt intact, undamaged
unbeschäftigt unemployed
unbeschränkt absolute, unlimited, unrestricted
unbesetzt (Stelle) vacant; (Ort, Platz) free, unoccupied
unbesonnen imprudent, rash
Unbesonnenheit *(f)* imprudence, rashness
unbestätigt unacknowledged, unconfirmed, unverified
unbestimmt uncertain, vague; (Daten etc.) indeterminate, indefinite
unbestritten undisputed
unbeteiligt not involved, uninvolved
unbeträchtlich negligible

unbewacht unguarded; (Parkplatz etc.) unattended
unbeweglich immobile, immovable, fixed; (geistig) inflexible
unbewusst inconscious
unbezahlt unpaid, unsettled
unbrauchbar useless, of no use, unusable; (Vorhaben) impracticable
unbrennbar nonflammable
undatiert undated
undeutlich indistinct, unclear
undicht leaking
undichte Stelle *(f)* leak
undurchführbar impracticable
undurchsichtig (Material) opaque; (obskur) obscure
uneben uneven, rough
Unebenheit *(f)* unevenness, roughness
uneingeschränkt unlimited, unrestricted, unconditional
uneinheitlich not uniform
unempfindlich insensitive
unentbehrlich indispensable
unentgeltlich free, free of charge
unentschlossen irresolute, undecided, indecisive
Unentschlossenheit *(f)* indecision, irresolution
unentschuldbar inexcusable
unerfahren inexperienced
unerheblich insignificant
unerlässlich essential, imperative, indispensable
unerlaubt forbidden, illicit, not allowed, unauthorized
unerlaubterweise without permission
unerledigt unsettled, unfulfilled
unerprobt untested, untried
unerträglich unbearable
unerwünscht unwelcome, undesirable
unfähig unable, incapable, incompetent, unqualified
Unfallmeldung *(f)* notice of accident
Unfallrisiko *(m)* accident risk, risk of accident

Unfallschaden *(m)* accident damage
Unfallschutz *(m)* accident prevention, prevention of accidents
Unfallstation *(f)* accident ward, first-aid station, first-aid post
Unfallverhütung *(f)* prevention of accidents, accident prevention
Unfallverhütungsvorschriften *(f, pl)* accident prevention regulations, safety codes and regulations, regulations concerning accident prevention
Unfallversicherung *(f)* accident insurance, casualty insurance
ungebräuchlich unusual, uncommon
ungebraucht unused
ungebunden independent
Ungeduld *(f)* impatience
ungeeignet inappropriate, ineligible, unsuitable, unsuited, unqualified
ungefährlich harmless, not dangerous
ungefragt unasked
ungeheuer enormous, immense
ungehindert unhindered
ungelegen inconvenient
ungenau inaccurate, inexact
Ungenauigkeit *(f)* inaccuracy
ungenügend insufficient, unsatisfactory, poor
ungerade uneven, odd
ungerechtfertigt unjustified, unjustly, unwarranted, unfair
Ungerechtigkeit *(f)* injustice
ungeregelt unregulated, irregular
ungesetzlich illegal, unlawful; (verboten) illicit
Ungesetzlichkeit *(f)* illegality
ungesichert unhedged
ungestört undisturbed
ungewiss uncertain
Ungewissheit *(f)* uncertainty
ungewöhnlich unusual
ungewollt unintentional
ungezählt countless, uncounted
ungiftig nontoxic

unglaubwürdig unreliable, untrustworthy
ungleich unequal, dissimilar, unlike
ungleichmäßig asymmetric, asymmetrical
ungültig void, invalid
Ungültigkeit *(f)* invalidity
ungünstig adverse, infavorable (US), infavourable (GB)
unhöflich impolite
Unhöflichkeit *(f)* impoliteness
universal universal
Universaladaptor *(m)* universal adapter, universal adaptor
Universalmesse *(f)* general trade fair
universell universal
Unkenntnis *(f)* ignorance
unklar unclear, not clear
unkompliziert uncomplicated; (einfach) straigtforward
unkonventionell unconventional, unorthodox
Unkosten *(pl)* costs, expenses, overhead costs, overheads
unlauter dishonest, unfair
unlogisch illogical
unmaßgeblich inconsequential, unauthoritative
unmodern old-fashioned, out of fashion
Unmöglichkeit *(f)* impossibility
unnachgiebig intransigent, uncompromising, unyielding; (Material) inflexible
unnatürlich unnatural
unnötig unnecessary
unnütz useless
Unordnung *(f)* disorder, mess
unpersönlich impersonal
unpraktisch impractical
unproblematisch unproblematic
unpünktlich unpunctual
Unpünktlichkeit *(f)* unpunctuality
unqualifiziert unqualified
Unrat *(m)* refuse, rubbish, filth

Unrecht *(n)* injustice
unrechtmäßig illegal, illegitimate, unlawful, wrongful
unregelmäßig irregular
unrentabel unprofitable, uneconomic, uneconomical
unrichtig false, incorrect, wrong
unsachgemäß improper
unsachlich unobjective, irrelevant
unschädlich harmless
unscharf (Bild) blurred; (unklar) poorly defined
unscheinbar insignificant, inconspicuous
unschlüssig undecided
unselbstständig dependent
Unselbstständigkeit *(f)* dependence
unsicher insecure, instable, uncertain, unsafe
Unsicherheit *(f)* insecurity, instability, uncertainty
unsichtbar invisible
unsymmetrisch assymetrical
unsympathisch disagreeable, unpleasant
untätig inactive, idle, passive
Untätigkeit *(f)* inactivity
unten below, underneath
Unteraussteller *(m)* subexhibitor
Unterbau *(m)* foundations
unterbelichtet underexposed
unterbesetzt shorthanded, short-staffed, understaffed
unterbewertet undervalued
unterbieten underbid, undercut, underquote
unterbrechen interrupt, disrupt, suspend; (Technik) break, cut off, disconnect
Unterbrechung *(f)* interruption, disruption, suspension; (Technik) break, disconnection
Unterbringungsmöglichkeit *(f)* accommodation
unterentwickelt underdeveloped

Unterflurhydrant *(m)* underfloor hydrant
Unterflurverlegung *(f)* underfloor installation
Unterführung *(f)* underpass, subway
Untergebene(r) *(f/m)* subordinate
untergeordnet inferior, subordinate
Untergeschoss *(n)* basement
Untergestell *(n)* underframe
Untergrund *(m)* subsoil
Untergurt *(m)* (Treppe, Brüstung) lower girder
unterhalb below, under, underneath
unterhalten (Gespräch) talk; (Gäste) entertain; (Anlage etc.) maintain
Unterhaltung *(f)* (Gespräch) conversation, talk; (Schau) entertainment; (Anlage etc.) maintenance
Unterhaltungsmusik *(f)* light music
Unterhändler *(m)* negotiator
unterirdisch subterranean
Unterkunft *(f)* accomodation
Unterlage *(f)* (Dokument) document; (Schreibtisch) pad
Unternehmen *(n)* firm, business, enterprise, concern, corporation, company, organization
Unternehmen *(n)*, **verbundenes** affiliate company, associated company
Unternehmen *(n)*, **zusätzlich vertretenes** additionally represented company
Unternehmensberater(in) *(m/f)* management consultant
Unternehmensbereich *(m)* division
Unternehmensdaten *(pl)* company figures
Unternehmensform *(f)* business form, form of business, form of business organisation
Unternehmensforschung *(f)* operations research, operational research
Unternehmensführung *(f)* management, business management

Unternehmensgewinn *(m)* corporate profit
Unternehmensgruppe *(f)* group, group of companies
Unternehmensimage *(n)* corporate image
Unternehmensleiter(in) *(m/f)* business executive, top manager
Unternehmensleitung *(f)* corporate management
Unternehmenspolitik *(f)* company policy, corporate policy
Unternehmensspitze *(f)* top management
Unternehmensverband *(m)* trade association
Unternehmensvorstand *(m)* board, board of directors
Unternehmenswerbung *(f)* corporate advertising
Unternehmer(in) *(m/f)* businessman, businesswoman, entrepreneur, operator
unternehmerisch enterprising, entrepreneurial
Unterredung *(f)* conversation, discussion, talk
Unterrichtung *(f)* instruction, information
Untersatz *(m)* mat
unterscheiden differ, differentiate, distinguish
Unterschied *(m)* difference, distinction, variance
unterschiedlich different, varying
Unterschrank *(m)* sideboard, base cabinet
unterschreiben sign, undersign
Unterschrift *(f)* signature
Unterschrift *(f)*, **rechtsgültige** legally binding signature
Unterschrift *(f)*, **rechtsverbindliche** authorized signature, legally binding signature
unterstehen be subordinate, report to s.o.

unterstützen aid, assist, back up, encourage, help, promote, subsidize, support
Unterstützung *(f)* aid, assistance, backing, backup, encouragement, promotion, sponsorship, subsidization, support
untersuchen analyze, enquire, examine, inspect, investigate, study, survey, scrutinize
Untersuchung *(f)* analysis, enquiry, examination, investigation, study, survey
Untersuchungsbericht *(m)* report, survey
unterteilen subdivide
Unterteilung *(f)* subdivision
Untertitel *(m)* subtitle, subhead
untervermieten sublet
Untervermietung *(f)* sublease, subletting
Unterverteilung *(f)* (Strom) subdistribution
unterweisen instruct
Unterweisung *(f)* instruction
unterzeichnen sign, undersign
Unterzeichner *(m)* signatory
Unterzeichnung *(f)* signature, signing
unübersehbar immense, vast
unübersichtlich badly arranged, confused, unclear
unumgänglich essential, unavoidable
unverantwortlich irresponsible
unverbindlich not binding, without engagement, witout obligation
unverbindliche Preisempfehlung *(f)* recommended retail price (RRP)
unverkäuflich not for sale, unsaleable, unmarketable
unverpackt loose, unpackaged
unversehens unexpectedly, all of a sudden
unversichert unassured, uninsured
unversteuert untaxed
unverzollt duty unpaid, duty-free

unverzüglich immediate, prompt, witout delay
unvollständig incomplete
unvollständige Lieferung incomplete delivery
unvorbereitet unprepared
unvorhergesehen unforeseen
unvorschriftsmäßig irregular, against the regulations, contrary to the regulations
unvorsichtig careless, incautious
Unvorsichtigkeit *(f)* carelessness, incautiousness
unwahrscheinlich improbable, unlikely
unwesentlich irrelevant, unimportant
unwichtig irrelevant, unimportant
unwiderruflich irrevocable, irreversible
unwirksam ineffective
unwirtschaftlich inefficient, uneconomic, uneconomical
unzeitgemäß untimely; (altmodisch) old-fashioned
unzerbrechlich unbreakable
unzerreißbar untearable
unzerstörbar indestructible
unzufrieden dissatisfied, discontended
unzulänglich insufficient, inadequate
unzulässig unsuitable; (rechtlich) illegal, inadmissible
unzureichend insufficient, unsatisfactory
unzutreffend incorrect
unzuverlässig unreliable
Unzuverlässigkeit *(f)* unreliability
unzweckmäßig inexpedient, unsuitable
U-Profil *(n)* channel section
Urheber *(m)* creator, originator; (Verfasser) author
Urheberrecht *(n)* copyright
Urheberrechte *(n, pl)*, **Schutz der** protection of proprietary rights
urheberrechtlich on copyright
urheberrechtlich geschützt proprietary, copyrighted, protected by copyright, copyright reserved

Urheberrechtsgesetz *(n)* copyright act, copyright law
Urkunde *(f)* document; (Bescheinigung) certificate, instrument; (Vertrag) deed
Ursache *(f)* cause, reason
Ursprung *(m)* origin, source
Ursprungsland *(n)* country of origin
urteilen adjudicate, judge

V

vakuumverpackt vacuum-packed
Vakuumverpackung *(f)* vacuum packaging
Valuta *(f)* value, currency, foreign currency
variabel adjustable, subject to change, variable
Variante *(f)* variant, version
variieren vary
Vase *(f)* vase
VDE-Vorschrift *(f)* VDE standard
Vegetarier(in) *(m/f)* vegetarian
Vegetarierrestaurant *(n)* vegetarian restaurant
vegetarisch vegetarian
Vektor *(m)* vector
Ventilator *(m)* ventilator, fan, ventilating fan
verabreden agree upon, arrange; (Termin etc.) appoint
Verabredung *(f)* appointment, arrangement, date
Verabredung *(f)* **einhalten** keep an appointment
verabschieden say goodbye to, bid s.o. good-bye
verallgemeinern generalize
Verallgemeinerung *(f)* generalization
veraltet obsolete, out of date, outdated, dated, outmoded

veränderlich variable
verändern alter, change, modify
Veränderung *(f)* alteration, change, variance, variation
verankern (festmachen) anchor; (rechtlich etc.) enshrine, embody, establish, lay down
Verankerung *(f)* **im Hallenboden** hall floor anchoring
veranlassen cause, arrange, bring about, order
Veranlassung *(f)* cause, occasion, reason, instigation
veranschaulichen illustrate, visualize
veranschlagen estimate
veranstalten arrange, organize, stage, hold
Veranstalter *(m)* organizer, promoter
Veranstaltung *(f)* arrangement, event, meeting, performance
Veranstaltungsbedingungen *(f, pl)* event conditions, show conditions
Veranstaltungsbedingungen *(f, pl)*, **allgemeine** general event conditions, general show conditions
Veranstaltungsdauer *(f)* event duration, show duration
Veranstaltungsgelände *(n)* show site, exhibition grounds, fair grounds
Veranstaltungsgesellschaft *(f)* managing organization
Veranstaltungskalender *(m)* calendar of events
Veranstaltungslaufzeit *(f)* duration of the event, show time
Veranstaltungsort *(m)* venue
Veranstaltungstitel *(m)* title of the event
Veranstaltungszeiten *(f, pl)* event schedule, show schedule
verantworten be responsible, be liable
verantwortlich accountable, answerable, responsible
verantwortlich machen hold s.o. responsible, hold s.o. accountable, blame s.o.

Verantwortlichkeit *(f)* responsibility, accountability
Verantwortung *(f)* responsibility
verantwortungsbewusst responsible
Verantwortungsbewusstsein *(n)* sense of responsibility
verantwortungslos irresponsible
verarbeiten process
Verarbeitung *(f)* (Material, Daten) processing; (Industrie) manufacturing
Verband *(m)* (Verletzung) bandage, dressing; (Vereinigung) association, union, federation, league
Verbandskasten *(m)* first-aid kit
Verbandsmaterial *(n)* dressing, dressing material, first-aid supplies
Verbesserung *(f)* advance, enhancement, betterment, improvement; (Fehler) correction
verbiegen bend
verbilligen cheapen, reduce the price
verbilligt cheap, reduced, at a reduced price
Verbinder *(m)* connector
verbindlich authentic, binding, firm, obligatory
Verbindlichkeit *(f)* commitment, liability, obligation, obligingness
Verbindlichkeiten *(f, pl)* accounts payable, liabilities
Verbindung *(f)* combination, connection, link
Verbindungsrohr *(n)* connecting rod
Verbindungsstück *(n)* connecting piece, connector, adapter, adaptor
Verbot *(n)* ban, prohibition; (Recht) interdiction
verboten forbidden, prohibited; (ungesetzlich) illegal
Verbrauch *(m)* consumption; (Geld) expenditure
verbrauchen consume; (aufbrauchen) use up; (abnutzen) wear out
Verbraucher(in) *(m/f)* consumer

Verbraucherbefragung *(f)* consumer survey
Verbrauchermesse *(f)* consumer show, consumer goods show, consumer fair
Verbraucherschutz *(m)* consumer protection
Verbraucherumfrage *(f)* consumer survey
Verbraucherverhalten *(n)* consumer behavior (US), consumer behaviour (GB)
Verbrauchsgüter *(n, pl)* consumer goods, consumable goods, consumption products
Verbrauchsmaterialien *(n, pl)* articles of consumption
verbreiten spread, distribute, circulate
Verbringung *(f)* **von Exponaten** carriage of exhibits
verbuchen book, enter in the books, post, recognize
verbunden connected; (geschäftlich) affiliated, associated
Verbundglas *(n)* laminated glass
Verbundwerbung *(f)* joint advertising
Verdacht *(m)* suspicion
verdächtig suspect, suspicious
Verdampfer *(m)* evaporator
verdanken owe
verdanken, jdm. etw. owe sth. to s.o.
Verdienst *(m)* (Einkommen) earnings, income; (Lohn) wages; (Gehalt) salary
verdienstvoll deserving
verdrahten wire
Verdrängungswettbewerb *(m)* destructive competition, crowding-out competition, cutthroat competition
verdunkeln darken
Verdunkelung *(f)* darkening
Verdünner *(m)* thinner
Verdunster *(m)* humidifier
Verdunstung *(f)* evaporation
Verein *(m)* association, club, society, union
vereinbaren agree; (Termin etc.) arrange
Vereinbarung *(f)* agreement, arrangement
Vereinbarung *(f)* **treffen** make an agreement, make an arrangement, enter into an agreement, reach an agreement
Vereinbarung *(f)***, laut** as agreed
vereinbarungsgemäß as per agreement
vereinfachen simplify
Vereinfachung *(f)* simplification
vereinheitlichen standardize, unify
Vereinheitlichung *(f)* standardization, unification
vereinigen combine, unit, join together
Vereinigung *(f)* association, grouping, organization, unification
Verfahren *(n)* procedure; (Methode) method; (Technik) process
Verfallsdatum *(n)* date of expiry, expiration date, expiry date; (Lebensmittel) best before date, sell-by date
Verflüssiger *(m)* condenser
Verflüssigungssatz *(m)* condensing unit
verfrachten transport, freight, ship
Verfrachtung *(f)* shipment
verfügbar available, disposable
Verfügbarkeit *(f)* availability
Vergabe *(f)* (Auftrag etc.) placing, award; (Zuweisung) allocation
vergeben (Auftrag etc.) place, award; (zuweisen) allocate
vergeblich in vain, futile
vergesslich forgetful
verglasen glaze
Verglasung *(f)* glazing
Vergleich *(m)* comparison, arrangement; (Recht) settlement
Vergleich *(m)* **zu, im** compared to, in comparison with
vergleichbar comparable
Vergleichbarkeit *(f)* comparability
Vergleichsjahr *(n)* base year

vergleichsweise comparatively
Vergleichszahl *(f)* comparative figure
vergriffen (Ware) sold out, out of stock
vergrößern enlarge, expand, extend, increase; (Bild) enlarge, blow up
Vergrößerung *(f)* augmentation, enlargement, expansion, increase; (Foto) enlargement
Vergünstigung *(f)* concession, privilege, benefit; (Steuer) allowance
Vergütung *(f)* refunding, reimbursement, remuneration
Verhalten *(n)* behavior (US), behaviour (GB), conduct, reaction
Verhaltensweise *(f)* behavior (US), behaviour (GB)
verhältnismäßig comparatively, proportionally, relatively
verhandeln negotiate
Verhandlung *(f)* negotiation, bargaining
Verhandlungsbasis *(f)* basis for negotiations
Verhandlungsführer *(m)* negotiator, chief negotiator
Verhandlungsposition *(f)* bargaining position, negotiating position
Verhandlungssache *(f)* negotiable matter
verhängen cover, drape
verhindern prevent, provide against, avert
Verhinderung *(f)* prevention, avertion
verkabeln cable; (Geräte) connect
Verkabelung *(f)* cabling
verkalkulieren miscalculate
Verkäufer(in) *(m/f)* seller, salesman, saleswoman, salesperson, vendor
Verkäufermarkt *(m)* seller's market
Verkäuferstab *(m)* sales force
verkäuflich marketable, saleable, vendible, merchantable, on sale
Verkaufsabteilung *(f)* sales department
Verkaufsaktion *(f)* sales campaign

Verkaufsangebot *(n)* offer, offer to sell
Verkaufsargument *(n)* sales argument, selling point, selling proposition, sales pitch
Verkaufsauflage *(f)* paid circulation
Verkaufsausstellung *(f)* sales exhibition
Verkaufsbedingungen *(f, pl)* conditions of sale, terms of sale
Verkaufserfolg *(m)* sales record
Verkaufserlös *(m)* sales receipts, sales returns, sales revenue
Verkaufsförderung *(m)* promotion, sales promotion
Verkaufsgespräch *(n)* sales talk
Verkaufshilfen *(f, pl)* sales aids
Verkaufskühlautomat *(m)* refrigerated vending machine
Verkaufskühlmöbel *(n)*, **steckerfertiges** plug-in type refrigerated sales cabinet
Verkaufsleiter(in) *(m/f)* sales executive, sales manager
Verkaufsmöglichkeiten *(f, pl)* sales opportunities
Verkaufspersonal *(n)* sales force, sales personnel, sales staff
Verkaufspreis *(m)* retail price, sales price, selling price
Verkaufsprospekt *(m)* sales literature
Verkaufsstelle *(f)* outlet
Verkaufsunterlagen *(f, pl)* sales documentation
Verkaufszahlen *(f, pl)* sales figures
Verkaufsziel *(n)* sales goal, sales objective, sales target
Verkehr *(m)* **im Messegelände** site traffic
Verkehr *(m)*, **öffentlicher** public transport, public transportation
Verkehrsablauf *(m)*, **reibungsloser** smooth flow of traffic
Verkehrsdurchsage *(f)* traffic announcement
Verkehrsfluss *(m)* flow of traffic, traffic flow
Verkehrsleitfaden *(m)* traffic guidelines

Verkehrsleitsystem *(n)* traffic guidance system
Verkehrsmittel *(n)* means of transport, means of transportation
Verkehrsmittel *(n, pl)*, **öffentliche** public transport, public transportation
Verkehrsmittelwerbung *(f)* transport advertising
Verkehrsregeln *(f, pl)*, **allgemeine** general traffic regulations
Verkehrsstau *(m)* traffic jam, traffic congestion
Verkleidung *(f)* sheathing, jacketing, casing; (Holzverkleidung) pannelling
verkleinern make smaller, reduce in size; (Maßstab etc.) scale down; (Bild) reduce; (Personal) downsize
verkünden announce, proclaim
verkürzen shorten, cut down, reduce; (Text etc.) abridge
Verladekosten *(pl)* loading charges
verladen load, ship
Verladestelle *(f)* loading point
Verladung *(f)* loading, shipment
Verlag *(m)* publishing house, publishing company, publisher
verlängern lengthen; (Frist etc.) prolong; (Kredit etc.) extend; (Ausweis etc.) renew
Verlängerung *(f)* lengthening; (Frist etc.) prolongation; (Kredit etc.) extension; (Ausweis etc.) renewal
Verlängerungskabel *(n)* extension cable, extension cord, extension flex, extension lead
verlässlich reliable
Verlässlichkeit *(f)* realibility
Verlauf *(m)* (Ablauf) course, run; (Entwicklung) progress, development
verlegen transfer, move; (Firma etc.) relocate; (Kabel, Teppichboden) lay; (Buch etc.) publish
Verleih *(m)* hire service, rental service
verleihen lend, rent (US), hire (GB), hire out (GB)

verleimen glue together
verletzen (verwunden) hurt, injure, wound; (Recht) infringe, violate
Verletzung *(f)* (Verwundung) injury, wound, wounding; (Recht) infringement, violation
Verletzungsgefahr *(f)* danger of injuring
verlorengehen get lost, be lost
verlosen draw lots for; (Tombola) raffle
Verlosung *(f)* prize draw, drawing lots, raffle
verlöten solder
Verlust *(m)* loss, wastage
Verlustanzeige *(f)* notice of a loss, report of a loss
Verlustgeschäft *(n)* money-losing deal, losing bargain
vermarkten market, commercialize
Vermarktung *(f)* marketing, commercialization
vermeiden avoid
vermengen mix
Vermerk *(m)* entry, note, remark
vermessen measure
Vermessung *(f)* measurement
vermieten let, lease, rent, rent out
Vermietung *(f)* lease, let, letting, renting
Vermittlung *(f)* (Geschäft etc.) negotiation; (Arbeit) employment, placement; (Termin etc.) arrangement; (Schlichtung) mediation
vernageln nail up
Vernunft *(f)* good sense, reason
vernünftig rational, reasonable, sensible
veröffentlichen publish, issue, release
Veröffentlichung *(f)* publication
Verordnung *(f)* **über Getränkeschankanlagen** Ordinance on Drinks Dispensing Systems
verpacken pack, wrap, wrap up
Verpackung *(f)* packing, packaging, wrapping
Verpackung *(f)*, **seemäßige** sea-proof packing, seaworthy packing
Verpackungseinheit *(f)* packing unit

Verpackungskosten *(pl)* packing cost, packing charges
Verpackungsmaterial *(n)* packing, packing material, packaging
Verpackungsverordnung *(f)* Packaging Ordinance
verpflegen feed, cater for
Verpflegung *(f)* food, food supply, catering
verpflichtend obligatory
verpflichtet committed, obligated, obliged
Verpflichtung *(f)* commitment, obligation, liability, engagement
Verrechnung *(f)* setting of account, clearing
Verrechnungsscheck *(m)* crossed check (US), crossed cheque (GB), non-negotiable check (US), non-negotiable cheque (GB), account-only
verringern diminish, reduce, scale down, decrease
Verringerung *(f)* decrease, reduction, scaling down
versagen fail
Versagen *(n)* failure, fault; (Technik) break down
Versammlung *(f)* assembly, convention, gathering, meeting
Versammlung *(f)* **abhalten** hold a meeting
Versammlung *(f)* **einberufen** convene a meeting
Versand *(m)* consignment, dispatch, dispatching, forwarding, shipment
Versandanschrift *(f)* dispatch note, parcel address
Versandanzeige *(f)* dispatch note
Versandgewicht *(n)* shipment weight
Versandkosten *(pl)* delivery costs, dispatching costs, forwarding costs, shipping costs
Versandpapiere *(n, pl)* dispatch papers, shipping documents

verschicken dispatch, send, send out, ship
verschiebbar movable
verschieben move, remove, shift; (zeitlich) defer, postpone
Verschiebung *(f)* postponement
verschieden different, diverse
verschieden sein differ, vary
verschiedentlich (mehrmals) several times, repeatedly; (gelegentlich) occasionally
verschließbar (Behälter etc.) closeable; (Tür etc.) lockable
verschließen shut, close; (abschließen) lock, lock up
Verschluss *(m)* fastener, lock; (Kamera) shutter
Verschlusstechnik *(f)* interlocking technique
verschönern brighten up, embellish
Verschönerung *(f)* embellishment
verschrauben bolt, screw up
verschrotten scrap
verschulden (verursachen) cause, be to blame for
verschulden, sich get into debt, run into debt, incur
verschweißen weld together
verschwinden disappear, vanish
Versehen *(n)* oversight, mistake; (Irrtum) error
Versehen *(n)***, aus** by mistake, inadvertently
versehentlich by mistake, inadvertently
versenden consign, convey, dispatch, forward, send, send out, ship
Versendung *(f)* consignment, conveyance, dispatch, dispatching, shipment, shipping
Versicherer *(m)* insurer, insurance company, underwriter
versichern (gegen Schaden) insure, underwrite; (behaupten) declare; (beteuern) affirm, protest; (bestätigen) assure

Versicherung *(f)* insurance; (Bekräftigung) assurance
Versicherungsbeitrag *(m)* insurance charge, insurance contribution, insurance premium
Versicherungsfall *(m)* insured event
Versicherungsgesellschaft *(f)* insurance company
Versicherungsnehmer(in) *(m/f)* policyholder, insurant
Versicherungspolice *(f)* insurance policy
Versicherungsprämie *(f)* insurance premium
Versicherungsschutz *(m)* insurance cover, insurance coverage, insurance protection
Versicherungssumme *(f)* sum insured
Versicherungswert *(m)* insurable value
versorgen (beliefern) supply, provide; (sich kümmern) look after, take care of
Versorgung *(f)* (Lieferung) supply; (Nahrungsmittel, Getränke) catering, provision
Versorgungskanal *(m)* services trench, utilities trench, supply channel, supply duct
Versorgungsleitung *(f)* service line, supply line
Versorgungsnetz *(n)* utilities network, services grid, supply network
Versorgungstechnik *(f)* utilities engineering
verspäten be late, be delayed
verspätet belated, late
Verspätung *(f)* delay, lateness
versperren bar, block; (Sicht etc.) obstruct
versprechen, etw. promise sth.
versprechen, sich make a slip
Verständigung *(f)* (Kommunikation) communication; (Übereinkunft) agreement, understanding

Verständigungsschwierigkeiten *(f, pl)* communication problems
Verständnis *(n)* understanding, comprehension
verständnislos uncomprehending
verständnisvoll understanding
verstärken increase, reinforce, strengthen; (Technik) amplify
Verstärker *(m)* amplifier
Verstärkung *(f)* reinforcement, support; (Intensivierung) intensification; (Technik) amplification
verstauben gather dust, get dusty
verstellbar adjustable
Verstellbarkeit *(f)* adjustability
Verstellfuß *(m)* adjustable foot, leveller foot
Verstellschraube *(f)* adjusting screw
versteuert tax-paid, net of taxes
Versteuerung *(f)* payment of tax, taxation
Verstoß *(m)* (Recht etc.) breach, infringement, offence, violation
verstoßen (Recht etc.) offend against, violate
Versuch *(m)* attempt, experiment, trial; (Test) test
vertagen adjourn, postpone
Vertagung *(f)* adjournment, postponement
verteilen distribute, hand out
Verteilerkasten *(m)* electric distribution box
Verteilung *(f)* distribution, allotment
vertikal vertical
Vertikalfuge *(f)* vertical gap
Vertrag *(m)* agreement, contract, pact, treaty
Vertrag *(m)* **abschließen** make a contract, enter into a contract
Vertrag *(m)* **zur Ausstellungsbeteiligung** exhibition participation contract, fair participation contract, show participation contract

Vertrag *(m)* **zur Messebeteiligung** exhibition participation contract, fair participation contract, show participation contract
vertraglich contractual
Vertragsabschluss *(m)* completion of a contract, conclusion of a contract
Vertragsbedingungen *(f, pl)* conditions of contract, terms of contract
Vertragsbruch *(m)* breach of contract, breach of agreement
Vertragsentwurf *(m)* draft agreement, draft contract
Vertragsinstallateur(in) *(m/f)* official utilities contractor
Vertragspartei *(f)* contract party, contracting party, party to an agreement, party to a contract
Vertragspartner *(m)* partner to a contract, contract party
Vertragsunternehmen *(n)* official contractor, contracting company
vertragswidrig contrary to the agreement, contrary to the contract
vertrauenswürdig trustworthy, reliable
vertraulich confidential, strictly confidential
Vertraulichkeit *(f)* confidence, confidentiality
Vertreter(in) *(m/f)* (Repräsentant(in)) agent, representative; (Stellvertreter(in)) substitute
Vertretung *(f)* (Firma) agency, representation; (Ersatz) replacement
Vertrieb *(m)* (Verkauf) distribution, sales; (Abteilung) marketing department, sales department
Vertriebskanal *(m)* distribution channel, sales channel
Vertriebskosten *(pl)* cost of sales, distribution costs, sales costs, sales expenses, selling expenses
Vertriebsleiter(in) *(m/f)* sales manager

Vertriebsnetz *(n)* distribution network
Vertriebspartner *(m)* sales partner
Vertriebsweg *(m)* distribution channel
verunglücken have an accident
verursachen cause, create
vervielfältigen copy, duplicate
Vervielfältigung *(f)* copy, duplication
vervollständigen complete
Vervollständigung *(f)* completion
verwackeln (Foto) blur
verwahren keep
Verwaltung *(f)* administration
Verwaltungsgebühr *(f)* administrative charge, administrative fee
Verwaltungskosten *(pl)* administrative costs, administrative expenses
Verwarnung *(f)* admonition
verwenden apply, use, make use of, utilize, employ
Verwendungszweck *(m)* purpose of use
verzählen count wrong, miscount
Verzehr *(m)* consumption
Verzeichnis *(n)* directory, list, register
verzögern delay, lag
Verzögerung *(f)* delay, lag
Verzögerungstaktik *(f)* delaying tactics
verzollen pay duty, clear, clear through customs, declare
verzollt duty-paid
Verzollung *(f)* clearance, customs clearance, payment of duty
Verzug *(m)* default, delay
Vibrationsalarm *(m)* vibration alarm
Videoaufzeichnung *(f)* video recording, video cassette recording, videotape recording
Videoband *(n)* videotape
Videoeingang *(m)* (Anschluss) video input
Videofilm *(m)* video film
Videogerät *(n)* video player, video recorder, video set
Videokamera *(f)* video camera
Videokassette *(f)* video cassette

Videokassettenrekorder *(m)* video cassette recorder
Videokonferenz *(f)* video conference, video conferencing
Videoproduktionsgesellschaft *(f)* video production company
Videorekorder *(m)* video recorder
Videosystem *(n)* video system
Videovorführung *(f)* video presentation
Videowand *(f)* video wall
Videowiedergabe *(f)* video playback
Vieleck *(n)* polygon
vielfach multiple
Vielfalt *(f)* variety, great variety
vielseitig (räumlich) many-sided; (Mensch) versatile; (Interessen) varied; (Fähigkeiten) all-round
Viereck *(n)* quadrangle, square
viereckig quadrangular, square
Vierfarbendruck *(m)* four-color printing (US), four-colour printing (GB), four-color process (US), four-colour process (GB); (Bild) four-color print (US), four-colour print (GB)
Vierkanteisen *(n)* square steel bar
vierkantig square, squareheaded
Viertelkreis *(m)* quarter-circle
Viertelseite *(f)* quarter page
V.I.P. *(m/f)* Very Important Person
virtuell virtual
virtuelle Messe *(f)* virtual trade fair
virtueller Markt *(m)* virtual market place
virtueller Raum *(m)* cyberspace
Vision *(f)* vision
visionär visionary
Visitenkarte *(f)* business card, visiting card
visuell visual
Vitrine *(f)* showcase
vollautomatisch fully automatic
vollelektronisch fully electronic
vollenden accomplish, achieve, complete, finish, finalize

vollkommen perfect; (vollendet) accomplished; (vollständig) complete
Vollkosten *(pl)* full cost
Vollkostenrechnung *(f)* absorption costing, full cost accounting, full costing
Vollmacht *(f)* authority, authorization, power, power of attorney
Vollmacht *(f)* **erteilen** authorize
Vollmacht *(f)* **haben** be authorized
Vollständigkeit *(f)* completeness
vollzählig complete
Volt *(n)* volt
Voltmeter *(n)* voltmeter
Voltzahl *(f)* voltage
Volumen *(n)* volume; (Fassungsvermögen) capacity
Vorabend *(m)* evening before, eve
Vorabend *(m)***, am** on the eve
Vorankündigung *(f)* advance notice, previous notice
Voranmeldung *(f)* advance reservation, booking, booking in advance; (Termin) appointment
Voranschlag *(m)* estimate, cost estimate
vorausbezahlt prepaid, paid in advance
vorausplanen plan ahead, preplan
Vorausplanung *(f)* advance planning, foreward planning
Voraussage *(f)* prediction, prognosis, forecast, forecasting
Voraussetzung *(f)* assumption, supposition; (Vorbedingung) precondition, premise, prerequisite, presupposition; (Bedingung) condition, requirement
voraussichtlich expected, prospective; (wahrscheinlich) probable; (vermutlich) presumable
Vorauszahlung *(f)* advance payment, payment in advance, prepayment

Vorauszahlung *(f)* **für Serviceleistungen** advance service charge, advanced payment for services
Vorbemerkung *(f)* preliminary note, preliminary remark, preliminary statement
vorbereiten prepare
Vorbereitung *(f)* preparation
vorbestellen book, order in advance
Vorbestellung *(f)* advance booking, advance order
Vorbestellung *(f)* **von Mitarbeitern** advance booking of staff
Vorbestellung *(f)* **von Standpersonal** advance booking of stand personnel
vorbildlich exemplary
Vordach *(n)* canopy
Vorderansicht *(f)* front view
Vorderfront *(f)* frontage
Vordergrund *(m)* foreground
Vorderseite *(f)* (Stand etc.) front; (Messekatalog etc.) front, front cover
Vordruck *(m)* form
vorführen demonstrate, perform, present; (Film) show
Vorführmodell *(n)* demonstration model
Vorführung *(f)* demonstration, presentation, performance, show
Vorgabe *(f)* (Bedingung) precondition; (Auflage) stipulation; (Ziel) performance target, given data, set data
vorgefertigt prefabricated
Vorgesetzte(r) *(f/m)* chief, superior, boss
Vorhaben *(n)* intention, plan, project
Vorhalle *(f)* entrance hall, vestibule
Vorhang *(m)* curtain
Vorhängeschloss *(n)* padlock
vorherrschend predominant
Vorhersage *(f)* forecast, prediction, projection
vorhersehbar foreseeable, predictable
Vorjahr *(n)* preceding year, previous year

Vorkalkulation *(f)* preliminary calculation, preliminary costing
Vorkasse *(f)* cash in advance, advance payment
Vorkehrung *(f)* precaution
vorläufig interim, provisional
vormachen show how to do
vormerken make a note of, note down
vornehm distinguished, prestigious; (edel) noble
Vorrat *(m)* stock, stockpile, supply; (Lebensmittel) provisions
vorrätig available; (auf Lager) in stock
Vorratsbehälter *(m)* storage container, storage tank
Vorratslager *(n)* stock in the hand, buffer stock
Vorratsraum *(m)* stockroom, storeroom
Vorraum *(m)* anteroom; (Theater etc.) foyer
vorregistrieren preregister
Vorregistrierung *(f)* preregistration
Vorreinigung *(f)* preliminary cleaning
Vorrichtung *(f)* appliance, device, gadget
Vorsatz *(m)* intent, intention
vorsätzlich deliberate, intentional
Vorschaltgerät *(n)* main electrical device
Vorschau *(f)* forecast, preview, prognostication, projection
Vorschlag *(m)* proposal, suggestion
vorschlagen propose, suggest
Vorschrift *(f)* direction, instruction, provision, regulation, rule
vorschriftsmäßig according to the regulations, correct, as prescribed, in due form
Vorschuss *(m)* advance, advance payment
Vorsicht *(f)* care
Vorsicht! Caution!, Take care!

vorsichtig careful, cautious
vorsichtshalber as a precaution
Vorsichtsmaßnahme *(f)* precaution
Vorsitzende(r) *(f/m)* chairman, chairwoman, president
Vorsprung *(m)* (Bau etc.) projection, ledge; (Vorteil) advantage; (Führung) lead
Vorsprung *(m)* **haben** be ahead, have a head start
Vorstand *(m)* board of directors, board of management, managing directors, executive board
Vorstandsmitglied *(n)* member of the board
vorstellen (einführen) introduce; (vorführen) present, show
Vorstellung *(f)* (Einführung) introduction; (Vision) vision; (Theater etc.) performance, showing; (Vorführung) presentation
Vorteil *(m)* advantage, benefit, profit
vorteilhaft advantageous, beneficial, profitable
Vortrag *(m)* lecture
Vortrag *(m)* **halten** give a lecture
vortragen report, present, state
vorübergehen pass, pass by
vorübergehend momentary, passing, transient
Vorverkauf *(m)* advance sale, advance booking
Vorverkaufsstelle *(f)* booking office, advance booking offic
Vorverstärker *(m)* preamplifier
Vorvertrag *(m)* precontract, preliminary agreement, letter of understanding
Vorwahlnummer *(f)* area code, dialling code
Vorwort *(n)* foreword; (Buch) preface
vorzeitig premature, anticipated, ahead of schedule
Vorzugspreis *(m)* bargain price, special price

W

waagerecht horizontal
Wachdienst *(m)* guard, security service, security staff
Wache *(f)* guard
wachen watch, guard
Wachlokal *(n)* guard-house, guardroom
Wachmann *(m)* watchman
Wachpersonal *(n)* security guards
Wachstum *(n)* growth, increase
Wachstumspotenzial *(n)* growth potential
Wachstumsrate *(f)* growth rate
Wächter *(m)* guard, guardian, watchman
Wagenwinde *(f)* lifting jack
Wahl *(f)* choice; (polit.) election
wählen choose, select; (Telefon) dial; (polit.) elect
wahlweise alternatively
Wahlwiederholung *(f)* phone redial
wahrnehmen notice, perceive, observe
Wahrnehmung *(f)* notice, perception, apprehension
Wahrscheinlichkeit *(f)* probability, likelihood, chance
Währung *(f)* currency
Währungsrisiko *(n)* currency exchange risk, foreign exchange risk
Währungsschwankungen *(f, pl)* monetary fluctuations, exchange fluctuations
Wand *(f)* wall
Wand *(f)***, doppelschalige** double layer wall
Wand *(f)***, einschalige** single layer wall
Wand *(f)***, freistehende** self-supporting wall
Wandbau *(m)* wall construction
Wandbreite *(f)* width of wall
Wandeinschubprofil *(n)* wall insert extrusion
Wandelement *(n)* wall element

Wanderausstellung *(f)* touring fair, travelling show
Wandermesse *(f)* touring fair, travelling show
Wandfüllung *(f)* infilling frame, infill panel
Wandleuchte *(f)* wall lamp, wall light
Wandmontage *(f)* wall mounting
Wandplatte *(f)* wall panel
Wandschaukasten *(n)* wall-mounted showcase
Wandschrank *(m)* wall cupboard
Wandstrahler *(m)* wall light
Wandverkleidung *(f)* panelling, wall panelling
Wandverlauf *(m)* wall's path
Wange *(f)* (Treppe) stringboard
Waren *(f, pl)* products, articles, goods, commodities, merchandise
Waren *(f, pl)*, **verderbliche** perishables
Warenangebot *(n)* range of goods
Warenbestand *(m)* inventories, stock on hand, stock in hand, stock of goods
Warengruppe *(f)* product category, product group
Warengruppenverzeichnis *(n)* product group index
Warenlager *(n)* depot, goods depot, warehouse
Warenmuster *(n)* commercial sample
Warenpräsentation *(f)* presentation of the products
Warenprobe *(f)* merchandise sample, trade sample
Warensortiment *(n)* assortment of goods, line of goods, range of goods
Warenverzeichnis *(n)* product index, list of goods
Warenwert *(m)* price of goods
Warenzeichen *(n)* trademark, mark, brand
Warenzeichen *(n)*, **eingetragenes** registered mark, registered trademark
Warenzeichenschutz *(m)* trademark protection

Wärmedämmung *(f)* insulation, heat insulation
Warmhalteplatte *(f)* plate warmer
Warmhalteschrank *(m)* heated cupboard
Warmhaltewagen *(m)* hotplate cart
Warmwasserbereiter *(m)* water heater
Warmwasserspeicher *(m)* hot-water tank
Warnanlage *(f)* warning device
Warnblinkanlage *(f)* warning flasher, warning flasher device
Warnleuchte *(f)* warning light
Warnlicht *(n)* warning light
Warnschild *(n)* danger sign, warning sign
Warnung *(f)* admonition
Warteliste *(f)* waiting list
Warteraum *(m)* waiting room
Wartung *(f)* maintenance, servicing
Wartungsdienst *(m)* maintenance service
wartungsfrei maintenance-free
Wartungsvertrag *(m)* maintenance contract, service contract
Waschbecken *(n)* washbasin
Wäscherei *(f)* laundry
Wäscheverleih *(m)* linen hire
Waschraum *(m)* washroom
Wasserableitung *(f)* water outlet pipe
Wasseranschluss *(m)* water connection, water supply
wasserdicht waterproof, watertight
Wasserhahn *(m)* water tap
Wasserinstallation *(f)* plumbing
Wasserkocher *(m)* water boiler
Wasserleitung *(f)* water pipe
Wasserleitung *(f)*, **flexible** flexible pipe
Wassernebenanschluss *(m)* auxiliary connection, secondary water supply
Wasserrohr *(n)* water pipe
Wasserrücklauf *(m)* water drain, water discharge
Wasserschaden *(m)* water damage
Wasserschlauch *(m)* water hose

Wasseruhr *(f)* water meter
Wasserverbrauch *(m)* water consumption
Wasserversorgung *(f)* water supply
Wasserverunreinigung *(f)* water pollution
Wasserwaage *(f)* spirit level
Wasserzähler *(m)* water meter
Wasserzapfstelle *(f)* water tap
Wasserzuleitung *(f)* water inlet pipe
Watt *(n)* watt
Wattstunde *(f)* watt-hour
Wattzahl *(f)* wattage
Webadresse *(f)* web address
Webdienst *(m)* web service
Webseite *(f)* web site
Wechsel *(m)* (Abwechseln) alternation, change, rotation; (Bank) bill (US), bill of exchange (US), draft (GB), note (GB), paper
Wechselautomat *(m)* change dispenser, change machine
Wechselfestplatte *(f)* interchangeable hard disk
Wechselgeld *(n)* change, small change
Wechselkurs *(m)* exchange rate, rate of exchange
Wechselkursgebühr *(n)* exchange charge
Wechselkursschwankung *(f)* exchange rate fluctuation
wechseln (abwechseln) alternate, change, rotate; (Geld) change, exchange
Wechselrahmen *(m)* interchangeable picture frame
wechselseitig mutual, reciprocal
Wechselstrom *(m)* alternating current (A.C.)
Wechselstube *(f)* exchange office
wegräumen clear away
wegtragen carry away
Wegweiser *(m)* sign, signpost; (in Gebäuden) directory

wegwerfen throw away
Wegwerfgesellschaft *(f)* throwaway society, waste society
Weichzeichner *(m)* (Kamera) soft-focus lens
Weinflasche *(f)* wine bottle
Weinglas *(n)* wineglass
Weinkühlschrank *(m)* wine cooling cabinet
Weinsorte *(f)* sort of wine
Weißwein *(m)* white wine
Weisung *(f)* direction, directive, instruction, order
weisungsgemäß as directed, as instructed
weiterempfehlen recommend
weiterentwickeln develop, develop further
weiterleiten pass on, transmit, forward
Weiterverkauf *(m)* resale
weiterverkaufen resell
Weitwinkelobjektiv *(n)* wide-angle lens
wellenförmig wave-like, wavy
Wellpappe *(f)* corrugated cardboard
Weltausstellung *(f)* world exhibition, world fair
weltbekannt world-famous
weltberühmt world-famous, world-renowned
Weltfachmesse *(f)* world trade fair
Weltfirma *(f)* world-renowned firm
Weltmarkt *(m)* world market, global market
weltweit world-wide, global, all over the world
Weltwirtschaft *(f)* global economy, world economy
Wendefläche *(f)* (Verkehr) turning area
Wendeltreppe *(f)* spiral staircase
Werbeabteilung *(f)* advertising department, publicity department
Werbeagentur *(f)* advertising agency, publicity agency

Werbeaktion *(f)* advertising campaign, publicity campaign, promotional activities
Werbeartikel *(m)* advertising article
Werbeaufwand *(m)* advertising expenditure, advertising expense
Werbeausgaben *(f, pl)* publicity expenses
Werbeaussage *(f)* advertising message
Werbebeilage *(f)* advertising supplement, magazine insert, stuffer
Werbebeitrag *(m)* advertising charge, advertising contribution
Werbebotschaft *(f)* advertising message
Werbebrief *(m)* advertising letter, sales letter
Werbebudget *(n)* advertising budget
Werbeetat *(m)* advertising budget, promotional budget, publicity budget
Werbeetikett *(n)* advertising sticker
Werbefachfrau *(f)* advertising expert
Werbefachmann *(m)* advertising expert
Werbefahne *(f)* advertising flag; (Banner, Wimpel) pennant
Werbefernsehen *(n)* commercial TV
Werbefilm *(m)* advertising film, promotion film, promotional film
Werbefläche *(f)* advertising space, poster panel, poster surface
Werbefunk *(m)* commercial radio
Werbegag *(m)* advertising gimmick, publicity stunt
Werbegeschenk *(n)* advertising gift, promotional gift, free gift, giveaway
Werbegrafik *(f)* artwork, graphic design
Werbehilfen *(f, pl)* sales aids
Werbekampagne *(f)* advertising campaign, publicity campaign
Werbekonzept *(n)* copy platform
Werbekosten *(pl)* advertising costs, advertising expenses, advertising expenditure, publicity expenditure

Werbeleiter(in) *(m/f)* advertising manager, publicity manager
Werbematerial *(n)* advertising material, publicity matter, sales literature
Werbemedien *(n, pl)* advertising media
Werbemittel *(n, pl)* advertising media, means of advertising
werben advertise, canvass, promote, publize
Werbeplakat *(n)* advertising poster
Werbeplan *(m)* advertising schedule
Werbeprospekt *(m)* advertising leaflet, advertising brochure, leaflet, publicity leaflet, publicity brochure, handout
Werberundschreiben *(n)* advertising circular
Werbeslogan *(m)* advertising slogan, publicity slogan
Werbespot *(m)* advertising spot, commercial, commercial spot
Werbespruch *(m)* slogan, advertising slogan
Werbetarif *(m)* advertising rates
Werbetext *(m)* advertising copy, advertising text
Werbetexter(in) *(m/f)* copywriter
Werbeträger *(m)* advertising medium
Werbeversand *(m)* mail-out
werbewirksam effective for advertising purposes
Werbewirksamkeit *(f)* advertising effectiveness
Werbewirkung *(f)* advertising effect, message effect, impact of advertising
Werbezettel *(m)* flyer, leaflet
Werbung *(f)* advertising, promotion, publicity; (Anzeige) ad, advertisement
Werbung *(f)* **im Messegelände** site advertising, advertising on the fair grounds
Werbung *(f)*, **vergleichende** comparative advertising
Werkstoff *(m)* material
Werkzeug *(n)* tool
Werkzeugkasten *(m)* tool box

Werkzeugtasche *(f)* tool bag
Wert *(m)* worth, value
Wertangabe *(f)* declaration of value, declared value
Wertsachen *(f, pl)* items of value, valuables
wertvoll valuable
Wertzeichen *(n)* stamp, postage stamp
Westeuropäische Zeit *(f)* **(WEZ)** Western European Time (WET)
Wettbewerb *(m)* competition, contest
Wettbewerb *(m)* **der Messeveranstalter** competition of exhibition organizers
Wettbewerber *(m)* competitor
Wettbewerbsbeschränkung *(f)* restraint of trade
wettbewerbsfähig competitive
Wettbewerbsfähigkeit *(f)* competitiveness
Wettbewerbsvorteil *(m)* competitive advantage
wetterfest weatherproof
wichtig important, significant
Wichtigkeit *(f)* importance
wickeln (einwickeln) wrap; (umwickeln) wind round
widerrechtlich illegal, unlawful
Widerruf *(m)* cancellation, revocation, withdrawal
Widerruf *(m)* **der Zulassung** cancellation of admission
widerrufen cancel, revoke, withdraw
wiederbeschaffen replace
Wiederbeschaffung *(f)* replacement
Wiederbeschaffungswert *(m)* replacement value
wiedererkennen recognize
Wiedererkennungstest *(m)* recognition test
Wiedergabe *(f)*, **audiovisuelle** audiovisual performance
Wiedergabe *(f)*, **musikalische** music performance
wiederherstellen restore, redress, reestablish
Wiederverkauf *(m)* resale
wiederverkaufen resell
Wiederverkäufer *(m)* reseller; (Einzelhandel) retailer
Wiederverkaufswert *(m)* resale value
wiederverwendbar reusable
Wiederverwendung *(f)* reuse, reutilization
Wiederverwertung *(f)* reutilization, (Wertstoffe) recycling
willkommen heißen welcome
Wimpel *(m)* pennant
Winde *(f)* winch, hoist
Windverband *(m)* windbracing
Winkel *(m)* angle
Winkel *(m)*, **rechter** right angle
Winkel *(m)*, **spitzer** acute angle
Winkeleisen *(n)* angle iron
Winkelelement *(n)* corner link
Winkelkupplung *(f)* right angle coupler
Winkelmaß *(n)* angular measure, square
Winkelmesser *(m)* protractor
Winkelschlüssel *(m)* Allen wrench
winkelverstellbar adjustable of angle
wirksam effective, effectual
Wirksamkeit *(f)* effect, effectiveness, efficiency
Wirkung *(f)* effect; (Eindruck) impression
wirkungslos ineffective
wirkungsvoll effective, efficacious
Wirtschaft *(f)* economy; (gewerblich) trade and industry
wirtschaftlich economic, efficient
Wirtschaftlichkeit *(f)* economic efficiency, cost effectiveness
Wirtschaftsabkommen *(n)* economic agreement, trade agreement
Wirtschaftsbeziehungen *(f, pl)* business relations
Wirtschaftsjahr *(n)* business year, financial year
Wirtschaftslage *(f)* business situation, economic situation
Wirtschaftspolitik *(f)* economic policy
Wirtschaftspresse *(f)* business press

Wirtschaftsverband *(m)* trade association
Wirtschaftswachstum *(n)* economic growth
Wirtschaftszeitung *(f)* business paper
Wirtschaftszweig *(m)* branch of industry, branch of trade, trade, business sector, industry segment
wischen wipe
Wischtuch *(n)* cloth
Wissen *(n)* knowledge; (spezifisch) know-how
wissenschaftlich scientific
wissenswert worth knowing
witterungsbeständig weatherproof
WLAN-Einwahlknoten *(m)* hot spot
wohlbekannt well-known
wohldurchdacht well thought-out
wölben arch, curve
Wölbung *(f)* arch, curvature
Wunde *(f)* wound; (Schnittwunde) cut
Wundpflaster *(n)* adhesive plaster
Wunsch *(m)*, **auf** on request
Würfel *(m)* cube
Würfeleisbereiter *(m)* ice-cube maker, ice-cube machine
Würfeleisspender *(m)* ice-cube dispenser
würfelförmig cubic, cube-shaped
Würfelknoten *(m)* cube-type node
Würfelzucker *(m)* cube sugar, lump sugar
Wurfsendung *(f)* circular mailing piece, door drop
Würstchenwärmer *(m)* hot-dog heater

Z

zahlbar due, payable, due and payable
zählbar countable
zahlbar bei Auftragsvergabe *(f)* cash with order

Zahlenschloss *(n)* combination lock
Zähler *(m)* meter
Zählerstand *(m)* meter reading
zahlreich numerous
Zahlung *(f)* clearance, payment, settlement
Zahlung *(f)* **bei Auftragserteilung** cash with order (C.W.O.)
Zahlung *(f)* **bei Erhalt der Rechnung** payment on receipt of invoice
Zahlung *(f)* **bei Erhalt der Ware** payment on receipt of goods
Zahlung *(f)* **ohne Abzug** net cash
Zahlung *(f)*, **sofortige** prompt payment
Zahlungsabkommen *(n)* payments agreement
Zahlungsanweisung *(f)* order to pay; (Bank) giro transfer order
Zahlungsaufforderung *(f)* request for payment
Zahlungsaufschub *(m)* extension of credit, moratorium, respite
Zahlungsbedingungen *(f, pl)* conditions of payment, terms of payment, payment terms
Zahlungsempfänger(in) *(m/f)* creditor beneficiary, payee
zahlungsfähig able to pay, solvent
Zahlungsfrist *(f)* period of payment, term of payment, time allowed for payment, time fixed for payment, time limit for payment, payment deadline
Zahlungsmittel *(n)* currency, means of payment
Zahlungsmodus *(m)* mode of payment, payment method
Zahlungsort *(m)* place of payment
zahlungspflichtig liable to pay, obliged to pay
Zahlungsschwierigkeiten *(f, pl)* financial difficulties
Zahlungstermin *(m)* date of payment, payment date, payment due date

Zahlungsverpflichtung *(f)* liability to pay, obligation to pay
Zahlungsverzug *(m)* default in payment, failure to pay on due date
Zahlungsweise *(f)* method of payment, mode of payment
Zange *(f)* pliers, pincers
Zapfanlage *(f)* beverage tap system, dispensing tap system
Zapfhahn *(m)* tap
Zarge *(f)* frame; (Türzarge) bricked-in door frame
Zeichen *(n)* sign, symbol; (Hinweis) signal
Zeichendreieck *(n)* triangle (US), set square (GB)
Zeichengenerator *(m)* character generator
Zeichenpapier *(n)* drawing paper
Zeichnung *(f)* drawing; (Illustration) illustration
Zeichnung *(f)*, **maßstabsgerechte** scale drawing
zeigen show; (Film etc.) present; (ausstellen) diplay, exhibit; (anzeigen) indicate; (deuten) point
Zeigestab *(m)* pointer
Zeile *(f)* line
Zeilenpreis *(m)* line rate
Zeitarbeit *(f)* temporary employment, temporary work, temporary job
Zeitarbeiter(in) *(m/f)* temporary worker, (coll.) temp
Zeitarbeitsfirma *(f)* temporary employment agency, temporary help agency, temporary help service
Zeitarbeitskraft *(f)* temporary worker, (coll.) temp
zeitaufwändig time-consuming
Zeitdauer *(f)* duration, period
Zeitdruck *(m)* time pressure, pressure of time
zeitgemäß timely, up to date
Zeitkarte *(f)* season ticket, commutation ticket

Zeitpersonal *(n)* temporary staff
Zeitpersonalvermittlung *(f)* temporary staff recruitment
Zeitplan *(m)* timetable, timescale, schedule
Zeitpunkt *(m)* (Termin) time; (Moment) moment
zeitraubend time-consuming
Zeitraum *(m)* time span, period, period of time
Zeitschaltuhr *(f)* time switch
Zeitschrift *(f)* magazine, journal, periodical
Zeitschriftenbeilage *(f)* magazine supplement
zeitsparend time-saving
Zeitungsanzeige *(f)* newspaper advertisement
Zeitungsausschnittdienst *(m)* clipping service
Zeitungsbeilage *(f)* newspaper supplement, insert
Zeitungswerbung *(f)* newspaper advertising
Zeitverlust *(m)* loss of time
Zeitverschiebung *(f)* time lag
Zeitverschwendung *(f)* waste of time
zeitweilig temporary; (gelegentlich) occasional
zeitweise at times, for a time
Zeltbauten *(pl)* tent constructions, tent structures
Zeltdach *(n)* tent roof
Zentrale *(f)* (Unternehmen) company headquarters
Zentralverwaltung *(f)* (Unternehmen) administrative center (US), administrative centre (GB), head office
zerbrechlich breakable, fragile
Zettel *(m)* piece of paper, slip, slip of paper
ziehen draw, pull, drag
Ziel *(n)* target, goal, objective; (Zweck) aim; (Reise) destination

Zielgruppe *(f)* focus group, target group
Zielmarkt *(m)* target market
Zielpublikum *(n)* target audience
Zielsetzung *(f)* goal setting, objective, objective setting, target; (kurzfristig) short-term objective; (langfristig) long-term objective
Ziffer *(f)* figure, number
Zimmernachweis *(m)* accomodation service
Zimmerreservierung *(f)* hotel reservation, room reservation
Zimmervermittlung *(f)* accomodation service; (Agentur) accomodation agency
Zins *(m)* interest
Zoll *(m)* customs, customs duty
Zollabfertigung *(f)* clearance, customs clearance
Zollamt *(n)* customs house
Zollbegleitpapiere *(n, pl)* customs documents
Zollbehörde *(f)* customs authority
Zollbestimmungen *(f, pl)* customs regulations
Zolldeklaration *(f)* customs declaration, customs report
Zollerklärung *(f)* customs declaration, bill of entry, customs entry
Zollerstattung *(f)* duty drawback
Zollfaktura *(f)* customs invoice
Zollformalitäten *(f, pl)* customs formalities
zollfrei duty-free, tax-free, free of duty
Zollgebühr *(f)* customs duty, customs tariff
Zollkontrolle *(f)* customs check, customs control, customs inspection
Zolllager *(n)* bond store, bonded warehouse
zollpflichtig dutiable, liable to duty, liable to customs duty
Zollrückvergütung *(f)* duty drawback
Zollstock *(m)* folding rule, ruler

Zolltarif *(m)* customs tariff, tariff schedule
Zollverschluss *(m)* customs seal
Zollverschluss *(m)*, **unter** bonded, in bond
Zollvorschriften *(f, pl)* customs regulations
Zollwert *(m)* customs value
Zoomobjektiv *(n)* zoom lense
Zubehör *(n)* accessories, trimmings
Zubehörtasche *(f)* accessory bag
Zubereitung *(f)* preparation
Zubringerbus *(m)* feeder bus, shuttle bus, bus service
Zubringerdienst *(m)* feeder service, shuttle service
Zuckeraustauschstoff *(m)* sugar substitute
Zufahrt *(f)* access, approach
Zufahrt *(f)* **zum Ausstellungsgelände** site access, access to the exhibition grounds
Zufahrt *(f)* **zum Messegelände** site access, access to the fair grounds
Zufahrtstraße *(f)* acces road
Zufall *(m)* accident, chance, coincidence
zufällig accidental, incidental
Zufallsauswahl *(f)* random selection
Zuflussleitung *(f)* supply pipe
zufrieden content, contented, satisfied, pleased
Zufriedenheit *(f)* contentment, contentedness, satisfaction
zufriedenstellen please, satisfy
zufriedenstellend satisfactory
Zugabe *(f)* bonus, bonus pack, free gift
Zugabenangebot *(n)* premium offer
Zugang *(m)* access; (Internet) access point
zugänglich accessible, open to the public; (persönlich) approachable
Zugangsberechtigung *(f)* access authorization
Zugangssperre *(f)* acces barrier

zugelassen authorized, approved
Zugeständnis *(n)* acknowledgement, admission, concession
zugestehen concede, grant; (zugeben) admit
Zugfahrplan *(f)* railroad timetable (US), railway timetable (GB)
Zugluft *(f)* draft (US), draught (GB)
Zugriff *(m)* (EDV) access
Zugriffsberechtigung *(f)* (EDV) acces right, access privileges
Zugriffsmöglichkeit *(f)* (EDV) accessibility
Zugriffszeit *(f)* (EDV) access time
Zugstange *(f)* tensile rod
Zuhörer *(m, pl)* audience
Zuhörer(in) *(m/f)* listener
Zuhörerraum *(m)* auditorium
Zuhörerschaft *(f)* audience
Zukauf *(m)* complementary purchase
zukünftig future, in future, prospective
Zukunftsaussichten *(f, pl)* future prospects
Zukunftsperspektive *(f)* future prospects
Zukunftspläne *(m, pl)* plans for the future
zukunftssicher with a safe future
Zukunftstechnologie *(f)* new technology
zukunftsweisend forward-looking
Zulage *(f)* allowance, bonus, extra pay, premium
zulässig admissible, allowable, allowed, permissible, permitted
zulässige Belastung *(f)* safe load
zulässiges Gesamtgewicht *(n)* license weight (US), licence weight (GB)
Zulassung *(f)* admission, admittance, approval, license (US), licence (GB)
Zulassungsbedingungen *(f, pl)* admission requirements, conditions of admission
Zulassungsbeschränkung *(f)* restriction of admissions, admission restriction

Zulassungsbestätigung *(f)* confirmation of acceptance, confirmation of admission, notification of acceptance, notification of admission
Zulassungsgebühr *(f)* admission fee
Zulassungsvoraussetzungen *(f, pl)* acceptance requirements; (Messe) exhibitor qualification conditions
Zuleitung *(f)* feeding line, supply line; (Rohr) feeding pipe, supply pipe
Zulieferer *(m)* supplier, subcontractor
Zum Wohl! Cheers!
zunageln nail up
Zunahme *(f)* augmentation, increase, rise
zuoberst at the top, on the top, right at the top, right on the top
zurückbezahlen pay back, repay
zurückerstatten refund, reimburse, repay
zurückgeben give back, return
zurückgehen (nachlassen) decline, decrease, go back, go down, retrogress
zurücknehmen take back
zurücksenden send back, return
zurückzahlen pay back, repay, refund; (Schulden) pay off
Zusage *(f)* promise, commitment; (Zustimmung) assent, consent; (Bestätigung) confirmation
zusagen promise; (bestätigen) confirm; (sich verpflichten) commit
Zusammenarbeit *(f)* cooperation
zusammenarbeiten cooperate, work together
Zusammenbau *(m)* assembly, assemblage, fitting together, mounting
zusammenbauen assemble, mount, set up
zusammenfassen summarize, sum up
Zusammenfassung *(f)* recapitulation, sum, summary, conspectus
Zusammenhang *(m)* coherence, connection, context

zusammenklappbar folding, collapsible
zusammenkommen come together, meet
Zusammenkunft *(f)* gathering, meeting
Zusammenschluss *(m)* combination, combining, joining together; (Bündnis) alliance; (Vereinigung, Fusion) amalgamation, merger
zusammenschrauben bolt together, screw together
Zusammensein *(n)* gathering, get-together, meeting
Zusammenstellung *(f)* (Arrangement) arrangement; (Aufstellung) compilation; (Übersicht) survey
zusammenstürzen collapse, tumble down
zusammentreffen (Personen) meet; (Ereignisse) coincide
Zusammentreffen *(n)* (Personen) meeting; (Ereignisse) coincidence
Zusatzausstattung *(f)* additional equipment, add-on equipment, extra equipment
Zusatzgerät *(n)* add-on equipment, attachment
Zusatzkosten *(pl)* additional costs, add-on costs
Zuschauer *(m, pl)* audience
Zuschauer(in) *(m/f)* onlooker, spectator, viewer
Zuschauerraum *(m)* auditorium, demonstration room, presentation room
Zuschlag *(m)* (Aufgeld) additional charge, extra charge, supplementary charge, surcharge
zuschließen lock, lock up
zuschneiden cut to size
Zuschnitt *(m)* cutting
zuschrauben screw shut; (Deckel etc.) screw on
Zuschuss *(m)* contribution, grant, subsidy
zusehen look on, watch

zusperren lock
zuständig competent, in charge, responsible
Zuständigkeit *(f)* competence, responsibility
Zustelldienst *(m)* delivery service, delivery agent
zustellen deliver
zustimmen agree; (billigen) approve, consent
Zustimmung *(f)* agreement, assent; (Billigung) approval, consent
Zutritt *(m)* access, admission, admittance
Zutritt verboten! Off limits!, No admittance!, No entry!
zuunterst right at the bottom
zuverlässig reliable
Zuwachs *(m)* increase, growth, gain
Zuwachsrate *(f)* growth rate, rate of growth, rate of increase
Zuwiderhandlung *(f)* contravention, violation
zwanglos informal, casual, unconstrained; (Verhalten) free and easy
zwangsläufig inevitable
Zweck *(m)* aim, purpose
zweckmäßig practical; (passend) suitable; (nützlich) useful; (funktionell) functional; (vernünftig) rational
Zweigniederlassung *(f)* branch, subsidiary
zweiseitig bilateral
zweitklassig inferior, second-class, second-rate
zweitrangig secondary, second-rate
Zwiegespräch *(n)* dialog (US), dialogue (GB)
Zwinge *(f)* clamp, screw clamp, cramp
Zwischenaufenthalt *(m)* intermediate stop
Zwischenbescheid *(m)* provisional notification

Zwischenboden *(m)* (Regal etc.) intermediate shelf
Zwischendecke *(f)* false ceiling
Zwischenergebnis *(n)* interim result, provisional result
Zwischenfall *(m)* incident
Zwischenlagerung *(f)* in-transit storage, intermediate storage, temporary warehousing
Zwischenpodest *(n)* intermediate pedestal
Zwischenraum *(m)* space; (Lücke) gap
Zwischenreinigung *(f)* interim cleaning
Zwischenstecker *(m)* adapter, adaptor
Zwischenwand *(f)* dividing wall
zyklisch cyclic
Zyklus *(m)* cycle
Zylinderschloss *(n)* cylinder lock
zylindrisch cylindric

2 English – German
Englisch – Deutsch

Part II: English – German
Teil II: Englisch – Deutsch

The English-German part of the dictionary includes the following abbreviations:

Gender labels:　　m – masculine (der)
　　　　　　　　　f　– feminine (die)
　　　　　　　　　n　– neuter (das)
　　　　　　　　　pl – plural (die)

as well as　　　　GB – British English
　　　　　　　　　US – American English

A

a piece pro Stück *(n)*
ability Fähigkeit *(f)*, Können *(n)*, Talent *(n)*
abrasion Abschaben *(n)*, Abschleifen *(n)*, Schürfwunde *(f)*
abridgement Kürzung *(f)*
abrupt schlagartig
absence Abwesenheit *(f)*
absolute absolut, unumschränkt, völlig, vollkommen
absorption costing Vollkostenrechnung *(f)*
acceptance Annahme *(f)*, Einwilligung *(f)*, Zusage *(f)*, Zustimmung *(f)*
acceptance requirements Zulassungsvoraussetzungen *(f, pl)*
access Zugang *(m)*, Zufahrt *(f)*, Zutritt *(m)*; (EDV) Zugriff *(m)*
access authorization Zugangsberechtigung *(f)*
access barrier Zugangssperre *(f)*
access hatch Zugangsluke *(f)*
access road Zufahrtstraße *(f)*
access to the exhibition grounds Zufahrt *(f)* zum Ausstellungsegelände
access to the fair grounds Zufahrt *(f)* zum Messegelände
accessibility Erreichbarkeit *(f)*; (EDV) Zugriffsmöglichkeit *(f)*
accessible erreichbar, zugänglich
accessory Zubehör *(n)*
accessory charges Nebenausgaben *(f, pl)*, Nebengebühren *(f, pl)*
accident Unfall *(m)*, Unglück *(n)*
accident damage Unfallschaden *(m)*
accident insurance Unfallversicherung *(f)*
accident prevention Unfallschutz *(m)*, Unfallverhütung *(f)*
accident prevention regulations Unfallverhütungsvorschriften *(f, pl)*
accident risk Unfallrisiko *(m)*
accident ward Unfallstation *(f)*
accident, industrial Arbeitsunfall *(m)*, Betriebsunfall *(m)*
accidental versehentlich, unabsichtlich, zufällig
accommodate beherbergen, unterbringen
accommodation Unterbringung *(f)*, Unterkunft *(f)*; Einigung *(f)*, Übereinkunft *(f)*; Gefälligkeit *(f)*
accommodation service Quartiernachweis *(m)*
accompany begleiten
accomplish ausführen, erfüllen, leisten, verrichten, verwirklichen, vollbringen, vollenden
accord Abkommen *(n)*, Übereinstimmung *(f)*
accord gewähren, zugestehen; übereinstimmen
accordance Übereinstimmung *(f)*
according to laut, nach, entsprechend, gemäß
according to plan planmäßig
according to the regulations vorschriftsmäßig
according to the rules ordnungsgemäß
according to the statutes satzungsgemäß
account Rechnung *(f)*, Berechnung *(f)*, Etat *(m)*; Konto *(n)*, Guthaben *(n)*; Bericht *(m)*, Rechenschaft *(f)*
account balance Saldo *(m)*
account for Rechenschaft *(f)* ablegen über, Bericht *(m)* erstatten über, etwas erklären
account, final Schlussabrechnung *(f)*
account, itemized spezifizierte Abrechnung *(f)*
accountable verantwortlich
accounting Abrechnung *(f)*
accounting day Abrechnungstag *(m)*

accounting period
Abrechnungszeitraum *(m)*
accumulation Anhäufung *(f)*, Ansammlung *(f)*
accumulator Akkumulator *(m)*, Akku *(m)*
accuracy Genauigkeit *(f)*
accurate exact, genau
ache Schmerz *(m)*, Schmerzen *(m, pl)*
ache schmerzen, weh tun
achieve (Ziel) erreichen; (Ergebnis) erzielen, verwirklichen
aching muscles Muskelkater *(m)*
acknowledgement Anerkennung *(f)*, Bestätigung *(f)*
acknowledgement, written schriftliche Bestätigung *(f)*
acoustic nuisance Geräuschbelästigung *(f)*
acoustics Akustik *(f)*
acquaintance Bekannte(r) *(f/m)*, Bekanntschaft *(f)*
acquire anschaffen, aufkaufen, erlangen, erwerben
acquisition Akquisition *(f)*, Anschaffung *(f)*, Aufkauf *(m)*, Erwerb *(m)*, Übernahme *(f)*
acrylic glass Acrylglas *(n)*
act of God höhere Gewalt *(f)*
acting geschäftsführend, stellvertretend
action for damages Schadenersatzklage *(f)*
activity, commercial gewerbliche Tätigkeit *(f)*
acute-angled spitzwinklig
adapt anpassen
adapter Adapter *(m)*, Passstück *(n)*, Verbindungsstück *(n)*, Zwischenstecker *(m)*
adapter for lighting tracks Stromschienenadapter *(m)*
adapter, multiple Mehrfachstecker *(m)*
adapter, two-way Doppelstecker *(m)*
adapter, universal Universaladapter *(m)*
adaption Anpassung *(f)*, Bearbeitung *(f)*

adaptor Adapter *(m)*, Passstück *(n)*, Verbindungsstück *(n)*, Zwischenstecker *(m)*
adaptor for lighting tracks Stromschienenadapter *(m)*
adaptor, multiple Mehrfachstecker *(m)*
adaptor, two-way Doppelstecker *(m)*
adaptor, universal Universaladapter *(m)*
add hinzuzählen, hinzufügen, hinzusetzen
add up addieren, zusammenzählen
additional zusätzlich, ergänzend
address Adresse *(f)*, Anschrift *(f)*, Aufschrift *(f)*; Ansprache *(f)*, Rede *(f)*
address adressieren, anreden, ansprechen; Ansprache *(f)* halten
address label Adressanhänger *(m)*
address list Adressenverzeichnis *(n)*
address system, public Ausrufanlage *(f)*, Durchsageanlage *(f)*
address, forwarding Nachsendeadresse *(f)*
address, full vollständige Adresse *(f)*
address, gummed Aufklebeadresse *(f)*
address, inaugural Eröffnungsrede *(f)*
addressee Adressat(in) *(m/f)*, Empfänger(in) *(m/f)*
adhere haften, kleben, ankleben, festhalten
adhesive Klebstoff *(m)*
adhesive label Selbstklebeetikett *(n)*
adhesive plaster Heftpflaster *(n)*
adhesive strip Klebestreifen *(m)*
adhesive tape Klebeband *(n)*
adjourn vertagen
adjournment Vertagung *(f)*, Verschiebung *(f)*
adjust abstimmen, anpassen, angleichen, einstellen, regulieren, justieren, richtig stellen, in Ordnung *(f)* bringen
adjustable einstellbar, regulierbar, verstellbar

adjustable of angle
   winkelverstellbar
adjustment   Einstellung *(f)*,
   Regulierung *(f)*, Anpassung *(f)*
adjustment, fine   Feineinstellung *(f)*
adjustment, vertical
   Höhenjustierbarkeit *(f)*,
   Höheneinstellung *(f)*
administration   Verwaltung *(f)*,
   Unternehmensführung *(f)*,
   Unternehmensleitung *(f)*
admission   Einlass *(m)*, Eintritt *(m)*,
   Zutritt *(m)*, Aufnahme *(f)*,
   Eintrittsgeld *(n)*, Eintrittspreis *(m)*
admission card   Eintrittskarte *(f)*
admission fee   Eintrittspreis *(m)*,
   Zulassungsgebühr *(f)*
Admission free!   Eintritt frei!
admission number
   Zulassungsnummer *(f)*
admission pass   Eintrittsausweis *(m)*
admission requirements
   Zulassungsbedingungen *(f, pl)*
admission ticket   Eintrittskarte *(f)*,
   Einlasskarte *(f)*
admission voucher
   Eintrittskartengutschein *(m)*
admit   eingestehen, zugeben,
   zugestehen, gestatten, hereinlassen,
   aufnehmen
admittance   Einlass *(m)*, Eintritt *(m)*,
   Zutritt *(m)*
admittance regulation
   Einlassregelung *(f)*, Zutrittsregelung *(f)*
admittance rules   Einlassregelung *(f)*,
   Zutrittsbestimmungen *(f, pl)*
admonish   ermahnen, warnen,
   verwarnen
admonition   Ermahnung *(f)*, Warnung *(f)*,
   Verwarnung *(f)*
advance   anführen, vorbringen,
   vorrücken, vorankommen;
   vorauszahlen; steigen, ansteigen;
   fördern, befördern, Fortschritte *(m, pl)*
   machen

advance   Anzahlung *(f)*, Darlehen *(n)*,
   Kredit *(m)*; Aufstieg *(m)*,
   Verbesserung *(f)*, Fortschritt *(m)*,
   Vorsprung *(m)*; Erhöhung *(f)*,
   Steigerung *(f)*; Vorschuss *(m)*,
   Vorauszahlung *(f)*
advance booking   Vorbestellung *(f)*,
   Vorbuchung *(f)*, Vorverkauf *(m)*
advance booking office
   Vorverkaufsstelle *(f)*
advance notice   Vorankündigung *(f)*
advance payment   Anzahlung *(f)*,
   Vorauszahlung *(f)*, Vorschuss *(m)*,
   Vorkasse *(f)*
advance reservation   Voranmeldung *(f)*
advance sale   Vorverkauf *(m)*
advanced, highly   äußerst
   fortschrittlich, hochentwickelt
advantage   Überlegenheit *(f)*, Vorteil *(m)*,
   Vorzug *(m)*
advantageous   vorteilhaft
adverse   nachteilig, ungünstig
advertise   ankündigen, anzeigen,
   annoncieren, inserieren, Werbung *(f)*
   betreiben, werben, Reklame *(f)*
   machen
advertisement   Annonce *(f)*, Anzeige *(f)*,
   Inserat *(n)*, Reklame *(f)*, Werbung *(f)*
advertisement column
   Anzeigenspalte *(f)*
advertiser   Inserent(in) *(m/f)*, Anzeigen-
   kunde *(m)*, Anzeigenkundin *(f)*,
   Werbungtreibende(r) *(f/m)*
advertising   Reklame *(f)*, Werbung *(f)*
advertising agency   Werbeagentur *(f)*
advertising article   Werbeartikel *(m)*
advertising budget   Werbebudget *(n)*,
   Werbeetat *(m)*
advertising campaign
   Anzeigenkampagne *(f)*,
   Werbekampagne *(f)*
advertising charge   Werbeabgabe *(f)*,
   Werbegebühr *(f)*, Werbekosten *(pl)*
advertising circular
   Werberundschreiben *(n)*

advertising contribution
   Werbebeitrag *(m)*
advertising copy Werbetext *(m)*
advertising costs Werbekosten *(pl)*
advertising department
   Werbeabteilung *(f)*
advertising effect Werbewirkung *(f)*
advertising effectiveness
   Werbewirksamkeit *(f)*
advertising expenditure
   Werbeaufwand *(m)*, Werbeausgabe *(f)*,
   Werbeausgaben *(f, pl)*
advertising expense
   Werbeaufwendungen *(f, pl)*,
   Werbekosten *(pl)*
advertising expert Werbefachmann *(m)*,
   Werbefachfrau *(f)*
advertising film Werbefilm *(m)*
advertising gift Werbegeschenk *(n)*
advertising gimmick Werbegag *(m)*
advertising journal Werbezeitung *(f)*,
   Anzeigenmagazin *(n)*
advertising manager
   Werbeleiter(in) *(m/f)*
advertising material Werbematerial *(n)*
advertising media Werbemedien *(n, pl)*,
   Werbemittel *(n, pl)*
advertising medium Werbeträger *(m)*
advertising message Werbeaussage *(f)*,
   Werbebotschaft *(f)*
advertising paper Anzeigenblatt *(n)*
advertising poster Werbeplakat *(n)*
advertising rate Anzeigentarif *(m)*,
   Anzeigenkosten *(pl)*, Anzeigenpreis *(m)*
advertising schedule Werbeplan *(m)*
advertising slogan Werbeslogan *(m)*,
   Werbespruch *(m)*
advertising space Anzeigenraum *(m)*,
   Werbefläche *(f)*
advertising spot Werbespot *(m)*
advertising sticker Werbeetikett *(n)*
advertising supplement
   Werbebeilage *(f)*
advertising, camouflaged
   Schleichwerbung *(f)*

advertising, direct-mail
   Briefwerbung *(f)*
advertising, follow-up
   Nachfasswerbung *(f)*
advertising, illuminated
   Leuchtreklame *(f)*, Leuchtwerbung *(f)*
advertising, luminous
   Leuchtreklame *(f)*
advertising, word-of-mouth
   Mund-zu-Mund-Werbung *(f)*
advice Rat *(m)*, Ratschlag *(m)*,
   Beratung *(f)*; Bescheinigung *(f)*,
   Benachrichtigung *(f)*
advice raten, empfehlen;
   benachrichtigen
advice of delivery
   Empfangsbescheinigung *(f)*
advice, legal Rechtsberatung *(f)*
advice, technical Fachberatung *(f)*
advisable ratsam, empfehlenswert
adviser, technical Fachberater(in) *(m/f)*
advisory board Beirat *(m)*
advisory council Beirat *(m)*, beratender
   Ausschuss *(m)*
advocate Anwalt *(m)*, Anwältin *(f)*,
   Fürsprecher(in) *(m/f)*,
   Rechtsbeistand *(m)*
aerial (GB) Antenne *(f)*
aerial connection (GB)
   Antennenanschluss *(m)*
aerosole can Sprühdose *(f)*
aesthetic ästhetisch
affiliated angegliedert, eingegliedert,
   verbunden
affiliated company
   Tochtergesellschaft *(f)*
affiliated firm Zweigfirma *(f)*,
   Zweigniederlassung *(f)*
affirm erklären, bestätigen, versichern
after-effect Nachwirkung *(f)*
after-sales service Kundendienst *(m)*
afterwards danach, später
age group Altersgruppe *(f)*
agency Agentur *(f)*
agency fee Agenturkosten *(pl)*

agency, commercial
  Handelsvertretung *(f)*
agency, forwarding
  Transportunternehmen *(n)*,
  Speditionsfirma *(f)*
agency, sole Alleinvertretung *(f)*
agenda Tagesordnung *(f)*
agenda item Tagesordnungspunkt *(m)*
agent Vertreter(in) *(m/f)*,
  Handelsvertreter(in) *(m/f)*,
  Beauftragte(r) *(f/m)*,
  Bevollmächtigte(r) *(f/m)*,
  Agent(in) *(m/f)*, Repräsentant(in) *(m/f)*;
  Mittel *(n)*, Wirkstoff *(m)*
agent, forwarding Spediteur *(m)*
aggregate Aggregat *(n)*, Anhäufung *(f)*,
  Gesamtbetrag *(m)*, Summe *(f)*,
  Masse *(f)*, Menge *(f)*
aggregate anhäufen, ansammeln,
  sich belaufen auf
agile agil, beweglich, wendig
agree vereinbaren, einwilligen, sich
  einigen, einverstanden sein
agreement Abmachung *(m)*,
  Abkommen *(n)*, Vereinbarung *(f)*,
  Übereinkunft *(f)*, Zustimmung *(f)*,
  Einigung *(f)*, Einverständnis *(n)*
agreement, come to an Abkommen *(n)*
  treffen
agreement, make an Vereinbarung *(f)*
  treffen
agreement, preliminary Vorvertrag *(m)*
agricultural fair
  Landwirtschaftsausstellung *(f)*,
  Landwirtschaftsmesse *(f)*
aid helfen, unterstützen
aid Hilfe *(f)*, Beistand *(m)*,
  Unterstützung *(f)*
aim Absicht *(f)*, Bestrebung *(f)*, Ziel *(n)*,
  Zweck *(m)*
aim at beabsichtigen, bezwecken,
  zielen auf
aimless ziellos
air bill of lading Luftfrachtbrief *(m)*
air booking Flugbuchung *(f)*

air cargo Luftfracht *(f)*
air conditioner Klimagerät *(n)*
air conditioning Klimatisierung *(f)*
air conditioning system
  Klimaanlage *(f)*
air connection Flugverbindung *(f)*
air connection, compressed
  Druckluftanschluss *(m)*
air cooler Luftkühler *(m)*
air fare Flugpreis *(m)*
air freight Luftfracht *(f)*
air freight charges
  Luftfrachtgebühren *(f, pl)*
air freight costs Luftfrachtkosten *(pl)*
air journey Flugreise *(f)*
air journey, inclusive
  Flugpauschalreise *(f)*
air letter Luftpostbrief *(m)*
air parcel Luftpostpaket *(n)*
air passenger Flugpassagier *(m)*,
  Fluggast *(m)*
air route Flugstrecke *(f)*
air shaft Luftschacht *(m)*
air supply, compressed
  Druckluftversorgung *(f)*
air ticket Flugschein *(m)*
air ticket issuing office
  Flugscheinverkaufsstelle *(f)*
air waybill Luftfrachtbrief *(m)*
air, compressed Druckluft *(f)*
air-conditioned klimatisiert
air-cooled luftgekühlt
airing Lüftung *(f)*
airline Fluglinie *(f)*, Fluggesellschaft *(f)*
airline company
  Luftfahrtgesellschaft *(f)*,
  Luftverkehrsgesellschaft *(f)*
airmail Luftpost *(f)*
airport Flughafen *(m)*
airport charges
  Flughafengebühren *(f, pl)*
airport transfer Flughafentransfer *(m)*
air-supported building Traglufthalle *(f)*
airtight luftdicht
aisle Gang *(m)*

aisle number (Messehalle) Gangnummer *(f)*
alarm system Alarmanlage *(f)*
alcohol Alkohol *(m)*
ale englisches Bier *(n)*
ale, pale englisches Bier *(n)*
align in Linie *(f)* ausrichten
alignment Ausrichtung *(f)*
Allen key Inbusschlüssel *(m)*
Allen screw Inbusschraube *(f)*
Allen wrench Sechskant-Schraubenzieher *(m)*, Winkelschlüssel *(m)*
allocate anweisen, zuteilen, zuweisen
allocation of stand space, start for Aufplanungsbeginn *(m)*
allow anerkennen, erlauben, bewilligen, gestatten, gewähren, stattgeben, zulassen
allowance Bewilligung *(f)*, Genehmigung *(f)*, Unterstützung *(f)*, Zuschuss *(m)*; Abzug *(m)*, Nachlass *(m)*, Rabatt *(m)*, Steuerfreibetrag *(m)*
allowance, make an Rabatt *(m)* gewähren
all-purpose Allzweck-
almanac Almanach *(m)*, Kalender *(m)*
alter ändern, sich ändern, sich verändern
alteration Änderung *(f)*, Abänderung *(f)*, Umänderung *(f)*, Umbau *(m)*
alteration fee Änderungsgebühr *(f)*
alternating abwechselnd
alternating current (A.C.) Wechselstrom *(m)*
alternation Abwechslung *(f)*, Wechsel *(m)*
alternative Alternative *(f)*, alternativ
aluminium foil Alufolie *(f)*
ambulance Krankenwagen *(m)*
amendment Änderung *(f)*, Richtigstellung *(f)*
amendment fee Änderungsgebühr *(f)*
ammeter Amperemeter *(n)*

amortization Abschreibung *(f)*, Amortisation *(f)*, Tilgung *(f)*, Rückzahlung *(f)*, Schuldentilgung *(f)*
amount Anzahl *(f)*, Betrag *(m)*, Menge *(f)*, Summe *(f)*
amount to ausmachen, betragen, sich belaufen auf, erreichen
amount, partial Teilbetrag *(m)*
ampere Ampere *(n)*
ampere-hour Amperestunde *(f)*
amplification Verstärkung *(f)*, Ausdehnung *(f)*, Erweiterung *(f)*
amplifier Verstärker *(m)*
amplify verstärken, ausdehnen, erweitern, vergrößern
analog and ISDN telephone connections (US) T-Net ISDN-Anschluss *(m)*
analog telephone connection (US) analoger Telefonanschluss *(m)*
analogue and ISDN telephone connections (GB) T-Net ISDN-Anschluss *(m)*
analogue telephone connection (GB) analoger Telefonanschluss *(m)*
analyse (GB) analysieren
analysis Analyse *(f)*, Auswertung *(f)*, Untersuchung *(f)*
analysis report, structural statischer Nachweis *(m)*
analyze (US) analysieren
anchor ankern, verankern
anchoring Verankerung *(f)*
angle ausrichten, abbiegen, umbiegen
angle Winkel *(m)*, Ecke *(f)*, Seite *(f)*; Aspekt *(m)*, Standpunkt *(m)*
angle connector Gelenkverbinder *(m)*, Gelenkprofil *(n)*
angle iron Winkeleisen *(n)*
angle of inclination Neigungswinkel *(m)*
angle, acute spitzer Winkel *(m)*
angle, connecting Anschlusswinkel *(m)*
angle, right rechter Winkel *(m)*
angular eckig, winklig

angular measure Winkelmaß *(n)*
animated view animierte Ansicht *(f)*, Animation *(f)*
announce ankündigen, ansagen, anzeigen, bekannt geben, durchsagen, melden, verkünden
announcement Ankündigung *(f)*, Ansage *(f)*, Durchsage *(f)*, Bekanntmachung *(f)*
annual Jahrbuch *(n)*
annual jährlich
annual accounts Bilanz *(f)*, Jahresabschluss *(m)*
annual balance sheet Jahresbilanz *(f)*
annual earnings Jahresgewinn *(m)*
annual report Jahresbericht *(m)*, Geschäftsbericht *(m)*
annual sales Jahresumsatz *(m)*
annual statement of accounts Jahresabschluss *(m)*
annual turnover Jahresumsatz *(m)*
annul annullieren; (Anordnung etc.) aufheben, für ungültig erklären
anodized eloxiert
answer Antwort *(f)*, Erwiderung *(f)*
answer antworten, erwidern
antenna (US) Antenne *(f)*
antenna connection (US) Antennenanschluss *(m)*
anticipate antizipieren, erwarten, erhoffen; vorwegnehmen, voraussehen, vorausberechnen, zuvorkommen
anti-glare ring (Lampe) Blendring *(m)*
aperture Kamerablende *(f)*
aperture control, automatic (Kamera) Blendenautomatik *(f)*
aperture setting Blendeneinstellung *(f)*
apologize sich entschuldigen
apparent augenscheinlich, offenbar, scheinbar
apparently anscheinend
appeal, with strong publikumswirksam

appearance Auftritt *(m)*, Aussehen *(n)*, Äußeres *(n)*, Erscheinen *(n)*, Erscheinungsbild *(n)*
appendix Anhang *(m)*, Zusatz *(m)*
applaud Beifall *(m)* spenden
applause Applaus *(m)*, Beifall *(m)*
appliance Apparat *(m)*, Gerät *(n)*, Vorrichtung *(f)*
appliances, electrical elektrische Geräte *(n, pl)*
applicant Bewerber(in) *(m/f)*, Antragsteller(in) *(m/f)*
application Antrag *(m)*, Anmeldung *(f)*, Bewerbung *(f)*, Gesuch *(n)*; Anwendung *(f)*, Verwendung *(f)*, Gebrauch *(m)*
application fee Anmeldegebühr *(f)*
application for admission Aufnahmeantrag *(m)*, Zulassungsantrag *(m)*
application for listing Zulassungsantrag *(m)*
application form Anmeldeformular *(n)*, Antragsformular *(n)*
application to the performing rights society GEMA Anmeldung *(f)* von Musikwiedergabe bei der GEMA
application, make an Antrag *(m)* stellen
apply anwenden, benutzen, verwenden, betätigen
apply for beantragen, sich bewerben um
appoint ernennen, berufen, festsetzen, verabreden, vereinbaren; ausstatten, einrichten
appointment Ernennung *(f)*, Bestellung *(f)*, Anstellung *(f)*, Termin *(m)*, Verabredung *(f)*, Vereinbarung *(f)*; Ausstattung *(f)*
appointment book Terminkalender *(m)*
appointment, make an Verabredung *(f)* treffen
appraise schätzen, abschätzen; taxieren
appreciate anerkennen, schätzen; einschätzen; dankbar sein; würdigen

approach Annäherung *(f)*; Zugang *(m)*, Zufahrtsstraße *(f)*; Methode *(f)*, Verfahren *(n)*
approach herangehen, sich nähern, zugehen auf
approval Anerkennung *(f)*, Billigung *(f)*, Genehmigung *(f)*, Beifall *(m)*, Zustimmung *(f)*
approval stamp Genehmigungsvermerk *(m)*
approval, official amtliche Genehmigung *(f)*
approval, written schriftliche Zustimmung *(f)*, schriftliche Genehmigung *(f)*
approve billigen, genehmigen, zustimmen, einverstanden sein
approved bestätigt, gebilligt, zugelassen
approximate annähernd, ungefähr
architect Architekt(in) *(m/f)*
architect's plan Bauplan *(m)*
architectural architektonisch
area Bereich *(m)*, Gebiet *(n)*, Fläche *(f)*, Raum *(m)*
area code (US) Vorwahlnummer *(f)*, Ortsnetzkennzahl *(f)*
area loading Flächenlast *(f)*
area manager Bezirksleiter(in) *(m/f)*
area, industrial Industriegebiet *(n)*, Gewerbegebiet *(n)*, Industriegelände *(n)*
area, rentable (US) vermietbare Fläche *(f)*
area, usable Nutzfläche *(f)*
argue argumentieren, ausführen, behaupten, darlegen, diskutieren, sich auseinandersetzen, streiten
argument Argument *(n)*; Erörterung *(f)*, Debatte *(f)*
armchair Sessel *(m)*
arrange arrangieren, anordnen, aufstellen, einrichten, ordnen; (Veranstaltung etc.) ansetzen, festsetzen, planen, regeln, umsetzen, verabreden, vereinbaren

arrangement Arrangement *(n)*, Anordnung *(f)*, Gruppierung *(f)*, Ordnung *(f)*; Abmachung *(f)*, Absprache *(f)*, Einigung *(f)*, Vereinbarung *(f)*, Übereinkunft *(f)*; Gebinde *(n)*
arrangement, make an Vereinbarung *(f)* treffen
arrangement, special Spezialarrangement *(n)*
arrangements, make disponieren
arrival Ankunft *(f)*, Eingang *(m)*
art Kunst *(f)*, Geschicklichkeit *(f)*
article Artikel *(m)*, Gegenstand *(m)*, Ware *(f)*; Abschnitt *(m)*, Klausel *(f)*, Paragraf *(m)*
article, mass-produced Massenartikel *(m)*
articles, high-quality Qualitätsware *(f)*
artificial künstlich, gekünstelt
artificial light Kunstlicht *(n)*
artificial plant Kunststoffpflanze *(f)*
artist Künstler(in) *(m/f)*, Könner(in) *(m/f)*
artistic künstlerisch, geschmackvoll
artwork Bildmaterial *(n)*, Werbegrafik *(f)*
as agreed laut Vereinbarung *(f)*
as per agreement vereinbarungsgemäß
as prescribed vorschriftsmäßig
ashtray Aschenbecher *(m)*, Ascher *(m)*
ashtray stand Standaschenbecher *(m)*
assemble montieren, zusammensetzen, versammeln, sich versammeln
assembler Monteur(in) *(m/f)*
assembly Montage *(f)*, Zusammensetzen *(n)*; Versammlung *(f)*, Zusammenkunft *(f)*
assembly instructions Montageanleitung *(f)*
assembly program (US) Montageplan *(m)*
assembly programme (GB) Montageplan *(m)*

assembly regulation Montagevorschrift *(f)*
assembly, final Fertigmontage *(f)*
assess einschätzen, schätzen, bewerten, veranschlagen, feststellen, festsetzen
assessment Einschätzung *(f)*, Bewertung *(f)*, Feststellung *(f)*, Veranlagung *(f)*
assignment Zuteilung *(f)*, Zuweisung *(f)*, Übertragung *(f)*
assignment of the stand Zuweisung *(f)* des Stands, Übertragung *(f)* des Stands
assist helfen, behilflich sein, unterstützen, mitwirken, teilnehmen
assistance Hilfe *(f)*, Unterstützung *(f)*
associate Gesellschafter(in) *(m/f)*, Teilhaber(in) *(m/f)*, Partner(in) *(m/f)*
associate vereinigen, verbinden, zusammenschließen, zuordnen, sich vereinigen, sich verbinden, sich zusammenschließen; assoziieren
associate verwandt, verbündet, beigeordnet
associated company verbundenes Unternehmen *(n)*
association Gesellschaft *(f)*, Vereinigung *(f)*, Verein *(m)*, Verband *(m)*, Interessenverband *(m)*; Gedankenverbindung *(f)*, Assoziation *(f)*
assortment Auswahl *(f)*, Sortiment *(n)*
assumption Annahme *(f)*, Voraussetzung *(f)*
assurance Gewissheit *(f)*, Sicherheit *(f)*, Vertrauen *(n)*, Versicherung *(f)*, Zusicherung *(f)*
assure versichern, garantieren, zusichern
asymmetric asymmetrisch, ungleichmäßig
asymmetrical asymmetrisch, ungleichmäßig

attach anheften, anbringen, ankleben, befestigen; beifügen, beilegen; beimessen, zuschreiben
attachment Befestigung *(f)*, Bindung *(f)*; Anhängsel *(n)*, Beilage *(f)*, Anlage *(f)*, Zusatzgerät *(n)*, Zusatzvorrichtung *(f)*
attempt Versuch *(m)*; (Attentat) Anschlag *(m)*
attempt versuchen, sich bemühen, in Angriff *(m)* nehmen
attend besuchen, begleiten, teilnehmen, anwesend sein, erscheinen; betreuen, pflegen, behandeln
attendance Anwesenheit *(f)*, Besuch *(m)*, Besucher *(m, pl)*, Teilnehmer *(m, pl)*, Zuhörerschaft *(f)*, Beteiligung *(f)*, Begleitung *(f)*, Erscheinen *(n)*
attendance analysis Besucheranalyse *(f)*
attendance list Besucherliste *(f)*
attendance promotion Besucherwerbung *(f)*
attendance statistics Besucherzahl *(f)*
attendant anwesend; begleitend, verbunden
attendant Aufseher(in) *(m/f)*, Wärter(in) *(m/f)*, Begleiter(in) *(m/f)*, Anwesende(r) *(f/m)*
attendees, international Auslandsbesucher *(m, pl)*
attention Aufmerksamkeit *(f)*, Beachtung *(f)*
attentive aufmerksam, zuvorkommend
attestation Bescheinigung *(f)*, Bestätigung *(f)*, Beglaubigung *(f)*, Beweis *(m)*, Zeugnis *(n)*
attraction Attraktion *(f)*, Anziehung *(f)*, Reiz *(m)*
attractive attraktiv, anziehend, verlockend
audible hörbar, vernehmlich
audience Publikum *(n)*, Besucher *(m, pl)*, Hörer *(m, pl)*, Zuhörerschaft *(f)*, Zuschauer *(m, pl)*

audience profile
Besucherstruktur *(f)*
audience qualification
Besuchereignung *(f)*,
Besucherqualität *(f)*
audience rating Einschaltquote *(f)*
audio- Ton-
audio conference
Telefonkonferenz *(f)*
audio mixer Tonmischer *(m)*
audio set Audioanlage *(f)*
audiovisual audiovisuell
audiovisual slide show Tonbildschau *(f)*
audit prüfen
audit Prüfung *(f)*, Buchprüfung *(f)*, Rechnungsprüfung *(f)*
audited show statistics geprüfte Messe- und Ausstellungsdaten *(pl)*
auditing of show statistics
Kontrolle *(m)* von Messe- und Ausstellungszahlen
auditorium Auditorium *(n)*, Zuhörerraum *(m)*, Zuschauerraum *(m)*, Vortragssaal *(m)*
augment aufbessern, steigern, vergrößern, vermehren, zunehmen
augmentation Aufbesserung *(f)*, Ausweitung *(f)*, Vergrößerung *(f)*, Vermehrung *(f)*, Steigerung *(f)*, Zunahme *(f)*
AUMA Ausstellungs- und Messe-Ausschuss *(m)* der Deutschen Wirtschaft e.V. (AUMA)
AUMA fee AUMA-Gebühr *(f)*
authority Autorität *(f)*, Ansehen *(n)*, Befugnis *(f)*, Vollmacht *(f)*, Amtsgewalt *(f)*, Befehlsgewalt *(f)*; Behörde *(n)*
authority to act and sign, limited
Handlungsvollmacht *(f)*
authority, domestic häusliche Befehlsgewalt *(f)*, Hausrecht *(n)*
authority, limited commercial
Handlungsvollmacht *(f)*

authority, local örtliche Behörde *(f)*
authority, without
unberechtigterweise
authorization Befugnis *(f)*, Erlaubnis *(f)*, Ermächtigung *(f)*, Genehmigung *(f)*, Bevollmächtigung *(f)*
authorization, written schriftliche Ermächtigung *(f)*
authorize autorisieren, ermächtigen, bevollmächtigen, bewilligen, genehmigen, Befugnis *(f)* erteilen
automatic automatisch, selbsttätig
automatic, fully vollautomatisch
autumn exhibition (GB)
Herbstmesse *(f)*
autumn fair (GB) Herbstmesse *(f)*
availability Verfügbarkeit *(f)*
available lieferbar, verfügbar
average Durchschnitt *(m)*
average durchschnittlich
average value
Durchschnittswert *(m)*
avoid meiden, vermeiden, ausweichen, aus dem Weg *(m)* gehen; (Strafe etc.) entgehen; (Recht etc.) umgehen
avoidable vermeidbar
award Auszeichnung *(f)*, Preis *(m)*, Verleihung *(f)*; Gutachten *(n)*
award a prize to (Preis) verleihen, prämieren
award to, give an (Preis) verleihen, prämieren
awareness Bekanntheit *(f)*, Bewusstsein *(n)*
awning Plane *(f)*, Markise *(f)*
ax (US) Axt *(f)*, Beil *(n)*, Hacke *(f)*
ax (US) zusammenstreichen, kürzen, abbauen
axe (GB) Axt *(f)*, Beil *(n)*, Hacke *(f)*
axe (GB) zusammenstreichen, kürzen, abbauen
axis, longitudinal Längsachse *(f)*
axle load Achslast *(f)*

B

back Rücken *(m)*, Rückseite *(f)*,
Kehrseite *(f)*, Hinterseite *(f)*,
Hintergrund *(m)*, rückwärtiger Teil *(m)*;
Lehne *(f)*
back rückwärts, zurück; hinter,
rückwärtig; abgelegen, fern;
rückständig
back cover, inside innere
Rückeneinbandseite *(f)*
back door Hintertür *(f)*
back freight Rückfracht *(f)*
back page (Katalog etc.)
Rückseite *(m)*
back payment Rückzahlung *(f)*
back up unterstützen
back view Rückansicht *(f)*
back wall Rückwand *(f)*
backdate rückdatieren
background Hintergrund *(m)*
background music Hintergrundmusik *(f)*,
musikalische Untermalung *(f)*
background noise Geräuschkulisse *(f)*
backlog demand Nachholbedarf *(m)*
backup Rückgriff *(m)*, Unterstützung *(f)*;
(EDV) Sicherung *(f)*, Sicherungskopie *(f)*
backwardness Rückständigkeit *(f)*
backwards rückwärts
badge Abzeichen *(n)*, Kennzeichen *(n)*,
Button *(m)*, Plakette *(f)*
bag Beutel *(m)*, Tasche *(f)*,
Tragetasche *(f)*, Handgepäck *(n)*
bag holder Taschenhalter *(m)*
baggage (US) Gepäck *(n)*
baggage (US), free Freigepäck *(n)*
baggage (US), item of Gepäckstück *(n)*
baggage allowance (US), free
Freigepäck *(n)*
baggage check (US) Gepäckschein *(m)*,
Aufbewahrungsschein *(m)*;
Gepäckkontrolle *(f)*
baggage claim (US) Gepäckausgabe *(f)*

baggage insurance (US)
Gepäckversicherung *(f)*
baggage locker (US)
Gepäckschließfach *(n)*
baggage processing (US)
Gepäckabfertigung *(f)*
baggage ticket (US)
Aufbewahrungsschein *(m)*
bait Verlockung *(f)*, Lockartikel *(m)*,
Lockvogelangebot *(n)*
bait advertising Lockvogelwerbung *(f)*
bait and switch advertising
Lockvogelwerbung *(f)*
balance abwägen, balancieren,
im Gleichgewicht *(n)* halten,
ausgleichen, saldieren
balance Ausgeglichenheit *(f)*,
Gleichgewicht *(n)*; Waage *(f)*; Bilanz *(f)*,
Guthaben *(n)*, Kontostand *(m)*,
Kontoabschluss *(m)*, Saldo *(m)*
balance sheet Bilanz *(f)*
balloon Luftballon *(m)*
balloons, gas-filled gasgefüllte
Luftballons *(m, pl)*
ballpoint pen Kugelschreiber *(m)*
balustrade Ballustrade *(f)*, Brüstung *(f)*
ban verbieten
ban Verbot *(n)*, Sperre *(f)*
band Band *(n)*, Ring *(m)*, Streifen *(m)*,
Leiste *(f)*, Gurt *(m)*; Musikkapelle *(f)*
band zusammenbinden
bandage Bandage *(f)*, Verband *(m)*
band-saw Bandsäge *(f)*
banisters Treppengeländer *(n)*
bank account Bankkonto *(n)*
bank charge Bankgebühr *(f)*
bank code Bankleitzahl *(f)*
bank transfer Banküberweisung *(f)*
banknote (GB) Banknote *(f)*
bankrupt, go Pleite *(f)* machen
bankruptcy Pleite *(f)*
banner Banner *(n)*, Spruchband *(n)*,
Transparent *(n)*
banquet Bankett *(n)*, Festessen *(n)*
banquet hall Festsaal *(m)*

167

bar abgesehen von, außer
bar Stab *(m)*, Stange *(f)*, Riegel *(m)*, Schranke *(f)*, Sperre *(f)*; Bar *(f)*, Theke *(f)*; Büfett *(n)*
bar schließen, verriegeln, zusperren; hindern, untersagen
bar chart Balkendiagramm *(n)*, Säulendiagramm *(n)*, Stabdiagramm *(n)*
bar code Strichcode *(m)*
bar counter Bartheke *(f)*
bar stool Barhocker *(m)*
bar stool with backrest Barhocker *(m)* mit Lehne
bare unmöbliert, leer
bargain Handel *(m)*, Geschäft *(n)*, Geschäftsabschluss *(m)*, Vereinbarung *(f)*; Gelegenheitskauf *(m)*; Sonderangebot *(n)*
bargain handeln, verhandeln, abmachen, feilschen
bargain price Sonderpreis *(m)*, Vorzugspreis *(m)*
barrier Barriere *(f)*, Schranke *(f)*, Sperre *(f)*
base basieren, gründen, stützen
base Basis *(f)*, Ausgangspunkt *(m)*, Grundlage *(f)*, Fundament *(n)*, Fuß *(m)*, Sockel *(m)*; Stützpunkt *(m)*
base gewöhnlich, minderwertig, niedrig
base cabinet Unterschrank *(m)*
base cover plate Sockelblende *(f)*
base line Schlusszeile *(f)*
base year Basisjahr *(n)*, Vergleichsjahr *(n)*
basement Fundament *(n)*, Kellergeschoss *(n)*
basic fundamental, grundsätzlich, grundlegend, prinzipiell
basis Basis *(f)*, Grundlage *(f)*, Fundament *(n)*
batch Stapel *(m)*, Stoß *(m)*
battery Batterie *(f)*
battery charger Batterieladegerät *(n)*
battery operated batteriebetrieben

beam Balken *(m)*, Querbalken *(m)*; (Übertragungstechnik) Richtstrahl *(m)*
beam strahlen, ausstrahlen, senden
beam of light Lichtstrahl *(m)*
bear tragen, ertragen, halten, aushalten, dulden, gestatten, zulassen; (Amt etc.) ausüben; (Zinsen etc.) einbringen; Richtung *(f)* einschlagen; sich stützen, sich drücken
bear the name Namen *(m)* führen
bearing Bedeutung *(f)*, Tragweite *(f)*
bearing capacity Tragkraft *(f)*
bedroom, single Einzelzimmer *(n)*, Einbettzimmer *(n)*
beer Bier *(n)*
beer barrel Bierfass *(n)*
beer bottle Bierflasche *(f)*
beer can Bierdose *(f)*
beer crate Bierkasten *(m)*
beer garden Biergarten *(m)*
beer mat Bierdeckel *(m)*
beer on tap Bier *(n)* vom Fass
beer, bottled Flaschenbier *(n)*
beer, canned Dosenbier *(n)*
beer, dark dunkles Bier *(n)*
beer, draft (US) Bier *(n)* vom Fass
beer, draught (GB) Bier *(n)* vom Fass
beer, light helles Bier *(n)*
behavior (US) Benehmen *(n)*, Betragen *(n)*, Verhalten *(n)*
behaviour (GB) Benehmen *(n)*, Betragen *(n)*, Verhalten *(n)*
behind hinten, hinter, dahinter, nach hinten, im Rückstand *(m)*
belated verspätet
below unten, hinunter, nach unten, abwärts, unter, unterhalb
belt anschnallen
belt Riemen *(m)*, Gurt *(m)*, Gürtel *(m)*
benchmark Benchmark *(f)*, Bezugsmarke *(f)*
benchmarking Leistungsvergleich *(m)*
bend biegen, krümmen, sich biegen, sich krümmen, abbiegen, durchbiegen, knicken, sich neigen

bend Biegung *(f)*, Krümmung *(f)*, Kurve *(f)*
benefit begünstigen, fördern, nützen, unterstützen
benefit Gewinn *(m)*, Nutzen *(m)*, Vorteil *(m)*; Hilfe *(f)*, Beihilfe *(f)*, Unterstützung *(f)*, Sondervergütung *(f)*
beverage Getränk *(n)*
beverage dispensing facility Getränkeschankeinrichtung *(f)*
beverage dispensing system Getränkeschankanlage *(f)*
beverage tap system Getränkezapfanlage *(f)*
bid bieten, Angebot *(n)* machen, sich bewerben
bid Gebot *(n)*, Kaufangebot *(n)*, Übernahmeangebot *(n)*, Offerte *(f)*, Bewerbung *(f)*
bilateral zweiseitig
bill Rechnung *(f)*, Bescheinigung *(f)*; Anschlag *(m)*, Plakat *(n)*; Programmzettel *(m)*; Frachtbrief *(m)*
bill ankündigen, (durch Anschlag) bekannt machen
bill (US) Banknote *(f)*, Wechsel *(m)*
bill of exchange (US) Wechsel *(m)*
bill of lading Ladeschein *(m)*
billboard Anschlagtafel *(f)*, Plakattafel *(f)*
billboard advertising Großflächenwerbung *(f)*
billing Abrechnung *(f)*
bind binden, verbinden, befestigen; verpflichten
binder, loose Schnellhefter *(m)*
binding, generally allgemeinverbindlich
binding, legally rechtsverbindlich
biscuit (GB) Keks *(m)*
black-and-white Schwarzweiß-
blame Tadel *(m)*, Verweis *(m)*, Schuld *(f)*, Verantwortung *(f)*
blame tadeln, Vorwürfe *(m, pl)* machen, die Schuld *(f)* geben
blank weiß, leer

blister pack Schrumpffolienverpackung *(f)*
block aufhalten, blockieren, versperren
block Klotz *(m)*, Hackklotz *(m)*, Richtblock *(m)*; Hindernis *(n)*; Flaschenzug *(m)*
block letter Blockbuchstabe *(m)*
block letters Blockschrift *(f)*
blocking period Sperrfrist *(f)*
blow up aufblasen, aufpumpen, sprengen; (Foto) vergrößern
blueprint Blaupause *(f)*, Entwurf *(m)*, Plan *(m)*, Projektstudie *(f)*
blur unklar, unscharf
blur verwischen, verschwimmen, trüben, undeutlich machen; (Foto) verwackeln
blurred verschwommen, unklar, unscharf
board Brett *(n)*, Diele *(f)*, Tafel *(f)*, Platte *(f)*, Planke *(f)*; Karton *(m)*, Pappe *(f)*; Behörde *(f)*, Ausschuss *(m)*, Beirat *(m)*, Verwaltungsrat *(m)*, Vorstand *(m)*
board täfeln, verschalen
board of directors Vorstand *(m)*, Unternehmensleitung *(f)*, Verwaltungsrat *(m)*, Direktorium *(n)*, Direktion *(f)*
boarding house Pension *(f)*
bodily injury Körperverletzung *(f)*
body Körper *(m)*, Leib *(m)*; Rumpf *(m)*, Karosserie *(f)*; Ansammlung *(f)*, Gruppe *(f)*, Masse *(f)*; Gremium *(n)*, Körperschaft *(f)*, Organ *(n)*
body language Körpersprache *(f)*
boiler, electric Elektroboiler *(m)*
bold mutig, kühn, gewagt; fortschrittlich; ausdrucksvoll; (Druck) fett
bold print Fettdruck *(m)*
bold typeface Fettschrift *(f)*
bolt Bolzen *(m)*, Schraube *(f)* mit Mutter; Riegel *(m)*; Blitz *(m)*
bolt festschrauben, verriegeln, zuriegeln; davonstürzen

bolt nut Schraubenmutter *(f)*
bolt setter Bolzenschussgerät *(n)*
bond Bund *(m)*, Verbindung *(f)*, Verbindlichkeit *(f)*; Obligation *(f)*, Schuldverschreibung *(f)*, Wertpapier *(n)*; Zollverschluss *(m)*
bonus Bonus *(m)*, Extradividende *(f)*, Gratifikation *(f)*, Prämie *(f)*, Sondervergütung *(f)*
bonus pack Zugabe *(f)*
book Buch *(n)*, Geschäftsbuch *(n)*, Block *(m)*, Heft *(n)*
book buchen, verbuchen, notieren, vormerken, vorbestellen, eintragen, reservieren
book in sich anmelden, sich eintragen, reservieren lassen, einchecken
bookkeeping Buchhaltung *(f)*
booklet Broschüre *(f)*, Prospekt *(m)*
bookshelf Buchablage *(f)*
boom Boom *(m)*, Aufschwung *(m)*, Hausse *(f)*, Hochkonjunktur *(f)*; (Kran) Ausleger *(m)*; Ladebaum *(m)*; (Mikrofon) Galgen *(m)*
boom rapide steigen, einen Aufschwung *(m)* nehmen; brausen, hallen, dröhnen
booth Messestand *(m)*
booth, in-line Reihenstand *(m)*
border einfassen, begrenzen
border Einfassung *(f)*, Kante *(f)*, Rand *(m)*, Umrandung *(f)*, Grenze *(f)*
bore bohren, aushöhlen
borer Bohrer *(m)*
borrow borgen, leihen
borrower Entleiher(in) *(m/f)*, Darlehensnehmer(in) *(m/f)*, Kreditnehmer(in) *(m/f)*
bottle Flasche *(f)*
bottle in Flaschen *(f, pl)* füllen
bottle cooling cabinet Flaschenkühlschrank *(m)*
bottle deposit Flaschenpfand *(n)*
bottle opener Flaschenöffner *(m)*
bottle screw Korkenzieher *(m)*

bottle, one-way Einwegflasche *(f)*
bottleneck Engpass *(m)*
bottom, false doppelter Boden *(m)*
bouquet Bukett *(n)*, Blumenstrauß *(m)*
box in eine Schachtel *(f)* packen
box Schachtel *(f)*, Karton *(m)*, Behälter *(m)*, Büchse *(f)*, Gehäuse *(n)*, Kasten *(m)*, Kiste *(f)*; Postfach *(n)*
box spanner Steckschlüssel *(m)*
bracket einklammern
bracket Konsole *(f)*; Träger *(m)*, Stütze *(f)*; Intervall *(m)*; typografische Klammer *(f)*; Steuerklasse *(f)*
bracket support Konsolenträger *(m)*
bracket, inclined Schrägkonsole *(f)*
branch Branche *(f)*, Filiale *(f)*, Geschäftsstelle *(f)*, Niederlassung *(f)*, Sparte *(f)*, Zweig *(m)*, Zweigstelle *(f)*, Abzweigung *(f)*
branch manager Filialleiter(in) *(m/f)*
branch of industry Industriezweig *(m)*
branch of trade Wirtschaftszweig *(m)*, Handelszweig *(m)*, Gewerbezweig *(m)*
branch office Filiale *(f)*, Niederlassung *(f)*
branch, local Filiale *(f)*, Zweigstelle *(f)*
brand Marke *(f)*, Handelsmarke *(f)*, Warenzeichen *(n)*, Fabrikat *(n)*, Sorte *(f)*
brand kennzeichnen, markieren, mit Warenzeichen *(n)* versehen
brand awareness Markenbekanntheit *(f)*
brand image Markenimage *(n)*, Markenprofil *(n)*
brand leader Markenführer *(m)*, Spitzenmarke *(f)*
brand name Markenzeichen *(n)*, Gütezeichen *(n)*
brand recognition Markenwiedererkennung *(f)*
brand, own Eigenmarke *(f)*
brand-new ganz neu, nagelneu
brandy Weinbrand *(m)*

breach Bruch *(m)*, Verstoß *(m)*, Verletzung *(f)*; Bresche *(f)*
breadth Breite *(f)*, Weite *(f)*
break abbrechen, aufbrechen, durchbrechen, zerbrechen, kaputt machen, zerreißen, zerschlagen; (Recht etc.) verletzen
break Bruch *(m)*, Bruchstelle *(f)*, Lücke *(f)*, Riss *(m)*, Sprung *(m)*; Unterbrechung *(f)*, Pause *(f)*; Wende *(f)*; (Text) Absatz *(m)*
break bulk cargo Stückgut *(n)*
break down ausfallen, abbrechen, abreißen, scheitern, versagen, kaputt gehen, eine Panne *(f)* haben
break even kostendeckend wirtschaften
breakdown Ausfall *(m)*, Betriebsunterbrechung *(f)*, Störung *(f)*
breakeven point Break-Even-Punkt *(m)*, Ertragsschwelle *(f)*, Gewinnschwelle *(f)*
breakfast room Frühstücksraum *(m)*
breakproof bruchsicher
brief Anweisung *(f)* geben, einweisen, instruieren
brief Auftrag *(m)*, Instruktion *(f)*; Kurzbericht *(m)*; Schriftsatz *(m)*
brief kurz, kurz angebunden, knapp
briefcase Aktentasche *(f)*, Aktenmappe *(f)*
briefing Briefing *(n)*, Einweisung *(f)*, Instruktion *(f)*
bright hell, leuchtend, strahlend, glänzend; glücklich, heiter; vielversprechend; gescheit, klug
brighten up aufhellen, erhellen, aufheitern, aufpolieren
brightness Helligkeit *(f)*, Leuchtkraft *(f)*, Glanz *(m)*, Klarheit *(f)*; Heiterkeit *(f)*
brilliant brillant, glänzend, geistreich, hell leuchtend
broad breit, weit, ausgedehnt, weitreichend, allgemein; deutlich, klar
broadband cable Breitbandkabel *(f)*

broadband distribution network Breitbandverteilernetz *(n)*
broadcast Rundfunkübertragung *(f)*, Fernsehübertragung *(f)*
broadcast senden, übertragen
brochure Broschüre *(f)*, Druckschrift *(f)*, Prospekt *(m)*
brochure dispenser Prospektspender *(m)*
brochure rack Prospektständer *(m)*, Prospektregal *(n)*
brochure stand Prospektständer *(m)*
broom Besen *(m)*
brush Bürste *(f)*; Pinsel *(m)*
brush bürsten; fegen, kehren
bucket Eimer *(m)*, Kübel *(m)*
buckle Schnalle *(f)*, Spange *(f)*
budget Budget *(n)*, Etat *(m)*, Finanzplan *(m)*
budget budgetieren, Etat *(m)* aufstellen
budgetary control Budgetkontrolle *(f)*
budgetary costs Budgetkosten *(pl)*, Sollkosten *(pl)*, Vorgabekosten *(pl)*
budgeting Budgetierung *(f)*, Finanzplanung *(f)*
buffet, cold kaltes Büffet *(n)*
build bauen, aufbauen, errichten, herstellen
build in einbauen
build up aufbauen; steigern, erhöhen; entstehen
building Bau *(m)*, Bauen *(n)*, Bauwesen *(n)*, Gebäude *(n)*
building authority Bauordnungsamt *(n)*
building component Bauelement *(n)*
building description Baubeschreibung *(f)*
building permission Baugenehmigung *(f)*
building permit Baugenehmigung *(f)*
building plan Bauplan *(m)*
building request Bauanfrage *(f)*
building site Baustelle *(f)*
building specification Baubeschreibung *(f)*

building waste

building waste Bauschutt *(m)*
building, adjoining
  Nebengebäude *(n)*
build-up period Aufbauzeit *(f)*
built-in eingebaut, Einbau-
built-in dishwasher
  Einbauspülmaschine *(f)*
built-in freezer Einbaugefriergerät *(n)*
built-in microphone
  Einbaumikrofon *(n)*
built-in refrigerator
  Einbaukühlschrank *(m)*
built-in spotlight Einbaustrahler *(m)*
bulb Glühbirne *(f)*
bulb, globe-type Großkolbenlampe *(f)*
bulk Masse *(f)*, Menge *(f)*, Größe *(f)*,
  Umfang *(m)*, Volumen *(n)*, Mehrzahl *(f)*
bulk baggage sperriges Gepäck *(n)*
bulk business Massengeschäft *(n)*
bulk buyer Großeinkäufer *(m)*
bulk discount Mengenrabatt *(m)*
bulk goods Schüttgut *(n)*, lose
  Waren *(f, pl)*
bulk mail Postwurfsendung *(f)*
bulk material Schüttgut *(n)*
bulk order Großauftrag *(m)*,
  Sammelauftrag *(m)*
bulk price Mengenpreis *(m)*
bulk purchaser Großabnehmer *(m)*
bulk quantity discount
  Mengenrabatt *(m)*
bulk rubbish Sperrmüll *(m)*
bulk volume discount
  Mengenrabatt *(m)*
bulky sperrig, massig, umfangreich
bulky goods Sperrgut *(n)*
bulky refuse Sperrmüll *(m)*
bulldozer Planierraupe *(f)*
bulletin Bulletin *(n)*, amtlicher
  Bericht *(m)*
bunch Bündel *(n)*, Bund *(m)*,
  Gruppe *(f)*, Haufen *(m)*
burglar Einbrecher(in) *(m/f)*
burglarproof einbruchsicher
burglary Einbruch *(m)*

burglary insurance
  Einbruchsversicherung *(f)*
burglary prevention
  Einbruchsverhütung *(f)*
burn anzünden, brennen, verbrennen,
  versengen
burn Verbrennung *(f)*
burst Ausbruch *(m)*, Explosion *(f)*,
  Bersten *(n)*, Platzen *(n)*
burst bersten, platzen, zerspringen,
  sprengen, aufsprengen, explodieren,
  ausbrechen
burst pipe Rohrbruch *(m)*
bus line Buslinie *(f)*, Busstrecke *(f)*
bus route Busroute *(f)*, Buslinie *(f)*
bus station Busbahnhof *(m)*
bus stop Bushaltestelle *(f)*
business Geschäft *(n)*, Handel *(m)*,
  Gewerbe *(n)*, Betrieb *(m)*,
  Geschäftsbetrieb *(m)*,
  Unternehmen *(n)*, Firma *(f)*;
  Beruf *(m)*, Beschäftigung *(f)*,
  Angelegenheit *(f)*, Aufgabe *(f)*,
  Sache *(f)*, Tätigkeit *(f)*
business acquaintance
  Geschäftsfreund *(m)*,
  Geschäftsbekanntschaft *(f)*
business activity Geschäftstätigkeit *(f)*
business address Geschäftsadresse *(f)*
business associate Geschäftpartner *(m)*
business call Geschäftsbesuch *(m)*
business card Geschäftskarte *(f)*,
  Visitenkarte *(f)*
business conditions
  Geschäftsbedingungen *(f, pl)*
business connection
  Geschäftsverbindung *(f)*
business dealings Geschäfte *(n, pl)*
business executive
  Unternehmensleiter(in) *(m/f)*
business form Unternehmensform *(f)*;
  Geschäftsformular *(n)*
business gain
  Unternehmensgewinn *(m)*,
  Geschäftsgewinn *(m)*

business gift Werbegeschenk *(n)*
business hours Geschäftszeiten *(f, pl)*, Schalterstunden *(f, pl)*
business letter Geschäftsbrief *(m)*
business line Geschäftszweig *(m)*
business lunch Geschäftsessen *(n)*
business outlook Geschäftsaussichten *(f, pl)*, Konjunkturaussichten *(f, pl)*
business paper Wirtschaftszeitung *(f)*, Handelswechsel *(m)*
business press Wirtschaftspresse *(f)*
business profit Geschäftsgewinn *(m)*
business recession Geschäftsrückgang *(m)*
business relations Geschäftsbeziehungen *(f, pl)*, Wirtschaftsbeziehungen *(f, pl)*
business report Geschäftsbericht *(m)*
business sector Wirtschaftszweig *(m)*
business segment Geschäftsfeld *(n)*, Unternehmensbereich *(m)*, Sparte *(f)*
business trip Geschäftsreise *(f)*
business year Geschäftsjahr *(n)*
business, commercial Handelsgeschäft *(n)*
business, domestic Inlandsgeschäft *(n)*
business, main Hauptgeschäft *(n)*, Kerngeschäft *(n)*
business, private Privatangelegenheit *(f)*, Privatsache *(f)*
business, terms of Geschäftsbedingungen *(f, pl)*
businessman Geschäftsmann *(m)*, Kaufmann *(m)*, Unternehmer *(m)*
businesspeople Geschäftsleute *(pl)*
businesswoman Geschäftsfrau *(f)*, Kauffrau *(f)*
busy beschäftigt, geschäftig, fleißig, tätig; belebt
button Knopf *(m)*, Abzeichen *(n)*, Plakette *(f)*
button zuknöpfen
buttress Stützpfeiler *(m)*

buy kaufen, einkaufen, erwerben, anschaffen; (Fahrkarte etc.) lösen
buyer Käufer(in) *(m/f)*, Einkäufer(in) *(m/f)*, Erwerber(in) *(m/f)*
buyer, prospective Kaufinteressent(in) *(m/f)*
buyer, ultimate Endabnehmer(in) *(m/f)*
buyer's pass Einkäuferausweis *(m)*
buyers' show Ordermesse *(f)*
buzz summen, surren, brummen
bypass umfahren, umgehen, umleiten
bypass Umleitung *(f)*, Umgehungsstraße *(f)*
by-product Nebenprodukt *(n)*

C

cab Taxi *(n)*, Taxe *(f)*; Fahrerhaus *(n)*, Führerhaus *(n)*
cab stand Taxistand *(m)*
cabin Kabine *(f)*, Kajüte *(f)*
cable Kabel *(n)*, Leitung *(f)*, Drahtseil *(n)*, Tau *(n)*, Trosse *(f)*
cable verkabeln, telegrafieren
cable bracing Seilverspannung *(f)*
cable clamp Kabelklemme *(f)*
cable clip Kabelbinder *(m)*
cable connection Kabelanschluss *(m)*
cable node Seilknoten *(m)*
cable remote control Kabelfernbedienung *(f)*
cable subtension Seilunterspannung *(f)*
cable support Seilstütze *(f)*
cable suspension Seilabhängung *(f)*
cable tension Seilabspannung *(f)*
cable trench Kabelgraben *(m)*
cable, connecting Anschlusskabel *(n)*
cable, electric Elektrokabel *(n)*
cable, flat Flachleitung *(f)*
cable, high-voltage Hochspannungskabel *(n)*

cafeteria Cafeteria *(f)*,
Selbstbedienungsrestaurant *(n)*
cake Kuchen *(m)*, Torte *(f)*; Stück *(n)*,
Tafel *(f)*, Riegel *(m)*
cakes Gebäck *(n)*
calculate kalkulieren, rechnen,
berechnen, errechnen, durchrechnen,
ausrechnen, veranschlagen
calculation Kalkulation *(f)*, Rechnung *(f)*,
Berechnung *(f)*, Berechnen *(n)*
calculation report, structural statischer
Nachweis *(m)*
calculation, preliminary
Vorkalkulation *(f)*
calculation, rough
Überschlagsrechnung *(f)*
calendar Kalender *(m)*,
Terminkalender *(m)*; Liste *(f)*,
Register *(n)*, Verzeichnis *(n)*
calendar of events
Veranstaltungskalender *(m)*
calendar week Kalenderwoche *(f)*
calendar year Kalenderjahr *(n)*
call Ruf *(m)*, Anruf *(m)*,
Telefongespräch *(n)*; Aufruf *(m)*,
Aufforderung *(f)*, Bitte *(f)*;
Kurzbesuch *(m)*
call rufen, anrufen, aufrufen,
herbeirufen, kommen lassen; kurz
besuchen; bezeichnen, nennen
call back zurückrufen
call box, public öffentliche
Fernsprechzelle *(f)*
call charge Telefongebühr *(f)*
call charge display
Gebührenanzeige *(f)*
call charge indicator
Gebührenanzeiger *(m)*
call for fragen nach
call frequency Besuchshäufigkeit *(f)*
call planning Besuchsplanung *(f)*
call, international
Auslandstelefongespräch *(n)*
call, local Ortsgespräch *(n)*
call, long-distance Ferngespräch *(n)*

callus Schwiele *(f)*
calm beruhigen
calm Ruhe *(f)*, Stille *(f)*, Flaute *(f)*
calm ruhig, still, friedlich, gelassen
calmness Ruhe *(f)*, Stille *(f)*
camcorder Camcorder *(m)*
camera Kamera *(f)*, Fotoapparat *(m)*
camera shot Kameraeinstellung *(f)*,
Kameraaufnahme *(f)*,
Schnappschuss *(m)*
camouflage tarnen, verschleiern
camouflage Tarnung *(f)*,
Verschleierung *(f)*
campaign Kampagne *(f)*, Aktion *(f)*
campaign, follow-up Nachfassaktion *(f)*
campaign, introductory
Einführungskampagne *(f)*
can eindosen
can Kanne *(f)*, Kanister *(m)*,
Konservendose *(f)*, Behälter *(m)*;
Mülleimer *(m)*
can opener (US) Büchsenöffner *(m)*,
Dosenöffner *(m)*
canal Kanal *(m)*
canalization Kanalisation *(f)*
cancel abbestellen, absagen,
annullieren, rückgängig machen,
ungültig machen, stornieren,
abbrechen; (Veranstaltung etc.)
ausfallen lassen; (Zulassung etc.)
widerrufen
cancellation Absage *(f)*,
Abbestellung *(f)*, Annullierung *(f)*,
Aufhebung *(f)*, Auflösung *(f)*,
Entwertung *(f)*, Kündigung *(f)*,
Stornierung *(f)*, Rückbuchung *(f)*,
Rückgängigmachung *(f)*, Streichung *(f)*,
Widerruf *(m)*
cancellation costs Stornokosten *(pl)*
cancellation fee Rücktrittsgebühr *(f)*,
Stornierungsgebühr *(f)*
cancellation of admission Widerruf *(m)*
der Zulassung
cancellation of registration
Zurücknahme *(f)* der Anmeldung

canned eingedost, Büchsen-, Dosen-
canopy Baldachin *(m)*, Vordach *(n)*, Überdachung *(f)*
canteen Kantine *(f)*
cantilever Ausleger *(m)*, Kragarm *(m)*, Konsolenträger *(m)*
cantilever spotlight Auslegestrahler *(m)*
canvass Kunden *(m, pl)* werben, Aufträge *(m, pl)* hereinholen; sich bewerben
canvass Kundenwerbung *(f)*, Werbefeldzug *(m)*
cap Kapsel *(f)*, Verschluss *(m)*, Deckel *(m)*, Aufsatz, *(m)*, Haube *(f)*, Schutzkappe *(f)*
cap mit einer Abdeckung *(f)* versehen
capable fähig, befähigt, geeignet, tüchtig
capacity Kapazität *(f)*, Rauminhalt *(m)*, Fassungsvermögen *(n)*, Volumen *(n)*; Befähigung *(f)*, Fähigkeit *(f)*, Funktion *(f)*, Stellung *(f)*, Leistung *(f)*; Leistungsfähigkeit *(f)*, Tragkraft *(f)*
capital Kapital *(n)*, Grundkapital *(n)*, Vermögen *(n)*; Großbuchstabe *(m)*; Kapitell *(n)*; Hauptstadt *(f)*
capital hauptsächlich, Haupt-, Kapital-
capital goods Anlagegüter *(n, pl)*, Investitionsgüter *(n, pl)*
capital goods exhibition Investitionsgütermesse *(f)*
capital goods fair Investitionsgütermesse *(f)*
capital letter Großbuchstabe *(m)*
caption mit Überschrift *(f)* versehen
caption Überschrift *(f)*, Schlagzeile *(f)*, Titel *(m)*, Kopf *(m)*; Bildunterschrift *(f)*; (Film) Untertitel *(m)*
car hire (GB) Autovermietung *(f)*, Autoverleih *(m)*
car park (GB), multi-storey Parkhaus *(n)*, Hochgarage *(f)*
car park (GB), underground Tiefgarage *(f)*

car park reservation ticket Parkplatzkarte *(f)*
car park ticket Parkplatzkarte *(f)*
car pool Fahrgemeinschaft *(f)*, Fuhrpark *(m)*
car rental (US) Autovermietung *(f)*, Autoverleih *(m)*
car rental service (US) Autovermietung *(f)*
carbon-copy pad Durchschreibeblock *(m)*
card Karte *(f)*, Geschäftskarte *(f)*, Visitenkarte *(f)*; Pappe *(f)*
card index Kartei *(f)*
cardboard Pappe *(f)*
cardboard box Pappschachtel *(f)*, Pappkarton *(m)*, Stülpkarton *(m)*
cardboard, corrugated Wellpappe *(f)*
care sich sorgen
care Sorge *(f)*, Sorgfalt *(f)*, Achtsamkeit *(f)*, Aufsicht *(f)*, Vorsicht *(f)*, Betreuung *(f)*, Fürsorge *(f)*
care for aufpassen auf, sich kümmern um, betreuen
carefree sorglos
careful achtsam, sorgfältig
careless gleichgültig, sorglos, nachlässig, gedankenlos, unachtsam, unvorsichtig
cargo Fracht *(f)*, Ladung *(f)*, Beförderungsgut *(n)*, Transportgut *(n)*
cargo charges Luftfrachtgebühren *(f, pl)*
cargo clearance Frachtabfertigung *(f)*
cargo costs Luftfrachtkosten *(pl)*
cargo, loose Stückgut *(n)*
carousel slide projector Diaprojektor *(m)* mit Rundummagazin
carousel slide tray (Diaprojektor) Rundummagazin *(n)*
carpenter Schreiner(in) *(m/f)*, Tischler(in) *(m/f)*, Zimmermann *(m)*
carpet mit Teppich *(m)* belegen
carpet Teppich *(m)*
carpet adhesive tape Teppichklebeband *(n)*
carpet tile Teppichfliese *(f)*

carpet, reusable Mehrwegteppich *(m)*
carpeting Teppich *(m)*,
 Teppichboden *(m)*
carpeting, off-the-roll
 Teppichbahnenware *(f)*
carriage Beförderung *(f)*, Fracht *(f)*,
 Transport *(m)*, Frachtkosten *(pl)*,
 Frachtgebühr *(f)*, Spediteurkosten *(pl)*,
 Transportgebühr *(f)*, Rollgeld *(n)*;
 Wagen *(m)*
carriage of exhibits Verbringung *(f)*
 von Exponaten
carrier Spediteur *(m)*, Transportunternehmer *(m)*, Frachtführer *(m)*,
 Lufttransportgesellschaft *(f)*; Bote *(m)*,
 Botin *(f)*
carrier's receipt Ladeschein *(m)*
carrying charge Speditionskosten *(pl)*
cart Karren *(m)*, Handwagen *(m)*
carton Karton *(m)*, Pappkarton *(m)*,
 Pappschachtel *(f)*, Zigarettenstange *(f)*
cartridge Patrone *(f)*
case Fall *(m)*, Sache *(f)*, Prozess *(m)*;
 Behälter *(m)*, Gehäuse *(n)*, Tasche *(f)*,
 Hülle *(f)*, Kasten *(m)*, Kiste *(f)*,
 Schachtel *(f)*; Überzug *(m)*,
 Verkleidung *(f)*
case überziehen, ummanteln,
 verkleiden
case study Fallstudie *(f)*
case, illuminated Leuchtkasten *(m)*
case, special Sonderfall *(m)*
cash Bargeld *(n)*, Geldmittel *(n, pl)*,
 Kasse *(f)*, Barzahlung *(f)*
cash kassieren, einziehen, einlösen,
 einwechseln
cash box Kasse *(f)*
cash card Geldautomatenkarte *(f)*
cash cow products ertragsstarke
 Produkte *(n, pl)*
cash desk Kasse *(f)*, Kassenschalter *(m)*
cash discount Skonto *(n)*
cash dispenser Geldautomat *(m)*
cash flow Barmittelfluss *(m)*
cash in advance Vorkasse *(f)*

cash on delivery (C.O.D.) Barzahlung *(f)*
 bei Lieferung, Nachnahme *(f)*
cash on delivery charge (C.O.D. charge)
 Nachnahmegebühr *(f)*
cash on delivery parcel (C.O.D. parcel)
 Nachnahmesendung *(f)*
cash payment Barzahlung *(f)*
cash price Barpreis *(m)*
cash sale Barverkauf *(m)*
cash voucher Kassenbeleg *(m)*
cash with order (C.W.O.) Zahlung *(f)*
 bei Auftragserteilung
cashdesk Kasse *(f)*, Kassenschalter *(m)*
cashier Kassierer(in) *(m/f)*
cashless bargeldlos
cask Fass *(n)*, Tonne *(f)*
castor Laufrolle *(f)*, Transportrolle *(f)*;
 Salzstreuer *(m)*
casual zwanglos, lässig; unerwartet,
 zufällig, gelegentlich, flüchtig
casualty insurance
 Schadenversicherung *(f)*
catalog (US) Katalog *(m)*,
 Verzeichnis *(f)*, Prospekt *(m)*
catalog (US) katalogisieren
catalog (US), free
 Katalogfreiexemplar *(n)*
catalog advertisement (US)
 Kataloganzeige *(f)*
catalog back cover (US)
 Katalogrückseite *(f)*
catalog editor (US) Katalogredaktion *(f)*
catalog entry (US) Katalogeintragung *(f)*
catalog entry (US), basic
 Grundeintrag *(m)* im Katalog
catalog flap (US) Katalogklappseite *(f)*
catalog page (US) Katalogseite *(f)*
catalog price (US) Katalogpreis *(m)*
catalog supplement (US)
 Katalognachtrag *(m)*, Katalogbeilage *(f)*
catalogue (GB) Katalog *(m)*,
 Verzeichnis *(f)*, Prospekt *(m)*
catalogue (GB) katalogisieren
catalogue (GB), free
 Katalogfreiexemplar *(n)*

catalogue advertisement (GB)
  Kataloganzeige *(f)*
catalogue back cover (GB)
  Katalogrückseite *(f)*
catalogue editor (GB)
  Katalogredaktion *(f)*
catalogue entry (GB)
  Katalogeintragung *(f)*
catalogue entry (GB), basic
  Grundeintrag *(m)* im Katalog
catalogue flap (GB)
  Katalogklappseite *(f)*
catalogue page (GB) Katalogseite *(f)*
catalogue price (GB) Katalogpreis *(m)*
catalogue supplement (GB)
  Katalognachtrag *(m)*,
  Katalogbeilage *(f)*
cater Speisen *(f, pl)* und Getränke *(n, pl)* liefern, für Verpflegung *(f)* sorgen, liefern, beschaffen
caterer Cateringunternehmen *(n)*
catering Verpflegung *(f)*, Versorgung *(f)*, Bewirtung *(f)*, Gastronomie *(f)*
catering waste Bewirtungsabfall *(m)*
cause Anlass *(m)*, Grund *(m)*, Motiv *(n)*, Ursache *(f)*, Veranlassung *(f)*, Angelegenheit *(f)*, Sache *(f)*; Prozess *(m)*
cause veranlassen, verursachen, (Schaden) anrichten
caution Vorsicht *(f)*, Warnung *(f)*, Umsicht *(f)*
cautious achtsam, umsichtig, vorsichtig
Cave automatic virtual environment
  Cave-Technik *(f)*, virtuelle Darstellungstechnik *(f)*
CD player CD-Spieler *(m)*
CE mark CE-Zeichen *(n)*
CE symbol CE-Zeichen *(n)*
ceiling (Raum) Decke *(f)*; Höchstgrenze *(f)*
ceiling beam Deckenbalken *(m)*
ceiling cell Deckenelement *(n)*
ceiling construction
  Deckenkonstruktion *(f)*

ceiling floodlight Deckenfluter *(m)*
ceiling lamp Deckenleuchte *(f)*
ceiling lighting Deckenbeleuchtung *(f)*
ceiling mounted spotlight
  Deckenstrahler *(m)*
ceiling panel Deckenplatte *(f)*, Deckenfüllung *(f)*
ceiling panel, square quadratisches Deckenfeld *(n)*
ceiling panel, triangular dreieckiges Deckenfeld *(n)*
ceiling suspension
  Deckenabhängung *(f)*
ceiling, closed geschlossene Decke *(f)*
ceiling, false Zwischendecke *(f)*
ceiling, luminous Lichtdecke *(f)*
cell phone (US) Mobiltelefon *(n)*, Handy *(n)*
cellulose thinner Nitroverdünner *(m)*
center (US) Zentrum *(n)*, Kern *(m)*, Mitte *(f)*, Mittelpunkt *(m)*, Mittelstück *(n)*; Sitz *(m)*, Zentrale *(f)*
Central Office of German Travel
  Deutsche Zentrale *(f)* für Fremdenverkehr
central railway station
  Hauptbahnhof *(m)*
central station Hauptbahnhof *(m)*
centre (GB) Zentrum *(n)*, Kern *(m)*, Mitte *(f)*, Mittelpunkt *(m)*, Mittelstück *(n)*; Sitz *(m)*, Zentrale *(f)*
CEO (chief executive officer)
  Generaldirektor(in) *(m/f)*,
  Hauptgeschäftsführer(in) *(m/f)*,
  Vorstandsvorsitzende(r) *(f/m)*
ceremony Zeremonie *(f)*, Feierlichkeit *(f)*, Festakt *(m)*
certificate bescheinigen, beurkunden
certificate Zertifikat *(n)*, Attest *(n)*, Bescheinigung *(f)*, Bestätigung *(f)*, Urkunde *(f)*, Zeugnis *(n)*
certificate of origin Herkunfts-zertifikat *(n)*, Ursprungszeugnis *(n)*
certificate of vaccination
  Impfzeugnis *(n)*

certification Bescheinigung *(f)*, Beglaubigung *(f)*
certify bescheinigen, bestätigen, beurkunden
chain saw Kettensäge *(f)*
chair bestuhlen; den Vorsitz *(m)* führen
chair Stuhl *(m)*, Sessel *(m)*; Gesprächsleiter(in) *(m/f)*, Vorsitz *(m)*, Vorsitzende(r) *(f/m)*
chair, easy Sessel *(m)*
chairman Vorsitzender *(m)*, Präsident *(m)*
chairwoman Vorsitzende *(f)*, Präsidentin *(f)*
challenge auffordern, herausfordern, verlangen, reizen; bestreiten, bezweifeln, in Frage *(f)* stellen, anfechten, ablehnen
challenge Aufforderung *(f)*, reizvolle Aufgabe *(f)*, Herausforderung *(f)*, Probe *(f)*, Wettstreit *(m)*; Infragestellen *(n)*, Ablehnung *(f)*
Chamber of Commerce Handelskammer *(f)*
Chamber of Handicrafts Handwerkskammer *(f)*
Chamber of Industry and Commerce Industrie- und Handelskammer *(f)*
champagne Champagner *(m)*
champagne flute Sektglas *(n)*, Sektkelch *(m)*
chance Chance *(f)*, Gelegenheit *(f)*, Aussicht *(f)*, Möglichkeit *(f)*, Wahrscheinlichkeit *(f)*; Zufall *(m)*, Wagnis *(n)*, Risiko *(n)*
chance riskieren
chance zufällig
chances of success Erfolgsaussichten *(f, pl)*
change ändern, verändern, verwandeln, austauschen, umtauschen, umwandeln, umschalten; umsteigen; sich ändern, sich verändern; sich umziehen; (Geld, Teile etc.) wechseln

change Änderung *(f)*, Abwechslung *(f)*, Wandel *(m)*, Wandlung *(f)*, Verwandlung *(f)*, Austausch *(m)*, Umtausch *(m)*, Umschwung *(m)*; Kleingeld *(n)*, Wechselgeld *(n)*
change dispenser Wechselautomat *(m)*
change in prices Preisänderung *(f)*
change one's clothes sich umkleiden
changing room Umkleideraum *(m)*
channel Kanal *(m)*, Graben *(m)*, Rinne *(f)*, Hohlkehle *(f)*, Verbindung *(f)*; Rundfunkkanal *(m)*, Fernsehkanal *(m)*
channel kanalisieren, hinleiten
channel of communication Kommunikationsweg *(m)*
channel section Verbindungsteil *(n)*, U-Profilteil *(n)*
character Charakter *(m)*, Wesen *(n)*, Persönlichkeit *(f)*, Gestalt *(f)*, Ruf *(m)*, Eigenschaft *(f)*; Stellung *(f)*, Rang *(m)*; Kennzeichen *(n)*; Schriftzeichen *(n)*, Buchstabe *(m)*; Zeugnis *(n)*
character generator Zeichengenerator *(m)*
characteristic Besonderheit *(f)*, Kennzeichen *(n)*, Merkmal *(n)*
characteristic charakteristisch, typisch
characters Schrift *(f)*
charge Abgabe *(f)*, Anrechnung *(f)*; Anklage *(f)*, Beschuldigung *(f)*, Belastung *(f)*; Einsatz *(m)*, Gebühr *(f)*, Kosten *(pl)*, Preis *(m)*, Taxe *(f)*, Lastschrift *(f)*, Forderung *(f)*; Verpflichtung *(f)*; Aufsicht *(f)*, Überwachung *(f)*; Ladung *(f)*, Lasten *(f, pl)*, Beschickung *(f)*
charge anrechnen, abbuchen, berechnen, in Rechnung *(f)* stellen, belasten; beladen, beschicken; befehlen, fordern, anweisen; anklagen, ermahnen, vorwerfen, verlangen; (Batterie) aufladen
charge for handling Bearbeitungsgebühr *(f)*

charge, additional Aufgeld *(n)*, Aufschlag *(m)*, Aufpreis *(m)*, Zuschlag *(m)*, Zusatzgebühr *(f)*
charge, inclusive Pauschale *(f)*
chargeable gebührenpflichtig, kostenpflichtig, abgabepflichtig, anrechenbar, zu verantworten
charges Aufwendungen *(f, pl)*, Gebühren *(f, pl)*
chart Schaubild *(n)*, Diagramm *(n)*, Übersicht *(f)*, tabellarische Darstellung *(f)*
charwoman Putzfrau *(f)*
chase Nute *(f)*
cheap billig, preiswert, minderwertig
check checken, prüfen, überprüfen, kontrollieren; hemmen, hindern, drosseln, bremsen, zum Stillstand *(m)* bringen
check Kontrolle *(f)*, Prüfung *(f)*, Überprüfung *(f)*; Hemmnis *(n)*, Hindernis *(n)*; Kassenbon *(m)*, Rechnung *(f)*
check card (US) Scheckkarte *(f)*
check in einchecken, sich anmelden, sich eintragen
check list Checkliste *(f)*, Kontrollliste *(f)*
check out (Flug, Hotel), sich abmelden, Hotelrechnung *(f)* bezahlen und abreisen
check-in (Flug, Hotel) Abfertigung *(f)*
check-out Kasse *(f)*; Abfertigung *(f)*
check-up Überprüfung *(f)*
checkroom (US) Garderobe *(f)*, Toilette *(f)*
checkroom attendant (US) Garderobenfrau *(f)*
checkroom ticket (US) Garderobenmarke *(f)*
Cheers! Prost!, Zum Wohl!
Chemical Prohibition Ordinance Chemikalien-Verbotsverordnung *(f)*
cheque card (GB) Scheckkarte *(f)*
chest Truhe *(f)*, Kiste *(f)*, Kasten *(m)*

chest freezer Gefriertruhe *(f)*, Tiefkühltruhe *(f)*
chic schick, elegant
chief Chef(in) *(m/f)*, Leiter(in) *(m/f)*, Vorgesetzte(r) *(f/m)*
chief designer Chefkonstrukteur(in) *(m/f)*
chief editor Chefredakteur(in) *(m/f)*
chief engineer technische(r) Leiter(in) *(m/f)*
chief executive oberste Führungsspitze *(f)*, Generaldirektor(in) *(m/f)*, Hauptgeschäftsführer(in) *(m/f)*, Vorstandsvorsitzende(r) *(f/m)*
chief executive officer (CEO) Generaldirektor(in) *(m/f)*, Hauptgeschäftsführer(in) *(m/f)*, Vorstandsvorsitzende(r) *(f/m)*
chief of protocol Protokollchef(in) *(m/f)*
chiefly besonders, hauptsächlich
chill Kälte *(f)*, Kühle *(f)*
chill kühlen, abkühlen
china Porzellan *(n)*, Porzellangeschirr *(n)*
chip spalten; (Geschirr etc.) lädieren
chip Splitter *(m)*, Scherbe *(f)*, Span *(m)*, Schnitzel *(n)*; (EDV) Chip *(m)*
chipboard Spanplatte *(f)*
choice auserlesen, ausgezeichnet, ausgesucht, ausgewählt, vorzüglich
choice Wahl *(f)*, Auswahl *(f)*, Auslese *(f)*, das Beste *(n)*
choice of location Standortwahl *(f)*
church center (US) Kirchencenter *(n)*
church centre (GB) Kirchencenter *(n)*
cinematic Film-
circle Kreis *(m)*, Ring *(m)*, Reif *(m)*; Wirkungskreis *(m)*, Gebiet *(n)*
circle umkreisen, umfahren, sich bewegen um
circuit Stromkreis *(m)*, Schaltkreis *(m)*, Schaltung *(f)*; Umfang *(m)*, Umkreis *(m)*, Runde *(f)*; Rundgang *(m)*, Rundfahrt *(f)*; Kreislauf *(m)*
circuit umfahren, umkreisen, sich im Kreis *(m)* bewegen

circuit breaker Stromkreisunterbrecher *(m)*, Ausschalter *(m)*
circuit breaker, automatic (Strom) Sicherungsautomat *(m)*
circular Rundschreiben *(n)*
circular rund, kreisrund, kreisförmig
circular letter Rundschreiben *(n)*
circular mailing Wurfsendung *(f)*
circular main Ringleitung *(f)*
circular saw Kreissäge *(f)*
circulate zirkulieren, umlaufen, in Umlauf *(m)* setzen
circulation Auflage *(f)*
circulation, paid Verkaufsauflage *(f)*
circumstance Umstand *(m)*, Umstände *(m, pl)*, Sachverhalt *(m)*, Tatsache *(f)*
city center (US) Stadtzentrum *(n)*
city centre (GB) Stadtzentrum *(n)*
city map Stadtplan *(m)*
city railway (GB) Stadtbahn *(f)*
city sightseeing tour Stadtrundfahrt *(f)*
city tour Stadtrundfahrt *(f)*
claim Anrecht *(n)*, Anspruch *(m)*, Beanspruchung *(f)*, Behauptung *(f)*, Forderung *(f)*; Schaden *(m)*, Klage *(f)*, Reklamation *(f)*
claim beanspruchen, Anspruch *(m)* erheben, behaupten, versichern, fordern, verlangen
claim for damages Schadenersatzanspruch *(m)*
claim for idemnification Ersatzanspruch *(m)*
claim of compensation Entschädigungsanspruch *(m)*, Schadenersatzanspruch *(m)*
claim of settlement Schadenregulierung *(f)*
claim, legal Rechtsanspruch *(m)*
clamp spannen, einspannen, festklemmen, klammern
clamp Klammer *(f)*, Klemme *(f)*, Schelle *(f)*, Zwinge *(f)*
clamping device Spannvorrichtung *(f)*

clamping extrusion Klemmprofil *(n)*
clamping spring Klemmfeder *(f)*
clamp-on floodlight Kragarmleuchte *(f)*
clarify abklären, aufklären, klarstellen, klar werden, sich aufklären
clarity Deutlichkeit *(f)*, Klarheit *(f)*
clasp einhaken, festhaken, zuhaken, ergreifen, fassen, umfassen, umklammern
clasp Haken *(m)*, Klammer *(f)*, Schnalle *(f)*, Spange *(f)*, Schließe *(f)*, Umklammerung *(f)*
classified ad Kleinanzeige *(f)*
classified directory Branchenverzeichnis *(n)*
classified telephone directory Branchentelefonbuch *(n)*
classify klassifizieren, einstufen, aufgliedern, einordnen, sortieren
clause Klausel *(f)*, Vertragsbestimmung *(f)*, Satz *(m)*, Absatz *(m)*, Paragraf *(m)*
clean reinigen, säubern, putzen
clean sauber, frisch, rein, einwandfrei, anständig, tadellos, makellos, vollkommen; schuldenfrei
clean down abwaschen, abwischen, abbürsten
clean out aufräumen, ausräumen, beseitigen
clean up sauber machen, aufräumen, aufwischen
cleaner Reiniger *(m)*, Reinemachefrau *(f)*
cleaners, team of Putzkolonne *(f)*
cleaning Reinigung *(f)*, Säuberung *(f)*
cleaning agent Putzmittel *(n)*
cleaning expenses Reinigungskosten *(pl)*
cleaning lady Reinmachefrau *(f)*, Raumpflegerin *(f)*
cleaning personnel Reinigungspersonal *(n)*
cleaning supply Reinigungsmittel *(n)*
cleaning things Putzzeug *(n)*

cleaning woman Reinmachefrau *(f)*, Raumpflegerin *(f)*
cleaning work Reinigungsarbeiten *(f, pl)*
cleaning, daily tägliche Reinigung *(f)*
cleaning, final Endreinigung *(f)*
cleaning, preliminary Vorreinigung *(f)*
cleaning, special Sonderreinigung *(f)*
clear aufhellen, deutlich werden, deutlich machen; freimachen, räumen, abräumen, säubern
clear klar, hell, heiter, rein, scharf, deutlich; ganz, völlig, vollständig; offensichtlich, verständlich, eindeutig, anschaulich, übersichtlich; frei, offen; zuversichtlich
clear away räumen, wegräumen
clear out ausräumen
clear through customs verzollen
clear up aufräumen, in Ordnung *(f)* bringen
clearance freier Raum *(m)*, lichte Höhe *(f)*, Abstand *(m)*, Zwischenraum *(m)*; Beseitigung *(f)*, Räumung *(f)*, Abfertigung *(f)*; Abrechnung *(f)*, Tilgung *(f)*; Freigabe *(f)*, Genehmigung *(f)*; Verzollung *(f)*, Zollabfertigung *(f)*
clearance height Durchfahrtshöhe *(f)*
clearance, vertical lichte Höhe *(f)*
clearing Clearing *(n)*, Abrechnung *(f)*, Verrechnung *(f)*, Räumung *(f)*
client Auftraggeber(in) *(m/f)*, Kunde *(m)*, Kundin *(f)*
clientele Kundenkreis *(m)*, Kundschaft *(f)*
climate, economic Konjunkturklima *(n)*, Wirtschaftsklima *(n)*
climb Aufstieg *(m)*, Steigung *(f)*
climb steigen, klettern
clip Klammer *(f)*, Büroklammer *(f)*, Halter *(m)*, Schelle *(f)*, Spange *(f)*
clip schneiden, ausschneiden, kürzen, klammern, festklemmen
clip, fixing Halteklammer *(f)*
clipboard Klemmbrett *(n)*

clipping service Presseausschnittdienst *(m)*, Zeitungsausschnittdienst *(m)*
cloakroom (GB) Garderobe *(f)*, Toilette *(f)*
cloakroom attendant (GB) Garderobenfrau *(f)*
cloakroom ticket (GB) Garderobenmarke *(f)*
close Ende *(n)*, Schluss *(m)*, Abschluss *(m)*
close eng, begrenzt, dicht, nah, knapp; gründlich; gespannt; geschlossen, verschlossen
close schließen, abschließen, zuschließen, zumachen, sperren; enden, beenden, einstellen, sich schließen, geschlossen werden, aufhören
close down Betrieb *(m)* zumachen, stilllegen
close of the exhibition Ausstellungsschluss *(m)*
close of the fair Ausstellungsschluss *(m)*
close-up Nahaufnahme *(f)*, Großaufnahme *(f)*
closing (Veranstaltung etc.) Abschluss *(m)*, Beendigung *(f)*, Schließung *(f)*
closing date Schlusstermin *(m)*, letzter Termin *(m)*
closing day Schlusstag *(m)*
closing down Stilllegung *(f)*
closing hour Geschäftsschluss *(m)*, Sperrstunde *(f)*
closing time Geschäftsschluss *(m)*, Sperrstunde *(f)*
closing words Schlusswort *(n)*
closure (Veranstaltung etc.) Schließung *(f)*; (Betrieb) Stilllegung *(f)*
cloth Tuch *(n)*, Stoff *(m)*, Lappen *(m)*
cloth cover Stoffbezug *(m)*
clothe kleiden, ankleiden, einkleiden, anziehen

clothes Kleider *(n, pl)*, Kleidung *(f)*, Wäsche *(f)*
clothes hanger Kleiderbügel *(m)*
clothes rod Garderobenstange *(f)*
clothing out Einkleidung *(f)*
clothing stand Konfektionsständer *(m)*
clue Anhaltspunkt *(m)*, Fingerzeig *(m)*, Hinweis *(m)*
coach Reisebus *(m)*, Eisenbahnwagen *(m)*; Trainer(in) *(m/f)*, Nachhilfelehrer(in) *(m/f)*
coach trainieren, Nachhilfeunterricht *(m)* geben
coat anstreichen, überstreichen; beschichten, bedecken, mit einem Überzug *(m)* versehen, umhüllen
coat Jacke *(f)*, Jackett *(n)*, Mantel *(m)*, Sakko *(n)*; Decke *(f)*; Hülle *(f)*; Anstrich *(m)*; Schicht *(f)*, Überzug *(m)*
coat hanger Kleiderbügel *(m)*
coat hook Kleiderhaken *(m)*
coat rack Garderobenständer *(m)*
coating Überzug *(m)*, Hülle *(f)*, äußere Schicht *(f)*, Belag *(m)*, Anstrich *(m)*, Putz *(m)*
coaxial cable Koaxialkabel *(f)*
cocktail glass Cocktailglas *(n)*
code Code *(m)*, Chiffre *(f)*; Kodex *(m)*, Gesetzbuch *(n)*
code name Deckname *(m)*
code number Kennnummer *(f)*, Kennziffer *(f)*
code of practice Verhaltenskodex *(m)*, Verhaltensregeln *(f, pl)*
co-exhibitor Mitaussteller *(m)*
co-exhibitor charge Mitausstellergebühr *(f)*
co-exhibitor fee Mitausstellergebühr *(f)*
coffee bar Café *(n)*, Imbissstube *(f)*
coffee break Kaffeepause *(f)*
coffee cup Kaffeetasse *(f)*
coffee machine Kaffeeautomat *(m)*
coffee maker Kaffeemaschine *(f)*
coffee pot Kaffeekanne *(f)*
coffee spoon Kaffeelöffel *(m)*

coffee table Couchtisch *(m)*
coffee without caffeine koffeinfreier Kaffee *(m)*
coffee, make Kaffee *(m)* kochen
coin Münze *(f)*
coin slot Münzeinwurf *(m)*
coincide übereinstimmen, sich decken, zusammentreffen, zusammenfallen
coincidence Übereinstimmung *(f)*, Zusammentreffen *(n)*, Zusammenfallen *(n)*, Zufall *(m)*
cold kalt, kühl, unfreundlich, sachlich
cold Kälte *(f)*, Erkältung *(f)*
cold cuts kalter Aufschnitt *(m)*, kalte Patte *(f)*
cold room Kühlraum *(m)*
cold room, portable Kühlzelle *(f)*
cold storage Kühlraumlagerung *(f)*, Kühlhauslagerung *(f)*
cold storage depot Kühlhaus *(n)*
cold storage room Kühlraum *(m)*
cold store Kühlhaus *(n)*
collaborate mitarbeiten, zusammenarbeiten
collaboration Mitarbeit *(f)*
colleague Kollege *(m)*, Kollegin *(f)*
collect sammeln, einsammeln, beschaffen, kassieren, zusammentragen; jmd. abholen; sich versammeln, sich ansammeln
collection Kollektion *(f)*, Sammeln *(n)*, Sammlung *(f)*, Beschaffung *(f)*, Einzug *(m)*, Einkassieren *(n)*, Inkasso *(n)*, Erhebung *(f)*
colloquial speech Umgangssprache *(f)*
color (US) Farbe *(f)*, Färbung *(f)*, Farbton *(m)*
color (US) färben, kolorieren, sich verfärben
color card (US) Farbkarte *(f)*
color chart (US) Farbskala *(f)*
color film (US) Farbfilm *(m)*
color photo (US) Farbaufnahme *(f)*, Farbfoto *(n)*

color photocopier (US)
Farbkopierer *(m)*
color photography (US)
Farbfotografie *(f)*
color print (US) Farbabzug *(m)*,
Farbdruck *(m)*
color printing (US) Farbdruck *(m)*
color proof (US) Farbandruck *(m)*
color range (US) Farbpalette *(f)*
color supplement (US) Farbbeilage *(f)*
color swatch (US) Farbmuster *(n)*
color TV (US) Farbfernsehen *(n)*,
Farbfernseher *(m)*
colored (US) farbig
colorfast (US) farbecht
coloring (US) Farbgebung *(f)*
colour (GB) Farbe *(f)*, Färbung *(f)*,
Farbton *(m)*
colour (GB) färben, kolorieren,
sich verfärben
colour card (GB) Farbkarte *(f)*
colour chart (GB) Farbskala *(f)*
colour film (GB) Farbfilm *(m)*
colour monitor (GB) Farbmonitor *(m)*
colour photocopier (GB)
Farbkopierer *(m)*
colour photography (GB)
Farbfotografie *(f)*
colour print (GB) Farbabzug *(m)*,
Farbdruck *(m)*
colour printing (GB) Farbdruck *(m)*
colour proof (GB) Farbandruck *(m)*
colour supplement (GB) Farbbeilage *(f)*
colour TV (GB) Farbfernsehen *(n)*,
Farbfernseher *(m)*
coloured (GB) farbig
colourfast (GB) farbecht
colouring (GB) Farbgebung *(f)*
column Säule *(f)*, Spalte *(f)*
column, luminous Lichtsäule *(f)*
combination Kombination *(f)*,
Zusammensetzung *(f)*,
Zusammenwirken *(n)*,
Zusammenschluss *(m)*,
Verbindung *(f)*, Verband *(m)*

combination freezer-refrigeration
Kühl-/Gefrierkombination *(f)*,
Kühl-/Gefriergerät *(n)*
combination lock Zahlenschloss *(n)*
combustible brennbar, entzündlich
comfort beruhigen
comfort Komfort *(m)*,
Bequemlichkeit *(f)*, Behaglichkeit *(f)*;
Hilfe *(f)*, Beruhigung *(f)*
comfortable komfortabel, behaglich,
bequem; sorgenfrei
comment bemerken, äußern
comment Kommentar *(m)*,
Bemerkung *(f)*, Stellungnahme *(f)*,
Erklärung *(f)*
commentary Kommentar *(m)*
commerce Handel *(m)*,
Handelsverkehr *(m)*,
Geschäftsverkehr *(m)*
commercial Funkwerbung *(f)*,
Fernsehwerbung *(f)*, Werbespot *(m)*
commercial kommerziell, geschäftlich,
geschäftsmäßig, gewerblich,
kaufmännisch, wirtschaftlich
commercialize auf den Markt *(m)*
bringen, vermarkten
commercially viable rentabel
commission beauftragen, in Auftrag *(m)*
geben, bestellen, ermächtigen,
bevollmächtigen
commission Kommission *(f)*,
Gremium *(n)*, Ausschuss *(m)*;
Auftrag *(m)*, Bestellung *(f)*, Order *(f)*,
Instruktion *(f)*, Funktion *(f)*;
Provision *(f)*
commit anvertrauen, übergeben,
verpflichten, festlegen; (Tat) begehen
commitment Verpflichtung *(f)*,
Festlegung *(f)*, Engagement *(n)*;
Verbindlichkeit *(f)*, Verbundenheit *(f)*,
Zusage *(f)*
committee Komitee *(n)*, Ausschuss *(m)*,
Gremium *(n)*, Kommission *(f)*
committee member Komitee-
mitglied *(n)*, Ausschussmitglied *(n)*

commodities Waren *(f, pl)*,
Produkte *(n, pl)*, Rohstoffe *(m, pl)*
common gemeinsam, gemeinschaftlich;
allgemein, öffentlich, alltäglich, häufig,
gewöhnlich
communication Kommunikation *(f)*,
Mitteilung *(f)*, Nachricht *(f)*,
Unterredung *(f)*, Besprechung *(f)*,
Übertragung *(f)*, Verbindung *(f)*
companies represented
Firmenvertretungen *(f, pl)*
company Firma *(f)*, Gesellschaft *(f)*,
Unternehmen *(n)*; Begleitung *(f)*,
Besuch *(m)*, Gäste *(m, pl)*,
Umgang *(m)*
company details Firmenangaben *(f, pl)*
company entry, basic
Firmengrundeintrag *(m)*
company figures
Unternehmensdaten *(pl)*
company headquarters Firmensitz *(m)*,
Firmenzentrale *(f)*, Stammhaus *(n)*
company logo Firmenlogo *(n)*
company name Firmenname *(m)*
company objective
Unternehmensziel *(n)*
company portrait Firmenporträt *(n)*
company profile Firmenprofil *(n)*
company results
Geschäftsergebnis *(n)*
company strategy
Unternehmensstrategie *(f)*
company trading result
Betriebsergebnis *(n)*,
Geschäftsergebnis *(n)*,
Handelsergebnis *(f)*
company website
Firmenhomepage *(f)*
company, additionally represented
zusätzlich vertretenes Unternehmen *(n)*
company, commercial
Handelsgesellschaft *(f)*
company, forwarding
Transportunternehmen *(n)*,
Speditionsfirma *(f)*

company, private
Privatunternehmen *(n)*, Gesellschaft *(f)*
mit beschränkter Haftung (GmbH)
company's report Geschäftsbericht *(m)*
comparability Vergleichbarkeit *(f)*
comparative vergleichend, relativ,
verhältnismäßig
comparative advertising
vergleichende Werbung *(f)*
comparative figure Vergleichszahl *(f)*
comparatively vergleichsweise
compare vergleichen, sich vergleichen,
sich vergleichen lassen, gleichsetzen,
auf eine Stufe *(f)* stellen
compared to im Vergleich *(m)* zu
comparison Vergleich *(m)*
comparison with, in im Vergleich *(m)* zu
compatibility Kompatibilität *(f)*,
Vereinbarkeit *(f)*, Verträglichkeit *(f)*
compensation Kompensation *(f)*,
Ausgleich *(m)*, Ersatz *(m)*,
Schadenersatz *(m)*, Entschädigung *(f)*;
Vergütung *(f)*, Entlohnung *(f)*
compensation for immaterial damage
Schmerzensgeld *(n)*
compensation for non-pecunary
damage Schmerzensgeld *(n)*
compensation for personal suffering
Schmerzensgeld *(n)*
compete konkurrieren, wetteifern,
rivalisieren
competence Kompetenz *(f)*,
Befähigung *(f)*, Geschick *(n)*,
Können *(n)*, Qualifikation *(f)*,
Zuständigkeit *(f)*
competent kompetent, fähig, geschickt,
qualifiziert, zuständig
competent to contract
geschäftsfähig
competent, legally geschäftsfähig
competing product
Konkurrenzprodukt *(n)*
competition Wettbewerb *(m)*,
Konkurrenz *(f)*, Konkurrenzkampf *(m)*,
Preisausschreiben *(n)*

competition of exhibition organizers
Wettbewerb *(m)* der Messeveranstalter
competition, crowding-out
Verdrängungswettbewerb *(m)*
competition, cutthroat ruinöse
Konkurrenz *(f)*,
Verdrängungswettbewerb *(m)*
competition, destructive
Verdrängungswettbewerb *(m)*
competitive konkurrierend,
konkurrenzfähig, wettbewerbsfähig
competitive advantage
Wettbewerbsvorteil *(m)*
competitiveness
Konkurrenzfähigkeit *(f)*
competitor Mitbewerber(in) *(m/f)*,
Konkurrent(in) *(m/f)*
compilation Aufstellung *(f)*,
Verzeichnis *(n)*
compile zusammenstellen,
zusammentragen
complain klagen, sich beklagen,
reklamieren
complaint Beanstandung *(f)*,
Beschwerde *(f)*, Reklamation *(f)*
complementary ergänzend,
sich ergänzend
complete abschließen, beenden, fertig
stellen, vollenden, vervollständigen;
(Formular) ausfüllen
complete komplett, vollständig,
vollkommen, vollzählig, völlig, ganz,
beendet, vollendet
completion Fertigstellung *(f)*,
Vervollständigung *(f)*, Abschluss *(m)*,
Erledigung *(f)*, Ergänzung *(f)*,
Erfüllung *(f)*; (Formular) Ausfüllung *(f)*
complicate komplizieren, schwieriger
machen
complication Komplikation *(f)*,
Kompliziertheit *(f)*
component einzeln, Einzel-, Teil-
component Komponente *(f)*,
Bestandteil *(m)*, Bauteil *(n)*,
Werkstück *(n)*

composition Anordnung *(f)*,
Gestaltung *(f)*, Komposition *(f)*,
Zusammensetzung *(f)*
compress komprimieren,
zusammendrücken, pressen
compressor Kompressor *(m)*
compulsory bindend, obligatorisch,
zwingend
computer Computer *(m)*, Rechner *(m)*,
Datenverarbeitungsanlage *(f)*
computer center (US)
Rechenzentrum *(n)*
computer centre (GB)
Rechenzentrum *(n)*
computer file Computerdatei *(f)*
computer graphics
Computergrafik *(f)*
computer language
Computersprache *(f)*
computer listing
Computerausdruck *(m)*
computer program
Computerprogramm *(n)*
computer time Rechnerzeit *(f)*
computer typesetting
Computersatz *(m)*
computer virus Computervirus *(m)*
computer-aided computergestützt,
rechnergestützt
computer-aided design (CAD)
rechnergestützte Entwicklung *(f)*,
rechnergestützte Konstruktion *(f)*,
rechnergestützte Zeichnung *(f)*
computer-controlled
computergesteuert,
rechnergesteuert
computer-cut types
computergeschnittene
Schriften *(f, pl)*
computer-readable maschinenlesbar
computing speed
Rechnergeschwindigkeit *(f)*
concede anerkennen, einräumen,
zugestehen, nachgeben, sich
geschlagen geben

concentrate Konzentrat *(n)*
concentrate konzentrieren, verdichten, bündeln; sich konzentrieren, sich sammeln
concentrated load Punktlast *(f)*
concept Plan *(m)*, Entwurf *(m)*, Idee *(f)*, Gedanke *(m)*, Vorstellung *(f)*
conception Plan *(m)*, Entwurf *(m)*, Idee *(f)*, Gedanke *(m)*, Begriff *(m)*, Vorstellung *(f)*, Konzept *(n)*
concern angehen, betreffen
concern Angelegenheit *(f)*, Geschäft *(n)*; Unternehmen *(n)*
concession Bewilligung *(f)*, Genehmigung *(f)*, Konzession *(f)*, Entgegenkommen *(n)*, Zugeständnis *(n)*
conclusion Abschluss *(m)*, Schluss *(m)*, Beendigung *(f)*, Beschluss *(m)*; Rückschluss *(m)*, Entscheidung *(f)*, Folgerung *(f)*
condenser Verflüssiger *(m)*
condensing unit Verflüssigungssatz *(m)*
condition Bedingung *(f)*, Voraussetzung *(f)*, Beschaffenheit *(f)*, Zustand *(m)*; Stellung *(f)*, Rang *(m)*
condition bestimmen, regeln, zur Bedingung *(f)* machen; in Form *(f)* bringen
conditions for participation, acceptance of the Anerkennung *(f)* der Teilnahmebedingungen
conditions for participation, general section of the allgemeiner Teil *(m)* der Teilnahmebedingungen
conditions of admission Zulassungsbedingungen *(f, pl)*
conditions of contract Vertragsbedingungen *(f, pl)*
conditions of participation Teilnahmebedingungen *(f, pl)*
conditions of participation, basic grundsätzliche Teilnahmebedingungen *(f, pl)*
conditions of participation, general allgemeine Teilnahmebedingungen *(f, pl)*
conditions of participation, special besondere Teilnahmebedingungen *(f, pl)*
conditions, basic Rahmenbedingungen *(f, pl)*
conditions, economic Konjunkturlage *(f)*, Wirtschaftslage *(f)*
conditions, special Sonderkonditionen *(f, pl)*
conductive leitfähig, leitend
conduit box Abzweigdose *(f)*
conference Konferenz *(f)*, Tagung *(f)*, Sitzung *(f)*, Besprechung *(f)*, Verhandlung *(f)*
conference and exhibition Ausstellungstagung *(f)*
conference cabin Besprechungskabine *(f)*
conference circuit Konferenzschaltung *(f)*
conference hall Tagungshalle *(f)*, Sitzungssaal *(m)*
conference room Tagungsraum *(m)*, Sitzungsraum *(m)*
confidence Vertrauen *(n)*, Zutrauen *(n)*, Zuversicht *(f)*; Geheimnis *(f)*, vertrauliche Mitteilung *(f)*
confidential geheim, vertraulich, vertraut
confirm bestätigen, bekräftigen, bestärken, festigen
confirmation Bestätigung *(f)*, Bekräftigung *(f)*, Bestärkung *(f)*, Billigung *(f)*
confirmation of admission Zulassungsbestätigung *(f)*
confirmation of participation Teilnahmebestätigung *(f)*
conformity Übereinstimmung *(f)*
confusion Durcheinander *(n)*, Verwirrung *(f)*, Verwechslung *(f)*, Tumult *(m)*

congestion Anhäufung *(f)*, Überfüllung *(f)*, Stockung *(f)*, Verstopfung *(f)*
conglomerate Mischkonzern *(m)*
conglomerate verschmelzen, sich zusammenballen
congress Kongress *(m)*, Tagung *(f)*, Zusammenkunft *(f)*
congress and exhibition Kongressausstellung *(f)*
congress program (US) Kongressprogramm *(n)*
congress programme (GB) Kongressprogramm *(n)*
connect anschließen, anhängen, ankuppeln, koppeln, verbinden, in Verbindung *(f)* bringen, zuschalten
connection Anschluss *(m)*, Verbindung *(f)*, Zusammenhang *(m)*, Beziehungen *(f, pl)*; Querverbindung *(f)*; Verkehrsverbindung *(f)*
connection activation (Leitung) Freischaltung *(f)*
connection fitting Anschlussarmatur *(f)*
connection line Anschlussleitung *(f)*
connection piece Anschlussstück *(n)*
connection piece, main Einspeisungsstück *(n)*
connection pipe Anschlussleitung *(f)*, Anschlussrohr *(n)*
connection price Anschlusspreis *(m)*
connection price, electrical Elektroanschlusspreis *(m)*
connection release (Leitung) Freischaltung *(f)*
connection spline Verbindungsfeder *(f)*
connection to the mains Stromanschluss *(m)*
connection, electrical Elektroanschluss *(m)*
connector Verbinder *(m)*, Verbindungsstück *(n)*, Lüsterklemme *(f)*
consensus Übereinstimmung *(f)*
consent einverstanden sein, einwilligen, sich bereit erklären, zustimmen
consent Einverständnis *(n)*, Einwilligung *(f)*, Zustimmung *(f)*
consequence Konsequenz *(f)*, Ergebnis *(n)*, Folge *(f)*, Folgerung *(f)*, Schluss *(m)*, Bedeutung *(f)*, Wichtigkeit *(f)*
consequently folglich, daher, somit
consider bedenken, betrachten, berücksichtigen, in Betracht *(m)* ziehen, erwägen, nachdenken über, denken an, sich überlegen; betrachten als, ansehen als, halten für; prüfen
considerable beachtlich, beträchtlich, bedeutend, wichtig
considerate aufmerksam, rücksichtsvoll
consideration Erwägung *(f)*, Überlegung *(f)*, Anlass *(m)*, Beweggrund *(m)*, Umstand *(m)*, Berücksichtigung *(f)*, Rücksichtnahme *(f)*, Aufmerksamkeit *(f)*; Entgelt *(n)*, Gegenleistung *(f)*
consign Waren *(f, pl)* zusenden, übergeben
consignee Empfänger *(m)*
consignment Aushändigung *(f)*, Sendung *(f)*, Versendung *(f)*, Versand *(m)*, Zustellung *(f)*
consignment note Frachtbrief *(m)*, Ladeschein *(f)*, Versandanzeige *(f)*, Warenbegleitschein *(m)*
console Konsole *(f)*, Wandgestell *(n)*, Gehäuse *(n)*, Schaltpult *(n)*, Steuerpult *(n)*
consolidation Konsolidierung *(f)*, Festigung *(f)*, Stärkung *(f)*, Verbindung *(f)*, Vereinigung *(f)*, Fusion *(f)*, Zusammenlegung *(f)*, Zusammenschluss *(m)*, Verdichtung *(f)*, Verschmelzung *(f)*
constancy Stabilität *(f)*, Beständigkeit *(f)*, Dauerhaftigkeit *(f)*

constant konstant, beständig, dauernd, fortwährend, ununterbrochen, gleichbleibend
construct konstruieren, bauen, errichten, entwickeln, gestalten
construction Konstruktion *(f)*, Bau *(m)*, Aufbau *(m)*, Errichtung *(f)*, Bauweise *(f)*, Bauwerk *(n)*, Gebäude *(n)*, Anlage *(f)*, Gestaltung *(f)*, Auslegung *(f)*
construction debris Bauschutt *(m)*
construction height Bauhöhe *(f)*, Aufbauhöhe *(f)*
construction materials classification Baustoffklassen *(f, pl)*
construction pass Ausweis *(m)* für den Aufbau
construction permission Baugenehmigung *(f)*
construction regulations Aufbaubestimmungen *(f, pl)*
construction site Baustelle *(f)*
construction waste disposal Entsorgung *(f)* von Bauabfallstoffen, Entsorgung *(f)* von Produktionsabfällen
construction work Bauarbeiten *(f, pl)*
construction, special Sonderkonstuktion *(f)*
construction, start of Aufbaubeginn *(m)*
construction, type of Bauweise *(f)*
constructions, portable fliegende Bauten *(m, pl)*
consultation Konsultation *(f)*, Beratung *(f)*, Befragung *(f)*, Sitzung *(f)*
consume konsumieren, aufbrauchen, verbrauchen, verzehren, verschwenden, in Anspruch *(m)* nehmen; vernichten, zerstören
consumer Konsument(in) *(m/f)*, Verbraucher(in) *(m/f)*
consumer advertising Verbraucherwerbung *(f)*
consumer behavior (US) Verbraucherverhalten *(n)*

consumer behaviour (GB) Verbraucherverhalten *(n)*
consumer benefit Verbrauchernutzen *(m)*
consumer demand Verbrauchernachfrage *(f)*
consumer durables Gebrauchsgüter *(n, pl)*
consumer exhibition Verbraucherausstellung *(f)*, Verbrauchermesse *(f)*
consumer expenditure Konsumausgaben *(f, pl)*, Verbrauchsausgaben *(f, pl)*
consumer fair Verbraucherausstellung *(f)*, Verbrauchermesse *(f)*
consumer goods Konsumgüter *(n, pl)*, Verbrauchsgüter *(n, pl)*
consumer goods fair Konsumgüterausstellung *(f)*, Konsumgütermesse *(f)*
consumer patterns Verbraucherverhalten *(n)*
consumer products Konsumgüter *(n, pl)*, Verbrauchsgüter *(n, pl)*
consumer research Verbraucherforschung *(f)*, Konsumentenforschung *(f)*
consumer show Verbraucherausstellung *(f)*, Verbrauchermesse *(f)*
consumer spending Verbraucherausgaben *(f, pl)*
consumer survey Konsumforschung *(f)*, Konsumentenbefragung *(f)*, Verbraucherbefragung *(f)*, Verbraucherumfrage *(f)*
consumption Konsum *(m)*, Verbrauch *(m)*, Verzehr *(m)*
consumption, articles of Verbrauchsartikel *(m, pl)*
consumption, electrical Stromverbrauch *(m)*

contact Kontakt (m), Berührung (f), Verbindung (f)
contact Kontakt (m) aufnehmen mit, in Verbindung (f) treten mit
contact generation Kontaktanbahnung (f)
contact partner Ansprechpartner(in) (m/f)
container Container (m), Behälter (m), Kanister (m)
container berth Containerliegeplatz (m)
container carrier truck Containerstapler (m)
container load Containerladung (f)
container space Containerstellfläche (f)
container stand Containerstand (m)
container terminal Containerterminal (n)
content befriedigen, zufrieden stellen
content Fassungsvermögen (n), Rauminhalt (m), Volumen (n), Inhalt (m); Gehalt (m), Aussage (f); Zufriedenheit (f)
content zufrieden, bereit, gewillt
contented zufrieden
contest Streit (m), Kampf (m), Wettkampf (m), Wettbewerb (m)
contest streiten, bestreiten; kämpfen, kämpfen um, wetteifern um, sich bewerben
continue fortsetzen, fortfahren, fortführen, fortbestehen, beibehalten, weitermachen, andauern, sich fortsetzen, verlängern
continuity Kontinuität (f), Dauer (f), Beständigkeit (f), Stetigkeit (f)
continuous kontinuierlich, durchgehend, stetig, beständig, dauernd, ununterbrochen, fortlaufend, zusammenhängend
contour drawing Umrisszeichnung (f)
contract kontrahieren, sich verpflichten, sich vertraglich verpflichten; sich zuziehen, bekommen, annehmen, übernehmen
contract Kontrakt (m), Abkommen (n), Vertrag (m), Vereinbarung (f), Übereinkunft (f)
contract negotiations Vertragsverhandlung (f)
contract of carriage Transportvertrag (m)
contract of employment Arbeitsvertrag (m)
contract of sale Kaufvertrag (m)
contract party Vertragspartei (f)
contract, commercial Handelsvertrag (m)
contract, make a Vertrag (m) abschließen
contract, terms of Vertragsbedingungen (f, pl)
contract, violation of Vertragsverletzung (f)
contracting company Vertragsunternehmen (n)
contracting party Vertragspartei (f)
contractor, official Vertragsunternehmer (m), Vertragslieferant (m)
contractor, official electrical Vertragselektriker(in) (m/f)
contractual vertraglich
contrary entgegengesetzt, gegenteilig, gegen, entgegen
contrary Gegenteil (n)
contrast entgegensetzen, in Gegensatz (m) stellen, einen Gegensatz (m) bilden, sich abheben; vergleichen
contrast Gegensatz (m), Kontrast (m)
contrast control Kontrastregler (m), Kontrastregelung (f)
contrast ratio Kontrastverhältnis (n)
contravention Verstoß (m), Zuwiderhandlung (f)
contribution Beitrag (m), Mitwirkung (f), Umlage (f), Spende (f), Einlage (f), Zuschuss (m)
contribution pricing Deckungsbeitrag (m)

contributions, social
Sozialabgaben *(f, pl)*
contributor Beitragszahler(in) *(m/f)*,
Spender(in) *(m/f)*
contributory negligence
Mitverschulden *(n)*
control Kontrolle *(f)*, Aufsicht *(f)*,
Überwachung *(f)*, Macht *(f)*, Gewalt *(f)*,
Beherrschung *(f)*, Führung *(f)*,
Leitung *(f)*; Lenkung *(f)*, Steuerung *(f)*,
Bedienung *(f)*, Regler *(m)*,
Regelung *(f)*, Regulierung *(f)*
control kontrollieren, prüfen,
beaufsichtigen, beherrschen,
überwachen, leiten; lenken, steuern,
regeln, regulieren
control desk Steuerpult *(n)*
control key Steuertaste *(f)*
control knob Einstellknopf *(m)*
control question Kontrollfrage *(f)*
control system Steuerung *(f)*
controller Regler *(m)*, Steuergerät *(n)*
controlling device Kontollgerät *(n)*
controversy Kontroverse *(f)*, Disput *(m)*,
Streit *(m)*, Streitfrage *(f)*
convection oven Heißluftherd *(m)*
convenience Annehmlichkeit *(f)*,
Bequemlichkeit *(f)*, Komfort *(m)*;
Toilette *(f)*
convenience goods
Convenienceprodukte *(n, pl)*,
Verbrauchsgüter *(n, pl)* des täglichen
Bedarfs
convenient bequem, praktisch,
günstig, geeignet, gelegen, passend,
leicht zu handhaben
convention Konvention *(f)*, Tagung *(f)*,
Kongress *(m)*, Versammlung *(f)*,
Abkommen *(n)*, Übereinkommen *(n)*,
Vereinbarung *(f)*, Vertrag *(m)*;
Brauch *(m)*, Gewohnheit *(f)*
convention center (US)
Tagungszentrum *(n)*
convention centre (GB)
Tagungszentrum *(n)*

convention room Tagungsraum *(m)*,
Versammlungsraum *(m)*
conversation Konversation *(f)*,
Gespräch *(n)*, Unterhaltung *(f)*,
Unterredung *(f)*
conversation, private
Privatgespräch *(n)*
conversion Umbau *(m)*, Umrüstung *(f)*,
Umstellung *(f)*; Umrechnung *(f)*;
Umwandlung *(f)*, Verwandlung *(f)*
conversion rate Umrechnungskurs *(m)*
conversion table
Umrechnungstabelle *(f)*
convey befördern, transportieren,
verfrachten, überbringen, übersenden,
übermitteln; übertragen, übereignen,
umschreiben
conveyance Beförderung *(f)*,
Transport *(m)*, Transportmittel *(n)*,
Spedition *(f)*, Versendung *(f)*,
Überbringung *(f)*, Übermittlung *(f)*,
Mitteilung *(f)*; Übertragung *(f)*,
Abtretung *(f)*
conveyor belt Beförderungsband *(n)*,
Transportband *(n)*
convince überzeugen
cooker, electric Elektroherd *(m)*
cookies (US) Kekse *(m, pl)*
cool abkühlen, kühl werden, abkühlen
lassen
cool kühl, frisch; ablehnend, gelassen,
zurückhaltend
cool Kühle *(f)*, Frische *(f)*
cooling Kühlung *(f)*, Abkühlung *(f)*
cooling container Kühlbehälter *(m)*
cooling fan Kühlgebläse *(n)*,
Lüfter *(m)*
cooling system Kühlanlage *(f)*
cooperate kooperieren, mitarbeiten,
mitwirken, zusammenarbeiten
cooperation Kooperation *(f)*,
Zusammenarbeit *(f)*, Mitwirkung *(f)*,
Zusammenschluss *(m)*,
Genossenschaft *(f)*
cooperative Genossenschaft *(f)*

cooperative kooperativ, hilfsbereit, zusammenarbeitend, mitwirkend; genossenschaftlich, Gemeinschafts-, Genossenschafts-
cooperative advertising Gemeinschaftswerbung *(f)*
copier Kopierer *(m)*, Kopiergerät *(n)*
copy Kopie *(f)*, Abschrift *(f)*, Abdruck *(m)*, Exemplar *(n)*, Abzug *(m)*, Nachbildung *(f)*; Durchschrift *(f)*, Text *(m)*, Manuskript *(n)*, Zeitungsausgabe *(f)*, Werbetext *(m)*, Zeitungstext *(m)*
copy kopieren, abschreiben, Kopie *(f)* herstellen, Abzug *(m)* herstellen, abpausen, durchpausen, nachbilden, nachahmen
copy shop Kopierladen *(m)*
copy, free Freiexemplar *(n)*
copying service Kopierdienst *(m)*
copyright Copyright *(n)*, Urheberrecht *(n)*
copyright urheberrechtlich
copyright act Urheberrechtsgesetz *(n)*
copyright law Urheberrechtsgesetz *(n)*
copyright reserved urheberrechtlich geschützt
copywriter Texter(in) *(m/f)*, Werbetexter(in) *(m/f)*
cord Schnur *(f)*, Seil *(n)*, Strick *(m)*, Kordel *(f)*, Leine *(f)*, Kabel *(n)*
corner Ecke *(f)*, Winkel *(m)*
corner in die Enge *(f)* treiben; aufkaufen
corner booth Eckstand *(m)*
corner connector Eckverbinder *(m)*
corner link Winkelelement *(n)*
corner panel Eckplatte *(f)*
corner stand Eckstand *(m)*
corner, external Außenecke *(f)*
corner, inner Innenecke *(f)*
corner, inside Innenecke *(f)*
corner, internal Innenecke *(f)*

corner, outer Außenecke *(f)*
corporate gemeinsam, gemeinschaftlich, vereinigt, zusammengeschlossen, gesellschaftlich, korporativ, körperschaftlich, Firmen-, Unternehmens-
corporate advertising Firmenwerbung *(f)*
corporate behavior (US) Unternehmensverhaltensweise *(f)*
corporate behaviour (GB) Unternehmensverhaltensweise *(f)*
corporate client Firmenkunde *(m)*, Firmenkundin *(f)*
corporate customer Firmenkunde *(m)*, Firmenkundin *(f)*
corporate design audiovisuelles Unternehmenserscheinungsbild *(n)*
corporate goal Firmenziel *(n)*, Unternehmensziel *(n)*
corporate governance Untermehmensführung *(f)*
corporate identity Unternehmensselbstverständnis *(n)* und Erscheinungsbild *(n)*
corporate image Firmenimage *(n)*, Unternehmensimage *(n)*
corporate management Unternehmensleitung *(f)*, Firmenleitung *(f)*
corporate name Firmenname *(m)*
corporate objective Unternehmensziel *(n)*, Unternehmenszielvorstellung *(f)*
corporate policy Unternehmenspolitik *(f)*
corporate profit Unternehmensgewinn *(m)*
corporate strategy Firmenstrategie *(f)*, Unternehmensstrategie *(f)*
corporate tax Körperschaftssteuer *(f)*
corporation Unternehmen *(n)*, Kapitalgesellschaft *(f)*, Aktiengesellschaft *(f)*, Körperschaft *(f)*, juristische Person *(f)*

correction Korrektur *(f)*, Berichtigung *(f)*, Verbesserung *(f)*, Richtigstellung *(f)*, Zurechtweisung *(f)*, Tadel *(m)*
correspond korrespondieren, entsprechen, übereinstimmen
correspondence Korrespondenz *(f)*, Briefwechsel *(m)*, Schriftverkehr *(m)*, Einklang *(m)*, Entsprechung *(f)*, Übereinstimmung *(f)*, Verbindung *(f)*, Zusammenhang *(m)*
correspondence, commercial Handelskorrespondenz *(f)*
corresponding korrespondierend, entsprechend, gemäß
cost kosten, erfordern, (Kosten etc.) verursachen, einbringen
cost Kosten *(pl)*, Selbstkosten *(pl)*, Ausgaben *(f, pl)*, Aufwand *(m)*, Preis *(m)*
cost accounting Kostenrechnung *(f)*
cost allocation Kostenaufteilung *(f)*, Kostenumlage *(f)*, Kostenverrechnung *(f)*
cost awareness Kostenbewusstsein *(n)*
cost center (US) Kostenstelle *(f)*
cost centre (GB) Kostenstelle *(f)*
cost control Kostenkontrolle *(f)*
cost estimate Kostenvoranschlag *(m)*
cost factor Kostenfaktor *(m)*
cost forecast Kostenvoranschlag *(m)*
cost increase Kostensteigerung *(f)*
cost monitoring Kostenkontrolle *(f)*
cost objective Kostenvorgabe *(f)*
cost of living Lebenshaltungskosten *(pl)*
cost of repairs Reparaturkosten *(pl)*
cost of sales Verkaufskosten *(pl)*, Vertriebskosten *(pl)*, Umsatzaufwendungen *(m, pl)*
cost planning Kostenplanung *(f)*
cost price Einstandspreis *(m)*, Selbstkostenpreis *(m)*
cost reduction Kostensenkung *(f)*
cost saving Kostenersparnis *(f)*
cost sharing Kostenbeteiligung *(f)*
cost, own Selbstkosten *(pl)*

cost-benefit analysis Kosten-Nutzen-Analyse *(f)*
cost-covering kostendeckend
cost-cutting Kostensenkung *(f)*, Kosteneinsparung *(f)*
cost-effective kostengünstig
cost-efficient kosteneffektiv, rentabel
costing Kalkulation *(f)*, Kostenberechnung *(f)*
costing, direct Deckungsbeitragsrechnung *(f)*
costly teuer
costs of the exhibition Ausstellungskosten *(pl)*, Messekosten *(pl)*
costs of the fair Ausstellungskosten *(pl)*, Messekosten *(pl)*
costs, actual Ist-Kosten *(pl)*
costs, additional Zusatzkosten *(pl)*
costs, fixed fixe Kosten *(pl)*, Fixkosten *(pl)*, Gemeinkosten *(pl)*
costs, follow-up Folgekosten *(pl)*
costs, forwarding Versandkosten *(pl)*
costs, full Vollkosten *(pl)*
costs, marginal Grenzkosten *(pl)*
costs, total Gesamtkosten *(pl)*
cost-saving kostensparend
counsel beraten, Rat *(m)* erteilen, empfehlen
counsel Beratung *(f)*, Ratschlag *(m)*; Anwalt *(m)*, Anwältin *(f)*
counsel, legal Anwalt *(m)*, Anwältin *(f)*
counselling, legal Rechtsberatung *(f)*
counter entgegen, zuwider, in gegensätzlicher Richtung *(f)*
counter kontern, entgegnen, entgegenwirken, zuwiderhandeln
counter Theke *(f)*, Ladentisch *(m)*, Schalter *(m)*; Büfett *(n)*; Zähler *(m)*
counterproposal Gegenvorschlag *(m)*
countersign gegenzeichnen
countersunk screw Senkschraube *(f)*
countless unzählig, zahllos
countries, foreign Ausland *(n)*

country of origin Herkunftsland *(n)*, Ursprungsland *(n)*
coupling part Kupplungsteil *(n)*, Verbindungsstück *(n)*
coupling stud Kupplungsstutzen *(m)*
coupon Coupon *(m)*, Gutschein *(m)*
courier Kurier *(m)*, Eilbote *(m)*; Reiseleiter(in) *(m/f)*
courier service Kurierdienst *(m)*, Eilbotenservice *(m)*
course Kurs *(m)*, Richtung *(f)*, Strecke *(f)*, Weg *(m)*, Lauf *(m)*, Ablauf *(m)*, Verlauf *(m)*, Reihe *(f)*, Folge *(f)*; Lehrgang *(m)*; Zyklus *(m)*; (Menü) Gang *(m)*
course of training Schulungskurs *(m)*
course, main Hauptgang *(m)*, Hauptgericht *(n)*
courteous höflich, gefällig, freundlich, nett, aufmerksam, liebenswürdig
courtesy Höflichkeit *(f)*, Gefälligkeit *(f)*, Freundlichkeit *(f)*, Liebenswürdigkeit *(f)*
cover Deckel *(m)*, Einband *(m)*, Hülle *(f)*, Umschlag *(m)*, Titelseite *(f)*; Bezug *(m)*, Überzug *(m)*, Schutz *(m)*; Abdeckhaube *(f)*, Schutzhaube *(f)*
cover verdecken, bedecken, überdecken, zudecken, verhüllen, einschließen, einwickeln, umhüllen, schützen; versichern
cover charge Gedeckpreis *(m)*
cover page Umschlagseite *(f)*, Einbandseite *(f)*
cover picture Titelbild *(n)*
cover profile Abdeckprofil *(n)*
coverage Reichweite *(f)*, Sendebereich *(m)*; Anwendungsbereich *(m)*, Geltungsbereich *(m)*; Berichterstattung *(f)*; (Versicherung) Deckung *(f)*
crack erstklassig, großartig, phantastisch
crack Knall *(m)*, Krach *(m)*; Riss *(m)*, Ritze *(f)*, Spalt *(m)*, Sprung *(m)*; Schlag *(m)*, Stoß *(m)*

crack krachen, aufplatzen, rissig werden, bersten, brechen, zerbrechen, zerspringen, platzen
craft Handwerk *(n)*, Gewerbe *(n)*; Geschicklichkeit *(f)*, Fertigkeit *(f)*; Schiff *(n)*, Schiffe *(n, pl)*; Flugzeug *(n)*, Flugzeuge *(n, pl)*
craftsman Handwerker *(m)*
craftswoman Handwerkerin *(f)*
cramp Klammer *(f)*, Krampe *(f)*, Zwinge *(f)*
cramp klammern, anklammern
crane Kran *(m)*
cranes and lifting equipment Kran- und Hebefahrzeuge *(n, pl)*
craneway Kranbahn *(f)*
crank ankurbeln
crank Kurbel *(f)*
crate Lattenkiste *(f)*, Lattenverschlag *(m)*, Kasten *(m)*
create schaffen, erschaffen, herstellen, bewirken, machen, errichten, gründen, hervorrufen, verursachen
creative kreativ, schöpferisch, produktiv
credible glaubwürdig, zuverlässig
credit Kredit *(m)*, Guthaben *(n)*, Gutschrift *(f)*; Ansehen *(n)*, Geltung *(f)*; Verdienst *(n)*
credit vertrauen; gutschreiben, kreditieren
credit card Kreditkarte *(f)*
credit conditions Kreditbedingungen *(f, pl)*
credit sale Kauf *(m)* auf Kredit, Abzahlungskauf *(m)*
credit standing Bonität *(f)*
credit worthiness Bonität *(f)*, Kreditwürdigkeit *(f)*
creditor Gläubiger(in) *(m/f)*
creditor beneficiary Zahlungsempfänger(in) *(m/f)*, Begünstigte(r) *(f/m)*
crew Crew *(f)*, Mannschaft *(f)*, Besatzung *(f)*, Gruppe *(f)*, Trupp *(m)*, Kolonne *(f)*

criterion Kriterium *(n)*
critical kritisch, bedenklich; anspruchsvoll; missbilligend, tadelnd
criticism Kritik *(f)*, kritische Beurteilung *(f)*, Tadel *(m)*, Vorwurf *(m)*
crook biegen, sich biegen, krümmen
crook Haken *(m)*, Biegung *(f)*, Krümmung *(f)*
cross reference Querverweis *(m)*
cross section Schnittbild *(n)*, Querschnitt *(m)*
crossways kreuzweise, quer
crosswise kreuzweise, quer
crowbar Stemmeisen *(n)*, Brecheisen *(n)*
crowd Menschenmenge *(f)*, Masse *(f)*, Ansammlung *(f)*, Haufen *(m)*, Gedränge *(n)*, Gewimmel *(n)*; Gesellschaft *(f)*, Verein *(m)*
crowd sich ansammeln, zusammenströmen, drängen, sich drängen, vollpfropfen, schieben
crush Gedränge *(n)*, Gewühl *(n)*, Menschenmenge *(f)*, Massen *(f, pl)*, Haufen *(m)*
cube Würfel *(m)*
cube sugar Würfelzucker *(m)*
cube-shaped würfelförmig
cube-type node (Messebausystem) Würfelknoten *(m)*
cubic kubisch, würfelförmig, Kubik-, Raum-
cubic meter (US) Kubikmeter *(m)*
cubic metre (GB) Kubikmeter *(m)*
cubicle Kabine *(f)*
culpable schuldhaft, strafbar
cup Tasse *(f)*, Becher *(m)*; Pokal *(m)*
cupboard Schrank *(m)*, Büfett *(n)*
cupboard showcase Schrankvitrine *(f)*
cupboard, heated Warmhalteschrank *(m)*
cupola Kuppel *(f)*
currency Währung *(f)*, Valuta *(f)*, Zahlungsmittel *(n)*; Laufzeit *(f)*, Gültigkeit *(f)*
currency exchange Geldwechsel *(m)*

currency restrictions Devisenbeschränkungen *(f, pl)*
currency risk Währungsrisiko *(n)*
currency, foreign Fremdwährung *(f)*
currency, national Landeswährung *(f)*
current aktuell, augenblicklich, gegenwärtig, laufend, gebräuchlich, üblich, gültig
current (Elektrizität) Strom *(m)*; Strömung *(f)*, Ablauf *(m)*, Richtung *(f)*
current intensity Stromstärke *(f)*
current, 3-phase Drehstrom *(m)*
current, continuous Gleichstrom *(m)*
current, cut-off Abschaltstrom *(m)*
current, direct Gleichstrom *(m)*
current, heavy Starkstrom *(m)*
current, high-voltage Starkstrom *(m)*
current, three-phase Drehstrom *(m)*
curtain Gardine *(f)*, Vorhang *(m)*
curve biegen, sich biegen, krümmen, sich krümmen, wölben, sich wölben
curve Kurve *(f)*, Biegung *(f)*, Krümmung *(f)*, Rundung *(f)*
cushion polstern, abfedern, dämpfen
cushion Sitzkissen *(n)*, Polster *(n)*, Dämpfer *(m)*, Puffer *(m)*
custom Brauch *(m)*, Gewohnheit *(f)*, Sitte *(f)*, Handelsbrauch *(m)*, Gewohnheitsrecht *(n)*; Kundschaft *(f)*, Kunden *(m, pl)*
custom clearance Zollabfertigung *(f)*
custom stand construction Messestandbau *(m)* durch den Aussteller
customary gebräuchlich, üblich
customer Kunde *(m)*, Kundin *(f)*, Auftraggeber(in) *(m/f)*, Abnehmer(in) *(m/f)*, Käufer(in) *(m/f)*
customer advisory service Kundenberatung *(f)*
customer assitance Gästebetreuung *(f)*
customer care Kundenbetreuung *(f)*
customer needs Kundenbedürfnisse *(n, pl)*

customer satisfaction
  Kundenzufriedenheit *(f)*
customer service Kundendienst *(m)*
customer support Kundenbetreuung *(f)*
customer value Kundennutzen *(m)*
customer, casual Laufkunde *(m)*,
  Laufkundin *(f)*
customer, foreign Auslandskunde *(m)*,
  Auslandskundin *(f)*
customer, potential
  Interessent(in) *(m/f)*, potenzieller
  Kunde *(m)*, potenzielle Kundin *(f)*
customer, prospective potenzieller
  Kunde *(m)*, potenzielle Kundin *(f)*,
  Kaufinteressent(in) *(m/f)*
customer, regular Stammkunde *(m)*,
  Stammkundin *(f)*
customer's request
  Kundenwunsch *(m)*
customer's solvency Kundenbonität *(f)*
customs Zoll *(m)*, Tarif *(m)*,
  Einfuhrzölle *(m, pl)*
customs authority Zollbehörde *(f)*
customs check Zollkontrolle *(f)*
customs clearance Verzollung *(f)*,
  Zollabfertigung *(f)*
customs control Zollkontrolle *(f)*
customs declaration Zolldeklaration *(f)*,
  Zollerklärung *(f)*, Zollabfertigung *(f)*
customs documents
  Zollbegleitpapiere *(n, pl)*
customs duty Zollabgabe *(f)*,
  Zollgebühr *(f)*
customs examination Zollkontrolle *(f)*
customs formalities
  Zollformalitäten *(f, pl)*
customs house Zollamt *(n)*
customs inspection Zollkontrolle *(f)*
customs investigation Zollfahndung *(f)*
customs regulations
  Zollbestimmungen *(f, pl)*,
  Zollvorschriften *(f, pl)*
customs seal Zollverschluss *(m)*
customs tariff Zolltarif *(m)*
customs value Zollwert *(m)*

cut schneiden, abschneiden,
  zuschneiden, zurechtschneiden,
  trennen, zerteilen; reduzieren,
  ermäßigen, herabsetzen, verringern;
  Schluss *(m)* machen; verdünnen;
  (Gehalt etc.) kürzen
cut Schnitt *(m)*, Schnittwunde *(f)*,
  Einschnitt *(m)*, Stich *(m)*;
  Zuschnitt *(m)*; Kürzung *(f)*,
  Senkung *(f)*, Verringerung *(f)*
cut off abschneiden, abtrennen,
  abstellen, abschalten, unterbrechen
cutting torch Schneidbrenner *(m)*
cyberspace virtueller Raum *(m)*
cycle Zyklus *(m)*, Kreis *(m)*, Periode *(f)*
cylinder lock Zylinderschloss *(n)*
cylindrical zylindrisch

D

damage beschädigen, schaden
damage Schädigung *(f)*, Schaden *(m)*,
  Verlust *(m)*
damage claim
  Schadenersatzanspruch *(m)*
damage in transit
  Transportschaden *(m)*
damage limitation
  Schadensbegrenzung *(f)*
damage to property Sachschaden *(m)*
damage, consequential
  Folgeschaden *(m)*
damage, extend of Schadenhöhe *(f)*
damage, malicious mutwillige
  Beschädigung *(f)*
damage, material Sachschaden *(m)*
damage, partial Teilschaden *(m)*
damages Schadenersatz *(m)*;
  Abfindung *(f)*, Entschädigung *(f)*
damp anfeuchten, befeuchten;
  dämpfen
damp feucht

damp Feuchtigkeit *(f)*
danger Gefahr *(f)*
danger of explosion
 Explosionsgefahr *(f)*
danger of fire Feuergefahr *(f)*,
 Brandgefahr *(f)*
danger of injuring Verletzungsgefahr *(f)*
dangerous goods Gefahrgut *(n)*,
 Gefahrgüter *(n, pl)*
dangerous substance Gefahrstoff *(m)*
Dangerous Substances Ordinance
 Gefahrstoffverordnung *(f)*
dangerous, extremely
 lebensgefährlich
darken verdunkeln
darkening Verdunkelung *(f)*
data Daten *(pl)*, Angaben *(f, pl)*,
 Einzelheiten *(f, pl)*
data acquisition Datenerfassung *(f)*
data bank Datenbank *(f)*
data carrier Datenträger *(m)*
data collection Datenerfassung *(f)*
data connection Datenanschluss *(m)*
data exchange Datenaustausch *(m)*
data input Dateneingabe *(f)*
data integrity Datensicherheit *(f)*
data output Datenausgabe *(f)*
data processing Datenverarbeitung *(f)*
data protection Datenschutz *(m)*
data retrieval Datenabruf *(m)*
data storage Datenspeicherung *(f)*
data transfer Datenübermittlung *(f)*
data transmission Datenübertragung *(f)*
data transmission speed
 Datenübertragungsgeschwindigkeit *(f)*
data, secondary Sekundärdaten *(pl)*
date datieren, zeitlich festlegen,
 sich verabreden
date Datum *(n)*; Termin *(m)*,
 Verabredung *(f)*, Zeitpunkt *(m)*
date of arrival Ankunftsdatum *(n)*
date of delivery Liefertermin *(m)*
date of departure Abreisedatum *(n)*
date of expiry Verfallsdatum *(n)*
date of invoice Rechnungsdatum *(n)*

date of receipt Eingangsdatum *(n)*
dates for dismantling (Messestand)
 Abbautermin *(m)*
day nursery Kindertagesstätte *(f)*
day of arrival Anreisetag *(m)*
day of departure Abreisetag *(m)*
day of rest Ruhetag *(m)*
day ticket Tageskarte *(f)*
daylight Tageslicht *(n)*
daylight projector
 Tageslichtprojektor *(m)*
daytime shot (Foto) Tagesaufnahme *(f)*
dazzle blenden
dead loss Totalausfall *(m)*
dead weight Leergewicht *(n)*
deadline letzter Termin *(m)*,
 Schlusstermin *(m)*,
 Anmeldeschluss *(m)*;
 Anzeigenschluss *(m)*;
 Einsendeschluss *(m)*;
 Redaktionsschluss *(m)*
deadline for application
 Anmeldeschluss *(m)*,
 Schlusstermin *(m)* für einen Antrag,
 Schlusstermin *(m)* für eine
 Bewerbung
deadline for entries Anmeldeschluss *(m)*, Eintragungsschluss *(m)*,
 Schlusstermin *(m)* zur Einreise
deadline for registration
 Anmeldeschluss *(m)*,
 Eintragungsschluss *(m)*,
 Registrierungsschluss *(m)*
deadweight Leergewicht *(n)*
deadweight cargo Schwergut *(n)*
deal Abmachung *(f)*, Abschluss *(m)*,
 Geschäft *(n)*, Geschäftsabschluss *(m)*,
 Handel *(m)*, Verfahren *(n)*
deal with Handel *(m)* treiben mit,
 Geschäfte *(n, pl)* machen mit;
 sich beschäftigen mit
dealer Händler *(m)*
dear lieb, teuer
debate Debatte *(f)*, Diskussion *(f)*
debate debattieren, diskutieren

debit Debet *(n)*, Soll *(n)*, Sollseite *(f)*, Belastung *(f)*, Lastschrift *(f)*
debit (Konto) belasten
debit card Geldkarte *(f)*, Kundenkarte *(f)*, Zahlungskarte *(f)*
debit interest Schuldzinsen *(m, pl)*, Sollzinsen *(m, pl)*
debt Schuld *(f)*, Schulden *(f, pl)*
debt, get into Schulden *(f, pl)* machen
debtor Schuldner(in) *(m/f)*
deceive täuschen, trügen, irreführen
decent anständig, ordentlich, passabel
deception Täuschung *(f)*, Betrug *(m)*, Irreführung *(f)*
deception package Mogelpackung *(f)*
decibel Dezibel *(n)*
decibel level Phonzahl *(f)*
decide entscheiden, sich entscheiden, beschließen, sich entschließen, bestimmen
deciding factor Entscheidungskriterium *(n)*
decision Entscheidung *(f)*, Entschluss *(m)*, Beschluss *(m)*, Entschlossenheit *(f)*
decision-maker Entscheidungsträger(in) *(m/f)*
decision-making process Entscheidungsprozess *(m)*
decisive ausschlaggebend, entscheidend; entschlussfreudig, entschieden, entschlossen
declaration Deklaration *(f)*, Aussage *(f)*, Erklärung *(f)*, Festsetzung *(f)*
declaration of conformity Konformitätserklärung *(f)*
declaration of origin Ursprungserklärung *(f)*
declaration of value Wertangabe *(f)*
declare angeben, erklären, bekanntgeben; (Zoll) deklarieren
decline Abnahme *(f)*, Rückgang *(m)*, Niedergang *(m)*, Neigung *(f)*, Senkung *(f)*, Schwächung *(f)*, Verfall *(m)*

decline abnehmen, geringer werden, nachlassen, zurückgehen, fallen, verfallen, sinken, sich neigen, sich senken, zur Neige *(f)* gehen; ablehnen
decor Dekor *(n)*, Ausstattung *(f)*, Dekoration *(f)*
decorate dekorieren, schmücken, ausschmücken, verzieren, streichen, tapezieren; (mit Orden etc.) auszeichnen
decoration Dekoration *(f)*, Verzierung *(f)*, Schmuck *(m)*; Auszeichnung *(f)*, Orden *(m)*
decorative element Dekoelement *(n)*
decorative material Dekorationsmaterial *(n)*
decorator Dokorateur(in) *(m/f)*, Maler(in) *(m/f)*, Tapezierer(in) *(m/f)*
decrease Abnahme *(f)*, Rückgang *(m)*, Verringerung *(f)*
decrease abnehmen, zurückgehen, nachlassen, herabsetzen, reduzieren, verringern, sich verringern, sich vermindern
deduct abziehen, einbehalten
deduction Abzug *(m)*, Rabatt *(m)*, Nachlass *(m)*
deep-frozen tiefgefroren
default im Verzug *(m)* sein, seinen Verpflichtungen *(f, pl)* nicht nachkommen, nicht antreten
default Unterlassung *(f)*, Nichterfüllung *(f)*, Säumnis *(f)*, Versäumnis *(n)*, Verzug *(m)*, Nichterscheinen *(n)*
default in delivery Lieferverzug *(m)*
default in payment Zahlungsverzug *(m)*
defect defekt, fehlerhaft, schadhaft
defect Defekt *(m)*, Fehler *(m)*, Mangel *(m)*
deficit Defizit *(n)*, Fehlbetrag *(m)*
definition Definition *(f)*, Bestimmung *(f)*, Erklärung *(f)*, Festlegung *(f)*

defrost (Kühlgerät etc.) abtauen; (Tiefkühlkost etc.) auftauen
delay aufschieben, verschieben, hinausschieben, verzögern, verschleppen, aufhalten
delay Verspätung (f), Verschiebung (f), Aufschub (m), Aufenthalt (m), Stockung (f), Säumnis (f), Verzögerung (f), Verzug (m)
delay penalty Säumnisstrafgeld (n)
delaying tactics Verzögerungstaktik (f)
delegation Abordnung (f), Delegation (f)
delete streichen, löschen
Delete where non-applicable! Nichtzutreffendes streichen!
Delete which is inapplicable! Nichtzutreffendes streichen!
deliberate absichtlich, bewusst, überlegt
deliberate bedenken, erwägen, nachdenken
deliver liefern, anliefern, aushändigen, übergeben, überbringen, zustellen, versorgen; Rede (f) halten
delivery Lieferung (f), Aushändigung (f), Auslieferung (f), Überbringung (f), Übergabe (f), Zustellung (f), Versorgung (f); Vortrag (m)
delivery charge Zustellgebühr (f), Zustellkosten (pl)
delivery contract Liefervertrag (m)
delivery costs Lieferkosten (pl)
delivery date Liefertermin (m)
delivery fee Zustellgebühr (f)
delivery note Lieferschein (m)
delivery of exhibition materials Anlieferung (f) von Messegut
delivery order Lieferauftrag (m)
delivery receipt Lieferbestätigung (f)
delivery service Zustelldienst (m)
delivery terms Lieferbedingungen (f, pl)
delivery time Lieferzeit (f)
delivery versus payment Lieferung (f) gegen Bezahlung
delivery, free kostenfreie Anlieferung (f)

demand beanspruchen, fordern, erfordern, nachfragen, verlangen
demand Forderung (f), Anforderung (f), Aufforderung (f), Bedarf (m), Nachfrage (f), Verlangen (n)
demand analysis Bedarfsanalyse (f), Nachfrageanalyse (f)
demand note Zahlungsaufforderung (f)
demand-oriented bedarfsgerecht, nachfragegerecht
demand, domestic Inlandsnachfrage (f)
demand, effective tatsächliche Nachfrage (f)
demand, potential potenzielle Nachfrage (f)
demo tape Demokassette (f)
demonstration Demonstration (f), Vorführung (f)
demurrage Liegegeld (n)
dent Beule (f), Delle (f)
deny bestreiten, abstreiten, dementieren, leugnen, verleugnen, ablehnen, verweigern
department Abteilung (n), Ressort (n), Fach (n), Gebiet (n), Fachbereich (m)
department head Abteilungsleiter(in) (m/f)
department manager Abteilungsleiter(in) (m/f)
department manageress Abteilungsleiterin (f)
department, legal Rechtsabteilung (f)
departure Abfahrt (f), Abreise (f), Abflug (m), Aufbruch (m); Abweichen (n)
departure date Abfahrtsdatum (n), Abreisedatum (n), Abflugdatum (n)
dependence Abhängigkeit (f); Vertrauen (n)
dependent abhängig, angewiesen
deposit Anzahlung (f), Einzahlung (f), Einlage (f), Guthaben (n), Hinterlegung (f), Verwahrung (f), Pfand (n), Kaution (f)

deposit hinterlegen, deponieren, einzahlen
depot Depot *(n)*, Lager *(n)*, Warenlager *(n)*, Magazin *(n)*
depreciate abschreiben, abwerten, entwerten
depreciation Abschreibung *(f)*, Abwertung *(f)*, Entwertung *(f)*, Wertverlust *(m)*, Verschlechterung *(f)*
depreciation, rate of Abschreibungssatz *(m)*
depth Tiefe *(f)*
depth of field (Foto) Tiefenschärfe *(f)*
depth of focus (Foto) Tiefenschärfe *(f)*
description Beschreibung *(f)*, Schilderung *(f)*, Bezeichnung *(f)*
design Design *(n)*, Entwurf *(m)*, Skizze *(f)*, Zeichnung *(f)*, Konstruktion *(f)*, Konstruktionszeichnung *(f)*, Gestaltung *(f)*, Modell *(n)*, Muster *(n)*; Plan *(m)*, Vorhaben *(n)*
design entwerfen, Entwürfe *(m, pl)* machen, planen, vorsehen, gestalten, skizzieren, zeichnen, konstruieren
design engineer Konstrukteur(in) *(m/f)*
design, registered eingetragenes Gebrauchsmuster *(n)*
designer Designer(in) *(m/f)*, Konzeptioner *(m)*, Konstrukteur(in) *(m/f)*
desk Schreibtisch *(m)*, Pult *(n)*; Kasse *(f)*; Rezeption *(f)*
desk pad Schreibunterlage *(f)*
desk research Sekundärforschung *(f)*
desk work Schreibarbeit *(f)*
destination Reiseziel *(n)*, Bestimmungsort *(m)*
destructive destruktiv, zerstörerisch
detail ausführlich berichten, einzeln aufführen
detail Detail *(n)*, Einzelheit *(f)*, Ausschnitt *(m)*
detergent Reinigungsmittel *(n)*

determine bestimmen, festsetzen, feststellen, entscheiden, beschließen, ermitteln
detour umleiten
detour Umweg *(m)*, Umleitung *(f)*
detract schmälern, beeinträchtigen; (Aufmerksamkeit etc.) ablenken
devaluate abwerten
devalue abwerten
develop entwickeln, sich entwickeln, entfalten, sich entfalten, sich herausstellen, ausweiten, ausbauen, ausarbeiten, weiterentwickeln
develop further weiterentwickeln
developed, highly hochentwickelt
development Entwicklung *(f)*, Entfaltung *(f)*, Wachstum *(n)*; Ausbau *(m)*, Ausführung *(f)*, Erschließung *(f)*
development, commercial wirtschaftliche Entwicklung *(f)*
development, economic Konjunkturentwicklung *(f)*, Wirtschaftsentwicklung *(f)*
development, undesirable Fehlentwicklung *(f)*
deviation Abweichung *(f)*
device Gerät *(n)*, Vorrichtung *(f)*; Kunstgriff *(m)*, Trick *(m)*
devices, technical technische Einrichtungen *(f, pl)*
diagonal diagonal
diagonal Diagonale *(f)*
diagram Diagramm *(n)*, Schaubild *(n)*, grafische Darstellung *(f)*
dial Skala *(f)*, Ziffernblatt *(n)*; Wählscheibe *(f)*
dial (Telefonnummer) wählen
dial tone (US) (Telefon) Freizeichen *(n)*
dialling code (GB) Vorwahlnummer *(f)*
dialling tone (GB) (Telefon) Freizeichen *(n)*
dialog (US) Dialog *(m)*, Zwiegespräch *(n)*

dialog marketing (US)
Dialogmarketing *(n)*
dialogue (GB) Dialog *(m)*,
Zwiegespräch *(n)*
dialogue marketing (US)
Dialogmarketing *(n)*
diameter Durchmesser *(m)*
diary Terminkalender *(m)*
dictionary, specialized
Fachwörterbuch *(n)*
differ sich unterscheiden, verschieden sein; anderer Meinung *(f)* sein; abweichen
difference Differenz *(f)*, Verschiedenheit *(f)*, Besonderheit *(f)*, Unterschied *(m)*, Unterscheidung *(f);* Meinungsverschiedenheit *(f)*
different unterschiedlich, verschieden, verschiedenartig, anders
differentiate differenzieren, unterscheiden, sich unterscheiden, trennen
difficult diffizil, schwierig, heikel, schwer, anspruchsvoll
difficulties, financial
Zahlungsschwierigkeiten *(f, pl)*
difficulty Schwierikeit *(f)*
digital digital
digital camera Digitalkamera *(f)*
digital display Digitalanzeige *(f)*
digitize digitalisieren
dim abdunkeln, verdunkeln, abblenden, abschwächen
dim trübe, dunkel, matt, blass, undeutlich, verschwommen
dimension Dimension *(f)*, Abmessung *(f)*, Ausdehnung *(f)*, Maß *(n)*, Ausmaß *(n)*, Umfang *(m)*, Größe *(f)*
dimension, clear lichtes Maß *(n)*
diminish vermindern, sich vermindern, verringern, sich verringern, abnehmen, herabsetzen
dimmer Dimmer *(m)*
dimmer switch Dimmerschalter *(m)*

dinner Diner *(n)*, Essen *(n)*, Abendessen *(n)*
dinner jacket Smoking *(m)*
dinner party Abendgesellschaft *(f)*
dinner suit Abendanzug *(m)*
direct direkt, gerade, genau, durchgehend, stufenlos, unmittelbar, deutlich
direct führen, leiten, lenken, regeln, anweisen, anordnen, verfügen, beauftragen; adressieren, schicken; (Worte) richten
direction Richtung *(f)*, Führung *(f)*, Leitung *(f)*, Anleitung *(f)*, Anweisung *(f)*, Anordnung *(f)*
directions for use
Gebrauchsanweisung *(f)*
directive Anweisung *(f)*, Direktive *(f)*, Richtlinie *(f)*, Weisung *(f)*
director Direktor(in) *(m/f)*, Leiter(in) *(m/f)*, Geschäftsführer(in) *(m/f)*, Vorstandsmitglied *(n)*
directory Adressbuch *(n)*, Verzeichnis *(n)*
directory, commercial
Branchenadressbuch *(n)*
dirt Schmutz *(m)*, Dreck *(m)*
disabled arbeitsunfähig, behindert, nicht rechtsfähig
disabled person Behinderte(r) *(f/m)*
disadvantage benachteiligen
disadvantage Nachteil *(m)*, Schaden *(m)*
disagree nicht übereinstimmen, nicht einverstanden sein, unzuträglich sein, sich streiten
disagreement Unstimmigkeit *(f)*, Meinungsverschiedenheit *(f)*, Streit *(m)*
disappear verschwinden, entschwinden
disapprove dagegen sein, missbilligen
disassembly Demontage *(f)*, Zerlegung *(f)*
disconnect trennen, abschalten, abstellen, abklemmen, ausschalten

discount Diskont *(m)*, Nachlass *(m)*, Preisnachlass *(m)*, Rabatt *(m)*, Skonto *(m/n)*
discount Rabatt *(m)* gewähren
discount terms Rabattbedingungen *(f, pl)*, Rabattbestimmungen *(f, pl)*
discount, special Sonderrabatt *(m)*
discuss diskutieren, besprechen, erörtern
discussion Diskussion *(f)*, Beratung *(f)*, Besprechung *(f)*, Erörterung *(f)*
disease Krankheit *(f)*
diseased krank
dish Speise *(f)*, Gericht *(n)*; Geschirr *(n)*, Schüssel *(f)*, Schale *(f)*, Platte *(f)*
dish (Speisen) anrichten
dish of the day Tagesgericht *(n)*
dish washer, commercial gewerbliche Geschirrspülmaschine *(f)*
dish, main Hauptgang *(m)*, Hauptgericht *(n)*
dishes, cold kalte Speisen *(f, pl)*
dishonest unredlich, unehrlich
dishwasher Geschirrspülmaschine *(f)*
disk Scheibe *(f)*, Platte *(f)*, Diskette *(f)*
disk drive Diskettenlaufwerk *(n)*
disk, magnetic Magnetplatte *(f)*
dismantle abbauen, auseinander nehmen, zerlegen, demontieren, ausräumen
dismantle deadline Abbauende *(n)*
dismantle rules Abbaurichtlinien *(f, pl)*
dismantle time extension verlängerte Abbauzeit *(f)*
dismantling Abbau *(m)*, Demontage *(f)*
dismantling pass Abbauausweis *(m)*
dismantling period Abbauzeit *(f)*, Abbauzeitraum *(m)*, Abbaufrist *(f)*
dismantling personnel Abbaupersonal *(n)*
dismantling staff Abbaupersonal *(n)*, Mitarbeiterstab *(m)* für den Abbau
dismantling ticket Abbaukarte *(f)*
dismantling time, end of Abbauende *(n)*

dismantling times Abbauzeiten *(f, pl)*
disorder Unordnung *(f)*
dispatch abfertigen, absenden, abschicken, schicken, aufgeben, befördern, versenden, erledigen
dispatch Abschicken *(n)*, Abfertigung *(f)*, Absendung *(f)*, Absenden *(n)*, Erledigung *(f)*, Versand *(m)*, Versendung *(f)*
dispatch note Frachtzettel *(m)*, Versandanzeige *(f)*, Versandschein *(m)*
dispatch papers Versandpapiere *(n, pl)*
dispatcher Absender *(m)*
dispatching Versand *(m)*
dispatching costs Versandkosten *(pl)*
dispenser (Automat) Spender *(m)*
display Display *(n)*, Auslage *(f)*, Warenauslage *(f)*, Ausstellung *(f)*, Zurschaustellung *(f)*; (EDV) Anzeige *(f)*
display zur Schau *(f)* stellen, zeigen, ausstellen, vorführen
display article Ausstellungsstück *(n)*
display cabinet Schaukasten *(m)*, Vitrine *(f)*
display case Schaukasten *(m)*, Vitrine *(f)*
display pack Schaupackung *(f)*
display system Display System *(n)*, Präsentationssystem *(n)*
display terminal, visual Datensichtgerät *(n)*, Bildschirmgerät *(n)*
display wall Displaywand *(f)*, Präsentationswand *(f)*
display window Schaufenster *(n)*
display, rotating drehendes Display *(n)*
disposable verfügbar; wegwerfbar, Einweg-, Wegwerf-
disposable carpet Einwegteppich *(m)*
disposable dishes Einweggeschirr *(n)*
disposal Beseitigung *(f)*, Erledigung *(f)*; Veräußerung *(f)*; Übergabe *(f)*; Verfügung *(f)*, Anordnung *(f)*; Arrangement *(n)*
dispose anordnen, aufstellen, bewegen

dispute Disput *(m)*,
Meinungsverschiedenheit *(f)*,
Kontroverse *(f)*, Streit *(m)*
dispute disputieren, streiten, bestreiten,
bezweifeln, sich streiten, anfechten,
kämpfen
disregard nicht beachten, missachten,
ignorieren
disregard Nichtbeachtung *(f)*,
Missachtung *(f)*, Ignorierung *(f)*
disruption Störung *(f)*,
Unterbrechung *(f)*
dissolve auflösen, sich auflösen;
(Projektion) überblenden
dissolve control unit
Überblendsteuereinheit *(f)*
dissolve projection
Überblendprojektion *(f)*
distance Distanz *(f)*, Abstand *(m)*,
Entfernung *(f)*, Ferne *(f)*, Strecke *(f)*
distance distanzieren, hinter sich
lassen; übertreffen
distance beam Distanzzarge *(f)*
distance connector Verbinder *(m)*
distance piece Abstandshalter *(m)*,
Distanzhalter *(m)*
distinction Unterschied *(m)*,
Unterscheidung *(f)*; Auszeichnung *(f)*,
Ehrung *(f)*; Rang *(m)*
distinctive charakteristisch,
kennzeichnend, unverwechselbar
distinguish auseinander halten,
unterscheiden, erkennen,
wahrnehmen, kennzeichnen,
sich auszeichnen, sich hervortun
distribute verteilen, verbreiten,
vertreiben
distribution Distribution *(f)*, Absatz *(m)*,
Vertrieb *(m)*, Verteilung *(f)*,
Verbreitung *(f)*, Streuung *(f)*
distribution area Absatzgebiet *(n)*
distribution box (Strom)
Verteilerkasten *(m)*
distribution box, electric
Elektroverteilerkasten *(m)*

distribution channel Absatzkanal *(m)*,
Vertriebsweg *(m)*
distribution network Vertriebsnetz *(n)*
distribution of cost Umlage *(f)*
distribution policy Absatzpolitik *(f)*,
Vertriebspolitik *(f)*
distribution, electrical
Elektroverteilung *(f)*
district Gebiet *(n)*, Landstrich *(m)*,
Stadtviertel *(n)*
disturb stören, unterbrechen,
beunruhigen
disturbance Störung *(f)*,
Ruhestörung *(f)*, Unruhe *(f)*
diverse verschieden, verschiedenartig,
ungleich, andersartig
diversification Diversifikation *(f)*,
Streuung *(f)*, Verschiedenartigkeit *(f)*
diversify diversifizieren,
abwechslungsreich gestalten
diversion Umleitung *(f)*, Ablenkung *(f)*,
Zerstreuung *(f)*
divert umleiten, ablenken, zerstreuen
divide teilen, aufteilen, verteilen,
zerteilen, trennen, spalten, zerfallen,
sich teilen, sich aufteilen
dividing groove Trennfuge *(f)*
dividing line Trennlinie *(f)*
dividing wall Trennwand *(f)*,
Zwischenwand *(f)*
divine service Gottesdienst *(m)*
divisible teilbar
division Abteilung *(f)*,
Unternehmensbereich *(m)*; Fach *(n)*,
Sparte *(f)*; Teilung *(f)*, Aufteilung *(f)*;
Grenze *(f)*, Trennlinie *(f)*; Spaltung *(f)*,
Entzweiung *(f)*, Uneinigkeit *(f)*
division of labor (US)
Arbeitsteilung *(f)*
division of labour (GB)
Arbeitsteilung *(f)*
DIY kit Heimwerkerbausatz *(m)*,
Selbstbausatz *(m)*
doctor on call Notarzt *(m)*,
Notärztin *(f)*

doctor's certificate ärztliches Attest *(n)*
document Dokument *(n)*, Beleg *(m)*, Urkunde *(f)*, Beurkundung *(f)*, Akten *(f, pl)*
document dokumentieren, beurkunden
document, accompanying Transportpapier *(n)*, Begleitschein *(m)*
do-it-yourself kit Heimwerkerbausatz *(m)*, Selbstbausatz *(m)*
domestic einheimisch, inländisch, häuslich, Haushalts-, Inlands-, Innen-, Binnen-
Don't touch! Nicht berühren!
door Tür *(f)*, Tor *(n)*, Pforte *(f)*
door drop Wurfsendung *(f)*
door frame Türrahmen *(m)*
door handle Türgriff *(m)*, Türklinke *(f)*
door handle set Drückergarnitur *(f)*
door hinge Türangel *(f)*, Türscharnier *(n)*
door knob Türknopf *(m)*
door lock Türschloss *(n)*
door man Pförtner *(m)*, Portier *(m)*
door plate Türschild *(n)*
door post Türpfosten *(m)*
door stop Türanschlag *(m)*
door stop extrusion Türanschlagprofil *(n)*
door, double Flügeltür *(f)*
dot Punkt *(m)*, Pünktchen *(n)*, Tupfen *(m)*, Tüpfelchen *(n)*
dot punktieren, sprenkeln
dotmatrix printer Nadeldrucker *(m)*
double doppelt, zweifach, verdoppelt, Doppel-
double Doppeltes *(n)*, Zweifaches *(n)*; Doppel *(n)*; Doppelgänger(in) *(m/f)*, Duplikat *(n)*
double verdoppeln, sich verdoppeln; sich falten lassen
double-sided doppelseitig, beidseitig
doubtful unsicher, ungewiss, zweifelhaft
douche Dusche *(f)*
dowel Dübel *(m)*
down herunter, hinunter, nach unten, abwärts

downward geneigt, absteigend
draft Ausarbeitung *(f)*, Entwurf *(m)*, Skizze *(f)*; Bankscheck *(m)*, Wechsel *(m)*
draft entwerfen, skizzieren
draft (US) Luftzug *(m)*
draft agreement Vereinbarungsentwurf *(m)*, Vertragsentwurf *(m)*
draft contract Vertragsentwurf *(m)*
drag Hindernis *(n)*, Hemmklotz *(m)*; Schleppen *(n)*, Zerren *(n)*
drag ziehen, zerren, schleppen, schleifen, sich in die Länge *(f)* ziehen
drain entwässern, kanalisieren, leeren, Wasser *(n)* ablassen
drain Rohr *(n)*, Abflussrohr *(n)*
drain connection Abwasseranschluss *(m)*
drainage Abzugskanal *(m)*, Abfluss *(m)*, Ableitung *(f)*, Entwässerung *(f)*, Kanalisation *(f)*
drainpipe Abflussrohr *(n)*
draught (GB) Durchzug *(m)*, Luftzug *(m)*, Zugluft *(f)*; Fassbier *(n)*
draw auslosen; (Linie etc.) ziehen, zeichnen; (Text etc.) abfassen, ausarbeiten; anlocken, anziehen; (Interesse) wecken
draw Verlosung *(f)*, Auslosung *(f)*, Ziehen *(n)*, Ziehung *(f)*; Zugkraft *(f)*; Attraktion *(f)*
drawer Zeichner(in) *(m/f)*; Schublade *(f)*, Schubfach *(n)*
drawing Zeichnung *(f)*
drawing board Reißbrett *(n)*, Zeichenbrett *(n)*
drawing lots Verlosung *(f)*
drawing pad Zeichenblock *(m)*
drawing paper Zeichenpapier *(n)*
drawing pin Reißzwecke *(f)*
drawing, dimensional vermaßte Zeichnung *(f)*
drawing, perspective perspektivische Zeichnung *(f)*

drawing, sectional Schnittzeichnung *(f)*, Querschnittszeichnung *(f)*
drayage Rollgeld *(n)*
drayage contractor Spedition *(f)*
dress anziehen, einkleiden, sich anziehen; dekorieren, schmücken
dress Kleid *(n)*, Kleidung *(f)*
dressing material Verbandsmaterial *(n)*
drill bohren
drill Bohrer *(m)*
drill hole Bohrloch *(n)*
drilling Bohrung *(f)*
drilling jig Bohrvorrichtung *(f)*
drilling template Bohrschablone *(f)*
drink Drink *(m)*, Getränk *(n)*; Schluck *(m)*
drink trinken
drink dispenser Getränkeautomat *(m)*
drinking cup Getränkebecher *(m)*
drinking water cooler Trinkwasserkühler *(m)*
drip tropfen, tröpfeln
drip Tropfen *(m)*, Tröpfeln *(n)*
drip tray Abtropfwanne *(f)*
drive, electric Elektroantrieb *(m)*
driver's license (US) Führerschein *(m)*
driver's license (US), revocation of the Führerscheinentzug *(m)*
driveway Zufahrt *(f)*, Zufahrtsstraße *(f)*
driving licence (GB) Führerschein *(m)*
driving licence (GB), revocation of the Führerscheinentzug *(m)*
drop tropfen, herabtropfen, fallen, fallen lassen, niederlegen; (Fahrgäste) absetzen; (Sache) aufgeben
drop Tropfen *(m)*; Fall *(m)*, Fallen *(n)*, Sturz *(m)*; Sinken *(n)*, Rückgang *(m)*
drop in orders Auftragsrückgang *(m)*
drop in pressure Druckabfall *(m)*
drop in prices Preisrückgang *(m)*, Preissturz *(m)*
drop in sales Umsatzrückgang *(m)*
dry trocken, ausgetrocknet
dry trocknen, abtrocknen
dry ice Trockeneis *(n)*

duct Rohr *(n)*, Röhre *(f)*, Leitung *(f)*, Kanal *(m)*
due fällig, unbeglichen, zahlbar; gebührend, angemessen, passend, richtig
due date Fälligkeitstermin *(m)*, Abgabefrist *(f)*, Verfallsdatum *(n)*
dues Abgaben *(f, pl)*, Gebühren *(f, pl)*, Zoll *(m)*, Zollgebühren *(f, pl)*
dummy Schaupackung *(f)*, Attrappe *(f)*
duplex doppelt
duplicate doppelt, zweifach
duplicate Duplikat *(n)*, Kopie *(f)*
duplicate kopieren, vervielfältigen
duplicate key Nachschlüssel *(m)*
durability Dauer *(f)*, Dauerhaftigkeit *(f)*, Haltbarkeit *(f)*, Widerstandsfähigkeit *(f)*
durable haltbar, dauerhaft, langlebig, widerstandsfähig
durable goods Gebrauchsgüter *(n, pl)*
durables Gebrauchsgüter *(n, pl)*
duration Dauer *(f)*, Laufzeit *(f)*
duration of guarantee Garantiedauer *(f)*
duration of the event Veranstaltungsdauer *(f)*, Veranstaltungslaufzeit *(f)*
duration of the exhibition Ausstellungsdauer *(f)*
duration of the fair Messedauer *(f)*
dusky dämmrig, düster
dust abstauben, Staub *(m)* wischen
dust Staub *(m)*
dustbin Mülltonne *(f)*
dust-proof rail Staubschutzleiste *(f)*
dust-trap Schmutzkante *(f)*
duty Zoll *(m)*, Steuer *(f)*; Pflicht *(f)*, Aufgabe *(f)*, Dienst *(m)*
duty drawback Zollerstattung *(f)*, Zollrückvergütung *(f)*
duty of supervision Aufsichtspflicht *(f)*
duty-free zollfrei
duty-paid verzollt
DVD drive DVD-Laufwerk *(n)*
DVD player DVD-Spieler *(m)*

E

ear protectors Gehörschutz *(m)*
earnings Arbeitslohn *(m)*, Einkommen *(n)*, Einnahme *(f)*, Einkünfte *(f, pl)*, Verdienst *(m)*, Ertrag *(m)*, Gewinn *(m)*
earnings before taxes Gewinn *(m)* vor Steuern
earth Erde *(f)*, Erdboden *(m)*, Land *(n)*
earth erden
ecological ökologisch
ecologically compatible umweltverträglich
ecologically friendly umweltfreundlich
ecologically harmful umweltschädlich
ecologically harmless umweltverträglich
economic ökonomisch, wirtschaftlich, volkswirtschaftlich
economical sparsam
economy Wirtschaft *(m)*, Volkswirtschaft *(f)*, Wirtschaftlichkeit *(f)*, Sparsamkeit *(f)*
economy class Touristenklasse *(f)*
economy measure Sparmaßnahme *(f)*
economy pack Sparpackung *(f)*
edge einfassen, säumen; schleifen, schärfen; schieben, drängen, vorrücken
edge Kante *(f)*, Ecke *(f)*, Rand *(m)*; Schneide *(f)*, Schärfe *(f)*; Vorteil *(m)*
edge protection Kantenschutz *(m)*
edge protection extrusion Kantenschutzprofil *(n)*
edge, radiussed abgerundete Kante *(f)*
edgeway seitwärts, hochkant
edgewise seitwärts, hochkant
edit (Buch) herausgeben, redigieren; (Daten) aufbereiten
edit control unit Schnittsteuereinheit *(f)*
edition Ausgabe *(f)*, Auflage *(f)*
edition, new Neuauflage *(f)*
edition, special Sonderausgabe *(f)*, Sondernummer *(f)*
editor Herausgeber(in) *(m/f)*, Redakteur(in) *(m/f)*
editorial redaktionell
editorial department Redaktion *(f)*, Redaktionsbüro *(n)*
editorial staff Redaktionsstab *(f)*
editor-in-chief Chefredakteur(in) *(m/f)*
EDP (electronic data processing) EDV (elektronische Datenverarbeitung)
EDP equipment EDV-Anlage *(f)*
EDP system EDV-System *(n)*
effect bewirken, auswirken, zu Stande *(m)* bringen, ausführen, tätigen
effect Effekt *(m)*, Wirkung *(f)*, Auswirkung *(f)*, Wirksamkeit *(f)*, Ergebnis *(n)*, Folge *(f)*, Erfolg *(m)*, Eindruck *(m)*
effect lighting Effektbeleuchtung *(f)*
effective effektiv, effektvoll, tatsächlich, erfolgreich, eindrucksvoll, wirksam, wirkungsvoll
effective for advertising purposes werbewirksam
effectiveness Effektivität *(f)*, Wirksamkeit *(f)*
efficiency Effizienz *(f)*, Leistungsfähigkeit *(f)*, Tüchtigkeit *(f)*, Wirkungsgrad *(m)*, Wirtschaftlichkeit *(f)*
efficiency review Erfolgskontrolle *(f)*
efficiency, economic Wirtschaftlichkeit *(f)*
efficient effizient, wirksam, wirtschaftlich, rationell, leistungsfähig, tüchtig
elastic elastisch, biegsam, dehnbar
electric elektrisch
electrical device, main (Strom) Vorschaltgerät *(n)*
electrical loading, total (Strom) Anschlussleistung *(f)*
electrician Elektriker(in) *(m/f)*
electricity bill Stromrechnung *(f)*

electricity consumption Stromverbrauch *(m)*
electro control panel Elektroschaltanlage *(f)*
electronic data processing (EDP) elektronische Datenverarbeitung *(f)* (EDV)
electronic, fully vollelektronisch
electronics Elektronik *(f)*
electroshock Elektroschock *(m)*
element Element *(n)*, Bestandteil *(m)*, Grundstoff *(m)*, wesentlicher Faktor *(m)*, wesentlicher Umstand *(m)*
element elementar, Elementar-, natürlich, ursprünglich, grundlegend, wesentlich
element, fixing Befestigungselement *(n)*
elevation Anhöhe *(f)*, Erhebung *(f)*; Erhabenheit *(f)*, Würde *(f)*; (Zeichnung) Aufriss *(m)*
elevenses Brotzeit *(f)*
eligible berechtigt, teilnahmeberechtigt, geeignet
eloquent beredt, redegewandt, ausdrucksvoll
e-mail E-Mail *(f)*
e-mail address E-Mail-Adresse *(f)*
embassy Botschaft *(f)*
embellish verschönern, ausschmücken
embellishment Verschönerung *(f)*
emergency Notfall *(m)*, Notlage *(f)*
emergency aid Soforthilfe *(f)*
emergency ambulance Notarztwagen *(m)*
emergency call Notruf *(m)*
emergency doctor Notarzt *(m)*
emergency dressing Notverband *(m)*
emergency evacuation Notfallräumung *(f)*
emergency exit Notausgang *(m)*
emergency generating set Notstromaggregat *(n)*
emergency generator Notstromaggregat *(n)*
emergency help Nothilfe *(f)*

emergency lighting Notbeleuchtung *(f)*
emergency measure Notmaßnahme *(f)*
emergency phone number Notrufnummer *(f)*
emergency power supply Notstromversorgung *(f)*
emergency route Rettungsweg *(m)*
emergency service Notdienst *(m)*, Hilfsdienst *(m)*
emergency services movement zone Bewegungszone *(f)* für Rettungsfahrzeuge
emergency telephone Notruftelefon *(n)*, Notrufsäule *(f)*
emphasis Betonung *(f)*, Nachdruck *(m)*
emphasize hervorheben, unterstreichen, Nachdruck *(m)* legen auf
emphatic emphatisch, betont, nachdrücklich, eindringlich, entscheidend
employ anstellen, einstellen, beschäftigen; anwenden, benutzen, gebrauchen, verwenden
employee Angestellte(r) *(f/m)*, Arbeitnehmer(in) *(m/f)*, Beschäftigte(r) *(f/m)*, Mitarbeiter(in) *(m/f)*
employer Arbeitgeber(in) *(m/f)*, Unternehmer(in) *(m/f)*
employment Arbeitsverhältnis *(n)*, Beschäftigung *(f)*, Stellung *(f)*
employment agency Arbeitsvermittlung *(f)*, Arbeitsvermittlungsagentur *(f)*, Stellenvermittlung *(f)*, Personalvermittlungsbüro *(n)*
employment agency, temporary Zeitarbeitsfirma *(f)*, Leiharbeitsfirma *(f)*
employment costs Personalkosten *(pl)*
employment expenses Personalaufwendungen *(f, pl)*, Personalkosten *(pl)*
employment security Arbeitsplatzsicherheit *(f)*

employment, temporary Zeitarbeit *(f)*, Aushilfsarbeit *(f)*
employment, unrecorded Schwarzarbeit *(f)*
empties Leergut *(n)*
empties handling Leergutmanipulation *(f)*
empty leer, leerstehend
empty leeren, ausleeren, entleeren, sich leeren, ausräumen, austrinken
empty weight Leergewicht *(n)*
encircle umschließen, umgeben, umfassen, einkreisen
enclose einschließen, umgeben, umringen; beifügen, beilegen
encourage ermuntern, ermutigen, fördern, bestärken, unterstützen
encouragement Ermunterung *(f)*, Ermutigung *(f)*, Förderung *(f)*, Bestärkung *(f)*, Unterstützung *(f)*
end Ende *(n)*, Schluss *(m)*, Rest *(m)*, Absicht *(f)*, Zweck *(m)*, Ziel *(n)*, Ergebnis *(n)*, Konsequenz *(f)*
end enden, beenden, zu Ende *(n)* gehen, zu Ende *(n)* bringen, aufhören, Schluss *(m)* machen; beschließen
end cap Endkappe *(f)*, Abdeckkappe *(f)*
end consumer Endverbraucher(in) *(m/f)*
end current load circuit Endstromverbraucherkreis *(m)*
end panel Abschlussplatte *(f)*, Randplatte *(f)*
end piece Endstück *(n)*
end plate Abschlussplatte *(f)*, Endplatte *(f)*
end, open offenes Ende *(n)*
endanger gefährden
end-of-show party Messe-Abschlussparty *(f)*
end-up hochkant
enduser Endabnehmer(in) *(m/f)*, Endverbraucher(in) *(m/f)*, Endanwender(in) *(m/f)*
energy consumption Energieverbrauch *(m)*

energy cost lump sum Energiekostenpauschale *(f)*
energy costs Energiekosten *(pl)*
energy demand Energiebedarf *(m)*
energy supply Energieversorgung *(f)*
engaged signal (Telefon) Besetztzeichen *(n)*
engaged tone (Telefon) Besetztzeichen *(n)*
engagement Engagement *(n)*, Anstellung *(f)*, Beschäftigung *(f)*, Stelle *(f)*; Abmachung *(f)*, Verabredung *(f)*, Vereinbarung *(f)*, Verpflichtung *(f)*
engine Maschine *(f)*, Motor *(m)*
engine failure Maschinenschaden *(m)*
engineer Ingenieur(in) *(m/f)*, Techniker(in) *(m/f)*, Maschinist(in) *(m/f)*, Mechaniker(in) *(m/f)*
engineer konstruieren, planen, bauen
engineering Technik *(f)*, Ingenieurwesen *(n)*
engineering, advanced neueste Technik *(f)*
engineering, electrical Elektrotechnik *(f)*
enlarge vergrößern, sich vergrößern, erweitern, sich erweitern, verbreitern, ausdehnen, sich ausdehnen, ausweiten, sich ausweiten
enlargement Ausdehnung *(f)*, Erweiterung *(f)*; (Foto etc.) Vergrößerung *(f)*
enormous enorm, gewaltig, riesig, ungeheuer
enquire (GB) sich erkundigen, fragen
enquiry (GB) Anfrage *(f)*, Befragung *(f)*, Erhebung *(f)*, Erkundigung *(f)*, Prüfung *(f)*, Untersuchung *(f)*
ensure sichern, sicherstellen, versichern, garantieren, schützen
enter eintreten, betreten, hineingehen, hereinkommen, einsteigen, eindringen, einreisen, einschreiben, eintragen, sich einschreiben; (EDV) sich anmelden, eingeben

enterprise Unternehmen *(n)*,
Unternehmung *(f)*, Betrieb *(m)*,
Geschäft *(n)*, Vorhaben *(n)*
enterprise, medium-sized
mittelständischer Betrieb *(m)*
entertain unterhalten, belustigen,
bewirten
entertainer Entertainer(in) *(m/f)*,
Unterhalter(in) *(m/f)*
entertainment Darbietung *(f)*,
Unterhaltung *(f)*, Vergnügung *(f)*,
Bewirtung *(f)*
entitle berechtigen
entrance Eingang *(m)*, Eintreten *(n)*,
Eintritt *(m)*, Eintrittsgeld *(n)*,
Zugang *(m)*, Einfahrt *(f)*
entrance fee Eintrittsgeld *(n)*,
Eintrittsgebühr *(f)*,
Aufnahmegebühr *(f)*
entrance form Anmeldeformular *(n)*
entrance gate Einfahrtstor *(n)*,
Toreinfahrt *(f)*
entrance hall Vorhalle *(f)*
entrance pass Eintrittsausweis *(m)*,
Einfahrtschein *(m)*,
Passierschein *(m)*
entrance permit
Eintrittsgenehmigung *(f)*,
Einfahrtsgenehmigung *(f)*,
Zulassungsgenehmigung *(f)*
entrance regulations
Einfahrtsregelung *(f)*,
Zugangsregelung *(f)*,
Zulassungsregelung *(f)*
entrance requirement
Zulassungsanforderung *(f)*
entrance, main Haupteingang *(m)*,
Haupteinfahrt *(f)*
entrepreneur
Unternehmer(in) *(m/f)*
entry Einlass *(m)*, Eintritt *(m)*,
Eingang *(m)*, Einfahrt *(f)*, Einreise *(f)*,
Zugang *(m)*, Zutritt *(m)*, Beitritt *(m)*;
Buchung *(f)*; (Katalog etc.)
Eintragung *(f)*, Vermerk *(m)*

entry fee Eintrittsgeld *(n)*,
Eintrittsgebühr *(f)*,
Aufnahmegebühr *(f)*,
Anmeldegebühr *(f)*
entry form Anmeldeformular *(n)*
entry permit Zutrittsgenehmigung *(f)*,
Einfahrtsgenehmigung *(f)*,
Einreisegenehmigung *(f)*
entry regulations
Zugangsbestimmungen *(f, pl)*,
Einreisebestimmungen *(f, pl)*
entry, false Falschbuchung *(f)*
entry, make an buchen, Eintragung *(f)*
vornehmen
enumerate aufzählen, aufführen
enumeration Aufzählung *(f)*
envelope einschlagen, einwickeln,
verhüllen
envelope Umschlag *(m)*, Kuvert *(n)*;
Decke *(f)*, Hülle *(f)*
environment Umwelt *(f)*,
Umgebung *(f)*,
Rahmenbedingungen *(f, pl)*
environmental awareness
Umweltbewusstsein *(n)*
environmental conservation
Umweltschutz *(m)*
environmental damage
Umweltschäden *(m, pl)*
environmental pollution
Umweltverschmutzung *(f)*
environmental protection
Umweltschutz *(m)*
environmental protection law
Umweltschutzgesetz *(n)*
environmental regulations
Umweltrichtlinien *(f, pl)*
environmentally beneficial
umweltfreundlich, umweltgünstig
environmentally conscious
umweltbewusst
environmentally friendly
umweltfreundlich
equip ausrüsten, ausstatten,
bestücken, einrichten, vorbereiten

equipment Ausrüstung *(f)*, Ausstattung *(f)*, Einrichtung *(f)*, Bestückung *(f)*, Gerätschaften *(f, pl)*, Anlage *(f)*
equipment safety law Gerätesicherheitsgesetz *(n)*
equipment, additional Zusatzausstattung *(f)*
equipment, add-on Zusatzgerät *(n)*
equipment, basic Grundausstattung *(f)*
equipment, high-frequency Hochfrequenzgerät *(n)*
equity capital Eigenkapital *(n)*
erase ausradieren, auslöschen, tilgen, entfernen; (Daten) löschen
erect aufrecht, aufgerichtet, senkrecht
erect aufrichten, errichten, senkrecht stellen, montieren, aufbauen
erection Errichtung *(f)*, Aufstellung *(f)*, Bau *(m)*, Montage *(f)*; Bauwerk *(n)*
error Irrtum *(m)*, Fehler *(m)*, Versehen *(n)*
error in translation Übersetzungsfehler *(m)*
error rate Fehlerquote *(f)*
error, typographical Druckfehler *(m)*
escalate ansteigen, ausweiten, eskalieren
escalation clause Preisgleitklausel *(f)*
escalator Rolltreppe *(f)*
escape fliehen, entfliehen, flüchten, entkommen, entgehen, sich retten; ausströmen, auslaufen, entweichen
escape Flucht *(f)*, Fluchtweg *(m)*, Entkommen *(n)*, Rettung *(f)*; Entweichen *(n)*, Ausströmen *(n)*
escape hatch Notausstiegsöffnung *(f)*, Notausstiegsluke *(f)*
escape period Rücktrittsfrist *(f)*
escape route Fluchtweg *(m)*
espresso machine Espressomaschine *(f)*
espresso maker Espressomaschine *(f)*
essential wesentlich, grundlegend, unerlässlich, unentbehrlich

essential Wesentliches *(n)*, Voraussetzung *(f)*, Notewendigstes *(n)*, Hauptsache *(f)*
essentially wesentlich, im Wesentlichen
estate, industrial Industriegebiet *(n)*, Industriegelände *(n)*, Industriepark *(m)*, Gewerbegebiet *(n)*, Gewerbefläche *(f)*, Gewerbepark *(m)*
estimate beurteilen, veranschlagen, schätzen, taxieren
estimate Bewertung *(f)*, Beurteilung *(f)*, Schätzung *(f)*, Voranschlag *(m)*
EU (European Union) EU (Europäische Union)
EU directive EU-Richtlinie *(f)*
EU member state EU-Mitgliedsland *(n)*
EU standard EU-Norm *(f)*
Eurocheck (US) Euroscheck *(m)*
Eurocheck card (US) Euroscheckkarte *(f)*
Eurocheque (GB) Euroscheck *(m)*
Eurocheque card (GB) Euroscheckkarte *(f)*
evacuate evakuieren, räumen
evacuation Evakuierung *(f)*, Räumung *(f)*
evaluate auswerten, bewerten, schätzen, beurteilen
evaluation Auswertung *(f)*, Bewertung *(f)*, Schätzung *(f)*, Taxierung *(f)*
evaporation Verdunstung *(f)*
evening before Vorabend *(m)*
evening dress Abendkleidung *(f)*
event Event *(m)*, Begebenheit *(f)*, Ereignis *(n)*, Veranstaltung *(f)*; Fall *(m)*
event conditions, general allgemeine Veranstaltungsbedingungen *(f, pl)*
event conditions, specific besondere Messeteilnahmebedingungen *(f, pl)*
event of loss Schadenfall *(m)*
evidence Beweis *(m)*, Beweismaterial *(n)*, Aussage *(f)*, Nachweis *(m)*, Anhaltspunkt *(m)*, Anzeichen *(n)*

evident augenscheinlich, offenkundig, offensichtlich
exact exakt, gewissenhaft, pünktlich
examine prüfen, untersuchen
example Beispiel *(n)*, Vorbild *(n)*
example of use Anwendungsbeispiel *(n)*
excavator Bagger *(m)*
excellent ausgezeichnet, hervorragend
except ausnehmen, ausschließen, sich vorbehalten
except außer, ausgenommen, mit Ausnahme *(f)* von
exception Ausnahme *(f)*, Einwand *(f)*, Vorbehalt *(m)*
exceptional außergewöhnlich, ungewöhnlich
excess baggage (US) Übergepäck *(n)*
excess baggage fee (US) Übergepäckgebühr *(f)*, Übergepäckzuschlag *(m)*
excess capacity Überkapazität *(f)*
excess luggage (GB) Übergepäck *(n)*
excess luggage fee (GB) Übergepäckgebühr *(f)*, Übergepäckzuschlag *(m)*
excessive übermäßig, übertrieben
exchange Tausch *(m)*, Austausch *(m)*, Umtausch *(m)*, Tauschgeschäft *(n)*, Wechseln *(n)*; Valuta *(f)*, Devisen *(f, pl)*; Börse *(f)*
exchange tauschen, austauschen, eintauschen, umtauschen, vertauschen, wechseln, auswechseln
exchange charges Wechselkosten *(pl)*, Wechselgebühr *(f)*
exchange fluctuations Kursschwankungen *(f, pl)*
exchange of experience Erfahrungsaustausch *(m)*
exchange of ideas Gedankenaustausch *(m)*
exchange of money Geldumtausch *(m)*
exchange of place (Messestand) Platztausch *(m)*

exchange of stands Standtausch *(m)*
exchange of views Meinungsaustausch *(m)*
exchange office Wechselstube *(f)*
exchange rate Wechselkurs *(m)*
exchange rate fluctuation Wechselkursschwankung *(f)*
exchange, foreign Devisen *(pl)*
exchange, rate of Devisenkurs *(m)*, Wechselkurs *(m)*
exchangeable austauschbar
excisable goods verbrauchssteuerpflichtige Güter *(n, pl)*
excise Verbrauchssteuer *(f)*, Warensteuer *(f)*
excite erregen, aufregen, anregen, reizen, begeistern
excitement Aufregung *(f)*, Erregung *(f)*
exclusion Ausschluss *(m)*
exclusion of warranty Ausschluss *(m)* der Gewährleistung
exclusion of exhibitors Ausschluss *(m)* von Ausstellern
exclusion of exhibits Ausschluss *(m)* von Exponaten
exclusion of liability Haftungsausschluss *(m)*
exclusion of seller's warranty Ausschluss *(m)* der Gewährleistung
exclusive exklusiv, ausschließlich; elegant, vornehm
exclusive right Ausschlussrecht *(n)*, Exklusivrecht *(n)*
excuse entschuldigen, verzeihen, rechtfertigen
excuse Entschuldigung *(f)*, Rechtfertigung *(f)*, Ausrede *(f)*, Ausflucht *(f)*
executive Führungskraft *(f)*, leitende(r) Angestellte(r) *(f/m)*
executive leitend, verfügend
executive assistant Chefsekretär(in) *(m/f)*
executive board Vorstand *(m)*

executive committee leitendes Gremium *(n)*, Vorstand *(m)*
executive director geschäftsführende(r) Direktor(in) *(m/f)*, Generaldirektor(in) *(m/f)*
executive functions Führungsaufgaben *(f, pl)*
executive manager leitende(r) Angestellte(r) *(f/m)*
executive secretary Chefsekretär(in) *(m/f)*
executive, top-level Spitzenkraft *(f)*
exemplary exemplarisch, musterhaft, mustergültig, vorbildlich; warnend, abschreckend
exempt from tax steuerfrei
exempt from VAT mehrwertsteuerfrei
exhaust emission, with low abgasarm
exhaust pipe Abgasleitung *(f)*
exhaust steam Abdampf *(m)*
exhibit ausstellen, zeigen, zur Schau *(f)* stellen; (Ware) auslegen
exhibit Ausstellungsstück *(n)*, Ausstellungsgegenstand *(m)*, Exponat *(n)*
exhibit a fair Messe *(f)* beschicken
exhibit insurance Exponatversicherung *(f)*
exhibit sign Exponatschild *(n)*
exhibition Ausstellung *(f)*, Messe *(f)*, Auslage *(f)*, Vorführung *(f)*
exhibition advisory council Messebeirat *(m)*
exhibition architect Messearchitekt(in) *(m/f)*
exhibition area Ausstellungsfläche *(f)*
exhibition area, rented (US) vermietete Ausstellungsfläche *(f)*
exhibition area, booked vorbestellte Ausstellungsfläche *(f)*
exhibition area, leased vermietete Ausstellungsfläche *(f)*
exhibition area, open Messefreigelände *(n)*

exhibition area, uncovered Messefreigelände *(n)*
exhibition authorities Ausstellungsleitung *(f)*, Messeleitung *(f)*
exhibition benefit check Messenutzencheck *(m)*
exhibition booth Ausstellungsstand *(m)*, Messestand *(m)*
exhibition budget Messebudget *(n)*, Ausstellungsetat *(m)*
exhibition building Ausstellungsgebäude *(n)*, Messegebäude *(n)*
exhibition building, multistorey (GB) mehrgeschossiges Messegebäude *(n)*
exhibition building, multistoried mehrgeschossiges Messegebäude *(n)*
exhibition building, multistory (US) mehrgeschossiges Messegebäude *(n)*
exhibition calendar Ausstellungskalender *(m)*, Messekalender *(m)*
exhibition catalog (US) Ausstellungskatalog *(m)*, Messekatalog *(m)*
exhibition catalogue (GB) Ausstellungskatalog *(m)*, Messekatalog *(m)*
exhibition committee Ausstellungskomitee *(n)*, Messekomitee *(n)*
exhibition company Ausstellungsgesellschaft *(f)*, Messegesellschaft *(f)*
exhibition concept Ausstellungskonzept, Messekonzept *(n)*
exhibition congress Ausstellungstagung *(f)*, Messetagung *(f)*
exhibition consultant Ausstellungsberater(in) *(m/f)*, Messeberater(in) *(m/f)*
exhibition corporation Ausstellungsgesellschaft *(f)*, Messegesellschaft *(f)*

exhibition corporations, major
Großmesseunternehmen *(n, pl)*
exhibition daily Ausstellungszeitung *(f)*, Messezeitung *(f)*
exhibition date Ausstellungstermin *(m)*, Messetermin *(m)*
exhibition display
Ausstellungsdisplay *(n)*, Messedisplay *(n)*
exhibition follow-up work
Ausstellungsnacharbeit *(f)*, Messenacharbeit *(f)*
exhibition form
Ausstellungsformblatt *(n)*, Messeformblatt *(n)*
exhibition functions
Ausstellungsfunktionen *(f, pl)*, Messefunktionen *(f, pl)*
exhibition goods Ausstellungsgut *(n)*, Messegut *(n)*
exhibition grounds
Ausstellungsgelände *(n)*, Messegelände *(n)*
exhibition hall Ausstellungshalle *(f)*, Messehalle *(f)*
exhibition infrastructure
Ausstellungsinfrastruktur *(f)*, Messeinfrastruktur *(f)*
exhibition innovation Ausstellungsneuheit *(f)*, Messeneuheit *(f)*
exhibition insurance
Ausstellungsversicherung *(f)*, Messeversicherung *(f)*
exhibition labor office (US)
Messearbeitsamt *(n)*
exhibition labour office (GB)
Messearbeitsamt *(n)*
exhibition logistics Messelogistik *(f)*
exhibition magazine Messemagazin *(n)*, Messezeitschrift *(f)*
exhibition management
Ausstellungsleitung *(f)*, Messeleitung *(f)*
exhibition management office
Ausstellungsbüro *(n)*, Messebüro *(n)*

exhibition marketing
Ausstellungsmarketing *(n)*, Messemarketing *(n)*
exhibition materials
Ausstellungsgut *(n)*, Messegut *(n)*
exhibition organizer
Ausstellungsveranstalter *(m)*, Messeveranstalter *(m)*
exhibition overview
Ausstellungsüberblick *(m)*, Messeüberblick *(m)*
exhibition participation
Ausstellungsbeteiligung *(f)*, Messebeteiligung *(f)*
exhibition participation contract
Vertrag *(m)* zur Ausstellungsbeteiligung, Vertrag *(m)* zur Messebeteiligung
exhibition pass
Ausstellungsausweis *(m)*, Messeausweis *(m)*
exhibition period
Ausstellungslaufzeit *(f)*, Messedauer *(f)*
exhibition photographer, official
offizielle(r) Messefotograf(in) *(m/f)*
exhibition program (US)
Ausstellungsprogramm *(n)*, Messeprogramm *(n)*
exhibition programme (GB)
Ausstellungsprogramm *(n)*, Messeprogramm *(n)*
exhibition project
Ausstellungsvorhaben *(n)*, Messevorhaben *(n)*
exhibition promoter
Ausstellungsveranstalter *(m)*, Messeveranstalter *(m)*
exhibition rankings, international
internationales Messeranking *(n)*
exhibition restaurant
Messerestaurant *(n)*
exhibition rules and regulations
Ausstellungsvorschriften *(f, pl)*, Messeregularien *(f, pl)*

exhibition sections
Ausstellungsbereiche *(m, pl)*,
Messebereiche *(m, pl)*
exhibition shuttle Messeshuttle *(n)*,
Messependelverkehr *(m)*
exhibition site Ausstellungsgelände *(n)*,
Messegelände *(n)*
exhibition space Ausstellungsraum *(m)*,
Ausstellungsfläche *(f)*
exhibition space, leased vermieteter
Ausstellungsplatz *(m)*
exhibition space, rented (US)
vermieteter Ausstellungsraum *(m)*,
vermietete Ausstellungsfläche *(f)*
exhibition stand Ausstellungsstand *(m)*,
Messestand *(m)*
exhibition stand construction
Messestandbau *(m)*
exhibition system manufacturer
Systemmessebauhersteller *(m)*
exhibition targets Ausstellungsziele *(n, pl)*, Messeziele *(n, pl)*
exhibition targets, definition of
Festlegung *(f)* der Ausstellungsziele
exhibition targets, quantitative
quantitative Messeziele *(n, pl)*
exhibition targets, strategic
strategische Messeziele *(n, pl)*
exhibition venues, major
Hauptmesseplätze *(m, pl)*,
Großmesseplätze *(m, pl)*
exhibition, competitive
Leistungsschau *(f)*
exhibition, foreign Auslandsmesse *(f)*
exhibition, industrial Gewerbeausstellung *(f)*, Industriemesse *(f)*
exhibition, international
internationale Ausstellung *(f)*,
internationale Messe *(f)*
exhibition, local regionale
Ausstellung *(f)*, regionale Messe *(f)*
exhibition, national nationale
Ausstellung *(f)*, nationale Messe *(f)*
exhibition, outdoor Messe *(f)* im
Freigelände

exhibition, permanent
Dauerausstellung *(f)*
exhibition, regional regionale
Ausstellung *(f)*
exhibition, special-interest
Fachausstellung *(f)*, Fachmesse *(f)*
exhibition, supraregional
überregionale Messe *(f)*
exhibition, technical technische Messe
(f), Fachausstellung *(f)*, Fachmesse *(f)*
exhibitions program (US), foreign
Auslandsmesseprogramm *(n)*
exhibitions programme (GB), foreign
Auslandsmesseprogramm *(n)*
exhibitions sponsoring, foreign
Auslandsmesseförderung *(f)*
exhibitor Aussteller(in) *(m/f)*
exhibitor advisory board
Ausstellerbeirat *(m)*
exhibitor advisory committee
Ausstellerfachbeirat *(m)*,
Messebeirat *(m)*
exhibitor analysis Ausstelleranalyse *(f)*,
Ausstelleruntersuchung *(f)*,
Ausstellerauswertung *(f)*
exhibitor badge Ausstellerabzeichen *(n)*,
Ausstellerkennzeichen *(n)*,
Ausstellerbutton *(m)*
exhibitor carpark Ausstellerparkplatz *(m)*
exhibitor list Verzeichnis *(n)* der
Aussteller, Ausstellerliste *(f)*
exhibitor participation frequency
Häufigkeit *(f)* der Ausstellerteilnahme,
Ausstellerfrequenz *(f)*
exhibitor pass Ausstellerausweis *(m)*
exhibitor pass, additional zusätzlicher
Ausstellerausweis *(m)*
exhibitor qualification conditions
Zulassungsvoraussetzungen *(f, pl)* für
Aussteller
exhibitor security staff firmeneigene
Standwache *(f)*
exhibitor structure Ausstellerstruktur *(f)*, Zusammensetzung *(f)* der
Aussteller

exhibitor survey Ausstellererhebung (f), Ausstelleruntersuchung (f), Ausstellerumfrage (f)
exhibitor ticket Ausstellereintrittskarte (f)
exhibitor ticket, additional zusätzliche Ausstellerkarte (f)
exhibitor, individual Einzelaussteller (m)
exhibitor, main Hauptaussteller (m)
exhibitor, new Erstaussteller (m)
exhibitor, secondary Mitaussteller (m)
exhibitor's liability insurance Ausstellerhaftpflichtversicherung (f)
exhibitor's own security personnel firmeneigene Standwache (f)
exhibitors invitation Ausstellereinladung (f)
exhibitors, foreign ausländische Aussteller (m, pl)
exhibitors, international ausländische Aussteller (m, pl)
exhibitors' service kit Ausstellerservicemappe (f)
exhibits, agreed vereinbarte Ausstellungsgüter (n, pl)
exit Ausgang (m), Ausfahrt (f), Ausreise (f)
exit drive Autoausfahrt (f)
exit gate Ausgangstor (n), Ausfahrtstor (n)
exit, main Hauptausgang (m)
expand ausbreiten, sich ausbreiten, ausdehnen, sich ausdehnen, erweitern, sich erweitern, vergrößern, sich vergrößern, zunehmen
expansion Expansion (f), Ausbreitung (f), Ausdehnung (f), Erweiterung (f)
expect erwarten, annehmen, meinen, vermuten, glauben, rechnen mit
expectation Erwartung (f)
expenditure Aufwand (m), Aufwendungen (f, pl), Ausgaben (f, pl), Kosten (pl)

expenditure, additional Mehrausgaben (f, pl)
expense Ausgabe (f), Aufwand (m), Kosten (pl)
expense allowance Aufwandsentschädigung (f)
expense control Kostenüberwachung (f)
expenses Auslagen (f, pl), Aufwendungen (f, pl), Geschäftsausgaben (pl f), Kosten (pl), Spesen (pl)
expenses, extraordinary außerordentliche Aufwendungen (f, pl)
expenses, fixed fixe Kosten (pl), Fixkosten (pl), Gemeinkosten (pl)
expensive teuer
experience erfahren, erleben, kennenlernen
experience Erfahrung (f), Praxis (f), Fachkenntnis (f), Routine (f), Erlebnis (n)
expert Experte (m), Expertin (f), Fachmann (m), Fachfrau (f), Gutachter(in) (m/f), Sachverständige(r) (f/m)
expert advice sachkundige Beratung (f)
expert guidance sachkundige Anleitung (f), sachkundige Führung (f)
expert knowledge Fachkenntnis (f), Sachkenntnis (f), Fachwissen (n)
expert, independent unabhängiger Experte (m), unabhängige Expertin (f), unabhängige(r) Sachverständige(r) (m/f)
expertise Expertise (f), Gutachten (n)
expiration date Ablauftermin (m), Verfallsdatum (n)
expiry date Ablauftermin (m)
expiry of the deadline Ablauf (m) der Frist
explain erklären, erläutern, begründen, rechtfertigen

explanation Erklärung *(f)*, Begründung *(f)*
explosion Explosion *(f)*, Ausbruch *(m)*
explosion protection document Explosionsschutzdokument *(n)*
explosive explosiv, aufbrausend
explosive Sprengstoff *(m)*
explosive materials explosionsgefährliche Stoffe *(m, pl)*
explosive substances explosionsgefährliche Stoffe *(m, pl)*
expo industry Messewirtschaft *(f)*
export article Exportartikel *(m)*
export declaration Ausfuhrerklärung *(f)*
export documents Ausfuhrpapiere *(n, pl)*
export duty Exportzoll *(m)*
export figures Exportzahlen *(f, pl)*
export goods exhibition Exportgüterausstellung *(m)*, Exportgütermesse *(f)*
export goods fair Exportgüterausstellung *(m)*, Exportgütermesse *(f)*
export item Exportartikel *(m)*
export licence (GB) Ausfuhrlizenz *(f)*
export license (US) Ausfuhrlizenz *(f)*
export manager Exportleiter(in) *(m/f)*
export permit Exportgenehmigung *(f)*
export terms Exportbedingungen *(f, pl)*
exporter Exporteur *(m)*
exposition Ausstellung *(f)*, Schau *(f)*; Erklärung *(f)*, Darlegung *(f)*, Darstellung *(f)*
exposure Enthüllung *(f)*, Preisgabe *(f)*, Bloßstellung *(f)*; (Kamera) Belichtung *(f)*; (Gebäude etc.) Lage *(f)*
express ausdrücklich, unmissverständlich; Eil-, Express-,
express Eilbote *(m)*; Eilbeförderung *(f)*; Schnellzug *(m)*
express zum Ausdruck *(m)* bringen, äußern, sich äußern, bezeichnen

extend ausbreiten, ausbauen, ausdehnen, erweitern, strecken, sich erstrecken, verlängern, Frist *(f)* verlängern, prolongieren
extension Ausdehnung *(f)*, Erweiterung *(f)*, Vergrößerung *(f)*, Verlängerung *(f)*, Fristverlängerung *(f)*, Ausbau *(m)*; Nebenanschluss *(m)*, Apparat *(m)*
extension cable Verlängerungskabel *(n)*
extension cord Verlängerungsschnur *(f)*, Verlängerungskabel *(n)*
extension flex Verlängerungskabel *(n)*
extension ladder Ausziehleiter *(f)*
extension lead Verlängerungskabel *(n)*
extension of product range Sortimentserweiterung *(f)*
extensive ausgedehnt, umfassend, beträchtlich
external extern, äußere(-r/-s), äußerlich, Außen-, außerbetrieblich
extinguish auslöschen, Feuer *(n)* löschen, abschalten
extinguisher Feuerlöscher *(m)*
extra bulb Ersatzlampe *(f)*
extra charge Aufgeld *(n)*, Aufschlag *(m)*, Zuschlag *(m)*, Preisaufschlag *(m)*
extra demand Mehrbedarf *(m)*
extra pay Gehaltszulage *(f)*
extra work Mehrarbeit *(f)*
extractor hood Abzugshaube *(f)*, Dunstabzugshaube *(f)*
extraordinary außerordentlich, außergewöhnlich, ungewöhnlich, seltsam
extreme extrem, äußerst, höchst, radikal
extreme Extrem *(n)*, Äußerstes *(n)*
eye contact Blickkontakt *(m)*, Sichtkontakt *(m)*
eyebolt Augenschraube *(f)*
eye-catcher Blickfang *(m)*
eyelet Öse *(f)*

F

fabricate fabrizieren, herstellen, erfinden
fabrication Fabrikation *(f)*, Herstellung *(f)*, Erfindung *(f)*
facade Fassade *(f)*
face ansehen, entgegentreten; gegenüberstehen, gegenüberliegen, gegenübersitzen
face Gesicht *(n)*, Miene *(f)*, Vorderseite *(f)*
fact Faktum *(n)*, Tatsache *(f)*, Realität *(f)*, Umstand *(m)*
factory Fabrik *(f)*, Fabrikanlage *(f)*, Fabrikgebäude *(n)*, Betrieb *(m)*, Werk *(n)*
factual sachlich, tatsächlich
fade in einblenden
fade over (Projektion) überblenden
fade-in Einblendung *(f)*
fail fehlschlagen, scheitern, erfolglos sein, misslingen, ausfallen, versagen
failure Fehler *(m)*, Fehlschlag *(m)*, Misserfolg *(m)*, Scheitern *(n)*, Ausfall *(m)*, Versagen *(n)*; Insolvenz *(f)*
failure to pay on due date Zahlungsverzug *(m)*
fair Ausstellung *(f)*, Messe *(f)*, Jahrmarkt *(m)*
fair fair, gerecht, anständig; reell; hübsch, schön; hell, klar, heiter; blond
fair attendance Ausstellungsbesuch *(m)*, Messebesuch *(m)*
fair carrier Messefrachtführer *(m)*, Messespediteur *(m)*
fair forwarder Messespediteur *(m)*
fair guest Ausstellungsgast *(m)*, Messegast *(m)*
fair guest card Ausstellungsgastkarte *(f)*, Messegastkarte *(f)*
fair management Ausstellungsleitung *(f)*, Messeverwaltung *(f)*

fair photographer, official offizielle(r) Messefotograf(in) *(m/f)*
fair site Ausstellungsgelände *(n)*, Messegelände *(n)*
fair, commercial Handelsmesse *(f)*
fair, industrial Gewerbeausstellung *(f)*, Industriemesse *(f)*
fair, local regionale Ausstellung *(f)*, regionale Messe *(f)*
fair, national nationale Ausstellung *(f)*, nationale Messe *(f)*
fair, outdoor Messe *(f)* im Freigelände
fair, regional regionale Messe *(f)*
fair, special-interest Fachausstellung *(f)*, Fachmesse *(f)*
fair, supraregional überregionale Messe *(f)*
fair, technical technische Messe *(f)*, Fachausstellung *(f)*, Fachmesse *(f)*
fairgoer Ausstellungsbesucher(in) *(m/f)*, Messebesucher(in) *(m/f)*
fairground Ausstellungsgelände *(n)*, Messegelände *(n)*
fake fälschen, vortäuschen
fake Fälschung *(f)*
fall exhibition (US) Herbstmesse *(f)*
fall fair (US) Herbstmesse *(f)*
fallacy Irrtum *(m)*, Trugschluss *(m)*
falsification Fälschung *(f)*
fan Ventilator *(m)*, Gebläse *(n)*
fan heater Heizlüfter *(m)*
fare Fahrgeld *(n)*, Fahrpreis *(m)*
fare reduction Fahrpreisermäßigung *(f)*
fascia Armaturenbrett *(n)*; (Messestand etc.) Blende *(f)*
fascia board Blendentafel *(f)*, Blendenbrett *(n)*
fascia inscription Blendenbeschriftung *(f)*
fascia panel Blendentafel *(f)*
fashion formen, gestalten
fashion Mode *(f)*, Stil *(m)*, Art und Weise *(f)*, Brauch *(m)*
fashionable elegant, modern, modisch

fast schnell; fest, widerstandsfähig; (Film) hochempfindlich; (Objektiv) lichtstark
fast food restaurant Schnellgaststätte *(f)*
fasten befestigen, festmachen, sich festmachen, zumachen
fastener Verschluss *(m)*
faucet Wasserhahn *(m)*
fault Fehler *(m)*, Defekt *(m)*, Mangel *(m)*, Schuld *(f)*, Verschulden *(n)*, Fahrlässigkeit *(f)*
fault indicator Störungsanzeiger *(m)*
faultless fehlerfrei, tadellos
faulty fehlerhaft, falsch, mangelhaft, defekt
favor (US) favorisieren, begünstigen, bevorzugen, fördern, unterstützen
favor (US) Gunst *(f)*, Gefälligkeit *(f)*
favour (GB) favorisieren, begünstigen, bevorzugen, fördern, unterstützen
favour (GB) Gunst *(f)*, Gefälligkeit *(f)*
fax Fax *(n)*, Telefax *(n)*, Telefaxgerät *(n)*
fax faxen
fax machine Telefaxgerät *(n)*
fax on demand Faxabruf *(m)*
fax subscriber Telefaxteilnehmer(in) *(m/f)*
feasibility Machbarkeit *(f)*, Realisierbarkeit *(f)*, Durchführbarkeit *(f)*
feasibility study Machbarkeitsuntersuchung *(f)*, Projektstudie *(f)*
feasibility survey Machbarkeitsuntersuchung *(f)*, Machbarkeitsprüfung *(f)*
feasible machbar, realisierbar, plausibel
feature Merkmal *(n)*, Charakteristikum *(n)*, Kennzeichen *(n)*; Attraktion *(f)*
feature spielen, darstellen; als Attraktion *(f)* zeigen, groß herausbringen
Federal Emissions Control Act Bundesimmissionsschutzgesetz *(n)*

federation of industries Industrieverband *(m)*
fee Gebühr *(f)*, Honorar *(n)*, Gage *(f)*, Beitrag *(m)*, Bezüge *(m, pl)*
feed Beschickung *(f)*, Versorgung *(f)*, Eingabe *(f)*; Fütterung *(f)*; Mahlzeit *(f)*
feed verpflegen, ernähren, sich ernähren, beschicken, versorgen
feed connector piece Einspeisungsstück *(n)*
feedback Feedback *(n)*, Rückkopplung *(f)*, Rückmeldung *(f)*
feeder Einspeiser *(m)*
feeder bridge Einspeiserbrücke *(f)*
feeder bus Zubringerbus *(m)*
feeding line Versorgungsleitung *(f)*, Zuleitung *(f)*
feeding pipe Versorgungsleitung *(f)*, Versorgungsrohr *(n)*
felt pen Filzstift *(m)*
felt-tip pen Filzstift *(m)*
fetch holen, herbeiholen, bringen, herbringen; (Preis etc.) erzielen
FI protective switch Fi-Schutzschalter *(m)*
fiberboard (US) Faserplatte *(f)*
fibreboard (GB) Faserplatte *(f)*
fiduciary Treuhänder(in) *(m/f)*
fiduciary treuhänderisch
field Gebiet *(n)*, Fachgebiet *(n)*, Bereich *(m)*, Sektor *(m)*
field force Außendienstmitarbeiter *(m, pl)*
field of activity Arbeitsbereich *(m)*, Tätigkeitsgebiet *(n)*
field research Marktforschung *(f)* vor Ort, Primärforschung *(f)*
field service Außendienst *(m)*
field survey Marktforschung *(f)*
field worker Außendienstmitarbeiter(in) *(m/f)*
fierce erbittert, grimmig heftig, scharf, stark
figure darstellen, formen, gestalten

figure Figur *(f)*, Form *(f)*, Gestalt *(f)*, Abbildung *(f)*, Illustration *(f)*; Persönlichkeit *(f)*; Zahl *(f)*, Ziffer *(f)*, Betrag *(m)*
figure out ausrechnen, berechnen; begreifen, verstehen
file abheften, ablegen, feilen
file Akte *(f)*, Aktenordner *(m)*, Hefter *(m)*; Feile *(f)*; (EDV) Datei *(f)*
file a medical certificate krankschreiben
file, attached (EDV) angehängte Datei *(f)*
fill in (Formular etc.) ausfüllen
fill out (Formular etc.) ausfüllen
filter Filter *(m)*
filter filtern, durchsickern
filter cigarette Filterzigarette *(f)*
filter coffee Filterkaffee *(m)*
filter paper Filterpapier *(n)*
filtered coffee Filterkaffee *(m)*
filter-tipped cigarette Filterzigarette *(f)*
filth Dreck *(m)*, Schmutz *(m)*, Unrat *(m)*
filthy schmutzig, dreckig
final Finale *(n)*; (Zeitung) Spätausgabe *(f)*
final letztendlich, endgültig, End-, Schluss-
finalize abschließen, beenden, vollenden
finally endlich, schließlich, endültig
finance finanzieren
finance Finanzierung *(f)*
financing Finanzierung *(f)*
find finden, ausfindig machen, bemerken, feststellen, herausfinden
find Fund *(m)*
finder's reward Finderlohn *(m)*
fine Bußgeld *(n)*, Geldstrafe *(f)*
fine fein, schön, ausgezeichnet, hervorragend, in Ordnung *(m)*, sehr gut, bestens
fine mit einer Geldstrafe *(f)* belegen

finish aufhören, enden, beenden, fertig stellen, fertig sein, fertig machen, vollenden
finish Ende *(n)*, Schluss *(m)*, Vollendung *(f)*
fire anzünden, in Brand *(m)* stecken, befeuern, anfeuern; entlassen, feuern
fire Feuer *(n)*, Brand *(m)*
fire alarm Feueralarm *(m)*, Feuermelder *(m)*
fire brigade Feuerwehr *(f)*
fire damage Brandschaden *(m)*, Feuerschaden *(m)*
fire detector Feuermelder *(m)*
fire engine Feuerwehrauto *(n)*, Löschfahrzeug *(n)*
fire escape Feuerleiter *(f)*, Feuertreppe *(f)*
fire extinguisher Feuerlöscher *(m)*
fire extinguisher, hand-held Handfeuerlöscher *(m)*
fire hazard Brandgefahr *(f)*, Feuergefahr *(f)*
fire house Feuerwache *(f)*
fire insurance Feuerversicherung *(f)*
fire plug Hydrant *(m)*
fire precautions Brandschutz *(m)*
fire prevention Brandschutz *(m)*
fire prevention regulations brandschutztechnische Bestimmungen *(f, pl)*
fire properties classification Klassifizierung *(f)* des Brandverhaltens
fire protection equipment brandschutztechnische Einrichtungen *(f, pl)*
fire risk Brandgefahr *(f)*, Feuergefahr *(f)*
fire safety door Brandschutztor *(n)*, Brandschutztür *(f)*
fire safety protection regulations Brandschutzbestimmungen *(f, pl)*
fire service movement zone Feuerwehrbewegungszone *(f)*
fire station Feuerwache *(f)*
firefighter Feuerwehrmann *(m)*
firefighting equipment feuerschutztechnische Geräte *(n, pl)*

fireman Feuerwehrmann *(m)*
fire-resistant schwer entflammbar
fire-resistant materials schwer entflammbare Stoffe *(m, pl)*
firm beständig, fest, hart, stabil
firm Firma *(f)*, Unternehmen *(n)*
firmness Festigkeit *(f)*, Beständigkeit *(f)*
first aid erste Hilfe *(f)*
first-aid attendant Sanitäter(in) *(m/f)*
first-aid box Verbandskasten *(m)*
first-aid dressing Notverband *(m)*
first-aid kit Verbandskasten *(m)*, Reiseapotheke *(f)*
first-aid post Sanitätsstation *(f)*
first-aid supplies Verbandzeug *(n)*
fit anbringen, anpassen, einbauen, montieren; passen, zusammenpassen
fit geeignet, tauglich, passend; angebracht, ratsam; gesund, in Form *(f)*
fit Passform *(f)*
fit for work arbeitsfähig
fit in einbauen, einpassen, unterbringen; harmonieren
fit out ausrüsten, ausstatten
fit together zusammenpassen
fit up ausrüsten, einrichten, möblieren, montieren
fitted carpet Teppichboden *(m)*
fitter Monteur *(m)*, Installateur *(m)*
fitting geeignet, passend
fitting Installation *(f)*, Montage *(f)*, Zubehörteil *(n)*, Armatur *(f)*
fix fixieren, anbringen, befestigen, festmachen, festsetzen; festlegen, abmachen, vereinbaren, anberaumen
fix Klemme *(f)*
fixing to the hall floor Befestigung *(f)* im Hallenboden
flag beflaggen
flag Flagge *(f)*, Fahne *(f)*
flag, national Nationalflagge *(f)*
flagpole Fahnenmast *(m)*
flagship fair Leitmesse *(f)*

flake ice maker Scherbeneiserzeuger *(m)*
flame, naked offene Flamme *(f)*
flameproof materials schwerentflammbare Stoffe *(m, pl)*
flameproofing agents Feuerschutzmittel *(n, pl)*
flammability of construction materials and components, DIN 4102 Brandverhalten *(n)* von Baustoffen und Bauteilen, DIN 4102
flammable brennbar, leichtentzündlich, feuergefährlich
flammable liquids brennbare Flüssigkeiten *(f, pl)*
flammable material, highly leichtentflammbares Material *(n)*, leicht entflammbare Baustoffe *(m, pl)*
flammable material, readily leichtentflammbares Material *(n)*
flammable materials brennbare Stoffe *(m, pl)*
flammable, highly leicht entflammbar
flange Flansch *(m)*
flash Aufblinken *(n)*, Blinken *(f)*, Aufblitzen *(n)*, Aufleuchten *(n)*, Blitz *(m)*, Blitzlicht *(n)*, Blitzen *(n)*; Stichflamme *(f)*; Kurzmeldung *(f)*
flash blinken, funkeln, blitzen, aufblitzen, aufleuchten, aufflammen
flash memory card Flash-memory-Karte *(f)*
flash shot Blitzlichtaufnahme *(f)*
flashback Rückblende *(f)*
flashlight Blitzlicht *(n)*, Blinklicht *(n)*
flat flach, eben, platt, fade, matt; pauschal, einheitlich, Einheits-, Pauschal-; entschieden; kategorisch
flat Fläche *(f)*, Ebene *(f)*
flat rate Einheitstarif *(m)*, Pauschale *(f)*
flat screen Flachbildschirm *(m)*
flat truss section Flachträger *(m)*
flatten abflachen
flexible flexibel, elastisch, biegsam, anpassungsfähig

flier Handzettel *(m)*, Flugblatt *(n)*
flight Flug *(m)*, Fliegen *(n)*, Schwarm *(m)*
flight cancellation Flugausfall *(m)*
flight delay Flugverspätung *(f)*
flight destination Flugziel *(n)*
flight schedule, change of Flugplanänderung *(f)*
flight, direct Direktflug *(m)*
flight, scheduled Linienflug *(m)*
flip chart Flip Chart *(n)*
floodlight anstrahlen, beleuchten
floodlight Scheinwerfer *(m)*, Flutlicht *(n)*
floor Boden *(m)*, Fußboden *(m)*; Stockwerk *(n)*, Geschoss *(n)*
floor Boden *(m)* legen; verblüffen, umhauen, niederschlagen
floor anchoring Befestigung *(m)* im Hallenboden
floor covering Bodenbelag *(m)*
floor coverings Auslegware *(f)*
floor duct Bodenkanal *(m)*
floor load Bodenbelastung *(f)*
floor plan Flächenbelegungsplan *(m)*, Raumaufteilungsplan *(m)*, Grundrissplan *(m)*, Stockwerksplan *(m)*
floor showcase Standvitrine *(f)*
floor space Bodenfläche *(f)*, Grundfläche *(f)*
floor space required benötigte Grundfläche *(f)*, Flächenbedarf *(f)*
floor space, usable Nutzfläche *(f)*
floor weight capacity Tragfägigkeit *(f)* des Bodens, Tragfähigkeit *(f)* des Stockwerks
floor, adjustable Ausgleichsboden *(m)*
floor, double Doppelboden *(m)*
floor, first Erdgeschoss *(n)*, Parterre *(n)*
floor, upper Obergeschoss *(n)*
flooring Fußbodenbelag *(m)*
flop durchfallen, ein Reinfall *(m)* sein
flop Flop *(m)*, Reinfall *(m)*, Misserfolg *(m)*, Pleite *(f)*
floral decoration Blumendekoration *(f)*

flow chart Fließgrafik *(f)*, Fließschaubild *(n)*
flow diagram Flussdiagramm *(n)*
flow graph Fließgrafik *(f)*
flow of traffic, smooth reibungsloser Verkehrsablauf *(m)*
flow off abfließen
flower bowl Blumenschale *(f)*
fluoresce fluoreszieren
flush bündig, in Fluchtlinie *(f)*
flush bolt Kantenriegel *(m)*
flyer Handzettel *(m)*, Flugblatt *(n)*
flying time Flugzeit *(f)*
foam fire extinguisher Schaumfeuerlöscher *(m)*
foam material Schaumstoff *(m)*
focal length (Objektiv) Brennweite *(f)*
focus Brennpunkt *(m)*, Mittelpunkt *(m)*, Zentrum *(n)*; (Kamera) Scharfeinstellung *(f)*
focus konzentrieren; (Kamera) scharf einstellen
focusing (US) (Kamera) Scharfeinstellung *(f)*
focussing (GB) (Kamera) Scharfeinstellung *(f)*
fog machine Nebelmaschine *(f)*
foil Folie *(f)*
folder Faltblatt *(n)*, Faltprospekt *(m)*, Broschüre *(f)*; Aktendeckel *(m)*; Schnellhefter *(m)*
folding klappbar, zusammenklappbar
folding cardboard box Faltkarton *(m)*
folding display Faltdisplay *(n)*
folding door Falttür *(f)*
folding rule Zollstock *(m)*
folding table Klapptisch *(m)*
follow folgen, befolgen, nachfolgen, verfolgen, sich anschließen, mitmachen
follow up nachgehen, nachfassen, weiterverfolgen, fortsetzen
follow-up Weiterverfolgen *(n)*, Nachfassaktivität *(f)*, nachfassende Untersuchung *(f)*

food Essen *(n)*, Nahrung *(f)*, Nahrungsmittel *(n)*, Verpflegung *(f)*
food hot display unit Heiße Theke *(f)*, Warmhaltetheke *(f)*
Food Hygiene Ordinance Lebensmittel-Hygiene-Verordnung *(f)*
food service gastronomische Versorgung *(f)*
food service disposal Entsorgung *(f)* von Bewirtungsabfällen
food shop (GB) Lebensmittelgeschäft *(n)*
food store (US) Lebensmittelladen *(m)*
food supervision Lebensmittelüberwachung *(f)*
food transport box Speisentransportkiste *(f)*
foodstuffs Lebensmittel *(n, pl)*, Nahrungsmittel *(n, pl)*
foot bracket Fußausleger *(m)*
foot, adjustable verstellbarer Fuß *(m)*
footlights Rampenlicht *(n)*
footpath Gehweg *(m)*, Fußweg *(m)*
footplate Fußteller *(m)*
force Gewalt *(f)*, Kraft *(f)*, Stärke *(f)*, Macht *(f)*, Wucht *(f)*; Zwang *(m)*
force zwingen, erzwingen, nötigen, mit Gewalt *(f)* durchsetzen
force majeure höhere Gewalt *(f)*
force of attraction Anziehungskraft *(f)*
forecast Voraussage *(f)*, Vorhersage *(f)*, Prognose *(f)*
forecast vorhersagen, vorhersehen, vorausplanen, prognostizieren
forecast, medium-term mittelfristige Prognose *(f)*
forecast, short-term kurzfristige Prognose *(f)*
foreground Vordergrund *(m)*
foreign fremd, ausländisch, auswärtig, Auslands-
foreigner Ausländer(in) *(m/f)*
foreseeable absehbar, vorhersehbar
foreword Vorwort *(n)*
forfeit Buße *(f)*, Einbuße *(f)*, Strafe *(f)*
forfeit verfallen, verlieren, verwirken, einbüßen
fork Gabel *(f)*
forklift Stapler *(m)*
forklift truck Gabelstapler *(m)*
form bilden, formen, gestalten; (Gedanken etc.) entwickeln; (Firma etc.) bilden, gründen
form Form *(f)*, Umgangsform *(f)*, Art *(f)*; Fassung *(f)*, Figur *(f)*, Gestalt *(f)*, Schema *(n)*; Formblatt *(n)*, Formular *(n)*, Vordruck *(m)*
formality Formalität *(f)*, Formsache *(f)*
format Format *(n)*, Aufmachung *(f)*
format formatieren
format, large Großformat *(n)*
format, vertical Hochformat *(n)*
formulation Formulierung *(f)*
forum Forum *(n)*
forward befördern, fördern, versenden, nachsenden, schicken, transportieren, übersenden, weiterleiten; unterstützen
forward fortschrittlich, frühzeitig, vorzeitig, Vorwärts-, vorwärts, nach vorn
forwarder Spediteur *(m)*
forwarding Beförderung *(f)*, Nachsendung *(f)*, Versand *(m)*, Spedition *(f)*
foundation Fundament *(n)*, Grundlage *(f)*, Basis *(f)*; Gründung *(f)*, Errichtung *(f)*; Stiftung *(f)*
four-color print (US) Vierfarbendruck *(m)*
four-colour print (GB) Vierfarbendruck *(m)*
foyer Foyer *(n)*, Empfangshalle *(f)*, Vorraum *(m)*
fragile empfindlich, schwach, zerbrechlich
frame rahmen, einrahmen, umrahmen
frame Rahmen *(m)*, Fassung *(f)*, Gestell *(n)*, Gerüst *(n)*, Gestalt *(f)*
frame construction Rahmenkonstruktion *(f)*, Skelettkonstruktion *(f)*

frame girder Gitterträger *(m)*
framework, general
  Rahmenbedingungen *(f, pl)*
free of charge gebührenfrei, gratis, kostenlos, umsonst, unentgeltlich, ohne Berechnung *(f)*
freelance freiberuflich
freelance freiberuflich tätig sein
freelance worker freie(r) Mitarbeiter(in) *(m/f)*
freelancer freie(r) Mitarbeiter(in) *(m/f)*
freeze frieren, gefrieren, einfrieren, tiefkühlen, erstarren
freeze Frost *(m)*, Einfrieren *(n)*
freezer Gefriermöbel *(n)*, Tiefkühlmöbel *(n)*
freezer, deep Gefriertruhe *(f)*
freezing compartment Tiefkühlfach *(n)*
freight beladen, befrachten, verfrachten
freight Fracht *(f)*, Frachtgut *(n)*, Ladung *(f)*, Frachtgebühr *(f)*, Frachtkosten *(pl)*
freight charges Frachtgebühren *(f, pl)*, Frachtkosten *(pl)*
freight costs Frachtkosten *(pl)*
freight door height
  Tordurchfahrtshöhe *(f)* für Frachtgut
freight elevator (US) Lastenaufzug *(m)*
freight forwarder Spediteur *(m)*
freight forwarding legislation
  Speditionsrecht *(n)*
freight lift (GB) Lastenaufzug *(m)*
frequency Frequenz *(f)*, Häufigkeit *(f)*
frequency, horizontal
  Horizontalfrequenz *(f)*
fret saw Stichsäge *(f)*
friction Reibung *(f)*
fridge Kühlschrank *(m)*
friendly freundlich, freundschaftlich
fringe program (US)
  Rahmenprogramm *(n)*
fringe programme (GB)
  Rahmenprogramm *(n)*
front erste(-r/-s), vorderste(-r/-s), Front-, Vorder-

front Front *(f)*, Vorderfront *(f)*, Vordergrund *(m)*, Vorderseite *(f)*, Stirnseite *(f)*, Fassade *(f)*
front gegenüberstehen, gegenüberliegen
front cover (Messekatalog) Vorderseite *(f)*, vordere Einbandseite *(f)*
front cover, inside innere Fronteinbandseite *(f)*
front page Titelseite *(f)*
front suspension part
  Frontabhänger *(m)*
front view Vorderansicht *(f)*
frontage Vorderfront *(f)*, Frontseite *(f)*
frontier formalities
  Grenzformalitäten *(f, pl)*
frosted glass Mattglas *(n)*, Milchglas *(n)*
frozen food Tiefkühlkost *(f)*
frozen food counter Tiefkühltheke *(f)*
frozen food island site cabinet
  Tiefkühlinsel *(f)*
frozen food multi-deck cabinet
  Tiefkühlregal *(n)*
frozen food room, portable
  Tiefkühlzelle *(f)*
frozen food storage cabinet
  Tiefkühllagermöbel *(n)*
frozen food storage room
  Tiefkühllagerraum *(m)*
frozen food vehicle Tiefkühlfahrzeug *(n)*
fruit juice Fruchtsaft *(m)*
fuel Kraftstoff *(m)*, Treibstoff *(m)*
full of ideas ideenreich
full service agency
  Fullservice-Agentur *(f)*
full time ganztägig, vollberuflich
full up voll besetzt
full-page ganzseitig
function Funktion *(f)*, Aufgabe *(f)*, Tätigkeit *(f)*
function funktionieren, arbeiten, laufen
functional funktionell, zweckmäßig
fundamental Basis *(f)*, Grundlage *(f)*
fundamental fundamental, elementar, grundlegend, hauptsächlich, wesentlich
funnel Trichter *(m)*

furnish einrichten, möblieren
furnishing Möblierung *(f)*
furnishings Einrichtung *(f)*, Mobiliar *(n)*
furniture Mobiliar *(n)*, Möbel *(n, pl)*
furniture rent company
  Mietmöbel-Verleihfirma *(f)*
furniture rental Mietmobiliar *(n)*
fuse box Sicherungskasten *(m)*
fuse, main Hauptsicherung *(f)*
future prospects
  Zukunftsaussichten *(f, pl)*
future, with a safe zukunftssicher

G

gadget Apparat *(m)*, Gerät *(n)*,
  Vorrichtung *(f)*
gain erlangen, erreichen, erwerben,
  gewinnen, verdienen
gain Steigerung *(f)*, Zunahme *(f)*,
  Zuwachs *(m)*; Vorteil *(m)*, Gewinn *(m)*
gallery Galerie *(f)*, Empore *(f)*, Tribüne *(f)*
galley-proof Fahnenabzug *(m)*
gangplank Steg *(m)*
gap Abstand *(m)*, Lücke *(f)*, Spalte *(f)*,
  Kluft *(f)*, Loch *(n)*, Unterbrechung *(f)*
gap in the market Marktlücke *(f)*
gap, horizontal Horizontalfuge *(f)*
gaps, without lückenlos
garage, multi-storey (GB)
  Hochgarage *(f)*
garage, multi-story (US) Hochgarage *(f)*
garbage (US) Müll *(m)*
garbage can (US) Mülleimer *(m)*,
  Mülltonne *(f)*
garbage collection (US) Müllabfuhr *(f)*
garbage disposal (US)
  Müllbeseitigung *(f)*
garbage separation (US)
  Mülltrennung *(f)*
gas connection Gasanschluss *(m)*
gas cylinder Gasflasche *(f)*

**gas equipment, compressed and
  liquefied** Druck- und
  Flüssiggasanlagen *(f, pl)*
gas lighter Gasfeuerzeug *(n)*
gas main Gasleitung *(f)*
gas pipe Gasleitung *(f)*
gastronomy Gastronomie *(f)*
gate Tor *(n)*, Pforte *(f)*, Zugang *(m)*,
  Durchfahrt *(f)*, Schranke *(f)*,
  Flugsteig *(m)*
gate security Torwache *(f)*
gate staff Torwache *(f)*
gatekeeper Pförtner(in) *(m/f)*
gateman Pförtner *(m)*
gateway Einfahrt *(m)*
gather dust verstauben
gathering Versammlung *(f)*
GDP (Gross Domestic Product) BIP *(n)*
  (Bruttoinlandsprodukt)
GEMA fees GEMA-Gebühren *(f, pl)*
generalization Verallgemeinerung *(f)*
generalize verallgemeinern
generator Generator *(m)*,
  Stromerzeuger *(m)*
gentlemen's cloakroom (GB)
  Herrentoilette *(f)*
gentlemen's lavatory (GB)
  Herrentoilette *(f)*
gents (GB) Herrentoilette *(f)*
German business events, special
  Sonderveranstaltungen *(f, pl)* der
  deutschen Wirtschaft
German Commercial Code
  Handelsgesetzbuch *(n)* (HGB)
**German Hotel and Catering
  Association** Deutscher Hotel- und
  Gaststättenverband *(m)*
German Tourist Association Deutscher
  Fremdenverkehrsverband *(m)*
get lost verlorengehen, abhanden
  kommen
get to know kennenlernen
gift Geschenk *(n)*, Schenkung *(f)*,
  Spende *(f)*; Gabe *(f)*, Begabung *(f)*,
  Talent *(n)*, Veranlagung *(f)*

gift coupon Geschenkgutschein *(m)*
gift voucher Geschenkgutschein *(m)*
gift, free Werbegeschenk *(n)*
girder Balken *(m)*, Träger *(m)*, Binder *(m)*
girder, lower (Treppe, Brüstung) Untergurt *(m)*
girder, middle (Treppe, Brüstung) Mittelgurt *(m)*
giro transfer order Zahlungsanweisung *(f)*
give geben, schenken, spenden; bewilligen
give a receipt for quittieren
give as a present schenken
give away verschenken, weggeben
give back zurückgeben
give in einreichen, eintragen
give out verteilen, veröffentlichen
give over abliefern, übergeben, aushändigen
give up aufgeben, aufhören, verzichten
giveaway Werbegeschenk *(n)*
glass Glas *(n)*, Trinkglas *(n)*; Scheibe *(f)*
glass board Glasboden *(m)*
glass cupboard Schauvitrine *(f)*
glass cut Glaszuschnitt *(m)*
glass display cabinet, large Hochvitrine *(f)*
glass display showcase, large Hochvitrine *(f)*
glass display system Display-Glasbausystem *(n)*
glass pane Glasscheibe *(f)*
glass railing Glasbrüstung *(f)*
glass retainer Glashalter *(m)*
glass showcase Glasvitrine *(f)*
glass, laminated Verbundglas *(n)*
glass-washing machine Gläserspülmaschine *(f)*
glass-washing machine, commercial gewerbliche Gläserspülmaschine *(f)*
gleam Lichtschein *(m)*, Schimmer *(m)*
gleam scheinen, schimmern, strahlen, leuchten, aufleuchten, blinken

glimmer glimmen, schimmern
glimmer Glimmen *(n)*, Schimmer *(m)*
glitter Glanz *(m)*, Glitzern *(n)*, Schimmer *(m)*, Funkeln *(n)*
glitter glitzern, glänzen, funkeln, schimmern
global global, umfassend, weltweit
globular kugelförmig
gloss Glanz *(m)*, Schein *(m)*; Erläuterung *(f)*, Anmerkung *(f)*; Glosse *(f)*
gloss paint Glanzlack *(m)*
glossy glänzend, Glanz-
glue kleben, leimen
glue Klebstoff *(m)*, Leim *(m)*
GNP (Gross National Product) Bruttosozialprodukt *(n)* (BSP)
goal Ziel *(n)*
goal setting Zielsetzung *(f)*
going Abgang *(m)*, Abreise*(f)*, Abfahrt *(f)*, Fortbewegung *(f)*
going gängig, in Betrieb *(f)*, funktionierend, florierend
going to press Drucklegung *(f)*
goods depot Warenlager *(n)*
goods elevator (US) Lastenaufzug *(m)*
goods lift (GB) Lastenaufzug *(m)*
goods on hand Lagerbestand *(m)*
goods, fancy Modeartikel *(m, pl)*
goods, high-quality Qualitätsware *(f)*
goodwill Firmenansehen *(n)*, ideeller Firmenwert *(m)*, Geschäftswert *(m)*
gourmet restaurant Feinschmeckerrestaurant *(n)*
grab ergreifen, packen; (Zuschauer etc.) fesseln
grade bewerten, einstufen, klassifizieren, einteilen, sortieren
grade Grad *(m)*, Rang *(m)*, Stufe *(f)*; Klasse *(f)*, Sorte *(f)*; Qualität *(f)*, Handelsklasse *(f)*; Gefälle *(n)*, Steigung *(f)*
grade up verbessern
gradient Steigung *(f)*, Gefälle *(n)*, Neigung *(f)*
graduate einstufen, staffeln

graduated price Staffelpreis *(m)*
grand groß, großartig, grandios, prächtig, fantastisch, bedeutend, berühmt, wichtig
graph grafisch darstellen
graph grafische Darstellung *(f)*, Schaubild *(n)*
graph paper Millimeterpapier *(n)*
graphic grafisch
graphic artist Grafiker(in) *(m/f)*
graphic designer Grafiker(in) *(m/f)*
graphical user interface grafische Benutzeroberfläche *(f)*
gratis unentgeltlich, kostenlos, gratis, umsonst, Gratis-
gratuitous kostenlos; grundlos, unbegründet; überflüssig, unnötig
grave ernst, besorgniserregend, schwerwiegend, wichtig
grease einfetten, schmieren, abschmieren
grease Fett *(n)*, Schmierfett *(n)*
green tax Ökosteuer *(f)*
grid Gitter *(n)*, Rost *(m)*; Netz *(n)*, Versorgungsnetz *(n)*, Leitungsnetz *(n)*, Stromnetz *(n)*
grid ceiling Rasterdecke *(f)*
grid panel Gitterfeld *(n)*, Gitterplatte *(f)*
grind schleifen
grind down abschleifen, zermahlen, zerreiben, zerkleinern
grinding machine Schleifmaschine *(f)*
grip greifen, ergreifen, fassen, festhalten, packen
grip Griff *(m)*, Greifen *(n)*, Handgriff *(m)*, Zugriff *(m)*, Packen *(n)*
grocer's Lebensmittelgeschäft *(n)*
groceries Lebensmittel *(n, pl)*
grocery (GB) Lebensmittelgeschäft *(n)*
grocery store (US) Lebensmittelgeschäft *(n)*
groove auskehlen, nuten, rillen
groove Hohlkehle *(f)*, Furche *(f)*, Rille *(f)*, Rinne *(f)*, Nut *(f)*, Tonspur *(f)*
groove profile Hohlkehlprofil *(n)*

gross amount Bruttobetrag *(m)*, Gesamtbetrag *(m)*
gross circulation Bruttoauflagenhöhe *(f)*
Gross Domestic Product (GDP) Bruttoinlandsprodukt *(n)* (BIP)
gross earnings Bruttoerlös *(m)*, Bruttoeinkommen *(n)*
gross exhibition area Bruttoausstellungsfläche *(f)*
gross exhibition space Bruttoausstellungsplatz *(m)*
gross hall space Hallenbruttofläche *(f)*
gross income Bruttoeinkommen *(n)*
gross margin Bruttogewinn *(m)*, Bruttospanne *(f)*
Gross National Product (GNP) Bruttosozialprodukt *(n)*
gross negligence grobe Fahrlässigkeit *(f)*
gross profit Bruttogewinn *(m)*, Rohgewinn *(m)*
gross retail price Bruttoeinzelhandelspreis *(m)*
gross return Bruttorendite *(f)*, Bruttoertrag *(m)*
gross sales Bruttoumsatz *(m)*
gross weight Bruttogewicht *(n)*
ground Grund *(m)*, Erdboden *(m)*, Erde *(f)*, Erdung *(f)*, Gebiet *(n)*, Grundbesitz *(m)*; Basis *(f)*, Grundlage *(f)*; Standpunkt *(m)*, Ursache *(f)*, Motiv *(n)*
ground gründen, basieren; begünden; stützen; erden
ground clearance Bodenfreiheit *(f)*
ground floor Erdgeschoss *(n)*
ground plan Grundriss *(m)*
ground plan, dimensional vermaßter Grundriss *(m)*
groundless unbegründet, ungerechtfertigt
group Gruppe *(f)*, Unternehmensgruppe *(f)*, Konsortium *(n)*, Konzern *(m)*

group gruppieren, eingruppieren, sich gruppieren, anordnen
group advertising Gemeinschaftswerbung *(f)*
group buying Sammeleinkauf *(m)*
group discount Gruppenermäßigung *(f)*
group discussion Gruppendiskussion *(f)*
group excursion Gruppenreise *(f)*, Gesellschaftsreise *(f)*
group journey Gruppenreise *(f)*
group leader Gruppenleiter(in) *(m/f)*
group of buyers Käuferschicht *(f)*
group of companies Unternehmensgruppe *(f)*
group rate Gruppentarif *(m)*
group stand Gemeinschaftsstand *(m)*
group ticket Sammelfahrschein *(m)*
group tour Gruppenführung *(f)*
group travel Gruppenreise *(f)*
group visit Gruppenbesichtigung *(f)*
groupage Sammelladung *(f)*
grouping Gruppierung *(f)*, Eingruppierung *(f)*, Anordnung *(f)*, Vereinigung *(f)*
growth Wachsen *(n)*, Wachstum *(n)*, Wuchs *(m)*, Entwicklung *(f)*, Zunahme *(f)*, Zuwachs *(m)*, Größe *(f)*
growth potential Wachstumspotenzial *(n)*
growth rate Wachstumsrate *(f)*
growth, rate of Zuwachsrate *(f)*
GS safety mark GS-Zeichen *(n)*
guarantee Garantie *(f)*, Gewährleistung *(f)*, Bürgschaft *(f)*, Kaution *(f)*, Sicherheit *(f)*
guarantee garantieren, Garantie *(f)* leisten, gewährleisten, bürgen, sich verbürgen, sicherstellen, zusichern
guard Wache *(f)*, Bewachung *(f)*, Wachsamkeit *(f)*, Wachmann *(m)*, Wachposten *(m)*, Wächter *(m)*, Wachmannschaft *(f)*; Zugschaffner *(m)*
guard wachen, bewachen, beaufsichtigen, behüten, sich hüten, schützen

guard duty Wachdienst *(m)*
guardhouse Wachlokal *(n)*, Wache *(f)*
guardian Wächter(in) *(m/f)*
guarding, special Sonderbewachung *(f)*
guess Annahme *(f)*, Vermutung *(f)*, Schätzung *(f)*
guess annehmen, raten, meinen, schätzen, vermuten
guest Gast *(m)*
guest house Pension *(f)*, Gästehaus *(n)*
guest nation Gastnation *(f)*
guest of honor (US) Ehrengast *(m)*
guest of honour (GB) Ehrengast *(m)*
guest pass Gastausweis *(m)*, Gastkarte *(f)*
guidance Anleitung *(f)*, Beratung *(f)*
guide Fremdenführer(in) *(m/f)*, Reiseführer(in) *(m/f)*; Leitfaden *(m)*, Handbuch *(n)*
guide führen, leiten, anleiten, beraten
guide book Reiseführer *(m)*
guide price Richtpreis *(m)*
guide rail Laufschiene *(f)*
guide track Laufschiene *(f)*
guide value Richtwert *(m)*
guided gelenkt, gesteuert, ferngesteuert
guided tour Führung *(f)*
guideline Richtlinie *(f)*, Richtwert *(m)*
guidelines, technical technische Richtlinien *(f, pl)*

H

haggle feilschen, streiten
half halb, zur Hälfte *(f)*, halbwegs, fast
half Hälfte *(f)*
half-dark halbdunkel
half-day halbtags
half-high halbhoch
half-page halbseitig
half-pension Halbpension *(f)*
half-year Halbjahr *(n)*

hall Halle (f), Saal (m)
hall access route Hallenzufahrt (f)
hall aisle Hallengang (m)
hall arrangement Hallengliederung (f)
hall capacity Hallenkapazität (f)
hall column Hallensäule (f)
hall crane Hallenkran (m)
hall dimensions Hallenmaß (n), Hallenmaße (n, pl)
hall door Hallentor (n)
hall door dimensions Hallentormaße (n, pl)
hall electrical contractor, official offizielle(r) Hallenelektriker(in) (m/f), offizielle(r) Vertragshallen-elektriker(in) (m/f)
hall electrician Hallenelektriker (m)
hall elevator Hallenaufzug (m)
hall entrance Halleneingang (m), Halleneinfahrt (f)
hall floor Hallenboden (m)
hall floor anchoring Verankerung (m) im Hallenboden
hall floor load-bearing capacity Belastbarkeit (f) des Hallenbodens
hall floor loading Belastbarkeit (f) des Hallenbodens
hall gangway Hallengang (m)
hall height Hallenhöhe (f)
hall information system Halleninformationssystem (n)
hall inspector Halleninspektor (m), Hallenmeister (m)
hall lift Hallenaufzug (m)
hall number Hallennummer (f)
hall passage Hallengang (m)
hall pillar Hallenpfeiler (m), Hallensäule (f)
hall plan, general Hallenübersichtsplan (m)
hall planning Hallenaufplanung (f)
hall power supply Hallenstromversorgung (f)
hall reservation plan Hallenbelegungsplan (m)

hall section Hallenbereich (m)
hall security Hallensicherheit (f), Hallenaufsicht (f)
hall space assignment plan Hallenplatzzuteilungsplan (m), Hallenbelegungsplan (m)
hall space layout planning Hallenplatzanordnungsplan (m), Hallenaufplanung (f)
hall support Hallenstütze (f)
hall wall Hallenwand (f)
halogen spotlight Halogenstrahler (m)
hammer Hammer (m)
hammer hämmern
hand baggage (US) Handgepäck (n)
hand luggage (GB) Handgepäck (n)
handbill Handzettel (m), Reklamezettel (m), Flugblatt (n)
handbook Handbuch (n), Reiseführer (m)
handle bedienen, handhaben, hantieren, erledigen, abwickeln, durchführen, sich befassen mit, umgehen mit
handle Griff (m), Henkel (m), Kurbel (f), Klinke (f), Drücker (m), Stiel (m); Handhabe (f)
handling Handhabung (f), Behandlung (f), Bearbeitung (f), Manipulation (f)
handling charge Bearbeitungsgebühr (f), Bearbeitungskosten (pl)
handling fee Bearbeitungsgebühr (f)
handout Werbeprospekt (m)
handrail Handlauf (m), Geländer (n)
handrail extrusion Handlaufprofil (n)
handrail wall fixing bracket Handlauf-Wandbefestigung (f)
handwritten handschriftlich
handy handlich
hard disk Festplatte (f)
hard disk drive Festplattenlaufwerk (n)
hard disk, interchangeable Wechselfestplatte (f)

hardboard Hartfaserplatte *(f)*, Pressspanplatte *(f)*
harm Schaden *(m)*, Verletzung *(f)*
harmful schädlich, nachteilig
harmful to the environment umweltschädlich
harmless harmlos, unschädlich
hasty hastig, überhastet, eilig, voreilig, schnell
hat shelf Hutablage *(f)*
hatch escape Fluchtluke *(f)*, Fluchtöffnung *(f)*
haulage Beförderung *(f)*, Transport *(m)*; Beförderungskosten *(pl)*, Transportkosten *(pl)*, Rollgeld *(n)*
haulage business Speditionsunternehmen *(n)*, Transportunternehmen *(n)*
haulage company Fuhrunternehmen *(n)*, Transportunternehmen *(n)*
haulage contractor Transportunternehmen *(n)*, Fernspediteur *(m)*
haulage costs Speditionskosten *(pl)*
haulage firm Speditionsfirma *(f)*, Transportunternehmen *(n)*
hauler Spediteur *(m)*, Transportunternehmer *(m)*, Fuhrunternehmer *(m)*, Fuhrunternehmen *(n)*
haulier Spediteur *(m)*, Transportunternehmer *(m)*, Fuhrunternehmer *(m)*, Fuhrunternehmen *(n)*
hazard Risiko *(n)*, Gefahr *(f)*
hazard wagen, riskieren, aufs Spiel *(n)* setzen
hazardous gefährlich, gewagt, riskant
hazy unklar, vage, verschwommen, nebelhaft, dunstig, diesig
head anführen, vorangehen, leiten, lenken
head Kopf *(m)*; Führer(in) *(m/f)*, Führung *(f)*, Leitung *(f)*, Spitze *(f)*, Vorgesetzte(r) *(f/m)*, Chef(in) *(m/f)*; Verstand *(m)*; Kopfende *(n)*; Überschrift *(f)*, Schlagzeile *(f)*

head office Hauptsitz *(m)*, Hauptverwaltung *(f)*, Zentralverwaltung *(f)*, Stammhaus *(n)*
headache Kopfweh *(n)*, Kopfschmerzen *(m, pl)*; Sorgen *(f, pl)*
headache tablet Kopfschmerztablette *(f)*
header hanger Blendenhaken *(m)*
heading Titel *(m)*, Überschrift *(f)*, Thema *(n)*, Gesprächspunkt *(m)*
headline Schlagzeile *(f)*
headphone panel Kopfhörerleiste *(f)*
headphones Kopfhörer *(m)*
headquarters Hauptsitz *(m)*, Hauptverwaltung *(f)*, Firmensitz *(m)*, Firmenzentrale *(f)*
health and safety regulations Arbeitsschutzvorschriften *(f, pl)*
health insurance Krankenversicherung *(f)*
health insurance company Krankenkasse *(f)*
health insurance for abroad Auslandskrankenversicherung *(f)*
heat heizen, beheizen, erhitzen, warm machen, warm werden
heat Hitze *(f)*, Wärme *(f)*; Eifer *(m)*
heat exchanger Wärmetauscher *(m)*
heat insulation Wärmedämmung *(f)*
heating Heizung *(f)*, Erwärmung *(f)*
heating system Heizanlage *(f)*
heavy goods vehicle (GB) Lastkraftwagen *(m)*
heavy load panel Schwerlastplatte *(f)*
heavy-current engineering Starkstromtechnik *(f)*
heavy-duty strapazierfähig, Hochleistungs-
height erhöhen, sich erhöhen, vergrößern, zunehmen
height Höhe *(f)*, Größe *(f)*; Anhöhe *(f)*, Erhebung *(f)*, Höhepunkt *(m)*
height adjustment Höheneinstellung *(f)*
height of stand structures Standbauhöhe *(f)*

hotel accommodation

height, clear usable lichte Nutzhöhe *(f)*
help, temporary Aushilfe *(f)*, Hilfskraft *(f)*
helper Helfer(in) *(m/f)*, Hilfskraft *(f)*
hexagon Sechseck *(n)*
hexagon nut Sechskantmutter *(f)*
hexagonal recess Innensechskant *(m)*, Innensechskantschlüssel *(m)*
high back rest upholstered Polstersessel *(m)*
high-grade erstklassig
highlight Glanzlicht *(n)*, Höhepunkt *(m)*
high polish Hochglanz *(m)*
high technology Hochtechnologie *(f)*
hinder hindern, behindern, aufhalten, verhindern, verhüten
hinge drehbar einhängen
hinge Gelenk *(n)*, Scharnier *(n)*, Türangel *(f)*
hinge plate Türband *(n)*
hinged profile Gelenkprofil *(n)*
hire (GB) Miete *(f)*, Mietpreis *(m)*, Mieten *(n)*, Leihen *(n)*
hire (GB) mieten, chartern, leihen
hire (US) einstellen, engagieren
hire charge (GB) Leihgebühr *(f)*
hire purchase (GB) Ratenkauf *(m)*, Mietkauf *(m)*
hire service (GB) Verleih *(m)*
hoist hochziehen
hoist Flaschenzug *(m)*, Kran *(m)*, Lastenaufzug *(m)*, Winde *(f)*
hoisting equipment Hebevorrichtung *(f)*
hold festhalten, aushalten
hold Griff *(m)*, Halt *(m)*, Stütze *(f)*
holding company Holdinggesellschaft *(f)*, Dachgesellschaft *(f)*, Muttergesellschaft *(f)*
holding device Halterung *(f)*
holding pin Haltedorn *(m)*
holding ring Haltering *(f)*
hole durchbohren, durchlöchern
hole Loch *(n)*, Lücke *(f)*, Öffnung *(f)*
holiday, national Nationalfeiertag *(m)*
hollow Loch *(n)*, Vertiefung *(f)*, Mulde *(f)*

hollow hohl
hollow space Hohlraum *(m)*
holograph Hologramm *(n)*
holography Holografie *(f)*
home address Heimatanschrift *(f)*, Privatanschrift *(f)*, Privatadresse *(f)*
home computer Heimcomputer *(m)*
home market Binnenmarkt *(m)*, Inlandsmarkt *(m)*
home page Homepage *(f)*, Startseite *(f)*
home sales Inlandsabsatz *(m)*
honest aufrichtig, ehrlich, ehrenhaft, vertrauenswürdig, zuverlässig
hood Haube *(f)*, Aufsatz *(m)*, Verdeck *(n)*
hook anhaken, festhaken, zuhaken, anhängen
hook Haken *(m)*
horizontal horizontal, waagerecht
hose abspritzen
hose Schlauch *(m)*
hose connector Schlauchverbinder *(m)*
hospitable gastlich, gastfreundlich
hospital Klinik *(f)*, Krankenhaus *(n)*
hospitality Gastfreundschaft, *(f)* Gastlichkeit *(f)*
hospitality area Bewirtungsbereich *(m)*
hospitality expenses Bewirtungskosten *(pl)*
hospitality waste disposal Entsorgung *(m)* von Bewirtungsabfällen
host Gastgeber *(m)*
hostess Hostess *(f)*, Gastgeberin *(f)*
hostess service Hostessendienst *(m)*
hot air Heißluft *(f)*
hot spot Nachtlokal *(n)*; (EDV) WLAN-Einwahlknoten *(m)*
hot water Heißwasser *(n)*, Warmwasser *(n)*
hot water tank Warmwasserspeicher *(m)*
hot-dog heater Würstchenwärmer *(m)*
hotel accommodation Hotelunterbringung *(f)*, Hotelunterkunft *(f)*

229

hotel and restaurant guide
Hotel- und Gaststättenführer *(m)*
hotel bill Hotelrechnung *(f)*
hotel booking Hotelreservierung *(f)*
hotel chain Hotelkette *(f)*
hotel costs Hotelkosten *(pl)*
hotel diningroom Hotelrestaurant *(n)*
hotel guest Hotelgast *(m)*
hotel guide Hotelführer *(m)*
hotel information service
Hotelnachweis *(m)*
hotel management Hotelleitung *(f)*, Hoteldirektion *(f)*
hotel occupancy Hotelbelegung *(f)*
hotel of international standard
Hotel *(n)* internationaler Klasse
hotel package Hotelarrangement *(n)*
hotel register Hotelverzeichnis *(n)*
hotel reservation
Hotelzimmerreservierung *(f)*
hotel reservation service
Zimmerreservierungsservice *(m)*, Hotelreservierungsdienst *(m)*
hotel, private Hotelpension *(f)*
hotel, residential Hotel *(n)* garni
hotel, upper-bracket Hotel *(n)* der gehobenen Mittelklasse
hotplate Heizplatte *(f)*, Kochplatte *(f)*
hotplate cart Warmhaltewagen *(m)*
hotplate, electric Elektrokochplatte *(f)*
hourly stündlich
house journal Hauszeitschrift *(f)*
house magazine Hauszeitung *(f)*, Hauszeitschrift *(f)*
house rules Hausordnung *(f)*
household refrigerator
Haushaltskühlschrank *(m)*
housing cover Gehäuseabdeckung *(f)*
hue Farbton *(m)*, Färbung *(f)*, Tönung *(f)*, Schattierung *(f)*
humid feucht
humidifier Verdunster *(m)*, Luftbefeuchtungsanlage *(f)*
humidity Feuchtigkeit *(f)*
humorous humorvoll

HV bulb Hochvoltlampe *(f)*
hydrant Hydrant *(m)*
hydraulics Hydraulik *(f)*
hygienic hygienisch

I

icebox (US) Kühlschrank *(m)*
ice cube Eiswürfel *(m)*
ice cube dispenser
Würfeleisspender *(m)*
ice cube machine
Eiswürfelbereiter *(m)*
ice cube maker Eiswürfelbereiter *(m)*
ice-cream Eiscreme *(f)*, Speiseeis *(n)*
idea Idee *(f)*, Gedanke *(m)*, Meinung *(f)*, Vorstellung *(f)*; Absicht *(f)*
idemnify (Versicherung)
Schadenersatz *(m)* leisten
identification card Personalausweis *(m)*, Ausweis *(m)*, Ausweiskarte *(f)*
identification papers
Ausweispapiere *(n, pl)*, Personalpapiere *(n, pl)*
identify identifizieren, erkennen
identity Identität *(f)*, Übereinstimmung *(f)*
identity card Personalausweis *(m)*
ignorance Ignoranz *(f)*, Unkenntnis *(f)*
illegal illegal, ungesetzlich, rechtswidrig, unerlaubt
illegality Illegalität *(f)*, Gesetzwidrigkeit *(f)*, Rechtswidrigkeit *(f)*
illegitimate gesetzwidrig, ungesetzlich, unrechtmäßig, unzulässig
illicit unerlaubt, verboten
illicit work Schwarzarbeit *(f)*
illness Krankheit *(f)*
illuminate illuminieren, beleuchten, festlich beleuchten, erleuchten, erhellen; erklären, erläutern

illumination Illumination *(f)*, Beleuchtung *(f)*, Ausleuchtung *(f)*, Festbeleuchtung *(f)*; Erklärung *(f)*, Erläuterung *(f)*
illumination design Lichtdesign *(n)*
illumination effect Beleuchtungseffekt *(m)*
illumination level Beleuchtungsstärke *(f)*
illustrate illustrieren, veranschaulichen, bebildern, erklären
illustration Illustration *(f)*, Abbildung *(f)*, Bebilderung *(f)*, Erklärung *(f)*, Veranschaulichung *(f)*
image Image *(n)*; Bild *(n)*, Abbild *(n)*, Vorstellung *(f)*, Verkörperung *(f)*, Sinnbild *(n)*
image building appearance imagebildender Auftritt *(m)*
image cultivation Imagepflege *(f)*
image processing Bildverarbeitung *(f)*
image splitting system (Multivision) Bildteilersystem *(n)*
image, three-dimensional dreidimensionales Bild *(n)*
imagination Fantasie *(f)*, Einbildung *(f)*, Vorstellung *(f)*
imaging input device Bildeingabegerät *(n)*
imaging output device Bildausgabegerät *(n)*
imitate imitieren, nachahmen, nachmachen, fälschen
imitate unecht, künstlich
imitation Imitation *(f)*, Nachahmung *(f)*, Fälschung *(f)*
immediate umgehend, unmittelbar, direkt, sofortig, prompt
immediate action Sofortmaßnahme *(f)*
immediate delivery Sofortlieferung *(f)*
immense immens, enorm, riesig, ungeheuer
immobile unbeweglich

impact Eindruck *(m)*, Einfluss *(m)*, Wirkung *(f)*, Auswirkung *(f)*; Aufprall *(m)*, Einschlag *(m)*
impassable unpassierbar, unüberwindbar
impatience Ungeduld *(f)*, Unduldsamkeit *(f)*
impatient ungeduldig
impersonal unpersönlich, sachlich
impolite unhöflich
impoliteness Unhöflichkeit *(f)*
import Import *(m)*, Einfuhr *(f)*
import importieren, einführen
import ban Einfuhrverbot *(n)*
import duty Einfuhrzoll *(m)*
import licence (GB) Importlizenz *(f)*, Importbewilligung *(f)*, Importgenehmigung *(f)*, Einfuhrbewilligung *(f)*, Einfuhrgenehmigung *(f)*
import license (US) Importlizenz *(f)*, Importbewilligung *(f)*, Importgenehmigung *(f)*, Einfuhrbewilligung *(f)*, Einfuhrgenehmigung *(f)*
import permit Importerlaubnis *(f)*, Einfuhrgenehmigung *(f)*
importance Bedeutung *(f)*, Ansehen *(n)*, Wichtigkeit *(f)*, Gewicht *(n)*
importance of exhibitions Bedeutung *(f)* von Messen
important wichtig, einflussreich
importer Importeur *(m)*
impossibility Unmöglichkeit *(f)*
impossible unmöglich
impracticable impraktikabel, praxisfern, undurchführbar, unpassierbar
impractical unpraktisch, undurchführbar
impregnate imprägnieren, tränken, durchdringen
impress beeindrucken, imponieren, prägen, einprägen, eindrucken, einschärfen
impression Abdruck *(m)*, Prägung *(f)*; Eindruck *(m)*, Vermutung *(f)*
impression, general Gesamteindruck *(m)*

impressive eindrucksvoll
imprint bedrucken, prägen, einprägen
imprint Aufdruck *(m)*, Abdruck *(m)*, Eindruck *(m)*; Druckvermerk *(m)*, Impressum *(n)*
improbable unwahrscheinlich
improper unangebracht, unpassend, ungeeignet, unrichtig, unschicklich
improve bessern, verbessern, sich verbessern, erhöhen, steigern, Fortschritte *(m, pl)* machen
improvement Fortschritt *(m)*, Aufbesserung *(f)*, Verbesserung *(f)*, Steigerung *(f)*, Vervollkommnung *(f)*
improvisation Improvisation *(f)*
improvise improvisieren
imprudence Unverschämtheit *(f)*, Frechheit *(f)*
imprudent unklug, unvorsichtig, unverschämt, frech
impulse Impuls *(m)*, Antrieb *(m)*, Anstoß *(m)*, Anreiz *(m)*, Drang *(m)*, Trieb *(m)*
impulse buy Impulskauf *(m)*, Spontankauf *(m)*
impulsive impulsiv, spontan
in due form vorschriftsmäßig
inaccuracy Ungenauigkeit *(f)*, Unrichtigkeit *(f)*
inaccurate ungenau, unrichtig
inactive untätig, müßig
inactivity Untätigkeit *(f)*, Lustlosigkeit *(f)*, Flaute *(f)*
inadequate unangemessen, unzulänglich, unzureichend, ungenügend, nicht geeignet
inadvertent unabsichtlich, unbeabsichtigt, ungewollt, versehentlich
inappropriate unangebracht, unangemessen, ungelegen
inattention Unaufmerksamkeit *(f)*
inattentive unaufmerksam
incalculable unabsehbar, unberechenbar, unschätzbar

incautious unvorsichtig, unbedacht
incidence Häufigkeit *(f)*, Verbreitung *(f)*, Vorkommen *(n)*
incident Ereignis *(n)*, Vorfall *(m)*, Zwischenfall *(m)*
incidental beiläufig, nebensächlich, zufällig
incidentally nebenbei bemerkt, übrigens
incidentals Nebenausgaben *(f, pl)*, Nebenkosten *(pl)*
inclination Neigung *(f)*, Hang *(m)*; Zuneigung *(f)*; Gefälle *(n)*
incline Gefälle *(n)*, Schräge *(f)*, Abhang *(m)*
incline neigen, sich neigen, abfallen
include einschließen, einbeziehen, enthalten, umfassen
inclusive inklusive, eingerechnet, einschließlich
income Einkommen *(n)*, Einkünfte *(f, pl)*, Einnahmen *(f, pl)*, Ertrag *(m)*, Erträge *(m, pl)*
incomplete unvollständig
incomprehensible unbegreiflich, unverständlich
inconscious unbewusst
inconsequential belanglos, unwichtig, unmaßgeblich
inconsiderate unaufmerksam, rücksichtslos
inconspicious unauffällig, unscheinbar
inconvenient ungelegen, ungünstig, unbequem, unpraktisch
incorrect inkorrekt, falsch, fehlerhaft, unzutreffend
increase Anwachsen *(n)*, Erhöhung *(f)*, Steigerung *(f)*, Vergrößerung *(f)*, Wachstum *(n)*, Zunahme *(f)*, Zuwachs *(m)*
increase wachsen, anwachsen, steigen, ansteigen, erhöhen, sich erhöhen, zunehmen, vermehren, verstärken, vergrößern, sich vergrößern
increase in turnover Umsatzplus *(n)*, Umsatzzuwachs *(m)*

increase of efficiency
  Ertragssteigerung *(f)*
increase, rate of Zuwachsrate *(f)*
indecision Unentschlossenheit *(f)*
indemnity Abfindung *(f)*,
  Absicherung *(f)*, Entschädigung *(f)*,
  Schadenversicherung *(f)*,
  Haftungsausschluss *(f)*
independence Unabhängigkeit *(f)*,
  Selbstständigkeit *(f)*
independent unabhängig,
  selbstständig
index Index *(m)*, Katalog *(m)*,
  Register *(n)*, Verzeichnis *(n)*
indicate anzeigen, hinweisen auf,
  deuten auf, zeigen auf, zu erkennen
  geben
indicator Indikator *(m)*, Zeichen *(n)*,
  Anzeichen *(n)*, Andeutung *(f)*,
  Hinweis *(m)*
indifferent indifferent, gleichgültig,
  desinteressiert; durchschnittlich,
  mittelmäßig
indirect indirekt
indispensable unerlässlich,
  unentbehrlich, unbedingt notwendig
indistinct undeutlich, unscharf,
  verschwommen
individual individuell, persönlich,
  einzeln, Einzel-
individual Individuum *(n)*,
  Einzelne(r) *(f/m)*, Einzelperson *(f)*
industrial industriell, gewerblich,
  Industrie-, Arbeits-, Betriebs-
Industrial Safety Ordinance
  Betriebssicherheitsverordnung *(f)*
industries exhibition
  Gewerbeausstellung *(f)*,
  Industrieausstellung *(f)*,
  Industriemesse *(f)*
industries fair Gewerbeausstellung *(f)*,
  Industrieausstellung *(f)*,
  Industriemesse *(f)*
ineffective unwirksam, wirkungslos,
  unfähig, untauglich

inefficient ineffizient, unrationell,
  unrentabel, unwirtschaftlich,
  untüchtig
inevitable unvermeidlich, zwangsläufig
inexact ungenau
inexcusable unentschuldbar,
  unverzeihlich
inexpedient unangebracht,
  unzweckmäßig
inexperienced unerfahren
inferior Untergebene(r) *(f/m)*
inferior weniger wert, minderwertig,
  mittelmäßig, niedriger, untergeordnet
infill materials Ausfachmaterial *(n)*
inflammable entflammbar, leicht
  entzündbar, feuergefährlich, reizbar
inflation, rate of Inflationsrate *(f)*
inflexible unflexibel, unbeweglich,
  starr, steif, unnachgiebig
informal inoffiziell, informell, formlos,
  zwanglos
information Information *(f)*,
  Auskunft *(f)*, Nachricht *(f)*,
  Benachrichtigung *(f)*, Mitteilung *(f)*,
  Bescheid *(m)*, Unterrichtung *(f)*
information brochure
  Informationsbroschüre *(f)*
information center (US)
  Informationszentrum *(n)*
information centre (GB)
  Informationszentrum *(n)*
information counter Infotheke *(f)*,
  Auskunftsschalter *(m)*
information desk Infotheke *(f)*,
  Auskunftsschalter *(m)*
information service
  Informationsdienst *(m)*
information stand
  Informationsstand *(m)*
information superhighway
  Datenautobahn *(f)*
information system, electronic
  elektronisches Informationssystem *(n)*
information technology
  Informationstechnik *(f)*

information, private vertrauliche
Mitteilung *(f)*
infrastructure Infrastruktur *(f)*
infringement Verstoß *(m)*,
Übertretung *(f)*, Verletzung *(f)*
in-house innerbetrieblich
injure verletzen, verwunden, kränken
injurious to health
gesundheitsschädlich
injury Verletzung *(f)*, Kränkung *(f)*,
Beeinträchtigung *(f)*
injustice Ungerechtigkeit *(f)*, Unrecht *(n)*
inn (GB) Gasthaus *(n)*, Wirtshaus *(n)*
innovation Innovation *(f)*,
Neuentwicklung *(f)*, Neuerung *(f)*,
Neuheit *(f)*
inoculation Impfung *(f)*
inoculation requirements
Impfbestimmungen *(f, pl)*
input data Eingabedaten *(pl)*
input device Eingabegerät *(n)*
inquire (US) sich erkundigen,
nachfragen
inquiry (US) Anfrage *(f)*, Befragung *(f)*,
Erhebung *(f)*, Erkundigung *(f)*,
Prüfung *(f)*, Untersuchung *(f)*
inscribe (in Liste etc.) eintragen
inscription Aufschrift *(f)*, Inschrift *(f)*,
Beschriftung *(f)*, Widmung *(f)*
insecure unsicher
insecurity Unsicherheit *(f)*
insert Inserat *(n)*, Anzeige *(f)*,
Einlage *(f)*, Beilage *(f)*
insert inserieren; einfügen, einsetzen,
einschalten, einschieben, einwerfen
insert profile (Messbau)
Einschubprofil *(n)*
insertion Anzeige *(f)*, Inserat *(n)*;
Einschaltung *(f)*, Einfügung *(f)*,
Platzierung *(f)*; (Automat etc.)
Einwurf *(m)*
inside Innenseite *(f)*, Inneres *(n)*
inside Innen-, innen, drinnen,
innere(-r/-s), hinein, innerhalb,
im Inneren *(n)*

insignificant bedeutungslos,
geringfügig, unbedeutend, unerheblich
insolvency Insolvenz *(f)*,
Überschuldung *(f)*,
Zahlungsunfähigkeit *(f)*
inspect inspizieren, kontrollieren,
prüfen, untersuchen, besichtigen
inspection Inspektion *(f)*,
Untersuchung *(f)*, Besichtigung *(f)*,
Prüfung *(f)*, Kontrolle *(f)*
inspection certificate Prüfzeugnis *(n)*,
Abnahmebescheinigung *(f)*
inspection mark legislation
Prüfzeichenverordnung *(f)*
inspection of exhibition materials
Abnahme *(m)* von Messegut
inspection opening Revisionsöffnung *(f)*
inspection report Prüfbescheid *(m)*
instability Instabilität *(f)*,
Unbeständigkeit *(f)*
install installieren, einbauen, einsetzen,
anschließen; (Leitung etc.) legen
installation Installation *(f)*,
Einrichtung *(f)*, Anschluss *(m)*,
Anlage *(f)*, Aufbau *(m)*, Einbau *(m)*,
Einsetzung *(f)*
installation dates Aufbautermine *(m, pl)*
installation deadline Aufbauschluss *(m)*
installation labor pass (US)
Aufbauausweis *(m)*
installation labour pass (GB)
Aufbauausweis *(m)*
installation pass Aufbauausweis *(m)*
installation rules Aufbaurichtlinien *(f, pl)*
installation start Aufbaubeginn *(m)*
installation time extension
verlängerte Aufbauzeit *(f)*
installations, electrical
Elektroinstallation *(f)*,
Elektroanschluss *(m)*
installment (US) Rate *(f)*, Teilzahlung *(f)*
instalment (GB) Rate *(f)*, Teilzahlung *(f)*
instance Instanz *(f)*; Fall *(m)*, Beispiel *(n)*
instead statt dessen, dafür
instead of statt, anstatt, an Stelle *(f)* von

instigation Anstiftung (f), Betreiben (n), Veranlassung (f)
instruct anleiten, anweisen, belehren, informieren; unterrichten, unterweisen, ausbilden
instruction Instruktion (f), Unterrichtung (f), Anordnung (m), Anweisung (m), Belehrung (f); Vorschrift (f); Ausbildung (f), Schulung (f), Unterricht (m)
instruction book Bedienungsanleitung (f), Gebrauchsanweisung (f)
instruction leaflet Merkblatt (n), Beipackzettel (m)
instructions for use Bedienungsanleitung (f), Gebrauchsanweisung (f)
instrument Instrument (n), Werkzeug (n), Gerät (n), Mittel (n), Dokument (n), Urkunde (f)
instrument panel Instrumentenbrett (n)
insufficient ungenügend, untauglich, unzulänglich, unbefriedigend
insulate isolieren
insulating tape Isolierband (n)
insulation Isolierung (f), Wärmedämmung (f)
insurable value Versicherungswert (m)
insurance Versicherung (f)
insurance against theft Diebstahlversicherung (f)
insurance charge Versicherungskosten (pl), Versicherungsgebühr (f)
insurance company Versicherungsgesellschaft (f)
insurance cover Versicherungsschutz (m), Deckung (f), Deckungsumfang (m)
insurance coverage Versicherungsschutz (m), Deckung (f), Deckungsumfang (m)
insurance policy Versicherungspolice (f)
insurance premium Versicherungsprämie (f)
insurance, social Sozialversicherung (f)
insure versichern
insured event Versicherungsfall (m)
insurer Versicherer (m), Assekurant (m)
integrate integrieren, eingliedern
integrated frame display Rahmendisplay (n)
intend beabsichtigen, vorhaben, Vorsatz (m) haben
intense intensiv, heftig, stark, durchdringend; hell, grell; dringend
intense activity Hochbetrieb (m)
intensify intensivieren, verstärken, vertiefen
intent Absicht (f), Vorsatz (m), Zweck (m)
intent aufmerksam, gespannt
intention Absicht (f), Vorhaben (n), Vorsatz (m)
interchangeable austauschbar, auswechselbar
intercom Gegensprechanlage (f)
intercommunication system Sprechanlage (f)
intercourse, commercial Geschäftsverkehr (m)
interdict amtlich verbieten, untersagen
interdict amtliches Verbot (n)
interest Interesse (n), Bedeutung (f), Wichtigkeit (f); Anteil (m), Beteiligung (f), Zins (m), Zinsen (m, pl)
interest interessieren
interface Interface (n), Schnittstelle (f)
interference Beeinträchtigung (f), Störung (f), Eingriff (m), Einmischung (f), Intervention (f)
interim einstweilig, vorläufig, Interims-, Zwischen-
interim Zwischenzeit (f)
interim cleaning Zwischenreinigung (f), Laufzeitreinigung (f)
interim result Zwischenergebnis (n)

interior Innen-, inner-, Binnen-
interior Inneres *(n)*, Innenraum *(m)*, Innenseite *(f)*; Innenaufnahme *(f)*, Studioaufnahme *(f)*
interior decoration Innenausstattung *(f)*, Raumausstattung *(f)*
interior design Innenarchitektur *(f)*, Raumgestaltung *(f)*
interior designer Innenarchitekt(in) *(m/f)*
interior lighting Innenbeleuchtung *(f)*
interior space umbauter Raum *(m)*
interior view Innenansicht *(f)*
intermediate Zwischen-, dazwischenliegend
internet access Internetzugang *(m)*
internet page Internetseite *(f)*, Webseite *(f)*
internet presence Internetpräsenz *(f)*, Internetauftritt *(m)*
internet press box Internetpressefach *(n)*
interpret interpretieren, auslegen, erklären; dolmetschen
interpreter Dolmetscher(in) *(m/f)*
interpreter, simultaneous Simultandolmetscher(in) *(m/f)*
interrupt unterbrechen, hindern, stören
interruption Unterbrechung *(f)*, Störung *(f)*
interval Abstand *(m)*, Zwischenraum *(m)*, Pause *(f)*
interview Interview *(n)*, Befragung *(f)*, Unterredung *(f)*
interview interviewen
interviewee Interviewte(r) *(f/m)*, Befragte(r) *(f/m)*
interviewer Interviewer(in) *(m/f)*
intranet Intranet *(n)*
intransigent unnachgiebig
introduce einführen, beginnen, einleiten, eröffnen; zur Sprache *(f)* bringen; (Person) vorstellen

introduce into the market auf den Markt *(m)* bringen
introduction Einführung *(f)*, Einleitung *(f)*, Vorwort *(n)*; Vorstellung *(f)*
invalid invalide, krank; ungültig, nicht zulässig
invalid Invalide(r) *(f/m)*, Körperbehinderte(r) *(f/m)*
invalidity Nichtigkeit *(f)*, Ungültigkeit *(f)*
inventory Inventar *(n)*, Inventarverzeichnis *(n)*, Inventur *(f)*, Bestandsaufnahme *(f)*, Lagerbestände *(m, pl)*
invest investieren, anlegen
investigate ermitteln, recherchieren, untersuchen, überprüfen, Nachforschungen *(f, pl)* anstellen
investigation Aufklärung *(f)*, Ermittlung *(f)*, Nachforschung *(f)*, Recherche *(f)*, Untersuchung *(f)*, Überprüfung *(f)*
investment Investition *(f)*, Anlage *(f)*
invitation Einladung *(f)*; Aufforderung *(f)*, Ersuchen *(n)*
invitation action Einladungsaktion *(f)*
invitation campaign Einladungskampagne *(f)*, Einladungsaktion *(f)*
invitation to bid öffentliche Ausschreibung *(f)*
invitation to make an offer öffentliche Ausschreibung *(f)*
invite einladen; ermuntern, ersuchen, auffordern, bitten
invite tenders (Projekt etc.) ausschreiben
invoice in Rechnung *(f)* stellen, fakturieren
invoice Rechnung *(f)*, Faktur *(f)*
invoice amount Rechnungsbetrag *(m)*
invoice price Rechnungspreis *(m)*
invoice, final Schlussrechnung *(f)*

invoicing Abrechnung *(f)*,
Fakturierung *(f)*,
Rechnungsstellung *(f)*
invoicing address
Rechnungsanschrift *(f)*
involve einbeziehen, hineinziehen,
verwickeln, zur Folge *(f)* haben, nach
sich ziehen
inward innere(-r/-s), innerlich,
einwärts, nach innen
inwards mission
Auslandsdelegation *(f)*
irregular irregulär, unregelmäßig,
unvorschriftsmäßig,
vorschriftswidrig
irrelevant irrelevant, belanglos,
nebensächlich, unerheblich,
unwesentlich
irresolute unentschlossen,
unschlüssig
irresponsible unverantwortlich,
verantwortungslos
irreversible unabänderlich,
unwiderruflich
irrevocable unwiderruflich
ISDN (Integrated Services Digital Network) ISDN
island site Blockstand *(m)*
island stand Blockstand *(m)*
issue Ausgabe *(f)*, Auflage *(f)*;
Emission *(f)*; Erlass *(m)*;
Ergebnis *(n)*; Problem *(n)*,
Streitfrage *(f)*
issue ausgeben, ausfertigen, begeben,
auflegen, veröffentlichen,
herausgeben; erlassen
item Artikel *(m)*, Gegenstand *(m)*,
Stück *(n)*; Punkt *(m)*; Posten *(m)*;
Notiz *(f)*; Nachricht *(f)*, Meldung *(f)*
item, special Sonderposten *(m)*
itemize aufgliedern, einzeln aufführen,
spezifizieren
items of value Wertsachen *(f, pl)*
itinerary Reiseführer *(m)*, Reiseplan *(m)*,
Straßenkarte *(f)*

J

jacket Sakko *(n)*
jam einklemmen, festklemmen, sich
verklemmen, quetschen, drücken,
hineinzwängen, drängen, sich hinein-
drängen; schieben, stoßen; blockieren
jam Gedränge *(n)*, Blockierung *(f)*;
Klemme *(f)*, Verklemmung *(f)*
jet of flame Stichflamme *(f)*
jewellery (GB) Schmuck *(m)*
jewelry (US) Schmuck *(m)*
jewels Schmuck *(m)*
job Arbeit *(f)*, Aufgabe *(f)*, Tätigkeit *(f)*,
Beschäftigung *(f)*, Beruf *(m)*,
Stellung *(f)*, Posten *(m)*, Pflicht *(f)*
job jobben, Gelegenheitsarbeit *(f)*
übernehmen
job assignment Aufgabenverteilung *(f)*
job fair Jobmesse *(f)*, Messe *(f)* für
den Berufseinstieg
job instruction Arbeitsunterweisung *(f)*
job, temporary Zeitarbeit *(f)*
join in mitmachen
joiner Tischler(in) *(m/f)*,
Schreiner(in) *(m/f)*
joiner panel Tischlerplatte *(f)*
joint gemeinsam, gemeinschaftlich,
Gemeinschafts-
joint Naht *(f)*, Fuge *(f)*, Scharnier *(n)*,
Verbindungsstelle *(f)*
joint advertising Verbundwerbung *(f)*
joint exhibit
Firmengemeinschaftsausstellung *(f)*
joint exhibition
Firmengemeinschaftsausstellung *(f)*
joint exhibition stand
Gemeinschaftsmessestand *(m)*
joint responsibility Mitverantwortung *(f)*
joint stand Gemeinschaftsstand *(m)*
joint stand organizer Gemeinschaftsstandorganisator *(m)*, Veranstalter *(m)*
des Gemeinschaftsstands

joint stand participant
Gemeinschaftsstandteilnehmer *(m)*
joint stand participation Gemeinschaftsbeteiligung *(f)* an einem Stand
joint venture Gemeinschaftsunternehmen *(n)*, Arbeitsgemeinschaft *(f)*, Beteiligungsgeschäft *(n)*
joke Scherz *(m)*
joke scherzen, spaßen
journal Journal *(n)*, Zeitschrift *(f)*, Magazin *(n)*
journalist Journalist(in) *(m/f)*
journey Reise *(f)*
journey reisen
joystick Joystick *(m)*
judge Richter(in) *(m/f)*; Preisrichter(in) *(m/f)*; Schiedsrichter(in) *(m/f)*; Sachverständige(r) *(f/m)*
judge urteilen, beurteilen, einschätzen, entscheiden, richten, verhandeln
jug Krug *(m)*, Kanne *(f)*, Kännchen *(n)*
juice entsaften
juice Saft *(m)*
juice extractor Saftpresse *(f)*
junk mail Reklamepostsendung *(f)*
jury Jury *(f)*, Preisgericht *(n)*
just for fun spaßeshalber
justification Rechtfertigung *(f)*
justify rechtfertigen, begründen
jut out hervorstehen, herausragen, vorspringen

K

keep Unterhalt *(m)*
keep halten, behalten, aufheben, bewahren, vorrätig haben; einhalten, befolgen; lassen; jdn. aufhalten; bleiben; betreiben, beschäftigen, veranstalten, führen; ernähren, unterhalten
keep ahead vorne bleiben

keep away wegbleiben
Keep clear! Freihalten!
keep in stock bevorraten
keep out abhalten, fernhalten, nicht hereinlassen, draußen bleiben
Keep out! Eintritt verboten!
Keep quiet! Ruhe bewahren!
keep the minutes Protokoll *(n)* führen
keep up aufrecht halten, hochhalten, fortfahren, weitermachen, ausharren, sich behaupten
keeping Aufbewahrung *(f)*, Verwahrung *(f)*; Befolgen *(n)*, Einhalten *(n)*
key Schlüssel *(m)*; Lösung *(f)*; Taste *(f)*
key button Tastenknopf *(m)*
key lighting Akzentbeleuchtung *(f)*
key position Schlüsselposition *(f)*
key staff leitende Angestellte *(m, pl)*
keyboard Tastatur *(f)*
keynote Grundgedanke *(m)*
kilowatt Kilowatt *(n)*
kilowatt hour Kilowattstunde *(f)*
kind Art *(f)*, Sorte *(f)*, Gattung *(f)*, Klasse *(f)*, Wesen *(n)*
kind freundlich, liebenswürdig, nett, entgegenkommend
kindergarten Kindergarten *(m)*
king-size großformatig
kitchen fittings Küchenausstattung *(f)*
kitchen furniture and fittings Kücheneinrichtung *(f)*
kitchen garbage (US) Küchenabfall *(m)*
kitchen help Küchenhilfe *(f)*
kitchen personnel Küchenpersonal *(n)*
kitchen staff Küchenpersonal *(n)*
kitchen towel Geschirrtuch *(n)*
kitchen utensils Küchengeräte *(n, pl)*
kitchen waste Küchenabfall *(m)*
kitchen waste disposal Entsorgung *(f)* von Küchenabfällen
kitchenette Kochnische *(f)*, vorgefertigte Kücheneinheit *(f)*, Kompaktküche *(f)*
kitchenmaid Küchenhilfe *(f)*

kitchenware Küchengeschirr *(n)*
knock klopfen; schlagen, stoßen; umstoßen
knock Klopfen *(n)*, Anklopfen *(n)*; Pochen *(n)*; Schlag *(m)*, Stoß *(m)*
know-how Know-how *(n)*, Fachwissen *(n)*, Fachkenntnisse *(f, pl)*, Erfahrung *(f)*, Können *(n)*
knowledge Kenntnis *(f)*, Wissen *(n)*
knowledge of languages Sprachkenntnisse *(pl)*
knowledge, specialized Fachwissen *(n)*
kw consumption kW-Anschlussleistung *(f)*, kW-Verbrauch *(m)*

L

label Etikett *(n)*, Anhängezettel *(m)*, Schildchen *(n)*, Aufschrift *(f)*, Beschriftung *(f)*, Kennzeichnung *(f)*
label etikettieren, kennzeichnen, beschriften
label, self-sticking Selbstklebeetikett *(n)*
labeling (US) Preisauszeichnung *(f)*, Etikettierung *(f)*, Markierung *(f)*
labelling (GB) Preisauszeichnung *(f)*, Etikettierung *(f)*, Markierung *(f)*
labor (US) Arbeit *(f)*, Aufgabe *(f)*, Anstrengung *(f)*, Mühe *(f)*; Arbeitnehmer *(m, pl)*, Arbeitskräfte *(f, pl)*
labor (US), heavy Schwerarbeit *(f)*
labor (US), unskilled ungelernte Arbeitskräfte *(f, pl)*
laborer (US), casual Gelegenheitsarbeiter(in) *(m/f)*
labor-intensive (US) arbeitsintensiv
labor-saving (US) arbeitssparend
labour (GB) Arbeit *(f)*, Aufgabe *(f)*, Anstrengung *(f)*, Mühe *(f)*, Arbeitnehmer *(m, pl)*, Arbeitskräfte *(f, pl)*
labour (GB), heavy Schwerarbeit *(f)*

labour (GB), unskilled ungelernte Arbeitskräfte *(f, pl)*
labourer (GB), casual Gelegenheitsarbeiter(in) *(m/f)*
labour-intensive (GB) arbeitsintensiv
labour-saving (GB) arbeitssparend
lack fehlen, nicht genug haben, Mangel *(m)* haben
lack Mangel *(m)*
lack of interest Desinteresse *(n)*
lack of space Platzmangel *(m)*
lacquer Lack *(m)*, Firnis *(m)*
lacquer lackieren
ladder Leiter *(m)*, Stehleiter *(f)*, Stufenleiter *(f)*
ladies Damentoilette *(f)*
ladies' lavatory (GB) Damentoilette *(f)*
ladies' room (US) Damentoilette *(f)*
ladies' toilet (GB) Damentoilette *(f)*
lager helles Bier *(n)*
lamella Lamelle *(f)*
laminate laminieren; (überziehen) kaschieren
lamp Lampe *(f)*, Leuchte *(f)*
lamp connector Leuchtenanschluss *(m)*
lamp, fluorescent Leuchtstofflampe *(f)*
lamp, hanging Hängelampe *(f)*, Hängeleuchte *(f)*
landing Landen *(n)*, Landung *(f)*, Treppenabsatz *(m)*
language, national Landessprache *(f)*
laser equipment Laseranlage *(f)*
laserpointer Laserzeiger *(m)*
lateness Verspätung *(f)*
lateral seitlich
lath Latte *(f)*, Leiste *(f)*
lattice Gitter *(n)*, Gitterwerk *(n)*
lattice vergittern
lattice beam girder Holzbalkengitter *(n)*
laundry Wäscherei *(f)*
lavatory (GB) Toilette *(f)*
lavatory (GB), public öffentliche Toilette *(f)*
law on equipment safety Gerätesicherheitsgesetz *(n)*

Law on the Promotion of Closed-Loop Recycling Systems and Safeguarding of Environmentally Compatible Waste Materials Disposal Gesetz *(m)* zur Förderung der Kreislaufwirtschaft und Sicherung der umweltverträglichen Beseitigung von Abfällen
law, commercial Handelsrecht *(n)*, Handelsgesetz *(n)*
law, industrial Arbeitsrecht *(n)*
lawful legitim, gesetzmäßig, rechtmäßig
lawfulness Gesetzmäßigkeit *(f)*, Rechtmäßigkeit *(f)*
lawsuit Rechtsstreit *(m)*, Prozess *(m)*
lay out entwerfen, planen, auslegen; zur Schau *(f)* stellen
lay-by Parkstreifen *(m)*, Parkbucht *(f)*
layer Schicht *(f)*, Lage *(f)*
layout Layout *(n)*, Anordnung *(f)*, Ausgestaltung *(f)*, Entwurf *(m)*, Plan *(m)*, Grundriss *(m)*
lead führen, anführen, leiten; veranlassen
lead Führung *(f)*, Leitung *(f)*, führende Stelle *(f)*; Spitze *(f)*, Vorsprung *(m)*; Leitbild *(n)*
lead fair Leitmesse *(f)*
leaflet Faltblatt *(n)*, Flugblatt *(n)*, Handzettel *(m)*, Prospekt *(m)*
leak Leck *(f)*, undichte Stelle *(f)*, Auslaufen *(n)*
leak lecken, leck sein, undicht sein, tropfen
leak indicator Leckanzeiger *(m)*
leakage Leckage *(f)*, Auslaufen *(n)*
lean-on table Stehtisch *(m)*
lease Miete *(f)*, Vermietung *(f)*, Mietvertrag *(m)*, Pacht *(f)*, Verpachtung *(f)*, Pachtvertrag *(m)*
lease mieten, pachten
leasing Leasing *(n)*
leasing agreement Leasingvertrag *(m)*
leave open aussparen
lecture Vorlesung *(f)*, Vortrag *(m)*, Referat *(n)*

lecture Vortrag *(m)* halten
LED display LED-Anzeige *(f)*
LED screen LED-Bildschirm *(m)*
ledge Leiste *(f)*, Sims *(m)*
left-luggage locker Gepäckschließfach *(n)*
left-luggage office Gepäckaufbewahrung *(f)*
leftover waste Restabfall *(m)*
legal legal, gesetzlich, gesetzmäßig, rechtlich, rechtmäßig, rechtsgültig, Rechts-, juristisch
legality Legalität *(f)*, Gesetzmäßigkeit *(f)*, Rechtmäßigkeit *(f)*
legislation, industrial Gewerbeordnung *(f)*
legitimacy Legitimität *(f)*, Gesetzmäßigkeit *(f)*, Rechtmäßigkeit *(f)*, Berechtigung *(f)*
legitimate legitim, gesetzlich, gesetzmäßig, rechtmäßig, berechtigt
legitimation Legitimierung *(f)*
lend leihen, ausleihen, verleihen, gewähren
lender Kreditgeber(in) *(m/f)*, Darlehensgeber(in) *(m/f)*
length Länge *(f)*, Strecke *(f)*, Dauer *(f)*
length, exceptional Überlänge *(f)*
length, special Sonderlänge *(f)*
lengthen verlängern, sich verlängern, länger machen, länger werden
lens Linse *(f)*, Objektiv *(n)*
lens, wide-angle Weitwinkelobjektiv *(n)*
lense, fixed focal (Kamera) Festbrennweite *(f)*
lessor Vermieter(in) *(m/f)*, Verpächter(in) *(m/f)*
lessor's lien Vermieterpfandrecht *(n)*
letter Brief *(m)*, Schreiben *(n)*; Buchstabe *(m)*, Type *(f)*
letter head Briefkopf *(m)*
letter of intent Absichtserklärung *(f)*
letter of invitation Einladungsbrief *(m)*
letter of recommendation Empfehlungsschreiben *(f)*

letter rate Briefgebühr *(f)*
letter service Schreibbüro *(n)*
letter, follow-up Nachfassbrief *(m)*,
  Erinnerungsschreiben *(n)*,
  Folgebrief *(m)*
letter, registered Einschreibebrief *(m)*
letters, illuminated Leuchtschrift *(f)*
level eben, flach, waagerecht; gleich,
  gleichwertig, ausgeglichen, ruhig
level Ebene *(f)*, Höhe *(f)*; Niveau *(n)*,
  Pegel *(m)*, Stufe *(f)*; Geschoss *(n)*;
  Wasserwaage *(f)*
level ebnen, planieren, nivellieren
level down herabsetzen, senken, nach
  unten ausgleichen
level of sound Geräuschpegel *(m)*,
  Tonstärke *(f)*
level up erhöhen, nach oben
  ausgleichen
levelfoot Stellfuß *(m)*
leveller foot Verstellfuß *(m)*
lever Hebel *(m)*; Brechstange *(f)*;
  Druckmittel *(n)*
lever bolt lock Hebelriegelschloss *(n)*
levy Abgabe *(f)*, Erhebung *(f)*,
  Umlage *(f)*, Steuer *(f)*;
  Beschlagnahme *(f)*, Eintreibung *(f)*
levy erheben, eintreiben, pfänden
liability Haftung *(f)*, Haftbarkeit *(f)*,
  Haftpflicht *(f)*; Belastung *(f)*,
  Schuld *(f)*, Verantwortung *(f)*,
  Verpflichtung *(f)*; Verbindlichkeit *(f)*
liability for damages
  Schadenhaftung *(f)*
liability for material defects
  Sachmängelhaftung *(f)*
liability insurance
  Haftpflichtversicherung *(f)*
liability to pay Zahlungsverpflichtung *(f)*
liability, extend of Haftungsumfang *(m)*
liability, limited beschränkte Haftung *(f)*
liability, unlimited unbeschränkte
  Haftung *(f)*
liable haftbar, haftpflichtig, verpflichtet,
  unterworfen

liable for compensation
  regresspflichtig
liable for damages
  schadenersatzpflichtig
liable to customs duty zollpflichtig
liable to duty zollpflichtig
liable to pay zahlungspflichtig
liable to recourse regresspflichtig
library picture Archivbild *(n)*
licence (GB) Lizenz *(f)*, Bewilligung *(f)*,
  Erlaubnis *(f)*, Genehmigung *(f)*,
  Zulassung *(f)*, Konzession *(f)*
licence holder (GB)
  Lizenzinhaber(in) *(m/f)*
licence weight (GB) zulässiges
  Gesamtgewicht *(n)*
license (US) Lizenz *(f)*, Bewilligung *(f)*,
  Erlaubnis *(f)*, Genehmigung *(f)*,
  Zulassung *(f)*, Konzession *(f)*
license holder (US)
  Lizenzinhaber(in) *(m/f)*
license weight (US) zulässiges
  Gesamtgewicht *(n)*
licensing agreement Lizenzvertrag *(m)*
lid Deckel *(m)*
lift heben, hochheben, erheben, sich
  heben; steigen, erhöhen
lift Heben *(n)*, Hochheben *(n)*, Hub *(m)*
lift (GB) Lift *(m)*, Aufzug *(m)*,
  Fahrstuhl *(m)*
lift truck Flurförderzeug *(n)*
lifting capacity Hubkraft *(f)*
lifting device Hubgerät *(n)*
lifting equipment Hebevorrichtung *(f)*
lifting gear Hebezeug *(n)*
lifting jack Wagenwinde *(f)*
lifting platform Hebebühne *(f)*
light anstrahlen, leuchten, beleuchten,
  anzünden
light licht, hell, leuchtend; leicht, locker
light Licht *(n)*
light box Leuchtkasten *(m)*
light box for slides Dialeuchtkasten *(m)*
light box for transparencies
  Dialeuchtkasten *(m)*

light circuit Lichtleitung *(f)*
light grid Lichtraster *(n)*
light switch Lichtschalter *(m)*
light up aufleuchten, beleuchten, Licht *(n)* anmachen
light, fluorescent Langfeldleuchte *(f)*
light, hanging Hängeleuchte *(f)*
lightcase Lichtgehäuse *(n)*
lighter Anzünder *(m)*, Feuerzeug *(n)*
lighting Beleuchtung *(f)*
lighting appliance Beleuchtungskörper *(m)*
lighting concept Beleuchtungskonzept *(n)*
lighting conditions Lichtverhältnisse *(n, pl)*
lighting design Lichtgestaltung *(f)*
lighting effect Lichteffekt *(m)*, Beleuchtungseffekt *(m)*
lighting inlet Beleuchtungseinspeisung *(f)*
lighting track Stromschiene *(f)*
lighting tube Lichtstab *(m)*
lighting, general Grundbeleuchtung *(f)*, Allgemeinbeleuchtung *(f)*
lightweight element Leichtbauelement *(n)*
limit Limit *(n)*, Grenze *(f)*, Preisgrenze *(f)*, Frist *(f)*, Beschränkung *(f)*, Endpunkt *(m)*
limit limitieren, beschränken, begrenzen, einschränken
limitation Begrenzung *(f)*, Beschränkung *(f)*, Einschränkung *(f)*; Verjährung *(f)*
limitation of liability Haftungsbeschränkung *(f)*
limitation on access Zugangsbeschränkung *(f)*
limited limitiert, begrenzt, beschränkt
limited commercial partnership Kommanditgesellschaft *(f)* (KG)
limited company (Ltd.) Gesellschaft mit beschränkter Haftung *(f)* (GmbH)

limited liability company (Ltd.) Gesellschaft mit beschränkter Haftung *(f)* (GmbH)
limited partnership Kommanditgesellschaft *(f)* (KG)
line Linie *(f)*, Grenzlinie *(f)*, Strich *(m)*; Fahrstrecke *(f)*, Flugstrecke *(f)*, Route *(f)*; Fluggesellschaft *(f)*; Gleis *(n)*; Zeile *(f)*, Text *(m)*; Schnur *(f)*, Leitung *(f)*, Telefonleitung *(f)*; Reihe *(f)*, Kette *(f)*; Richtung *(f)*; Vorgehen *(n)*, Methode *(f)*, Richtlinien *(f, pl)*; Branche *(f)*, Fach *(n)*, Gebiet *(n)*
line liniieren, zeichnen, skizzieren
line chart Strichdiagramm *(n)*
line drawing Strichzeichnung *(f)*
line graph Strichzeichnung *(f)*
line illustration Strichzeichnung *(f)*
line rate Zeilenpreis *(m)*
line up sich aufstellen, sich anstellen, aufreihen
linear measure Längenmaß *(n)*
linen hire Wäscheverleih *(m)*
link anschließen, verbinden, verketten, vernetzen
link Verbindungsstück *(n)*, Glied *(n)*, Bindeglied *(n)*, Verbindung *(f)*, Lasche *(f)*
liquidity Liquidität *(f)*, Zahlungsfähigkeit *(f)*
list aufzählen, aufschreiben, einschreiben, eintragen, registrieren, katalogisieren, verzeichnen
list Liste *(f)*, Aufstellung *(f)*, Verzeichnis *(n)*
list of beverages Getränkekarte *(f)*
list of contents Inhaltserklärung *(f)*
list of customers Kundenkartei *(f)*
list of exhibitors Ausstellerverzeichnis *(n)*
list of exhibitors, alphabetical alphabetisches Ausstellerverzeichnis *(n)*
list of materials Stückliste *(f)*
list of participants Teilnehmerliste *(f)*
list price Listenpreis *(m)*

list, itemized Einzelaufstellung *(f)*
listener Zuhörer(in) *(m/f)*
listeners Hörerschaft *(f)*
liter (US) Liter *(m)*
literature Literatur *(f)*; Informationsmaterial *(n)*, Prospekte *(m, pl)*
literature dispenser Prospektspender *(m)*
literature, technical Fachliteratur *(f)*
litre (GB) Liter *(m)*
litter bin (GB) Abfalleimer *(m)*
live wire stromführend
load laden, beladen, verladen; überladen, überlasten, überhäufen; (Film) einlegen
load Last *(f)*, Belastung *(f)*, Ladung *(f)*, Fracht *(m)*; technische Leistung *(f)*, Spannung *(f)*
load capacity Tragfähigkeit *(f)*
load distribution Lastenverteilung *(f)*
load up aufladen, beladen
load, connected (Strom) Anschlusswert *(m)*
load, distributed Flächenlast *(f)*
load-bearing capacity Belastbarkeit *(f)*, Tragfähigkeit *(f)*, Traglast *(f)*
loading Ladung *(f)*, Fracht *(f)*
loading charges Verladekosten *(pl)*
loading point Verladestelle *(f)*
loading ramp Laderampe *(f)*
loading, electrical elektrische Leistung *(f)*
loadspeaker Lautsprecher *(m)*
loan leihen, ausleihen, verleihen, als Darlehen *(n)* geben
loan Leihen *(n)*, Verleihen *(n)*, Leihgabe *(f)*, Anleihe *(f)*, Darlehen *(n)*
lobby Lobby *(f)*, Interessensgruppe *(f)*, Interessenvertretung *(f)*; Eingangshalle *(f)*, Foyer *(n)*
local lokal, hiesig, örtlich, ortsansässig
local Lokal *(n)*; Einheimische(r) *(f/m)*, Ortsansässige(r) *(f/m)*
Local Area Network (LAN) lokales Netzwerk *(n)*

locality Lokalität *(f)*, Örtlichkeit *(f)*, Lage *(f)*
location Lage *(f)*, Standort *(m)*, Stelle *(f)*, Platz *(m)*, Ortsangabe *(f)*; Ortung *(f)*; Drehort *(m)*
location of goods Lagerort *(m)*
location, high-traffic Auflaufposition *(f)*, Lage *(f)* mit viel Publikumsverkehr
lock schließen, sperren
lock Schloss *(n)*, Verschluss *(m)*, Sperrvorrichtung *(f)*
lock up einschließen, verschließen, zuschließen, zusperren
lockable abschließbar, verschließbar
locker Schließfach *(n)*, Spind *(m)*
locknut Spannmutter *(f)*
locksmith Schlosser *(m)*
lodging house Pension *(f)*
logistics Logistik *(f)*
logo Logo *(n)*, Firmenlogo *(n)*, Firmenemblem *(n)*, Firmenschriftzug *(m)*, Firmenzeichen *(n)*
logotype Logo *(n)*, Firmenemblem *(n)*, Firmenlogo *(n)*, Firmenschriftzug *(m)*
longish ziemlich lang, länglich
longitude Länge *(f)*
long-range langfristig, weit reichend, weit vorausschauend
long-term langfristig
look after nachsehen, nachschauen, aufpassen, überwachen; betreuen, sich kümmern um
look ahead vorausschauen, nach vorn schauen
look around sich umsehen
look at anschauen, betrachten, sich ansehen, überprüfen, überlegen
look back zurückschauen
look for suchen, erwarten
look forward to sich freuen auf
look in einen kurzen Besuch *(m)* abstatten
look on ansehen, betrachten, zusehen
look round sich umsehen
look through durchsehen, prüfen

look upon ansehen, betrachten, zusehen
loom over ragen über
loop Schleife *(f)*, Schlinge *(f)*, Schlaufe *(f)*, Öse *(f)*, Windung *(f)*
loop schlingen, winden
loose lockern, loslassen, freilassen, befreien,
loose lose, locker, frei, ungebunden, unverpackt; ungenau, nachlässig
lorry (GB) Lastwagen *(m)*
loss Verlust *(m)*, Ausfall *(m)*, Einbuße *(f)*, Abnahme *(f)*, Schwund *(m)*, Nachteil *(m)*, Schaden *(m)*
loss in time Zeitverlust *(m)*
loss in transport Transportverlust *(m)*
loss leader Lockartikel *(m)*, Lockvogel *(m)*
loss of sound Tonausfall *(m)*
lost-property office Fundbüro *(n)*
loud laut, geräuschvoll, auffallend, grell, schreiend
loudness Lautstärke *(f)*, Auffälligkeit *(f)*, Aufdringlichkeit *(f)*
loudspeaker Lautsprecher *(m)*
lounge Foyer *(n)*, Aufenthaltsraum *(m)*, Gesellschaftsraum *(m)*, Salon *(m)*, Hotelhalle *(f)*, Wartehalle *(f)*
low niedrig, tief, tiefgelegen, flach; knapp, schwach, schlecht, dürftig, gering, geringfügig
low-cut filter Trittschallfilter *(m)*
lower herabsetzen, ermäßigen, senken, sich senken, sinken, fallen, abnehmen, nachlassen, sich vermindern
low-grade minderwertig
low-noise rauschfrei, laufruhig
low-priced preiswert, billig
low-voltage bulb Niedervoltlampe *(f)*
low-voltage current Schwachstrom *(m)*
low-voltage system Niedervoltanlage *(f)*
lubricant Schmiere *(f)*, Schmiermittel *(n)*
lubricate ölen, einölen, schmieren, abschmieren, einschmieren

luggage allowance (GB), free Freigepäck *(n)*
luggage claim (GB) Gepäckausgabe *(f)*
luggage insurance (GB) Gepäckversicherung *(f)*
luggage locker (GB) Gepäckschließfach *(n)*
luggage room (GB) Gepäckaufbewahrung *(f)*
luggage ticket (GB) Aufbewahrungsschein *(m)*
luggage (GB) Gepäck *(n)*
luggage (GB), free Freigepäck *(n)*
luggage (GB), item of Gepäckstück *(n)*
luminous leuchtend, Leucht-
lump sugar Würfelzucker *(m)*
lump sum Pauschale *(f)*, Pauschalbetrag *(m)*
lunch Mittagessen *(n)*
lunch zu Mittag *(m)* essen
lunch break Mittagspause *(f)*
lunch hour Mittagspause *(f)*
luncheon voucher Essensbon *(m)*, Essensgutschein *(m)*
lunchtime Mittag *(m)*, Mittagszeit *(f)*
luxurious luxuriös, verschwenderisch, üppig
luxury Luxus *(m)*
luxury goods Luxusgüter *(n, pl)*

M

machine Maschine *(f)*, Apparat *(m)*, Automat *(m)*
machinery Apparat *(m)*, Maschinen *(f, pl)*
magazine Magazin *(n)*, Lagerhaus *(n)*, Zeitschrift *(f)*
magazine supplement Zeitschriftenbeilage *(f)*
mail (US) mit der Post *(f)* versenden, aufgeben

mail (US) Post *(f)*
mailing piece (US) Postwurfsendung *(f)*
mail-out Werbeversand *(m)*
main Hauptleitung *(f)*, Hauptschalter *(m)*
main Haupt-
main connection, electric Strom-Hauptanschluss *(m)*
mains Hauptgasleitung *(f)*, Hauptwasserleitung *(f)*, Stromnetz *(n)*, Versorgungsnetz *(n)*
mains adapter Netzteil *(n)*
mains connection Netzanschluss *(m)*
mains plug Netzstecker *(m)*
mains system Leitungsnetz *(n)*
mains unit Netzteil *(n)*
mains voltage Netzspannung *(f)*
maintain erhalten, beibehalten; unterhalten, instand halten, pflegen, warten; (Preis etc.) halten
maintenance Erhaltung *(f)*, Beibehaltung *(f)*, Aufrechterhaltung *(f)*; Instandhaltung *(f)*, Pflege *(f)*, Wartung *(f)*; Unterhalt *(m)*
maintenance contract Wartungsvertrag *(m)*
maintenance department Serviceabteilung *(f)*
maintenance of industrial health and safety standards Arbeitsschutz *(m)*
maintenance service Wartungsdienst *(m)*
maintenance-free wartungsfrei
major bedeutend, wichtig, größer, Haupt-
make ausführen, ausfertigen, anfertigen, erledigen, herstellen, machen, schaffen; bewirken, veranlassen, verursachen; zubereiten
make Marke *(f)*; Ausführung *(f)*, Machart *(f)*; Erzeugnis *(n)*, Fabrikat *(n)*, Sorte *(f)*
make out ausfindig machen, herausbekommen, vorwärtskommen; (Rechnung etc.) ausstellen, aufstellen

make over überarbeiten, umbauen, übertragen
make up bilden, zusammenstellen, zusammensetzen, vervollständigen, vollenden; (Bericht etc.) abfassen; (Liste etc.) anfertigen, aufstellen; (Rechnung etc.) begleichen, ausgleichen; (Streit etc.) beilegen; wieder gutmachen, ersetzen, entschädigen; schminken, sich schminken
make-up Aufmachung *(f)*, Verfassung *(f)*, Struktur *(f)*, Zusammensetzung *(f)*
malicious arglistig, böswillig, vorsätzlich
mallet Hammer *(m)*
man hour Arbeitsstunde *(f)*
manage managen, führen, leiten, verwalten; fertigbringen, schaffen
management Management *(n)*, Führung *(f)*, Leitung *(f)*, Betriebsleitung *(f)*, Firmenleitung *(f)*, Unternehmensleitung *(f)*, Verwaltung *(f)*
management, general Gesamtgeschäftsführung *(f)*, allgemeine Verwaltung *(f)*
manager Manager(in) *(m/f)*, Leiter(in) *(m/f)*, Betriebsleiter(in) *(m/f)*, Geschäftsführer(in) *(m/f)*, Direktor(in) *(m/f)*, Verwalter(in) *(m/f)*
manager, commercial kaufmännische(r) Leiter(in) *(m/f)*
manager, general Generaldirektor(in) *(m/f)*
manager, registered Handlungsbevollmächtigte(r) *(f/m)*
manageress Managerin *(f)*, Direktorin *(f)*, Geschäftsführerin *(f)*, Leiterin *(f)*, Betriebsleiterin *(f)*
managing geschäftsführend, leitend
managing director Geschäftsführer(in) *(m/f)*, Generaldirektor(in) *(m/f)*, Betriebsleiter(in) *(m/f)*

managing organization
Veranstaltungsgesellschaft *(f)*
mandatory verbindlich, obligatorisch, zwingend
manpower Arbeitskräfte *(f, pl)*, Arbeitspotenzial *(n)*, Mitarbeiter *(m, pl)*, Personalbestand *(m)*
manpower planning Personalplanung *(f)*
manpower requirement Personalbedarf *(m)*
manpower shortage Personalengpass *(m)*
manual Handbuch *(n)*
manual manuell, körperlich
manufacture Fabrikation *(f)*, Fertigung *(f)*, Herstellung *(f)*, Produktion *(f)*, Erzeugnis *(n)*, Fabrikat *(n)*, Produkt *(n)*
manufacture fabrizieren, herstellen, produzieren
manufactured goods Industriegüter *(n, pl)*
manufacturer Hersteller *(m)*, Fabrikant *(m)*, Produzent *(m)*
manufacturer's recommended price empfohlener Herstellerpreis *(m)*
manufacturing costs Fertigungskosten *(pl)*, Herstellungskosten *(pl)*, Produktionskosten *(pl)*
manufacturing method Herstellungsverfahren *(n)*
manufacturing process Herstellungsprozess *(m)*
manufacturing program (US) Fertigungsprogramm *(n)*, Herstellungsprogramm *(n)*
manufacturing programme (GB) Fertigungsprogramm *(n)*, Herstellungsprogramm *(n)*
MARATEL screen MARATEL-Bildschirm *(m)*, MARATEL-Scheibe *(f)*

margin Marge *(f)*, Spanne *(f)*, Gewinnspanne *(f)*, Handelsspanne *(f)*, Verdienstspanne *(f)*; Rand *(m)*, Seitenrand *(m)*, Satzkante *(f)*; Spielraum *(m)*; Grenze *(f)*
margin Rand-, Grenz-, geringfügig
margin, operating Handelsspanne *(f)*
margin, operating price Handelsspanne *(f)*
marginal geringfügig, unwesentlich, Rand-
mark Marke *(f)*; Markierung *(f)*, Mal *(n)*, Merkmal *(n)*, Fleck *(m)*; Etikett *(n)*, Zeichen *(n)*, Warenmarke *(f)*, Warenzeichen *(n)*, Handelsmarke *(f)*, Handelszeichen *(n)*, Schutzmarke *(f)*; Auszeichnung *(f)*, Note *(f)*, Zensur *(f)*
mark markieren, kennzeichnen, bezeichnen, beschriften, auszeichnen, verzeichnen, anzeigen; herausstellen, hervorheben; aufzeigen, notieren; bewerten; charakterisieren
mark down notieren; (Preise) herabsetzen, reduzieren
mark of quality Gütezeichen *(n)*
mark up (Preis) heraufsetzen
mark, registered eingetragenes Firmenzeichen *(n)*, eingetragenes Warenzeichen *(n)*
markdown Preissenkung *(f)*, Preisreduzierung *(f)*
market Markt *(m)*, Marktplatz *(m)*, Absatzmarkt *(m)*; Börse *(f)*
market vertreiben, auf den Markt *(m)* bringen
market analysis Marktanalyse *(f)*
market area Marktgebiet *(n)*, Absatzgebiet *(n)*
market coverage Marktanteil *(m)*
market demand Marktnachfrage *(f)*
market development Marktentwicklung *(f)*
market forecast Marktprognose *(f)*
market leader Marktführer *(m)*
market niche Marktlücke *(f)*

market opportunities
Absatzmöglichkeiten *(f, pl)*
market place, virtual virtueller
Marktplatz *(m)*
market potential Marktpotenzial *(n)*
market price Marktpreis *(m)*,
Marktwert *(m)*
market research Marktforschung *(f)*
market segment Marktsegment *(n)*
market share Marktanteil *(m)*
market study Marktbeobachtung *(f)*,
Marktuntersuchung *(f)*
market survey Marktuntersuchung *(f)*,
Marktbefragung *(f)*, Marktumfrage *(f)*
market trend Markttrend *(m)*,
Markttendenz *(f)*
market, domestic Binnenmarkt *(m)*,
Inlandsmarkt *(m)*
market, global Weltmarkt *(m)*
market, potential potenzieller
Markt *(m)*
marketable marktfähig, absatzfähig,
verkäuflich
marketer Marketingfachmann *(m)*,
Marketingfachfrau *(f)*
marketing Marketing *(n)*, Absatz *(m)*,
Absatzwirtschaft *(f)*, Absatzlehre *(f)*,
Vertrieb *(m)*
marketing budget Marketingbudget *(n)*,
Marketingetat *(m)*
marketing channel Absatzkanal *(m)*
marketing concept
Marketingkonzept *(n)*,
Absatzkonzept *(n)*
marketing department
Marketingabteilung *(f)*,
Vertriebsabteilung *(f)*
marketing manager
Marketingleiter(in) *(m/f)*,
Absatzleiter(in) *(m/f)*
marketing mix Marketingmix *(n)*
marketing objective Absatzziel *(n)*
marketing research Marktforschung *(f)*,
Absatzforschung *(f)*,
Absatzanalyse *(f)*

marketing specialist
Marketingfachmann *(m)*,
Marketingfachfrau *(f)*
marketing strategy
Marketingstrategie *(f)*
marking Markierung *(f)*,
Kennzeichnung *(f)*, Beschriftung *(f)*,
Notierung *(f)*
marvellous (GB) wunderbar,
erstaunlich, fabelhaft, fantastisch
marvelous (US) wunderbar,
erstaunlich, fabelhaft, fantastisch
mask Schutzmaske *(f)*
mask, protective Schutzmaske *(f)*
mass Masse *(f)*, Mehrzahl *(f)*, Menge *(f)*
mass ansammeln, sich ansammeln,
sich zusammenballen, anhäufen,
sich anhäufen
mass audience Besuchermasse *(f)*
mass-produced in Serie *(f)* gefertigt
mass production Massenfertigung *(f)*
mast Mast *(m)*
master Original *(n)*; Leiter *(m)*,
Meister *(m)*, Herr *(m)*, Lehrherr *(m)*
master key Hauptschlüssel *(m)*,
Generalschlüssel *(m)*
mat Matte *(f)*, Abtreter *(m)*,
Untersatz *(m)*, Untersetzer *(m)*,
Unterlage *(f)*
mat (Foto) matt, mattiert
material Material *(n)*, Stoff *(m)*,
Baustoff *(m)*
material materiell, Material-, physisch;
ausschlaggebend, erheblich, wesentlich
materials handling
Materialtransport *(m)*
maturity Fälligkeit *(f)*,
Fälligkeitstermin *(m)*
maximum maximal, Höchst-
maximum Maximum *(n)*
maximum exhibit height maximale
Exponathöhe *(f)*
maximum fee Höchstgebühr *(f)*
maximum floor load maximale
Bodenbelastung *(f)*

maximum height of stand structures maximale Standbauhöhe *(f)*
maximum load Nutzlast *(f)*, Höchstlast *(f)*
maximum noise level Maximalgeräuschpegel *(m)*
maximum price Höchstpreis *(m)*
maximum speed Höchstgeschwindigkeit *(f)*
maximum stand height maximale Standbauhöhe *(f)*
meal ticket Essensmarke *(f)*
meal voucher Essensgutschein *(m)*
mean level Mittelungspegel *(m)*
means Mittel *(n)*
means of advertising Werbemittel *(n, pl)*
means of payment Zahlungsmittel *(n, pl)*
means of transport Beförderungsmittel *(n, pl)*, Transportmittel *(n, pl)*, Verkehrsmittel *(n, pl)*
means of transportation Beförderungsmittel *(n, pl)*, Transportmittel *(n, pl)*, Verkehrsmittel *(n, pl)*
measure Maß *(n)*, Maßeinheit *(f)*, Maßstab *(m)*, Ausmaß *(n)*, Grad *(m)*, Umfang *(m)*; Maßnahme *(f)*; Messgerät *(n)*
measure messen, ausmessen, abmessen, vermessen, nachmessen, Maß *(n)* nehmen, vergleichen
measure of length Längenmaß *(n)*
measurement Messung *(f)*, Vermessung *(f)*, Maß *(n)*, Maßstab *(m)*, Abmessungen *(f, pl)*
measurement on site Aufmaß *(n)* vor Ort
measures, set of Maßnahmenpaket *(n)*
measuring instrument Messinstrument *(n)*
measuring tape Bandmaß *(n)*, Maßband *(n)*
mechanical mechanich, automatisch

mechanical breakdown Maschinenschaden *(m)*
media Medien *(n, pl)*
media coverage Medienberichterstattung *(f)*
media mix Medienmix *(m)*, Medienmischung *(f)*
media plan Mediaplan *(m)*
media, electronic elektronische Medien *(n, pl)*
media, new neue Medien *(n, pl)*
medical assistance ärztliche Fürsorge *(f)*, ärztliche Hilfe *(f)*
medical care ärztliche Betreuung *(f)*
medical center (US) Sanitätsstation *(f)*
medical centre (GB) Sanitätsstation *(f)*
medical certificate ärztliches Attest *(n)*
medical insurance Krankenversicherung *(f)*
medicine case, portable Reiseapotheke *(f)*
medium Medium *(n)*, Träger *(m)*, Werkzeug *(n)*, Mittel *(n)*; Mitte *(f)*
medium mittel-, mittlere(-r,-s), mittelmäßig
medium high halbhoch
medium-term mittelfristig
meeting Begegnung *(f)*, Treffen *(n)*; Besprechung *(f)*, Sitzung *(f)*, Tagung *(f)*, Konferenz *(f)*, Veranstaltung *(f)*, Versammlung *(f)*, Zusammenkunft *(f)*
meeting place Sammelstelle *(f)*, Tagungsort *(m)*, Versammlungsort *(m)*, Treffpunkt *(m)*
meeting room Besprechungszimmer *(n)*, Sitzungszimmer *(n)*, Tagungsraum *(m)*, Konferenzraum *(m)*, Versammlungsraum *(m)*
megashow Großveranstaltung *(f)*
member Mitglied *(n)*, Angehörige(r) *(f/m)*
member of the board Vorstandsmitglied *(n)*
member of the top management Mitglied *(n)* der Geschäftsleitung

membership Mitgliedschaft *(f)*
memorandum Notiz *(f)*, Mitteilung *(f)*, Vermerk *(m)*, Denkschrift *(f)*
memory Gedächtnis *(n)*, Erinnerung *(f)*, Andenken *(n)*
memory capacity (EDV) Speicherkapazität *(f)*
memory function (EDV) Speicherfunktion *(f)*
men's lavatory (GB) Herrentoilette *(f)*
men's restroom (US) Herrentoilette *(f)*
men's toilet Herrentoilette *(f)*
mend ausbessern, bessern, verbessern, berichtigen, reparieren; sich bessern
menu Speisekarte *(f)*, Menü *(n)*
menu-driven (EDV) menügesteuert
merchandise Waren *(f, pl)*
merchandise for resale Handelsware *(f)*
merchandise samples Warenproben *(f, pl)*
merchant Händler *(m)*, Großhändler *(m)*, Kaufmann *(m)*
merchantable verkäuflich
merge fusionieren, miteinander verbinden, verschmelzen, sich zusammenschließen
merger Fusion *(f)*, Unternehmenszusammenschluss *(m)*, Verschmelzung *(f)*
mess Unordnung *(f)*, Durcheinander *(n)*, Schlamassel *(m)*; Schmutz *(m)*; schwierige Lage *(f)*, Klemme *(f)*, Patsche *(f)*
mess around herumbasteln, herumhantieren
message Mitteilung *(f)*, Meldung *(f)*, Benachrichtigung *(f)*, Nachricht *(f)*, Botschaft *(f)*
meter messen
meter Messgerät *(n)*, Zähler *(m)*
meter (US) Meter *(m)*
meter reading Zählerstand *(m)*
meter, electric Stromzähler *(m)*

method Methode *(f)*, Verfahren *(n)*, Verfahrensweise *(f)*, Arbeitsweise *(f)*; System *(n)*, Prozess *(m)*
method methodisch, planmäßig, systematisch
method of payment Zahlungsweise *(f)*
method of testing Prüfverfahren *(n)*
metre (GB) Meter *(m)*
metric scale metrisches Maß *(n)*
microphone Mikrofon *(n)*
microphone boom Tonangel *(f)*
microphone, wireless drahtloses Mikrofon *(n)*
microprocessor Mikroprozessor *(m)*
microwave Mikrowelle *(f)*
microwave oven Mikrowellengerät *(n)*
middle Mitte *(f)*, mittlerer Teil *(m)*, Mittelstück *(n)*
middle mittlere(-r,-s), mittel-
mileage account Meilenkonto *(n)*
mileage balance Meilenguthaben *(n)*
milk jug Milchkännchen *(n)*
milk, canned (US) Dosenmilch *(f)*
milk, tinned (GB) Dosenmilch *(f)*
mill fräsen
mill-cut fräsen
milling machine Fräse *(f)*
mineral water Mineralwasser *(n)*
minibus Kleinbus *(m)*
minimum mindest-
minimum Minimum *(n)*
minimum amount Mindestbetrag *(m)*
minimum charge Mindestgebühr *(f)*, Mindestkosten *(pl)*
minimum contribution Mindestbeitrag *(m)*
minimum diameter Mindestquerschnitt *(m)*
minimum fee Mindestgebühr *(f)*
minimum lighting Mindestbeleuchtung *(f)*
minimum number Mindestzahl *(f)*
minimum requirement Mindestanforderung *(f)*

minimum stand size
 Mindeststandgröße (f)
minimum width Mindestbreite (f)
minor minderjährig; kleiner, geringer; unbedeutend, unwichtig
minor Minderjährige(r) (f/m)
minor matter Nebensache (f)
minute Minute (f), Augenblick (m)
minute minuziös, ganz genau
minutes Protokoll (n), Niederschrift (f), Sitzungsbericht (m)
mirror Spiegel (m), Spiegelbild (n)
mirror spiegeln, widerspiegeln
mirror foil Spiegelfolie (f)
miscalculate verkalkulieren, falsch rechnen, falsch berechnen, sich verrechnen
misfortune Missgeschick (n), Unglück (n), Unglücksfall (m)
misprint Druckfehler (m)
mistake falsch verstehen, missverstehen, verkennen, verwechseln, sich irren
mistake Fehler (m), Irrtum (m), Missverständnis (n), Versehen (n)
misunderstanding Missverständnis (n), Meinungsverschiedenheit (f), Differenz (f)
miter (US) Gehrung (f)
mitre (GB) Gehrung (f)
mix mischen, vermischen, sich vermischen, mengen, vermengen, verbinden, durcheinander bringen
mix Mischung (f), Durcheinander (n)
mixing amplifier Mischverstärker (m)
mixing desk Mischpult (n)
mixture Mixtur (f), Mischung (f), Gemisch (n)
mobile mobil, beweglich, fahrbar, wendig; lebhaft
mobile phone (GB) Handy (n), Mobiltelefon (n)
mobile stand mobiler Stand (m)
mock-up Modell (n), Attrappe (f)
model beispielhaft, musterhaft, vorbildlich, modell-, muster-

model formen, modellieren, vorführen
model Modell (n), Muster (n), Typ (m); Vorbild (n), Vorlage (f); Fotomodell (n), Mannequin (n), Dressman (m)
model, follow-up Nachfolgemodell (n)
modem Modem (n)
moderate abschwächen, mäßigen, mildern; moderieren
moderate angemessen, gemäßigt, gering, bescheiden, vernünftig, mäßig, maßvoll
moderation Mäßigung (f), Milderung (f), Abschwächung (f); Moderation (f)
modernize modernisieren
modification Modifizierung (f), Abänderung (f), Abwandlung (f)
modify modifizieren, ändern, abändern, verändern, mäßigen
modular modular, modul-
modular stand construction Modulstandkonstruktion (f), Systemmessestandbau (m)
modular system Modulsystem (n), Baukastensystem (n)
moisture Feuchtigkeit (f)
moment of inertia Trägheitsmoment (n)
momentary momentan, flüchtig
money transfer Geldüberweisung (f)
money, loose Kleingeld (n)
monitor Monitor (m)
monitor split wall Monitorsplitwand (f)
monitor wall Monitorwand (f)
monkey wrench Universalschraubenschlüssel (m), Engländer (m)
mono input Monoeingang (m)
monopoly Monopol (n)
monopoly position Monopolstellung (f)
moonlighter Schwarzarbeiter(in) (m/f)
mortise chisel Stemmeisen (n)
motivate motivieren, anspornen
motivation Motivation (f), Ansporn (m), Antrieb (m)

motivational research
Motivforschung (f)
motor insurance card, international
Grüne Versicherungskarte (f)
motor transport
Lastwagentransport (m)
motor truck (US) Lastwagen (m)
motor vehicle Kraftfahrzeug (n)
motor, electric Elektromotor (m)
motor-driven motorgetrieben, motorbetrieben
motto Motto (n), Wahlspruch (f)
mould fräsen
mount aufsteigen; aufstellen, errichten, befestigen, montieren, zusammenbauen, rahmen
mount Gestell (n), Rahmen (m), Sockel (m), Fassung (f); Berg (m)
mounting Aufstellung (f), Montage (f), Beschlag (m)
mouse click Mausklick (m)
movable beweglich, verschiebbar, transportierbar
movable Mobiliar (n)
movable hinge Gelenkverbinder (m)
move bewegen, sich bewegen, rücken, rühren, umstellen, transportieren, wegschaffen; (Wohnsitz) umziehen
move Bewegung (f); Umzug (m); Schritt (m), Maßnahme (f); Wechsel (m); (Schach) Zug (m)
move-in deadline (Stand) Bezugsschluss (m), Einbringungsschluss (m)
movie performance (US)
Filmvorführung (f)
movie show (US) Filmvorführung (f)
multicolored (US) mehrfarbig
multicoloured (GB) mehrfarbig
multi-deck refrigerated cabinet
Kühlregal (n)
multi-device connection
Mehrgeräteanschluss (m)
multilingual mehrsprachig
multimedia show Multimediaschau (f)

multiple vielfach, mehrfach, vielfältig, mannigfaltig, Merfach-, Vielfach-
multiple Vielfaches (n); Einzelhandelskette (f)
multiply multiplizieren, vervielfältigen, vermehren
multipurpose Mehrzweck-
multi-storey (GB) mehrgeschossig
multi-story (US) mehrgeschossig
multivision Multivision (f)
multivision show Multivisionsschau (f)
music performance Musikwiedergabe (f), Musikaufführung (f)
music, incidental Begleitmusik (f), Musikuntermalung (f)
music, light U-Musik (f), Unterhaltungsmusik (f)
musical musikalisch, Musik-
musical presentation musikalische Aufführung (f)
musician Musiker(in) (m/f)
mutual gegenseitig, wechselseitig, beiderseitig, gemeinsam

N

nail up vernageln, zunageln
name Name (m), Handelsname (m), Firma (f), Ruf (m)
name nennen, benennen, ernennen, bezeichnen; bekanntgeben; vorschlagen
nameplate Namensschild (n)
napkin Serviette (f)
narrow eng, schmal; beschränkt, eingeschränkt, knapp; eingehend, gründlich, sorgfältig
narrow enger werden, sich verengen, knapper werden, enger machen
national national, staatlich, öffentlich, inländisch, landesweit, überregional, National-, Volks-, Staats-, Landes-

national Staatsangehörige(r) *(f/m)*
national anthem Nationalhymne *(f)*
nationwide landesweit
native Einheimische(r) *(f/m)*
native inländisch, einheimisch, Heimat-, Mutter-
native language Muttersprache *(f)*
native town Heimatstadt *(f)*
natural natürlich, naturgetreu, naturgemäß, Natur-
naturally natürlich, von Natur *(f)* aus, instinktiv, spontan
nature Natur *(f)*, Beschaffenheit *(f)*; Veranlagung *(f)*; Wesen *(n)*
nearby nahe gelegen, in der Nähe *(f)*
necessary nötig, notwendig, erforderlich, unerlässlich; unvermeidlich, unausweichlich, zwangsläufig
necessity Notwendigkeit *(f)*, Bedürfnis *(n)*
need benötigen, brauchen, müssen
need Notwendigkeit *(f)*, Bedürfnis *(n)*, Bedarf *(m)*; Mangel *(m)*, Not *(f)*, Notlage *(f)*
negligence Nachlässigkeit *(f)*, Unachtsamkeit *(f)*, Fahrlässigkeit *(f)*
negligent nachlässig, unachtsam, fahrlässig
negligible geringfügig, unbedeutend, unerheblich, unbeträchtlich, unwesentlich, nebensächlich
negotiate verhandeln, aushandeln, unterhandeln; überwinden, meistern
negotiating position Verhandlungsposition *(f)*
negotiation Verhandlung *(f)*, Aushandeln *(n)*, Begebung *(f)*; Überwindung *(f)*
negotiator Unterhändler(in) *(m/f)*
neighbor (US) Nachbar(in) *(m/f)*
neighborhood (US) Nachbarschaft *(f)*
neighbour (GB) Nachbar(in) *(m/f)*
neighbourhood (GB) Nachbarschaft *(f)*
neon light Neonlicht *(f)*

neon sign Neonschrift *(f)*, Leuchtreklame *(f)*
net netto, rein, per saldo
net Netz *(n)*
net verrechnen, aufrechnen, ausgleichen; netto einnehmen, netto verdienen
net amount Nettobetrag *(m)*
net cash Zahlung *(f)* ohne Abzug
net cover Nettoreichweite *(f)*
net earnings Nettoverdienst *(m)*
net exhibition area Nettoausstellungsfläche *(f)*
net exhibition space Nettoausstellungsplatz *(m)*, Nettoausstellungsraum *(m)*
net income Nettogewinn *(m)*, Reingewinn *(m)*
net margin Nettomarge *(f)*
net paid circulation verkaufte Auflage *(f)*
net price Nettopreis *(m)*
net profit Reingewinn *(m)*, Reinerlös *(m)*, Nettogewinn *(m)*
net reach Nettoreichweite *(f)*
net result Endergebnis *(n)*
net revenue Nettoerlös *(m)*
net sales Nettoabsatz *(m)*, Nettoauftragseingang *(m)*
net weight Nettogewicht *(n)*, Eigengewicht *(n)*
net yield Nettorendite *(f)*, Reinertrag *(m)*
network Netz *(n)*, Netzwerk *(n)*, Sendenetz *(n)*
network planning technique Netzplantechnik *(f)*
network provider Netzbetreiber *(m)*
network, external externes Datennetz *(n)*
news agency Nachrichtenagentur *(f)*
news service Nachrichtendienst *(m)*
newspaper Zeitung *(f)*
newspaper advertisement Zeitungsanzeige *(f)*, Zeitungswerbung *(f)*
newspaper clipping service Zeitungsausschnittdienst *(m)*

newspaper supplement Zeitungsbeilage *(f)*
newspaper, local Lokalzeitung *(f)*
niche Nische *(f)*
night concierge Nachtportier *(m)*
night duty Nachtwache *(f)*
night flight Nachtflug *(m)*
night porter Nachtportier *(m)*
night rate Nachttarif *(m)*
night tariff Nachttarif *(m)*
night-time Nachtzeit *(f)*
night watch Nachtwache *(f)*
night watchman Nachtwächter *(m)*
night's rest Nachtruhe *(f)*
nightcleaner Nachtreinigungspersonal *(n)*
nightclub Nachtlokal *(n)*, Nachtklub *(m)*
nightshift Nachtschicht *(f)*
nighttime Nachtzeit *(f)*
nightwork Nachtarbeit *(f)*
nightwork permit Nachtarbeitserlaubnis *(f)*
night-working permit Nachtarbeitserlaubnis *(f)*
No admittance! Zutritt verboten!
No entry! Eintritt verboten!, Zutritt verboten!, Einfahrt verboten!
No parking! Parken verboten!
No smoking! Rauchen verboten!
no stopping sign Halteverbotszeichen *(n)*
no stopping zone Halteverbotszone *(f)*
node Knoten *(m)*
node axis Knotenachse *(f)*
noise Geräusch *(n)*, Krach *(m)*, Lärm *(m)*; Rauschen *(n)*
noise disturbance Lärmstörung *(f)*
noise level Geräuschpegel *(m)*, Lärmpegel *(m)*
noise molestation Geräuschbelästigung *(f)*, Lärmbelästigung *(f)*
noise pollution Geräuschbelästigung *(f)*, Lärmbelästigung *(f)*

noise reduction Geräuschverminderung *(f)*, Lärmsenkung *(f)*
noiseless geräuschlos, lautlos
noisy laut, lärmend, geräuschvoll, lebhaft
nominal capacity (Strom) Nennleistung *(f)*
nonalcoholic alkoholfrei
non-deductible nicht abzugsfähig
non-deforming formstabil
nonflammable nicht brennbar, unbrennbar
nonflammable materials nichtbrennbare Stoffe *(m, pl)*
nonpolluting umweltfreundlich
non-returnable bottle Einwegflasche *(f)*
non-returnable packing Einwegverpackung *(f)*
nonslip rutschsicher
non-smoker Nichtraucher(in) *(m/f)*
non-smoking area Nichtraucherbereich *(m)*
nonstop operation Dauerbetrieb *(m)*
nontoxic ungiftig
noose Schlaufe *(f)*, Schlinge *(f)*
normal case Normalfall *(m)*
normal distribution Normalverteilung *(f)*
normal height Normalhöhe *(f)*
normal state Normalzustand *(m)*
normal working hours Normalarbeitszeit *(f)*
normal-flammability materials normalentflammbare Stoffe *(m, pl)*
normalize normalisieren, sich normalisieren, wiederherstellen
normally normalerweise, gewöhnlich
not binding unverbindlich
notable angesehen, bedeutend, beachtenswert, bemerkenswert, beachtlich, beträchtlich
notable prominente Persönlichkeit *(f)*
note Anmerkung *(f)*, Aufzeichnung *(f)*, Notiz *(f)*, Vermerk *(m)*, kurze Mitteilung *(f)*

note (GB) Banknote *(f)*, Geldschein *(m)*, Wechsel *(m)*
note of, make a vormerken
note, marginal Randbemerkung *(f)*
notebook Notizbuch *(n)*
notice achten, beachten, bemerken, wahrnehmen, zur Kenntnis *(f)* nehmen
notice Benachrichtigung *(f)*, Bescheid *(m)*, Mitteilung *(f)*, Ankündigung *(f)*, Bekanntmachung *(f)*; Beachtung *(f)*, Wahrnehmung *(f)*
notice of accident Unfallmeldung *(f)*
notice of claim Schadensanzeige *(f)*
notice of defect Mängelrüge *(f)*
notice of loss Verlustanzeige *(f)*
notice to exhibitors Hinweis *(m)* für Aussteller
notice, preliminary Voranzeige *(f)*
noticeboard Anschlagbrett *(n)*
notification Anzeige *(f)*, Meldung *(f)*, Mitteilung *(f)*, Benachrichtigung *(f)*
notification of illness Krankmeldung *(f)*
notification, provisional Zwischenbescheid *(m)*
notify benachrichtigen, melden, mitteilen, unterrichten
novel neu, neuartig
novelty Neuheit *(f)*, Neuheiten *(f, pl)*, Neues *(n)*
nozzle Düse *(f)*
nuisance Belästigung *(f)*, Plage *(f)*; Missstand *(m)*
null nichtig, ungültig
null and void null und nichtig
nullify annullieren, aufheben, für null und nichtig erklären, ungültig machen
number nummerieren, zählen, abzählen, rechnen; einordnen, klassifizieren
number Nummer *(f)*, Zahl *(f)*, Anzahl *(f)*, Ziffer *(f)*; Seitenzahl *(f)*; Ausgabe *(f)*
number of exhibitors Zahl *(f)* der Aussteller

number of items Stückzahl *(f)*, Artikelzahl *(f)*, Anzahl *(f)* der Posten
number of participants Teilnehmerzahl *(f)*
number of pieces Stückzahl *(f)*
number of visitors Besucherzahl *(f)*
number, total Gesamtzahl *(f)*
numerous zahlreich

O

object einwenden
object Objekt *(n)*, Gegenstand *(m)*; Ziel *(n)*, Zweck *(m)*
object of interest Sehenswürdigkeit *(f)*
objection Einwand *(m)*, Einspruch *(m)*, Abneigung *(f)*
objective objektiv, tatsächlich, sachlich, wirklich
objective Ziel *(n)*, Zielsetzung *(f)*, Zielvorstellung *(f)*, Zweck *(m)*; Objektiv *(n)*
objective setting Zielsetzung *(f)*
objectives of participation Beteiligungsziele *(n, pl)*
objectivity Objektivität *(f)*
obligate verpflichten
obligation Pflicht *(f)*, Verpflichtung *(f)*, Verbindlichkeit *(f)*
obligation to pay Zahlungsverpflichtung *(f)*
obligation, without unverbindlich
obligatory obligatorisch, verbindlich, verpflichtend
obligatory supervision Aufsichtspflicht *(f)*
oblige verpflichten, nötigen, zwingen; gefällig sein
oblique geneigt, schief, schräg
oblique stroke Schrägstrich *(m)*
oblong Rechteck *(n)*
oblong rechteckig

obscure undurchsichtig
observe beachten, beobachten, zusehen; überwachen; bemerken, wahrnehmen; äußern, feststellen
obsolete veraltet, überholt
obstruct obstruieren, hindern, behindern, blockieren, hemmen, sperren, versperren
obstruction Behinderung *(f)*, Blockierung *(f)*, Versperrung *(f)*, Verstopfung *(f)*, Hemmung *(f)*, Hindernis *(n)*
obvious offenbar, offensichtlich, offenkundig, augenfällig, einleuchtend, nahe liegend, klar
occasion Anlass *(m)*, Gelegenheit *(f)*, Möglichkeit *(f)*; Grund *(m)*, Veranlassung *(f)*; Ereignis *(n)*
occasion veranlassen, verursachen; Anlass *(m)* sein
occasional gelegentlich, hin und wieder, Gelegenheits-
occasionally gelegentlich, hin und wieder
occupation Beruf *(m)*, Beschäftigung *(f)*, Tätigkeit *(f)*, Besetzung *(f)*
occupational health and safety Arbeitssicherheit *(f)*
occupy besetzen, belegen, einnehmen, innehaben, beschäftigen
occurrence Ereignis *(n)*, Begebenheit *(f)*, Vorkommen *(n)*, Vorfall *(m)*
ocean freight Seefracht *(f)*
octagon Achteck *(n)*
octagonal achteckig
oddments Reststücke *(n, pl)*, Einzelstücke *(n, pl)*
odor (US) Geruch *(m)*
odor molestation (US) Geruchsbelästigung *(f)*
odor nuisance (US) Geruchsbelästigung *(f)*
odour (GB) Geruch *(m)*
odour molestation (GB) Geruchsbelästigung *(f)*
odour nuisance (GB) Geruchsbelästigung *(f)*
Off limits! Zutritt verboten!
offend beleidigen, kränken, verletzen, verstoßen
offensive offensiv, angreifend, anstößig, beleidigend, kränkend; widerlich
offensive Offensive *(f)*, Angriff *(m)*
offer offerieren, anbieten, bieten, vorschlagen
offer Offerte *(f)*, Angebot *(n)*, Antrag *(m)*, Gebot *(n)*
offer, introductory Einführungsangebot *(n)*
offer, limited beschränktes Angebot *(n)*
offer, special Sonderangebot *(n)*
office supplies Büromaterial *(n)*
office work Innendienst *(m)*
office worker Innendienstmitarbeiter(in) *(m/f)*
official Beamter *(m)*, Beamtin *(f)*
official offiziell, amtlich, dienstlich
offset printing Offsetdruck *(m)*
off-the-cuff aus dem Stehgreif *(m)*
off-the-cuff speech, make an aus dem Stehgreif *(m)* reden
ohm Ohm *(n)*
oil color (US) Ölfarbe *(f)*
oil colour (GB) Ölfarbe *(f)*
oil paint Ölfarbe *(f)*
oil pressure Öldruck *(m)*
old-fashioned altmodisch
omnibus survey Omnibusumfrage *(f)*
on end hochkant
on principle prinzipiell, grundsätzlich
on request auf Wunsch *(m)*
on schedule termingemäß, planmäßig
on the occasion of anlässlich
on top oben, obenauf
on top of the other übereinander
on trial probeweise
on trial basis probeweise
one-storey (GB) einstöckig
one-story (US) einstöckig

online application

online application Onlineantrag *(m)*,
 Onlineanmeldung *(f)*, Onlinegesuch *(n)*
online catalog (US) Onlinekatalog *(m)*
online catalogue (GB)
 Onlinekatalog *(m)*
online ordering system
 Onlinebestellsystem *(n)*
online purchasing Onlinekauf *(m)*
online registration Onlineanmeldung *(f)*, Onlinebuchung *(f)*
opal (Glühbirne) matt
opaque lichtundurchlässig,
 undurchsichtig, milchig, trüb
open to public geöffnet für das
 Publikum *(n)*
open-air grounds Freigelände *(n)*
open-air site Freigelände *(n)*
opener Öffner *(m)*
opening Eröffnung *(f)*, Beginn *(m)*,
 Anfang *(m)*; Öffnen *(n)*, Öffnung *(f)*,
 Aufmachen *(n)*; Loch *(n)*, Lücke *(f)*
opening ceremony
 Eröffnungsveranstaltung *(f)*
opening hours Öffnungszeiten *(f, pl)*
opening times Öffnungszeiten *(f, pl)*
operate (Gerät etc.) arbeiten, in
 Betrieb *(m)* sein, funktionieren,
 laufen, tätig sein; anwenden,
 betätigen, betreiben, bedienen
operating hours Betriebszeiten *(f, pl)*
operating instructions
 Arbeitsanleitung *(f)*,
 Bedienungsanleitung *(f)*,
 Betriebsanleitung *(f)*
operating manual Betriebsanleitung *(f)*,
 Benutzerhandbuch *(n)*
operating prohibition (Geräte,
 Anlagen) Betriebsverbot *(n)*
operating regulation (Geräte, Anlagen)
 Betriebsvorschrift *(f)*
operating system Betriebssystem *(n)*
operation Bedienung *(f)*, Betätigung *(f)*,
 Handhabung *(f)*, Arbeitsweise *(f)*,
 Funktionsweise *(f)*, Funktionieren *(n)*;
 Unternehmung *(f)*

operation, continuous
 Dauerbetrieb *(m)*
operational betriebsbereit, einsatzbereit, einsatzfähig, Betriebs-, Einsatz-
Operational Safety Ordinance
 Betriebssicherheitsverordnung *(f)*
opinion Meinung *(f)*, Ansicht *(f)*,
 Stellungnahme *(f)*; Gutachten *(n)*
opinion poll Meinungsumfrage *(f)*
opinion survey Meinungsumfrage *(f)*
opinion, current öffentliche Meinung *(f)*
opportunity Gelegenheit *(f)*,
 Möglichkeit *(f)*, Chance *(f)*
oppose opponieren, ablehnen, sich
 widersetzen, entgegensetzen
opposite entgegengesetzt, gegenüber,
 gegenüberliegend, gegensätzlich
opposite Gegenteil *(n)*, Gegensatz *(m)*
opt optieren, sich entscheiden, wählen
optical optisch
optics Optik *(f)*
optimization Optimierung *(f)*
opting-out Teilnahmeverzicht *(m)*
option Option *(f)*, Alternative *(f)*;
 frei Wahl *(f)*, Wahlmöglichkeit *(f)*;
 Vorkaufsrecht *(n)*
option deadline Optionsfrist *(f)*
optional extras Sonderleistungen *(f, pl)*,
 Sonderausstattung *(f)*
orange juice Orangensaft *(m)*
order ordern, bestellen, in Auftrag *(m)*
 geben; anordnen, befehlen, verordnen
order Order *(f)*, Auftrag *(m)*,
 Bestellung *(f)*; Anweisung *(f)*,
 Befehl *(m)*; Anordnung *(f)*,
 Ordnung *(f)*, Reihenfolge *(f)*;
 System *(n)*; Zustand *(m)*;
 Verfügung *(f)*, Weisung *(f)*
order book Auftragsbuch *(n)*
order form Bestellformular *(n)*,
 Bestellvordruck *(m)*
order in advance vorbestellen
order number Auftragsnummer *(f)*
order of ranking Rangfolge *(f)*
order to pay Zahlungsanweisung *(f)*

order, forwarding Speditionsauftrag *(m)*
orderly ordentlich, geordnet, geregelt, systematisch, friedlich, gesittet
orders, follow-up Anschlussaufträge *(m, pl)*
orders, incoming Auftragseingang *(m)*
Ordinance on Drinks Dispensing Systems Verordnung *(f)* über Getränkeschankanlagen
organization Organisation *(f)*, Struktur *(f)*, Aufbau *(m)*; Bildung *(f)*, Planung *(f)*, Einteilung *(f)*; Unternehmen *(n)*
organization chart Organisationsplan *(m)*, Geschäftsverteilungsplan *(m)*
organizational organisatorisch
organize organisieren, aufbauen, gestalten, einteilen, planen, sich organisieren
organize a fair Messe *(f)* veranstalten
organize a trade fair Messe *(f)* veranstalten
organize an exhibition Messe *(f)* veranstalten
organizer Organisator *(m)*, Veranstalter *(m)*
organizer's information office Auskunftsbüro *(n)* des Veranstalters
origin Ursprung *(m)*, Abstammung *(f)*, Herkunft *(f)*
original original, ursprünglich; originell
original Original *(n)*, Vorlage *(f)*
out of control außer Kontrolle *(f)*
out of date altmodisch, veraltet, unmodern
out of stock vergriffen
outdoor advertising Außenwerbung *(f)*
outdoor area Freigelände *(n)*
outdoor exhibition Messe *(f)* im Freigelände
outdoor exhibition area Messefreigelände *(n)*
outdoor fair Messe *(f)* im Freigelände
outdoor stand Messestand *(m)* im Freigelände

outdoors draußen, im Freien *(n)*
outfit Ausstattung *(f)*, Ausrüstung *(f)*; Geräte *(n, pl)*, Werkzeuge *(n, pl)*; Kleider *(n, pl)*, Kleidung *(f)*
outlet Abfluss *(m)*, Abzug *(m)*, Ausguss *(m)*; Absatzmöglichkeit *(f)*, Absatzgebiet *(n)*, Verkaufsstelle *(f)*; Händler *(m)*
outline Abriss *(m)*, Umriss *(m)*, Grundriss *(m)*, Kontur *(f)*, Silhouette *(f)*
outline umreißen, skizzieren
outlook, economic Konjunkturaussichten *(f, pl)*
output Ausstoß *(m)*, Ausgabe *(f)*, Leistung *(f)*, Arbeitsleistung *(f)*, Ertrag *(m)*, Förderung *(f)*, Fördermenge *(f)*, Produktion *(f)*, Produktionsmenge *(f)*
output amplifier Endverstärker *(m)*
output data (EDV) Ausgabedaten *(pl)*
output device (EDV) Ausgabegerät *(n)*
output, rated (Strom) Nennleistung *(f)*
outside außen, Außen-, äußere(-r,-s), äußerste(-r,-s); draußen, heraus, hinaus, außerhalb
outside Außenseite *(f)*
outstanding hervorragend, hervorstechend, auffallend, außerordentlich, überragend
outward and homeward voyage Hin- und Rückreise *(f)*
outward flight Hinflug *(m)*
oval oval
oven, electric Elektroofen *(m)*
oven, hot-air Heißluftofen *(m)*
overbook überbuchen, überbelegen
overcharge überladen, überlasten, zu viel berechnen
overestimate überschätzen
overexpose überbelichten
overexposure Überbelichtung *(f)*
overhead costs Gemeinkosten *(pl)*, Unkosten *(pl)*
overhead projector Tageslichtprojektor *(m)*

overheads Gemeinkosten *(pl)*
overheat überheizen, heißlaufen
overload Übergewicht *(n)*, Überlastung *(f)*, Überbelastung *(f)*
overload überladen, überbeladen, überlasten
overload protection switch (Strom) Überlastungsschutzschalter *(m)*
overnight accommodation Übernachtungsmöglichkeit *(f)*
overnight charge Übernachtungspreis *(m)*
overnight stay Übernachtung *(f)*
overprint eindrucken, überdrucken
overprint Überdrucken *(n)*, Überdruck *(m)*
overproduction Überproduktion *(f)*
overseas überseeisch, Übersee-, in Übersee, nach Übersee
overseas representation Auslandsvertretung *(f)*
overseas transfer Auslandsüberweisung *(f)*
oversight Versehen *(n)*; Aufsicht *(f)*, Beaufsichtigung *(f)*
oversized übergroß
overstretch überdehnen
oversupply Überangebot *(n)*
overtime Überstunden *(f, pl)*
overtime pay Überstundenvergütung *(f)*
overtime rate Überstundentarif *(m)*
overvalue überbewerten
overview Überblick *(m)*
overweight Übergewicht *(n)*
overweight übergewichtig, zu schwer
owe s.o. sth. jdm. etw. schulden, bei jdm. Schulden *(pl)* haben; jdm. etw. verdanken
owner Besitzer(in) *(m/f)*, Eigner(in) *(m/f)*, Eigentümer(in) *(m/f)*, Inhaber(in) *(m/f)*
owner of a company Geschäftsinhaber(in) *(m/f)*
oxygen cylinder Sauerstoffflasche *(f)*

P

P.O. box Postfach *(n)*
pack Pack *(m)*, Packen *(m)*, Paket *(n)*, Bündel *(n)*, Schachtel *(f)*
pack packen, abpacken, einpacken, verpacken; vollstopfen, zusammendrängen
pack label Kollizettel *(m)*
package Packung *(f)*, Päckchen *(n)*, Paket *(n)*, Schachtel *(f)*, Karton *(m)*
package verpacken
package deal Gesamtvereinbarung *(f)*, Verhandlungspaket *(n)*, Pauschalangebot *(n)*
package price Komplettpreis *(m)*
package tour Pauschalreise *(f)*
packaging Verpackung *(f)*, Packmaterial *(n)*
Packaging Ordinance Verpackungsverordnung *(f)*
packet Packung *(f)*, Päckchen *(n)*, Paket *(n)*, Schachtel *(f)*
packing charges Verpackungskosten *(pl)*
packing costs Verpackungskosten *(pl)*
packing list Versandliste *(f)*
packing slip Packzettel *(m)*
packing unit Verpackungseinheit *(f)*
packing, sea-proof seemäßige Verpackung *(f)*
pad Einlage *(f)*, Polster *(n)*, Füllung *(f)*, Schreibblock *(m)*, Unterlage *(f)*
pad polstern, auspolstern, ausstopfen
pad saw Blattsäge *(f)*
padlock Vorhängeschloss *(n)*
page Blatt *(n)*, Buchseite *(f)*; Hotelpage *(m)*
page paginieren, mit Seitenzahlen *(f, pl)* versehen; ausrufen
page rate Seitenpreis *(m)*
pager Personenrufgerät *(f)*
paging receiver Personenrufempfänger *(m)*

paging system Rufanlage *(f)*
pail Eimer *(m)*, Kübel *(m)*
pain Schmerz *(m)*, Schmerzen *(m, pl)*, Leid *(n)*, Leiden *(n)*; Angst *(f)*, Sorge *(f)*
pain schmerzen, weh tun
painkiller Schmerztablette *(f)*
paint Farbe *(f)*, Anstrich *(m)*, Farbanstrich *(m)*; Lack *(m)*; Schminke *(f)*
paint malen, anmalen, anstreichen; lackieren; schminken
paint over übermalen
paint, fluorescent Leuchtfarbe *(f)*
painter Anstreicher(in) *(m/f)*, Maler(in) *(m/f)*, Lackierer(in) *(m/f)*
painting Gemälde *(n)*; Malen *(n)*, Malerei *(f)*, Malerarbeit *(f)*; Anstreichen *(n)*, Anstrich *(m)*; Spritzlackieren *(n)*
pallet Palette *(f)*
palletize palettieren
pamphlet Broschüre *(f)*
pane Scheibe *(f)*, Fensterscheibe *(f)*
panel Panel *(n)*, Platte *(f)*, Tafel *(f)*; Türfüllung *(f)*; Schalttafel *(f)*, Kontrolltafel *(f)*; Ausschuss *(m)*, Gremium *(n)*, Diskussionsrunde *(f)*, Kommission *(f)*, Forum *(n)*, Fachgruppe *(f)*, Befragtengruppe *(f)*
panel täfeln
panel connector Panelhalter *(m)*, Plattenhalter *(m)*
panel construction Panelkonstruktion *(f)*, Plattenkonstruktion *(f)*
panel discussion Podiumsdiskussion *(f)*
panel thickness Panelstärke *(f)*, Plattenstärke *(f)*
panel width Panelbreite *(f)*, Plattenbreite *(f)*
panelling Wandverkleidung *(f)*
panorama Panorame *(n)*, Rundblick *(m)*, Übersicht *(f)*
paper Papier *(n)*, Blatt *(n)*; Abhandlung *(f)*, Referat *(n)*, Vortrag *(m)*; Zeitung *(f)*, Tapete *(f)*
paper tapezieren

paper bag Tüte *(f)*
paper carrier Papiertragetasche *(f)*
paper clip Heftklammer *(f)*
paper cup Pappbecher *(m)*
paper feed (Drucker) Papiereinzug *(m)*
paper jam (Drucker) Papierstau *(m)*
paper napkin Papierserviette *(f)*
paper plate Pappteller *(m)*
papers Papiere *(n, pl)*, Akten *(f, pl)*, Unterlagen *(f, pl)*
paperwork Schreibarbeit *(f)*
paragraph Abschnitt *(m)*, Absatz *(m)*
parallel parallel, entsprechend
parallel Parallele *(f)*, Entsprechung *(f)*
parameter Parameter *(m)*
parcel Paket *(n)*, Päckchen *(n)*; Aktienpaket *(n)*
parcel delivery service Paketzustelldienst *(m)*
parent company Muttergesellschaft *(f)*, Stammhaus *(n)*, Dachgesellschaft *(f)*
parking area Parkplatz *(m)*, Abstellplatz *(m)*
parking attendant Parkwächter(in) *(m/f)*
parking bay Pakbucht *(f)*
parking disc Parkscheibe *(f)*
parking facilities Parkmöglichkeit *(f)*
parking fee Parkgebühr *(f)*
parking gap Parklücke *(f)*
parking level Parkdeck *(n)*
parking meter Parkuhr *(f)*
parking permit Parkausweis *(m)*
parking place Parkplatz *(m)*, Abstellplatz *(f)*
parking space Parkraum *(m)*, Parkplatz *(m)*, Abstellfläche *(f)*, Abstellplatz *(m)*
parking ticket Strafzettel *(m)* für Falschparken
part teilen, sich teilen, trennen, sich trennen, sich lösen
part Teil *(m)*, Bauteil *(m)*, Anteil *(m)*, Abschnitt *(m)*, Stück *(f)*; Folge *(f)*, Fortsetzung *(f)*; Partei *(f)*; Partie *(f)*; (Theater) Rolle *(f)*

part teils, teilweise
part payment Abschlagszahlung *(f)*, Teilzahlung *(f)*
partial partiell, teilweise, Teil-; parteiisch, voreingenommen
participant Teilnehmer(in) *(m/f)*
participate teilnehmen, sich beteiligen, beteiligt sein
participation Beteiligung *(f)*, Teilnahme *(f)*, Mitwirkung *(f)*
participation costs Beteiligungskosten *(pl)*
participation fee Teilnahmegebühr *(f)*
participation forms Beteiligungsformen *(f, pl)*
participation goals Beteiligungsziele *(n, pl)*
participation promotion Beteiligungsförderung *(f)*
participation success Teilnahmeerfolg *(m)*
participation, foreign Auslandsbeteiligung *(f)*
participation, individual individuelle Beteiligung *(f)*
participation, international Auslandsbeteiligung *(f)*
participation, official offizielle Beteiligung *(f)*
participation, single Einzelbeteiligung *(f)*
particular besonders, bestimmt; speziell, eigen
particular Einzelheit *(f)*
particulars Näheres *(n)*, nähere Angaben *(f, pl)*, Personalien *(f, pl)*
particulary besonders, im Besonderen, insbesondere
partition teilen, aufteilen, verteilen
partition Teilung *(f)*, Aufteilung *(f)*; Stellwand *(f)*, Trennwand *(f)*, Zwischenwand *(f)*, Raumteiler *(m)*
partition wall Trennwand *(f)*, Zwischenwand *(f)*, Raumteiler *(m)*

partner Partner(in) *(m/f)*, Teilhaber(in) *(m/f)*, Gesellschafter(in) *(m/f)*, Beteiligte(r) *(f/m)*
partner to a contract Vertragspartner *(m)*
partnership Partnerschaft *(f)*, Personengesellschaft *(f)*, offene Handelsgesellschaft *(f)*, Gesellschaft *(f)* bürgerlichen Rechts, Gesellschaftsvertrag *(m)*
partnership, general Offene Handelsgesellschaft *(f)* (OHG)
partnership, general ordinary Offene Handelsgesellschaft *(f)* (OHG)
party Party *(f)*, Veranstaltung *(f)*; Partei *(f)*, Gesellschaft *(f)*, Gruppe *(f)*; Teilnehmer(in) *(m/f)*, Beteiligte(r) *(f/m)*
party tent Partyzelt *(n)*
pass Ausweis *(m)*, Passierschein *(m)*; (Prüfung etc.) Bestehen *(n)*
pass passieren, vorübergehen, vorbeifahren; geben, reichen, weitergeben; (Prüfung etc.) bestehen; durchkommen, durchgehen; übergehen; vergehen; übersehen
pass for dismantling staff Ausweis *(m)* für Abbaupersonal
pass on weitergeben, weiterreichen, weiterleiten, weitersagen
pass over (Thema wechseln) übergehen
pass through durchstecken, durchziehen, durchgehen, durchreisen; durchmachen
pass, all-days Dauerausweis *(f)*
pass, free kostenfreier Passierschein *(m)*
passable passabel, leidlich, befahrbar, begehbar
passage Passage *(f)*, Gang *(m)*, Korridor *(m)*, Weg *(m)*, Durchfahrt *(f)*; Durchreise *(f)*, Überfahrt *(f)*, Seefahrt *(f)*
passage pass Passierschein *(m)*, Durchfahrtsausweis *(m)*
passage ticket Passierschein *(m)*, Durchfahrtsschein *(m)*

passage way Durchgang *(m)*
passenger Passagier(in) *(m/f)*, Reisende(r) *(f/m)*, Fahrgast *(m)*, Mitfahrer(in) *(m/f)*
passenger carriage Personentransport *(m)*
passenger terminal Fluggastterminal *(m)*
passer-by Passant(in) *(m/f)*
pass-key Hauptschlüssel *(m)*, Generalschlüssel *(m)*
passport Reisepass *(m)*
passport control Passkontrolle *(f)*
passport inspection Passkontrolle *(f)*
password Passwort *(n)*
paste Paste *(f)*, Brei *(m)*, Aufstrich *(m)*; Kleister *(m)*
paste kleben, zukleben, zukleistern
paste up ankleben, aufkleben, zukleben
pasteboard Pappe *(f)*, Karton *(m)*
pastries Gebäck *(n)*
pastry Gebäck *(n)*
patent offenkundig, offensichtlich
patent Patent *(n)*, Konzession *(f)*
patent patentieren lassen
patent application Patentanmeldung *(f)*
patent applied for angemeldetes Patent *(n)*
patent claim Patentanspruch *(m)*
patent infringement Patentverletzung *(f)*
patent pending zum Patent *(n)* angemeldet
patented patentiert, durch Patent *(n)* geschützt
patron Schirmherr *(m)*
patronage Schirmherrschaft *(f)*
patroness Schirmherrin *(f)*
pattern Muster *(n)*, Schablone *(f)*, Schema *(n)*, Vorlage *(f)*, Vorbild *(n)*, Modell *(n)*, Probe *(f)*
pattern mustern, formen, gestalten
pause Pause *(f)*, Schweigen *(n)*
pause pausieren, anhalten, innehalten, verweilen, zögern

pave pflastern
paved area gepflasterter Bereich *(m)*
pavilion Pavillon *(m)*
pavilion, national Länderpavillon *(m)*
pay zahlen, bezahlen, begleichen, erstatten, Kosten *(pl)* tragen; sich lohnen, sich auszahlen
pay Zahlung *(f)*, Bezahlung *(f)*; Gehalt *(n)*, Lohn *(n)*
pay a fine Strafe *(f)* zahlen
pay attention Beachtung *(f)* schenken
pay back zurückzahlen, tilgen
pay cash bar zahlen
pay compensation Schadenersatz *(m)* leisten
pay extra nachzahlen
payable fällig, zahlbar
payment Zahlung *(f)*, Auszahlung *(f)*, Bezahlung *(f)*, Rückzahlung *(f)*, Einlösung *(f)*; Entlohnung *(f)*, Belohnung *(f)*; Lohn *(m)*, Gehalt *(n)*
payment by installment (US) Ratenzahlung *(f)*
payment by instalment (GB) Ratenzahlung *(f)*
payment date Zahlungstermin *(m)*
payment due date Zahlungstermin *(m)*
payment in advance Vorauszahlung *(f)*
payment on account Abschlagszahlung *(f)*, Akontozahlung *(f)*, Teilzahlung *(f)*
payment on receipt of goods Zahlung *(f)* bei Erhalt der Ware
payment on receipt of invoice Zahlung *(f)* bei Erhalt der Rechnung
payment, additional Nachzahlung *(f)*
payment, terms of Zahlungsbedingungen *(f, pl)*
peak Höchst-, Spitzen-
peak Höchststand *(m)* erreichen
peak Spitze *(f)*, Gipfel *(m)*, Höhepunkt *(m)*, Höchststand *(m)*
peak capacity Höchstleistungsgrenze *(f)*
peak hours Stoßzeit *(f)*, Spitzenbelastungszeit *(f)*, Hauptbelastungszeit *(f)*

peak load Spitzenbelastung *(f)*
peak period Spitzenzeit *(f)*
peak season Hochsaison *(f)*
peak time Spitzenzeit *(f)*
peak year Spitzenjahr *(n)*
pedestal Sockel *(m)*, Podest *(n)*
pedestal, intermediate Zwischenpodest *(n)*
pedestrian bridge Fußgängerbrücke *(f)*
peg anklammern, feststecken, festsetzen, stützen, halten, fixieren
peg Pflock *(m)*, Nagel *(m)*, Stift *(m)*, Dübel *(m)*, Keil *(m)*, Bolzen *(m)*, Haken *(m)*
penalty Strafe *(f)*, Geldbuße *(f)*
peninsula stand Kopfstand *(m)*
pennant Fähnchen *(n)*, Stander *(m)*, Wimpel *(m)*
per annum pro Jahr *(n)*
per capita pro Kopf *(m)*
per day pro Tag *(m)*
per diem allowance Reisespesentagessatz *(m)*
per hour pro Stunde *(f)*
per meter (US) pro Meter *(m)*
per metre (GB) pro Meter *(m)*
perceive wahrnehmen, erkennen, merken, bemerken, begreifen, verstehen
percentage Prozentsatz *(m)*, Anteil *(m)*, Provision *(f)*
perception Auffassung *(f)*, Einsicht *(f)*, Wahrnehmung *(f)*
percussion drill Schlagbohrer *(m)*
perfect perfekt, einwandfrei, fehlerlos, tadellos; vollkommen, vollständig, gänzlich; exakt, genau
perfect perfektionieren, vervollkommnen
perfection Perfektion *(f)*, Vervollkommnung *(f)*
perfectly shaped formvollendet
perforate perforieren, lochen, durchbohren, durchlöchern
perforated board (Regal etc.) Lochblechboden *(m)*

perforated panel Lochplatte *(f)*
perforated steel panel Lochblech *(n)*
perforation Lochung *(f)*
perform aufführen, vorführen, vortragen, darbieten, spielen; ausführen, durchführen, verrichten, erfüllen, vollziehen; (Verpflichtung) nachkommen
performance Aufführung *(f)*, Vorführung *(f)*, Vorstellung *(f)*, Vortrag *(m)*, Veranstaltung *(f)*; Ausführung *(f)*, Durchführung *(f)*, Erfüllung *(f)*; Effizienz *(f)*, Leistung *(f)*
performance, public öffentliche Darbietung *(f)*
performance, visual optische Darbietung *(f)*
period Periode *(f)*, Zeitdauer *(f)*, Zeitraum *(m)*, Dauer *(f)*, Frist *(f)*
period of time Zeitraum *(m)*
period of validity Geltungsdauer *(f)*, Gültigkeitsdauer *(f)*
period of withdrawal Rücktrittsfrist *(f)*
periodical Magazin *(n)*, Zeitschrift *(f)*
periodical periodisch, regelmäßig wiederkehrend
peripheral nebensächlich
peripheral Peripheriegerät *(n)*
perish (Ware) verderben
perishable verderblich, begrenzt haltbar
perishables verderbliche Waren *(f, pl)*
permanent ständig, beständig, dauernd, fortdauernd, dauerhaft, Dauer-
permissible zulässig
permission Erlaubnis *(f)*, Genehmigung *(f)*, Zustimmung *(f)*
permission, official amtliche Genehmigung *(f)*
permission, without unerlaubterweise
permission, written schriftliche Genehmigung *(f)*
permit erlauben, genehmigen, gestatten, zulassen

permit Erlaubnis *(f)*, Genehmigung *(f)*, Bewilligung *(f)*, Freigabe *(f)*, Konzession *(f)*, Lizenz *(f)*; Ausweis *(m)*, Passierschein *(m)*
permit application Genehmigungsantrag *(m)*
perpendicular senkrecht, lotrecht
perpendicular Senkrechte *(f)*
person, accompanying Begleitperson *(f)*
personal persönlich, privat; körperlich; Personal-
personal affair Privatangelegenheit *(f)*
personal assistant (PA) persönliche(r) Mitarbeiter(in) *(m/f)*, Privatsekretär(in) *(m/f)*, Chefsekretär(in) *(m/f)*
personal call Privatgespräch *(n)*
personal computer Personalcomputer *(m)*
personal data Personalien *(f, pl)*
personal identification number (PIN) persönliche Geheimzahl *(f)*, PIN *(f)*
personal injury Personenschaden *(m)*
personal organizer Terminplaner *(m)*
personality Persönlichkeit *(f)*
personnel costs Personalkosten *(pl)*
personnel department Personalabteilung *(f)*
perspective Perspektive *(f)*
persuade überreden, überzeugen, verleiten
persuasion Überredung *(f)*, Überzeugung *(f)*
persuasion, powers of Überredungskunst *(f)*
persuasive power Überzeugungskraft *(f)*
phase Phase *(f)*, Abschnitt *(m)*, Stadium *(n)*
phase schrittweise durchführen, stufenweise durchführen
phase out auslaufen lassen
phase-out model Auslaufmodell *(n)*

phone Telefon *(n)*
phone telefonieren
phone bill Telefonrechnung *(f)*
phone box Telefonzelle *(f)*
phone call Telefonanruf *(m)*
phone connection Telefonverbindung *(f)*
phone number Telefonnummer *(f)*
phone redial Wahlwiederholung *(f)*
phone, by telefonisch
phone, cordless schnurloses Telefon *(n)*
phone, over the telefonisch
phonecard Telefonkarte *(f)*
photo Foto *(n)*, Fotografie *(f)*
photo composition Fotosatz *(m)*
photo, large Großfoto *(n)*
photocopier Fotokopiergerät *(n)*
photocopy Fotokopie *(f)*
photocopy fotokopieren
photoelectric barrier Lichtschranke *(f)*
photograph Foto *(n)*, Fotografie *(f)*
photograph fotografieren
photographer Fotograf(in) *(m/f)*
Photographing not allowed! Fotografieren verboten!
photography Foto *(n)*, Fotografie *(f)*
photography and film permit Foto- und Filmerlaubnis *(f)*
photography and film restrictions Fotografier- und Filmverbot *(n)*
photography, digital digitale Fotografie *(f)*
photography, video and audio recording Bild- und Tonaufnahme *(f)*
photomontage Fotomontage *(f)*
photo-realistic view (Internet etc.) fotorealistische Betrachtung *(f)*
phototypesetting Photosatz *(m)*
phrase ausdrücken, formulieren, zum Ausdruck *(m)* bringen
phrase Phrase *(f)*, Ausdruck *(m)*, Redewendung *(f)*, Redensart *(f)*, Formulierung *(f)*
physician Arzt *(m)*, Ärztin *(f)*

pick aufhacken; auflesen, aufsammeln; auswählen, aussuchen
pick Hacke *(f)*, Pickel *(m)*; Auswahl *(f)*, Auslese *(f)*
pick axe Spitzhacke *(f)*
pick up service Abholdienst *(m)*
pickup Kleintransporter *(m)*, Lieferwagen *(m)*
pickup truck Kleintransporter *(m)*, Lieferwagen *(m)*
pictogram Piktogramm *(n)*
picture abbilden, darstellen, malen, zeichnen, sich vorstellen, beschreiben, schildern
picture Bild *(n)*, Abbildung *(f)*, Gemälde *(n)*, Illustration *(f)*; Aufnahme *(f)*; Vorstellung *(f)*; Darstellung *(f)*, Schilderung *(f)*, Wiedergabe *(f)*
picture definition Bildschärfe *(f)*
picture frame Bilderrahmen *(m)*
picture frame, interchangeable Wechselrahmen *(m)*
picture memory Bildspeicher *(m)*
picture resolution Bildauflösung *(f)*
picture storage system Bildspeichersystem *(n)*
pictures, digital treatment of digitale Bildbearbeitung *(f)*
pie chart Kreisdiagramm *(n)*
piece Stück *(n)*, Teil *(n)*, Einzelteil *(n)*, Einzelstück *(n)*, Abschnitt *(m)*; Zeitungsartikel *(m)*
piece of paper Zettel *(m)*
piece price Stückpreis *(m)*
piece, connecting Verbindungsstück *(n)*
piggy-back freight Huckepacktransport *(m)*
pile Pfahl *(m)*, Pfosten *(m)*
pillar Pfeiler *(m)*, Säule *(f)*
pilot lamp Kontrolllampe *(f)*
pin Nadel *(f)*, Anstecknadel *(f)*, Stift *(m)*, Bolzen *(m)*, Dorn *(m)*
pin stecken, anstecken, heften, festmachen, klemmen

pin connection modules Stecksystem *(n)*
pin socket panel Buchsenleiste *(f)*
pincers Kneifzange *(f)*, Beißzange *(f)*
pipe durch ein Rohr *(n)* leiten
pipe Rohr *(n)*, Röhre *(f)*, Leitung *(f)*; Pfeife *(f)*
pipe clamp Rohrschelle *(f)*
pipe wrench Rohrzange *(f)*
pipe, flexible flexible Wasserleitung *(f)*
pipe, main Hauptleitung *(f)*
pipeline Pipeline *(f)*, Rohrleitung *(f)*
piracy Piraterie *(f)*, Plagiat *(n)*, Raubkopieren *(n)*, Raubdruck *(m)*
pitch-monitoring Hinterbandkontrolle *(f)*
placard Plakat *(n)*, Anschlag *(m)*, Transparent *(n)*
placard plakatieren, Pakatwerbung *(f)* machen, anschlagen
place Platz *(m)*, Ort *(m)*, Stelle *(f)*; Wohnort *(m)*; Stellung *(f)*, Amt *(n)*, Rang *(m)*, Stand *(m)*
place platzieren, setzen, stellen, legen, aufstellen; (Bestellung) aufgeben; inserieren; übergeben, deponieren; vergeben; (Auftrag) erteilen
place an order Auftrag *(m)* erteilen
place of fulfillment (US) Erfüllungsort *(m)*
place of fulfillment and court of jurisdiction (US) Erfüllungsort *(m)* und Gerichtsstand *(m)*
place of fulfilment (GB) Erfüllungsort *(m)*
place of fulfilment and court of jurisdiction (GB) Erfüllungsort *(m)* und Gerichtsstand *(m)*
place of jurisdiction Gerichtsstand *(m)*
place of payment Zahlungsort *(m)*
place swap Platztausch *(m)*
placement Platzierung *(f)*, Unterbringung *(f)*, Anlage *(f)*, Investition *(f)*

plagiarism Plagiat *(n)*, unerlaubte Nachahmung *(f)*
plain Ebene *(f)*
plain einfach, schlicht, unscheinbar; klar, rein; offen, offensichtlich; einfarbig, uni
plan Plan *(m)*, Lageplan *(m)*, Vorhaben *(n)*, Projekt *(n)*, Entwurf *(m)*, Grundriss *(m)*
plan planen, beabsichtigen, vorhaben; ausarbeiten, entwerfen, skizzieren
plan ahead vorausplanen
plan view Grundriss *(m)*
plane eben, flach, plan
plane Ebene *(f)*, Niveau *(n)*, Stufe *(f)*; Hobel *(m)*; Flugzeug *(n)*
plane planieren, hobeln, glätten
plane off abhobeln, weghobeln
plane ticket Flugschein *(m)*
plank Planke *(f)*, Brett *(n)*, Bohle *(f)*
planning Planung *(f)*
planning department Entwicklungsabteilung *(f)*
planning stage Entwurfsstadium *(n)*
planning stage, in the im Planungsstadium *(n)*
planning, foreward Vorausplanung *(f)*
planning, short-term kurzfristige Planung *(f)*
plant Betriebsanlage *(f)*, Werk *(n)*, Anlage *(f)*, Einrichtung *(f)*; Pflanze *(f)*
plant pflanzen
plant management Betriebsleitung *(f)*
plant, potted Topfpflanze *(f)*
planter Übertopf *(m)*
plasma flat screen Plasma-Flachbildschirm *(m)*
plasma screen Plasma-Bildschirm *(m)*
plaster Pflaster *(n)*, Putz *(m)*
plaster verputzen, bekleben
plastic aus Plastik *(n)*, Plastik-; plastisch, formbar
plastic Plastik *(n)*, Kunststoff *(m)*
plastic bag Plastiktasche *(f)*, Plastiktüte *(f)*

plastic clip (Systemstandbau) Kunststoffclip *(m)*
plastic covering Abdeckfolie *(f)*
plastic folder, clear Klarsichthülle *(f)*
plastic set screw (Systemstandbau) Kunststoff-Klemmschraube *(f)*
plastic spacer (Systemstandbau) Kunststoff-Distanzstück *(n)*
plastic tube (Systemstandbau) Kunststoffstab *(m)*
plastic-coated kunststoffbeschichtet
plastic-laminated kunststoffbeschichtet
plate panzern, plattieren
plate Platte *(f)*, Schild *(n)*, Tafel *(f)*, Teller *(m)*
plate dispenser Tellerspender *(m)*
plate warmer Warmhalteplatte *(f)*
plate, fixing Fixierleiste *(f)*
platform Plattform *(f)*, Tribüne *(f)*, Podium *(n)*; Bahnsteig *(m)*, Gleis *(n)*
plausible plausibel, glaubhaft, überzeugend
please gefallen, zusagen, erfreuen, zufriedenstellen
pliers Beißzange *(f)*, Flachzange *(f)*
plug stecken, füllen, zustopfen, zuhalten
plug Stecker *(m)*, Steckdose *(f)*, Stöpsel *(m)*, Pfropfen *(m)*
plug in anschließen, einstecken
plug, earthed-pin Schukostecker *(m)*
plug, multiple Mehrfachstecker *(m)*
plug-in type refrigerated sales cabinet steckerfertiges Verkaufskühlmöbel *(n)*
plumber Klempner(in) *(m/f)*, Installateur(in) *(m/f)*
plumbing Klempnerarbeit *(f)*, Wasserinstallation *(f)*; Rohre *(n, pl)*, Rohrleitungen *(f, pl)*, sanitäre Anlagen *(f, pl)*
plywood Sperrholz *(n)*
pneumatic pneumatisch, Luft-
pocket einstecken, in die Tasche *(f)* stecken

pocket Tasche (f)
pocket calculator Taschenrechner (m)
pocket diary Taschenkalender (m)
pocket knife Taschenmesser (n)
podium Podest (n)
point Punkt (m), Spitze (f); Ort (m), Platz (m), Stelle (f); Augenblick (m), Moment (m), Zeitpunkt (m); Einzelheit (f), Detail (n), Wesentliches (n), Kernpunkt (m), Pointe (f); Sinn (m), Zweck (m), Ziel (n), Absicht (f); Steckdose (f), Anschluss (m)
point (mit dem Finger) zeigen, weisen, deuten, hinweisen; anspitzen, zuspitzen
point load Punktlaste (f)
point of view Blickwinkel (m), Standpunkt (m)
point out zeigen auf, hinweisen auf
point, main Hauptsache (f)
pointed spitz, scharf; treffend
pointer Zeiger (m), Zeigestab (m); Tipp (m)
police check Polizeikontrolle (f)
policy Politik (f), Methode (f), Verfahrensweise (f); Versicherungspolice (f)
policy holder Versicherungsnehmer(in) (m/f)
policy, economic Wirtschaftspolitik (f)
polish polieren, aufpolieren, glätten; (Schuhe) putzen
polish Politur (f), Putzmittel (n); Schuhcreme (f); Eleganz (f), Schliff (m)
polite höflich
politeness Höflichkeit (f)
pollster Meinungsforscher(in) (m/f)
pollutant Schadstoff (m)
pollution Verschmutzung (f), Verunreinigung (f)
pollution of the environment Umweltverschmutzung (f)
polygon Vieleck (n)
Polystyrene Styropor (n)

popular populär, populärwissenschaftlich, volkstümlich, allgemeinverständlich, beliebt, weitverbreitet
porcelain Porzellan (n)
porous porös, durchlässig
portable tragbar
portal Portal (n)
porter Portier (m), Pförtner (m), Dienstmann (m), Gepäckträger (m)
portion Portion (f), Abschnitt (m), Teil (m), Anteil (m)
position Position (f), Lage (f), Platz (m), Stelle (f), Standort (m); Standpunkt (m), Einstellung (f); Stellung (f), Rang (m); Situation (f)
position stellen, aufstellen, postieren
position, special Sonderstellung (f)
positive positiv, definitiv, eindeutig, ausdrücklich, bestimmt, fest, sicher, konkret
possibility Möglichkeit (f)
possibly möglicherweise, eventuell, vielleicht
post ankleben, anschlagen; versetzen
post Pfahl (m), Pfosten (m); Stelle (f), Arbeitsstelle (f), Posten (m); Post (f)
post (GB) aufgeben, abschicken
post office Postamt (n)
post profile Stützenprofil (n)
postage Postgebühr (f)
postage paid portofrei, Gebühr (f) bezahlt
postage rate Postgebühr (f)
postal charge Postgebühr (f)
postal rate Portogebühr (f)
postcode (GB) Postleitzahl (f)
poste restante postlagernd
poster Poster (n), Plakat (n), Großbild (n)
poster advertising Plakatwerbung (f)
poster panel Plakattafel (f), Anschlagtafel (f)
poster surface Plakatfläche (f), Werbefläche (f)
post-free stützenfrei; portofrei

post-free structure stützenfreie Konstruktion *(f)*, stützenfreie Überbauung *(f)*
postpone aufschieben, verschieben, verlegen, vertagen, zurückstellen
postponement Verschiebung *(f)*, Vertagung *(f)*, Verlagerung *(f)*
post-show business Nachmessegeschäft *(n)*
pot eintopfen, einlegen
pot Topf *(m)*, Kanne *(f)*, Krug *(m)*; Pokal *(m)*
potential Potenzial *(n)*
potential potenziell, möglich
potential, electric Spannung *(f)*
powder Pulver *(n)*, Puder *(n)*
powder pulverisieren
powder-coated einbrennlackiert
power Kraft *(f)*, Stärke *(f)*, Macht *(f)*, Vollmacht *(f)*, Gewalt *(f)*, Einfluss *(m)*, Befugnis *(f)*, Überzeugungskraft *(f)*; Leistung *(f)*, Energie *(f)*, Strom *(m)*
power antreiben
power cable Starkstromkabel *(n)*
power connection price, electric Elektroanschlusspreis *(m)*
power connection, electric Elektroanschluss *(m)*
power connection, three-phase Drehstromanschluss *(m)*
power connection, 3-phase Drehstromanschluss *(m)*
power consumption Leistungsaufnahme *(f)*
power current Starkstrom *(m)*
power failure Stromausfall *(m)*
power input Leistungsaufnahme *(f)*
power installation Stromanschluss *(m)*
power line Starkstromleitung *(f)*
power output Ausgangsleistung *(f)*
power plug Netzstecker *(m)*
power point Steckdose *(f)*
power saw Motorsäge *(f)*
power supply Elektrizitätsversorgung *(f)*, Stromversorgung *(f)*

power, electrical elektrische Leistung *(f)*
power, three-phase Drehstrom *(m)*
power, 3-phase Drehstrom *(m)*
powerful stark, mächtig, kräftig, einflussreich
practical praktisch, praxisorientiert
practically praktisch, in der Praxis *(f)*; so gut wie
practice Brauch *(m)*, Sitte *(f)*, Gewohnheit *(f)*; Praxis *(f)*, Praktik *(f)*, Übung *(f)*; Verfahrensweise *(f)*; Probe *(f)*
practice (GB) üben, ausüben, proben, praktizieren, tätig sein
practise (US) üben, ausüben, proben, praktizieren, tätig sein
pragmatic pragmatisch
prayer room Gebetsraum *(m)*
preamplifier Vorverstärker *(m)*
precaution Vorsicht *(f)*, Vorsichtsmaßnahme *(f)*, Vorkehrung *(f)*, Schutzmaßnahme *(f)*
precise präzis, exakt, genau, gewissenhaft, pünktlich
precision Präzision *(f)*, Exaktheit *(f)*, Genauigkeit *(f)*
precondition Bedingung *(f)*, Vorbedingung *(f)*, Voraussetzung *(f)*
precontract Vorvertrag *(m)*
predictable vorsehbar
prediction Vorhersage *(f)*, Prognose *(f)*
predominant vorherrschend, überwiegend
prefabricate vorfabrizieren, vorfertigen
prefabricated construction Fertigbauweise *(f)*
prefabricated part Fertigteil *(n)*
prefabricated stand vorgefertigter Stand *(m)*, Fertigstand *(m)*
preface Vorwort *(n)*
prefer bevorzugen, vorziehen
preference Präferenz *(f)*, Vorzug *(m)*, Bevorzugung *(f)*, Vorliebe *(f)*, Vorrecht *(n)*

preferred stand location bevorzugte Standlage *(f)*
preliminary einleitend, einstweilig, vorbereitend, Vor-
preliminary Vorbereitung *(f)*, vorbereitende Maßnahme *(f)*
premature vorzeitig, verfrüht
premise Prämisse *(f)*, Voraussetzung *(f)*
premium Prämie *(f)*, Preis *(m)*, Aufgeld *(n)*, Aufschlag *(m)*, Zulage *(f)*, Zuschlag *(m)*, Bonus *(m)*, Belohnung *(f)*; Vorzugsangebot *(n)*
premium offer Werbegeschenk *(n)*
pre-pack bracket Blisterhaken *(m)*
preparation Vorbereitung *(f)*, Zubereitung *(f)*
prepare vorbereiten, anfertigen, zubereiten
prepay vorauszahlen, frankieren
prepayment Anzahlung *(f)*, Vorauszahlung *(f)*
preregistration Vorregistrierung *(f)*, Voranmeldung *(f)*
prerequisite erforderlich, notwendig
prerequisite Voraussetzung *(m)*, Vorbedingung *(f)*
presence Präsenz *(f)*, Anwesenheit *(f)*, Gegenwart *(f)*
present anwesend, vorhanden, zugegen; augenblicklich, gegenwärtig, derzeitig, momentan
present Geschenk *(n)*, Präsent *(n)*; Präsenz *(f)*, Gegenwart *(f)*
present überreichen, schenken; präsentieren, moderieren, aufzeigen, vorführen, vorlegen, unterbreiten
presentation Präsentation *(f)*, Aufführung *(f)*, Darstellung *(f)*, Vorführung *(f)*, Vorstellung *(f)*, Moderation *(f)*; Überreichung *(f)*, Übergabe *(f)*
presentation technology Präsentationstechnik *(f)*
preserve bewahren, erhalten, beibehalten, schützen, konservieren

preserve Ressort *(n)*, Zuständigkeitsbereich *(m)*; Konserve *(f)*
presidency Präsidentschaft *(f)*, Vorsitz *(m)*
president Präsident(in) *(m/f)*, Vorsitzende(r) *(f/m)*
press Presse *(f)*, Druck *(m)*, Zeitungen *(f, pl)*; Andrang *(m)*, Gedränge *(n)*
press pressen, auspressen, drücken; drängen, bestehen auf; bügeln
press advertising Anzeigenwerbung *(f)*
press agency Nachrichtenagentur *(f)*
press briefing Presseinformation *(f)*
press card Presseausweis *(m)*
press center (US) Pressezentrum *(n)*
press centre (GB) Pressezentrum *(n)*
press clipping service Presseausschnittdienst *(m)*
press commentaries Pressestimmen *(f, pl)*
press conference Pressekonferenz *(f)*
press conference, closing Abschlusspressekonferenz *(f)*
press cutting agency Presseausschnittsagentur *(f)*
press cutting service Presseausschnittdienst *(m)*
press date Drucklegung *(f)*
press distribution box Pressefach *(n)*
press folder Pressemappe *(f)*
press guide Presseführer *(m)*
press kit Pressemappe *(f)*
press office Pressebüro *(n)*
press officer Pressesprecher(in) *(m/f)*, Pressereferent(in) *(m/f)*
press photo Pressefoto *(n)*
press photographer Pressefotograf(in) *(m/f)*
press reception Presseempfang *(m)*
press relations Pressearbeit *(f)*
press release Presseerklärung *(f)*, Pressemitteilung *(f)*

pricing

press report Pressemeldung *(f)*, Zeitungsbericht *(m)*
press review Pressespiegel *(m)*
press spokesman Pressesprecher *(m)*
press spokeswoman Pressesprecherin *(f)*
press, local Lokalpresse *(f)*
press, national überregionale Presse *(f)*
pressing service Bügelservice *(m)*
pressure Druck *(m)*, Zwang *(m)*
pressure container Druckbehälter *(m)*
Pressure Container Ordinance Druckgeräteverordnung *(f)*
pressure pipe Druckluftrohr *(n)*
pressurized gas Druckgas *(n)*
pressurized gas bottle Druckgasflasche *(f)*
pressurized gas system Druckgasanlage *(f)*
prestige Prestige *(n)*, Ansehen *(n)*
prestige advertising Repräsentationswerbung *(f)*
presupposition Voraussetzung *(f)*
pretax profit Gewinn *(m)* vor Steuern
prevent verhindern, verhüten, vermeiden, vorbeugen
prevention Verhinderung *(f)*, Verhütung *(f)*, Vermeidung *(f)*, Vorbeugung *(f)*
preview Vorbesichtigung *(f)*, Vorschau *(f)*
previous notice Vorankündigung *(f)*
price auszeichnen, den Preis *(m)* festsetzen, bewerten
price Preis *(m)*, Angebotspreis *(m)*, Kaufpreis *(m)*, Marktpreis *(m)*, Kurs *(m)*
price bid Preisangebot *(n)*
price calculation Kalkulation *(f)*, Preisgestaltung *(f)*
price category Preisklasse *(f)*
price ceiling Preisobergrenze *(f)*
price concession Preiszugeständnis *(n)*
price cut Preisreduzierung *(f)*, Preissenkung *(f)*

price differential Preisdifferenzierung *(f)*, Preisgefälle *(n)*, Preisunterschied *(m)*
price fixing Preisfestsetzung *(f)*, Preisbindung *(f)*, Preisabsprache *(f)*
price fluctuation Preisschwankung *(f)*
price incentive Preisanreiz *(m)*
price increase Preisanstieg *(m)*, Preissteigerung *(f)*, Preiserhöhung *(f)*
price increases, rate of Teuerungsrate *(f)*
price label Preisschild *(n)*
price leadership Preisführerschaft *(f)*
price level Preisniveau *(n)*
price list Preisliste *(f)*
price maintenance Preisbindung *(f)*, Preisbindung *(f)* der zweiten Hand
price policy Preispolitik *(f)*
price quotation Preisangebot *(n)*
price range Preislage *(f)*, Preisspanne *(f)*
price reduction Preisermäßigung *(f)*, Preisnachlass *(m)*
price spread Preisspanne *(f)*
price structure Preisgefüge *(n)*
price tag Preisschild *(n)*
price trend Preisentwicklung *(f)*
price, all-in Pauschalpreis *(m)*, Inklusivpreis *(m)*
price, competitive konkurrenzfähiger Preis *(m)*, Konkurrenzpreis *(m)*
price, fixed Festpreis *(m)*
price, inclusive Pauschalpreis *(m)*
price, reduced ermäßigter Preis *(m)*
price, special Sonderpreis *(m)*
prices on request Preise *(m, pl)* auf Anfrage
prices subject to alteration Preisänderungen *(f, pl)* vorbehalten
prices subject to change Preisänderungen *(f, pl)* vorbehalten
price-sensitive preisempfindlich
pricing Preisfestlegung *(f)*, Preiskalkulation *(f)*, Preisverhalten *(n)*

pricing, common Preisabsprache *(f)*
primary data Primärdaten *(pl)*
primary exhibitor Hauptaussteller *(m)*
priming coat Grundanstrich *(m)*
principally hauptsächlich, besonders, vor allem
principle Prinzip *(n)*, Grundsatz *(m)*
print Druck *(m)*, Gedrucktes *(n)*, Schrift *(f)*, Abdruck *(m)*; (Foto) Abzug *(m)*
print drucken, abdrucken, bedrucken; in Druckschrift *(f)* schreiben; (Foto) abziehen
print on aufdrucken
print out ausdrucken
printed form vorgedrucktes Formular *(n)*
printed in bold type fettgedruckt
printed letter Druckbuchstabe *(m)*
printed line Druckzeile *(f)*
printed matter Drucksache *(f)*
printed media Druckmedien *(n, pl)*
printed papers reduced rate ermäßigte Drucksachengebühr *(f)*
printer Drucker *(m)*
printer, high-speed Schnelldrucker *(m)*
printing Drucken *(n)*, Drucklegung *(f)*, Druckschrift *(f)*; Auflage *(f)*; (Foto) Abzug *(m)*
printing material Druckunterlage *(f)*
printing works Druckerei *(f)*
printout Ausdruck *(m)*
priority Priorität *(f)*, Vorrang *(m)*, Vorrecht *(n)*, Vorfahrt *(f)*
priority, first größte Dringlichkeit *(f)*, Vorrang *(m)*
private privat, Privat-, persönlich, individuell, vertraulich, ungestört
private affair Privatangelegenheit *(f)*, Privatsache *(f)*
private and confidential streng vertraulich
private limited partnership Kommanditgesellschaft *(f)* (KG)
private matter Privatangelegenheit *(f)*, Privatsache *(f)*
privilege Privileg *(n)*, Vorrang *(m)*, Vorrecht *(n)*; Ehre *(f)*
privilege privilegieren, bevorzugen, bevorrechten, bevorrechtigen
privileged privilegiert, bevorrechtigt
prize Siegespreis *(m)*, Gewinn *(m)*
prize hoch schätzen
prize draw Verlosung *(f)*
prizewinner Gewinner(in) *(m/f)*, Preisträger(in) *(m/f)*
prizewinning presentation Preisverleihung *(f)*
probability Wahrscheinlichkeit *(f)*
probable wahrscheinlich
problem Problem *(n)*, Problematik *(f)*
problematic problematisch
problem-free problemlos
procedure Verfahren *(n)*, Verfahrensweise *(f)*, Vorgehen *(n)*
procedure, legal Rechtsverfahren *(n)*
proceeds Erlös *(m)*, Einnahmen *(f, pl)*, Ertrag *(m)*
process bearbeiten, verarbeitem, abfertigen, behandeln; (Film) entwickeln
process Prozess *(m)*, Verfahren *(n)*, Vorgang *(m)*, Arbeitsablauf *(m)*, Verarbeitung *(f)*
process control Fertigungskontrolle *(f)*, Prozesssteuerung *(f)*, Prozessleitsystem *(n)*
process engineering Fertigungsplanung *(f)*, Verfahrenstechnik *(f)*
processing Bearbeitung *(f)*, Weiterverarbeitung *(f)*, Behandlung *(f)*, Veredelung *(f)*
processor (EDV) Prozessor *(m)*
procuration Vollmacht *(f)*, Bevollmächtigung *(f)*, Vertretungsmacht *(f)*, Prokura *(f)*
procurement Anschaffung *(f)*, Beschaffung *(f)*, Besorgung *(f)*, Vermittlung *(f)*

produce Erzeugnis *(n)*, Produkt *(n)*
produce produzieren, erzeugen, herstellen, schaffen; bewirken, hervorrufen; einbringen; (Gewinn etc.) abwerfen; (Dokument etc.) vorzeigen, beibringen; (Nachweis etc.) erbringen
producer Produzent *(m)*, Erzeuger *(m)*, Hersteller *(m)*, Fabrikant *(m)*
product Produkt *(n)*, Erzeugnis *(n)*, Fabrikat *(n)*, Artikel *(m)*, Ware *(f)*
product acceptance Produktakzeptanz *(f)*
product advertising Produktwerbung *(f)*
product awareness Produktbekanntheit *(f)*
product benefit Produktnutzen *(m)*, Produktvorteil *(m)*
product category Produktgruppe *(f)*, Warengruppe *(f)*, Warenkategorie *(f)*
product category index (Messekatalog) Produktgruppenverzeichnis *(n)*, Warengruppenverzeichnis *(n)*
product category listings (Messekatalog) Produktgruppeneintrag *(m)*, Warengruppeneintrag *(m)*
product design Produktgestaltung *(f)*
product development Produktentwicklung *(f)*
product differentiation Produktdifferenzierung *(f)*, Produktunterscheidung *(f)*
product features Produkteigenschaften *(f, pl)*
product group Produktgruppe *(f)*, Warengruppe *(f)*
product image Produktimage *(n)*
product improvement Produktverbesserung *(f)*
product index Warenverzeichnis *(n)*
product introduction Produkteinführung *(f)*
product liability Produkthaftung *(f)*

product life cycle Produktlebenszyklus *(m)*
product line Produktreihe *(f)*, Produktsortiment *(n)*
product management Produktmanagement *(n)*
product manager Produktmanager(in) *(m/f)*
product mix Produktmix *(n)*
product positioning Produktpositionierung *(f)*
product presentation Produktvorführung *(f)*
product range Produktpalette *(f)*, Sortimentsbreite *(f)*
product research Produktforschung *(f)*
product safety law Produktsicherheitsgesetz *(n)*
product strategy Produktstrategie *(f)*
product, competitive konkurrenzfähiges Produkt *(n)*, konkurrierendes Produkt *(n)*
product, high-quality Qualitätserzeugnis *(n)*
production Produktion *(f)*, Erzeugung *(f)*, Fabrikation *(f)*, Fertigung *(f)*, Herstellung *(f)*, Werk *(n)*
production capacity Produktionskapazität *(f)*
production costs Fertigungskosten *(pl)*, Herstellkosten *(pl)*
productive capacity Produktionskapazität *(f)*
productivity Produktivität *(f)*, Rentabilität *(f)*, Ergiebigkeit *(f)*, Ertragsfähigkeit *(f)*
profession Beruf *(m)*
professional professionell, fachmännisch, fachlich, berufsmäßig, Berufs-, Fach-
professional association Fachverband *(m)*
profile im Pofil *(n)* darstellen

profile Profil *(n)*, Längsschnitt *(m)*, Seitenansicht *(f)*, Querschnitt *(m)*; Kurzbeschreibung *(f)*
profile extension Profilverlängerung *(f)*
profile support Profilstütze *(f)*
profile, hook-in Einhängeprofil *(n)*
profile, tightening Spannprofil *(n)*
profit Profit *(m)*, Gewinn *(m)*, Ertrag *(m)*, Nutzen *(m)*, Vorteil *(m)*
profit profitieren, Gewinn *(m)* ziehen, Nutzen *(m)* ziehen
profit after-tax Gewinn *(m)* nach Steuern
profit and loss account Gewinn- und Verlustrechnung *(f)*
profit before taxes Gewinn *(m)* vor Steuern
profit center (US) Profit-Center *(n)*
profit centre (GB) Profit-Center *(n)*
profit improvement Gewinnverbesserung *(f)*
profit margin Gewinnspanne *(f)*, Umsatzrendite *(f)*
profit, clear Nettogewinn *(m)*
profitability Rentabilität *(f)*, Wirtschaftlichkeit *(f)*
profitable profitabel, rentabel, einträglich, gewinnbringend, nützlich, vorteilhaft
profit-making gewinnbringend, rentabel
proforma account Proformarechnung *(f)*
progam (US), follow-up Anschlussprogramm *(n)*
progamme (GB), follow-up Anschlussprogramm *(n)*
prognosis Prognose *(f)*
program (US) Programm *(n)*, Sendung *(f)*
program (US) programmieren
program (US), accompanying Rahmenprogramm *(n)*
program control (US) (EDV) Programmsteuerung *(f)*
program for data processing (US) Datenverarbeitungsprogramm *(n)*
program operation (US) programmierter Ablauf *(m)*
programmable programmierbar
programme (GB) Programm *(n)*, Sendung *(f)*
programme (GB) programmieren
programme (GB), accompanying Rahmenprogramm *(n)*
programme control (GB) (EDV) Programmsteuerung *(f)*
programme for data processing (GB) Datenverarbeitungsprogramm *(n)*
programme operation (GB) programmierter Ablauf *(m)*
programmes (GB), promotional Förderprogramme *(n, pl)*
programming Programmierung *(f)*
programming language Programmiersprache *(f)*
programs (US), promotional Förderprogramme *(n, pl)*
progress Fortschritt *(m)*, Fortschritte *(m, pl)*, Fortschreiten *(n)*
progress Fortschritte *(m, pl)* machen, vorranschreiten, vorrücken
progressive fortschrittlich
prohibit verbieten, untersagen, verhindern
prohibition Verbot *(n)*
prohibition of photography and film Fotografier- und Filmverbot *(n)*
project Projekt *(n)*, Vorhaben, Unternehmen *(n)*
project projektieren, planen; projizieren; vorspringen, vorstehen
project engineer Projektingenieur(in) *(m/f)*
project leader Projektleiter(in) *(m/f)*
project management Projektmanagement *(n)*, Projektleitung *(f)*
project manager Projektleiter(in) *(m/f)*

projection Projektion *(f)*, Entwurf *(m)*, Plan *(m)*, Planung *(f)*; Vorführung *(f)*; Vorausschau *(f)*, Vorhersage *(f)*, Prognose *(f)*; (Bau) Auskragung *(f)*, vorspringender Teil *(m)*
projection area Projektionsfläche *(f)*
projector Projektor *(m)*
prominent prominent, bekannt, berühmt, bedeutend, hervorragend; vorspringend, vorstehend
promise versprechen, andeuten
promise Versprechen *(n)*, Zusage *(f)*, Aussicht *(f)*, Hoffnung *(f)*
promising erfolgversprechend, vielversprechend, verheißungsvoll
promote fördern, befördern, befürworten, vorantreiben, unterstützen; werben
promoter Promoter(in) *(m/f)*, Förderer *(m)*, Förderin *(f)*, Befürworter(in) *(m/f)*, Veranstalter(in) *(m/f)*, Projektentwickler(in) *(m/f)*, Träger(in) *(m/f)*
promotion Promotion *(f)*, Förderung *(f)*, Beförderung *(f)*; Verkaufsförderung *(f)*, Reklame *(f)*, Werbung *(f)*; Unterstützung *(f)*
promotion mobile Ausstellungswagen *(m)*
promotional gift Werbegeschenk *(n)*
promotional material Werbematerial *(n)*
prompt anspornen, auffordern, veranlassen
prompt prompt, sofort, umgehend, unverzüglich; pünktlich
promtly pünktlich
proof fest, geschützt, sicher, undurchlässig, unempfindlich
proof imprägnieren
proof Probe *(f)*, Erprobung *(f)*; Probeabzug *(m)*, Korrekturfahne *(f)*; Beweis *(m)*, Nachweis *(m)*, Beleg *(m)*

proof of foreign medical coverage Auslandskrankenschein *(m)*
prop Pfosten *(f)*, Säule *(f)*, Stütze *(f)*
prop stützen, verstreben
propaganda Propaganda *(f)*
propaganda, verbal Mundpropaganda *(f)*
propagate propagieren, ausbreiten, verbreiten, sich verbreiten
propane Propan *(n)*, Propangas *(n)*
propane gas Propangas *(n)*
propensity Neigung *(f)*, Hang *(m)*
propensity to consume Konsumneigung *(f)*
property Eigentum *(n)*, Besitz *(m)*, Grundbesitz *(m)*, Grundstück *(n)*, Anlageobjekt *(n)*, Immobilien *(f, pl)*, Vermögen *(n)*
property damage Sachschaden *(m)*
property protection, industrial gewerblicher Rechtsschutz *(m)*
proportion anteilmäßig verteilen
proportion Proportion *(f)*, Quote *(f)*, Teil *(m)*, Anteil *(m)*, Verhältnis *(n)*, Größenverhältnisse *(n, pl)*
proportional proportional, anteilmäßig, verhältnismäßig
proposal Vorschlag *(m)*, Antrag *(m)*, Anregung *(f)*
propose vorschlagen, anregen, beabsichtigen, vorhaben; (Vorschlag etc.) einbringen
proprietary urheberrechtlich geschützt
proprietary brand Handelsname *(m)*, Markenname *(m)*
proprietary goods Markenartikel *(m, pl)*
proprietary make Markenfabrikat *(n)*
proprietary rights Eigentumsrechte *(n, pl)*
proprietor Eigentümer(in) *(m/f)*, Besitzer(in) *(m/f)*, Inhaber(in) *(m/f)*, Einzelunternehmer(in) *(m/f)*
prospect Aussicht *(f)*, Ausblick *(m)*
prospective voraussichtlich, zukünftig

prospects, economic
Konjunkturaussichten *(f, pl)*,
Wirtschaftsaussichten *(f, pl)*
prospectus Prospekt *(m)*,
Verzeichnis *(n)*
protect schützen, beschützen,
bewahren, verteidigen; (Rechte etc.)
wahren
protected by copyright
urheberrechtlich geschützt
protection Schutz *(m)*, Wahrung *(f)*
(von Interessen)
protection by copyright
Urheberrechtsschutz *(m)*
protection of industrial property rights gewerblicher Rechtsschutz *(m)*
protection of inventions
Patentschutz *(m)*
protection of nature Naturschutz *(m)*
protection of proprietary rights
Schutz *(m)* der Urheberrechte
protection of registered design
Gebrauchsmusterschutz *(m)*,
Geschmacksmusterschutz *(m)*
protection of trademarks
Markenschutz *(m)*,
Warenzeichenschutz *(m)*
protection, legal Rechtsschutz *(m)*
protective schützend
protective barrier Schutzgitter *(f)*
protective circuit breaker
Schutzschalter *(m)*
protective clothing Schutzkleidung *(f)*
protective cover Schutzhülle *(f)*
protective device Schutzeinrichtung *(f)*
protective glove
Schutzhandschuh *(m)*
protective goggles Schutzbrille *(f)*
protective sheeting Abdeckfolie *(f)*
protective strip Schutzleiste *(f)*
protective suit Schutzanzug *(m)*
protest Protest *(m)*
protest protestieren, Einspruch *(m)* erheben, beteuern
protocol Protokoll *(f)*

prototype Prototyp *(m)*
protractor Winkelmesser *(m)*
provable nachweislich
prove beweisen, nachweisen,
bestätigen, beglaubigen, erproben; sich
erweisen, (gut/schlecht etc.) ausfallen
proven bewährt, erprobt
provide beschaffen, heanschaffen,
liefern, beliefern, besorgen,
ausstatten, versehen, versorgen,
bereitstellen, vorsehen, Vorsorge *(f)*
treffen; (Recht) vorschreiben
provided that sofern
provider Lieferant *(m)*
provider of services Dienstleister *(m)*
provision Bestimmung *(f)*, Vorschrift *(f)*;
Beschaffung *(f)*, Bereitstellung *(f)*,
Bersorgung *(f)*, Vorsorge *(f)*,
Versorgung *(f)*, Verpflegung *(f)*;
Vorkehrung *(f)*
provision with stocks Bevorratung *(f)*
provision, special Sonderregelung *(f)*
provisional provisorisch, einstweilig,
vorläufig
provisions Proviant *(m)*, Verpflegung *(f)*,
Lebensmittel *(n, pl)*
provisions on construction
Aufbaubestimmungen *(f, pl)*
provisions on dismantling
Abbaubestimmungen *(f, pl)*
provisions on setting up
Aufbaubestimmungen *(f, pl)*
proximity Nähe *(f)*
pub (GB) Kneipe *(f)*, Wirtshaus *(n)*
pub crawl (GB) Kneipenbummel *(m)*
public öffentlich, allgemein bekannt
public Publikum *(n)*, Öffentlichkeit *(f)*,
Allgemeinheit *(f)*
public days Publikumstage *(m, pl)*
public house (GB) Bierlokal *(n)*,
Wirtshaus *(n)*
public relations (PR)
Öffentlichkeitsarbeit *(f)*, PR-Arbeit *(f)*
public relations campaign
PR-Kampagne *(f)*

public relations department
Abteilung *(f)* für Öffentlichkeitsarbeit, PR-Abteilung *(f)*
publication Publikation *(f)*, Veröffentlichung *(f)*, Druckschrift *(m)*
publication date Erscheinungsdatum *(n)*, Erscheinungstermin *(m)*
publicity Publizität *(f)*, Bekanntheit *(f)*; Publicity *(f)*, Reklame *(f)*, Werbung *(f)*
publicity budget Werbebudget *(n)*, Werbeetat *(m)*
publicity campaign Werbekampagne *(f)*, Werbefeldzug *(m)*
publicity costs Werbekosten *(pl)*
publicity expenses Werbeausgaben *(f, pl)*
publicity slogan Werbeslogan *(m)*
publish publizieren, bekannt machen, veröffentlichen, herausgeben, verlegen
publisher Verleger(in) *(m/f)*, Herausgeber(in) *(m/f)*, Verlag *(m)*
publishing company Verlag *(m)*
publishing house Verlagshaus *(m)*, Verlag *(m)*
pull zerren, ziehen, reißen
pull Ziehen *(n)*, Zug *(m)*, Ruck *(m)*; Anstieg *(m)*, Steigung *(f)*
pulley Flaschenzug *(m)*
pull-out shelf Auszugsplatte *(f)*
punch lochen, stanzen
punch Locher *(m)*, Lochzange *(f)*
punch pliers Lochzange *(f)*
punctual pünktlich
punishable strafbar
purchase Ankauf *(m)*, Kauf *(m)*, Anschaffung *(f)*, Erwerb *(m)*
purchase kaufen, einkaufen, ankaufen, anschaffen, erwerben
purchase cost Anschaffungskosten *(pl)*
purchase intention Kaufabsicht *(f)*
purchase invoice Einkaufsrechnung *(f)*
purchase option Kaufoption *(f)*
purchase order Auftrag *(m)*, Bestellung *(f)*

purchase price Kaufpreis *(m)*, Einkaufspreis *(m)*, Anschaffungspreis *(m)*
purchaser Käufer(in) *(m/f)*, Erwerber(in) *(m/f)*, Auftraggeber(in) *(m/f)*
purchasing manager Einkaufsleiter(in) *(m/f)*
pure pur, rein, sauber, fehlerlos, völlig
purity Reinheit *(f)*, Ehrlichkeit *(f)*
purpose Absicht *(f)*, Entschlossenheit *(f)*, Vorsatz *(m)*, Ziel *(n)*, Zweck *(m)*
purpose of participation Beteiligungsziel *(f)*
push Stoß *(m)*, Druck *(m)*, Schub *(m)*; werbliche Aktion *(f)*
push stoßen, schieben, drücken, drängen, antreiben; propagieren, Reklame *(f)* machen
put aside aufheben, zurücklegen
put back (an seinen Patz) zurücklegen
put down hinlegen, niederlegen, hinstellen, hinsetzen; aufschreiben
put in einsetzen, installieren, hineinbringen; (Bemerkung etc.) einwerfen
put in order ordnen
put into operation Inbetriebnahme *(f)*
put off abschalten; verschieben, zurückstellen; (Mantel etc.) ausziehen
put on (Licht) anmachen; (Mantel etc.) anziehen
put on the market auf den Markt *(m)* bringen
put out herstellen, produzieren; (Licht etc.) ausmachen
put out of action außer Betrieb *(m)* setzen
put right in Ordnung *(f)* bringen
put together zusammensetzen, aufbauen, montieren
put up aufbauen, aufstellen, errichten, hochziehen, installieren, montieren
pyramidal pyramidenförmig
pyramid-shaped pyramidenförmig

Q

quadrangle Viereck *(n)*
quadrangular viereckig
quadratic quadratisch
qualified personnel Fachpersonal *(n)*, Fachkräfte *(f, pl)*
quality Qualität *(f)*, Güte *(f)*, Güteklasse *(f)*; Ausführung *(f)*, Sorte *(f)*
quality articles Qualitätsware *(f)*
quality control Qualitätskontrolle *(f)*
quality goods Qualitätserzeugnisse *(n, pl)*, Qualitätswaren *(f, pl)*
quality label Gütezeichen *(n)*
quality mark Gütezeichen *(n)*, Gütesiegel *(n)*
quality product Qualitätserzeugnis *(n)*
quality protection Qualitätssicherung *(f)*
quality standard Qualitätsstandard *(m)*
quality work Qualitätsarbeit *(f)*
quality workmanship Qualitätsarbeit *(f)*
quality, first-class erstklassige Qualität *(f)*
quality, high-grade hochwertig
quality-conscious qualitätsbewusst
quantitative quantitativ
quantity Quantität *(f)*, Menge *(f)*
quarter Viertel *(n)*; Vierteljahr *(n)*, Quartal *(n)*; Himmelsrichtung *(f)*; Gegend *(f)*, Viertel *(n)*; Seite *(f)*, Stelle *(f)*
quarter vierteln; einquartieren, unterbringen
quarter page Viertelseite *(f)*
quarters Quartier *(n)*, Unterkunft *(f)*
question Frage *(f)*, Problem *(n)*, Zweifel *(m)*; Sache *(f)*
question fragen, verhören, bezweifeln, in Frage *(f)* stellen
question of costs Kostenfrage *(f)*
questionable fraglich, fragwürdig, zweifelhaft
questionnaire Fragebogen *(m)*
queue up Schlange *(f)* stehen
quick schnell, rasch, prompt, kurz; gewandt, geschickt, schlagfertig
quick lunch restaurant Schnellgaststätte *(f)*
quick-witted schlagfertig, geistesgegenwärtig
quiet Ruhe *(f)*, Stille *(f)*
quiet ruhig, still, leise, sanft, zurückhaltend, geheim, heimlich
quintessence Quintessenz *(f)*
quota Quantum *(n)*, Kontingent *(n)*, Anteil *(m)*
quotation Angebot *(n)*, Kostenanschlag *(m)*, Notierung *(f)*
quote Angebot *(n)*, Preisangebot *(n)*
quote veranschlagen, anführen, nennen, zitieren; (Kurs etc.) notieren

R

rack Ständer *(m)*, Gestell *(n)*, Regal *(n)*
radiation protection Strahlenschutz *(m)*
radio Radio *(n)*, Hörfunk *(m)*, Funkgerät *(n)*
radio über Funk *(m)* durchgeben
radio paging service Personenfunkdienst *(m)*
radio station Rundfunksender *(m)*
radio station, local Regionalsender *(m)*
radio, commercial Werbefunk *(m)*
radioactive radioaktiv
radioactive material radioaktives Material *(n)*
radioactive material, handling of Umgang *(m)* mit radioaktivem Material
Radiological Protection Order Strahlenschutzverordnung *(f)*
radiopager Funksprechgerät *(n)*, Personenrufgerät *(n)*
radiotelephone Sprechfunkgerät *(n)*

radiotelephone with audible alert
Personenrufgerät *(n)* mit akustischem Signal
radius Radius *(m)*, Aktionsradius *(m)*, Wirkungsbereich *(m)*
raffle Lotterie *(f)*, Tombola *(f)*
raffle off verlosen
rail, electrical Stromschiene *(f)*
rail, fixing Befestigungsschiene *(f)*
railing Geländer *(n)*, Zaun *(m)*
railroad guide (US) Kursbuch *(n)*
railroad rates (US) Bahntarif *(m)*
railroad station (US) Bahnhof *(m)*
railroad ticket (US) Bahnfahrkarte *(f)*
railroad timetable (US) Zugfahrplan *(m)*, Kursbuch *(n)*
railway guide (GB) Kursbuch *(n)*
railway rates (GB) Bahntarif *(m)*
railway station (GB) Bahnhof *(m)*
railway ticket (GB) Bahnfahrkarte *(f)*
railway timetable (GB) Zugfahrplan *(m)*, Kursbuch *(n)*
raise heben, anheben, erheben, hochheben, hochziehen, erhöhen, aufbringen, heraufsetzen; errichten
raise one's glass to s.o. jdm. zutrinken
raise one's voice die Stimme *(f)* erheben, lauter sprechen
raised floor Doppelboden *(m)*, Liftboden *(m)*
RAL color range (US) RAL-Farbkarte *(f)*
RAL colour range (GB) RAL-Farbkarte *(f)*
RAL special color (US) RAL-Sonderfarbe *(f)*
RAL special colour (GB) RAL-Sonderfarbe *(f)*
ramp Rampe *(f)*
random selection Zufallsauswahl *(f)*
range aufstellen, anordnen, ausrichten; sich bewegen; durchziehen, durchstreifen; schwanken
range Reihe *(f)*, Skala *(f)*; Sortiment *(n)*, Kollektion *(f)*; Spektrum *(n)*, Bereich *(m)*, Spielraum *(m)*, Reichweite *(f)*, Tragweite *(f)*; Angebot *(n)*

range of activity Tätigkeitsbereich *(m)*
range of application Einsatzmöglichkeit *(f)*
range of goods Produktsoriment *(n)*, Warensortiment *(n)*, Warenangebot *(n)*
range of products Produktpalette *(f)*
range, wide (Waren etc.) breite Palette *(f)*
ranged right rechtsbündig
rank Rang *(m)*, Reihe *(f)*, Glied *(n)*, Stellung *(f)*
rank rechnen, zählen, gelten, rangieren
ranking list Rangliste *(f)*
rapid rapide, rasch, schnell
rare rar, selten
rash unbesonnen
rashness Unbesonnenheit *(f)*
raster (Druck, TV) Raster *(n)*
raster screen (Druck, TV) Raster *(n)*
ratchet Rätsche *(f)*
rate einschätzen, halten für; veranlagen; verdienen
rate Rate *(f)*, Quote *(f)*, Satz *(m)*, Kurs *(m)*, Tarif *(m)*, Ziffer *(f)*; Geschwindigkeit *(f)*
rate of return Rendite *(f)*
rate, daily Tagessatz *(m)*
rational rational, vernünftig
rationalization Rationalisierung *(f)*
rationalize rationalisieren, rational erklären
raw roh, Roh-, rein, unbearbeitet, unverarbeitet
raw material Rohstoff *(m)*
reach reichen, sich erstrecken; erreichen, erlangen, erzielen
reach Reichweite *(f)*
reaction Reaktion *(f)*
read lesen, vorlesen, ablesen; anzeigen
Read Only Memory (ROM) (EDV) ROM
ready for occupancy bezugsfertig
ready for the scrap heap schrottreif
ready to help hilfsbereit
real time (EDV) Echtzeit *(f)*

realize realisieren, verwirklichen; veräußern, verkaufen; (Gewinn) erzielen; erkennen, begreifen, einsehen, sich bewusst werden
rear hintere(-r/-s), Heck-
rear building Rückgebäude *(n)*
rear of the stand Standrückseite *(f)*
rear projection Rückprojektion *(f)*
rear projection box Rückprojektionsbox *(f)*
rear projection split screen Rückprojektions-Splitwand *(f)*
rear wall Rückwand *(f)*
reason Grund *(m)*, Motiv *(n)*, Ursache *(f)*; Verstand *(m)*, Vernunft *(f)*
reason überlegen, durchdenken, folgern, schließen; vernünftig reden
reasonable vernünftig, angemessen, reell; ganz gut, ordentlich, berechtigt
rebate Rabatt *(m)*, Nachlass *(m)*, Preisnachlass *(m)*; Rückvergütung *(f)*, Rückerstattung *(f)*, Rückzahlung *(f)*
rebuild umbauen, wieder aufbauen, wieder herstellen
recall abberufen; sich erinnern
recall Erinnerung *(f)*, Gedächtnis *(n)*; Rückruf *(m)*, Rückforderung *(f)*, Abberufung *(f)*
recall test Erinnerungstest *(m)*
recapitulate rekapitulieren, kurz zusammenfassen
recapitulation Rekapitulation *(f)*, Wiederholung *(f)*, kurze Zusammenfassung *(f)*
receipt Annahme *(f)*, Empfang *(m)*, Erhalt *(m)*; Empfangsbestätigung *(f)*, Beleg *(m)*, Quittung *(f)*
receipt bescheinigen, quittieren
receipt book Quittungsblock *(m)*
receipt form Quittungsformular *(n)*
reception Rezeption *(f)*, Empfang *(m)*, Aufnahme *(f)*
reception area Empfangsbereich *(m)*
reception committee Empfangskomitee *(n)*
reception desk Rezeption *(f)*, Empfang *(m)*
receptionist Empfangschef(in) *(m/f)*, Empfangsdame *(f)*
recess Nische *(f)*; Pause *(f)*, Unterbrechung *(f)*
recess in eine Nische *(f)* stellen, einbauen
recessed head screw Kreuzschlitzschraube *(f)*
recession Rezession *(f)*, Rückgang *(m)*
recognition Erkennen *(n)*, Wiedererkennung *(f)*; Anerkennen *(n)*, Anerkennung *(f)*
recognition test Wiedererkennungstest *(m)*
recognize erkennen, wiedererkennen; anerkennen, eingestehen, zugeben
recommend empfehlen
recommendation Empfehlung *(f)*
recommended price Preisempfehlung *(f)*, Richtpreis *(m)*
recommended retail price (RRP) unverbindliche Preisempfehlung *(f)*
reconfirmation (Buchung etc.) Rückbestätigung *(f)*
record Aufnahme *(f)*, Aufzeichnung *(f)*, Liste *(f)*, Niederschrift *(f)*, Protokoll *(n)*, Datensatz *(m)*
record aufschreiben, aufzeichnen, protokollieren; aufnehmen, mitschneiden
recording (Film, Ton) Aufnahme *(f)*, Aufzeichnung *(f)*
recording studio Tonstudio *(n)*
recourse Rückgriff *(m)*, Regress *(m)*
recovery Belebung *(f)*, Erholung *(f)*; Wiedergewinnung *(f)*, Rückgewinnung *(f)*
recreation Erholung *(f)*, Arbeitsruhe *(f)*
recreation area Ruhezone *(f)*
recruitment agency Personalvermittlung *(f)*

recruitment of staff
  Personalbeschaffung *(f)*
rectangle Rechteck *(n)*
rectangular rechteckig, rechtwinklig
recyclability Recyclingfähigkeit *(f)*
recyclable materials
  wiederverwertbare Stoffe *(m, pl)*,
  recyclingfähige Stoffe *(m, pl)*
recyclable waste wiederverwertbarer
  Abfall *(m)*, recyclingfähiger Abfall *(m)*
recycle recyceln, rückgewinnen, wieder
  verwerten
recycling Recycling *(n)*,
  Rückgewinnung *(f)*,
  Wiederverwertung *(f)*
reduce reduzieren, ermäßigen,
  herabsetzen, heruntersetzen,
  abbauen, kürzen, verbilligen,
  vermindern, verringern, verkleinern,
  senken; drosseln, verlangsamen
reduce in size verkleinern
reduction Reduktion *(f)*,
  Reduzierung *(f)*, Ermäßigung *(f)*,
  Nachlass *(m)*, Rabatt *(m)*,
  Herabsetzung *(f)*, Senkung *(f)*,
  Verminderung *(f)*, Verringerung *(f)*,
  Verkleinerung *(f)*, Abbau *(m)*,
  Drosselung *(f)*, Kürzung *(f)*
reduction of the stand rental charge
  Ermäßigung *(f)* der Standmietkosten
reference Referenz *(f)*, Empfehlung *(f)*,
  Zeugnis *(n)*; Bezugnahme *(f)*;
  Geschäftszeichen *(n)*; Bemerkung *(f)*,
  Erwähnung *(f)*, Verweis *(m)*,
  Hinweis *(m)*, Quellenangabe *(f)*
reference number Kennziffer *(f)*,
  Aktenzeichen *(n)*
reflect nachdenken; reflektieren,
  zurückstrahlen, widerspiegeln
reflection Reflexion *(f)*, Spiegelung *(f)*,
  Spiegelbild *(n)*; Nachdenken *(n)*,
  Überlegung *(f)*
reflector Reflektor *(m)*, Rückstrahler *(m)*
reflector bulb Reflektorlampe *(f)*
reflex camera Spiegelreflexkamera *(f)*

reflexion Reflexion *(f)*, Spiegelung *(f)*,
  Spiegelbild *(n)*; Nachdenken *(n)*,
  Überlegung *(f)*
refreshment Erfrischung *(f)*
refrigerate kühlen
refrigerated cabinet Kühlmöbel *(m)*
refrigerated container
  Kühlcontainer *(m)*
refrigerated cupola Kühlkuppel *(f)*
refrigerated display Kühlauslage *(f)*
refrigerated display cabinet
  Kühlvitrine *(f)*
refrigerated display on trolley
  Kühlauslage *(f)* auf Rollgestell
refrigerated island site cabinet
  Kühlinsel *(f)*
refrigerated open top display cabinet
  Kühltruhe *(f)*
refrigerated service counter
  Kühltheke *(f)*
refrigerated trolley
  Kühlservierwagen *(m)*
refrigerated vending machine
  Verkaufskühlautomat *(m)*
refrigerated vertical cabinet
  Kühlregal *(n)*
refrigerating unit system
  Kältesatz *(m)*
refrigerating unit system, water-cooled
  (Kühlaggregat) wassergekühlter
  Kältesatz *(m)*
refrigeration Kühlung *(f)*
refrigeration plant Kälteanlage *(f)*
refrigerator Kühlschrank *(m)*
refrigerator with glazed door
  Kühlschrank *(m)* mit verglaster Tür
refrigerator with low temperature
  compartment Kühlschrank *(m)* mit
  Tiefkühlfach
refrigerator, commercial
  Gewerbekühlschrank *(m)*
refund erstatten, rückerstatten,
  rückvergüten, ersetzen, zurückzahlen
refund Rückerstattung *(f)*,
  Rückvergütung *(f)*, Rückzahlung *(f)*

refusal Ablehnung *(f)*, Weigerung *(f)*, Verweigerung *(f)*, Zurückweisung *(f)*
refuse ablehnen, abweisen, ausschlagen, verweigern
refuse (GB) Abfall *(m)*, Müll *(m)*
refuse bin (GB) Mülleimer *(m)*
refuse collection (GB) Müllabfuhr *(f)*
refuse disposal (GB) Müllbeseitigung *(f)*, Abfallentsorgung *(f)*
register Register *(n)*, Verzeichnis *(n)*, Liste *(f)*
register registrieren, eintragen, eintragen lassen, sich eintragen, einschreiben lassen, sich einschreiben, anmelden
register, commercial Handelsregister *(n)*
registered eingetragen, registriert
registration Registrierung *(f)*, Anmeldung *(f)*; (Katalog etc.) Eintragung *(f)*, Einschreibung *(f)*
registration certificate Eintragungsbescheinigung *(f)*
registration confirmation Anmeldebestätigung *(f)*
registration fee Anmeldegebühr *(f)*, Einschreibungsgebühr *(f)*, Eintragungsgebühr *(f)*
registration form Anmeldeformular *(n)*, Einschreibeformular *(n)*
registration number Anmeldungsnummer *(f)*, Einschreibenummer *(f)*
registration, withdrawal of Zurücknahme *(f)* der Anmeldung
regret bedauern
regret Bedauern *(n)*
regular regulär, regelmäßig, geregelt, geordnet, fahrplanmäßig, normal, gleichmäßig, gleichförmig; fest, Stamm-
regulate regeln, regulieren, steuern, einstellen
regulation Regelung *(f)*, Regulierung *(f)*, Vorschrift *(f)*; Einstellung *(f)*

regulation, legal gesetzliche Bestimmung *(f)*
regulations concerning accident prevention Unfallverhütungsvorschriften *(f, pl)*
regulations, technical technische Richtlinien *(f, pl)*
rehearsal (Theater etc.) Probe *(f)*
reimbursement Entschädigung *(f)*, Rückerstattung *(f)*, Ersatz *(m)*, Vergütung *(f)*
reinforce verstärken, untermauern, bestätigen, stützen
reinforcement Verstärkung *(f)*
reinforcing plate Sicherungsplatte *(f)*
reinforcing profile Aussteifungsprofil *(n)*
reinsurance Rückversicherung *(f)*
reinsure rückversichern
relation Beziehung *(f)*, Verhältnis *(n)*
relationship Beziehung *(f)*, Verhältnis *(n)*, Verbindung *(f)*
relaunch Relaunch *(m)*, Wiedereinführung *(f)*
relaunch wieder auflegen, wieder einführen
release befreien, freigeben, entlassen, lösen; (Kamera) auslösen; (Buch etc.) herausbringen, veröffentlichen
release Entlassung *(f)*, Befreiung *(f)*, Freigabe *(f)*; Veröffentlichung *(f)*
relevant relevant, bedeutsam, wichtig; zweckdienlich, zuständig
reliable verlässlich, vertrauenswürdig, zuverlässig, seriös
reload nachladen, umladen
reloading charge Umladegebühr *(f)*, Umladekosten *(pl)*
remain bleiben, bestehen, fortdauern, übrig bleiben
remain open offen bleiben
remaining restlich, übrig
remains Reste *(m, pl)*, Überreste *(m, pl)*
remark bemerken, äußern, wahrnehmen
remark Bemerkung *(f)*

remarkable bemerkenswert, beachtlich, außergewöhnlich
remarks, preliminary einleitende Bemerkung *(f)*, Vorbemerkung *(f)*
remind erinnern, mahnen
reminder Gedächtnisstütze *(f)*, Erinnerung *(f)*; Mahnung *(f)*, Mahnbescheid *(m)*
remnant Rest *(m)*, Überbleibsel *(n)*
remodel umbilden, umformen, umgestalten
remote control Fernbedienung *(f)*
remote-controlled ferngesteuert
removable abnehmbar, abtrennbar, herausnehmbar
removal Entfernung *(f)*, Entfernen *(n)*, Beseitigung *(f)*, Abbau *(m)*, Abnahme *(f)*; Umzug *(m)*
removal period Abbauzeitraum *(m)*
removal staff Abbaupersonal *(n)*
removal ticket Abbaukarte *(f)*
removal time Abbauzeit *(f)*
removal time, end of Ende *(n)* der Abbauzeit
remove beseitigen, entfernen, beheben, forträumen, abbauen, wegschaffen, transportieren; entlassen; umziehen
rent out (US) vermieten, verpachten
rent (US) Miete *(f)*, Pacht *(f)*
rent (US) mieten, pachten
rent (US), terms of Mietvereinbarung *(f)*
rental (US) Miete *(f)*, Pacht *(f)*, Leihgebühr *(f)*
rental charge (US) Leihgebühr *(f)*, Leihkosten *(pl)*
rental dinnerware (US) Leihgeschirr *(n)*
rental equipment (US) Leihausstattung *(f)*, Leiheinrichtung *(f)*, Mietausrüstung *(f)*, Mietgeräte *(n, pl)*
rental exhibition stand (US) Mietmessestand *(m)*
rental fee (US) Mietgebühr *(f)*, Leihgebühr *(f)*
rental furniture (US) Leihmöbel *(n, pl)*, Mietmöbel *(n, pl)*

rental rate (US) Mietpreis *(m)*
rental service (US) Verleih *(m)*
rental system stand (US) Mietsystemstand *(m)*
reorder nachbestellen
reorder Nachbestellung *(f)*
reorganization Neuorganisation *(f)*, Neugliederung *(f)*, Umstrukturierung *(f)*
repair reparieren, ausbessern, flicken, wiedergutmachen
repair Reparatur *(f)*, Ausbesserung *(f)*, Wiedergutmachung *(f)*
repair costs Reparaturkosten *(pl)*
reparable reparabel, ersetzbar
repay zurückzahlen, abzahlen, entschädigen; vergelten; Besuch *(m)* erwidern
repayable rückzahlbar
repayment Rückzahlung *(f)*, Vergütung *(f)*; Vergeltung *(f)*
repeat wiederholen
repeat Wiederholung *(f)*
replace austauschen, ersetzen, wiederbeschaffen; rückvergüten; zurücklegen, zurückstellen; (Telefonhörer) auflegen
replacement Ersatz *(m)*, Ersatzbeschaffung *(f)*, Wiederbeschaffung *(f)*; Vertretung *(f)*
replacement part Ersatzteil *(n)*
replacement value Wiederbeschaffungswert *(m)*
reply Antwort *(f)*, Rückantwort *(f)*, Erwiderung *(f)*
reply card Antwortkarte *(f)*
reply coupon Antwortcoupon *(m)*
report berichten, melden, vortragen; sich melden
report Reportage *(f)*, Bericht *(m)*, Rechenschaftsbericht *(m)*, Gutachten *(n)*; Referat *(n)*; Gerücht *(n)*
report on exhibition Messebericht *(m)*
report on trade fair Messebericht *(m)*
report, special Sonderbericht *(m)*

represent repräsentieren, vertreten, symbolisieren, darstellen, wiedergeben
representation Repräsentation *(f)*, Darstellung *(f);* Stellvertretung *(f)*, Vertretung *(f)*, Agentur *(f)*
representative Repräsentant(in) *(m/f)*, Beauftragte(r) *(f/m)*, Bevollmächtigte(r) *(f/m)*, Vertreter(in) *(m/f)*
representative repräsentativ, stellvertretend
reprint Nachdruck *(m)*, Neuauflage *(f)*
reprint nachdrucken, neu auflegen
reproduce reproduzieren, abdrucken, wiedergeben
reproduction Reproduktion *(f)*, Vervielfältigung *(f)*, Wiedergabe *(f)*, Abdruck *(m)*, Kopie *(f)*
reproduction proof Reprovorlage *(f)*
reputation Ansehen *(n)*, Name *(m)*, Ruf *(m)*, Renommee *(n)*
request Anforderung *(f)*, Aufforderung *(f)*, Verlangen *(n)*, Bitte *(f)*, Ersuchen *(n)*, Wunsch *(m)*
request bitten, ersuchen; Anspruch *(m)* erheben auf, beanspruchen, fordern, verlangen, geltend machen; behaupten, versichern
request for payment Zahlungsaufforderung *(f)*
require benötigen, brauchen, erfordern, wünschen, verlangen
requirement Anforderung *(f)*, Anspruch *(m)*, Bedürfnis *(n)*, Bedarf *(m)*, Erfordernis *(n)*, Wunsch *(m)*
resale Weiterverkauf *(m)*, Wiederverkauf *(m)*
resale price maintenance (RPM) Preisbindung *(f)* der zweiten Hand, vertikale Preisbindung *(f)*
resale value Wiederverkaufswert *(m)*
rescue retten
rescue Rettung *(f)*, Hilfe *(f)*
research forschen, erforschen, untersuchen

research Forschung *(f)*
reseller Wiederverkäufer *(m)*
reservation Reservierung *(f)*, Vorbestellung *(f)*, Vorbehalt *(m)*
reservation confirmation Reservierungsbestätigung *(f)*
reserve Reserve *(f)*, Vorrat *(m)*; Rücklage *(f)*; Reserviertheit *(f)*, Vorbehalt *(m)*, Zurückhaltung *(f)*
reserve reservieren, vorbestellen; sich vorbehalten, aufheben, aufsparen
resolution Resolution *(f)*, Beschluss *(m)*, Entschlossenheit *(f)*; (TV, EDV) Bildauflösung *(f)*
resolution, horizontal (TV, EDV) Horizontalauflösung *(f)*
resonance Resonanz *(f)*
respect Respekt *(m)*, Achtung *(f)*, Rücksicht *(f)*; Beziehung *(f)*, Hinsicht *(f)*
respect respektieren, achten, anerkennen, berücksichtigen
response Antwort *(f)*, Erwiderung *(f)*, Reaktion *(f)*
responsibility Verantwortung *(f)*, Pflicht *(f)*, Verpflichtung *(f)*
responsible verantwortlich, zuständig; verantwortungsbewusst, zuverlässig; haftbar
responsible, legally geschäftsfähig
rest Ausruhen *(n)*, Erholung *(f)*, Rast *(f)*, Ruhe *(f)*, Pause *(f)*; Rest *(m)*; Stütze *(f)*, Auflage *(f)*
rest ruhen, sich ausruhen, sich erholen, Pause *(f)* machen, pausieren; sich stützen
rest room Ruheraum *(m)*
restaurant Gaststätte *(f)*, Restaurant *(n)*
restless rastlos, ruhelos, unruhig
restore restaurieren, wiederherstellen, wieder einsetzen, zurückgeben, zurückerstatten
restraining clause Konkurrenzklausel *(f)*
restraint Beschränkung *(f)*, Einschränkung *(f)*
restraint clause Konkurrenzklausel *(f)*

restraint of trade
Wettbewerbsbeschränkung *(f)*
restrict beschränken, einschränken, begrenzen
restriction Beschränkung *(f)*, Einschränkung *(f)*, Begrenzung *(f)*
restriction of admissions
Zulassungsbeschränkung *(f)*
result Resultat *(n)*, Ergebnis *(n)*, Ausgang *(m)*, Erfolg *(m)*, Folge *(f)*, Wirkung *(f)*
result resultieren, sich ergeben
result, final Endergebnis *(n)*
retail Einzelhandel *(m)*
retail dealer Einzelhändler *(m)*
retail price Einzelhandelspreis *(m)*
retail shop Einzelhandelsgeschäft *(n)*
retail trade Einzelhandel *(m)*
retailer Wiederverkäufer *(m)*, Einzelhändler *(m)*
retouch retuschieren
retrenchment Einschränkung *(f)*, Kürzung *(f)*; Personalabbau *(m)*
retrospective Retrospektive *(f)*
retrospective rückblickend, rückschauend, rückwirkend
return Rückkehr *(f)*, Wiederkehr *(f)*, Rückfahrt *(f)*, Rückgabe *(f)*, Rücksendung *(f)*, Herausgabe *(f)*; Ertrag *(m)*, Gewinn *(m)*, Rendite *(f)*, Rentabilität *(f)*, Verzinsung *(f)*
return zurückkehren, zurückfahren, zurückbringen, zurückgeben, zurücksenden, rückliefern; zurückzahlen, rückerstatten; (Ertrag) abwerfen, einbringen
return address Absender *(m)*
return fare Hin- und Rückfahrpreis *(m)*
return flight Hin- und Rückflug *(m)*
return journey Rückfahrt *(f)*, Rückreise *(f)*
return on investment Ertrag *(m)*, Gewinn *(m)*, Verzinsung *(f)*
return ticket Rückfahrkarte *(f)*, Rückflugticket *(n)*

returnable rückgabepflichtig, Mehrweg-
returnable bottle Mehrwegflasche *(f)*, Pfandflasche *(f)*
reusable wiederverwendbar
reuse Wiederverwendung *(f)*
revenue Einkommen *(n)*, Einkünfte *(f, pl)*, Einnahmen *(f, pl)*, Erlös *(m)*, Ertrag *(m)*
revenue, additional
Mehreinnahmen *(f, pl)*
reversal Aufhebung *(f)*, Rückbuchung *(f)*, Stornierung *(f)*
reverse Gegenteil *(n)*, Kehrseite *(f)*, Rückseite *(f)*; Rückschlag *(m)*; Rückwärtsgang *(m)*
reverse umgekehrt, entgegengesetzt
reverse umkehren, umdrehen, wenden, rückwärts fahren; Reihenfolge *(f)* umkehren; annullieren, stornieren; (Recht) aufheben
reverse page Rückseite *(f)*
review Rückblick *(m)*; Überprüfung *(f)*, Inspektion *(f)*; Rezension *(f)*, Besprechung *(f)*, Kritik *(f)*
review überprüfen, besichtigen, besprechen, rezensieren, inspizieren
revise revidieren, überprüfen, wiederholen
revision Revision *(f)*, Überarbeitung *(f)*, Wiederholung *(f)*
revocation Widerruf *(m)*, Zurückziehen *(n)*, Aufhebung *(f)*, Entzug *(m)*
revoke (Erlaubnis etc.) widerrufen, rückgängig machen; (Gesetz etc.) aufheben; (Genehmigung etc.) entziehen
revolution Umdrehung *(f)*, Umlauf *(m)*, Rotation *(f)*; Revolution *(f)*
revolutions per minute
Umdrehungen *(f, pl)* pro Minute
revolve drehen, sich drehen
revolving door Drehtür *(f)*
revolving stage Drehbühne *(f)*
rhetoric Rhetorik *(f)*

rich reich; großartig, prächtig; kostbar; ertragreich; (Klang) voll; (Farbe) satt
ride, special Sonderfahrt *(f)*
right recht, richtig, korrekt, wahr, geeignet, in Ordnung *(f)*, genau; ganz, völlig; rechts; direkt
right Recht *(m)*, Anrecht *(n)*, Anspruch *(m)*
right angle coupler Winkelkupplung *(f)*
right at the bottom zuunterst
right in the middle mittendrin
right of rescission Widerrufsrecht *(n)*, Rücktrittsrecht *(n)*
right of return Rückgaberecht *(n)*
right of withrawal Rücktrittsrecht *(n)*
right-angled rechtwinklig
rights, domestic Hausrecht *(n)*
rights, domiciliary Hausrecht *(n)*
ring Ring *(m)*; Klang *(m)*, Klingeln *(n)*, Anruf *(m)*
ring umringen, einkreisen; klingeln, läuten, erklingen, tönen
ring binder Ringbuch *(n)*
ring node Ringknoten *(m)*
ring, adjustable Stellring *(m)*
rise steigen, ansteigen, aufstehen, sich heben, sich erheben, höher werden, wachsen, zunehmen
rise Anstieg *(m)*, Steigen *(n)*, Steigung *(f)*, Steigerung *(f)*, Erhöhung *(f)*, Aufstieg *(m)*, Aufschwung *(m)*, Zunahme *(f)*
rise in prices Preissteigerung *(f)*, Teuerung *(f)*
risk riskieren, wagen, aufs Spiel *(n)* setzen
risk Risiko *(n)*, Gefahr *(f)*, Wagnis *(n)*
risk-free risikolos
risky riskant, risikoreich, gewagt
rival Rivale *(m)*, Rivalin *(f)*, Konkurrent(in) *(m/f)*
rival rivalisieren, konkurrieren
rival brand Konkurrenzmarke *(f)*
rival firm Konkurrenzfirma *(f)*
rival product Konkurrenzprodukt *(n)*

rivalry Rivalität *(f)*
road accident Verkehrsunfall *(m)*
road map Straßenkarte *(f)*
road tractor Sattelschlepper *(m)*
road transport Straßentransport *(m)*
robust robust, kräftig, stabil, stark
rod Stab *(m)*, Stange *(f)*
rod bracket Rundstab *(m)*
rod, connecting Verbindungsrohr *(n)*
roll Rolle *(f)*, Rollen *(n)*, Ballen *(m)*, Bündel *(n)*; Liste *(f)*, Register *(n)*; Brötchen *(n)*
roll rollen, aufrollen, ausrollen; schlingern, schwanken; wälzen, walzen
roll cage Bügeltransportwagen *(m)*
roll container Rollbehälter *(m)*
roll out ausrollen
roll up aufrollen
roller Laufrolle *(f)*; Salzstreuer *(m)*
roof Dach *(n)*, Verdeck *(n)*
roof mit einem Dach *(n)* versehen
roof beam Dachbalken *(m)*
roof over überdachen
roof, trapezoid Trapezdach *(n)*
room Raum *(m)*, Platz *(m)*, Zimmer *(n)*
room divider Raumtrenner *(m)*, Raumteiler *(m)*
room height Raumhöhe *(f)*
room supplement, single Einzelzimmerzuschlag *(m)*
rope Seil *(n)*, Strick *(m)*, Strang *(m)*, Tau *(n)*
rope verschnüren
rostrum Tribüne *(f)*, Rednerpult *(n)*
rotatable drehbar
rotate rotieren, drehen, sich drehen, rotieren lassen, turnusmäßig wechseln
rotation Rotation *(f)*, Drehung *(f)*, Umdrehung *(f)*, Turnus *(m)*
rotunda Rundbau *(m)*
rough roh, Roh-, rauh, hart, grob, ungehobelt, stürmisch; ungefähr
rough Rohentwurf *(m)*

round Kreis *(m)*, Ring *(m)*, Scheibe *(f)*, Runde *(f)*, Rundgang *(m)*; (Bier etc.) Lage *(f)*
round rund, gerundet, rundum, rundherum
round runden, rund machen, abrunden; herumgehen, herumfahren, umfahren
round extrusion Rundrohr *(n)*
round-the-clock service Tag- und Nachtdienst *(m)*
route Route *(f)*, Strecke *(f)*, Weg *(m)*, Linie *(f)*, Runde *(f)*
route (Gepäck etc.) schicken
route to the exhibition Weg *(m)* zur Messe, Buslinie *(f)* zu Messe, Anfahrtsplan *(m)* zur Messe
routine Routine *(f)*
routine routinemäßig, gewohnheitsmäßig
row Reihe *(f)*; Lärm *(m)*, Krawall *(m)*, Streit *(m)*
row sich streiten
row booth Reihenstand *(m)*
row booth, end-of- Kopfstand *(m)*
row stand Reihenstand *(m)*
royalty Abgabe *(f)*, Nutzungsgebühr *(f)*, Lizenzgebühr *(f)*, Patentgebühr *(f)*; Tantieme *(f)*
rub reiben, abreiben, scheuern, polieren
rub off ausradieren, wegreiben
rubber Gummi *(n)*, Kautschuk *(m)*; Radiergummi *(m)*; Präservativ *(n)*
rubber bump Gummipuffer *(m)*
rubber o-ring Gummiring *(m)*
rubber pipe, steel-sheathed stahlummantelter Gummischlauch *(m)*
rubber stopper Gummistopfen *(m)*, Gummistöpsel *(m)*
rubbish (GB) Abfall *(m)*, Abfälle *(m, pl)*, Müll *(m)*, Schutt *(m)*; Blödsinn *(m)*
rubbish bin (GB) Abfalleimer *(m)*, Mülleimer *(m)*
rubbish collection (GB) Müllabfuhr *(f)*
rubbish container (GB) Müllcontainer *(m)*

rule entscheiden, festsetzen, verfügen, herrschen
rule Regel *(f)*, Normalfall *(m)*; Bestimmung *(f)*, Vorschrift *(f)*; Herrschaft *(f)*
ruler Lineal *(n)*, Maßstab *(m)*, Zollstock *(m)*
run out zu Ende *(n)* gehen, ablaufen
rush Andrang *(m)*, Ansturm *(m)*, Gedränge *(n)*; Eile *(f)*, Hast *(f)*, Hetze *(f)*
rush eilen, rennen, laufen, hasten, hetzen, stürmen, rasen, antreiben, drängen, schnell erledigen
rush hour Stoßzeit *(f)*, Hauptverkehrszeit *(f)*
rush order Eilauftrag *(m)*
rust Rost *(m)*
rust rosten
rustproof rostfrei

S

safe Safe *(m)*, Tresor *(m)*
safe sicher, ungefährlich, risikolos, zuverlässig
safe deposit box Schließfach *(n)*, Tresorfach *(n)*
safe distance Sicherheitsabstand *(m)*
safe load (Transport) zulässige Belastung *(f)*
safeguard Schutz *(m)*
safeguard schützen, sichern
safety Sicherheit *(f)*
safety clearance Sicherheitsabstand *(m)*
safety device Schutzvorrichtung *(f)*
safety equipment Sicherheitseinrichtung *(f)*, Sicherheitsvorrichtung *(f)*, sicherheitstechnische Einrichtungen *(f, pl)*
safety gate Sicherheitstor *(n)*

safety glass Sicherheitsglas *(n)*
safety goggles Schutzbrille *(f)*
safety helmet Schutzhelm *(m)*
safety lighting
 Sicherheitsbeleuchtung *(f)*
safety lock Sicherheitsschloss *(n)*
safety measure
 Sicherheitsmaßnahme *(f)*
safety plug Schukostecker *(m)*
safety precaution
 Sicherheitsmaßnahme *(f)*,
 Schutzmaßnahme *(f)*
safety regulations
 Sicherheitsvorschriften *(f, pl)*
safety regulations, technical technische
 Sicherheitsbestimmungen *(f, pl)*
safety rules
 Sicherheitsbestimmungen *(f, pl)*
safety, industrial Arbeitssicherheit *(f)*,
 Arbeitsschutz *(m)*,
 Betriebssicherheit *(f)*
salary Gehalt *(n)*
sale Verkauf *(m)*, Abverkauf *(m)*,
 Ausverkauf *(m)*, Schlussverkauf *(m)*;
 Veräußerung *(f)*, Abschluss *(m)*,
 Geschäft *(n)*
saleability Absatzfähigkeit *(f)*
sales Absatz *(m)*, Umsatz *(m)*
sales aids Verkaufshilfen *(f, pl)*
sales analysis Absatzanalyse *(f)*,
 Umsatzanalyse *(f)*
sales area Verkaufsgebiet *(n)*
sales argument Verkaufsargument *(n)*
sales campaign Absatzkampagne *(f)*,
 Verkaufsaktion *(f)*
sales chart Absatzdiagramm *(n)*,
 Umsatzdiagramm *(n)*
sales contract Kaufvertrag *(m)*
sales department Verkaufsabteilung *(f)*
sales discount Kundenrabatt *(m)*
sales documentation
 Verkaufsunterlagen *(f, pl)*
sales executive Verkaufsleiter(in) *(m/f)*,
 Verkaufsdirektor(in) *(m/f)*
sales exhibition Verkaufsausstellung *(f)*

sales figures Absatzzahlen *(f, pl)*,
 Umsatzzahlen *(f, pl)*,
 Verkaufszahlen *(f, pl)*
sales force Absatzorganisation *(f)*,
 Außendienst *(m)*, Verkäuferstab *(m)*
sales forecast Absatzprognose *(f)*,
 Umsatzprognose *(f)*,
 Verkaufsprognose *(f)*
sales goal Absatzziel *(n)*
sales increase Absatzsteigerung *(f)*,
 Umsatzsteigerung *(f)*
sales literature Verkaufsprospekt *(m)*,
 Werbematerial *(n)*
sales management Absatzleitung *(f)*
sales manager Vertriebsleiter(in) *(m/f)*,
 Vertriebsdirektor(in) *(m/f)*
sales manual Verkaufshandbuch *(n)*
sales opportunities
 Verkaufsmöglichkeiten *(f, pl)*
sales order Auftrag *(m)*
sales organization
 Verkaufsorganisation *(f)*
sales outlet Verkaufsstelle *(f)*
sales partner Vertriebspartner *(m)*
sales personnel Verkaufspersonal *(n)*
sales pitch Verkaufsargument *(n)*
sales plan Absatzplan *(m)*,
 Umsatzplan *(m)*
sales potential Absatzpotenzial *(n)*
sales promotion Verkaufsförderung *(f)*
sales prospects Absatzchancen *(f, pl)*,
 Verkaufsaussichten *(f, pl)*
sales push
 Verkaufsanstrengungen *(f, pl)*
sales receipt Kassenbeleg *(m)*,
 Verkaufserlös *(m)*
sales record Verkaufserfolg *(m)*
sales representative
 Handelsvertreter(in) *(m/f)*
sales returns Verkaufserlöse *(m, pl)*,
 Retouren *(f, pl)*
sales revenue Umsatzertrag *(m)*,
 Umsatzerlös *(m)*
sales service Kundendienst *(m)*
sales statistics Umsatzstatistik *(f)*

sales talk Verkaufsgespräch *(n)*
sales training Verkaufsschulung *(f)*
sales trend Umsatzentwicklung *(f)*
sales turnover Warenumsatz *(m)*
sales volume Absatz *(m)*, Absatzvolumen *(n)*, Verkaufsvolumen *(n)*
sales, domestic Inlandsabsatz *(m)*
salesman Verkäufer *(m)*
saleswoman Verkäuferin *(f)*
sample Beispiel *(n)*, Probe *(f)*, Stichprobe *(f)*, Auswahl *(f)*, Muster *(n)*
sample kosten, probieren
sample, commercial Warenmuster *(n)*
sample, free Gratisprobe *(f)*
sample, representative repräsentative Stichprobe *(f)*
samples fair Mustermesse *(f)*
sampling Mustersammlung *(f)*, Stichprobenverfahren *(n)*, Kostprobe *(f)*
sand abschmirgeln, schleifen
sand Sand *(m)*
sandpaper abschmirgeln, schleifen
sandpaper Schmirgelpapier *(n)*
sandwich einklemmen
sandwich Sandwich *(n)*
sandwich board Reklametafel *(f)*
sandwich panel Sandwichplatte *(f)*
sanitary sanitär, hygienisch, Gesundheits-
sanitary facilities sanitäre Einrichtungen *(f, pl)*
satellite television Satellitenfernsehen *(n)*
satisfactory zufriedenstellend, befriedigend, ausreichend, annehmbar
satisfy befriedigen, zufriedenstellen, erfüllen, entsprechen, genügen
saturation Sättigung *(f)*
saucepan Kochtopf *(m)*
sausages, hot heiße Würstchen *(n, pl)*
save retten; aufbewahren, aufheben; sparen, einsparen; ersparen; (EDV) abspeichern, sichern
saving Einsparung *(f)*, Ersparnis *(f)*
saw Säge *(f)*

saw sägen
saw blade Sägeblatt *(n)*
saw off absägen
scaffold Gerüst *(n)*
scale Skala *(f)*, Maßstab *(m)*, Maßeinteilung *(f)*, Gradeinteilung *(f)*; Tabelle *(f)*; Messgerät *(n)*, Waagschale *(f)*; Ausmaß *(n)*, Umfang *(m)*
scale down (Maßstab etc.) verkleinern, verringern
scale drawing maßstabsgerechte Zeichnung *(f)*
scale floor plan maßstabsgerechter Grundriss *(m)*
scale model maßstabsgerechtes Modell *(n)*
scale of prices Preisliste *(f)*
scale up aufstocken, erhöhen; (im Maßstab) vergrößern
scale, true to maßstabsgerecht
scarce selten, knapp, spärlich
scarcely kaum, wohl kaum, schwerlich
scarcity Knappheit *(f)*, Mangel *(m)*
scene Szene *(f)*, Schauplatz *(m)*, Anblick *(m)*
sceptical (GB) skeptisch, zweifelnd
schedule Zeitplan *(m)*, Fahrplan *(m)*, Flugplan *(m)*; Programm *(n)*, Aufstellung *(f)*, Verzeichnis *(n)*
schedule planen, (Zeit) ansetzen, Zeitplan *(m)* aufstellen
schematic schematisch
scheme Schema *(n)*, System *(n)*, Plan *(m)*, Programm *(n)*, Projekt *(n)*; Intrige *(f)*
scheme Pläne *(m, pl)* schmieden; intrigieren
scientific wissenschaftlich, systematisch
scissor platform lift Scherenarbeitsbühne *(f)*
scissors Schere *(f)*
scope Außmaß *(n)*, Reichweite *(f)*, Umfang *(m)*, Spielraum *(m)*, Möglichkeiten *(f, pl)*; Bereich *(m)*; Fassungsvermögen *(n)*

scope of services
Leistungsumfang *(m)*
scour scheueren, schrubben; absuchen, durchsuchen
scouring cloth Scheuerlappen *(m)*
scrap Fetzen *(m)*, Stückchen *(n)*; Altmaterial *(n)*, Altmetall *(n)*, Schrott *(m)*
scrap verschrotten, ausrangieren
scrape kratzen, abkratzen, ankratzen, bürsten, abbürsten, streifen, abschürfen, schaben, scheuern
scratch kratzen, ankratzen, ritzen
scratch Kratzer *(m)*, Schramme *(f)*
scratch-resistant kratzfest
screen abschirmen, abdecken, verdecken, verhüllen, verschleiern; überprüfen; (Film) vorführen; (Radio, TV) senden
screen Bildschirm *(m)*, Leinwand *(f)*; Trennwand *(f)*, Wandschirm *(m)*, Schutz *(m)*
screen line dimension Rastermaß *(n)*
screen print Siebdruck *(m)*
screen printing Siebdruck *(m)*
screen projector, large Großbildprojektor *(m)*
screen reader Bildschirmlesegerät *(n)*
screen test (Film) Probeaufnahme *(f)*
screen, large Großbildschirm *(m)*
screw Schraube *(f)*, Drehung *(f)*
screw schrauben
screw cap Schraubdeckel *(m)*
screw down anschrauben, festschrauben
screw in tight festschrauben
screw off abschrauben
screw on anschrauben, zuschrauben
screw on the outer side Außengewinde *(n)*
screw tap Gewindebohrer *(m)*
screw, adjusting Stellschraube *(f)*
screw, fixing Feststellschraube *(f)*
screwdriver Schraubendreher *(m)*, Schraubenzieher *(m)*

scrub scheuern, schrubben
scrubbing brush Scheuerbürste *(f)*, Schrubber *(m)*
seal Siegel *(n)*, Verschluss *(m)*, Plombe *(f)*, Dichtung *(f)*, Abdichtung *(f)*; Aufkleber *(m)*; Bestätigung *(f)*
seal verschließen, versiegeln, plombieren, abdichten, zukleben; bestätigen
sealing compound Dichtungsmaterial *(n)*
search Suche *(f)*, Nachforschung *(f)*
search suchen, durchsuchen, erforschen
search function (TV, EDV) Suchfunktion *(f)*
season ticket Dauerkarte *(f)*
seat setzen, einpassen
seat Sitz *(m)*, Sitzplatz *(m)*, Sitzgelegenheit *(f)*, Sitzfläche *(f)*; Firmensitz *(m)*
seating Bestuhlung *(f)*, Sitzplätze *(m, pl)*
seating accomodation Sitzgelegenheit *(f)*
seating arrangement Sitzordnung *(f)*
seating plan Sitzplan *(m)*, Bestuhlungsplan *(m)*
secondary zweitrangig, sekundär, untergeordnet
second-class zweitklassig, zweitrangig
second-rate zweitklassig, zweitrangig
secret number Geheimnummer *(f)*
secretary Sekretär(in) *(m/f)*, Schriftführer(in) *(m/f)*
secretary, private Privatsekretär(in) *(m/f)*
section Absatz *(m)*, Abschnitt *(m)*, Teil *(m)*, Paragraf *(m)*; Schnitt *(m)*
section teilen
section, legal Rechtsabteilung *(f)*
section, longitudinal Längsschnitt *(m)*
sectional view Schnittbild *(n)*
sector Sektor *(m)*
secure sicher, gesichert

secure sichern, fest verschließen, schützen, garantieren
security Sicherheit *(f)*, Schutz *(m)*, Bürgschaft *(f)*, Kaution *(f)*, Garantie *(f)*, Wertpapier *(n)*
security check Sicherheitskontrolle *(m)*
security company Bewachungsgesellschaft *(f)*
security guard Wache *(f)*, Wächter(in) *(m/f)*
security risk Sicherheitsrisiko *(n)*
security service Sicherheitsdienst *(m)*, Bewachungsunternehmen *(n)*
security staff Sicherheitspersonal *(n)*, Wachdienst *(m)*
segment Segment *(n)*, Kreisabschnitt *(m)*, Teil *(m)*, Stück *(n)*
segment segmentieren, zerlegen, zerteilen
seize ergreifen, packen, beschlagnahmen
select aussuchen, wählen, auswählen
select exklusiv, ausgesucht, ausgewählt, auserlesen
selection Wahl *(f)*, Auswahl *(f)*, Auslese *(f)*
selection of exhibitions Auswahl *(f)* von Messen
self-adhesive selbstklebend
self-employed selbstständig, freiberuflich, freischaffend
self-employment Selbstständigkeit *(f)*
self-evident selbstverständlich, offensichtlich
self-service Selbstbedienung *(f)*
self-service restaurant Selbstbedienungsrestaurant *(n)*
self-supporting selbsttragend
self-supporting wall freistehende Wand *(f)*
sell absetzen, verkaufen, vertreiben, veräußern, umsetzen
sell out ausverkaufen
sell-by date Mindesthaltbarkeitsdatum *(n)*, Verfallsdatum *(n)*

seller Verkäufer(in) *(m/f)*
selling Absatz *(m)*, Verkauf *(m)*, Vertrieb *(m)*
selling costs Vertriebskosten *(pl)*
selling price Verkaufspreis *(m)*
selling, direct Direktverkauf *(m)*
semi darkness Halbdunkel *(n)*
semi gloss seidenmatt
semiautomatic halbautomatisch
semicircle Halbkreis *(m)*, Halbrund *(n)*
semicircular halbkreisförmig
sense fühlen, spüren
sense Sinn *(m)*, Verstand *(m)*, Vernunft *(f)*, Gefühl *(n)*
sense of responsibility Verantwortungsbewusstsein *(n)*
sensitive empfindlich
sensitive to pressure druckempfindlich
sensitivity to light Lichtempfindlichkeit *(f)*
sensor Sensor *(m)*
separate separat, getrennt, abgetrennt, gesondert, extra, einzeln, verschieden
separate trennen, abtrennen, sich trennen, aufteilen, einteilen, zerteilen
separation Trennung *(f)*, Teilung *(f)*, Aufteilung *(f)*, Einteilung *(f)*, Zerteilung *(f)*
sequence Sequenz *(f)*, Folge *(f)*, Reihenfolge *(f)*
serialized in Serie *(f)* gefertigt
series Serie *(f)*, Reihe *(f)*, Sendereihe *(f)*, Folge *(f)*
serious seriös, ernst, ernsthaft, ernstlich, ernstgemeint, schwer, schlimm
serve dienen, bedienen, servieren; nützen; versorgen
service Service *(m)*, Dienst *(m)*, Dienstleistung *(f)*, Bedienung *(f)*; Wartung *(f)*, Inspektion *(f)*; Zustellung *(f)*
service (Auto etc.) warten
service booklet Servicebroschüre *(n)*
service charge Bedienungsgeld *(m)*, Bearbeitungsgebühr *(f)*

service connections technische Anschlüsse *(m, pl)*
service contract Dienstleistungsvertrag *(m)*
service engineer Kundendienstmechaniker(in) *(m/f)*
service included Bedienung *(f)* inbegriffen
service industries Dienstleistungsgewerbe *(n)*
service not included Bedienung *(f)* nicht inbegriffen
service provider Dienstleister *(m)*
service staff Bedienungspersonal *(n)*
service, fault-clearing Stördienst *(m)*
services Serviceleistungen *(f, pl)*
services for exhibitors Ausstellerservice *(m)*
services, technical technische Dienstleistungen *(f, pl)*
session, final Schlusssitzung *(f)*
set Bühnenbild *(n)*; Fernsehgerät *(n)*, Rundfunkgerät *(n)*; (Werkzeug etc.) Satz *(m)*, Paar *(n)*, Garnitur *(f)*, Reihe *(f)*, Serie *(f)*, Menge *(f)*
set festgesetzt, festgelegt, bereit, fertig; starr
set setzen, stellen, legen, einstellen; (Termin) festsetzen
set back behindern, verzögern, zurücksetzen, zurückwerfen
set down (Fahrgast) absetzen; (Sachen) absetzen, abstellen
set going in Gang *(m)* setzen
set square (GB) Zeichendreieck *(n)*
set up aufbauen, aufstellen, errichten, einrichten, arrangieren; gründen
set upright aufrichten
setback Rückschlag *(m)*
setting Schauplatz *(m)*, Umgebung *(f)*; technische Einstellung *(f)*
setting up, start of Aufbaubeginn *(m)*
setting-up personnel Aufbaupersonal *(n)*

setting-up staff Aufbaupersonal *(n)*, Aufbaustab *(m)*
setting-up ticket Aufbaukarte *(f)*
setting, general Rahmenbedingungen *(f, pl)*
settle aushandeln, ausmachen, regeln, klären, regulieren, festlegen, vereinbaren, sich einigen, entscheiden; schlichten, beilegen, beruhigen, sich beruhigen
settle an account Rechnung *(f)* bezahlen
settlement Abrechnung *(f)*, Zahlung *(f)*, Bezahlung *(f)*, Abfindung *(f)*; Regelung *(f)*, Regulierung *(f)*, Entscheidung *(f)*, Übereinkunft *(f)*; Schlichtung *(f)*, Klärung *(f)*, Beilegung *(f)*
settlement date Fälligkeitsdatum *(n)*
settlement day Abrechnungstag *(m)*
settlement of accounts Abrechnung *(f)*
sewage Abwasser *(n)*
sewage disposal Abwasserentsorgung *(f)*
sewerage Abwasserleitung *(f)*, Kanalisation *(f)*
sewing kit Nähzeug *(n)*
shade abschirmen
shade Schatten *(m)*, Schattierung *(f)*, Farbton *(m)*; Schild *(m)*; Lampenschirm *(m)*; Jalousie *(f)*, Markise *(f)*
shadow Schatten *(m)*
shadowy schattig, dunkel, schemenhaft, geheimnisvoll
shake schütteln, wackeln
shaker Shaker *(m)*, Mixbecher *(m)*
shape Form *(f)*, Gestalt *(f)*, Modell *(n)*, Muster *(n)*; Verfassung *(f)*, Zustand *(m)*
shape formen, gestalten, bilden, bearbeiten, entwickeln, prägen
shapeless formlos, gestaltlos
share Teil *(m)*, Anteil *(m)*, Geschäftsanteil *(m)*, Beteiligung *(f)*, Beitrag *(m)*
share teilen, sich teilen
share of the market Marktanteil *(m)*

sharing of costs Kostenbeteiligung *(f)*
sharp scharf, spitz; gescheit; deutlich, heftig; abrupt, unvermittelt, plötzlich
sharp-edged scharfkantig
sheathing Armierung *(m)*, Ummantelung *(f)*, Umhüllung *(f)*, Verkleidung *(f)*, Verschalung *(f)*
sheet Blatt *(n)*, Bogen *(m)*; Platte *(f)*, Scheibe *(f)*
sheet of glass Glasscheibe *(f)*
sheet of writing paper Briefbogen *(m)*
shelf Brett *(n)*, Bord *(n)*, Sims *(n)*, Regal *(n)*
shelf display Regalauslage *(f)*
shelf of glass Regalboden *(m)* aus Glas
shelf of perforated sheet metal Regalboden *(m)* aus Lochblech
shelf of timber Regalboden *(m)* aus Holz
shelf space Regalfläche *(f)*
shelf support Auflagebügel *(m)*, Fachbodenhalter *(m)*
shelf unit Regal *(n)*
shelf, intermediate (Regal) Zwischenboden *(m)*
shell Schale *(f)*, Muschel *(f)*; Rohbau *(m)*, Gemäuer *(n)*, Karosserie *(f)*, Rumpf *(m)*
shell scheme booth Blockstand *(m)*
shell stand Fertigstand *(m)*
shell-type chair upholstered Polsterschalenstuhl *(m)*
shelves Regal *(n)*
shelving Regale *(n, pl)*
shelving system Regalsystem *(f)*
shelving system component Regalsystemteil *(n)*
shift bewegen, sich bewegen, schieben, wegschieben, sich verschieben, verrücken, wegräumen, umschalten, verlegen, sich verlagern
shift Verschiebung *(f)*, Verlagerung *(f)*, Veränderung *(f)*, Wechsel *(m)*; Schicht *(f)*
shift-key (EDV) Umschalttaste *(f)*

shine Schein *(m)*, Glanz *(m)*, Politur *(f)*
shine scheinen, leuchten, funkeln, glänzen, glänzend machen; (Schuhe) putzen
shipment Beförderung *(f)*, Verladen *(n)*, Verladung *(f)*, Ladung *(f)*, Verfrachtung *(f)*, Versand *(m)*, Transport *(m)*, Sendung *(f)*, Verschiffung *(f)*
shipment weight Versandgewicht *(n)*
shipping documents Versandpapiere *(n, pl)*
shock, electric Stromstoß *(m)*
shockproof stoßfest, stoßsicher
shockproof plug Schukostecker *(m)*
shop Laden *(m)*, Geschäft *(n)*, Betrieb *(m)*, Werk *(n)*, Werkstatt *(f)*
shop window decoration Schaufensterdekoration *(f)*
shopfittings Ladeneinrichtung *(f)*
short kurz, kurzfristig, knapp; kurz angebunden, barsch; plötzlich, abrupt; (Wuchs) klein
short circuit Kurzschluss *(m)*
shortage Mangel *(m)*, Knappheit *(f)*
short-dated kurzfristig
shorten kürzen, verringern, sich verringern, vermindern, zusammenstreichen
shorthand Stenografie *(f)*
shorthand dictation Stenogramm *(n)*
short-staffed unterbesetzt
shovel Schaufel *(f)*
shovel schaufeln
show ausstellen, zeigen, zur Schau *(f)* stellen, vorführen, demonstrieren, erkennen lassen, darlegen, erklären, aufweisen, beweisen
show Schau *(f)*, Ausstellung *(f)*, Messe *(f)*, Aufführung *(f)*, Darbietung *(f)*, Vorführung *(f)*, Demonstration *(f)*; Sendung *(f)*
show and information center, special Sonderschau *(f)* mit Informationszentrum

show carrier Messespediteur *(m)*
show conditions Veranstaltungsbedingungen *(f, pl)*
show conditions, general allgemeine Veranstaltungsbedingungen *(f, pl)*
show duration Messedauer *(f)*
show forwarder Messespediteur *(m)*
show homepage Messehomepage *(f)*
show hostess Messehostess *(f)*
show impact and status Bedeutung *(f)* von Messen
show information system Ausstellungsinformationssystem *(n)*
show organizer Ausstellungsveranstalter *(m)*
show participation Ausstellungsbeteiligung *(f)*
show participation goals Ziele *(n)* der Ausstellungsbeteiligung
show participation sponsoring Förderung *(f)* von Messebeteiligungen
show participation targets Ziele *(n)* der Ausstellungsbeteiligung
show radio Messeradio *(n)*
show report Messebericht *(m)*
show rescheduling Messeturnusänderung *(f)*
show review Messerückblick *(m)*
show room Ausstellungsraum *(m)*
show schedule Veranstaltungsprogramm *(n)*, Veranstaltungszeitplan *(m)*
show site Messegelände *(n)*
show transparency Messetransparenz *(f)*
show, commercial Handelsmesse *(f)*
show, special Sonderschau *(f)*
show, special-interest Fachausstellung *(f)*, Fachmesse *(f)*
show, supraregional überregionale Messe *(f)*
show, virtual virtuelle Show *(f)*, virtuelle Schau *(f)*, virtuelle Vorführung *(f)*, virtuelle Messe *(f)*

showcase Präsentationsmöbel *(f)*, Vitrine *(f)*, Schauvitrine *(f)*, Schaukasten *(m)*
shower Schauer *(m)*; Fülle *(f)*, Schwall *(m)*; Dusche *(f)*
shower nass spritzen, überschütten; duschen
shrink schrumpfen, einlaufen, abnehmen, einschrumpfen lassen, nachlassen; zurückschrecken
shrink wrapping Schrumpfpackung *(f)*
shut geschlossen
shut schließen, zuschließen, zumachen, verriegeln, versperren, geschlossen werden
shut away einschließen, wegschließen
shut in einschließen, einsperren
shut off ausschließen, ausschalten, abschalten, abstellen, zudrehen
shut up verschließen, zuschließen; den Mund *(m)* halten
shutdown Stilllegung *(f)*
shutter release (Kamera) Auslöser *(m)*
shuttle pendeln, hin und her befördern
shuttle Pendelverkehr *(m)*
shuttle bus Pendelbus *(m)*
shuttle service Pendelverkehr *(m)*, Zubringerdienst *(m)*
sickness Krankheit *(f)*, Übelkeit *(f)*
side Seite *(f)*, Rand *(m)*, Wand *(f)*; Meinung *(f)*, Standpunkt *(m)*; Partei *(f)*, Mannschaft *(f)*
side neben, Neben-, Seiten-
side by side nebeneinander
side effect Nebeneffekt *(m)*
side entrance Seiteneingang *(m)*, Nebeneingang *(m)*
side exit Nebenausgang *(m)*, Seitenausgang *(m)*
side view Seitenansicht *(f)*
side wall Seitenwand *(f)*
sideward seitlich, seitwärts
sideways seitlich, seitwärts
sight screen Sichtschutz *(m)*

sign Zeichen *(n)*, Anzeichen *(n)*, Vorzeichen *(n)*, Schild *(n)*, Hinweisschild *(n)*, Wegweiser *(m)*, Symbol *(n)*
sign unterschreiben, unterzeichnen, sich eintragen, signieren
sign off Schluss *(m)* machen; (EDV) sich abmelden
signal Signal *(n)*, Zeichen *(n)*
signal Zeichen *(n)* geben, signalisieren
signal-to-noise ratio Signal-Rauschabstand *(m)*
signatory Unterzeichner(in) *(m/f)*
signature Signatur *(f)*, Unterschrift *(f)*, Unterzeichnung *(f)*; (Radio, TV) Erkennungsmelodie *(f)*
signature, authorized rechtsverbindliche Unterschrift *(f)*
signature, legally binding rechtsverbindliche Unterschrift *(f)*
significant bedeutend, bedeutsam, wichtig, vielsagend, bezeichnend
signpost ausschildern, beschildern
signpost Wegweiser *(m)*
silence Ruhe *(f)*, Stille *(f)*, Schweigen *(n)*
silence zum Schweigen *(n)* bringen
silent ruhig, still, schweigsam
silk screen printing Siebdruck *(m)*
similar ähnlich
simple simpel, einfach, leicht, unkompliziert, schlicht, natürlich, rein; einfältig; naiv
simplification Vereinfachung *(f)*
simplify vereinfachen
simultaneous gleichzeitig, Simultan-
single-storey (GB) eingeschossig
single-story (US) eingeschossig
sink sinken, versinken, sich senken, untergehen, nachlassen, schwächer werden, zurückgehen, fallen
sink Spülbecken *(n)*, Spüle *(f)*, Waschbecken *(n)*
sink unit Spüle *(f)*, Spültisch *(m)*
siphon ausheben, entleeren
siphon Siphon *(m)*, Saugheber *(m)*

site Lage *(f)*, Gelände *(n)*, Platz *(m)*, Ort *(m)*, Standort *(m)*, Stelle *(f)*, Stätte *(f)*, Sitz *(m)*; Baustelle *(f)*
site platzieren, legen
site access Zugang *(m)* zum Gelände, Zufahrt *(f)* zum Gelände
site advertising Werbung *(f)* im Messegelände
site catering Messegastronomie *(f)*
site depot Messelager *(n)*
site inspection Ortsbesichtigung *(f)*
site map Geländekarte *(f)*, Geländeplan *(m)*
site plan Geländeplan *(m)*, Lageplan *(m)*
site server Messeserver *(m)*
site traffic Verkehr *(m)* im Messegelände
site vacation deadline letzter Termin *(m)* zum Verlassen des Messegeländes
site warehouse Messelager *(n)*, Messelagerhaus *(n)*
size Größe *(f)*, Umfang *(m)*, Ausmaß *(n)*
size nach Größe *(f)* ordnen
size of cabin Kabinengröße *(f)*
size, large Großformat *(n)*
skeleton agreement Rahmenabkommen *(n)*
skeptical (US) skeptisch, zweifelnd
sketch Skizze *(f)*, Entwurf *(m)*
sketch skizzieren, entwerfen, umreißen
sketch in einzeichnen
sketch out grob skizzieren
sketchy skizzenhaft, flüchtig, oberflächlich
skirting board Scheuerleiste *(f)*, Sockelblende *(f)*
skirting component Sockelelement *(n)*
slant abschrägen, schräg stellen, kippen, sich neigen
slant Schräge *(f)*, Neigung *(f)*
slat Latte *(f)*, Leiste *(f)*, Lamelle *(f)*
slat profile Lamellenprofil *(n)*

sleeping accomodation
Schlafgelegenheit *(f)*
sleeve Muffe *(f)*, Manschette *(f)*,
Buchse *(f)*, Hülle *(f)*, Hülse *(f)*
slide Diapositiv *(n)*; Rutsche *(f)*
slide gleiten, rutschen, schieben
slide frame Diarahmen *(m)*
slide lecture Lichtbildvortrag *(m)*
slide presentation
Lichtbildvorführung *(f)*
slide projection Diaprojektion *(f)*
slide projector Diaprojektor *(m)*
slide projector, high-power
Hochleistungsdiaprojektor *(m)*
slide show Diaschau *(f)*,
Diavorführung *(f)*
sliding door Schiebetür *(f)*
slip Abschnitt *(m)*, Beleg *(m)*, Zettel *(m)*;
Fehler *(m)*, Irrtum *(m)*, Versehen *(n)*,
Versprechen *(n)*, Unglücksfall *(m)*
slip fallen, rutschen, ausrutschen,
gleiten, schlüpfen, schieben,
nachlassen; übersehen, sich vertun;
verpassen
slip of paper Zettel *(m)*
slipcase Schuber *(m)*
slip-proof rutschfest
slip-proof security
Rutschsicherung *(f)*
slogan Slogan *(m)*, Werbespruch *(m)*,
Schlagwort *(n)*
slope abfallen, neigen, sich neigen
slope Gefälle *(n)*, Neigung *(f)*,
Schräge *(f)*, Hang *(m)*
sloping abfallend, schräg, geneigt
sloping shelf (Regal) Schrägboden *(m)*
sloppiness Nachlässigkeit *(f)*
sloppy nachlässig
slot Kerbe *(f)*, Schlitz *(m)*,
Automateneinwurf *(m)*
slot in einfügen, einblenden,
unterbringen
slotted profile Schlitzprofil *(n)*,
Lochschiene *(f)*
slotted tube Schlitzstab *(m)*

**small and medium-sized enterprises
(SMEs)** Mittelstand *(m)*
small change Kleingeld *(n)*,
Wechselgeld *(n)*
small coin Kleingeld *(n)*
small handicrafts fair
Handwerksmesse *(f)*,
Gewerbemesse *(f)*
small industries fair
Handwerksmesse *(f)*
small print das Kleingedruckte *(n)*
small talk Geplauder *(n)*,
Konversation *(f)*
smart smart, flott, schnell, fix, klug,
schlau; vornehm, gepflegt, schick
smell Geruch *(m)*, Gestank *(m)*
smell riechen, stinken
smoke qualmen, rauchen
smoke Qualm *(m)*, Rauch *(m)*
smoke alarm Rauchmelder *(m)*
smoke outlet Rauchabzug *(m)*
smoke, formation of
Rauchentwicklung *(f)*
smoking ban Rauchverbot *(n)*
smooth eben, glatt, weich; ruhig,
reibungslos, flüssig; gepflegt,
geschliffen
smooth glätten, sich glätten,
besänftigen, sich beruhigen
snack Snack *(m)*, Imbiss *(m)*
snack bar Snackbar *(f)*, Imbissstube *(f)*,
Schnellgaststätte *(f)*
snapshot Schnappschuss *(m)*
snip Schnäppchen *(n)*, Schnipsel *(m)*
snow-white schneeweiß
sociable gesellig, kontaktfreudig,
umgänglich
social sozial, gesellig, umgänglich,
gesellschaftlich, Gesellschaft-, Sozial-
society Gesellschaft *(f)*, Verein *(m)*,
Vereinigung *(f)*, Verband *(m)*
socket Sockel *(m)*, Steckdose *(f)*,
Fassung *(f)*
socket bar Steckdosenleiste *(f)*
socket wrench Steckschlüssel *(m)*

soda water Selterswasser *(n)*
soft drink alkoholfreies Getränk *(n)*
soft-focus lens (Kamera) Weichzeichner *(m)*
software Software *(f)*
solar cell Solarzelle *(f)*
solar energy Solarenergie *(f)*
solar technology Solartechnik *(f)*
solder löten
solder Lötzinn *(n)*
soldering iron Lötkolben *(m)*
solid fest, stabil, dauerhaft; massiv, gewichtig; haltbar; stichhaltig, triftig; reell; verlässlich; gediegen; einmütig, geschlossen
solidity Haltbarkeit *(f)*, Festigkeit *(f)*, Stabilität *(f)*, Stichhaltigkeit *(f)*, Zuverlässigkeit *(f)*; Kreditfähigkeit *(f)*
solo Solo-, allein
solo entertainer Alleinunterhalter(in) *(m/f)*
solution Lösung *(f)*, Auflösung *(f)*, Klärung *(f)*
solution, individual individuelle Lösung *(f)*
solution, temporary Zwischenlösung *(f)*
solvency Solvenz *(f)*, Liquidität *(f)*, Zahlungsfähigkeit *(f)*
solvent Lösungsmittel *(n)*
solvent solvent, liquide, zahlungsfähig
sort Sorte *(f)*, Art *(f)*, Marke *(f)*, Gattung *(f)*, Güte *(f)*, Qualität *(f)*; Charakter *(m)*
sort sortieren
sound ertönen, klingen, erklingen, sich anhören
sound Sound *(m)*, Geräusch *(n)*, Klang *(m)*, Ton *(m)*, Schall *(m)*
sound absorbing schallschluckend
sound carrier Tonträger *(m)*
sound column Tonsäule *(f)*
sound deadening schalldämpfend
sound engineer Toningenieur(in) *(m/f)*, Tontechniker(in) *(m/f)*
sound head Tonkopf *(m)*
sound insulation Schalldämmung *(f)*
sound recording Tonaufnahme *(f)*
sound technician Tontechniker(in) *(m/f)*
sound track Tonspur *(f)*, Filmmusik *(f)*, Soundtrack *(m)*
sound volume Lautstärke *(f)*
source Ursprung *(m)*, Ursache *(f)*, Quelle *(f)*, Wurzel *(f)*
source of danger Gefahrenherd *(m)*
source of information Informationsquelle *(f)*
source of light Lichtquelle *(f)*
source of power Stromquelle *(f)*
space Raum *(m)*, Platz *(m)*, Stelle *(f)*; Abstand *(m)*, Lücke *(f)*, Zwischenraum *(m)*; Zeitraum *(m)*, Frist *(f)*
space verteilen, in Abständen *(m, pl)* anordnen
space assignment Platzzuteilung *(f)*
space assignment plan Platzzuteilungsplan *(m)*, Platzbelegungsplan *(m)*
space confirmation Platzbestätigung *(f)*
space hire (GB) Platzmiete *(f)*
space rate Platzpreis *(m)*, Platztarif *(m)*
space rate, basic Grundtarif *(m)* für den Standplatz
space rent (US) Platzmiete *(f)*
space rent (US), basic Grundmiete *(m)* für den Standplatz
space request Platzwunsch *(m)*
space swap Platztausch *(m)*
space-saving platzsparend, raumsparend
spacious geräumig
span Abstand *(m)*, Spanne *(f)*
span überspannen, sich erstrecken über
span length Spannweite *(f)*
spanner Schraubenschlüssel *(m)*
spar Rundholz *(n)*
spare entbehren, übrig haben, verzichten auf; verschonen
spare Ersatz-; übrig, überzählig
spare part Ersatzteil *(n)*

sparkle glitzern, funkeln; perlen, schäumen
sparkling wine Sekt *(m)*
spastic Rollstuhlfahrer(in) *(m/f)*
spatial räumlich
spatula Spachtel *(m)*, Spatel *(m)*
speach, make a Rede *(f)* halten
speaker Sprecher(in) *(m/f)*, Redner(in) *(m/f)*, Vorsitzende(r) *(f/m)*, Lautsprecher *(m)*
speaker, spherical Kugellautsprecher *(m)*
speakers'desk Rednerpult *(n)*
special Sonderdruck *(m)*, Sonderausgabe *(f)*
special speziell, Spezial-, Sonder-, besonders, außergewöhnlich, außerordentlich
specialist Spezialist(in) *(m/f)*, Fachmann *(m)*, Fachfrau *(f)*, Experte *(m)*, Expertin *(f)*
specialist dictionary Fachwörterbuch *(n)*
specialist report Sachverständigengutachten *(n)*
speciality (GB) Spezialität *(f)*
speciality contractor, licensed konzessionierte Fachfirma *(f)*
specialization Spezialisierung *(f)*
specialize spezialisieren, sich spezialisieren
specialty (US) Spezialität *(f)*
specific spezifisch, bestimmt, genau, charakteristisch, typisch, besonders
specification Spezifikation *(f)*, genaue Angabe *(f)*, genaue Beschreibung *(f)*, Baubeschreibung *(f)*; Bedingung *(f)*, Bestimmung *(f)*
specify spezifizieren, genau angeben, aufführen, beschreiben, festlegen
specimen Exemplar *(n)*, Muster *(n)*, Probe *(f)*
specimen copy Belegexemplar *(n)*
specimen page Probeseite *(f)*
spectator Zuschauer(in) *(m/f)*

spectrum Spektrum *(n)*
speech Sprache *(f)*, Ansprache *(f)*, Rede *(f)*
speed Geschwindigkeit *(f)*, Schnelligkeit *(f)*, Tempo *(n)*, Drehzahl *(f)*, Gang *(m)*; Filmempfindlichkeit *(f)*
speed rasch bringen; beschleunigen, rasen, zu schnell fahren
speed limit Tempolimit *(n)*, Geschwindigkeitsbeschränkung *(f)*
spherical kugelförmig
spill basin Auffangbehälter *(m)*
spin-off Nebenprodukt *(n)*
spiral Spirale *(f)*
spiral spiralförmig
spiral staircase Spindeltreppe *(f)*, Wendeltreppe *(f)*
spirit level Wasserwaage *(f)*
spirits Spirituosen *(f, pl)*
splash Spritzen *(n)*, Spritzer *(m)*, Farbfleck *(m)*
splash spritzen, bespritzen; klatschen, platschen, tropfen
splendid großartig, prachtvoll, prächtig, glanzvoll, ausgezeichnet
splinter spalten, sich spalten, zerhacken, zersplittern
splinter Span *(m)*, Splitter *(m)*
split screen Bildsplitwand *(f)*
spokesman Sprecher *(m)*, Pressesprecher *(m)*, Wortführer *(m)*
spokeswoman Sprecherin *(f)*, Pressesprecherin *(f)*, Wortführerin *(f)*
sponsor sponsern, fördern, unterstützen; Patenschaft *(f)* übernehmen
sponsor Sponsor(in) *(m/f)*, Förderer *(m)*, Förderin *(f)*, Geldgeber(in) *(m/f)*; Pate *(m)*, Patin *(f)*
sponsorship Sponsoring *(n)*, Sponsern *(n)*, Förderung *(f)*
spontaneous spontan, impulsiv
spoon Löffel *(m)*
sporadic sporadisch, gelegentlich
sports coat Sakko *(n)*

sports jacket Sakko *(n)*
spot ausmachen, erkennen, entdecken, sehen
spot Fleck *(m)*, Punkt *(m)*, Stelle *(f)*, Ort *(m)*, Platz *(m)*; Werbespot *(m)*, Werbekurzfilm *(m)*; Scheinwerfer *(m)*
spot load Punktlast *(f)*
spot mounted on arm Auslegestrahler *(m)*
spot, commercial Werbespot *(m)*, Werbekurzfilm *(m)*
spot, high Höhepunkt *(m)*
spotlight anstrahlen, aufmerksam machen
spotlight Punktstrahler *(m)*, Strahler *(m)*, Scheinwerfer *(m)*
spray sprühen, besprühen, spritzen, spritzlackieren, zerstäuben
spray Spray *(n)*, Besprühen *(n)*, Sprühnebel *(m)*, Gischt *(f)*
spray can Sprühdose *(f)*
spray gun Spritzpistole *(f)*
spray-paint spritzlackieren
spread ausbreiten, sich ausbreiten, erstrecken, sich erstrecken, verbreiten, verteilen, streuen; (Brot) bestreichen
spread Ausbreitung *(f)*, Ausdehnung *(f)*, Spanne *(f)*, Spannweite *(f)*, Spektrum *(n)*, Streuung *(f)*, Verteilung *(f)*; Doppelseite *(f)*
spring folder Schnellhefter *(m)*
spring-tighting device Federspannvorrichtung *(f)*
sprinkler system Sprinkleranlage *(f)*
square Quadrat *(n)*, Viereck *(n)*, Rechteck *(n)*, Karo *(n)*; Quadratzahl *(f)*; Zeichendreieck *(n)*, Winkelmaß *(n)*; Platz *(m)*
square quadratisch, viereckig, vierkantig, eckig, rechtwinklig; fair, gerecht, ordentlich, ehrlich
square quadratisch machen, rechtwinklig machen; (Schulden) begleichen, (Konto) ausgleichen; übereinstimmen

square measure Flächenmaß *(n)*
square meter (US) Quadratmeter *(m)*
square meter space rate (US) Quadratmeterpreis *(m)*
square metre (GB) Quadratmeter *(m)*
square metre space rate (GB) Quadratmeterpreis *(m)*
square steel bar Vierkanteisen *(n)*
squared paper Millimeterpapier *(n)*
squared timber Kantholz *(n)*
square-headed vierkantig
squeak quietschen
squeeze drücken, ausdrücken, auspressen, quetschen, ausquetschen; sich quetschen, sich zwängen
squeeze Drücken *(n)*, Pressen *(n)*; Gedränge *(n)*
squeezer Presse *(f)*
squirt Spritzer *(m)*
squirt spritzen, bespritzen
stability Stabilität *(f)*, Beständigkeit *(f)*, Dauerhaftigkeit *(f)*, Ausgeglichenheit *(f)*
stable stabil, fest, beständig, dauerhaft, sicher
stack Haufen *(m)*, Stapel *(m)*, Stoß *(m)*
stack stapeln, sich stapeln lassen
stackable stapelbar
staff Mitarbeiter *(m, pl)*, Mitarbeiterstab *(m)*, Personal *(n)*, Belegschaft *(f)*, Kollegium *(n)*, Stab *(m)*; Stütze *(f)*, Stock *(m)*
staff Personal *(n)* einstellen, Stelle *(f)* besetzen
staff agency Personalvermittlung *(f)*
staff briefing Personaleinweisung *(f)*
staff clothing (Standmitarbeiter) Einkleidung *(f)*
staff fitting (Standmitarbeiter) Einkleidung *(f)*
staff function Stabsfunktion *(f)*
staff outfitting (Standmitarbeiter) Einkleidung *(f)*
staff recruitment, temporary Zeitpersonalvermittlung *(f)*
staff requirements Personalbedarf *(m)*

staff resourcing
Personalbeschaffung *(f)*
staff shortage Personalengpass *(m)*
staff training Mitarbeiterschulung *(f)*, Personalschulung *(f)*
staff, own eigenes Personal *(n)*
staff, permanent Stammpersonal *(n)*
staff, temporary Zeitpersonal *(n)*, Zeitarbeitskräfte *(f, pl)*
stage aufführen, arrangieren, inszenieren, veranstalten
stage Stadium *(n)*, Etappe *(f)*, Phase *(f)*, Stufe *(f)*, Bühne *(f)*, Podium *(n)*
stage floodlight Bühnenleuchte *(f)*
stage lighting Bühnenbeleuchtung *(f)*
stage of development Entwicklungsstadium *(n)*
stage set Bühnenbild *(n)*
staging area Aktionszone *(f)*
stagnate stagnieren
stagnation Stagnation *(f)*
stainless steel Edelstahl *(m)*
stair Stufe *(f)*
stair rail Treppengeländer *(n)*
stair stringe Treppenwange *(f)*
staircase Treppe *(f)*, Treppenhaus *(n)*
staircase gradient Treppenneigung *(f)*
stairs Treppe *(f)*
stairs, form of Treppenform *(f)*
stairshape stufenförmig
stairway Treppenaufgang *(m)*
stall Verkaufsstand *(m)*, Messestand *(m)*
stall Zeit *(m)* schinden, hinauszögern; Motor *(m)* abwürgen
stamp Briefmarke *(f)*, Postwertzeichen *(n)*, Stempelmarke *(f)*, Stempel *(m)*, Aufkleber *(m)*
stamp frankieren, markieren, prägen, stempeln, abstempeln; stampfen, trampeln
stand Stand *(m)*, Messestand *(m)*
stand administration Standleitung *(f)*
stand allocation Standzuteilung *(f)*
stand ambience Standatmosphäre *(f)*

stand appearance, general Gesamterscheinungsbild *(n)* des Stands
stand approval Standgenehmigung *(f)*
stand area Standfläche *(f)*
stand area, required gewünschte Standfläche *(f)*
stand areas, closed-in geschlossene Standbereiche *(m)*
stand assembly Standmontage *(f)*
stand assembly instructions Standbaurichtlinien *(f, pl)*
stand assembly period Standaufbauzeit *(f)*
stand blueprint Standentwurf *(m)*
stand boundary Standgrenze *(f)*
stand building, individual individueller Messestandbau *(m)*
stand cabin Standkabine *(f)*
stand call report Standbesuchsbericht *(m)*
stand captain Standleiter(in) *(m/f)*
stand catering Standcatering *(n)*, Standversorgung *(f)*
stand ceiling Standdecke *(f)*
stand cleaning Standreinigung *(f)*
stand cleaning, daily tägliche Standreinigung *(f)*
stand components Standbauteile *(n, pl)*
stand components waste disposal Entsorgung *(f)* von Standbauteilen
stand concept Standkonzept *(n)*
stand confirmation Standbestätigung *(f)*
stand construction Standbau *(m)*, Standaufbau *(m)*, Standkonstruktion *(f)*
stand construction approval Standbaugenehmigung *(f)*
stand construction elements Standbauelemente *(n, pl)*
stand construction expense Standbaukosten *(pl)*
stand construction inspection Standbauabnahme *(f)*
stand construction instructions Standbaurichtlinien *(f, pl)*

stand construction materials
Standbaumaterialien *(n, pl)*
stand construction period
Standaufbauzeit *(f)*
stand construction regulations
Standbauvorschriften *(f, pl)*
stand construction symbols
Symbole *(n, pl)* im Standbau
stand construction system
Standbausystem *(n)*,
Messebausystem *(n)*
stand construction waste
Standbaureststoffe *(m, pl)*
stand constructions
Standaufbauten *(pl)*
stand constructor Standerbauer *(m)*
stand contractor
Standbauunternehmer *(m)*,
Messebauunternehmer *(m)*,
Messebaulieferant *(m)*
stand costs Standkosten *(pl)*
stand covering Standüberdachung *(f)*
stand cubicle Standkoje *(f)*
stand depth Standtiefe *(f)*
stand design Standdesign *(n)*,
Standskizze *(f)*, Standentwurf *(m)*,
Sandzeichnung *(f)*, Standplan *(m)*
stand design, high-image
repräsentative Standgestaltung *(m)*
stand dimensions Standgröße *(f)*,
Standabmessungen *(f, pl)*
stand dismantling time
Standabbauzeit *(f)*
stand dividing wall
Standtrennwand *(f)*
stand draft Standentwurf *(m)*,
Standskizze *(f)*
stand drawing Standzeichnung *(f)*
stand duty roster Standdienstplan *(m)*
stand equipment Standausstattung *(f)*,
Standeinrichtung *(f)*
stand equipment, additional
zusätzliche Standausstattung *(f)*
stand erection Standaufbau *(m)*,
Standerrichtung *(f)*, Standmontage *(f)*

stand fittings Standausstattung *(f)*,
Standeinrichtung *(f)*
stand furnishing Standausstattung *(f)*,
Standeinrichtung *(f)*
stand furnishings, additional
zusätzliche Standeinrichtung *(f)*,
zusätzliches Standmobiliar *(n)*
stand height Standhöhe *(f)*
stand help Standhilfe *(f)*
stand hospitality Standbewirtung *(f)*
stand installation Standaufbau *(m)*,
Standerrichtung *(f)*
stand insurance Standversicherung *(f)*
stand layout Standlayout *(n)*,
Standplan *(m)*, Standgrundriss *(m)*,
Standgestaltung *(f)*
stand layout plan Standplan *(m)*,
Standgrundrissplan *(m)*,
Standgestaltungsplan *(m)*
stand lettering Standbeschriftung *(f)*
stand limits Standgrenzen *(f, pl)*
stand location Standlage *(f)*
stand location, change of
Änderung *(m)* der Standplazierung,
Standplatzwechsel *(m)*
stand location, requirements for
Wünsche *(m, pl)* für die Standzuteilung
stand management Standleitung *(f)*
stand number Standnummer *(f)*
stand organization Standorganisation
(f), Standgliederung *(f)*
stand outfitting Standausstattung *(f)*
stand package, basic
Basisausstattung *(f)*
stand partition wall
Standbegrenzungswand *(f)*
stand personnel Standpersonal *(n)*,
Standmitarbeiter *(m, pl)*
stand photo Standaufnahme *(f)*
stand planning Standplanung *(f)*
stand reception desk
Standempfang *(m)*, Standrezeption *(f)*
stand reception point
Standempfang *(m)*, Standrezeption *(f)*
stand rent Standmiete *(f)*

stand rental charge Standmietpreis *(m)*
stand rental contract Standmietvertrag *(m)*
stand rental expenses Standmietkosten *(pl)*
stand rental fee Standmietpreis *(m)*
stand roof Standdach *(n)*, Standdecke *(f)*
stand roofing Standüberdachung *(f)*
stand running costs Standbetriebskosten *(pl)*
stand safety Standsicherheit *(f)*
stand scale model maßstäbliches Standmodell *(n)*
stand security Standsicherheit *(f)*, Standschutz *(m)*
stand security guard Standschutzwache *(f)*
stand security service, special Separatwachdienst *(m)*, Sonderwache *(f)*
stand setting-up period Standaufbauzeit *(f)*
stand setup Standaufbau *(m)*, Standerrichtung *(f)*
stand size Standgröße *(f)*
stand size, determination of Festlegung *(m)* der Standgröße
stand sketch Standskizze *(f)*, Standentwurf *(m)*
stand space Standplatz *(m)*
stand space allocation Standzuteilung *(f)*
stand space assignment Standzuteilung *(f)*
stand space request Standplatzwunsch *(m)*
stand space required gewünschter Standplatz *(m)*
stand space, raw reine Standfläche *(n)*, tatsächlich belegte Fläche *(f)*
stand space, rented (US) vermietete Standfläche *(f)*
stand staff Standpersonal *(n)*, Standmitarbeiter *(m, pl)*

stand staff training Schulung *(f)* des Standpersonals
stand structure, multistoried mehrgeschossiger Standaufbau *(m)*
stand structures Standaufbauten *(pl)*
stand subletting Überlassung *(f)* des Stands an Dritte
stand telephone Standtelefon *(n)*
stand type Standtyp *(m)*, Standart *(f)*
stand use Standnutzung *(f)*
stand view Standansicht *(f)*
stand visit report Standbesuchsbericht *(m)*
stand walkthrough Standeinweisung *(f)*
stand width Standbreite *(f)*
stand working expenses Standbetriebskosten *(pl)*
stand, complete Komplettstand, Komplettmessestand *(m)*, Fertigstand *(m)*
stand, double-decker zweigeschossiger Standbau *(m)*
stand, facing gegenüberliegender Stand *(m)*
stand, in-line Reihenstand *(m)*
stand, neighboring (US) Nachbarstand *(m)*
stand, neighbouring (GB) Nachbarstand *(m)*
stand, rear boundary of rückseitige Standgrenze *(f)*
stand, two-corner Kopfstand *(m)*
standard Norm *(f)*, Maßstab *(m)*, Niveau *(n)*, Standarte *(f)*, Flagge *(f)*
standard normal, Normal-, üblich, durchschnittlich, Durchschnitts-, serienmäßig, Serien-, Standard-
standard connection Standardanschluss *(m)*
standard conversion Normwandlung *(f)*
standard costing Normalkostenrechnung *(f)*
standard design Standardausführung *(f)*

standard equipment
Standardausstattung *(f)*
standard height Normalhöhe *(f)*
standard length Normlänge *(f)*
standard node Normknoten *(m)*
standard size Standardgröße *(f)*
standard unit Normelement *(n)*
standard working hours
Normalarbeitszeit *(f)*
standardization Standardisierung *(f)*,
Normung *(f)*, Vereinheitlichung *(f)*
standardize standardisieren, normen,
vereinheitlichen
standing Ansehen *(n)*, Position *(f)*,
Rang *(m)*, Ruf *(m)*, Stand *(m)*,
Stellung *(f)*
standing stehend, ständig
standing charge Grundgebühr *(f)*
standing place Stehplatz *(m)*
standing reception Stehempfang *(m)*
stands, single-storey (GB)
eingeschossige Standbauten *(pl)*
stands, single-story (US)
eingeschossige Standbauten *(pl)*
stapler Heftmaschine *(f)*, Hefter *(m)*
starting point Ausgangspunkt *(m)*
state darlegen, nennen
state Stand *(m)*, Zustand *(m)*; Rang *(m)*;
Staat *(m)*
statement Erklärung *(f)*, Feststellung *(f)*,
Darstellung *(f)*, Stellungnahme *(f)*,
Angabe *(f)*, Aussage *(f)*; Bilanz *(f)*;
Kontoauszug *(m)*
statement of accounts Abrechnung *(f)*
statement, preliminary einleitende
Erklärung *(f)*
static statisch, konstant
static calculation statische
Berechnung *(f)*
statistical statistisch
statistics Statistik *(f)*,
Statistiken *(f, pl)*
status Status *(m)*, Stellung *(f)*,
Prestige *(n)*
statutes Satzung *(f)*

statutory gesetzlich, rechtskräftig,
bestimmungsgemäß, satzungsgemäß
STD code Vorwahlnummer *(f)*
steady beruhigen, sich beruhigen,
sich festigen
steady fest, beständig,
ununterbrochen, zuverlässig, ruhig
steam Dampf *(m)*, Dunst *(m)*
steam dämpfen, dampfen, dünsten
steel cable Stahlseil *(n)*
steel furniture, tubular
Stahlrohrmöbel *(n, pl)*
steel girder Stahlträger *(m)*
steel loop Stahlbügel *(m)*
steel node Stahlknoten *(m)*
steel sink Edelstahlspüle *(f)*
steel strip Stahlband *(n)*
steel tube Stahlrohr *(n)*, Stahlstab *(m)*
stencil Schablone *(f)*, Matrize *(f)*
stencil mit Schablone *(f)* zeichnen,
auf Matrize *(f)* schreiben
step gehen; abstufen
step Stufe *(f)*, Sprosse *(f)*, Schritt *(m)*,
Abschnitt *(m)*; Maßnahme *(f)*
step aside Platz *(m)* machen
step on betreten
stepladder Trittleiter *(f)*, Stehleiter *(f)*
stereo input Stereoeingang *(m)*
stereo system Stereoanlage *(f)*
stereophonic stereofon
stick kleben, haften bleiben, stechen,
stecken, steckenbleiben, klemmen
stick Stück *(n)*, Stock *(m)*, Stange *(f)*,
Stiehl *(m)*, Stift *(m)*, Streifen *(m)*
stick down ankleben, zukleben
stick on aufkleben
sticker Aufkleber *(m)*,
Aufklebeschildchen *(n)*
stick-on letters
Folienbuchstaben *(m, pl)*
stimulate stimulieren, anregen, reizen,
anspornen
stimulation Stimulation *(f)*,
Anregung *(f)*, Erregung *(f)*, Anreiz *(m)*,
Ansporn *(m)*, Ankurbelung *(f)*

stipulate festsetzen, vorschreiben, auferlegen, verlangen, zur Auflage *(f)* machen, zur Bedingung *(f)* machen, vereinbaren
stipulation Auflage *(f)*, Bedingung *(f)*, Festsetzung *(f)*, Vereinbarung *(f)*
stock Vorrat *(m)*, Bestand *(m)*, Lager *(n)*; Aktie *(f)*, Anteil *(m)*, Anleihe *(f)*, Wertpapier *(n)*, Aktienkapital *(n)*; Stamm *(m)*, Abstammung *(f)*
stock vorrätig haben, (Waren) führen, (Lager etc.) füllen
stock in hand verfügbare Ware *(f)*, Warenbestand *(m)*
stock inventory Inventar *(n)*, Bestandsaufnahme *(f)*
stock of goods Warenbestand *(m)*
stock of materials Materiallager *(n)*
stock on hand verfügbare Ware *(f)*, Warenbestand *(m)*
stock, remaining Restposten *(m)*
stockroom Lager *(n)*, Lagerraum *(m)*
stool Hocker *(m)*, Schemel *(m)*
stop valve, main Hauptabsperrventil *(n)*
stop, intermediate Zwischenaufenthalt *(m)*
stopover Zwischenlandung *(f)*
storage Lager *(n)*, Lagerung *(f)*, Speicher *(m)*, Speicherung *(f)*, Aufbewahrung *(f)*, Einlagerung *(f)*; Lagergeld *(n)*, Lagerkosten *(pl)*
storage area for empties Lagerstelle *(f)* für Leergut
storage battery Akkumulator *(m)*, Akku *(m)*
storage battery screwdriver Akkuschrauber *(m)*
storage charge Lagergebühr *(f)*
storage container Vorratsbehälter *(m)*
storage location Lagerort *(m)*
storage of empties Leergutlagerung *(f)*
storage space Lagerraum *(m)*, Stauraum *(m)*; (EDV) Speicherplatz *(m)*

storage water heater Heißwasserspeicher *(m)*
storage, intermediate Zwischenlagerung *(f)*
store Lager *(n)*, Lagerhalle *(f)*, Lagerhaus *(n)*, Lagerraum *(m)*, Warenhaus *(n)*; Vorrat *(m)*, Bestände *(m, pl)*
store lagern, einlagern, aufbewahren; (EDV) abspeichern
store (US) Laden *(m)*, Geschäft *(n)*
storehouse Lager *(n)*, Depot *(n)*, Lagergebäude *(n)*, Lagerhaus *(n)*
storeroom Lager *(n)*, Lagerraum *(m)*, Vorratsraum *(m)*
storey (GB) Stockwerk *(n)*, Etage *(f)*
story (US) Stockwerk *(n)*, Etage *(f)*
storyboard Storyboard *(n)*
straight gerade, geradlinig, direkt; glatt; klar, offen, ehrlich; sofort
strainer Filter *(m)*, Sieb *(n)*
strap festschnallen, bandagieren
strap Gurt *(m)*, Riemen *(m)*, Haltegriff *(m)*, Schlaufe *(f)*, Träger *(m)*
strategic strategisch, taktisch, wichtig
strategy Strategie *(f)*, Taktik *(f)*
streamline rationalisieren, modernisieren, straffen
strength Kraft *(f)*, Kräfte *(f, pl)*, Stärke *(f)*, Stabilität *(f)*, Festigkeit *(f)*; Überzeugungskraft *(f)*
strengthen kräftigen, festigen, stärken, verstärken, stärker werden, sich verstärken
stress Stress *(m)*, Beanspruchung *(f)*, Belastung *(f)*; Betonung *(f)*, Akzent *(m)*
stretch ausbreiten, dehnen, sich dehnen, strecken, sich strecken, sich erstrecken, sich hinziehen, spannen, länger werden
stretch Strecken *(n)*, Dehnen *(n)*, Dehnbarkeit *(f)*, Elastizität *(f)*; Strecke *(f)*; Zeitraum *(m)*, Zeitspanne *(f)*

stretcher Trage *(f)*, Tragbahre *(f)*
stringboard Treppenwange *(f)*
strip abkratzen, abreißen, abziehen, abbeizen, ausziehen, demontieren
strip Streifen *(m)*
strip lighting Lichtband *(n)*
stroke Hieb *(m)*, Schlag *(m)*, Stoß *(m)*; Pinselstrich *(m)*
strong stark, kräftig, fest, robust, stabil, mächtig, groß, solide, ausgeprägt; überzeugt, überzeugend
structural integrity, violations of Eingriffe *(m, pl)* in die Bausubstanz
structure, hexagonal sechseckige Konstruktion *(m)*
structure, two-storey (GB) doppelstöckige Bauweise *(f)*, zweigeschossiger Bau *(m)*
structure, two-story (US) doppelstöckige Bauweise *(f)*, zweigeschossiger Bau *(m)*
structure, upper Oberbau *(m)*
structures, non-approved nicht genehmigte Bauten *(m, pl)*
structures, portable fliegende Bauten *(m, pl)*
structures, special Sonderaufbauten *(m, pl)*
strut Strebe *(f)*, Stütze *(f)*
study Studie *(f)*, Studium *(f)*, Untersuchung *(f)*, Lernen *(n)*, Beobachtung *(f)*
study studieren, lernen, erforschen; beobachten
stuffer Reklamebeilage *(f)*, Werbebeilage *(f)*
style entwerfen, gestalten
style Stil *(m)*, Art *(f)*, Ausführung *(f)*, Modell *(n)*
stylish stilvoll, elegant, modisch
subcontractor Subunternehmer *(m)*, Unterlieferant *(m)*
subdistribution (Stromanschluss etc.) Unterverteilung *(f)*
subdivide unterteilen, sich aufteilen

subdivision Unterteilung *(f)*, Unterabteilung *(f)*
subexhibitor Unteraussteller *(m)*
subject Subjekt *(n)*, Anlass *(m)*, Gegenstand *(m)*, Grund *(m)*, Thema *(n)*
subject of conversation Gesprächsthema *(n)*
sublease Untervermietung *(f)*, Unterverpachtung *(f)*
sublease untervermieten, unterverpachten
sublet untervermieten
subletting Untervermietung *(f)*
subordinate Untergebene(r) *(f/m)*
subordinate untergeordnet
subsidiary Tochtergesellschaft *(f)*, Zweigniederlassung *(f)*
subsidiary company Tochtergesellschaft *(f)*
subsidiary corporation Tochtergesellschaft *(f)*
subsidize subventionieren, finanziell unterstützen
subsidy Subvention *(f)*, Zuschuss *(m)*
subsoil Untergrund *(m)*
substance, harmful Schadstoff *(m)*
substancial kräftig, fest, solide; schlüssig, stichhaltig; bedeutend, beträchtlich, ansehnlich, wesentlich
substitute Ersatz *(m)*, Vertreter(in) *(m/f)*, Vertretung *(f)*, Nachahmung *(f)*, Surrogat *(n)*
substitute ersetzen, austauschen, auswechseln
subterranean unterirdisch
subtitle Untertitel *(m)*
subtitle mit Untertiteln *(m, pl)* versehen
suburban railroad (US) S-Bahn *(f)*
suburban railway (GB) S-Bahn *(f)*
suburban train S-Bahn *(f)*
subway Unterführung *(f)*, Untergrundbahn *(f)*
success Erfolg *(m)*
success survey Erfolgskontrolle *(f)*

success with the public Publikumserfolg *(m)*
success, great popular Publikumserfolg *(m)*
success, partial Teilerfolg *(m)*
successful erfolgreich
succession Folge *(f)*, Nachfolge *(f)*, Aufeinanderfolge *(f)*
successive aufeinanderfolgend
successor Nachfolger(in) *(m/f)*, Nachfolgemodell *(n)*
suck saugen
suck off absaugen
suction Sog *(m)*
suction pipe Saugrohr *(n)*
suction pump Saugpumpe *(f)*
sudden schlagartig
sugar substitute Zuckeraustauschstoff *(m)*
suggest anregen, vorschlagen, vorbringen, nahelegen, darauf hindeuten, hinweisen, andeuten
suggestion Anregung *(f)*, Vorschlag *(m)*, Andeutung *(f)*, Vermutung *(f)*, Unterstellung *(f)*, Vorstellung *(f)*, Eindruck *(m)*
suggestive question Suggestivfrage *(f)*
suit Anzug *(m)*, Kostüm *(n)*
suit passen, geeignet sein, gefallen, zufrieden stellen
suitable angemessen, geeignet, passend
sum Summe *(f)*, Betrag *(m)*, Ergebnis *(n)*, Resultat *(n)*
sum up zusammenfassen
sum, flat Pauschalbetrag *(m)*
summary Zusammenfassung *(f)*
Sunday working Sonntagsarbeit *(f)*
Sundays and public holidays Sonn- und Feiertage *(m, pl)*
superficial oberflächlich, scheinbar
superior besser, ausgezeichnet, hervorragend, überragend, ranghöher

superior Vorgesetzte(r) *(f/m)*, Chef(in) *(m/f)*
superstructure Überbau *(m)*, Aufbauten *(pl)*
supervise beaufsichtigen, überwachen
supervision Aufsicht *(f)*, Beaufsichtigung *(f)*, Überwachung *(f)*, Kontrolle *(f)*
supervisor Aufseher(in) *(m/f)*, Aufsichtsperson *(f)*
supper Abendessen *(n)*
supplement Anhang *(m)*, Ergänzung *(f)*, Nachtrag *(m)*, Beilage *(f)*, Aufschlag *(m)*
supplement ergänzen
supplement, special Sonderbeilage *(f)*
supplementary ergänzend, zusätzlich, Zusatz-
supplementary charge Zuschlag *(m)*, Zuzahlung *(f)*, Preisaufschlag *(m)*
supplier Anbieter *(m)*, Lieferant *(m)*
supply liefern, beliefern, bereitstellen, besorgen, versorgen, Bedarf *(m)* befriedigen
supply Lieferung *(f)*, Belieferung *(f)*, Versorgung *(f)*; Angebot *(n)*; Vorrat *(m)*
supply and demand Angebot *(n)* und Nachfrage *(f)*
supply channel Versorgungskanal *(m)*
supply duct Versorgungsrohr *(n)*, Versorgungsleitung *(f)*, Versorgungskanal *(m)*
supply line Versorgungsleitung *(f)*
supply line installation Leitungsinstallation *(f)*, Leitungsverlegung *(f)*
supply network Versorgungsnetz *(n)*
supply pipe Versorgungsrohr *(n)*, Zuflussleitung *(f)*
supply pressure Betriebsdruck *(m)*
supply price Angebotspreis *(m)*, Lieferpreis *(m)*
supply subsequently nachliefern

supply system Versorgungsnetz *(n)*
supply, electrical Elektroversorgung *(f)*
support Hilfestellung *(f)*, Unterstützung *(f)*; Stütze *(f)*, Stützbalken *(m)*, Stützpfeiler *(m)*
support tragen, stützen; unterstützen, fördern; erhärten, untermauern, beweisen
support clamp Stützschelle *(f)*
supporting angle Auflagewinkel *(m)*
supporting beam Stützbalken *(m)*
supporting event Rahmenveranstaltung *(f)*
supporting loop Haltebügel *(m)*
supporting wall Stützmauer *(f)*
supposition Annahme *(f)*, Vermutung *(f)*
surcharge Aufgeld *(n)*, Aufpreis *(n)*, Zuschlag *(m)*, Nachgebühr *(f)*, Strafgebühr *(f)*
sure instinct Fingerspitzengefühl *(n)*
surface Fläche *(f)*, Oberfläche *(f)*
surface finish Oberflächenausführung *(f)*
surface measurement Flächenmaß *(n)*
surplus Überschuss *(m)*, Überhang *(m)*, Mehrbetrag *(m)*, Mehreinnahme *(f)*, Gewinn *(m)*
surplus überschüssig
surround umgeben, umstellen
surroundings Umgebung *(f)*
surveillance Überwachung *(f)*
surveillance camera Überwachungskamera *(f)*
survey betrachten, begutachten, untersuchen; einen Überblick *(m)* geben
survey Überblick *(m)*, Untersuchung *(f)*, Umfrage *(f)*, Begutachtung *(f)*, Gutachten *(n)*
survey, general Gesamtübersicht *(f)*
suspension Suspendierung *(f)*; Einstellung *(f)*, Aufhängung *(f)*, Abhängung *(f)*

suspension cable Abhängeseil *(n)*
suspension clamp Hängeschelle *(f)*
suspension from the hall roof Hallendeckenabhängung *(f)*
suspension hook Einhängehaken *(m)* zur Abhängung
suspension point Auslasspunkt *(m)* für Abhängungen, Befestigungspunkt *(m)* für Abhängungen
suspension rod Abhängestab *(m)*
suspension strap Abhängegurt *(m)*, Abhängelasche *(f)*
suspension wire Abhängedraht *(m)*
suspicion Verdacht *(m)*, Vermutung *(f)*, Spur *(f)*; Argwohn *(m)*, Misstrauen *(n)*
suspicious verdächtig, argwöhnisch, misstrauisch
swap Tausch *(m)*, Tauschgeschäft *(n)*
swap tauschen, austauschen, eintauschen
sweep fegen, ausfegen, kehren; überspülen, überschwemmen; absuchen
sweet süß, anmutig, hübsch, reizend, freundlich, frisch
sweet Süßigkeit *(f)*, Nachtisch *(m)*
sweet dessert Süßspeise *(f)*
sweet dish Süßspeise *(f)*, Dessert *(n)*
sweetener Süßstoff *(m)*
swift flink, rasch, schnell
swing schwingen, sich schwingen, Schwung *(m)* haben, schaukeln, baumeln
swing Schwingen *(n)*, Schwung *(m)*, Umschwung *(m)*, Ausschlag *(m)*
swing door Pendeltür *(f)*
switch ändern, umschalten, umstellen, tauschen, vertauschen, wechseln, einwechseln
switch Schalter *(m)*; Umstellung *(f)*, Wechsel *(m)*; Kompensationsgeschäft *(n)*, Tauschgeschäft *(n)*

switch off abschalten, ausschalten, abstellen
switch on anschalten, einschalten
switch over umschalten, umstellen, überwechseln
switch, electric elektrischer Schalter *(m)*
switch, main Hauptschalter *(m)*
switchboard Schalttafel *(f)*
switching circuit Schaltkreis *(m)*
swivel Drehlager *(n)*
swivel schwenken, sich drehen, herumdrehen
swivel adaptor Schwenkadapter *(m)*
swivel chair Drehstuhl *(m)*
swivelling schwenkbar
symbol Symbol *(n)*, Zeichen *(n)*
symmetrical symmetrisch
symmetry Symmetrie *(f)*
sympathy Sympathie *(f)*, Mitgefühl *(n)*, Verständnis *(n)*
symposium Symposium *(n)*, Symposion *(n)*, Konferenz *(f)*
synchronization Synchronisierung *(f)*
synchronize synchronisieren, aufeinander abstimmen, übereinstimmen
synchronous synchron, gleichzeitig
synonymous synonym, gleichbedeutend
synthetic Kunststoff *(m)*
synthetic synthetisch, Kunst-
synthetic material Kunststoff *(m)*
system System *(n)*, Methode *(f)*
system component Systembauteil *(n)*
system exhibition stand Systemmessestand *(m)*, Messestand *(m)* aus Systembauteilen
system groove Systemnut *(f)*
system profile Systemprofil *(n)*
system wall Systemwand *(f)*
systematic systematisch

T

table tabellarisch zusammenstellen
table Tisch *(m)*; Liste *(f)*, Tabelle *(f)*, Verzeichnis *(n)*
table water Mineralwasser *(n)*
table, occasional Beistelltisch *(m)*
tablecloth Tischdecke *(f)*, Tischtuch *(n)*
tablet Tablette *(f)*; (Schokolade etc.) Tafel *(f)*; (Seife) Stück *(n)*
tabletop Tischplatte *(f)*
tabletop cooker Platten-Tischherd *(m)*
tabletop frozen food storage cabinet Tisch-Tiefkühlschrank *(m)*
tabletop refrigerator Tischkühlschrank *(m)*
tabular tabellarisch
tactical taktisch
tactics Taktik *(f)*
tag Etikett *(n)*, Preisschildchen *(n)*
tag etikettieren, (Ware) auszeichnen
tailor Schneider(in) *(m/f)*
tailor's Schneiderei *(f)*
take Einnahmen *(f, pl)*; (Film) Aufnahme *(f)*
take nehmen, annehmen, einnehmen, mitnehmen, wegnehmen; auf sich nehmen; ergreifen; begreifen; erringen; aushalten, hinnehmen, ertragen; dauern; (Foto, Film) aufnehmen
take action Maßnahmen *(f, pl)* ergreifen
take along mitnehmen
take apart auseinander nehmen
take away wegnehmen
take back zurücknehmen
Take care! Pass auf dich auf!, Mach's gut!
take down abbauen, auseinandernehmen, abnehmen, einreißen, herunternehmen; notieren
take into account anrechnen, einkalkulieren, berücksichtigen

take over (Geschäft etc.) aufkaufen, übernehmen
take part in teilnehmen, mitmachen
take the minutes protokollieren, Protokoll *(n)* führen
takeover Übernahme *(f)*
talk Gespräch *(n)*, Unterhaltung *(f)*, Gerede *(n)*, Besprechung *(f)*, Diskussion *(f)*, Vortrag *(m)*
talk reden, sprechen, sich unterhalten, schwatzen
talk shop fachsimpeln
talking key Sprechtaste *(f)*
tap (Fass) anzapfen, anstechen; (Telefon) abhören
tap Zapfhahn *(m)*
tape Band *(n)*, Isolierband *(n)*, Klebeband *(n)*, Streifen *(m)*; Tonband *(n)*, Videoband *(n)*, Bandaufnahme *(f)*
tape mit Band *(n)* befestigen, mit Klebeband *(n)* verkleben; auf Band *(n)* aufnehmen, aufzeichnen
tape cassette Tonbandkassette *(f)*
tape measure Bandmaß *(n)*, Maßband *(n)*
tape recorder Tonbandgerät *(n)*
tape recording Tonbandaufnahme *(f)*
tape, magnetic Magnetband *(n)*
taper spitz zulaufen, sich verjüngen
tape-record aufnehmen
tare Tara *(f)*
tare form Taraformular *(n)*
tare slip Taraschein *(m)*
target zielen, abzielen, gerichtet sein
target Ziel *(n)*, Zielscheibe *(f)*, Planziel *(n)*, Planziffer *(f)*, Soll *(n)*
target audience Zielpublikum *(n)*
target cost Sollkosten *(pl)*
target group Zielgruppe *(f)*
target market Zielmarkt *(m)*
target-actual comparison Soll-Ist-Vergleich *(m)*
tariff Tarif *(m)*, Gebührensatz *(m)*, Preisliste *(f)*
tarpaulin Plane *(f)*

task Aufgabe *(f)*
taste Geschmack *(m)*, Kostprobe *(f)*, Vorliebe *(f)*, Neigung *(f)*
taste kosten, schmecken, abschmecken, probieren, versuchen; erfahren, erleben
tax Abgabe *(f)*, Steuer *(f)*, Beitrag *(m)*, Gebühr *(f)*
tax allowance Steuerernachlass *(f)*
tax deduction Steuerabzug *(m)*
tax domicile steuerlicher Wohnsitz *(m)*
tax exemption Steuerbefreiung *(f)*
tax rate Steuersatz *(m)*
tax rebate Steuererstattung *(f)*
tax reduction Steuerermäßigung *(f)*
tax refund Steuerrückzahlung *(f)*
taxation, rate of Steuersatz *(m)*
tax-free zollfrei, steuerfrei
tax-free allowance Steuerfreibetrag *(m)*
taxi Taxi *(n)*, Taxe *(f)*
taxi charge Taxigebühr *(f)*
taxi driver Taxifahrer(in) *(m/f)*
tax-privileged steuerbegünstigt
tax-sheltered steuerbegünstigt
tea cakes Teegebäck *(n)*
tea towel Geschirrtuch *(n)*
teabag Teebeutel *(m)*
teacup Teetasse *(f)*
team Team *(n)*, Mannschaft *(f)*, Arbeitsgruppe *(f)*
teapot Teekanne *(f)*
tear reißen, zerreißen, einreißen, aufreißen, spalten; zerren
tear Riss *(m)*
tear away wegreißen
tear down abbrechen, abreißen, herunterreißen
tear off abreißen
technical technisch, fachlich
technical show technische Messe *(f)*, Fachausstellung *(f)*, Fachmesse *(f)*
technician Techniker(in) *(m/f)*
technique Technik *(f)*, Verfahren *(n)*
technological technisch, technologisch
technology Technik *(f)*, Technologie *(f)*
technology, advanced Spitzentechnik *(f)*

technology, clean umweltfreundliche Technik *(f)*
technology, high-advanced Spitzentechnologie *(f)*
technology, new neue Technologie *(f)*, Zukunftstechnologie *(f)*
TEE train TEE-Zug *(m)*
telecast Fernsehsendung *(f)*, Fernsehübertragung *(f)*
telecast im Fernsehen *(n)* senden, übertragen
telecommunication equipment Fernsprecheinrichtung *(f)*
telecommunications Telekommunikation *(f)*
telefax machine Telefaxgerät *(n)*
telefax subscriber Telefaxteilnehmer(in) *(m/f)*
telephone answering machine Anrufbeantworter *(m)*
telephone bill Telefonrechnung *(f)*
telephone box Telefonzelle *(f)*
telephone cable Telefonkabel *(n)*
telephone connection Telefonanschluss *(m)*, Telefonverbindung *(f)*
telephone connection, digital digitaler Telefonanschluss *(m)*
telephone conversation Telefongespräch *(n)*
telephone equipment Telefonanlage *(f)*
telephone extension Telefonnebenanschluss *(m)*
telephone installation Telefoneinrichtung *(f)*, Telefoninstallation *(f)*
telephone line Telefonleitung *(f)*
telephone number Telefonnummer *(f)*
telephone rates Fernsprechgebühren *(f, pl)*
telephone subscriber Fernsprechteilnehmer(in) *(m/f)*
telephonic telefonisch
telephoto lens Teleobjektiv *(n)*
teleprinter Fernschreiber *(m)*
teleprocessing Datenfernverarbeitung *(f)*
television Fernsehen *(n)*, Fernsehgerät *(n)*
television advertising Fernsehwerbung *(f)*
television ratings Fernseheinschaltquote *(f)*
television viewer Fernsehzuschauer(in) *(m/f)*
television, commercial Werbefernsehen *(n)*, Privatfernsehen *(n)*
temp (coll.) Zeitarbeitskraft *(f)*, Aushilfskraft *(f)*
template Schablone *(f)*
temporary temporär, zeitweilig, zeitlich begrenzt, vorübergehend, provisorisch
tend tendieren
tendency Tendenz *(f)*, Neigung *(f)*
tender Angebot *(n)*, Offerte *(f)*, Ausschreibeverfahren *(n)*, Submissionsangebot *(n)*
tender Angebot *(n)* machen, sich an Ausschreibung *(f)* beteiligen, anbieten, bieten
tender hook Spannhaken *(m)*
tensile rod Zugstange *(f)*
tension Spannung *(f)*; Stromspannung *(f)*; Anspannung *(f)*
tension lock Spannschloss *(n)*
tension lock, eccentric Exzenterspannschloss *(n)*
tension, high Hochspannung *(f)*
tent Zelt *(n)*
tent constructions Zeltbauten *(pl)*
tent structures Zeltbauten *(pl)*
term bezeichnen, benennen, nennen
term Terminus *(m)*, Ausdruck *(m)*, Begriff *(m)*, Fachbegriff *(m)*, Bezeichnung *(f)*; Dauer *(f)*, Laufzeit *(f)*, Zeitraum *(m)*, Frist *(f)*
term, technical Fachausdruck *(m)*, Fachbegriff *(m)*
terminal Terminal *(n)*, Endstation *(f)*, Endgerät *(n)*

terminal stop Endhaltestelle *(f)*
terminus Endstation *(f)*
terms Bedingungen *(f, pl)*
terms, special
 Sonderbedingungen *(f, pl)*
test erproben, prüfen, untersuchen
test Test *(m)*, Prüfung *(f)*,
 Prüfungsarbeit *(f)*; Untersuchung *(f)*,
 Probe *(f)*, Versuch *(m)*
test certificate Prüfzeugnis *(n)*
test mark Prüfzeichen *(n)*
test mark ordinance
 Prüfzeichenverordnung *(f)*
test run Probelauf *(m)*
testing procedure Prüfverfahren *(n)*
testing, method of Prüfverfahren *(n)*
theft Diebstahl *(m)*
theft protection
 Diebstahlsicherung *(f)*
theftproof diebstahlsicher
theme Thema *(n)*, Leitmotiv *(n)*
theory Theorie *(f)*
thermometer Thermometer *(n)*
thermostat Thermostat *(m)*
thesis These *(f)*, Behauptung *(f)*
thin dünn, dürr, schmal; dürftig, gering,
 schwach, fadenscheinig; schütter
thin verdünnen, dünner machen,
 dünner werden; schütter werden
thinner Verdünner *(m)*
thorough gründlich, eingehend,
 sorgfältig, genau; durchgreifend,
 völlig, vollständig
thoughtful nachdenklich, aufmerksam,
 rücksichtsvoll
thoughtless gedankenlos, unbedacht,
 rücksichtslos
thread Gewinde *(n)*; Strahl *(m)*;
 Faden *(m)*
thread mit Gewinde *(n)* versehen,
 aufreihen, einfädeln
threaded bolt Gewindestift *(m)*
threaded bushing Gewindebuchse *(f)*
threaded pin Gewindestift *(m)*
threaded plate Gewindeplättchen *(n)*

threaded sleeve Gewindehülse *(f)*
three-dimensional (3-D)
 dreidimensional (3-D), plastisch
3-D image 3-D-Bild *(n)*
threshold Schwelle *(f)*, Anfang *(m)*,
 Beginn *(f)*; Türschwelle *(f)*
thrift Sparsamkeit *(m)*
throng Andrang *(m)*, Gedränge *(n)*,
 Gewühl *(n)*, Schar *(f)*
throng drängen, strömen
throng of people Menschenmenge *(f)*
throw werfen, schmeißen, geben
throw away wegwerfen
throwaway society
 Wegwerfgesellschaft *(f)*
thrust Stoß *(m)*, Stich *(m)*, Schub *(m)*
thrust stoßen, stechen, durchbohren,
 drängen
thumbscrew Flügelschraube *(f)*
thumbtack Heftzwecke *(f)*,
 Reißnagel *(m)*
ticket etikettieren
ticket Ticket *(n)*, Fahrkarte *(f)*,
 Fahrschein *(m)*, Flugschein *(m)*,
 Eintrittskarte *(f)*; Schein *(m)*; Etikett *(n)*;
 Zettel *(m)*; Strafzettel *(m)*
ticket counter Kartenschalter *(m)*
ticket machine Fahrkartenautomat *(m)*
ticket machine, automatic
 Fahrkartenautomat *(m)*,
 Eintrittskartenautomat *(m)*
ticket office Fahrkartenschalter *(m)*,
 Eintrittskartenschalter *(m)*
ticket, free Freikarte *(f)*
ticket, reduced ermäßigte Eintrittskarte *(f)*, ermäßigte Fahrkarte *(f)*
tidy ordentlich, sauber
tidy up aufräumen, in Ordnung *(f)*
 bringen
tie Band *(n)*, Bindung *(f)*, Schnur *(f)*;
 Verpflichtung *(f)*; Krawatte *(f)*
tie binden, verbinden, verknüpfen,
 zusammenschnüren
tiepin Krawattennadel *(f)*
tight fest; dicht, eng, knapp; straff

tighten (Schraube etc.) anziehen; enger machen, enger werden, straffen; verschärfen
tile Kachel *(f)*, Fliese *(f)*, Ziegel *(m)*
tile kacheln, fliesen, mit Ziegeln *(m, pl)* decken
tiled floor Fliesenboden *(m)*
tiler Fliesenleger(in) *(m/f)*, Dachdecker(in) *(m/f)*
timber Bauholz *(n)*, Nutzholz *(n)*; Balken *(m)*
timber construction Holzkonstruktion *(f)*
timber-frame construction Holzrahmenkonstruktion *(f)*, Balkenkonstruktion *(f)*
timberwork Gebälk *(n)*, Fachwerk *(n)*
time timen; (Geschwindigkeit) messen; (Zeit) stoppen
time Zeit *(f)*, Uhrzeit *(f)*, Zeitdauer *(f)*, Zeitpunkt *(m)*, Zeitraum *(m)*, Frist *(f)*, Termin *(m)*; Mal *(n)*; Takt *(m)*, Tempo *(n)*, Geschwindigkeit *(f)*; Gelegenheit *(f)*
time limit Frist *(f)*
time of arrival Ankunftszeit *(f)*
time of departure Abfahrtszeit *(f)*
time pressure Zeitdruck *(m)*, Termindruck *(m)*
time scale zeitlicher Rahmen *(m)*, Zeitplan *(m)*
time span Zeitraum *(m)*
time switch Zeitschalter *(m)*, Zeitschaltuhr *(f)*
time, local Ortszeit *(f)*
time-consuming zeitaufwändig, zeitraubend
time-lag Zeitverschiebung *(f)*, Zeitunterschied *(m)*, Verzögerung *(f)*
timely rechtzeitig, zur rechten Zeit *(f)*
timer Schaltuhr *(f)*, Zeitmesser *(m)*
time-saving zeitsparend
timetable Fahrplan *(m)*, Flugplan *(m)*; Terminkalender *(m)*; Stundenplan *(m)*; Zeitplan *(m)*, Programm *(n)*

tin eindosen, einmachen
tin Zinn *(n)*, Weißblech *(n)*
tin (GB) Dose, Büchse *(f)*
tin opener (GB) Büchsenöffner *(m)*, Dosenöffner *(m)*
tip mit einer Spitze *(f)* versehen; Trinkgeld *(n)* geben; tippen auf, setzen auf; kippen, schütten, Schutt *(m)* abladen
tip Tipp *(m)*, Hinweis *(m)*; Spitze *(f)*, Gipfel *(m)*; Müllhalde *(f)*; Trinkgeld *(n)*
tissue Papiertaschentuch *(n)*
title Titel *(m)*, Überschrift *(f)*; Rechtsanspruch *(m)*
title of event Veranstaltungstitel *(m)*
title page Titelseite *(f)*, Titelblatt *(n)*
toast Toast *(m)*, Trinkspruch *(m)*
toilet Toilette *(f)*, Klosett *(n)*
tolerance Toleranz *(f)*, Duldung *(f)*
tolerate tolerieren, aushalten, dulden, ertragen
tombola Tombola *(f)*
ton (Gewicht) Tonne *(f)*
tone Ton *(m)*, Klang *(m)*, Note *(f)*; Farbton *(m)*
tone color (US) Klangfarbe *(f)*
tone colour (GB) Klangfarbe *(f)*
tone control Klangregler *(m)*, Tonregler *(m)*
tone down abschwächen, dämpfen
tonic water Tonic *(n)*
tonnage Tonnage *(f)*
tool Werkzeug *(n)*, Gerät *(n)*, Instrument *(n)*
tool bag Werkzeugtasche *(f)*
tool box Werkzeugkasten *(m)*
tool cleaning Arbeitsmittelreinigung *(f)*
top beste(-r/-s), oberste(-r/-s), höchste(-r/-s), Höchst-, Spitzen-
top die Spitze *(f)* bilden, übersteigen, an der Spitze *(f)* stehen; bedecken
top Spitze *(f)*, Gipfel *(m)*, Höhepunkt *(m)*, oberes Ende *(n)*, obere Seite *(f)*; Oberfläche *(f)*; Deckel *(m)*; Verdeck *(n)*

top edge Oberkante *(f)*
top executive leitende(r) Angestellte(r) *(f/m)*
top girder (Treppe, Brüstung) Obergurt *(m)*
top management Top-Management *(n)*, oberste Unternehmensführung *(f)*, Unternehmensspitze *(f)*
top quality Spitzenqualität *(f)*
top seller Spitzenreiter *(m)*, Verkaufsschlager *(m)*
topic Thema *(n)*
topic of conversation Gesprächsthema *(n)*
torx head screw Torxschraube *(f)*
torx head screw driver Torxschraubendreher *(m)*
torx head wrench Torxwinkelschlüssel *(m)*
total Summe *(f)*, Endsumme *(f)*, Gesamtbetrag *(m)*, Gesamtmenge *(f)*
total sich belaufen auf, zusammenzählen, zusammenrechnen
total total, ganz, vollständig, völlig, gesamt, Gesamt-
touch anfassen, berühren, sich berühren; grenzen an, erreichen; benutzen; treffen, betreffen
touch Berührung *(f)*, Empfindung *(f)*, Gefühl *(n)*, Tastsinn *(m)*; Verbindung *(f)*; Pinselstrich *(m)*
touch in einfügen
touch screen Kontaktbildschirm *(m)*
touch up auffrischen, nachbessern, überarbeiten, retuschieren
tour conductor Reiseleiter(in) *(m/f)*
tour manager Reiseleiter(in) *(m/f)*
tour operator Reiseveranstalter(in) *(m/f)*
tour organizer Reiseveranstalter(in) *(m/f)*
touring exhibition Wanderausstellung *(f)*, Wandermesse *(f)*
touring fair Wanderausstellung *(f)*, Wandermesse *(f)*

touring show Wanderausstellung *(f)*, Wandermesse *(f)*
tourism Tourismus *(m)*, Fremdenverkehr *(m)*
tourist Tourist(in) *(m/f)*
tourist agency Reisebüro *(n)*
tourist office Fremdenverkehrsbüro *(n)*, Fremdenverkehrsamt *(n)*
tow schleppen, abschleppen
towel Handtuch *(n)*
tower Turm *(m)*
tower ragen
tower above (Größe) überragen
town office Stadtbüro *(n)*
trade Handel *(m)*, Handwerk *(n)*, Gewerbe *(n)*, Wirtschaftszweig *(m)*, Branche *(f)*, Handelsverkehr *(m)*
trade handeln, Geschäfte *(n, pl)* machen
trade allowance Großhandelsrabatt *(m)*
trade and industry Handel *(m)* und Wirtschaft *(f)*, gewerbliche Wirtschaft *(f)*
trade association Fachverband *(m)*, Handelsverband *(m)*, Unternehmensverband *(m)*, Wirtschaftsverband *(m)*
trade attendance, international Auslandsfachbesucher *(m, pl)*
trade audience Fachpublikum *(n)*
trade channel Absatzkanal *(m)*
trade directory Branchenverzeichnis *(n)*, Firmenverzeichnis *(n)*
trade discount Händlerrabatt *(m)*
trade fair Messe *(f)*, Fachmesse *(f)*, Gewerbeausstellung *(f)*
trade fair and exhibition risk insurance Messe- und Ausstellungsversicherung *(f)*
trade fair participation Messebeteiligung *(f)*
trade fair targets, quantitative quantitative Messeziele *(n, pl)*
trade fair, general Universalmesse *(f)*
trade fair, international internationale Messe *(f)*

trade fair, virtual virtuelle Messe *(f)*
trade journal Fachzeitschrift *(f)*
trade knowledge Branchenkenntnis *(f)*
trade magazine Fachzeitschrift *(f)*
trade margin Handelsspanne *(f)*
trade name Markenname *(m)*, Handelsbezeichnung *(f)*, Firmenname *(m)*
trade press Fachpresse *(f)*
trade register Handelsregister *(n)*
trade show Fachausstellung *(f)*, Fachmesse *(f)*, Branchenmesse *(f)*, Gewerbeausstellung *(f)*, Handelsmesse *(f)*
trade show, in-house Hausausstellung *(f)*, Hausmesse *(f)*
trade sign Firmenzeichen *(n)*
trade union Gewerkschaft *(f)*
trade visitor Fachbesucher(in) *(m/f)*
trade visitor brochure Fachbesucherprospekt *(m)*
trade visitor day Fachbesuchertag *(m)*
trade visitors profile Fachbesucherprofil *(n)*
trade, external Außenhandel *(m)*
trade, foreign Außenhandel *(m)*
trade, international Außenhandel *(m)*
trademark Marke *(f)*, Markenzeichen *(n)*, Handelsmarke *(f)*, Handelszeichen *(n)*, Warenzeichen *(n)*, Schutzmarke *(f)*
trademark protection Markenzeichenschutz *(m)*, Warenzeichenschutz *(m)*
trademark, registered eingetragenes Firmenzeichen *(n)*, eingetragenes Warenzeichen *(n)*, eingetragene Schutzmarke *(f)*
trader Händler(in) *(m/f)*, Makler(in) *(m/f)*, Unternehmer(in) *(m/f)*, Geschäftsmann *(m)*, Geschäftsfrau *(f)*
trading channel Absatzweg *(m)*
traffic announcement Verkehrsdurchsage *(f)*, Verkehrsmeldung *(f)*
traffic congestion Verkehrsstau *(m)*
traffic control Verkehrsregelung *(f)*

traffic guidance system Verkehrsleitsystem *(n)*
traffic guidelines Verkehrsleitfaden *(m)*
traffic hold up Verkehrsstörung *(f)*
traffic jam Verkehrsstau *(m)*
traffic regulation Verkehrsregelung *(f)*
traffic regulations, general allgemeine Verkehrsregeln *(f, pl)*
traffic sign Verkehrszeichen *(n)*
traffic, local Nahverkehr *(m)*
trafficability Befahrbarkeit *(f)*
trailer Anhänger *(m)*; (Film) Vorschau *(f)*
trailer parking area Anhänger-Abstellplatz *(m)*
trailor-tractor unit Lastzug *(m)*
train trainieren, ausbilden, schulen
train Zug *(m)*, Wagenkolonne *(f)*; Gefolge *(n)*, Reihe *(f)*
trainee Auszubildende(r) *(f/m)*, Praktikant(in) *(m/f)*
trainer Trainer(in) *(m/f)*, Ausbilder(in) *(m/f)*
transaction Ausführung *(f)*, Abschluss *(m)*, Durchführung *(f)*, Transaktion *(f)*
transaction, legal Rechtsgeschäft *(n)*
transfer Transfer *(m)*, Übertragung *(f)*; Überweisung *(f)*; Umbuchung *(f)*; Umzug *(m)*; Verlegung *(f)*; Versetzung *(f)*; Veräußerung *(f)*
transfer transferieren, übertragen; überweisen; überschreiben; versetzen; veräußern; abtreten
transfer of stand space Übertragung *(f)* von Standfläche an Dritte
transferable übertragbar
transform transformieren, umformen, umwandeln, verwandeln
transformer Transformator *(m)*
transit Transit *(m)*, Durchfahrt *(f)*, Durchgangsverkehr *(m)*, Transport *(m)*
transit goods Transitgüter *(n, pl)*
transit lounge Transithalle *(f)*
transit traffic Transitverkehr *(m)*
translate übersetzen

translating agency
  Übersetzungsbüro *(n)*
translation Übersetzung *(f)*
translation service
  Übersetzungsdienst *(m)*
translator Übersetzer(in) *(m/f)*
translator, technical
  Fachübersetzer(in) *(m/f)*
transmitter, handheld Handsender *(m)*
transparency Transparenz *(f)*,
  Durchsichtigkeit *(f)*, Diapositiv *(n)*
transparent transparent, durchsichtig,
  durchschaubar, offensichtlich
transport Transport *(m)*, Beförderung *(f)*
transport transportieren, befördern
transport advertising
  Verkehrsmittelwerbung *(f)*
transport agent Spediteur *(m)*
transport case Transportkiste *(f)*
transport company
  Speditionsunternehmen *(n)*
transport facilities
  -Beförderungsmittel *(n, pl)*,
  Transportmöglichkeiten *(f, pl)*
transport insurance
  Transportversicherung *(f)*
transport means Transportmittel *(n, pl)*
transport, public öffentlicher Verkehr
  (m), öffentliche Verkehrsmittel *(n, pl)*
transportable transportierbar,
  versandfertig
transportation Transport *(m)*,
  Beförderung *(f)*, Versand *(m)*,
  Transportmittel *(n)*, Beförderungsmittel *(n)*; Transportkosten *(pl)*
transportation charges Transportkosten *(pl)*, Beförderungskosten *(pl)*
transportation document
  Transportdokument *(n)*,
  Transportpapiere *(n, pl)*
transporter Transportfahrzeug *(n)*
trash bag (US) Abfallbeutel *(m)*
trashcan (US) Abfalleimer *(m)*,
  Mülleimer *(m)*, Mülltonne *(f)*
travel Reise *(f)*, Reisen *(n)*

travel reisen, bereisen, fahren,
  sich bewegen, sich verbreiten
travel agency Reisebüro *(n)*
travel costs Reisekosten *(pl)*
travel expense statement
  Reisekostenabrechnung *(f)*
travel expenses Reisekosten *(pl)*
travel information Reiseauskunft *(f)*
travel insurance Reiseversicherung *(f)*
traveling allowance (US)
  Reisespesen *(pl)*
traveling crane (US) Laufkran *(m)*
traveling exhibition (US) Wanderausstellung *(f)*, Wandermesse *(f)*
traveling fair (US) Wanderausstellung *(f)*, Wandermesse *(f)*
traveling show (US) Wanderausstellung *(f)*, Wandermesse *(f)*
traveling (US) Reisen *(n)*
travelling allowance (GB)
  Reisespesen *(pl)*
travelling crane (GB) Laufkran *(m)*
travelling exhibition (GB) Wanderausstellung *(f)*, Wandermesse *(f)*
travelling fair (GB) Wanderausstellung *(f)*, Wandermesse *(f)*
travelling show (GB) Wanderausstellung *(f)*, Wandermesse *(f)*
travelling (GB) Reisen *(n)*
tray Tablett *(n)*, Ablage *(f)*, Schale *(f)*
treaty Abkommen *(n)*, Übereinkunft *(f)*,
  Vertrag *(m)*
treaty, violation of a Vertragsbruch *(m)*
treenail Dübel *(m)*
trench Graben *(m)*
trend tendieren, gerichtet sein
trend Trend *(m)*, Tendenz *(f)*,
  Richtung *(f)*, Entwicklung *(f)*,
  Verlauf *(m)*, Mode *(f)*
trend analysis Trendanalyse *(f)*
trend reversal Trendwende *(f)*
trend, economic Konjunkturtrend *(m)*,
  Konjunkturentwicklung *(f)*,
  Geschäftstrend *(m)*
trendsetting richtungsweisend

trial Versuch *(m)*, Prüfung *(f)*,
  Erprobung *(f)*, Probe *(f)*, Test *(m)*,
  Untersuchung *(f)*, Prozess *(m)*,
  Gerichtsverfahren *(n)*
trial package Probepackung *(f)*
triangle Dreieck *(n)*, Zeichendreieck *(n)*
triangle node Dreiecksknoten *(m)*
triangular dreieckig
trip, special Sonderfahrt *(f)*
tripod Stativ *(n)*
trouble beunruhigen, bedrücken;
  belästigen; bemühen, sich bemühen,
  Mühe *(f)* machen, sich
  Umstände *(m, pl)* machen;
  Umstände *(m, pl)* verursachen
trouble Schwierigkeit *(f)*,
  Schwierigkeiten *(f, pl)*,
  Unannehmlichkeiten *(f, pl)*,
  Problem *(n)*, Mühe *(f)*,
  Umstände *(m, pl)*; Durcheinander *(n)*;
  Defekt *(m)*, Störung *(f)*
truck (US) Lastwagen *(m)*, LKW *(m)*
truck (US) mit einem Lastwagen *(m)*
  transportieren
truck trailer (US) LKW-Anhänger *(m)*
truck trailer parking area (US)
  LKW-Anhängerabstellplatz *(m)*
truckage LKW-Transport *(m)*
trucking charges Rollgeld *(n)*
truss abstützen
truss Tragbalken *(m)*, Fachwerk *(n)*,
  Binder *(m)*, Klammer *(f)*
truss section, triangular
  Dreieckträgerteil *(m)*
trust vertrauen
trust Vertrauen *(n)*, Zutrauen *(n)*;
  Kartell *(n)*, Trust *(m)*, Konzern *(m)*
trustworthy vertrauenswürdig,
  glaubwürdig
try Versuch *(m)*
try versuchen, probieren, ausprobieren;
  (Sache) verhandeln
T-Shirt T-Shirt *(f)*
tube Tube *(f)*, Rohr *(n)*, Röhre *(f)*,
  Schlauch *(m)*

tube construction Rohrkonstruktion *(f)*
tube diameter Rohrdurchmesser *(m)*
tumble Sturz *(m)*, Durcheinander *(n)*
tumble stürzen, stark fallen
tuner (Radio, TV) Tuner *(m)*
tuning, fine Feinabstimmung *(f)*
tunnel Tunnel *(m)*, Unterführung *(f)*
turbulent turbulent, aufgeregt,
  stürmisch, unruhig
turn drehen, sich drehen,
  sich umdrehen; umblättern, wenden;
  zuwenden; abbiegen; verwandeln,
  sich verwandeln; umschlagen
turn Drehung *(f)*, Biegung *(f)*, Kurve *(f)*,
  Umdrehung *(f)*, Reihenfolge *(f)*,
  Tendenz *(f)*, Wende *(f)*, Wendung *(f)*
turn off abschalten, ausschalten,
  abstellen
turn on the lights Licht *(n)* anmachen
turn over umsetzen, umschlagen,
  verkaufen, ausliefern, sich umdrehen
turn round sich umdrehen, umkehren,
  wenden; abfertigen; in die
  Gewinnzone *(f)* bringen
turnable stage Drehbühne *(f)*
turnaround (Ware) Umschlag *(m)*
turnbuckle Spannschloss *(n)*
turning area Wendefläche *(f)*
turning circle Wendekreis *(m)*
turnkey bezugsfertig, schlüsselfertig
turnkey stand schlüsselfertiger
  Stand *(m)*
turnover Umsatz *(m)*,
  Lagerumschlag *(m)*, Fluktuation *(f)*,
  Volumen *(n)*
TV screen Fernsehbildschirm *(m)*
TV show coverage
  Messefernsehen *(n)*
TV spot Fernsehspot *(m)*
TV, commercial Werbefernsehen *(n)*,
  Privatfernsehen *(n)*
type bestimmen, klassifizieren;
  Schreibmaschine *(f)* schreiben, tippen
type Type *(f)*, Schrifttyp *(m)*; Art *(f)*,
  Sorte *(f)*

type area Satzspiegel *(m)*
type plate Typenschild *(n)*
typewriter Schreibmaschine *(f)*
typical typisch, charakteristisch, kennzeichnend
typing service Schreibdienst *(m)*

U

ultimate schließlich, endlich, endgültig, End-; grundlegend; perfekt; äußerste(-r/-s), letzte(-r/-s)
umbrella Schirm *(m)*, Schutz *(m)*, Abschirmung *(f)*
umbrella organization Dachorganisation *(f)*
umbrella stand Schirmständer *(m)*
unable unfähig, untauglich
unacceptable unannehmbar
unannounced unangemeldet
unanswered unbeantwortet
unasked ungefragt, ungebeten
unattended unbeaufsichtigt, unbewacht
unauthorized unbefugt, unberechtigt, nicht ermächtigt
unauthorized person Unbefugte(r) *(f/m)*
unavailability Nichtverfügbarkeit *(f)*
unbearable unerträglich, unausstehlich
unbreakable unzerbrechlich, unumstößlich
uncertain unbestimmt, ungewiss, ungenau, unsicher, unbeständig, vage, problematisch
uncertainty Ungewissheit *(f)*
unclear unklar
uncomfortable unbequem, unbehaglich
uncommon ungewöhnlich, außergewöhnlich, ungebräuchlich
unconcerned uninteressiert, gleichgültig, unbekümmert, unbeteiligt

unconditional bedingungslos, vorbehaltlos
unconfirmed unbestätigt
uncork entkorken
undamaged unbeschädigt
undecided unentschieden, unentschlossen, unschlüssig
underbid unterbieten
underdeveloped unterentwickelt
underexposed unterbelichtet
underfloor hydrant Unterflurhydrant *(m)*
underfloor installation Unterflurverlegung *(f)*
underframe Untergestell *(n)*
underground U-Bahn *(f)*
underground unterirdisch, Untergrund-
underline unterstreichen, hervorheben, betonen
underneath unter, darunter
underneath Unterseite *(f)*
underpass Unterführung *(f)*
understand verstehen, einsehen, erfahren, begreifen, annehmen, entnehmen, schließen; voraussetzen
understanding Verständnis *(n)*, Einsicht *(f)*, Übereinkommen *(n)*, Verständigung *(f)*; Voraussetzung *(f)*
undervalued unterbewertet
underwrite garantieren; unterstützen; versichern; (Anleihe etc.) zeichnen
underwriter Versicherer *(m)*, Versicherungsgeber *(m)*
undesirable unerwünscht
undisputed unbestritten
undisturbed ungestört
undoubtedly fraglos, zweifellos, gewiss
uneconomic unrentabel, unwirtschaftlich
uneconomical unrentabel, unwirtschaftlich
unemployed arbeitslos, erwerbslos, unbeschäftigt; ungenutzt
unequal ungleich

uneven uneben, ungleich, ungerade, ungleichmäßig, unregelmäßig, unausgeglichen
uneveness of the floor Bodenunebenheit *(f)*
unexpected unerwartet, unvorhergesehen
unexposed (Film) unbelichtet
unfair unfair, ungerecht, ungerechtfertigt, unlauter
unfamiliar ungewohnt, nicht vertraut
unforeseen unvorhergesehen
unfortunately unglücklicherweise, leider
unfriendly unfreundlich
unguarded unbewacht; nachlässig, sorglos
unhedget ungesichert
unicolored (US) einfarbig
unicoloured (GB) einfarbig
uniform einheitlich, einförmig, gleich, gleichförmig; übereinstimmend
uniform Uniform *(f)*
unilateral einseitig
unimportant unwichtig
uninsured unversichert
unintentional unbeabsichtigt, unabsichtlich
uninteresting uninteressant
uninterrupted ununterbrochen
unique einmalig, einzigartig
unit Einheit *(f)*, Element *(n)*, Stück *(n)*, Teil *(n)*; Anlage *(f)*; Abteilung *(f)*
unit cost Stückkosten *(pl)*
unit price Stückpreis *(m)*
unit weight Einzelgewicht *(n)*
universal universal, universell, allgemein, Welt-
unjust ungerecht
unknown fremd, unbekannt
unknown Unbekannte(r) *(f/m)*
unknown person Unbekannte(r) *(f/m)*
unlawful gesetzwidrig, rechtswidrig, ungesetzlich
unlike verschieden, ungleich, unähnlich

unlimited unbegrenzt, unbeschränkt, grenzenlos
unload abladen, ausladen, entladen, abstoßen
unlock aufschließen
unnecessary unnötig, überflüssig
unnoticed unbemerkt
unobserved unbeobachtet
unoccupied unbeschäftigt; unbewohnt, unbesetzt, leer stehend
unorthodox unkonventionell
unpack auspacken
unpackaged unverpackt
unpaid unbeglichen, unbezahlt, ehrenamtlich
unpleasant unangenehm, unerfreulich, unfreundlich
unpopular unpopulär, unbeliebt
unpredictable unberechenbar, unvorhersehbar
unprepared unvorbereitet
unprofitable unrentabel
unprotected schutzlos, ungeschützt
unpunctual unpünktlich
unqualified unqualifiziert, ungeeignet; uneingeschränkt
unreasonable unvernünftig, unangemessen, unsinnig; übertrieben
unregistered nicht registriert, nicht eingetragen, nicht angemeldet
unreliability Unzuverlässigkeit *(f)*
unreliable unzuverlässig
unrestricted unbeschränkt, unbegrenzt, uneingeschränkt
unrivaled (US) konkurrenzlos, einzigartig, unerreicht, unübertroffen
unrivalled (GB) konkurrenzlos, einzigartig, unerreicht, unübertroffen
unsafe unsicher, gefährlich
unsaleable unverkäuflich
unsatisfactory unbefriedigend
unscrew aufschrauben, losschrauben
unsettled unbeglichen, unbezahlt; ungeklärt; unbeständig, unsicher

unskilled ungelernt, ungeübt, ungeschickt
unsuccessful erfolglos, vergeblich
unsuitable ungeeignet, unangebracht, unpassend
untaxed steuerfrei, unbesteuert
untimely ungelegen, unpassend, verfrüht, vorzeitig
unused unbenutzt, ungebraucht, nicht beansprucht
unusual ungewöhnlich, selten
unwrap auswickeln, auspacken
up to date aktuell, neu, auf dem neuesten Stand *(m)*, modern
update aktualisieren, modernisieren, auf den neuesten Stand *(m)* bringen
update Aktualisierung *(f)*, neueste Information *(f)*
upholster polstern
upholstered chair Polsterstuhl *(m)*
upholstery Polster *(n)*
upright aufrecht, gerade, senkrecht
upright Ständer *(m)*, Pfosten *(m)*
upright freezer Gefrierschrank *(m)*
upright freezer with glassdoor Tiefkühlschrank *(m)* mit Glastür
upright profile Stützenprofil *(n)*
upwards nach oben, Aufwärts-, aufwärts
urge anspornen, antreiben, drängen
urge Bedürfnis *(n)*, Drang *(m)*, Verlangen *(n)*
urgency Dringlichkeit *(f)*
urgent dringend, vordringlich, eilig
usage Gebrauch *(m)*, Anwendung *(f)*; Behandlung *(f)*; Gewohnheit *(f)*, Sitte *(f)*, Brauch *(m)*
usage, common allgemeiner Brauch *(m)*
use benutzen, nutzen, gebrauchen, verwenden, anwenden, verwerten
use Benutzung *(f)*, Nutzung *(f)*, Gebrauch *(m)*, Anwendung *(f)*, Verwendung *(f)*, Verwertung *(f)*
useful nützlich, brauchbar, praktisch; tüchtig

useless nutzlos, unnütz, unbrauchbar, zwecklos
user Anwender(in) *(m/f)*, Benutzer(in) *(m/f)*, Nutzer(in) *(m/f)*, Bediener(in) *(m/f)*, Verbraucher(in) *(m/f)*
user's guide Benutzerhandbuch *(n)*
user's handbook Benutzerhandbuch *(n)*
user-friendly benutzerfreundlich
usual gewöhnlich, üblich
usually gewöhnlich, normalerweise, im Allgemeinen
utilities contractor, official offizieller Versorgungslieferant *(m)*
utilities engineering Versorgungstechnik *(f)*
utilities installations Versorgungseinrichtungen *(f, pl)*
utility Nützlichkeit *(f)*, Nutzen *(m)*
utility goods Gebrauchsgüter *(n, pl)*

V

vacant vakant, frei, leer stehend, unbesetzt, unbewohnt
vaccinate impfen
vaccination Impfung *(f)*
vacuum staubsaugen
vacuum Vakuum *(n)*
vacuum cleaner Staubsauger *(m)*
vacuum packaging Vakuumverpackung *(f)*
vacuum-packed vakuumverpackt
vague vage, unbestimmt, unklar, verschwommen
vain vergeblich, nutzlos, zwecklos; eingebildet
valid rechtsgültig, rechtskräftig, berechtigt, bindend, gültig; stichhaltig
validity Geltung *(f)*, Gültigkeit *(f)*, Berechtigung *(f)*, Rechtswirksamkeit *(f)*; Stichhaltigkeit *(f)*

valuation Bewertung *(f)*, Schätzung *(f)*, Veranschlagung *(f)*, Schätzwert *(m)*
value schätzen, abschätzen, bewerten
value Wert *(m)*, Nutzen *(m)*; Valuta *(f)*
value, good preiswert
value, high hochwertig
value-added tax (VAT) Mehrwertsteuer *(f)*
valve Ventil *(n)*; (TV) Röhre *(f)*
van Kleintransporter *(m)*, Lieferwagen *(m)*
vanish verschwinden, schwinden
variable variabel, veränderlich, unbeständig, schwankend, wechselnd; einstellbar, regulierbar
variable Variable *(f)*
variance Abweichung *(f)*, Streuung *(f)*, Unterschied *(m)*
variant abweichend, verschieden
variant Variante *(f)*
variety Vielfalt *(f)*, Abwechslung *(f)*; Auswahl *(f)*; Sortiment *(n)*
varnish Lack *(m)*, Firnis *(m)*, Politur *(f)*
varnish lackieren, mit Firnis *(m)* überziehen, polieren
vary variieren, abändern, verändern, sich verändern, sich wandeln, sich unterscheiden, verschieden sein
vase Vase *(f)*
VAT (value-added tax) Mehrwertsteuer *(f)*
VAT refund Vergütung *(f)* der Mehrwertsteuer, Mehrwertsteuerrückerstattung *(f)*
VAT refund application Antrag *(m)* auf Vergütung der Mehrwertsteuer
VAT, statutory gesetzliche Mehrwertsteuer *(f)*
vault Gewölbe *(n)*, Wölbung *(f)*
vaulted bogenförmig, gewölbt
VDE standard VDE-Vorschrift *(f)*
vegetarian Vegetarier(in) *(m/f)*
vegetarian vegetarisch
vehicle Fahrzeug *(n)*; Medium *(n)*, Mittel *(n)*

vehicle for refrigerated transport Kühlfahrzeug *(n)*
vending machine Verkaufsautomat *(m)*, Warenautomat *(m)*
veneer Furnier *(n)*
venetian blind Jalousie *(f)*
ventilate lüften, belüften
ventilation Belüftung *(f)*, Entlüftung *(f)*
ventilation and air conditioning systems Lüftungs- und Klimaanlagen *(f, pl)*
ventilation system Belüftungsanlage *(f)*, Entlüftungsanlage *(f)*
ventilator Ventilator *(m)*, Lüfter *(m)*
venue Austragungsort *(m)*, Begegnungsstätte *(f)*, Treffpunkt *(m)*, Verhandlungsort *(m)*, Schauplatz *(m)*
verifiable nachprüfbar, nachweisbar
verify prüfen, überprüfen, kontrollieren; beglaubigen, bestätigen, belegen, beweisen
veritable wahr, wahrhaft, wirklich
versatile vielseitig
versatility Vielseitigkeit *(f)*
version Version *(f)*, Darstellung *(f)*, Fassung *(f)*, Ausführung *(f)*; Übersetzung *(f)*
vertical vertikal, senkrecht, lotrecht
vertical Vertikale *(f)*, Senkrechte *(f)*
vertical frozen food display cabinet Tiefkühlkostvitrine *(f)*, verglaster Tiefkühlschrank *(m)*
vertical frozen food storage cabinet Tiefkühlkost-Lagerschrank *(m)*
vertically adjustable höhenverstellbar
vessel Gefäß *(n)*, Behälter *(m)*
vestibule Vorhalle *(f)*
vibration Vibrieren *(n)*, Vibration *(f)*, Schwingung *(f)*, Zittern *(n)*
vibration alarm Vibrationsalarm *(m)*
video camera Videokamera *(f)*
video cassette Videokassette *(f)*
video cassette recorder Video-Kassettenrekorder *(m)*

video cassette recording
  Videoaufzeichnung *(f)*
video conference Videokonferenz *(f)*
video disc Bildplatte *(f)*
video film Videofilm *(m)*
video input (Anschluss)
  Videoeingang *(m)*
video playback Videowiedergabe *(f)*
video presentation
  Videovorführung *(f)*
video production company
  Videoproduktionsgesellschaft *(f)*,
  Videoproduktionsfirma *(f)*
video recorder Videorekorder *(m)*,
  Videogerät *(n)*,
video set Videogerät *(n)*,
  Video-/Fernsehgerät *(n)*
video wall Videowand *(f)*
videotape aufnehmen
videotape Videoband *(n)*
videotape recording
  Videoaufzeichnung *(f)*
view ansehen, besichtigen, betrachten,
  beurteilen
view Sicht *(f)*, Ansicht *(f)*, Aussicht *(f)*,
  Blick *(m)*, Überblick *(m)*; Meinung *(f)*
view, general Gesamtansicht *(f)*
view, lateral Seitenansicht *(f)*
view, partial Teilansicht *(f)*
viewer Zuschauer(in) *(m/f)*,
  Fernsehzuschauer(in) *(m/f)*
viewfinder (Kamera) Sucher *(m)*
viewing platform
  Aussichtsplattform *(f)*
vindicate bestätigen, rechtfertigen;
  rehabilitieren
vindication Rechtfertigung *(f)*,
  Verteidigung *(f)*; Rehabilitation *(f)*
violation Verletzung *(f)*, Verstoß *(m)*,
  Rechtsbruch *(m)*, Übertretung *(f)*;
  Störung *(f)*
violence Gewalt *(f)*, Gewalttätigkeit *(f)*;
  Heftigkeit *(f)*, Stärke *(f)*
violent heftig, stark, leidenschaftlich;
  gewaltsam

VIP (Very Important Person)
  bedeutende Persönlichkeit *(f)*,
  wichtige Person *(f)*
virtual wirklich, tatsächlich; virtuell
visible sichtbar, sichtlich, ersichtlich,
  offensichtlich, deutlich
vision Vision *(f)*, Voraussicht *(f)*,
  Vorstellung *(f)*, Sehen *(n)*, Sehkraft *(f)*,
  Weitblick *(m)*
visionary visionär, hellseherisch,
  weitblickend; fantastisch, unwirklich
visit Besuch *(m)*; Besichtigung *(f)*;
  Kontrolle *(f)*
visit besuchen, aufsuchen; besichtigen,
visiting hours Besuchszeit *(f)*
visitor authorization
  Besucherzulassung *(f)*
visitor brochure Besucherprospekt *(m)*
visitor information system
  Besucherinformationssystem *(n)*
visitor interview Besucherbefragung *(f)*
visitor invitation
  Besuchereinladung *(f)*
visitor pass Besucherausweis *(m)*
visitor report Besuchsbericht *(m)*
visitor survey Besuchererhebung *(f)*,
  Besucherumfrage *(f)*,
  Besucherübersicht *(f)*
visitor, specialized
  Fachbesucher(in) *(m/f)*
visitors from abroad ausländische
  Besucher *(m, pl)*
visitors information
  Besucherinformation *(f)*
visitors leaflet Besucherprospekt *(m)*
visitors profile Besucherprofil *(n)*
visual visuell, optisch, Seh-
visual aids Anschauungsmaterial *(n)*,
  Lehrmittel *(n, pl)*
visual contact Blickkontakt *(m)*
visualize erwarten, sich vorstellen
void leer; nichtig, ungültig
void Leere *(f)*
volt Volt *(n)*
voltage Stromspannung *(f)*

voltage detector Spannungsprüfer *(m)*
voltage, high Hochspannung *(f)*
voltage, rated Nennspannung *(f)*
voltage, total (Strom) Anschlussleistung *(f)*
voltmeter Spannungsmesser *(m)*
volume Volumen *(n)*, Rauminhalt *(m)*; Umfang *(m)*; Lautstärke *(f)*, Klangfülle *(f)*; Band *(m)*, Buch *(n)*
volume control Lautstärkeregler *(m)*
volume discount Mengenrabatt *(m)*
voluntary freiwillig, spontan, vorsätzlich, willkürlich
voucher Beleg *(m)*, Bescheinigung *(m)*, Bon *(m)*; Gutschein *(m)*
voucher, free Gutschein *(m)*

W

wage Lohn *(m)*, Arbeitslohn *(m)*
wage tax Lohnsteuer *(f)*
waistband Gurtband *(n)*
wait on Gäste *(m, pl)* bedienen
waiter Kellner *(m)*, Ober *(m)*
waiting list Warteliste *(f)*
waiting room Warteraum *(m)*
waitress Kellnerin *(f)*
walkie-talkie Sprechfunkgerät *(n)*
wall mit einer Wand *(f)* umgeben
wall Wand *(m)*, Mauer *(f)*
wall cabinet Hängeschrank *(m)*
wall construction Wandbau *(m)*
wall cupboard Wandschrank *(m)*
wall insert extrusion Wandeinschubprofil *(n)*
wall lamp Wandlampe *(f)*, Wandleuchte *(f)*
wall light Wandlicht *(m)*
wall mounting Wandmontage *(f)*
wall panel Wandplatte *(f)*
wall panelling Wandverkleidung *(f)*

wall, double layer doppelschalige Wand *(f)*
wall, single layer einschalige Wand *(f)*
wall's path Wandverlauf *(m)*
wallet Brieftasche *(f)*
wall-mounted showcase Wandschaukasten *(m)*, Wandvitrine *(f)*
wallpaper Tapete *(f)*
wallpaper tapezieren
wallpaper paste Tapetenkleister *(m)*
warehouse Lager *(n)*, Lagerhaus *(n)*, Warenlager *(n)*, Depot *(n)*, Magazin *(n)*
warehouse, bonded Zolllager *(n)*
warehousing Lagerung *(f)*
warehousing, temporary Zwischenlagerung *(f)*
warn warnen
warn sign Warnzeichen *(n)*
warning flasher Warnblinkanlage *(f)*
warning flasher device Warnblinkanlage *(f)*
warning light Warnlicht *(n)*
warning sign Warnschild *(n)*
warp Biegung *(f)*
warp verbiegen, verziehen, sich verziehen
wash waschen, abwaschen, aufwischen, ausspülen; sich waschen
wash off abwaschen, wegwaschen
wash out auswaschen, ausspülen
wash up abwaschen, spülen, abspülen
washbasin Waschbecken *(f)*
washer Dichtungsscheibe *(f)*, Unterlegescheibe *(f)*
washing Wäsche *(f)*
washing liquid Spülmittel *(n)*
washing-up (Geschirr) Abwaschen *(n)*
washroom Waschraum *(m)*
waste Abfall *(m)*, Müll *(m)*; Verschwendung *(f)*
waste überschüssig, ungenutzt; Abfall-
waste verschwenden, vergeuden, vergeben, vertun; schwächen; verkümmern, verfallen; verwüsten
waste air Abluft *(f)*

waste bag Abfallbeutel *(m)*
waste bin (GB) Abfalleimer *(m)*
waste collection Müllabfuhr *(f)*
waste collection, presorted
  sortenreine Abfallsammlung *(f)*
waste container Abfallbehälter *(m)*
waste depot, hazardous
  Sondermülldeponie *(f)*
waste disposal Abfallbeseitigung *(f)*,
  Abfallentsorgung *(f)*,
  Müllbeseitigung *(f)*
waste disposal company
  Entsorgungsunternehmen *(n)*
waste disposal concept
  Entsorgungskonzept *(n)*
waste disposal costs
  Entsorgungskosten *(pl)*
waste disposal firm
  Entsorgungsunternehmen *(n)*,
  Entsorgungsfirma *(f)*
waste disposal, hazardous
  Entsorgung *(f)* von Sondermüll
waste fumes Abgase *(n, pl)*
  (auch Dampf und Rauch)
waste gases Abgase *(n, pl)*
waste heat Abwärme *(f)*
waste law Abfallgesetz *(n)*
waste management
  Abfallentsorgung *(f)*
waste of energy
  Energieverschwendung *(f)*
waste of time Zeitverschwendung *(f)*
waste paper basket Papierkorb *(m)*
waste pipe Abflussrohr *(n)*,
  Abflussleitung *(f)*
waste recycling, reusable
  Wertstoffentsorgung *(f)*
waste society Wegwerfgesellschaft *(f)*
waste sorting for collection
  sortenreine Abfallsammlung *(f)*
waste, hazardous Sonderabfall *(m)*,
  Sondermüll *(m)*
wastewater Abwasser *(n)*
wastewater disposal
  Abwasserbeseitigung *(f)*

watch Uhr *(f)*; Wache *(f)*,
  Bewachung *(f)*, Überwachung *(f)*;
  Wachsamkeit *(f)*; Wachmann *(m)*,
  Wächter(in) *(m/f)*
watch wachen, Wache *(f)* halten,
  bewachen, aufpassen; beobachten,
  zuschauen
watchman Wachmann *(m)*
water boiler Boiler *(m)*, Wasserkocher
  (m), Warmwasserbereiter *(m)*
water connection
  Wasseranschluss *(m)*
water connection, secondary
  Wassernebenanschluss *(m)*
water consumption
  Wasserverbrauch *(m)*
water damage Wasserschaden *(m)*
water discharge Wasserauslass *(m)*
water drain Wasserablauf *(m)*
water heater Heißwassergerät *(n)*,
  Warmwasserbereiter *(m)*
water heater, continuous-flow
  Durchlauferhitzer *(m)*
water heater, instantaneous
  Durchlauferhitzer *(m)*
water hose Wasserschlauch *(m)*
water inlet pipe Wasserzuleitung *(f)*
water main Hauptwasserleitung *(f)*
water main connection
  Hauptwasseranschluss *(m)*
water meter Wasseruhr *(f)*,
  Wasserzähler *(m)*
water outlet pipe
  Wasserabflussleitung *(f)*,
  Wasserabflussrohr *(n)*
water pipe Wasserleitung *(f)*,
  Wasserrohr *(n)*
water supply Wasserversorgung *(f)*
water supply, auxiliary
  Wassernebenanschluss *(m)*
water tap Wasserhahn *(m)*,
  Wasserzapfstelle *(f)*
waterproof wasserdicht, wasserfest
watertight wasserdicht
watt Watt *(n)*

wattage Wattleistung *(f)*, Wattzahl *(f)*
wavy wellenförmig
way Weg *(m)*, Strecke *(f)*, Richtung *(f)*, Entfernung *(f)*; Art *(f)*, Weise *(f)*, Verhaltensweise *(f)*; Gelegenheit *(f)*, Möglichkeit *(f)*; Hinsicht *(f)*
way back Rückweg *(m)*
way in Eingang *(m)*
way out Ausgang *(m)*
weak point Schwachstelle *(f)*
weakness Schwäche *(f)*
weatherproof wetterfest
web address Webadresse *(f)*
web site Webseite *(f)*
wedge Keil *(m)*
wedge-shaped keilförmig
weight (mit einem Gewicht) beschweren
weight Gewicht *(n)*, Last *(f)*; Bedeutung *(f)*, Wertigkeit *(f)*, Wichtigkeit *(f)*
weight limit Höchstgewicht *(n)*
weight per square meter (US) Gewicht *(n)* pro Quadratmeter
weight per square metre (GB) Gewicht *(n)* pro Quadratmeter
weight, distributed flächig aufgelagerte Last *(f)*
welcome begrüßen, willkommen heißen
welcome willkommen, gern gesehen; angenehm, erfreulich
welcome Willkommen *(n)*, Willkommensgruß *(m)*, Empfang *(m)*
welcome drink Begrüßungsgetränk *(n)*
welcoming speech Begrüßungsansprache *(f)*
weld schweißen
weld together verschweißen
welding torch Schweißbrenner *(m)*
well thought-out wohldurchdacht
well-known bekannt, wohlbekannt
well-tried bewährt
Western European Time (WET) Westeuropäische Zeit *(f)* (WEZ)

wet anfeuchten, nass machen
wet Nässe *(f)*, Feuchtigkeit *(f)*
wet nass, feucht, regnerisch; (Farbe) frisch
wheel drehen, fahren, schieben, rollen
wheel Rad *(n)*, Steuer *(n)*
wheelchair Rollstuhl *(m)*
wheelchairs, suitable for rollstuhlgerecht
whet schärfen, schleifen
whiskey Whisky *(m)*
white coffee Milchkaffee *(m)*
white wine Weißwein *(m)*
whitewash Tünche *(f)*
whitewash tünchen
wholesale Großhandel *(m)*
wholesale discount Großhandelsrabatt *(m)*
wholesale price Großhandelspreis *(m)*
wholesaler Großhändler *(m)*
width Breite *(f)*, Weite *(f)*, Vielfalt *(f)*
width, clear lichtes Maß *(n)*
winch Winde *(f)*
winch up hochwinden
wind drehen, wickeln, winden
wind Wind *(m)*; Drehung *(f)*, Biegung *(f)*, Windung *(f)*
wind round umwickeln
wind up abwickeln, aufwickeln, hochwinden; auslaufen lassen
windbracing Windverband *(m)*
window Fenster *(n)*, Schalter *(m)*
window display Schaufensterdekoration *(f)*
window dressing Schaufensterdekoration *(f)*
window pane Fensterscheibe *(f)*
window, high Oberlicht *(n)*
wine Wein *(m)*
wine bottle Weinflasche *(f)*
wine cooling cabinet Weinkühlschrank *(m)*
wine, bottled Flaschenwein *(m)*
wineglass Weinglas *(n)*
wing nut Flügelmutter *(f)*

wing screw Flügelschraube *(f)*
wipe wischen, abwischen, säubern, reinigen, putzen; abtrocknen
wire Draht *(m)*, Leitung *(f)*
wire Leitung *(f)* legen
wire cable Drahtseil *(n)*
wire model Drahtmodell *(n)*
Wireless LAN (WLAN) kabelloses lokales Netzwerk *(n)*
wiring Kabelnetz *(n)*, Verkabelung *(f)*
wiring diagram Schaltbild *(n)*
withdraw widerrufen, abberufen; zurücktreten; (Angebot etc.) zurückziehen, zurücknehmen; (Geld) abheben
withdrawal Ausstieg *(m)*, Ausscheiden *(n)*, Rücktritt *(m)*; Rücknahme *(f)*; Rückzug *(m)*, Widerruf *(m)*; (Geld) Abhebung *(f)*
withdrawal fee Rücktrittsgebühr *(f)*
woodchip paper Rauhfasertapete *(f)*
woodchip wallpaper Rauhfasertapete *(f)*
wooden board Holzbrett *(n)*, Holzplatte *(f)*; (Regal) Holzfachboden *(m)*
wooden ledge Holzleiste *(f)*
wooden strut Holzstrebe *(f)*, Holzstütze *(f)*
woodworking Holzbearbeitung *(f)*
word formulieren, ausdrücken; (Text) abfassen
word Wort *(n)*; Nachricht *(f)*; Text *(m)*; Äußerung *(f)*; Rede *(f)*; Zusage *(f)*
word processing Textverarbeitung *(f)*
word processing program (US) Textverarbeitungsprogramm *(n)*
word processing programme (GB) Textverarbeitungsprogramm *(n)*
word processing system Textverarbeitungssystem *(n)*
words of thanks Dankesworte *(n, pl)*
work climate Arbeitsklima *(n)*
work clothes Arbeitskleidung *(f)*
work in the black schwarzarbeiten

work in the black economy schwarzarbeiten
work on bearbeiten
work on the side schwarzarbeiten
work out ausarbeiten
work panel Arbeitsplatte *(f)*
work permit Arbeitserlaubnis *(f)*
work place Arbeitsplatz *(m)*
work sloppily schludern
work, high-quality Qualitätsarbeit *(f)*
work, temporary Zeitarbeit *(f)*
worker Arbeiter(in) *(m/f)*, Arbeitnehmer(in) *(m/f)*, Arbeitskraft *(f)*
worker, casual Gelegenheitsarbeiter(in) *(m/f)*, Leiharbeiter(in) *(m/f)*
worker, highly qualified Spitzenkraft *(f)*
worker, temporary Aushilfe *(f)*, Aushilfskraft *(f)*, Aushilfsarbeiter(in) *(m/f)*, Zeitarbeitnehmer(in) *(m/f)*
worker, unskilled Hilfsarbeiter(in) *(m/f)*, ungelernte Arbeitskraft *(f)*
workforce Arbeitskräfte *(f, pl)*, Arbeitskräftepotenzial *(n)*, Belegschaft *(f)*
working clothes Arbeitskleidung *(f)*
working conditions Arbeitsbedingungen *(f, pl)*
working day Arbeitstag *(m)*
working dinner Arbeitsessen *(n)*
working gloves Arbeitshandschuhe *(m, pl)*
working group Arbeitsgemeinschaft *(f)*
working hours Arbeitszeit *(f)*, Dienststunden *(f, pl)*
working lunch Arbeitsessen *(n)*
working pass Arbeitsausweis *(m)*
working platform Arbeitsbühne *(f)*
working pool Arbeitsgemeinschaft *(f)*
working time, regular Normalarbeitszeit *(f)*
workman Handwerker *(m)*
workmanlike fachmännisch
workmanship Arbeitsqualität *(f)*
workmanship, high-quality Qualitätsarbeit *(f)*

workshop Werkstatt *(f)*;
Arbeitsgruppe *(f)*, Arbeitskreis *(m)*,
Arbeitstreffen *(n)*; Kurs *(m)*
world exhibition Weltausstellung *(f)*,
Weltmesse *(f)*
world fair Weltausstellung *(f)*,
Weltmesse *(f)*
world-famous weltberühmt,
weltbekannt
world-renowned weltberühmt
world-renowned firm Weltfirma *(f)*
world trade fair
Weltfachausstellung *(f)*,
Weltfachmesse *(f)*
world wide weltweit
worry sich sorgen, sich Sorgen *(f, pl)*
machen; jdm. Sorgen *(f, pl)* machen,
beunruhigen
worry Sorge *(f)*
worth knowing wissenswert
worth mentioning nennenswert
worth seeing sehenswert
wound verwunden, verletzen
wound Wunde *(f)*, Verletzung *(f)*;
Kränkung *(f)*
wrap Umhang *(m)*
wrap wickeln, einwickeln, einpacken,
verpacken
wrap up einpacken, einwickeln,
einschlagen; unter Dach *(n)* und
Fach *(n)* bringen
wrapping Verpackung *(f)*
wrapping paper Packpapier *(n)*
wrench reißen, ziehen, zerren,
verrenken
wrench Schraubenschlüssel *(m)*;
Verrenkung *(f)*; Ruck *(m)*, Zerrung *(f)*
write shorthand stenographieren
writing Schrift *(f)*
written schriftlich
wrong beeinträchtigen, benachteiligen,
unrecht tun
wrong falsch, unrichtig, nicht richtig;
unrecht, nicht recht
wrong decision Fehlentscheidung *(f)*

X

X-ray equipment Röntgenanlage *(f)*
X-rays Röntgenstrahlen *(m, pl)*

Y

yardstick Kriterium *(n)*, Maßstab *(m)*
yardstick of performance
Erfolgsmaßstab *(m)*
year of foundation Gründungsjahr *(n)*
year of manufacture Baujahr *(n)*
yellow pages Branchenverzeichnis *(n)*,
Gelbe Seiten *(pl)*
young people junge Leute *(pl)*
young persons Jugendliche *(pl)*
Your health! Prost!
youth Jugend *(f)*, Jugendliche(r) *(f/m)*,
junge Leute *(pl)*

Z

zero Null *(f)*; Nullpunkt *(m)*; Tiefpunkt
(m); Gefrierpunkt *(m)*; Nichts *(n)*
zero growth Nullwachstum *(n)*
zero-rated von der Mehrwertsteuer *(f)*
befreit
ZIP code (US) Postleitzahl *(f)*
zone, marginal Randzone *(f)*,
Randbereich *(m)*
zone, neighboring (US)
Nachbarschaftsbereich *(m)*,
angrenzender Bereich *(m)*
zone, neighbouring (GB)
Nachbarschaftsbereich *(m)*,
angrenzender Bereich *(m)*
zoom lense Zoomobjektiv *(n)*